Financial
Econometrics

THE FRANK J. FABOZZI SERIES

Financial
Econometrics

From Basics to Advanced Modeling Techniques

SVETLOZAR T. RACHEV

STEFAN MITTNIK

FRANK J. FABOZZI

SERGIO M. FOCARDI

TEO JAŠIĆ

John Wiley & Sons, Inc.

ISBN-13 978-0-471-78450-0
ISBN-10 0-471-78450-8

Printed in the United States of America.

10 9 8 7 6 5 4 3 2 1

STR
To my children Boryana and Vladimir

SM
To Erika and Alissa

FJF
To my son Francesco Alfonso

SMF
To my parents

TJ
To my parents

Contents

Preface

This book is intended to provide a modern, up-to-date presentation of financial econometrics. It was written for students in finance and practitioners in the financial services sector.

Initially and primarily used in the derivative business, mathematical models have progressively conquered all areas of risk management and are now widely used also in portfolio construction. The choice of topics and walk-through examples in this book reflect the current use of modeling in all areas of investment management.

Financial econometrics is the science of modeling and forecasting financial time series. The development of financial econometrics was made possible by three fundamental enabling factors: (1) the availability of data at any desired frequency, including at the transaction level; (2) the availability of powerful desktop computers and the requisite IT infrastructure at an affordable cost; and (3) the availability of off-the-shelf econometric software. The combination of these three factors put advanced econometrics within the reach of most financial firms.

But purely theoretical developments have also greatly increased the power of financial econometrics. The theory of autoregressive and moving average processes reached maturity in the 1970s with the development of a complete analytical toolbox by Box and Jenkins. Multivariate extensions followed soon after; and the fundamental concepts of cointegration and of ARCH/GARCH modeling were introduced by Engle and Granger in the 1980s. Starting with the fundamental work of Benoit Mandelbrot in the 1960s, empirical studies established firmly that returns are not normally distributed and might exhibit "fat tails," leading to a renewed interest in distributional aspects and in models that might generate fat tails and stable distributions.

This book updates the presentation of these topics. It begins with the basics of econometrics and works its way through the most recent theoretical results as regards the properties of models and their estimation procedures. It discusses tests and estimation methods from the point of view of a user of modern econometric software—although we have not endorsed any software.

A distinguishing feature of this book is the wide use of walk-through examples in finance to explain the concepts that modelers and those that use model results encounter in their professional life. In particular, our objective is to show how to interpret the results obtained through econometric packages. The reader will find all the important concepts in this book—from stepwise regression to cointegration and the econometrics of stable distributions—illustrated with examples based on real-world data. The walk-through examples provided can be repeated by the reader, using any of the more popular econometric packages available and data of the reader's choice.

Here is a roadmap to the book. In Chapter 1, we informally introduce the concepts and methods of financial econometrics and outline how modeling fits into the investment management process. In Chapter 2, we summarize the basic statistical concepts that are used throughout the book.

Chapters 3 to 5 are devoted to regression analysis. We present different regression models and their estimation methods. In particular, we discuss a number of real-world applications of regression analysis as walk-through examples. Among the walk-through examples presented are:

- Computing and analyzing the characteristic line of common stocks and mutual funds
- Computing the empirical duration of common stocks
- Predicting the Treasury yield
- Predicting corporate bond yield spread
- Testing the characteristic line in different market environments
- Curve fitting to obtain the spot rate curve with the spline method
- Tests of market efficiency and tests of CAPM
- Evaluating manager performance
- Selecting benchmarks
- Style analysis of hedge-funds
- Rich-cheap analysis of bonds

Chapter 6 introduces the basic concepts of time series analysis. Chapter 7 discusses the properties and estimation methods of univariate autoregressive moving average models. Chapter 8 is an up-to-date presentation of ARCH/GARCH modeling with walk-through examples. We illustrate the concepts discussed, analyzing the properties of returns of the DAX stock index and of selected stock return processes.

Chapters 9 through 11 introduce autoregressive vector processes and cointegrated processes, including advanced estimation methods for cointegrated systems. Both processes are illustrated with real-world examples. Vector autoregressive (VAR) analysis is illustrated by fitting a

VAR model to three real-world stock indexes; a cointegration analysis is also performed on the same three indexes.

Chapter 12 covers robust estimation. With the broad diffusion of modeling, interest in robust estimation methods has grown: Robust estimation is used to make results more robust. The concepts of robust statistics are introduced and a detailed analysis of robust regressions is performed and illustrated with many examples. We provide a robust analysis of the returns of a Japanese stock and show the results of applying robust methods to some of the regression examples discussed in previous chapters.

Chapter 13 discusses Principal Components Analysis (PCA) and Factor Analysis, both now widely used in risk management and in equity and bond portfolio construction. We illustrate the application of both techniques on a portfolio of selected U.S. stocks and show an application of PCA to bond portfolio management, to control interest rate risk.

Chapters 14 and 15 introduce stable processes and autoregressive moving average (ARMA) and GARCH models with fat-tailed errors. We illustrate the concepts discussed with an example in currency modeling and equity return modeling.

We thank several individuals for their assistance in various aspects of this project:

- Christian Menn for allowing us to use material from the book he coauthored with Svetlozar Rachev and Frank Fabozzi to create the appendix to Chapter 14.
- Robert Scott of the Bank for International Settlements for providing data for the illustration on predicting the 10-year Treasury yield in Chapter 3 and the data and regression results for the illustration on the use of the spline method in Chapter 4.
- Raman Vardharaj of The Guardian for the mutual fund data and regression results for the characteristic line in Chapter 3.
- Katharina Schüller for proofreading several chapters.
- Anna Chernobai of Syracuse University and Douglas Martin of the University of Washington and *Finanalytica* for their review of Chapter 12 (Robust Estimation).
- Stoyan Stoyanov for reviewing several chapters.
- Markus Hoechstoetter for the illustration in Chapter 14.
- Martin Fridson and Greg Braylovskiy for the corporate bond spread data used for the illustration in Chapter 4.
- David Wright of Northern Illinois University for the data to compute the equity durations in Chapter 3.

Svetlozar Rachev's research was supported by grants from the Division of Mathematical, Life and Physical Sciences, College of Letters and Science, University of California, Santa Barbara, and the Deutschen Forschungsgemeinschaft. Stefan Mittnik's research was supported by the Deutsche Forschungsgemeinschaft (SFB 368) and the Institut für Quantitative Finanzanalyse (IQF) in Kiel, Germany.

Svetlozar T. Rachev
Stefan Mittnik
Frank J. Fabozzi
Sergio M. Focardi
Teo Jasic

Abbreviations and Acronyms

a.a.   almost always
ABS   asset-backed securities
ACF   autocorrelation function
ACovF   autocovariance function
ADF   augmented Dickey-Fuller (test)
AD-statistic   Anderson-Darling distance statistic
a.e.   almost everywhere
AIC   Akaike information criterion
AICC   Corrected Akaike information criterion
ALM   asset-liability management
APT   arbitrage pricing theory
AR   autoregressive
ARCH   autoregressive conditional heteroskedastic
ARDL   autoregressive distributed lag
ARIMA   autoregressive integrated moving average
ARMA   autoregressive moving average
ARMAX   autoregressive moving average with exogenous variables
a.s.   almost surely

BD   breakdown (as in BD bound/point)
BHHH   Berndt, Hall, Hall, and Hausmann (algorithm)
BIC   Bayesian information criterion
BIS   Bank of International Settlements
BLUE   best linear unbiased estimator

cap   capitalization
CAPM   capital asset pricing model
CCA   canonical correlation analysis
CD   certificate of deposit
CLF   concentrated likelihood function
CLT   central limit theorem

DA domain of attraction
DAX Deutscher Aktinenindex (German blue chip stock index)
DGP data generating process
DJIA Dow Jones Industrial Average
DF Dickey-Fuller
DS difference stationary

EBIT earnings before interest and taxes
EGARCH exponential generalized autoregressive conditional heteroskedastic
EGB2 exponential generalized beta distribution of the second kind
EBITDA earnings before interest, taxes, depreciation, and amortization
ECM error correction model

FA factor analysis
FARIMA fractional autoregressive integrated moving average
FFT fast Fourier transform
FIEGARCH fractionally integrated exponential generalized autoregressive conditional heteroskedastic
FIGARCH fractionally integrated generalized autoregressive conditional heteroskedastic
FPE final prediction error
FRC Frank Russell Company

GAAP generally accepted accounting principles
GARCH generalized autoregressive conditional heteroskedastic
GED generalized exponential distribution
GLS generalized least squares
GCLT generalized central limit theorem
GM General Motors
GNP gross national product

HFD high-frequency data
HFR Hedge Fund Research Company

IBM International Business Machines
IC information criterion/criteria
IC influence curve
IF influence function
IGARCH integrated generalized autoregressive conditional heteroskedastic
IID independent and identically distributed
IMA infinite moving average
IQR interquartile range

IR information ratio
IV instrumental variables (as in IV methods)
IVAR infinite variance autoregressive model

KD-statistic Kolmogorov distance statistic

L lag operator
LAD least absolute deviation
LCCA level canonical correlation analysis
LF likelihood function
LM Lagrange multipliers (as in LM test/statistics)
LMedS least median of squares (as in LMedS estimator)
LMGARCH long-memory generalized autoregressive conditional heteroskedastic
LRD long-range dependent
LS least squares (as in LS estimators)
LSE least squares estimator
LTS least trimmed of squares (as in LTS estimator)

MA moving average
MAD median absolute deviation
MAE mean absolute error
MAPE mean absolute percentage error
MBS mortgage-backed securities
MeanAD mean absolute deviation
Med median
ML maximum likelihood
MLE maximum likelihood estimator
MM method of moments
MSCI Morgan Stanley Composite Index
MSE mean squared error

OAS option-adjusted spread (as in OAS duration)
OLS ordinary least squares

PACF partial autocorrelation function
PC principal components
PCA principal components analysis
PDE partial differential equation
pdf probability density function
PMLE pseudo-maximum likelihood estimator

QMLE quasi-maximum likelihood estimator

RLS   reweighted least squares
RMSE   root mean squared error
ROI   return on investment

S&P   Standard & Poor
SACF (or SACovF)   sample autocorrelation function
SPACF   sample partial autocorrelation function
ss   self similar (as in ss-process)
SSB BIG Index   Salomon Smith Barney Broad Investment Grade Index

TS   trend stationary

VAR   vector autoregressive
VaR   value at risk
VARMA   vector autoregressive moving average
VDE   vector difference equation
VECH   multivariate GARCH model

YW   Yule-Walker (in Yule-Walker equations)

About the Authors

Svetlozar (Zari) T. Rachev completed his Ph.D. Degree in 1979 from Moscow State (Lomonosov) University, and his Doctor of Science Degree in 1986 from Steklov Mathematical Institute in Moscow. Currently he is Chair-Professor in Statistics, Econometrics and Mathematical Finance at the University of Karlsruhe in the School of Economics and Business Engineering. He is also Professor Emeritus at the University of California, Santa Barbara in the Department of Statistics and Applied Probability. He has published seven monographs, eight handbooks and special-edited volumes, and over 250 research articles. Professor Rachev is cofounder of Bravo Risk Management Group specializing in financial risk-management software. Bravo Group was recently acquired by FinAnalytica for which he currently serves as Chief-Scientist.

Stefan Mittnik studied at the Technical University Berlin, Germany, the University of Sussex, England, and at Washington University in St. Louis, where he received his doctorate degree in economics. He is now Professor of Financial Econometrics at the University of Munich, Germany, and research director at the Ifo Institute for Economic Research in Munich. Prior to joining the University of Munich he taught at SUNY-Stony Brook, New York, the University of Kiel, Germany, and held several visiting positions, including that of Fulbright Distinguished Chair at Washington University in St. Louis. His research focuses on financial econometrics, risk management, and portfolio optimization. In addition to purely academic interests, Professor Mittnik directs the risk management program at the Center for Financial Studies in Frankfurt, Germany, and is co-founder of the Institut für Quantitative Finanzanalyse (IQF) in Kiel, where he now chairs the scientific advisory board.

Frank J. Fabozzi is an Adjunct Professor of Finance and Becton Fellow in the School of Management at Yale University. Prior to joining the Yale faculty, he was a Visiting Professor of Finance in the Sloan School at MIT. Professor Fabozzi is a Fellow of the International Center for Finance at Yale University and on the Advisory Council for the Department of Operations Research and Financial Engineering at Princeton University. He is the editor of *The Journal of Portfolio Management* and an associate editor of the *The Journal of Fixed Income*. He earned a doctorate in economics from the City University of New York in 1972. In 2002 Professor Fabozzi was inducted into the Fixed Income Analysts Society's Hall of Fame. He earned the designation of Chartered Financial Analyst and Certified Public Accountant. He has authored and edited numerous books in finance.

Sergio Focardi is a partner of The Intertek Group and a member of the Editorial Board of the *Journal of Portfolio Management*. He is the (co-) author of numerous articles and books on financial modeling and risk management, including the CFA Institute's recent monograph *Trends in Quantitative Finance* (co-authors Fabozzi and Kolm) and the award-winning books *Financial Modeling of the Equity Market* (co-authors Fabozzi and Kolm, Wiley) and *The Mathematics of Financial Modeling and Investment Management* (co-author Fabozzi, Wiley). Mr. Focardi has implemented long-short portfolio construction applications based on dynamic factor analysis and conducts research in the econometrics of large equity portfolios and the modeling of regime changes. He holds a degree in Electronic Engineering from the University of Genoa and a post-graduate degree in Communications from the Galileo Ferraris Electro-technical Institute (Turin).

Teo Jašić earned his doctorate (Dr.rer.pol.) in economics from the University of Karlsruhe in 2006. He also holds an MSc degree from the National University of Singapore and a Dipl.-Ing. degree from the University of Zagreb. Currently, he is a Postdoctoral Research Fellow at the Chair of Statistics, Econometrics and Mathematical Finance at the University of Karlsruhe in the School of Economics and Business Engineering. He is also a senior manager in Financial & Risk Management Group of a leading international management consultancy firm in Frankfurt, Germany. His current professional and research interests are in the areas of asset management, risk management, and financial forecasting. Dr. Jašić has published more than a dozen research papers in internationally refereed journals.

CHAPTER 1

Financial Econometrics: Scope and Methods

Financial econometrics is the econometrics of financial markets. It is a quest for models that describe financial time series such as prices, returns, interest rates, financial ratios, defaults, and so on. The economic equivalent of the laws of physics, econometrics represents the quantitative, mathematical laws of economics. The development of a quantitative, mathematical approach to economics started at the end of the 19th century, in a period of great enthusiasm for the achievements of science and technology.

The World Exhibition held in Paris in 1889 testifies to the faith of that period in science and technology. The key attraction of the exhibition—the Eiffel Tower—was conceived by Gustave Eiffel, an architect and engineer who had already earned a reputation building large metal structures such as the 94-foot-high wrought-iron square skeleton that supports the Statue of Liberty.[1] With its 300-meter-high iron structure, Eiffel's tower was not only the tallest building of its time but also a

---

[1] Eiffel was a shrewd businessman as well as an accomplished engineer. When he learned that the funding for the 1889 World Exhibition tower would cover only one fourth of the cost, he struck a deal with the French government: He would raise the requisite funds in return for the right to exploit the tower commercially for 20 years. The deal made him wealthy. In the first year alone, revenues covered the entire cost of the project! Despite his sense of business, Eiffel's career was destroyed by the financial scandal surrounding the building of the Panama Canal, for which his firm was a major contractor. Though later cleared of accusations of corruption, Eiffel abandoned his business activities and devoted the last 30 years of his life to research.

monument to applied mathematics. To ensure that the tower would withstand strong winds, Eiffel wrote an integral equation to determine the tower's shape.[2]

The notion that mathematics is the language of nature dates back 2,000 years to the ancient Greeks and was forcefully expressed by Galileo. In his book *Il saggiatore* (*The Assayer*), published in 1623, Galileo wrote (translation by one of the authors of this book):

> [The universe] cannot be read until we have learnt the language and become familiar with the characters in which it is written. It is written in the language of mathematics; the letters are triangles, circles, and other geometrical figures, without which it is humanly impossible to comprehend a single word.

It was only when Newton published his *Principia* some 60 years later (1687) that this idea took its modern form. In introducing the concept of *instantaneous rate of change*[3] and formulating mechanics as laws that link variables and their rates of change, Newton made the basic leap forward on which all modern physical sciences are based. Linking variables to their rate of change is the principle of differential equations. Its importance can hardly be overestimated. Since Newton, differential equations have progressively conquered basically all the fields of the physical sciences, including mechanics, thermodynamics, electromagnetism, relativity, and quantum mechanics.

During the 19th century, physics based on differential equations revolutionized technology. It was translated into steam and electrical engines, the production and transmission of electrical power, the transmission of electrical signals, the chemical transformation of substances, and the ability to build ships, trains, and large buildings and bridges. It

---

[2] The design principles employed by Eiffel have been used in virtually every subsequent tall building. Eiffel's equation,

$$\frac{1}{2}\int_x^H f(x)^2 dx - c(H-x) = \int_x^H x w(x) f(x) dx$$

states that the torque from the wind on any part of the Tower from a given height to the top is equal to the torque of the weight of this same part.

[3] The instantaneous rate of change, "derivative" in mathematical terminology, is one of the basic concepts of calculus. Calculus was discovered independently by Newton and Leibniz, who were to clash bitterly in claiming priority in the discovery.

changed every aspect of the manufacture of goods and transportation. Faith in the power of science and technology reached a peak.[4]

Enthusiasm for science led to attempts to adopt the principles of the physical sciences to domains as varied as linguistics, the behavioral sciences, and economics. The notion of economic equilibrium had already been introduced by Stanley Jevons[5] and Carl Menger[6] when Leon Walras[7] and Vilfredo Pareto[8] made the first attempts to write comprehensive mathematical laws of the economy. Engineers by training, Walras and Pareto set themselves the task of explicitly writing down the equation of economic equilibrium. Their objective was well in advance on their time. A reasonable theoretical quantitative description of economic systems had to wait the full development of probability theory and statistics during the first half of the 20th century. And its practical application had to wait the development of fast computers. It was only in the second half of the 20th century that a quantitative description of economics became a mainstream discipline: econometrics (i.e., the quantitative science of economics) was born.

THE DATA GENERATING PROCESS

The basic principles for formulating quantitative laws in financial econometrics are the same as those that have characterized the development of quantitative science over the last four centuries. We write mathematical models, that is, relationships between different variables and/or variables in different moments and different places. The basic tenet of quantitative science is that there are relationships that do not change regardless of the

---

[4] The 19th century had a more enthusiastic and naive view of science and the linearity of its progress than we now have. There are two major differences. First, 19th century science believed in unlimited possibilities of future progress; modern science is profoundly influenced by the notion that uncertainty is not eliminable. Second, modern science is not even certain about its object. According to the standard interpretation of quantum mechanics, the laws of physics are considered mere recipes to predict experiments, void of any descriptive power.

[5] Stanley Jevons, *Theory of Political Economy* (London: Macmillan, 1871).

[6] Carl Menger, *Principles of Economics* (available online at http://www.mises.org/etexts/menger/Mengerprinciples.pdf). Translated by James Dingwall and Bert F. Hoselitz from *Grundsätze der Volkswirtschaftslehre* published in 1871.

[7] Léon Walras. *Eléments d'économie politique pure; ou, Théorie de la richesse sociale* (Elements of Pure Economics or The Theory of Social Wealth) (Lausanne: Rouge, 1874).

[8] Vilfredo Pareto, *Manuel d'économie Politique* (Manual of Political Economy), translated by Ann S. Schwier from the 1906 edition (New York: A.M. Kelley, 1906).

moment or the place under consideration. For example, while sea waves might look like an almost random movement, in every moment and location the basic laws of hydrodynamics hold without change. Similarly, asset price behavior might appear to be random, but econometric laws should hold in every moment and for every set of assets.

There are similarities between financial econometric models and models of the physical sciences but there are also important differences. The physical sciences aim at finding immutable laws of nature; econometric models model the economy or financial markets—artifacts subject to change. For example, financial markets in the form of stock exchanges have been in operation for two centuries. During this period, they have changed significantly both in the number of stocks listed and the type of trading. And the information available on transactions has also changed. Consider that in the 1950s, we had access only to daily closing prices and this typically the day after; now we have instantaneous information on every single transaction. Because the economy and financial markets are artifacts subject to change, econometric models are not unique representations valid throughout time; they must adapt to the changing environment.

While basic physical laws are expressed as differential equations, financial econometrics uses both continuous time and discrete time models. For example, continuous time models are used in modeling derivatives where both the underlying and the derivative price are represented by stochastic (i.e., random) differential equations. In order to solve stochastic differential equations with computerized numerical methods, derivatives are replaced with finite differences.[9] This process of discretization of time yields discrete time models. However, discrete time models used in financial econometrics are not necessarily the result of a process of discretization of continuous time models.

Let's focus on models in discrete time, the bread-and-butter of econometric models used in asset management. There are two types of discrete-time models: static and dynamic. Static models involve different variables at the same time. The well-known *capital asset pricing model* (CAPM), for example, is a static model. Dynamic models involve one or more vari-

---

[9] The stochastic nature of differential equations introduces fundamental mathematical complications. The definition of stochastic differential equations is a delicate mathematical process invented, independently, by the mathematicians Ito and Stratonovich. In the Ito-Stratonovich definition, the path of a stochastic differential equation is not the solution of a corresponding differential equation. However, the numerical solution procedure yields a discrete model that holds pathwise. See Sergio M. Focardi and Frank J. Fabozzi, *The Mathematics of Financial Modeling and Investment Management* (Hoboken, NJ: John Wiley & Sons, 2004) and the references therein for details.

ables at two or more moments.[10] Momentum models, for example, are dynamic models.

In a dynamic model, the mathematical relationship between variables at different times is called the *data generating process* (DGP). This terminology reflects the fact that, if we know the DGP of a process, we can simulate the process recursively, starting from initial conditions. Consider the time series of a stock price p_t, that is, the series formed with the prices of that stock taken at fixed points in time, say daily. Let's now write a simple econometric model of the prices of a stock as follows:[11]

$$p_{t+1} = \mu + \rho p_t + \varepsilon_{t+1}$$

This model tells us that if we consider any time $t + 1$, the price of that stock at time $t + 1$ is equal to a constant plus the price in the previous moment t multiplied by ρ plus a zero-mean random disturbance independent from the past, which always has the same statistical characteristics.[12] A random disturbance of this type is called a *white noise*.[13]

If we know the initial price p_0 at time $t = 0$, using a computer program to generate random numbers, we can simulate a path of the price process with the following recursive equations:

$$p_1 = \mu + \rho p_0 + \varepsilon_1$$
$$p_2 = \mu + \rho p_1 + \varepsilon_2$$
$$\vdots$$

That is, we can compute the price at time $t = 1$ from the initial price p_0 and a computer-generated random number ε_1 and then use this new price to compute the price at time $t = 2$, and so on.[14] It is clear that we

---

[10] This is true in discrete time. In continuous time, a dynamic model might involve variables and their derivatives at the same time.

[11] In this example, we denote prices with lower case p and assume that they follow a simple linear model. In the following chapters, we will make a distinction between prices, represented with upper case letter P and the logarithms of prices, represented by lower case letters. Due to the geometric compounding of returns, prices are assumed to follow nonlinear processes.

[12] If we want to apply this model to real-world price processes, the constants μ and ρ must be estimated. μ determines the trend and ρ defines the dependence between the prices. Typically ρ is less than but close to 1.

[13] The concept of white noise will be made precise in the following chapters where different types of white noise will be introduced.

[14] The ε_i are independent and identically distributed random variables with zero mean. Typical choices for the distribution of ε are normal distribution, t-distribution, and stable non-Gaussian distribution. The distribution parameters are estimated from the sample (see Chapter 3).

have a DGP as we can generate any path. An econometric model that involves two or more different times can be regarded as a DGP.

However, there is a more general way of looking at econometric models that encompasses both static and dynamic models. That is, we can look at econometric models from a perspective other than that of the recursive generation of stochastic paths. In fact, we can rewrite our previous model as follows:

$$p_{t+1} - \mu - \rho p_t = \varepsilon_{t+1}$$

This formulation shows that, if we consider any two consecutive instants of time, there is a combination of prices that behave as random noise. More in general, an econometric model can be regarded as a mathematical device that reconstructs a noise sequence from empirical data. This concept is visualized in Exhibit 1.1, which shows a time series of numbers p_t generated by a computer program according to the previous rule with $\rho = 0.9$ and $\mu = 1$ and the corresponding time series ε_t. If we choose any pair of consecutive points in time, say $t+1, t$, the differ-

EXHIBIT 1.1   DGP and Noise Terms

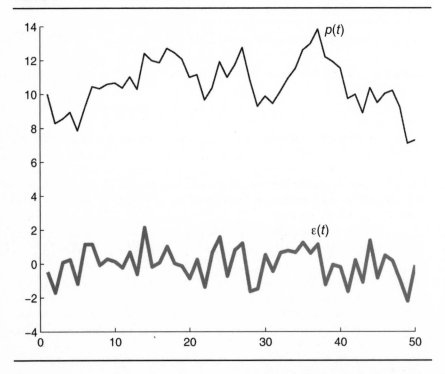

ence $p_{t+1} - \mu - \rho p_t$ is always equal to the series ε_{t+1}. For example, consider the points $p_{13} = 10.2918$, $p_{14} = 12.4065$. The difference $p_{14} - 0.9p_{13} - 1 = 2.1439$ has the same value as ε_{14}. If we move to a different pair we obtain the same result, that is, if we compute $p_{t+1} - 1 - 0.9p_t$, the result will always be the noise sequence ε_{t+1}.

To help intuition, imagine that our model is a test instrument: probing our time series with our test instrument, we always obtain the same reading. Actually, what we obtain is not a constant reading but a random reading with mean zero and fixed statistical characteristics. The objective of financial econometrics is to find possibly simple expressions of different financial variables such as prices, returns, or financial ratios in different moments that always yield, as a result, a zero-mean random disturbance.

Static models (i.e., models that involve only one instant) are used to express relationships between different variables at any given time. Static models are used, for example, to determine exposure to different risk factors. However, because they involve only one instant, static models cannot be used to make forecasts; forecasting requires models that link variables in two or more instants in time.

FINANCIAL ECONOMETRICS AT WORK

Applying financial econometrics involves three key steps:

1. Model selection
2. Model estimation
3. Model testing

In the first step, model selection, the modeler chooses (or might write *ex novo*) a family of models with given statistical properties. This entails the mathematical analysis of the model properties as well as economic theory to justify the model choice. It is in this step that the modeler decides to use, for example, regression on financial ratios or other variables to model returns.

In general, models include a number of free parameters that have to be estimated from sample data, the second step in applying financial econometrics. Suppose that we have decided to model returns with a regression model, a technique that we discuss in later chapters. This requires the estimation of the regression coefficients, performed using historical data. Estimation provides the link between reality and models. As econometric models are probabilistic models, any model can in principle describe our empirical data. We choose a family of models in the model selection phase and then determine the optimal model in the estimation phase.

As mentioned, model selection and estimation are performed on historical data. As models are adapted (or fitted) to historical data there is always the risk that the fitting process captures ephemeral features of the data. Thus there is the need to test the models on data different from the data on which the models were estimated. This is the third step in applying financial econometrics, model testing. We assess the performance of models on fresh data.

We can take a different approach to model selection and estimation, namely statistical learning. Statistical learning combines the two steps—model selection and model estimation—insofar as it makes use of a class of universal models that can fit any data. Neural networks are an example of universal models. The critical step in the statistical learning approach is estimation. This calls for methods to restrict model complexity (i.e., the number of parameters used in a model).

Within this basic scheme for applying financial econometrics, we can now identify a number of modeling issues, such as:

- How do we apply statistics given that there is only one realization of financial series?
- Given a sample of historical data, how do we choose between linear and nonlinear models, or the different distributional assumptions or different levels of model complexity?
- Can we exploit more data using, for example, high-frequency data?
- How can we make our models more robust, reducing model risk?
- How do we measure not only model performance but also the ability to realize profits?

Implications of Empirical Series with Only One Realization

As mentioned, econometric models are *probabilistic* models: Variables are random variables characterized by a probability distribution. Generally speaking, probability concepts cannot be applied to single "individuals."[15] Probabilistic models describe "populations" formed by many individuals. However, empirical financial time series have only one realization. For example, there is only one historical series of prices for each stock—and we have only one price at each instant of time. This makes problematic the application of probability concepts. How, for example, can we meaningfully discuss the distribution of prices at a specific time given that there is only one price observation? Applying probability concepts to perform estimation and testing would require populations made up of multi-

---

[15] At least, not if we use a frequentist concept of probability. See Chapter 2.

ple time series and samples made up of different time series that can be considered a random draw from some distribution.

As each financial time series is unique, the solution is to look at the single elements of the time series as the individuals of our population. For example, because there is only one realization of each stock's price time series, we have to look at the price of each stock at different moments. However, the price of a stock (or of any other asset) at different moments is not a random independent sample. For example, it makes little sense to consider the distribution of the prices of a single stock in different moments because the level of prices typically changes over time. Our initial time series of financial quantities must be transformed; that is, a unique time series must be transformed into populations of individuals to which statistical methods can be applied. This holds not only for prices but for any other financial variable.

Econometrics includes transformations of the above type as well as tests to verify that the transformation has obtained the desired result. The DGP is the most important of these transformations. Recall that we can interpret a DGP as a method for transforming a time series into a sequence of noise terms. The DGP, as we have seen, constructs a sequence of random disturbances starting from the original series; it allows one to go backwards and infer the statistical properties of the series from the noise terms and the DGP. However, these properties cannot be tested independently.

The DGP is not the only transformation that allows statistical estimates. Differencing time series, for example, is a process that, as we will see in Chapter 6, may transform nonstationary time series into stationary time series. A stationary time series has a constant mean that, under specific assumptions, can be estimated as an empirical average.

Determining the Model

As we have seen, econometric models are mathematical relationships between different variables at different times. An important question is whether these relationships are linear or nonlinear. Consider that every econometric model is an approximation. Thus the question is: Which approximation—linear or nonlinear—is better?

To answer this, it is generally necessary to consider jointly the linearity of models, the distributional assumptions, and the number of time lags to introduce. The simplest models are linear models with a small number of lags under the assumption that variables are normal variables. A widely used example of normal linear models are regression models where returns are linearly regressed on lagged factors under the assumption that noise terms are normally distributed. A model of this type can be written as:

$$r_{t+1} = \beta f_t + \varepsilon_{t+1}$$

where r_t are the returns at time t and f_t are factors, that is economic or financial variables. Given the linearity of the model, if factors and noise are jointly normally distributed, returns are also normally distributed.

However, the distribution of returns, at least at some time horizons, is not normal. If we postulate a nonlinear relationship between factors and returns, normally distributed factors yield a nonnormal return distribution. However, we can maintain the linearity of the regression relationship but assume a nonnormal distribution of noise terms and factors. Thus a nonlinear models transforms normally distributed noise into nonnormal variables but it is not true that nonnormal distributions of variables implies nonlinear models.

If we add lags (i.e., a time space backwards), the above model becomes sensitive to the shape of the factor paths. For example, a regression model with two lags will behave differently if the factor is going up or down. Adding lags makes models more flexible but more brittle. In general, the optimal number of lags is dictated not only by the complexity of the patterns that we want to model but also by the number of points in our sample. If sample data are abundant, we can estimate a rich model.

Typically there is a trade-off between model flexibility and the size of the data sample. By adding time lags and nonlinearities, we make our models more flexible, but the demands in terms of estimation data are greater. An optimal compromise has to be made between the flexibility given by nonlinear models and/or multiple lags and the limitations due to the size of the data sample.

TIME HORIZON OF MODELS

There are trade-offs between model flexibility and precision that depend on the size of sample data. To expand our sample data, we would like to use data with small time spacing in order to multiply the number of available samples. High-frequency data or HFD (i.e., data on individual transactions) have the highest possible frequency (i.e., each individual transaction) and are irregularly spaced. To give an idea of the ratio in terms of numbers, consider that there are approximately 2,100 ticks per day for the median stock in the Russell 3000.[16] Thus the size of the HDF data set of one day for a typical stock in the Russell 3000 is 2,100 times larger than the size of closing data for the same day!

---

[16] Thomas Neal Falkenberry, "High Frequency Data Filtering," Tick Data Inc., 2002.

In order to exploit all available data, we would like to adopt models that work over time intervals of the order of minutes and, from these models, compute the behavior of financial quantities over longer periods. Given the number of available sample data at high frequency, we could write much more precise laws than those established using longer time intervals. Note that the need to compute solutions over forecasting horizons much longer than the time spacing is a general problem which applies at any time interval. For example, as will be discussed in Chapter 5, in asset allocation we need to understand the behavior of financial quantities over long time horizons. The question we need to ask is if models estimated using daily intervals can correctly capture the process dynamics over longer periods, such as years.

It is not necessarily true that models estimated on short time intervals, say minutes, offer better forecasts at longer time horizons than models estimated on longer time intervals, say days. This is because financial variables might have a complex short-term dynamics superimposed on a long-term dynamics. It might be that using high-frequency data one captures the short-term dynamics without any improvement in the estimation of the long-term dynamics. That is, with high-frequency data it might be that models get more complex (and thus more data-hungry) because they describe short-term behavior superimposed on long-term behavior. This possibility must be resolved for each class of models.

Another question is if it is possible to use the *same* model at different time horizons. To do so is to imply that the behavior of financial quantities is similar at different time horizons. This conjecture was first made by Benoit Mandelbrot who observed that long series of cotton prices were very similar at different time aggregations.[17] This issue will be discussed in Chapter 14 where we review families of variables and processes that exhibit self-similarity.

Model Risk and Model Robustness

Not only are econometric models probabilistic models, as we have already noted; they are only *approximate* models. That is, the probability distributions themselves are only approximate and uncertain. The theory of model risk and model robustness assumes that all parameters of a model are subject to uncertainty, and attempts to determine the consequence of model uncertainty and strategies for mitigating errors.

The growing use of models in finance over the last decade has heightened the attention to model risk and model-risk mitigation techniques. Asset management firms are beginning to address the need to

---

[17] Benoit Mandelbrot, "The Variation of Certain Speculative Prices," *Journal of Business* 36 (1963), pp. 394–419.

implement methodologies that allow both robust estimation and robust optimization in the portfolio management process.

Performance Measurement of Models

It is not always easy to understand *ex ante* just how well (or how poorly) a forecasting model will perform. Because performance evaluations made on training data are not reliable, the evaluation of model performance requires separate data sets for training and for testing. Models are estimated on training data and tested on the test data. Poor performance might be due to model misspecification, that is, models might not reflect the true DGP of the data (assuming one exists), or there might simply be no DGP.

Various measures of model performance have been proposed. For example, one can compute the correlation coefficient between the forecasted variables and their actual realizations. Each performance measure is a single number and therefore conveys only one aspect of the forecasting performance. Often it is crucial to understand if errors can become individually very large or if they might be correlated. Note that a simple measure of model performance does not ensure the profitability of strategies. This can be due to a number of reasons, including, for example, the risk inherent in apparently profitable forecasts, market impact, and transaction costs.

APPLICATIONS

There has been a greater use of econometric models in investment management since the turn of the century. Application areas include:

- Portfolio construction and optimization
- Risk management
- Asset and liability management

Each type of application requires different modeling approaches. In the appendix to this chapter, we provide a more detailed description of the investment management process and some investment concepts that will be used in this book.

Portfolio Construction and Optimization

Portfolio construction and optimization require models to forecast returns: There is no way to escape the need to predict future returns. Passive strategies apparently eschew the need to forecast future returns of individual stocks by investing in broad indexes. They effectively shift the need to forecast to a higher level of analysis and to longer time horizons.

Until recently, the mainstream view was that financial econometric models could perform dynamic forecasts of volatility but not of expected returns. However, volatility forecasts are rarely used in portfolio management. With the exception of some proprietary applications, the most sophisticated models used in portfolio construction until recently were factor models where forecasts are not dynamic but consist in estimating a drift (i.e., a constant trend) plus a variance-covariance matrix.

Since the late 1990s, the possibility of making dynamic forecasts of both volatility and expected returns has gained broad acceptance. During the same period, it became more widely recognized that returns are not normally distributed, evidence that had been reported by Mandelbrot in the 1960s. Higher moments of distributions are therefore important in portfolio management. We discuss the representation and estimation of nonnormal distributions in Chapter 14.

As observed above, the ability to correctly forecast expected returns does not imply, per se, that there are profit opportunities. In fact, we have to take into consideration the interplay between expected returns, higher moments, and transaction costs. As dynamic forecasts typically involve higher portfolio turnover, transaction costs might wipe out profits. As a general comment, portfolio management based on dynamic forecasts calls for a more sophisticated framework for optimization and risk management with respect to portfolio management based on static forecasts.

At the writing of this book, regression models form the core of the modeling efforts to predict future returns at many asset management firms. Regression models regress returns on a number of predictors. Stated otherwise, future returns are a function of the value of present and past predictors. Predictors include financial ratios such as earning-to-price ratio or book-to-price ratio and other fundamental quantities; predictors might also include behavioral variables such as market sentiment. A typical formula of a regressive model is the following:

$$r_{i,\,t+1} = \alpha_i + \sum_{j=1}^{s} \beta_{ij} f_{j,\,t} + \varepsilon_{i,\,t+1}$$

where

$$r_{i,\,t+1} = \frac{P_{i,\,t+1} - P_{i,\,t}}{P_{i,\,t}}$$

is the return at time $t + 1$ of the i-th asset and the $f_{j,t}$ are factors observed at time t. While regressions are generally linear, nonlinear models are also used.

In general, the forecasting horizon in asset management varies from a few days for actively managed or hedge funds to several weeks for more traditionally managed funds. Dynamic models typically have a short forecasting horizon as they capture a short-term dynamics. This contrasts with static models, such as the widely used multifactor models, which tend to capture long-term trends and ignore short-term dynamics.

The evolution of forecasting models over the last two decades has also changed the way forecasts are used. A basic utilization of forecasts is in stock picking/ranking systems, which have been widely implemented at asset management firms. The portfolio manager builds his or her portfolio combining the model ranking with his or her personal views and within the constraints established by the firm. A drawback in using such an approach is the difficulty in properly considering the structure of correlations and the role of higher moments.

Alternatively, forecasts can be fed to an optimizer that automatically computes the portfolio weights. But because an optimizer implements an optimal trade-off between returns and some measure of risk, the forecasting model must produce not only returns forecasts but also measures of risk. If risk is measured by portfolio variance or standard deviation, the forecasting model must be able to provide an estimated variance-covariance matrix.

Estimating the variance-covariance matrix is the most delicate of the estimation tasks. Here is why. The number of entries of a variance-covariance matrix grows with the square of the number of stocks. As a consequence, the number of entries in a variance-covariance matrix rapidly becomes very large. For example, the variance-covariance matrix of the stocks in the S&P 500 is a symmetric matrix that includes some 125,000 entries. If our universe were the Russell 5000, the variance-covariance matrix would include more than 12,000,000 entries. The problem with estimating matrices of this size is that estimates are very noisy because the number of sample data is close to the number of parameters to estimate. For example, if we use three years of data for estimation, we have, on average, less than three data points per estimated entry in the case of the S&P 500; in the case of the Russell 5000, the number of data points would be one fourth of the number of entries to estimate! Robust estimation methods are called for.

Note that if we use forecasting models we typically have (1) an equilibrium variance-covariance matrix that represents the covariances of the long-run relationships between variables plus (2) a short-term, time-dependent, variance-covariance matrix. If returns are not normally distributed, optimizers might require the matrix of higher moments.

A third utilization of forecasting models and optimizers is to construct model portfolios. In other words, the output of the optimizer is used to construct not an actual but a model portfolio. This model portfolio is used as input by portfolio managers.

Risk Management

Risk management has different meanings in different contexts. In particular, when optimization is used, risk management is intrinsic to the optimization process, itself a risk-return trade-off optimization. In this case, risk management is an integral part of the portfolio construction process.

However, in most cases, the process of constructing portfolios is entrusted to human portfolio managers who might use various inputs including, as noted above, ranking systems or model portfolios. In these cases, portfolios might not be optimal from the point of view of risk management and it is therefore necessary to ensure independent risk oversight. This oversight might take various forms. One form is similar to the type of risk oversight adopted by banks. The objective is to assess potential deviations from expectations. In order to perform this task, the risk manager receives as input the composition of portfolios and makes return projections using static forecasting models.

Another form of risk oversight, perhaps the most diffused in portfolio management, assesses portfolio exposures to specific risk factors. As portfolio management is often performed relative to a benchmark and risk is defined as underperformance relative to the benchmark, it is important to understand the sensitivity of portfolios to different risk factors. This type of risk oversight does not entail the forecasting of returns. The risk manager uses various statistical techniques to estimate how portfolios move in function of different risk factors. In most cases, linear regressions are used. A typical model will have the following form:

$$r_{i,t} = \alpha_i + \sum_{j=1}^{s} \beta_{ij} f_{j,t} + \varepsilon_{i,t}$$

where

$$r_{i,t} = \frac{P_{i,t} - P_{i,t-1}}{P_{i,t-1}}$$

is the return observed at time t of the i-th asset and the $f_{j,t}$ are factors observed at time t. Note that this model is fundamentally different from a regressive model with time lags as written in the previous section.

Asset-Liability Management

Asset-liability management (ALM) is typical of those asset management applications that require the optimization of portfolio returns at some fixed time horizon plus a stream of consumption throughout the entire life of the portfolio. ALM is important for managing portfolios of institutional investors such as pension funds or foundations. It is also important for wealth management, where the objective is to cover the investor's financial needs over an extended period.

ALM requires forecasting models able to capture the asset behavior at short-, medium-, and long-term time horizons. Models of the long-term behavior of assets exist but are clearly difficult to test. Important questions related to these long-term forecasting models include:

- Do asset prices periodically revert to one or many common trends in the long run?
- Can we assume that the common trends (if they exist) are deterministic trends such as exponentials or are common trends stochastic (i.e., random) processes?
- Can we recognize regime shifts over long periods of time?

APPENDIX: INVESTMENT MANAGEMENT PROCESS

Finance is classified into two broad areas: investment management (or portfolio management) and corporate finance. While financial econometrics has been used in corporate finance primarily to test various theories having to do with the corporate policy, the major use has been in investment management. Accordingly, our primary focus in this book is on applications to investment management.

The investment management process involves the following five steps:

Step 1: Setting investment objectives
Step 2: Establishing an investment policy
Step 3: Selecting an investment strategy
Step 4: Selecting the specific assets
Step 5: Measuring and evaluating investment performance

The overview of the investment management process described below should help understand how the econometric tools presented in this book are employed by portfolio managers, analysts, plan sponsors, and researchers. In addition, we introduce concepts and investment terms that are used in the investment management area throughout this book.

Step 1: Setting Investment Objectives

The first step in the investment management process, setting investment objectives, begins with a thorough analysis of the investment objectives of the entity whose funds are being managed. These entities can be classified as *individual investors* and *institutional investors*. Within each of these broad classifications, there is a wide range of investment objectives.

The objectives of an individual investor may be to accumulate funds to purchase a home or other major acquisitions, to have sufficient funds to be able to retire at a specified age, or to accumulate funds to pay for college tuition for children. An individual investor may engage the services of a financial advisor/consultant in establishing investment objectives.

In general, we can classify institutional investors into two broad categories—those that have to meet contractually specified liabilities and those that do not. We can classify those in the first category as institutions with "liability-driven objectives" and those in the second category as institutions with "nonliability-driven objectives." Many firms have a wide range of investment products that they offer investors, some of which are liability-driven and others that are nonliability-driven. Once the investment objective is understood, it will then be possible to (1) establish a benchmark by which to evaluate the performance of the investment manager and (2) evaluate alternative investment strategies to assess the potential for realizing the specified investment objective.

Step 2: Establishing an Investment Policy

The second step in the investment management process is establishing policy guidelines to satisfy the investment objectives. Setting policy begins with the asset allocation decision. That is, a decision must be made as to how the funds to be invested should be distributed among the major classes of assets.

Asset Classes

Throughout this book we refer to certain categories of investment products as an "asset class." From the perspective of a U.S. investor, the convention is to refer the following as *traditional asset classes*:

- U.S. common stocks
- Non-U.S. (or foreign) common stocks
- U.S. bonds
- Non-U.S. (or foreign) bonds
- Cash equivalents
- Real estate

Cash equivalents are defined as short-term debt obligations that have little price volatility. Common stocks and bonds are further divided into asset classes. For U.S. common stocks (also referred to as U.S. equities), the following are classified as asset classes:

- Large capitalization stocks
- Mid-capitalization stocks
- Small capitalization stocks
- Growth stocks
- Value stocks

By "capitalization," it is meant the market capitalization of the company's common stock. This is equal to the total market value of all of the common stock outstanding for that company. For example, suppose that a company has 100 million shares of common stock outstanding and each share has a market value of $10. Then the capitalization of this company is $1 billion (100 million shares times $10 per share). The market capitalization of a company is commonly referred to as the "market cap" or simply "cap."

For U.S. bonds, also referred to as fixed-income securities, the following are classified as asset classes:

- U.S. government bonds
- Investment-grade corporate bonds
- High-yield corporate bonds
- U.S. municipal bonds (i.e., state and local bonds)
- Mortgage-backed securities
- Asset-backed securities

Corporate bonds are classified by the type of issuer. The four general classifications are (1) public utilities, (2) transportations, (3) banks/finance, and (4) industrials. Finer breakdowns are often made to create more homogeneous groupings. For example, public utilities are subdivided into electric power companies, gas distribution companies, water companies, and communication companies. Transportations are divided further into airlines, railroads, and trucking companies. Banks/finance include both money center banks and regional banks, savings and loans, brokerage firms, insurance companies, and finance companies. Industrials are the catchall class and the most heterogeneous of the groupings with respect to investment characteristics. Industrials include manufacturers, mining companies, merchandising, retailers, energy companies, and service-related industries.

Corporate bonds expose investors to credit risk. There are private companies that rate bonds with respect to their likelihood to default. They are Moody's, Standard & Poor's, and Fitch. These firms perform credit analysis and issue their conclusions about the credit risk of a company in the form of a rating. The rating systems use similar symbols. In all three systems, the term "high grade" means low credit risk, or conversely, high probability of future payments. The highest-grade bonds are designated by Moody's by the letters Aaa, and by the other two rating agencies by AAA. The next highest grade is Aa or AA; for the third grade all rating agencies use A. The next three grades are Baa or BBB, Ba or BB, and B, respectively. There are also C grades. Standard & Poor's and Fitch uses plus or minus signs to provide a narrower credit quality breakdown within each class, and Moody's uses 1, 2, or 3 for the same purpose. Bonds rated triple A (AAA or Aaa) are said to be prime; double A (AA or Aa) are of high quality; single A issues are called upper medium grade, and triple B are medium grade. Lower-rated bonds are said to have speculative elements or to be distinctly speculative.

Bond issues that are assigned a rating in the top four categories are referred to as investment-grade bonds. Issues that carry a rating below the top four categories are referred to as noninvestment-grade bonds, or more popularly as high-yield bonds or junk bonds. Thus, the corporate bond market can be divided into two sectors: the investment-grade and noninvestment-grade markets.

Mortgage-backed and asset-backed securities are referred to as securitized products. Agency mortgage-backed securities carry little credit risk and represent the largest spread sector in the bond market. By spread sector it is meant sectors of the bond market that offer a spread to U.S. Treasuries. The key use of econometric tools in analyzing mortgage-backed securities is to forecast prepayments. In the case of nonagency and asset-backed securities, econometric tools are used to forecast defaults and recoveries in addition to prepayments.

For non-U.S. stocks and bonds, the following are classified as asset classes:

- Developed market foreign stocks
- Emerging market foreign stocks
- Developed market foreign bonds
- Emerging market foreign bonds

In addition to the traditional asset classes, there are asset classes commonly referred to as *alternative investments*. Two of the more popular ones are hedge funds and private equity.

Constraints

There are some institutional investors that make the asset allocation decision based purely on their understanding of the risk-return characteristics of the various asset classes and expected returns. The asset allocation will take into consideration any investment constraints or restrictions. Asset allocation models are commercially available for assisting those individuals responsible for making this decision.

In the development of an investment policy, the following factors must be considered: client constraints, regulatory constraints, and tax and accounting issues.

Examples of client-imposed constraints would be restrictions that specify the types of securities in which a manager may invest and concentration limits on how much or little may be invested in a particular asset class or in a particular issuer. Where the objective is to meet the performance of a particular market or customized benchmark, there may be a restriction as to the degree to which the manager may deviate from some key characteristics of the benchmark.

There are many types of regulatory constraints. These involve constraints on the asset classes that are permissible and concentration limits on investments. Moreover, in making the asset allocation decision, consideration must be given to any risk-based capital requirements.

Step 3: Selecting a Portfolio Strategy

Selecting a portfolio strategy that is consistent with the investment objectives and investment policy guidelines of the client or institution is the third step in the investment management process. Portfolio strategies can be classified as either active or passive.

An *active portfolio strategy* uses available information and forecasting techniques to seek a better performance than a portfolio that is simply diversified broadly. Essential to all active strategies are expectations about the factors that have been found to influence the performance of an asset class. For example, with active common stock strategies this may include forecasts of future earnings, dividends, or price-earnings ratios. With bond portfolios that are actively managed, expectations may involve forecasts of future interest rates and sector spreads. Active portfolio strategies involving foreign securities may require forecasts of local interest rates and exchange rates.

A *passive portfolio strategy* involves minimal expectational input, and instead relies on diversification to match the performance of some market index. In effect, a passive strategy assumes that the marketplace will reflect all available information in the price paid for securities. Between these extremes of active and passive strategies, several strategies have sprung up that have elements of both. For example, the core of a portfolio may be passively managed with the balance actively managed.

In the bond area, several strategies classified as *structured portfolio strategies* have been commonly used. A structured portfolio strategy is one in which a portfolio is designed to achieve the performance of some predetermined liabilities that must be paid out. These strategies are frequently used when trying to match the funds received from an investment portfolio to the future liabilities that must be paid.

Given the choice among active and passive management, which should be selected? The answer depends on (1) the client's or money manager's view of how "price-efficient" the market is; (2) the client's risk tolerance; and (3) the nature of the client's liabilities. By marketplace price efficiency we mean how difficult it would be to earn a greater return than passive management after adjusting for the risk associated with a strategy and the transaction costs associated with implementing that strategy. Market efficiency is explained in Chapter 5. Econometric tools are used to test theories about market efficiency.

Step 4: Selecting the Specific Assets

Once a portfolio strategy is selected, the next step is to select the specific assets to be included in the portfolio. It is in this phase of the investment management process that the investor attempts to construct an *efficient portfolio*. An efficient portfolio is one that provides the greatest expected return for a given level of risk or, equivalently, the lowest risk for a given expected return.

Inputs Required

To construct an efficient portfolio, the investor must be able to quantify risk and provide the necessary inputs. As will be explained in the next chapter, there are three key inputs that are needed: future expected return (or simply expected return), variance of asset returns, and correlation (or covariance) of asset returns. Many of the financial econometric tools described in this book are intended to provide the investor with information with which to estimate these three inputs.

There are a wide range of approaches to obtain the expected return of assets. Investors can employ various econometric tools discussed in this book to derive the future expected return of an asset.

Approaches to Portfolio Construction

Based on the expected return for a portfolio (which depends on the expected returns of all the asset returns in the portfolio) and some risk measure of the portfolio's return (which depends on the covariance of returns between all pairs of assets in the portfolio) an efficient portfolio can be constructed. This approach also allows for the inclusion of constraints such as lower and upper bounds on particular assets or assets in particular industries or sectors. The end result of the analysis is a set of efficient portfolios—alternative portfolios from which the investor can select—that offer the maximum expected portfolio return for a given level of portfolio risk.

There are variations on this approach to portfolio construction. The analysis can be employed by estimating risk factors that historically have explained the variance of asset returns. The basic principle is that the value of an asset is driven by a number of systematic factors (or, equivalently, risk exposures) plus a component unique to a particular company or industry. A set of efficient portfolios can be identified based on the risk factors and the sensitivity of assets to these risk factors. This approach is referred to the "multifactor risk approach" to portfolio construction.

Step 5: Measuring and Evaluating Performance

The measurement and evaluation of investment performance is the last step in the investment management process. This step involves measuring the performance of the portfolio and then evaluating that performance relative to some benchmark. Econometric tools are used to construct models that can be employed to evaluate the performance of managers. We discuss this in Chapter 5.

**CONCEPTS EXPLAINED IN THIS CHAPTER
(IN ORDER OF PRESENTATION)**

Data generating process
White noise
High frequency data
Models
    Mathematical model
    Model estimation
    Model selection
    Model testing
    Static models
    Dynamic models
    Models as probes that recover IID sequences
    Linear and nonlinear models
    Model risk

Model robustness
Exact and approximate models
Model performance
Statistical learning
Stationary time series
Nonstationary time series
Differencing
Portfolio construction and optimizaiton
Risk management
Asset-liability management

CHAPTER 2

Review of Probability and Statistics

Financial econometrics draws on the fields of probability theory and statistics. Probability is the standard mathematical representation of uncertainty in finance. Probabilistic models have to be estimated from empirical data and this is where the concepts and methods of statistics come in. In this chapter, we provide a review of concepts of both probability and statistics.

CONCEPTS OF PROBABILITY

Because we cannot build purely deterministic models of the economy, we need a mathematical representation of uncertainty. *Probability theory* is the mathematical description of uncertainty that presently enjoys the broadest diffusion. It is the paradigm of choice for mainstream finance theory. But it is by no means the only way to describe uncertainty. Other mathematical paradigms for uncertainty include, for example, fuzzy measures.[1]

Though probability as a mathematical axiomatic theory is well known, its interpretation is still the subject of debate. There are three basic interpretations of probability:

- Probability as "intensity of belief" as suggested by John Maynard Keynes.[2]

---

[1] Lotfi A. Zadeh, "Fuzzy Sets," *Information and Control* 8 (1965), pp. 338–353.
[2] John Maynard Keynes, *Treatise on Probability* (London: McMillan, 1921).

- Probability as "relative frequency" as formulated by Richard von Mises.[3]
- Probability as an axiomatic system as formulated by Andrei N. Kolmogorov.[4]

The idea of probability as intensity of belief was introduced by John Maynard Keynes in his *Treatise on Probability*. In science, as in our daily lives, we have beliefs that we cannot strictly prove but to which we attribute various degrees of likelihood. We judge not only the likelihood of individual events but also the plausibility of explanations. If we espouse probability as intensity of belief, probability theory is then a set of rules for making consistent probability statements. The obvious difficulty here is that one can judge only the consistency of probability reasoning, not its truth. Bayesian probability theory (which we will discuss later in the chapter) is based on the interpretation of probability as intensity of belief.

Probability as relative frequency is the standard interpretation of probability in the physical sciences. Introduced by Richard Von Mises in 1928, probability as relative frequency was subsequently extended by Hans Reichenbach.[5] Essentially, it equates probability statements with statements about the frequency of events in large samples; an unlikely event is an event that occurs only a small number of times. The difficulty with this interpretation is that relative frequencies are themselves uncertain. If we accept a probability interpretation of reality, there is no way to leap to certainty. In practice, in the physical sciences we usually deal with very large numbers—so large that nobody expects probabilities to deviate from their relative frequency. Nevertheless, the conceptual difficulty exists. As the present state of affairs might be a very unlikely one, probability statements can never be proved empirically.

The two interpretations of probability—as intensity of belief and as relative frequency—are therefore complementary. We make probability statements such as statements of relative frequency that are, ultimately, based on an *a priori* evaluation of probability insofar as we rule out, in practice, highly unlikely events. This is evident in most procedures of statistical estimation. A statistical estimate is a rule to choose the probability scheme in which one has the greatest faith. In performing statistical estimation, one chooses the probabilistic model that yields the

---

[3] Richard von Mises, *Wahrscheinlichkeitsrechnung, Statistik unt Wahrheit* (Vienna: Verlag von Julius Spring, 1928). English edition published in 1939, *Probability, Statistics and Truth*.

[4] Andrei N. Kolmogorov, *Grundbegriffe der Wahrscheinlichkeitsrechnung* (Berlin: Springer, 1933). English edition published in 1950, *Foundations of the Theory of Probability*.

[5] At the time, both were German professors working in Constantinople.

highest probability on the observed sample. This is strictly evident in maximum likelihood estimates but it is implicit in every statistical estimate. Bayesian statistics allow one to complement such estimates with additional *a priori* probabilistic judgment.

The axiomatic theory of probability avoids the above problems by interpreting probability as an abstract mathematical quantity. Developed primarily by the Russian mathematician Andrei Kolmogorov, the axiomatic theory of probability eliminated the logical ambiguities that had plagued probabilistic reasoning prior to his work. The application of the axiomatic theory is, however, a matter of interpretation.

In economic and finance theory, probability might have two different meanings: (1) as a descriptive concept and (2) as a determinant of the agent decision-making process. As a descriptive concept, probability is used in the sense of relative frequency, similar to its use in the physical sciences: the probability of an event is assumed to be approximately equal to the relative frequency of its occurrence in a large number of experiments. There is one difficulty with this interpretation, which is peculiar to economics: empirical data (i.e., financial and economic time series) have only one realization. Every estimate is made on a single time-evolving series. If stationarity (or a well-defined time process) is not assumed, performing statistical estimation is impossible.[6]

Probability in a Nutshell

In making probability statements we must distinguish between outcomes and events. *Outcomes* are the possible results of an experiment or an observation, such as the price of a security at a given moment. However, probability statements are not made on outcomes but on *events*, which are sets of possible outcomes. Consider, for example, the probability that the price of a security be in a given range, say from \$10 to \$12 in a given period.

In a discrete probability model (i.e., a model based on a finite or at most a countable number of individual events), the distinction between outcomes and events is not essential as the probability of an event is the sum of the probabilities of its outcomes. If, as happens in practice, prices can vary by only one-hundredth of a dollar, there are only a countable number of possible prices and the probability of each event will be the sum of the individual probabilities of each admissible price.

However, the distinction between outcomes and events is essential when dealing with continuous probability models. In a continuous

---

[6] Actually the stronger requirement of ergodicity is needed. An ergodic process is a process where we can interchange time averages with expectations. However, we cannot assume that financial processes themselves are ergodic; for the most part we assume that the residuals in the fitted financial time series model are ergodic.

probability model, the probability of each individual outcome is zero though the probability of an event might be a finite number. For example, if we represent prices as continuous functions, the probability that a price assumes any particular real number is strictly zero, though the probability that prices fall in a given interval might be other than zero.

Probability theory is a set of rules for inferring the probability of an event from the probability of other events. The basic rules are surprisingly simple. The entire theory is based on a few simple assumptions. First, the universe of possible outcomes or measurements must be fixed. This is a conceptually important point. If we are dealing with the prices of an asset, the universe is all possible prices; if we are dealing with n assets, the universe is the set of all possible n-tuples of prices. If we want to link n asset prices with k economic quantities, the universe is all possible ($n + k$)-tuples made up of asset prices and values of economic quantities.

Second, as our objective is to interpret probability as relative frequencies (i.e., percentages), the scale of probability is set to the interval [0,1]. The maximum possible probability is one, which is the probability that any of the possible outcomes occurs. The probability that none of the outcomes occurs is 0. In continuous probability models, the converse is not true as there are nonempty sets of measure zero.

Third, and last, the probability of the union of countably many disjoint events is the sum of the probabilities of individual events.

All statements of probability theory are logical consequences of these basic rules. The simplicity of the logical structure of probability theory might be deceptive. In fact, the practical difficulty of probability theory consists in the description of events. For instance, derivative contracts link in possibly complex ways the events of the underlying with the events of the derivative contract. Though the probabilistic "dynamics" of the underlying phenomena can be simple, expressing the links between all possible contingencies renders the subject mathematically complex.

Probability theory is based on the possibility of assigning a precise uncertainty index to each event. This is a stringent requirement that might be too strong in many instances. In a number of cases we are simply uncertain without being able to quantify uncertainty. It might also happen that we can quantify uncertainty for some but not all events. There are representations of uncertainty that drop the strict requirement of a precise uncertainty index assigned to each event. Examples include fuzzy measures and the Dempster-Schafer theory of uncertainty.[7] The

---

[7] See G. Schafer, *A Mathematical Theory of Evidence* (Princeton, NJ: Princeton University Press, 1976); Judea Pearl, *Probabilistic Reasoning in Intelligent Systems: Networks of Plausible Beliefs* (San Mateo, CA: Morgan Kaufmann, 1988); and, Zadeh, "Fuzzy Sets."

latter representations of uncertainty have been widely used in Artificial Intelligence and engineering applications, but their use in economics and finance has so far been limited.

Let's now examine probability as the key representation of uncertainty, starting with a more formal account of probability theory.

Outcomes and Events

The axiomatic theory of probability is based on three fundamental concepts: (1) outcomes, (2) events, and (3) measure. The outcomes are the set of all possible results of an experiment or an observation. The set of all possible outcomes is often written as the set Ω. For instance, in the dice game a possible outcome is a pair of numbers, one for each face, such as 6 + 6 or 3 + 2. The space Ω is the set of all 36 possible outcomes.

Events are sets of outcomes. Continuing with the example of the dice game, a possible event is the set of all outcomes such that the sum of the numbers is 10. Probabilities are defined on events. To render definitions consistent, events must be a class $\Im$ of subsets of Ω with the following properties:

- *Property 1.* $\Im$ is not empty, $\Omega \in \Im$

- *Property 2.* If $A \in \Im$ then $A^C \in \Im$; A^C is the complement of A with respect to Ω, made up of all those elements of Ω that do not belong to A

- *Property 3.* If $A_i \in \Im$ for $i = 1,2,\ldots$ then $\bigcup_{i=1}^{\infty} A_i \in \Im$

Every such class is called a σ-algebra (sometimes also called, sigma-filed, or a tribe). Any class for which Property 3 is valid only for a finite number of sets is called an *algebra*.

Given a set Ω and a σ-algebra $\mathfrak{G}$ of subsets of Ω, any set $A \in \mathfrak{G}$ is said to be *measurable* with respect to $\mathfrak{G}$. The pair $(\Omega, \mathfrak{G})$ is said to be a *measurable space*. Consider a class $\mathfrak{G}$ of subsets of Ω and consider the smallest σ-algebra that contains $\mathfrak{G}$, defined as the intersection of all the σ-*algebras* that contain $\mathfrak{G}$. That σ-algebra is denoted by $\sigma\{\mathfrak{G}\}$ and is said to be the σ-algebra generated by $\mathfrak{G}$.

A particularly important space in probability is the *Euclidean space*. Consider first the real axis R (i.e., the Euclidean space R^1 in one dimension). Consider the collection formed by all intervals open to the left and closed to the right, for example, $(a,b]$. The σ-algebra generated by this set is called the 1-dimensional Borel σ-algebra and is denoted by $\mathfrak{B}$. The sets that belong to $\mathfrak{B}$ are called *Borel sets*.

Now consider the n-dimensional Euclidean space R^n, formed by n-tuples of real numbers. Consider the collection of all generalized rectangles open to the left and closed to the right, for example, $((a_1, b_1] \times \ldots \times (a_n, b_n])$. The σ-algebra generated by this collection is called the n-dimensional Borel σ-algebra and is denoted by $\mathfrak{B}^n$. The sets that belong to $\mathfrak{B}^n$ are called n-dimensional Borel sets.

The above construction is not the only possible one. The $\mathfrak{B}^n$, for any value of n, can also be generated by open or closed sets. As we will see later in this chapter, $\mathfrak{B}^n$ is fundamental to defining random variables and random vectors. It defines a class of subsets of the Euclidean space on which it is reasonable to impose a probability structure: the class of every subset would be too big while the class of, say, generalized rectangles would be too small. The $\mathfrak{B}^n$ is a sufficiently rich class.

Probability

Intuitively speaking, probability is a set function that associates to every event a number between 0 and 1. Probability is formally defined by a triple $(\Omega, \mathfrak{S}, P)$ called a *probability space*, where Ω is the set of all possible outcomes, $\mathfrak{S}$ the event σ-algebra or algebra, and P a probability measure.

A probability measure P is a set function from $\mathfrak{S}$ to R (the set of real numbers) that satisfies three conditions:

■ *Condition 1.* $0 \leq P(A)$, for all $A \in \mathfrak{S}$

■ *Condition 2.* $P(\Omega) = 1$

■ *Condition 3.* $P(\cup A_i) = \Sigma P(A_i)$ for every finite or countable collection of disjoint events $\{A_i\}$ such that $A_i \in \mathfrak{S}$

$\mathfrak{S}$ does not have to be a σ-algebra but can be an algebra. Here and in the rest of this book $C = A \cup B$ is the union of two sets that is the set formed by all elements that belong to A or B nonexclusively, while $C = A \cap B$ is the intersection of two sets, that is, the set formed by all elements that belong to A and B. The definition of a probability space can be limited to algebras of events. However it is possible to demonstrate that a probability defined over an algebra of events $\aleph$ can be extended in a unique way to the σ-algebra generated by $\aleph$.

Two events are said to be independent if

$$P(A \cap B) = P(A)P(B)$$

The (conditional) probability of event A given event B with $P(B) > 0$, written as $P(A|B)$, is defined as follows:

$$P(A|B) = \frac{P(A \cap B)}{P(B)}$$

It is possible to deduct from simple properties of set theory and from the disjoint additivity of probability that

$$P(A \cup B) = P(A) + P(B) - P(A \cap B) \leq P(A) + P(B)$$

$$P(A) = 1 - P(A^C)$$

Bayes theorem[8] is a rule that links conditional probabilities. It can be stated in the following way:

$$P(A|B) = \frac{P(A \cap B)}{P(B)} = \frac{P(A \cap B)P(A)}{P(B)P(A)} = P(B|A)\frac{P(A)}{P(B)}$$

Bayes theorem allows one to recover the probability of the event A given B from the probability of the individual events A, B, and the probability of B given A assuming that $P(A) > 0$, $P(B) > 0$.

Discrete probabilities are a special instance of probabilities. Defined over a finite or countable set of outcomes, discrete probabilities are nonzero over each outcome. The probability of an event is the sum of the probabilities of its outcomes. In the finite case, discrete probabilities are the usual combinatorial probabilities.

Random Variables

Probability is a set function defined over a space of events; *random variables* transfer probability from the original space Ω into the space of real numbers. Given a probability space $(\Omega, \mathfrak{I}, P)$, a random variable X is a function $X(\omega)$ defined over the set Ω that takes values in the set R of real numbers such that

$$(\omega: X(\omega) \leq x) \in \mathfrak{I}$$

for every real number x. In other words, the inverse image of any interval $(-\infty, x]$ is an event. It can be demonstrated that the inverse image of any Borel set is also an event.

---

[8] In this formulation, Bayes theorem is a simple theorem of elementary probability. Bayes theorem can be given a different interpretation as we will see later in this chapter in the section on Bayesian statistics.

A real-valued set function defined over Ω is said to be measurable with respect to a σ-algebra $\mathfrak{I}$ if the inverse image of any Borel set belongs to $\mathfrak{I}$. Random variables are real-valued measurable functions. A random variable that is measurable with respect to a σ-algebra cannot discriminate between events that are not in that σ-algebra. This is the primary reason why the abstract and rather difficult concept of measurability is important in probability theory. By restricting the set of events that can be identified by a random variable, measurability defines the "coarse graining" of information relative to that variable. A random variable X is said to generate $\mathfrak{G}$ if $\mathfrak{G}$ is the smallest σ-algebra in which it is measurable.

Distributions and Distribution Functions

Given a probability space $(\Omega, \mathfrak{I}, P)$ and a random variable X, consider a set $A \in \mathfrak{B}^1$. Recall that a random variable is a real-valued measurable function defined over the set of outcomes. Therefore, the inverse image of A, $X^{-1}(A)$ belongs to $\mathfrak{I}$ and has a well-defined probability $P(X^{-1}(A))$.

The measure P thus induces another measure on the real axis called *distribution* or *distribution law* of the random variable X given by: $\mu_X(A) = P(X^{-1}(A))$. It is easy to see that this measure is a probability measure on the Borel sets. A random variable therefore transfers the probability originally defined over the space Ω to the set of real numbers.

The function F defined by: $F(x) = P(X \leq x)$ for $x \in R$ is the *cumulative distribution function (c.d.f.)*, or simply *distribution function (d.f.)*, of the random variable X. Suppose that there is a function f such that

$$F(x) = \int_{-\infty}^{x} f(y)dy$$

or $F'(x) = f(x)$, then the function f is called the *probability density function* (p.d.f.), or simply density function, of the random variable X.

Random Vectors

After considering a single random variable, the next step is to consider not only one but a set of random variables referred to as *random vectors*. Random vectors are formed by n-tuples of random variables. Consider a probability space $(\Omega, \mathfrak{I}, P)$. A random variable is a measurable function from Ω to R^1; a random vector is a measurable function from Ω to R^n.

We can therefore write a random vector $\mathbf{X}$ as a vector-valued function

$$X(\omega) = [X_1(\omega), \ldots, X_n(\omega)]$$

Measurability is defined with respect to the Borel σ-algebra $\mathfrak{B}^n$. It can be demonstrated that the function X is measurable $\mathfrak{I}$ if and only if each component function $X_i(\omega)$ is measurable $\mathfrak{I}$.

Conceptually, the key issue is to define joint probabilities (i.e., the probabilities that the n variables are in a given set). For example, consider the joint probability that the inflation rate is in a given interval *and* the economic growth rate in another given interval.

Consider the Borel σ-algebra $\mathfrak{B}^n$ on the real n-dimensional space R^n. It can be demonstrated that a random vector formed by n random variables X_i, $i = 1,2,...,n$ induces a probability measure over $\mathfrak{B}^n$. In fact, the inverse image of every set of the σ-algebra $\mathfrak{B}^n$ belongs to the σ-algebra $\mathfrak{I}$: $(\omega \in \Omega \ (X_1(\omega),X_2(\omega),...,X_n(\omega)) \in H; H \in \mathfrak{B}^n) \in \mathfrak{I}$ (i.e.,). It is therefore possible to induce over every set H that belongs to $\mathfrak{B}^n$ a probability measure, which is the joint probability of the n random variables X_i. The function

$$F(x_1, ..., x_n) = P(X_1 \le x_1, ..., X_n \le x_n)$$

where $x_i \in R$ is called the n-*dimensional cumulative distribution function* or simply n-*dimensional distribution function* (*c.d.f., d.f.*). Suppose there exists a function $f(x_1,...,x_n)$ for which the following relationship holds:

$$F(x_1, ..., x_n) = \int\limits_{-\infty}^{x_1} ... \int\limits_{-\infty}^{x_n} f(u_1, u_{j-1}, y, u_{j+1}, ..., u_n) du_1 ... du_n$$

The function $f(x_1,...,x_n)$ is called the n-*dimensional probability density function* (*p.d.f.*) of the random vector X. Given a n-dimensional probability density function $f(x_1,...,x_n)$, if we integrate with respect to all variables except the j-th variable, we obtain the *marginal density* of that variable:

$$f_{X_j}(y) = \int\limits_{-\infty}^{\infty} ... \int\limits_{-\infty}^{\infty} f(u_1, ..., u_n) du_1 \cdot du_{j-1} du_{j+1} \cdot du_n$$

Given a n-dimensional d.f., we define the *marginal distribution function* with respect to the j-th variable, $F_{X_j}(y) = P(X_j \le y)$ as follows:

$$F_{x_j}(y) = \lim_{\substack{x_i \to \infty \\ i \ne j}} F(x_1, ..., x_{j-1}, y, x_{j+1}, ..., x_n)$$

If the distribution admits a density (short for "probability density"), we can also write

$$F_{X_j}(y) = \int_{-\infty}^{y} f_{X_j}(u)\,du$$

These definitions can be extended to any number of variables. Given a n-dimensional p.d.f., if we integrate with respect to k variables $(x_{i_1}, ..., x_{i_k})$ over R^k, we obtain the marginal density functions with respect to the remaining variables. Marginal distribution functions with respect to any subset of variables can be defined taking the infinite limit with respect to all other variables.

If the d.f. $F_X(u)$ has a density $f_X(u) = F'_X(u)$, then we can define the expectation of X (also called the mean of X) as follows:

$$E[X] = \int_{-\infty}^{\infty} u f(u)\,du$$

where the last integral is intended in the sense of Riemann. More in general, given a measurable function g the following relationship holds:

$$E[g(X)] = \int_{-\infty}^{\infty} g(u) f(u)\,du$$

This latter expression of expectation of $g(x)$ is the most widely used in practice.

In general, however, knowledge of the distributions and of distribution functions of each random variable of a random vector $X = (X_1, ..., X_n)$ is not sufficient to determine the joint probability distribution function.

Two random variables X, Y are said to be independent if

$$P(X \in A, Y \in B) = P(X \in A)P(Y \in B)$$

for all $A \in \mathfrak{B}$, $B \in \mathfrak{B}$. This definition generalizes in obvious ways to any number of variables and therefore to the components of a random vector. It can be shown that if the components of a random vector are independent, the joint probability distribution is the product of the marginal distributions. Therefore, if the variables $(X_1, ..., X_n)$ are all mutually independent, we can write the joint d.f. as a product of marginal distribution functions:

$$F(x_1, ..., x_n) = \prod_{j=1}^{n} F_{X_j}(x_j)$$

It can also be demonstrated that if a d.f. admits a joint p.d.f., the joint p.d.f. factorizes as follows:

$$f(x_1, ..., x_n) = \prod_{j=1}^{n} f_{X_j}(x_j)$$

Given the marginal p.d.f.s the joint d.f. can be recovered as follows:

$$F(x_1, ..., x_n) = \int_{-\infty}^{x_1} ... \int_{-\infty}^{x_n} f(u_1, ..., u_n) du_1 ... du_n$$

$$= \int_{-\infty}^{x_1} ... \int_{-\infty}^{x_n} \left[\prod_{j=1}^{n} f_{X_j}(u_j) \right] du_1 ... du_n$$

$$= \prod_{j=1}^{n} \int_{-\infty}^{x_j} f_{X_j}(u_j) du_j$$

$$= \prod_{j=1}^{n} F_{X_j}(x_j)$$

Stochastic Processes

Given a probability space $(\Omega, \mathfrak{F}, P)$ a stochastic process is a parameterized collection of random variables $\{X_t\}$, $t \in [0,T]$ that are measurable with respect to $\mathfrak{F}$. (This is the naive definition, the exact definition is given below.) The parameter t is often interpreted as time. The interval in which a stochastic process is defined might extend to infinity in both directions.

When it is necessary to emphasize the dependence of the random variable on both time t and the element ω, a stochastic process is explicitly written as a function of two variables: $X = X(t,\omega)$. Given ω, the function $X = X_t(\omega)$ is a function of time that is referred to as a *path* of the stochastic process.

The variable X might be a single random variable or a multidimensional random vector. We define an n-dimensional stochastic process as a function $X = X(t,\omega)$ from the product space $[0,T] \times \Omega$ into the n-dimensional real space R^n. Because to each ω corresponds a time path of the process—in general formed by a set of functions $X = X_t(\omega)$—it is possible to identify the space Ω with a subset of the real functions defined over an interval $[0,T]$.

Let's now discuss how to represent a stochastic process $X = X(t,\omega)$ and the conditions of identity of two stochastic processes. As a stochastic process is a function of two variables, we can define equality as pointwise identity for each couple (t,ω). However, as processes are defined over probability spaces, pointwise identity is seldom used. It is more fruitful to define equality modulo sets of measure zero or equality with respect to probability distributions. In general, two random variables X,Y will be considered equal if the equality $X(\omega) = Y(\omega)$ holds for every ω with the exception of a set of probability zero. In this case, it is said that the equality holds almost everywhere (denoted *a.e.*) or almost surely, a.s.

A rather general (but not complete) representation is given by the finite dimensional probability distributions. Given any set of indices $t_1,...,t_m$, consider the distributions

$$\mu_{t_1, ..., t_m}(H) = P[(X_{t_1}, ..., X_{t_m}) \in H, H \in \mathfrak{B}^n]$$

These probability measures are, for any choice of the t_i, the finite-dimensional joint probabilities of the process. They determine many, but not all, properties of a stochastic process. For example, the finite dimensional distributions of a Brownian motion do not determine whether or not the process paths are continuous.

Probabilistic Representation of Financial Markets

We are now in the position to summarize the probabilistic representation of financial markets. From a financial point of view, an *asset* is a contract which gives the right to receive a distribution of future cash flows. In the case of a common stock, the stream of cash flows will be uncertain. It includes the common stock dividends and the proceeds of the eventual liquidation of the firm. A *debt instrument* is a contract that gives its owner the right to receive periodic interest payments and the repayment of the principal by the maturity date. Except in the case of debt instruments of governments whose risk of default is perceived to be extremely low, payments are uncertain as the issuing entity might default.

Suppose that all payments are made at the trading dates and that no transactions take place between trading dates. Let's assume that all assets are traded (i.e., exchanged on the market) at either discrete fixed dates, variable dates, or continuously. At each trading date there is a market price for each asset. Each asset is therefore modeled with two time series, a series of market prices and a series of cash flows. As both series are subject to uncertainty, cash flows and prices are time-dependent random variables (i.e., they are stochastic processes). The time dependence of random variables in this probabilistic setting is a delicate question and will be examined shortly.

Following Kenneth Arrow[9] and using a framework now standard, the economy and the financial markets in a situation of uncertainty are described with the following basic concepts:

- It is assumed that the economy is in one of the states of a probability space $(\Omega, \Im, P)$.
- Every security is described by two stochastic processes formed by two time-dependent random variables $S_t(\omega)$ and $d_t(\omega)$ representing prices and cash flows of the asset.

This representation is completely general and is not linked to the assumption that the space of states is finite.

Conditional Probability and Conditional Expectation

Conditional probabilities and conditional averages are fundamental in the stochastic description of financial markets. For instance, one is generally interested in the probability distribution of the price of an asset at some date given its price at an earlier date. The widely used regression models are an example of conditional expectation models.

The *conditional probability* of event A given event B was defined earlier as

$$P(A|B) = \frac{P(A \cap B)}{P(B)}$$

This simple definition cannot be used in the context of continuous random variables because the conditioning event (i.e., one variable assuming a given value) has probability zero. To avoid this problem, we condition on σ-algebras and not on single zero-probability events. In general, as each instant is characterized by a σ-algebra $\Im_t$, the conditioning elements are the $\Im_t$.

It is possible to demonstrate that given two random variables X and Y with joint density $f(x,y)$, the conditional density of X given Y is

[9] Kenneth Arrow, "The Role of Securities in the Optimal Allocation of Risk Bearing," *Review of Economic Studies* 31 (April 1964), pp. 91–96.

$$f(x|y) = \frac{f(x, y)}{f_Y(y)}$$

where the marginal density, defined as

$$f_Y(y) = \int\limits_{-\infty}^{\infty} f(x, y)dx$$

is assumed to be strictly positive.

The conditional expectation $E[Y|X = x]$ is the expectation of the variable $(Y|X = x)$. It is another random variable defined on Ω:

$$E[Y|X = x] = \int\limits_{-\infty}^{+\infty} yf(y|x)dy$$

The *law of iterated expectations* states that

$$E[E[Y|X]] = E[Y]$$

In fact, we can write

$$E[Y] = \int\limits_{R^2} yf(x, y)dxdy = \int\limits_{-\infty}^{+\infty}\left(\int\limits_{-\infty}^{+\infty} y\frac{f(x, y)}{f_X(x)}dy\right)f_X(x)dx$$

$$= \int\limits_{-\infty}^{+\infty} E[Y|X = x]f_X(x)dx = E[E[Y|X]]$$

We can also prove that

$$E[XY] = E[XE[Y|X]]$$

In fact, we can write

$$E[XY] = \int\limits_{R^2} xyf(x, y)dxdy = \int\limits_{-\infty}^{+\infty} x\left(\int\limits_{-\infty}^{+\infty} y\frac{f(x, y)}{f_X(x)}dy\right)f_X(x)dx$$

$$= \int\limits_{-\infty}^{+\infty} xE[Y|X = x]f_X(x)dx = E[XE[Y|X]]$$

In the discrete case, the conditional expectation is a random variable that takes a constant value over the sets of the finite partition associated (see Appendix A for a definition of Information structures). Its value for each element of Ω is defined by the classical concept of conditional probability. Conditional expectation is simply the average over a partition assuming the classical conditional probabilities.

An important econometric concept related to conditional expectations is that of a *martingale*. Given a probability space $(\Omega, \Im, P)$ and a filitration I_t desribing the information flow (see Appendix B for an explanation of the concept of filtration) a sequence of random variables X_i with $E|X_i| < \infty$, is called a martingale with respect to the filtration I_i if the following condition holds:

$$E[X_{i+1} | I_i] = X_i$$

where I_t is the information set known at time t. The information set is usually embodied by the value of all variables known at time t. A martingale translates the idea of a "fair game" as the expected return of a fair game at the next trial should be zero given the current information, as the martingale property is equivalent to

$$E(X_{i+1} - X_i | I_i) = 0$$

Describing a Probability Distribution Function: Statistical Moments and Quantiles[10]

In describing a probability distribution function, it is common to summarize it by using various measures. The five most commonly used measures are: location, dispersion, asymmetry, concentration in tails, and quantiles. We will now describe each of these measures.

Location

The first way to describe a probability distribution function is by some measure of *central value* or *location*. The various measures that can be used are the mean or average value, the median, or the mode. The relationship among these three measures of location depends on the skewness of a probability distribution function that we will describe later. The most commonly used measure of location is the *mean* and is denoted by μ or EX or $E(X)$.

---

[10] The discussion in this section is adapted from Chapter 4 in Svetlozar T. Rachev, Christian Menn, and Frank J. Fabozzi, *Fat-Tailed and Skewed Asset Return Distributions: Implications for Risk Management, Portfolio Selection, and Option Pricing* (Hoboken, NJ: John Wiley & Sons, 2005).

Dispersion

Another measure that can help us to describe a probability distribution function is the dispersion or how spread out the values of the random variable can realize. Various measures of dispersion are range, variance, and mean absolute deviation. The most commonly used measure is the *variance*. The variance measures the dispersion of the values that the random variable can realize relative to the mean. It is the average of the squared deviations from the mean. The variance is in squared units. Taking the square root of the variance one obtains the *standard deviation*. In contrast to the variance, the *mean absolute deviation* takes the average of the absolute deviations from the mean.[11] In practice, the variance is used and is denoted by σ^2 or VX or $V(X)$ and the standard deviation by σ or $\sqrt{VX}$.

Asymmetry

A probability distribution may be symmetric or asymmetric around its mean. A popular measure for the asymmetry of a distribution is called its *skewness*. A negative skewness measure indicates that the distribution is skewed to the left; that is, compared to the right tail, the left tail is elongated. A positive skewness measure indicates that the distribution is skewed to the right; that is, compared to the left tail, the right tail is elongated.

Concentration in Tails

Additional information about a probability distribution function is provided by measuring the concentration (mass) of potential outcomes in its tails. The tails of a probability distribution function contain the extreme values. In financial applications, it is these tails that provide information about the potential for a financial fiasco or financial ruin. As we will see, the fatness of the tails of the distribution is related to the peakedness of the distribution around its mean or center. The joint measure of peakedness and tail fatness is called *kurtosis*.

Statistical Moments

In the parlance of the statistician, the four measures described above are called *statistical moments* or simply *moments*. The mean is the *first moment* and is also referred to as the *expected value*. The variance is the *second central moment*, skewness is a rescaled *third central moment*, and kurtosis is a rescaled *fourth central moment*. The general mathematical formula for the calculation of the four parameters is shown in Exhibit 2.1.

---

[11] It is also common to define the mean absolute deviation from the median because it minimizes the average absolute distance from an arbitrary point x.

EXHIBIT 2.1   General Formula for Parameters

Parameter	Discrete Probability Distribution	Continuous Probability Distribution
Mean	$EX = \sum_i x_i P(X = x_i)$	$EX = \int_{-\infty}^{\infty} x \cdot f(x)dx$
Variance	$VX = \sum_i (x_i - EX)^2 P(X = x_i)$	$VX = \int_{-\infty}^{\infty} (x - EX)^2 f(x)dx$
Skewness	$\varsigma = \dfrac{E(X - EX)^3}{(VX)^{\frac{3}{2}}}$	$\varsigma = \dfrac{E(X - EX)^3}{(VX)^{\frac{3}{2}}}$
Kurtosis	$\kappa = \dfrac{E(X - EX)^4}{(VX)^2}$	$\kappa = \dfrac{E(X - EX)^4}{(VX)^2}$

Exhibit 2.2 shows the mean, variance, and skewness for several probability distribution functions that have been used in financial modeling and risk management.

The definition of skewness and kurtosis is not as unified as for the mean and the variance. The skewness measure reported in Exhibit 2.2 is the so-called *Fisher's skewness*. Another possible way to define the measure is *Pearson's skewness,* which equals the square of Fisher's skewness. The same holds true for the kurtosis, where we have reported *Pearson's kurtosis. Fishers' kurtosis* (sometimes denoted as excess kurtosis) can be obtained by subtracting three from Pearson's kurtosis.

Quantiles

Sometimes not only are the four statistical moments described above used to summarize a probability distribution but a concept called α-quantile. The α-*quantile* gives us information where the first $\alpha\%$ of the distribution are located. Given an arbitrary observation of the considered probability distribution, this observation will be smaller than the α-quantile q_α in $\alpha\%$ of the cases and larger in $(100 - \alpha)\%$ of the cases.[12] For example, for the normal distribution with mean 7% and standard deviation 2.6%, the value 0% represents the 0.35% quantile.

---

[12] Formally, the α-quantile for a continuous probability distribution P with strictly increasing cumulative distribution function F is obtained as $q_\alpha = F^{-1}(\alpha)$.

EXHIBIT 2.2 Distributions and their Mean, Variance, and Skewness
Panel A. Distribution Descriptions

	Density Function	Parameters	Mean	Variance
Normal	$f(x) = \dfrac{1}{\sqrt{2\pi}\sigma}\, e^{-\frac{1}{2}\left(\frac{x-\mu}{\sigma}\right)^2}$	μ location σ scale $\sigma > 0$	μ	σ^2
Beta	$f(x) = \dfrac{x^{\alpha_1-1}(1-x)^{\alpha_2-1}}{B(\alpha_1, \alpha_2)}$	α_1 shape $\alpha_1 > 0$ α_2 shape $\alpha_2 > 0$	$\dfrac{\alpha_1}{\alpha_1 + \alpha_2}$	$\dfrac{\alpha_1\alpha_2}{(\alpha_1+\alpha_2)^2(\alpha_1+\alpha_2+1)}$
Exponential	$f(x) = \dfrac{e^{-x/\beta}}{\beta}$	β scale $\beta > 0$	β	β^2
Extreme Value	$f(x) = \dfrac{1}{b}\left(\dfrac{1}{e^{\frac{(x-a)}{b}+\exp\left(\frac{a-x}{b}\right)}}\right)$	a location b scale $b > 0$	$a + 0.577b$	$\dfrac{\pi^2 b^2}{6}$
Gamma	$f(x) = \dfrac{1}{\beta\Gamma(\alpha)}\left(\dfrac{x}{\beta}\right)^{\alpha-1} e^{-x/\beta}$	α location β scale $\beta > 0$	$\beta\alpha$	$\beta^2\alpha$

EXHIBIT 2.2 Panel A. Continued

	Density Function	Parameters	Mean	Variance
Logistic	$f(x) = \dfrac{e^{-(x-\alpha)/\beta}}{\beta(1 + e^{-(x-\alpha)/\beta})^2}$	α location β scale $\beta > 0$	α	$\dfrac{\pi^2\beta^2}{3}$
Lognormal	$f(X) = \dfrac{1}{x\sqrt{2\pi}\sigma}e^{-\frac{1}{2}\left(\frac{\ln x - \mu}{\sigma}\right)^2}$	$\mu > 0$ $\sigma > 0$	$e^{\mu + \frac{\sigma^2}{2}}$	$e^{2\mu}e^{\sigma^2}(e^{\sigma^2} - 1)$
Student-t	$f(x) = \dfrac{1}{\sqrt{\pi \cdot n}} \cdot \dfrac{\Gamma((n+1)/2)}{\Gamma(n/2)} \cdot \left(1 + \dfrac{x^2}{n}\right)^{-\frac{n+1}{2}}$	n degrees of freedom	0	$\dfrac{n}{n-2}$
Skewed Normal	$f(x) = \dfrac{2}{\sigma} \cdot \varphi\left(\dfrac{x-\mu}{\sigma}\right) \cdot \Phi\left(\alpha\dfrac{x-\mu}{\sigma}\right)$	μ location σ scale α shape	μ	σ^2
Weibull	$f(x) = \dfrac{\alpha x^{\alpha-1}}{\beta^{\alpha}}e^{-(x/\beta)^{\alpha}}$	α shape $\alpha > 0$ β scale $\beta > 0$	$\beta\Gamma\left(1 + \dfrac{1}{\alpha}\right)$	$\beta^2\left[\Gamma\left(1 + \dfrac{2}{\alpha}\right) - \Gamma^2\left(1 + \dfrac{1}{\alpha}\right)\right]$

EXHIBIT 2.2   (Continued)
Panel B. Domain and Symmetry

	Domain	Skewness
Normal	$-\infty < x < +\infty$	0
Beta	$0 < x < 1$	$2\dfrac{\alpha_2 - \alpha_1}{\alpha_1 + \alpha_2 + 2}\sqrt{\dfrac{\alpha_1 + \alpha_2 + 1}{\alpha_1 \alpha_2}}$
Exponential	$0 < x < +\infty$	2
Extreme Value	$-\infty < x < +\infty$	1.139547
Gamma	$0 < x < +\infty$	$\dfrac{2}{\sqrt{\alpha}}$
Logistic	$-\infty < x < +\infty$	0
Lognormal	$0 < x < +\infty$	$(w + 2)\sqrt{(w - 1)}$ where $w = e^{\alpha^2}$
Student's-t	$-\infty < x < +\infty$	0
Skewed Normal	$-\infty < x < +\infty$	a
Weibull	$0 < x < +\infty$	$\dfrac{\Gamma\left(1 + \dfrac{3}{\alpha}\right) + 3\Gamma\left(1 + \dfrac{2}{\alpha}\right)\Gamma\left(1 + \dfrac{1}{\alpha}\right) + 2\Gamma^3\left(1 + \dfrac{1}{\alpha}\right)}{\left[\Gamma\left(1 + \dfrac{2}{\alpha}\right) - \Gamma^2\left(1 + \dfrac{1}{\alpha}\right)\right]^{3/2}}$

Source: Adapted from Exhibit 1 in Haim Levy and R. Duchin, "Asset Return Distributions and the Investment Horizon Explaining Contradictions," *Journal of Portfolio Management* 30 (Summer 2004), pp. 47–62. For the sake of exposition and consistency we have sometimes used a slightly different notation and omitted some entries.

Some quantiles have special names. The 25%, 50%, and 75% quantile are referred to as the *first quartile*, *second quartile*, and *third quartile*, respectively. The 1%, 2%, ..., 98%, 99% quantiles are called *percentiles*.

Sample Moments

Above we introduced the four statistical moments mean, variance, skewness, and kurtosis. Given a probability density function *f* or a probability distribution *P*, we are able to calculate these statistical moments according to the formulae given in Exhibit 2.1. In practical applications however, we are faced with the situation that we observe realizations of a probability distribution (e.g., the daily return of the S&P 500 index over the last two years), but we do not know the distribution that generates these returns. Consequently we are not able to apply our knowledge about the calculation of statistical moments. But, having the observations $x_1, \ldots, x_n$, we can try to estimate the "true moments" out of the sample. The estimates are sometimes called *sample moments* to stress the fact that they are obtained out of a sample of observations.

The idea is quite simple: The empirical analogue for the mean of a random variable is the average of the observations:

$$EX \approx \frac{1}{n} \sum_{i=1}^{n} x_i$$

For large n it is reasonable to expect that the average of the observations will not be far from the mean of the probability distribution. Now, we observe that all theoretical formulae for the calculation of the four statistical moments are expressed as "means of something." This insight leads to the expression for the sample moments, summarized in Exhibit 2.3.[13]

EXHIBIT 2.3   Calculation of Sample Moments

Moment	Sample Moment
Mean EX	$\bar{x} = \dfrac{1}{n} \sum\limits_{i=1}^{n} x_i$
Variance VX	$s^2 = \dfrac{1}{n} \sum\limits_{i=1}^{n} (x_i - \bar{x})^2$
Skewness	$\hat{\varsigma} = \dfrac{\dfrac{1}{n} \sum\limits_{i=1}^{n} (x_i - \bar{x})^3}{(s^2)^{\frac{3}{2}}}$
Kurtosis	$\hat{\kappa} = \dfrac{\dfrac{1}{n} \sum\limits_{i=1}^{n} (x_i - \bar{x})^4}{(s^2)^2}$

---

[13] A "hat" on a parameter (like $\hat{\kappa}$) symbolizes the fact that the true parameter (in this case the kurtosis κ) is estimated.

Moments and Correlation

If X is a random variable on a probability space $(\Omega, \Im, P)$, the quantity $E[|X|^p]$, $p > 0$ is called the *p-th absolute moment* of X. If k is any positive integer, $E[X^k]$, if it exists ($E(Y)$ exists if $E(|Y|)$ is finite), is called the *k-th moment*. In the general case of a probability measure P, we can therefore write

■ $E[|X|^p] = \int_\Omega |X|^p dP$, $p > 0$, is the p-th absolute moment.

■ $E[X^k] = \int_\Omega X^k dP$, if it exists for k positive integer, is the k-th moment.

In the case of discrete probabilities p_i, $\Sigma p_i = 1$ the above expressions become

$$E[|X|^p] = \sum |x_i|^p p_i$$

and

$$E[X^k] = \sum x_i^k p_i$$

respectively. If the variable X is continuous and has a density $p(x)$ such that

$$\int_{-\infty}^{\infty} p(x)dx = 1$$

we can write

$$E[|X|^p] = \int_{-\infty}^{\infty} |x|^p p(x)dx$$

and

$$E[X^k] = \int_{-\infty}^{\infty} x^k p(x)dx$$

respectively.

The centered moments are the moments of the fluctuations of the variables around its mean. For example, the *variance* of a variable X is defined as the centered moment of second order:

$$\text{var}(X) = \sigma_x^2 = \sigma^2(X) = E[(X - \overline{X})^2]$$

$$= \int_{-\infty}^{\infty} (x - \overline{X})^2 p(x)dx = \int_{-\infty}^{\infty} x^2 p(x)dx - \left[\int_{-\infty}^{\infty} xp(x)dx\right]^2$$

where $\overline{X} = E[X]$.

The positive square root of the variance, σ_x is called the *standard deviation* of the variable.

We can now define the covariance and the correlation coefficient of a variable. *Correlation* is a quantitative measure of the strength of the dependence between two variables. Intuitively, two variables are dependent if they move together. If they move together, they will be above or below their respective means in the same state. Therefore, in this case, the product of their respective deviations from the means will have a positive mean. We call this mean the *covariance* of the two variables. The covariance divided by the product of the standard deviations is a dimensionless number called the *correlation coefficient*.

Given two random variables X, Y with finite variances, we can write the following definitions:

- $\text{cov}(X, Y) = \sigma_{X,Y} = E[(X - \overline{X})(Y - \overline{Y})]$ is the covariance of X, Y.

- $\rho_{X,Y} = \dfrac{\sigma_{X,Y}}{\sigma_X \sigma_Y}$ is the correlation coefficient of X, Y.

The correlation coefficient can assume values in the interval $[-1, 1]$. If two variables X, Y are independent, their correlation coefficient vanishes. However, uncorrelated variables (i.e., variables whose correlation coefficient is zero) are not necessarily independent.

It can be demonstrated that the following property of variances holds:

$$\text{var}\left(\sum_i X_i\right) = \sum_i \text{var}(X_i) + \sum_{i \neq j} \text{cov}(X_i, X_j)$$

Further, it can be demonstrated that the following properties hold:

$$\sigma_{X,Y} = E[XY] - E[X]E[Y]$$

$$\sigma_{X,Y} = \sigma_{Y,X}$$

$$\sigma_{aX,bY} = ab\sigma_{Y,X}$$

$$\sigma_{X+Y,Z} = \sigma_{X,Z} + \sigma_{Y,Z}$$

$$\text{cov}\left(\sum_i a_i X_i, \sum_i b_j Y_j\right) = \sum_i \sum_j a_i b_j \text{cov}(X_i, Y_j)$$

Sequences of Random Variables

Consider a probability space $(\Omega, \Im, P)$. A sequence of random variables is an infinite family of random variables X_i on $(\Omega, \Im, P)$ indexed by integer numbers: $i = 0,1,2,...,n...$ If the sequence extends to infinity in both directions, it is indexed by positive and negative integers: $i = ...,-n,..., 0,1,2,...,n....$

A sequence of random variables can *converge* to a *limit random variable*. Several different notions of the limit of a sequence of random variables can be defined. The simplest definition of convergence is that of pointwise convergence. A sequence of random variables X_i, $i \geq 1$ on $(\Omega, \Im, P)$, is said to *converge almost surely to a random variable X*, denoted

$$X_i \overset{a.s.}{\rightarrow} X$$

if the following relationship holds:

$$P\{\omega: \lim_{i \to \infty} X_i(\omega) = X(\omega)\} = 1$$

In other words, a sequence of random variables converges almost surely to a random variable X if the sequence of real numbers $X_i(\omega)$ converges to $X(\omega)$ for all ω except a set of measure zero.

A sequence of random variables X_i, $i \geq 1$ on $(\Omega, \Im, P)$, is said to *converge in mean of order p to a random variable X* if

$$\lim_{i \to \infty} E[|X_i(\omega) - X(\omega)|^p] = 0$$

provided that all expectations exist. Convergence in mean of order one and two are called convergence in mean and convergence in mean square, respectively.

A weaker concept of convergence is that of convergence in probability. A sequence of random variables X_i, $i \geq 1$ on $(\Omega, \Im, P)$ is said to *converge in probability to a random variable X*, denoted

$$X_i \xrightarrow{P} X$$

if the following relationship holds:

$$\lim_{i \to \infty} P\{\omega: |X_i(\omega) - X(\omega)| \leq \varepsilon\} = 1 \text{, for all } \varepsilon > 0$$

It can be demonstrated that if a sequence converges almost surely, then it also convergences in probability while the converse is not generally true. It can also be demonstrated that if a sequence converges in mean of order $p > 0$, then it also convergences in probability while the converse is not generally true.

A sequence of random variables X_i, $i \geq 1$ on $(\Omega, \mathfrak{S}, P)$ with distribution functions F_{X_i} is said to *converge in distribution to a random variable* X with distribution function F_X, denoted

$$X_i \xrightarrow{d} X$$

if

$$\lim_{i \to \infty} F_{X_i}(x) = F_X(x), x \in C$$

It can be demonstrated that if a sequence converges almost surely (and thus converges in probability) it also converges in distribution while the converse is not true in general. More precisely, convergence in distribution does not imply convergence in probability in general, however if X is a constant, then convergence in distribution is equivalent to convergence in probability.

Independent and Identically Distributed Sequences

Consider a probability space $(\Omega, \mathfrak{S}, P)$. A sequence of random variables X_i on $(\Omega, \mathfrak{S}, P)$ is called an *independent and identically distributed* (IID) *sequence* if the variables X_i have all the same distribution and are all mutually independent. An IID sequence is the strongest form of white noise. Note that in many applications white noise is defined as a sequence of uncorrelated variables.

An IID sequence is completely unforecastable in the sense that the past does not influence the present or the future in any possible sense. In an IID sequence all conditional distributions are identical to unconditional distributions. Note, however, that an IID sequence presents a simple form of reversion to the mean. In fact, suppose that a sequence X_i

assumes at a given time t a value larger than the common mean of all variables: $X_t > E[X]$. By definition of mean, it is more likely that X_t be followed by a smaller value: $P(X_{t+1} < X_t) > P(X_{t+1} > X_t)$.

Note that this type of mean reversion does not imply forecastability as the probability distribution of asset returns at time $t + 1$ is independent of the distribution at time t.

Sum of Variables

Given two random variables $X(\omega)$, $Y(\omega)$ on the same probability space $(\Omega, \mathfrak{S}, P)$, the *sum of variables* $Z(\omega) = X(\omega) + Y(\omega)$ is another random variable. The sum associates to each state ω a value $Z(\omega)$ equal to the sum of the values taken by the two variables X, Y. Let's suppose that the two variables $X(\omega)$, $Y(\omega)$ have a joint density $p(x,y)$ and marginal densities $p_X(x)$ and $p_Y(x)$, respectively. Let's call H the cumulative distribution of the variable Z. The following relationship holds

$$H(u) = P[Z(\omega) \leq u] = \iint_A p(x, y) dx dy$$

$$A = \{y \leq -x + u\}$$

In other words, the probability that the sum $X + Y$ be less than or equal to a real number u is given by the integral of the joint probability distribution function in the region A. The region A can be described as the region of the x,y plane below the straight line $y = -x + u$.

If we assume that the two variables are independent, then the distribution of the sum admits a simple representation. In fact, under the assumption of independence, the joint density is the product of the marginal densities: $p(x,y) = p_X(x)p_Y(x)$. Therefore, we can write

$$H(u) = P[Z(\omega) \leq u] = \iint_A p(x, y) dx dy = \int_{-\infty}^{\infty} \left\{ \int_{-\infty}^{u-y} p_X(x) dx \right\} p_Y(y) dy$$

We can now use a property of integrals called the *Leibnitz rule*, which allows one to write the following relationship:

$$\frac{dH}{du} = p_Z(u) = \int_{-\infty}^{\infty} p_X(u - y) p_Y(y) dy$$

The above formula is a convolution of the two marginal distributions. This formula can be reiterated for any number of summands: the density of the sum of n random variables is the convolution of their densities.

Computing directly the convolution of a number of functions might be very difficult or impossible. Given a function $f(x)$ the integral

$$F(s) = \frac{1}{2\sqrt{\pi}} \int_{-\infty}^{\infty} f(x)e^{-isx}dx$$

is called the *Fourier transform of the function* f. Fourier transforms admit inversion formulas as one can completely recover the function f from its transform with the inversion formula

$$f(x) = \frac{1}{2\sqrt{\pi}} \int_{-\infty}^{\infty} F(s)e^{isx}ds$$

If we take the Fourier transforms of the densities, $P_Z(s)$, $P_X(s)$, $P_Y(s)$ computations are substantially simplified as the transform of the convolution is the product of the transforms

$$p_Z(u) = \int_{-\infty}^{\infty} p_X(u-y)p_Y(y)dy \Rightarrow P_Z(s) = P_X(s) \times P_Y(s)$$

This relationship can be extended to any number of variables.

In probability theory, given a random variable X, the following expectation is called the *characteristic function (c.f.) of the variable* X

$$\varphi_X(t) = E[e^{itX}] = E[\cos tX] + iE[\sin tX]$$

If the variable X admits a d.f. $F_X(y)$, it can be demonstrated that the following relationship holds:

$$\varphi_X(t) = E[e^{itX}] = \int_{-\infty}^{\infty} e^{itX}dF_X(x) = \int_{-\infty}^{\infty} \cos tx\,dF_X(x) + i\int_{-\infty}^{\infty} \sin tx\,dF_X(x)$$

In this case, the characteristic function therefore coincides with the Fourier-Stieltjes transform. It can be demonstrated that there is a one-to-one correspondence between c.f and d.f.s. In fact, it is well known that the Fourier-Stieltjes transform can be uniquely inverted.

In probability theory convolution is defined, in a more general way, as follows. Given two d.f.s $F_X(y)$ and $F_Y(y)$, their convolution is defined as

$$F^*(u) = (F_X * F_Y)(u) = \int_{-\infty}^{\infty} F_X(u-y)dF_Y(y)$$

It can be demonstrated that the d.f. of the sum of two variables X, Y with d.f.s $F_X(y)$ and $F_Y(y)$ is the convolution of their respective d.f.s:

$$P(X+Y \le u) = F_{X+Y}(u) = (F_X * F_Y)(u) = \int_{-\infty}^{\infty} F_X(u-y)dF_Y(y)$$

If a d.f. admits a p.d.f., then the inversion formulas are those established earlier. Inversion formulas also exist in the case that a d.f. does not admit a density but these are more complex and will not be given here.[14]

We can therefore establish the following property: the characteristic function of the sum of n independent random variables is the product of the characteristic functions of each of the summands.

Gaussian Variables

Gaussian random variables are extremely important in probability theory and statistics. Their importance stems from the fact that any phenomenon made up of a large number of independent or weakly dependent variables has a *Gaussian distribution*. Gaussian distributions are also known as *normal distributions*. The name Gaussian derives from the German mathematician Gauss who introduced them.

Let's start with univariate variables. A *normal variable* is a variable whose probability distribution function has the following form:

$$f(x|\mu, \sigma^2) = \frac{1}{\sigma\sqrt{2\pi}} \exp\left\{ -\frac{(x-\mu)^2}{2\sigma^2} \right\}$$

The *univariate normal distribution* is a distribution characterized by only two parameters, (μ, σ^2), which represent, respectively, the mean and

---

[14] See Y.S. Chow and H. Teicher, *Probability Theory* (New York: Springer, 1997).

the variance of the distribution. We write $X \sim N(\mu,\sigma^2)$ to indicate that the variable X has a normal distribution with parameters (μ,σ^2). We define the *standard normal distribution* as the normal distribution with zero mean and unit variance. It can be demonstrated by direct calculation that if $X \sim N(\mu,\sigma^2)$ then the variable

$$Z = \frac{X - \mu}{\sigma}$$

is standard normal. The variable Z is called the *score* or *Z-score*. The cumulative distribution of a normal variable is generally indicated as

$$F(x) = \Phi\left(\frac{x - \mu}{\sigma}\right)$$

where $\Phi(x)$ is the cumulative distribution of the standard normal.

It can be demonstrated that the sum of n independent normal distributions is another normal distribution whose expected value is the sum of the expected values of the summands and whose variance is the sum of the variances of the summands.

The normal distribution has a typical bell-shaped graph symmetrical around the mean. Exhibit 2.4 shows the graph of a normal distribution.

Multivariate normal distributions are characterized by the same exponential functional form. However, a multivariate normal distribution in n variables is identified by n means, one for each axis, and by a $n \times n$ symmetrical variance-covariance matrix. For instance, a bivariate normal distribution is characterized by two expected values, two variances and one covariance. We can write the general expression of a bivariate normal distribution as follows:

$$f(x,y) = \frac{\exp\left\{-\frac{1}{2}Q\right\}}{2\pi\sigma_X\sigma_Y\sqrt{1-\rho^2}}$$

$$Q = \frac{1}{1-\rho^2}\left\{\left(\frac{x-\mu_X}{\sigma_X}\right)^2 - 2\rho\left(\frac{x-\mu_X}{\sigma_X}\right)\left(\frac{y-\mu_Y}{\sigma_Y}\right) + \left(\frac{y-\mu_Y}{\sigma_Y}\right)^2\right\}$$

where ρ is the correlation coefficient.

EXHIBIT 2.4 Graph of a Normal Variable with Zero Mean and $\sigma = 100$

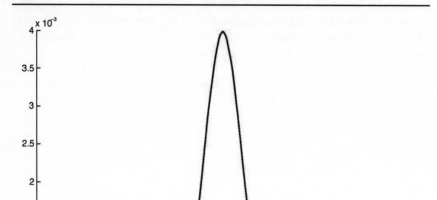

This expression generalizes to the case of n random variables. Using matrix notation, the joint normal probability distributions of the random n vector $V = \{X_i\}$, $i = 1,2,\ldots,n$ has the following expression:

$$V = \{X_i\} \sim N_n(\mu, \Sigma)$$

where

$$\mu_i = E[X_i]$$

and Σ is the variance-covariance matrix of the $\{X_i\}$,

$$\Sigma = E[(V - \mu)(V - \mu)^T]$$
$$f(v) = [(2\pi)^n |\Sigma|]^{-\frac{1}{2}} \exp[(-\frac{1}{2})(v - \mu)^T \Sigma^{-1}(v - \mu)]$$

where $|\Sigma| = \det\Sigma$, the determinant of Σ. Here we assume that V has nondegenerated normal distribution, that is the covariance matrix is strictly positive definite. If this is not the case we define the Gaussian distribution with the characteristic function.

For $n = 2$ we find the previous expression for bivariate normal, taking into account that variances and correlation coefficients have the following relationship

$$\sigma_{ij} = \rho_{ij}\sigma_i\sigma_j$$

It can be demonstrated that a linear combination

$$W = \sum_{i=1}^{n} \alpha_i X_i$$

of n jointly normal random variables $X_i \sim N(\mu_i, \sigma_i^2)$ with $\mathrm{cov}(X_i, X_j) = \sigma_{ij}$ is a normal random variable $W \sim N(\mu_W, \sigma_W^2)$ where

$$\mu_W = \sum_{i=1}^{n} \alpha_i \mu_i$$

$$\sigma_W^2 = \sum_{i=1}^{n}\sum_{j=1}^{n} \alpha_i \alpha_j \sigma_{ij}$$

Normal Distribution Revisited

Let's take another look at the normal distribution, especially at the four statistical moments for the normal distribution. The previously called location parameter μ actually equals the mean of the normal distribution; the parameter σ represents the standard deviation and consequently the variance coincides with the value of σ^2. This is consistent with our observations that the density is located and symmetric around μ and that the variation of the distribution increases with increasing values of σ. Because a normal distribution is symmetric, its skewness measure is zero. The kurtosis measure of all normal distributions is 3.

Exhibit 2.5 shows a normal distribution and a symmetric nonnormal distribution with a mean of zero. The symmetric nonnormal distribution has a higher peak at the mean (zero) than the normal distribution. A distribution that has this characteristic is said to be a *leptokurtic distribution* with the same mean of zero. Look at the result of the greater peakedness. The tails of the symmetric nonnormal distribution are "thicker" or "heavier" than the normal distribution. A probability distribution with this characteristics is said to be a "heavy-tailed distribu-

EXHIBIT 2.5   Illustration of Kurtosis: Difference Between a Standard Normal
Distribution and a Distribution with High Excess Kurtosis

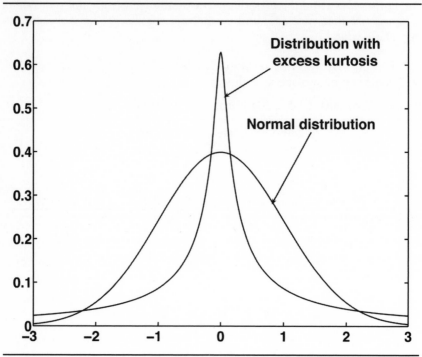

tion" or "fat tailed." The kurtosis measure for such a heavy-tailed
distribution will exceed 3. Statistical programs commonly report a measure called "excess kurtosis" or "Fisher's kurtosis." This is simply the
kurtosis for the distribution minus 3 (the kurtosis for the normal distribution) and will be a positive value for a heavy-tailed distribution. When
a distribution is less peaked than the normal distribution, it is said to be
platykurtic. This distribution is characterized by less probability in the
tails than the normal distribution. It will have a kurtosis that is less than
3 or, equivalently, an excess kurtosis that is negative.

Exponential, Chi-Square, *t*, and *F* distributions

In this section we briefly describe three distributions that play a basic
role in econometrics: exponential, Chi-square, *t*, and *F* distributions.

Exponential Distribution

The exponential distribution has the following form:

$$f(x) = \lambda e^{-\lambda x}, \quad x > 0$$

$$F(x) = \int_0^x f(x) dx = 1 - e^{-\lambda x}, \quad x > 0$$

If a positive variable is exponentially distributed, then its first four moments can be written as follows:

$$E(X) = \int_0^x x \lambda e^{-\lambda x} dx = 1/\lambda$$

$$E(X^2) = \int_0^x x^2 \lambda e^{-\lambda x} dx = 2/\lambda^2$$

$$E(X^3) = \int_0^x x^3 \lambda e^{-\lambda x} dx = 3!/\lambda^3$$

$$E(X^4) = \int_0^x x^4 \lambda e^{-\lambda x} dx = 4!/\lambda^4$$

The exponential distribution is called *memoryless* because if a waiting time for some event is exponentially distributed, the expected waiting time to the next event does not depend on the time elapsed since the last occurrence of the event. For example, if waiting times for a bus arrival were exponentially distributed, the expected time for the next arrival would be independent of how long we have been waiting for the bus.

Chi-Square Distribution

The Chi-square (χ^2) distribution is basic to the study of variance distributions. The Chi-square distribution with k degrees of freedom is defined as the distribution of the sum of the squares of k independent standard normal variables (i.e., normal variables with mean 0 and unitary standard deviation). It can be demonstrated that the Chi-square distribution has the following form:

$$f_{\chi^2}(x) = \frac{x^{k/2-1} e^{-x/2}}{2^{k/2} \Gamma\left(\dfrac{k}{2}\right)}$$

where Γ is the Γ-function. The Gamma function is defined as follows:

$$\Gamma(\alpha) = \int_0^\infty x^{\alpha-1} e^{-x} dx$$

The mean and variance of the Chi-square distribution are the following:

$$E(\chi^2) = k$$
$$\mathrm{var}(\chi^2) = 2k$$

The cumulative density function of the Chi-square distribution cannot be expressed as an elementary function.

F and t Distributions

The probability distribution function of a Student's t-distribution with m degrees of freedom is the following:

$$f_T(x) \propto \left(1 + \frac{x^2}{m}\right)^{-(m+1)/2}$$

When m $\to \infty$ the t-distribution tends to a normal distribution.

The F distribution is indexed with two parameters. The probability density function is the following:

$$f_F(x) \propto \frac{u^{k/2-1}}{(1 + ku/m)^{(k+m)/2}}$$

It can be demonstrated that the F distribution is the distribution of the ratio of independent Chi-square variables.

PRINCIPLES OF ESTIMATION

In making financial predictions, the interest is not in the raw distribution of financial quantities such as prices or returns but in the idealized, underlying mechanism that is supposed to generate the data, that is, the data generating process or data generating process (DGP). This means that a typical population in financial modeling is formed taking n-tuples of consecutive data, say n-tuples of consecutive prices or returns. The distribution of interest is the joint distribution of these data, or, better, the conditional distribution of present data given past data. Distributions of this type are assumed to be sufficiently time-invariant to be learnable from past data.

Whether or not there is indeed a true DGP impinges on whether the future repeats the past. This question is ever-present in the context of our ability to forecast financial values: Is past performance a guarantee of future performance? It should be remarked that, to make any knowledge possible, the future must somehow repeat the past. If the future does not repeat the past, at least at the level of DGP, no knowledge is possible. However, we cannot take a naive view that would have the future repeat the past in a simple sense. For example, we cannot assume that a stock price will keep going up because it has been going up for some time. What eventually remains stable is the generating mechanism, that is, the DGP. The problem with financial modeling is that we do not know what repeats what, that is, we do not know what the correct DGP is. In addition, any DGP is subject to possibly abrupt and unpredictable changes.

The starting point of financial modeling is generally a tentative DGP. The objective of the estimation process is (1) to estimate the model parameters and (2) to estimate the parameters of the distributions and of the noise term. One might or might not assume a specific form for the distributions.

This calls for the discussion of the following key statistical concepts: Estimators, sample distribution, and critical values and confidence intervals. Let us start with estimators.

Estimators

To estimate a statistical model is to estimate its parameters from sample data. For example, given a sample of historical stock returns R_t, $t = 1, 2, ..., T$, a portfolio manager might want to estimate the standard deviation of their distribution. The process of estimation can be described as follows. Suppose that a distribution f is given and that μ is a constant parameter or a vector of constant parameters of the distribution f. Now consider a sample of T observations X_t, $t = 1, 2, ..., T$ extracted from a population with distribution f. An estimator $\hat{\mu}$ of the parameter μ is a function $\hat{\mu} = g(X_1, ..., X_T)$ of the sample which produces numbers close to the parameter μ.

When we estimate the parameters of a model, we apply a slightly different concept of estimation. In fact, our estimators are those parameters that obtain the best fit to empirical data. See the discussion on estimation of regressions in Chapter 3.

Any estimator is characterized by several important properties, among which the following two are fundamental:

■ An estimator $\hat{\mu}$ is called *unbiased* if the mean of the estimator equals the true parameter μ: $E(\hat{\mu}) = \mu$ for any sample size.

■ An estimator $\hat{\mu}$ is called *consistent* if the limit in probability of the estimator equals the true parameter μ: plim $(\hat{\mu}) = \mu$.

Sampling Distributions

Any estimation process yields results that depend on the specific sample data. As sample data are random variables, estimated parameters that are functions of the sample data are also random variables. Consider, for example, the estimation of the following model:

$$X_t = a_{11}X_{t-1} + a_{12}Y_{t-1} + \varepsilon_{1,t}$$
$$Y_t = a_{21}X_{t-1} + a_{22}Y_{t-1} + \varepsilon_{2,t}$$
$$t = 1, 2, ..., T$$

from empirical time series data. (Models of this type, called *vector autoregressive models*, will be discussed in Chapter 6.) The empirical data that form the empirical time series must be considered a sample extracted from a population. As a consequence, the model parameters estimated on the sample (i.e., the a_{ij}) are random variables characterized by a probability distribution.

Sampling distributions are critical for testing and choosing hypotheses because, in general, we do not know if the model we are estimating is the correct model: Any model is only a scientific hypothesis. Often two competing models explain the same data. We have to choose which of the models is more faithful. We therefore formulate a hypothesis and decide on the basis of observations. For example, we formulate the hypothesis that a given time series is integrated. If a series is integrated, its autocorrelation coefficient is unity, that is, the correlation coefficient between the time series at time t and at time $t - 1$ is 1. But because samples vary, no observation will yield exactly unity, even if the series is indeed integrated. However, if we know the sampling distribution, we can formulate a decision rule which allows us to determine if a series is integrated even if the estimated autocorrelation parameter has a value other than one with predescribed probability (confidence).

The probability distributions of a model's parameters depend on the estimation method. In some cases, they can be expressed as explicit functions of the sample data. For example, as we will see in the section on regression, the regression parameters are algebraic functions of sample data. In other cases, however, it might be impossible to express estimators as explicit functions of sample data.

The probability distribution of estimators clearly depends on the probability distribution of sample data. Determining the distribution of parameters is a rather difficult task. In cases such as simple regressions, one might assume that variables have given distributions, for example normal distributions. However, in complex models, one cannot assume an arbitrary distribution for sample data.

We illustrate the problem of sampling distributions with the simple case of determining the parameters of a normal distribution. Consider a sample of T observations X_t, $t = 1, 2, ..., T$ extracted independently from a normally distributed population with distribution $N(\mu, \sigma^2)$. In this case, it is known that the empirical mean

$$\bar{\mu} = \frac{1}{T} \sum_{t=1}^{T} X_t$$

and the empirical variance

$$\bar{\sigma}^2 = \frac{1}{T} \sum_{t=1}^{T} (X_t - \bar{\mu})^2$$

are unbiased estimators of μ and σ^2 respectively.[15]

If we assume that the sample data are independent random draws from the sample population, then the empirical mean is the rescaled sum of normally distributed data and is therefore normally distributed. The empirical variance is the sum of the square of independent, normally distributed variables. As discussed earlier in this chapter, the distribution of the sum of the square of k independent normal variables is a Chi-square distribution with k degrees of freedom (or χ^2-distribution with k degrees of freedom). For large values of k, the χ^2 distribution is approximated by a normal distribution. Therefore, for large samples, both the empirical mean and the empirical variance are normally distributed.

To illustrate the above, we generated 2 million random numbers extracted from a normal distribution with mean 0 and unitary variance. We then computed the mean and variance on 100,000 samples of 20 points, each selected from the given population. Mean and variance change from sample to sample as shown in Exhibit 2.6. The distribution

---

[15] The empirical mean and the empirical variance are unbiased estimators of the true mean and variance not only for the normal distribution but also for any distribution with finite second moments.

EXHIBIT 2.6 Sampling Distribution of the Mean and Variance for a Sample of 20 Elements Each

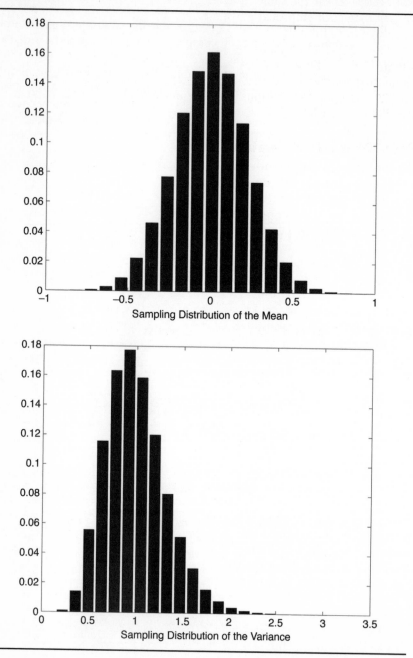

of sample variance is not normal but is approximated by a χ^2 distribution. If we repeat the same calculations on samples of 100 points each, we see that both empirical mean and variance are normally distributed as shown in Exhibit 2.7.

Though sampling distributions can be very complex, they typically simplify in the limit of very large samples. The asymptotic theory of estimators studies the distribution of estimators in large samples. We consider sample distributions for different models in our discussion of the models themselves.

Critical Values and Confidence Intervals

An estimator is a random variable characterized by a distribution that depends on the population distribution. If the estimator distribution is known, it is possible to determine *critical values*, that is, the numbers that allow one to reject or accept any hypothesis that bears on that estimator. The reasoning is the following. Suppose a statistical hypothesis on a given population depends on a parameter. In general, the parameter will vary with the sample.

For example, even if a process is truly integrated, its autoregressive parameter estimated from any given sample will be slightly different from 1. However, if we know the distribution of the autoregressive parameter, we can establish the interval within which any estimate of the autoregressive parameter falls with a given probability. For example, we can estimate in what interval around 1 the autoregressive parameter will fall with a 99% probability. If the autoregressive parameter falls outside of the critical value at 99%, we can conclude that the process is not integrated at a 99% confidence interval. If the estimated autoregressive parameter is less than the critical value, we cannot say that the process is integrated with 99% confidence. The process might in fact, follow a different dynamics that could produce the same result by chance.

Each estimated parameter is associated with a confidence interval, defined as the interval in which the estimated parameter will be within with a given probability. The confidence interval can be established *a priori* as in the case of testing if a series is integrated where, in fact, we were interested in the special value 1 for the autoregressive parameter. If we know the sample distribution of an estimated parameter, we can determine a confidence interval such that, if the model is correctly specified, the true parameter falls within that interval with a given probability. For example, suppose the estimated autoregressive parameter is 0.9. Given the sample distribution, we can determine the probability that the true autoregressive parameter falls between, say, 0.85 and 0.95. The assumption that the model is correctly specified is critical.

EXHIBIT 2.7 Sampling Distribution of the Mean and Variance for a Sample of 100 Elements Each

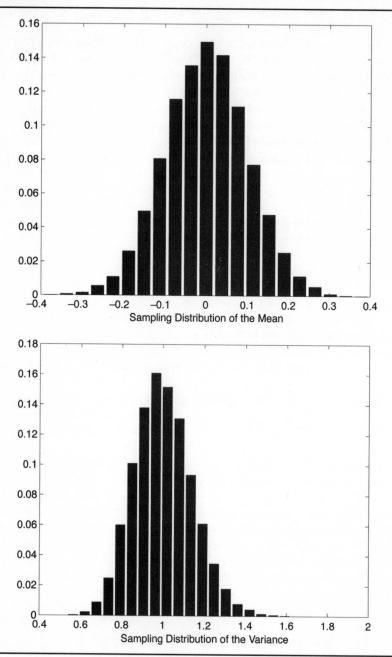

Significance Test

A common statistical procedure is to run a test to check whether a given hypothesis can be considered true or has to be rejected. A *test statistic* is a function of the sample and is therefore a random variable. Suppose we want to test an hypothesis H_0. The hypothesis to be tested is called the *null hypothesis* or simply the *null*. Consider a test statistic k relative to the hypothesis H_0. For example, suppose we want to test the null hypothesis that a regression parameter is zero.

Intuitively, we can reject the null that the regression coefficient is zero if the estimation yields a value of the parameter sufficiently distant from zero. In other words, how can we decide if the test is significant? Fisher introduced a method based on the p values.

Suppose we know the sampling distribution of a test statistic. For example, suppose we know the distribution of an estimated regression parameter. Given a sampling distribution and an observed value of a statistic, the p-value is the probability of the tail beyond the observed value. A small p-value is evidence against the null hypothesis. As a rule of thumb, a test is considered highly significant if its p-value is less than 0.01. A t-statistic to test the null hypothesis that regression parameter is zero is obtained by dividing the estimated parameter by its own standard deviation.

Maximum Likelihood, Ordinary Least Squares, and Regressions

We now discuss a fundamental principle, the *maximum likelihood* (ML) principle of estimation. In Chapter 3 on Regression we shall see its links with *ordinary least squares* (OLS) estimation. The ML principle is very intuitive. Suppose you flip a coin 1,000 times and you get 700 heads. Would you draw the conclusion that the coin is biased or that the coin is fair and that you have experienced a particularly unlikely stream of outcomes? It is reasonable to expect that you conclude that the coin is biased with a 70% probability of heads. In other words you rule out the possibility that very unlikely things occur in practice.

The ML principle generalizes the above idea. Suppose that a sample is randomly and independently extracted from a distribution which contains a number of parameters, for example a binomial distribution with an unknown probability parameter. The ML principle prescribes that the estimate of the distribution parameters should maximize the (*a priori*) probability of the sample given the distribution. In the previous example of the coin, it is easy to see that 0.7 is the binomial probability value that maximizes the probability of a sample with 700 heads and 300 tails.

It should be clear that the ML principle is a *decision rule*; it is not possible to demonstrate the ML principle. There is no theoretical reason why the sample we are considering should not be a low-probability sample. There is no way to go from a decision rule to a factual demonstration or, as stated in the preface of the book by Chow and Teicher: "Once one is in the world of probability, there is no way to get out of it."[16] One might be tempted to think that the systematic adoption of the ML principle reduces the number of mistakes in estimation over repeated estimation processes. However, it is easy to see that this reasoning is circular, as it simply assumes that sequences of unlikely events do not occur. Ultimately there is no way to demonstrate that we are not experiencing a very unlikely event.[17]

We now formally state the ML principle. Suppose that a sample of T observations $\mathbf{X}_t = (X_{1,t}, ..., X_{p,t})'$, $t = 1, 2, ..., T$ is given. Suppose that the sample is characterized by a global multivariate probability distribution density $f(\mathbf{X}_1, ..., \mathbf{X}_T; \alpha_1, ..., \alpha_q)$ which contains q parameters $\alpha_1,$ ..., α_q. The distribution parameters have to be estimated.

The *likelihood function L* is any function proportional to f:

$$L(\alpha_1, ..., \alpha_q | \mathbf{X}_1, ..., \mathbf{X}_T) \propto f(\mathbf{X}_1, ..., \mathbf{X}_T | \alpha_1, ..., \alpha_q)$$

In the sequel, we will choose the constant of proportionality equal to 1. If the sample is formed by random independent extractions from a population with a density f, then the likelihood function L is the product of f computed on the different elements of the sample:

$$L(\alpha_1, ..., \alpha_q | \mathbf{X}_1, ..., \mathbf{X}_T) = \prod_{t=1}^{T} f(\mathbf{X}_i ; \alpha_1, ..., \alpha_q)$$

---

[16] Chow and Teicher, *Probability Theory*, p. X.

[17] The ML principle touches upon questions of scientific methodology. The notion of uncertainty and estimation is different in economics and in the physical sciences. In general, the physical sciences tend to have a "deterministic" view of uncertainty in the sense that individual events are uncertain, but aggregates are certain and probability distributions are empirically ascertained with great precision given the astronomical size of the samples involved. In economics, uncertainty is more fundamental as the entire theory of economics is uncertain. However, there are theoretical subtleties in the physical sciences that we cannot discuss here. The interested reader can consult, for example, David Ruelle, *Hasard et Chaos* (Paris: Odile Jacob, 1991), Lawrence Sklar, *Physics and Chance: Philosophical Issues in the Foundations of Statistical Mechanics* (Cambridge: Cambridge University Press, 1993), or more technical treatises such as R. F. Streater, *Statistical Dynamics* (London: Imperial College Press, 1995).

The ML principle states that the optimal estimate of parameters $\alpha_1, ..., \alpha_q$ maximizes L:

$$(\hat{\alpha}_1, ..., \hat{\alpha}_q) = \text{argmax}(L(\alpha_1, ..., \alpha_q))$$

As the log function is strictly monotone, we can replace the likelihood function with the log-likelihood defined as the logarithm of L. The ML principle states equivalently that the optimal estimate of parameters $\alpha_1, ..., \alpha_q$ maximizes the log-likelihood $\log L$:

$$(\hat{\alpha}_1, ..., \hat{\alpha}_q) = \text{argmax}(\log L(\alpha_1, ..., \alpha_q))$$

In the case of independent samples, the transformation to the logarithms has the advantage of replacing a product with a sum, which is easier to compute.

$$\log(L(\alpha_1, ..., \alpha_q)) = \log \prod_{i=1}^{N} f(\mathbf{X}_{1,i}, ..., X_{p,i}\,;\,\alpha_1, ..., \alpha_q)$$
$$= \sum_{i=1}^{N} \log f(\mathbf{X}_{1,i}, ..., X_{p,i}\,;\,\alpha_1, ..., \alpha_q)$$

Observe that if the distribution is continuous, the probability of an individual sample is zero. Maximizing the probability of an individual sample is thus meaningless. However, we can approximate the probability of a small interval around any observed value with the product of the density times the size of the interval. We can now maximize the probability of small fixed intervals, which entails the likelihood maximization as stated above.

The Fisher Information Matrix and the Cramer-Rao Bound

ML estimators are usually biased. This is a consequence of the equivariance property of ML estimators: a function of an estimator is the estimator of the function. An interesting aspect of unbiased ML estimators is the possibility to estimate, in advance, bounds to the precision of estimates. Consider the q-vector $\boldsymbol{\alpha} = (\alpha_1, ..., \alpha_q)'$ of parameters that determine the population distribution $f(\mathbf{X}_1, ..., \mathbf{X}_N; \alpha_1, ..., \alpha_q)$. Suppose that $\hat{\boldsymbol{\alpha}}$ is an unbiased ML estimator of $\boldsymbol{\alpha}$. Then it can be demonstrated that the variance of the sampling distribution of $\hat{\boldsymbol{\alpha}}$ has a lower limit given by the Cramer-Rao bound,

$$\text{var}(\hat{\alpha}) \geq \{J^{-1}(\alpha)\}$$

where $\{J^{-1}(\alpha)\}$ are the diagonal elements of the inverse $J^{-1}(\alpha)$ of the *Fisher information matrix* $J(\alpha)$.

To define the Fisher information matrix, let's first define the *score*. The score q is defined as the vector formed by the first derivatives of the log-likelihood with respect to the parameters α, that is,

$$q(\hat{\alpha}) = \frac{\partial(l(\alpha|X))}{\partial \alpha}$$

The score is a random vector. It can be demonstrated that the expectation of the score is zero:

$$E(q(\hat{\alpha})) = 0$$

The covariance matrix of the score is the Fisher information matrix (also called the *Fisher information*):

$$J(\hat{\alpha}) = E[qq']$$

It can be demonstrated that the Fisher information matrix is also the expected value of the Hessian of the log-likelihood:

$$J(\hat{\alpha}) = -E\left[\left.\frac{\partial^2 l}{\partial \alpha_i \partial \alpha_j}\right|_{\alpha = \hat{\alpha}}\right]_{1 \leq i \leq q, 1 \leq j \leq q}$$

Intuitively, Fisher information is the amount of information that an observable random variable carries about a nonobservable parameter. There is a deep connection between Fisher information and Shannon information.[18]

---

[18] See Chapter 17 in Sergio M. Focardi and Frank J. Fabozzi, *The Mathematics of Financial Modeling and Investment Management* (Hoboken, NJ: John Wiley & Sons, 2004).

BAYESIAN MODELING

The Bayesian approach to dynamic modeling is based on Bayesian statistics. Therefore, we will begin our discussion of Bayesian modeling with a brief introduction to Bayesian statistics.

Bayesian Statistics

Bayesian statistics is perhaps the most difficult area in the science of statistics. The difficulty is not mathematical but conceptual: it resides in the Bayesian interpretation of probability. Classical statistics adopts a *frequentist* interpretation of probability; that is to say, the probability of an event is essentially the relative frequency of its appearance in large samples. However, it is well known that pure relative frequency is not a tenable basis for probability: One cannot strictly identify probability with relative frequency. What is needed is some *bridging principle* that links probability, which is an abstract concept, to empirical relative frequency. Bridging principles have been widely discussed in the literature, especially in the philosophical strain of statistical literature but, in practice, classical statistics identifies probability with relative frequency in large samples. When large samples are not available, for example in analyzing tail events, classical statistics adopts theoretical considerations.

The frequentist interpretation is behind most of today's estimation methods. When statisticians compute empirical probability distributions, they effectively equate probability and relative frequency. The concept is also implicit in estimation methods based on likelihood. In fact, maximum likelihood estimates of distribution parameters can be interpreted as those parameters that align the distribution as close as possible to the empirical distribution. When we compute empirical moments, we also adhere to a frequentist interpretation of probability.

In classical statistics, the probability distributions that embody a given statistical model are not subject to uncertainty. The perspective of classical statistics is that a given population has a *true* distribution: the objective of statistics is to infer the true distribution from a population sample.

Although most mathematical methods are similar to those of classical statistics, Bayesian statistics is based on a different set of concepts.[19] In particular, the following three concepts characterize Bayesian statistics:

---

[19] For a complete exposition of Bayesian statistics, see: D. A. Berry, *Statistics: A Bayesian Perspective* (Belmont, CA: Wadsworth, 1996); Thomas Leonard and John Hsu, *Bayesian Methods: An Analysis for Statisticians and Interdisciplinary Researchers* (Cambridge: Cambridge University Press, 1999) for a basic discussion; and J. M. Bernardo and A. F. M Smith, *Bayesian Theory* (Chichester: John Wiley & Sons, 2000) for a more advanced discussion.

- Statistical models are uncertain and subject to modification when new information is acquired.
- There is a distinction between prior probability (or prior distribution), which conveys the best estimate of probabilities given initial available information, and the posterior probability, which is the modification of the prior probability consequent to the acquisition of new information.
- The mathematical link between prior and posterior probabilities is given by Bayes' theorem.

The main difficulty is in grasping the meaning of these statements. On one side, the first two statements seem mere educated common sense, while the third is a rather simple mathematical statement that we illustrate in the following paragraphs. However, common sense does not make science. The usual scientific interpretation is that Bayesian statistics is essentially a rigorous method for making decisions based on the *subjectivistic* interpretation of probability.

In Bayesian statistics, probability is intended as subjective judgment guided by data. While a full exposé of Bayesian statistics is beyond the scope of this book, the crux of the problem can be summarized as follows. Bayesian statistics is rooted in data as probability judgments are updated with new data or information. However, according to Bayesian statistics there is an ineliminable subjective element; the subjective element is given by the initial prior probabilities that cannot be justified within the Bayesian theory.

It would be a mistake to think that Bayesian statistics is only a rigorous way to perform subjective uncertain reasoning while classical statistics is about real data.[20] Bayesian statistics explicitly recognizes that there is some ineliminable subjectivity in probability statements and attempts to reduce such subjectivity by updating probabilities. Classical statistics implicitly recognizes the same subjectivity when setting rules that bridge from data to probabilities.

In a nutshell, the conceptual problem of both classical and Bayesian statistics is that a probability statement does not per se correspond to any empirical reality. One cannot observe probabilities, only events that are interpreted in a probabilistic sense. The real problem, both in classical and Bayesian statistics, is how to link probability statements to empirical data. If mathematically sound and interpretable probability statements are to be constructed, bridging principles are required.

---

[20] Bayesian theories of uncertain reasoning are important in machine learning and artificial intelligence. See, for example, J. Pearl, *Probabilistic Reasoning in Intelligent Systems: Networks of Plausible Inference* (San Francisco: Morgan Kaufmann, 1988).

Before leaving the subject of Bayesian statistics, note that in financial econometrics there is a strain of literature and related methodologies based on Empirical Bayesian Statistics. In Empirical Bayesian Statistics, priors are estimated with the usual classical methods and then updated with new information. We will come back to this subject later in this chapter.

Bayes' Theorem

Let's now discuss Bayes' theorem, for which there are two interpretations. One interpretation is a simple accounting of probabilities in the classical sense. Given two events A and B, the following properties, called *Bayes' theorem*, hold:

$$P(A|B) = \frac{P(B|A)P(A)}{P(B)}$$

$$P(B|A) = \frac{P(A|B)P(B)}{P(A)}$$

These properties are an elementary consequence of the definitions of conditional probabilities:

$$P(AB) = P(A|B)P(B) = P(B|A)P(A)$$

In the second interpretation of Bayes' theorem, we replace the event A with a statistical hypothesis H and the event B with the data and write

$$P(H|\text{data}) = \frac{P(\text{data}|H)P(H)}{P(\text{data})}$$

This form of Bayes' theorem is the mathematical basis of Bayesian statistics. Given that $P(\text{data})$ is unconditional and does not depend on H, we can write the previous equation as

$$P(H|\text{data}) \propto P(\text{data}|H)P(H)$$

The probability $P(H)$ is called the *prior probability*, while the probability $P(H|\text{data})$ is called the *posterior probability*. The probability $P(\text{data}|H)$ of the data given H is called the *likelihood*.

Bayes' theorem can be expressed in a different form in terms of odds. The odds of H is the probability that H is false, written as $P(H^C)$. Bayes' theorem is written in terms of odds as follows:

$$\frac{P(H|\text{data})}{P(H^C|\text{data})} = \frac{P(\text{data}|H)P(H)}{P(\text{data}|H^C)P(H^C)}$$

The second interpretation of Bayes' theorem is not a logical consequence of Bayes' theorem in the first interpretation; it is an independent principle that assigns probabilities to statistical assumptions.

When applied to modeling, Bayes' theorem is expressed in terms of distributions, not probabilities. Bayes' theorem can be stated in terms of distributions as follows:

$$p(\vartheta|y) \propto L(y|\vartheta)\pi(\vartheta)$$

In this formulation, y represents the data, ϑ is the parameter set, $p(\vartheta|y)$ is the posterior distribution, $L(y|\vartheta)$ is the likelihood function, and $\pi(\vartheta)$ is the prior distribution.

A key issue in Bayesian statistics is how to determine the prior. Though considered subjective, the prior is not arbitrary. If it were, the estimation exercise would be futile. The prior represents the basic knowledge before specific measurements are taken into account. Two types of priors are often used: diffuse priors and conjugate priors. The *diffuse prior* assumes that we do not have any prior knowledge of the phenomena. A diffuse prior is a uniform distribution over an unspecified range. The *conjugate prior* is a prior such that, for a given likelihood, the prior and the posterior distribution type coincide.

APPENDIX A: INFORMATION STRUCTURES

Let's now turn our attention to the question of time. The previous discussion considered a space formed by states in an abstract sense. We must now introduce an appropriate representation of time as well as rules that describe the evolution of information, that is, *information propagation*, over time. The concepts of information and information propagation are fundamental in economics and finance theory.

The concept of information in finance is different from both the intuitive notion of information and that of information theory in which information is a quantitative measure related to the *a priori* probability of messages. In our context, information means the (progressive) revelation of the set of events to which the current state of the economy belongs. Though somewhat technical, this concept of information sheds light on the probabilistic structure of finance theory. The point is the following. Assets prices and returns are represented by stochastic processes, that is, time-dependent random variables. But the probabilistic states on which these random variables are defined represent entire histories of the economy. To embed time into the probabilistic structure of states in a coherent way calls for information structures and filtrations (a concept we explain in Appendix B of this chapter).

Recall that it is assumed that the economy is in one of many possible states and that there is uncertainty on the state that has been realized. Consider a time period of the economy. At the beginning of the period, there is complete uncertainty on the state of the economy (i.e., there is complete uncertainty on what path the economy will take). Different events have different probabilities, but there is no certainty. As time passes, uncertainty is reduced as the number of states to which the economy can belong is progressively reduced. Intuitively, revelation of information means the progressive reduction of the number of possible states; at the end of the period, the realized state is fully revealed. In continuous time and continuous states, the number of events is infinite at each instant. Thus its cardinality remains the same. We cannot properly say that the number of events shrinks. A more formal definition is required.

The progressive reduction of the set of possible states is formally expressed in the concepts of information structure and filtration. Let's start with *information structures*. Information structures apply only to discrete probabilities defined over a discrete set of states. At the initial instant T_0, there is complete uncertainty on the state of the economy; the actual state is known only to belong to the largest possible event (that is, the entire space Ω). At the following instant T_1, assuming that instants are discrete, the states are separated into a *partition*, a partition being a denumerable class of disjoint sets whose union is the space itself. The actual state belongs to one of the sets of the partitions. The revelation of information consists in ruling out all sets but one. For all the states of each partition, and only for these, random variables assume the same values.

Suppose, to exemplify, that only two assets exist in the economy and that each can assume only two possible prices and pay only two possible cash flows. At every moment there are 16 possible price-cash flow combinations. We can thus see that at the moment T_1 all the states are partitioned into 16 sets, each containing only one state. Each partition includes all the states that have a given set of prices and cash distributions at the moment T_1. The same reasoning can be applied to each instant. The evolution of information can thus be represented by a tree structure in which every path represents a state and every point a partition. Obviously the tree structure does not have to develop as symmetrically as in the above example; the tree might have a very generic structure of branches.

APPENDIX B: FILTRATION

The concept of information structure based on partitions provides a rather intuitive representation of the propagation of information through a tree of progressively finer partitions. However, this structure is not sufficient to describe the propagation of information in a general probabilistic context. In fact, the set of possible events is much richer than the set of partitions. It is therefore necessary to identify not only partitions but also a structure of events. The structure of events used to define the propagation of information is called a *filtration*. In the discrete case, however, the two concepts—information structure and filtration—are equivalent.

The concept of filtration is based on identifying all events that are known at any given instant. It is assumed that it is possible to associate to each trading moment t a σ-algebra of events $\Im_t \subset \Im$ formed by all events that are known prior to or at time t. It is assumed that events are never "forgotten," that is, that $\Im_t \subset \Im_s$, if $t < s$. An ordering of time is thus created. This ordering is formed by an increasing sequence of σ-algebras, each associated to the time at which all its events are known. This sequence is a filtration. Indicated as $\{\Im_t\}$, a filtration is therefore an increasing sequence of all σ-algebras $\Im_t$, each associated to an instant t.

In the finite case, it is possible to create a mutual correspondence between filtrations and information structures. In fact, given an information structure, it is possible to associate to each partition the algebra generated by the same partition. Observe that a tree information structure is formed by partitions that create increasing refinement: By going from one instant to the next, every set of the partition is decomposed. One can then conclude that the algebras generated by an information structure form a filtration.

On the other hand, given a filtration $\{\Im_t\}$, it is possible to associate a partition to each $\Im_t$. In fact, given any element that belongs to Ω, consider any other element that belongs to Ω such that, for each set of $\Im_t$, both either belong to or are outside this set. It is easy to see that classes of equivalence are thus formed, that these create a partition, and that the σ-algebra generated by each such partition is precisely the $\Im_t$ that has generated the partition.

A stochastic process is said to be adapted to the filtration $\{\Im_t\}$ if the variable X_t is measurable with respect to the σ-algebra $\Im_t$. It is assumed that the price and cash distribution processes $S_t(\omega)$ and $d_t(\omega)$ of every asset are adapted to $\{\Im_t\}$. This means that, for each t, no measurement of any price or cash distribution variable can identify events not included in the respective algebra or σ-algebra. Every random variable is a partial image of the set of states seen from a given point of view and at a given moment.

The concepts of filtration and of processes adapted to a filtration are fundamental. They ensure that information is revealed without anticipation. Consider the economy and associate at every instant a partition and an algebra generated by the partition. Every random variable defined at that moment assumes a value constant on each set of the partition. The knowledge of the realized values of the random variables does not allow identifying sets of events finer than partitions.

One might well ask: Why introduce the complex structure of σ-algebras as opposed to simply defining random variables? The point is that, from a logical point of view, the primitive concept is that of states and events. The evolution of time has to be defined on the primitive structure—it cannot simply be imposed on random variables. In practice, filtrations become an important concept when dealing with conditional probabilities in a continuous environment. As the probability that a continuous random variable assumes a specific value is zero, the definition of conditional probabilities requires the machinery of filtration.

CONCEPTS EXPLAINED IN THIS CHAPTER (IN ORDER OF PRESENTATION)

Probability
   Relative frequency
   Outcomes and events
   Algebras and sigma-algebras
   Measurable spaces
   Borel sets
   Probability space
   Probability measure
Independent events
Bayes theorem
Discrete probabilities
Random variables
Measurable functions
Cumulative distribution function
Probability density function
Random vectors
N-dimensional distribution functions and density functions
Marginal density and marginal distribution
Expectation
Independent random variables
Stochastic processes

Stochastic representation of financial markets
Conditional expectations
Law of iterated expectations
Martingale
Location
Dispersion
Skewness
Concentration in the tails
Kurtosis
Moments
Alpha quantiles
Sample moments
Correlation and covariance
Sequences of random variables
Limit
Concepts of convergence
Independent and identically distributed (IID) sequences
Sum of random variables
Convolution
Fourier transform
Characteristic function
Normal distribution
Score
Chi square distribution
t distribution
F distributions
Estimators
Sampling distributions
Critical values
Confidence intervals
Significance test
Test statistic
Null hypothesis
p-values
t-statistics
Maximum likelihood estimation
Likelihood function
Log-likelihood function
Cramer-Rao bound
Score
Fisher information matrix

Bayesian statistics
  Frequentist interpretation of probability
  Subjectivistic interpretation of probability
  Bayes' Theorem
  Prior probability
  Posterior probability
  Likelihood
  Diffuse priors
  Conjugate priors
Information propagation
Information structure
Filtration

CHAPTER 3

Regression Analysis: Theory and Estimation

Having covered the background information in the previous chapter, we are ready to turn to our first basic tool in econometrics: regression analysis. In regression analysis, we estimate the relationship between a random variable Y and one or more variables X_i. The variables X_i can be either deterministic variables or random variables. The variable Y is said to be the *dependent variable* because its value is assumed to be dependent on the value of the X_i's. The X_i's are referred to as the *independent variables, regressor variables,* or *explanatory variables.* Our primary focus in this book is on the *linear regression model.* We will be more precise about what we mean by a "linear" regression model later in this chapter. Let's begin with a discussion of the concept of dependence.

THE CONCEPT OF DEPENDENCE

Regressions are about *dependence* between variables. In this section we provide a brief discussion of how dependence is represented in both a deterministic setting and a probabilistic setting. In a deterministic setting, the concept of dependence is embodied in the mathematical notion of *function*. A function is a correspondence between the individuals of a given *domain A* and the individuals of a given *range B*. In particular, numerical functions establish a correspondence between numbers in a domain A and numbers in a range B.

In quantitative science, we work with variables obtained through a process of observation or measurement. For example, price is the observation of a transaction, time is the reading of a clock, position is determined with measurements of the coordinates, and so on. In quantitative science, we are interested in numerical functions $y = f(x_1, ..., x_n)$ that link the results of measurements so that by measuring the independent variables $(x_1, ..., x_n)$ we can predict the value of the dependent variable y. Being the results of measurements, variables are themselves functions that link a set Ω of unobserved "states of the world" to observations. Different states of the world result in different values for the variables but the link among the variables remains constant. For example, a column of mercury in a thermometer is a physical object that can be in different "states." If we measure the length and the temperature of the column (in steady conditions), we observe that the two measurements are linked by a well-defined (approximately linear) function. Thus, by measuring the length, we can predict the temperature.[1]

In order to model uncertainty, we keep the logical structure of variables as real-valued functions defined on a set Ω of unknown states of the world. However, we add to the set Ω the structure of a probability space as we have seen in Chapter 2. A probability space is a triple formed by a set of individuals (the states of the world), a structure of events, and a probability function: $(\Omega, \Im, P)$. Random variables represent measurements as in the deterministic case, but with the addition of a probability structure that represents uncertainty. In financial econometrics, a "state of the world" should be intended as a complete history of the underlying economy, not as an instantaneous state.

Our objective is to represent dependence between random variables, as we did in the deterministic case, so that we can infer the value of one variable from the measurement of the other. In particular, we want to infer the future values of variables from present and past observations. The probabilistic structure offers different possibilities. For simplicity, let's consider only two variables X and Y; our reasoning extends immediately to multiple variables. The first case of interest is the case when the dependent variable Y is a random variable while the independent variable X is deterministic. This situation is typical of an experimental setting where we can fix the conditions of the experiment while the outcome of the experiment is uncertain.

---

[1] The nature of the relationship between variables and the underlying reality has been (and still is) the subject of philosophical and scientific debate. In the classical view of science, variables represent an objective material reality. At the turn of the 19th century, logical positivists, in particular Michael Ayers and Rudolph Carnap, introduced the concept that the meaning of our assertions on the external world resides in the process of observation. This notion, introduced by Percy Bridgman, became the operational point of view of physics. The School of Copenhagen formed around Niels Bohr introduced the standard interpretation of quantum mechanics that follows the operational point of view.

In this case, the dependent variable Y has to be thought of as a family of random variables Y_x, all defined on the same probability space $(\Omega, \Im, P)$, indexed with the independent variable x. Dependence means that *the probability distribution of the dependent random variable depends on the value of the deterministic independent value.* To represent this dependence we use the notation $F(y|x)$ to emphasize the fact that x enters as a parameter in the distribution. An obvious example is the dependence of a price random variable on a time variable in a stochastic price process.

In this setting, where the independent variable is deterministic, the distributions $F(y|x)$ can be arbitrarily defined. Important for the discussion of linear regressions in this chapter is the case when the shape of the distribution $F(y|x)$ remains constant and only the mean of the distribution changes as a function of x.

Consider now the case where both X and Y are random variables. For example, Y might be the uncertain price of IBM stock tomorrow and X the uncertain level of the S&P 500 tomorrow. One way to express the link between these two variables is through their joint distribution $F(x,y)$ and, if it exists, their joint density $f(x,y)$. We define the joint and marginal distributions as follows:

$$F_{XY}(x, y) = P(X \leq x, Y \leq y), \; F_X(x) = P(X \leq x), \; F_Y(y) = P(Y \leq y)$$

$$F_{XY}(x, y) = \int\limits_{-\infty}^{+\infty} \int\limits_{-\infty}^{+\infty} f(x, y)\,dx\,dy$$

$$F_X(x) = \int\limits_{-\infty}^{x} \int\limits_{-\infty}^{-\infty} f(u, y)\,du\,dy = \int\limits_{-\infty}^{x} \left(\int\limits_{-\infty}^{-\infty} f(u, y)\,dy \right) du = \int\limits_{-\infty}^{x} f_X(u)\,du$$

$$F_Y(y) = \int\limits_{-\infty}^{-\infty} \int\limits_{-\infty}^{y} f(x, v)\,dx\,dv = \int\limits_{-\infty}^{y} \left(\int\limits_{-\infty}^{-\infty} f(x, v)\,dx \right) dv = \int\limits_{-\infty}^{x} f_Y(v)\,dv$$

$$f(x|y) = \frac{f(x, y)}{f_Y(y)}, \; f(y|x) = \frac{f(x, y)}{f_X(x)}$$

We will also use the short notation:

$$f_X(x) = f(x), \; f_Y(y) = f(y), \; f_{X|Y}(x|y) = f(x|y), \; f_{Y|X}(y|x) = f(y|x)$$

Given a joint density $f(x,y)$, we can also represent the functional link between the two variables as the dependence of the distribution of one variable on the value assumed by the other variable. In fact, we can write the joint density $f(x,y)$ as the product of two factors, the conditional density $f(y|x)$ and the marginal density $f_X(x)$:

$$f(x, y) = f(y|x)f_X(x) \qquad (3.1)$$

This *factorization*—that is, expressing a joint density as a product of a marginal density and a conditional density—is the conceptual basis of financial econometrics (see Chapter 1). There are significant differences in cases where both variables X and Y are random variables, compared to the case where the variable X is deterministic. First, as both variables are uncertain, we cannot fix the value of one variable as if it were independent. We have to adopt a framework of *conditioning* where our knowledge of one variable influences our knowledge of the other variable.

The impossibility of making experiments is a major issue in econometrics. In the physical sciences, the ability to create the desired experimental setting allows the scientist to isolate the effects of single variables. The experimenter tries to create an environment where the effects of variables other than those under study are minimized. In economics, however, all the variables change together and cannot be controlled. Back in the 1950s, there were serious doubts that econometrics was possible. In fact, it was believed that estimation required the independence of samples while economic samples are never independent.

However, the framework of conditioning addresses this problem. After conditioning, the joint densities of a process are factorized into initial and conditional densities that behave as independent distributions. This notion was anticipated in Chapter 1: An econometric model is a probe that extracts independent samples—the noise terms—from highly dependent variables.

Let's briefly see, at the heuristic level, how conditioning works. Suppose we learn that the random variable X has the value x, that is, $X = x$. Recall that X is a random variable that is a real-valued function defined over the set Ω. If we know that $X = x$, we do not know the present state of the world but we do know that it must be in the subspace ($\omega \in \Omega$: $X(\omega) = x$). We call ($Y|X = x$) the variable Y defined on this subspace. If we let x vary, we create a family of random variables defined on the family of subspaces ($\omega \in \Omega$: $X(\omega) = x$) and indexed by the value assumed by the variable X.

It can be demonstrated that the sets ($\omega \in \Omega$: $X(\omega) = x$) can be given a structure of probability space, that the variables ($Y|X = x$) are indeed random variables on these probability spaces, and that they have (if they exist) the conditional densities:

$$f(y|x) = \frac{f(x, y)}{f_X(x)} \tag{3.2}$$

for $f_X(x) > 0$. In the discrete setting we can write

$$f(y|x) = P(Y = y|X = x)$$
$$f(x,y) = P(X = x, Y = y)$$

The conditional expectation $E[Y|X = x]$ is the expectation of the variable $(Y|X = x)$. Consider the previous example of the IBM stock price tomorrow and of the S&P 500 level tomorrow. Both variables have unconditional expectations. These are the expectations of IBM's stock tomorrow and of S&P 500's level tomorrow considering every possible state of the world. However, we might be interested in computing the expected value of IBM's stock price tomorrow if we know S&P 500's value tomorrow. This is the case if, for example, we are creating scenarios based on S&P 500's value.

If we know the level of the S&P 500, we do not know the present state of the world but we do know the subset of states of the world in which the present state of the world is. If we only know the value of the S&P 500, IBM's stock price is not known because it is different in each state that belongs to this restricted set. IBM's stock price is a random variable on this restricted space and we can compute its expected value.

If we consider a discrete setting, that is, if we consider only a discrete set of possible IBM stock prices and S&P 500 values, then the computation of the conditional expectation can be performed using the standard definition of conditional probability. In particular, the conditional expectation of a random variable Y given the event B is equal to the unconditional expectation of the variable Y set to zero outside of B and divided by the probability of B: $E[Y|B] = E[1_B Y]/P(B)$, where 1_B is the indicator function of the set B, equal to 1 for all elements of B, zero elsewhere. Thus, in this example,

$E[\text{IBM stock price}|\text{S\&P 500 value} = s]$
$= E[1_{(\text{S\&P 500 value} = s)}(\text{IBM stock price})]/P(\text{S\&P 500 value} = s)$

However, in a continuous-state setting there is a fundamental difficulty: The set of states of the world corresponding to any given value of the S&P 500 has probability zero; therefore we cannot normalize dividing by $P(B)$. As a consequence we cannot use the standard definition of conditional probability to compute directly the conditional expectation.

To overcome this difficulty, we define the conditional expectation indirectly, using only unconditional expectations. We define the conditional expectation of IBM's stock price given the S&P 500 level as that variable that has the same unconditional expectation as IBM's stock price on each set that can be identified by for the value of the S&P 500. This is a random variable which is uniquely defined for each state of the world up to a set of probability zero.[2]

If the conditional density exists, conditional expectation is computed as follows:

$$E[Y|X = x] = \int_{-\infty}^{+\infty} yf(y|x)dy \qquad (3.3)$$

We know from Chapter 2 that the *law of iterated expectations* holds

$$E[E[Y|X = x]] = E[Y] \qquad (3.4)$$

and that the following relationship also holds

$$E[XY] = E[XE[Y|X]] \qquad (3.5)$$

Rigorously proving all these results requires a considerable body of mathematics and the rather difficult language and notation of σ-algebras. However, the key ideas should be sufficiently clear.

What is the bearing of the above on the discussion of regressions in this chapter? Regressions have a twofold nature: they can be either (1) the representation of dependence in terms of conditional expectations and conditional distributions or (2) the representation of dependence of

---

[2] In rigorous terms, conditioning is defined with respect to a σ-algebra. Consider a random variable X defined on the probability space $(\Omega, \Im, P)$. Suppose that $G \subset \Im$ is a sub-σ-algebra of $\Im$ and that P_G is the probability measure P restricted to G. Then we define the conditional expectation of X given G as that random variable $E[X|G]$, measurable G, such that, for every $A \in G$:

$$E[1_A X] = \int_{\Omega} 1_A E[X|G]dP_G = E[1_A E[X|G]]$$

It can be demonstrated that the conditional expectation exists for any integrable random variable. The conditional expectation is not uniquely defined. For each integrable random variable, there are infinite conditional expectations defined up to P_G only almost surely (a.s.). Conditioning with respect to another variable is therefore conditioning with respect to the σ-algebra generated by that variable.

random variables on deterministic parameters. The above discussion clarifies the probabilistic meaning of both.

REGRESSIONS AND LINEAR MODELS

In this section we discuss regressions and, in particular, linear regressions.

Case Where All Regressors Are Random Variables

Let's start our discussion of regression with the case where all regressors are random variables. Given a set of random variables $X = (Y, X_1,..., X_N)'$, with a joint probability density $f(y, x_1,..., x_N)$, consider the conditional expectation of Y given the other variables $(X_1,..., X_N)'$:

$$Y = E[Y|X_1, ..., X_N]$$

As we saw in the previous section, the conditional expectation is a random variable. We can therefore consider the *residual*:

$$\varepsilon = Y - E[Y|X_1, ..., X_N]$$

The residual is another random variable defined over the set Ω. We can rewrite the above equation as a *regression equation*:

$$Y = E[Y|X_1, ..., X_N] + \varepsilon \tag{3.6}$$

The deterministic function $y = \varphi(z)$ where

$$y = \varphi(z) = E[Y|X_1 = z_1,..., X_N = z_N] \tag{3.7}$$

is called the *regression function*.

The following properties of regression equations hold.

Property 1. The conditional mean of the residual is zero: $E[\varepsilon|X_1,..., X_N] = 0$. In fact, taking conditional expectations on both sides of equation (3.7), we can write

$$E[Y|X_1,..., X_N] = E[E[Y|X_1,..., X_N]|X_1,..., X_N] + E[\varepsilon|X_1,..., X_N]$$

Because

$$E[E[Y|X_1,..., X_N]|X_1,..., X_N] = E[Y|X_1,..., X_N]$$

is a property that follows from the law of iterated expectations, we can conclude that $E[\varepsilon|X_1,..., X_N] = 0$.

Property 2. The unconditional mean of the residual is zero: $E[\varepsilon] = 0$. This property follows immediately from the multivariate formulation of the law of iterated expectations (3.4): $E[E[Y|X_1,..., X_N]] = E[Y]$. In fact, taking expectation of both sides of equation (3.7) we can write

$$E[Y] = E[E[Y|X_1,..., X_N]] + E[\varepsilon]$$

hence $E[\varepsilon] = 0$.

Property 3: The residuals are uncorrelated with the variables $X_1,..., X_N$: $E[\varepsilon X] = 0$. This follows from equation (3.6) by multiplying both sides of equation (3.7) by $X_1,..., X_N$ and taking expectations. Note however, that the residuals are not necessarily independent of the regressor X.

If the regression function is linear, we can write the following *linear regression equation*:

$$Y = a + \sum_{i=1}^{N} b_i X_i + \varepsilon \tag{3.8}$$

and the following linear regression function:

$$y = a + \sum_{i=1}^{N} b_i x_i \tag{3.9}$$

The rest of this chapter deals with linear regressions. If the vector $Z = (Y, X_1,..., X_N)'$ is jointly normally distributed, then the regression function is linear. To see this, partition z, the vector of means μ, and the covariance matrix Σ conformably in the following way:

$$Z = \begin{pmatrix} Y \\ X \end{pmatrix}, z = \begin{pmatrix} y \\ x \end{pmatrix}, \mu = \begin{pmatrix} \mu_y \\ \mu_x \end{pmatrix}, \Sigma = \begin{pmatrix} \sigma_{yy} & \sigma_{xy} \\ \sigma_{yx} & \Sigma_{xx} \end{pmatrix}$$

where μ is the vector of means and Σ is the covariance matrix. It can be demonstrated that the conditional density $(Y|X = x)$ has the following expression:

$$(Y|X = x) \sim N(\alpha + \beta'x, \sigma^2) \qquad (3.10)$$

where

$$\begin{aligned} \beta &= \Sigma_{xx}^{-1}\sigma_{xy} \\ \alpha &= \mu_y - \beta'\mu_x \\ \sigma^2 &= \sigma_{yy}^2 - \sigma_{yx}\Sigma_{xx}^{-1}\sigma_{xy} \end{aligned} \qquad (3.11)$$

The regression function can be written as follows:

$$y = \alpha + \beta'x, \text{ or explicitly: } y = \alpha + \sum_{i=1}^{N} \beta_i x_i \qquad (3.12)$$

The normal distribution is not the only joint distribution that yields linear regressions. Spherical and elliptical distributions also yield linear regressions. Spherical distributions extend the multivariate normal distribution $N(0,I)$ (i.e., the joint distribution of independent normal variables). Spherical distributions are characterized by the property that their density is constant on a sphere, so that their joint density can be written as

$$f(x_1, ..., x_N) = g(x_1^2 + \cdots + x_N^2)$$

for some function g.

Spherical distributions have the property that their marginal distributions are uncorrelated but not independent, and can be viewed as multivariate normal random variables, with a random covariance matrix. An example of a spherical distribution used in financial econometrics is the multivariate t-distribution with m degrees of freedom, whose density has the following form:

$$f(x_1, ..., x_N) = c\left[1 + \frac{1}{m}(x_1^2 + \cdots + x_N^2)\right]^{-\frac{m+N}{2}}$$

The multivariate t-distribution is important in econometrics for several reasons. First, some sampling distributions are actually a t-distribution (we will see this in the following chapters). Second, the t-distribution proved to be an adequate description of fat-tailed error terms in some econometrics models, as we will see in Chapter 14 (although not as good as the stable Paretian distribution described in Chapter 14).

Elliptical distributions generalize the multivariate normal distribution $N(0,\Sigma)$.[3] Because they are constant on an ellipsoid, their joint density can be written as

$$f(\mathbf{x}) = g((\mathbf{x}-\boldsymbol{\mu})'\Sigma(\mathbf{x}-\boldsymbol{\mu})), \; \mathbf{x}' = (x_1,...,x_N)$$

where $\boldsymbol{\mu}$ is a vector of constants and Σ is a strictly positive-definite matrix. Spherical distributions are a subset of elliptical distributions. Conditional distributions and linear combinations of elliptical distributions are also elliptical.

The fact that elliptical distributions yield linear regressions is closely related to the fact that the linear correlation coefficient is a meaningful measure of dependence only for elliptical distributions. There are distributions that do not factorize as linear regressions. The linear correlation coefficient is not a meaningful measure of dependence for these distributions. The copula function of a given random vector $X = (X_1,...,X_N)'$ completely describes the dependence structure of the joint distribution of random variables X_i, $i = 1,...,N$.[4]

Linear Models and Linear Regressions

Let's now discuss the relationship between linear regressions and linear models. In applied work, we are given a set of multivariate data that we want to explain through a model of their dependence. Suppose we want to explain the data through a linear model of the type:

$$Y = \alpha + \sum_{i=1}^{N} \beta_i X_i + \varepsilon$$

We might know from theoretical reasoning that linear models are appropriate or we might want to try a linear approximation to nonlin-

---

[3] Brendan O. Bradley and Murad S. Taqqu, "Financial Risk and Heavy Tails," in Svetlozar T. Rachev (ed.), *Handbook of Heavy Tailed Distributions in Finance* (Amsterdam: Elsevier/North Holland, 2003), pp. 35–103.

[4] Paul Embrechts, Alexander McNeil, and Daniel Straumann, "Correlation and Dependence in Risk Management: Properties and Pitfalls," in Michael Dempster (ed.), *Risk Management: Value at Risk and Beyond* (Cambridge: Cambridge University Press, 2002), pp. 176–223.

ear models. A linear model such as the above is not, per se, a linear regression unless we apply appropriate constraints. In fact, linear regressions must satisfy the three properties mentioned above. We call linear regressions linear models of the above type that satisfy the following set of assumptions such that

$$\alpha + \sum_{i=1}^{N} \beta_i X_i$$

is the conditional expectation of Y.

Assumption 1. The conditional mean of the residual is zero: $E[\varepsilon | X_1,..., X_N]$.

Assumption 2. The unconditional mean of the residual is zero: $E[\varepsilon] = 0$.

Assumption 3: The correlation between the residuals and the variables $X_1,..., X_N$ is zero: $E[\varepsilon X] = 0$.

The above set of assumptions is not the full set of assumptions used when estimating a linear model as a regression but only consistency conditions to interpret a linear model as a regression. We will introduce additional assumptions relative to how the model is sampled in the section on estimation. Note that the linear regression equation does not fully specify the joint conditional distribution of the dependent variables and the regressors.[5]

Case Where Regressors Are Deterministic Variables

In many applications of interest to the financial modeler, the regressors are deterministic variables. Conceptually, regressions with deterministic regressors are different from cases where regressors are random variables. In particular, as we have seen in a previous section, one cannot consider the regression as a conditional expectation. However, we can write a linear regression equation:

$$Y = \alpha + \sum_{i=1}^{N} \beta_i x_i + \varepsilon \qquad (3.13)$$

---

[5] This point is a rather subtle point related to concept of exogeneity of variables. See David F. Hendry, *Dynamic Econometrics* (Oxford: Oxford University Press, 1995) for a discussion of these questions.

and the following linear regression function:

$$y = \alpha + \sum_{i=1}^{N} \beta_i x_i \qquad (3.14)$$

where the regressors are deterministic variables. As we will see in the following section, in both cases the least squares estimators are the same though the variances of the regression parameters as functions of the samples are different.

ESTIMATION OF LINEAR REGRESSIONS

In this section, we discuss how to estimate the linear regression parameters. We consider two main estimation techniques: maximum likelihood and least squares methods. A discussion of the sampling distributions of linear regression parameters follow. The method of moments and the instrumental variables method are discussed in Chapter 4.

Maximum Likelihood Estimates

Let's reformulate the regression problem in a matrix form that is standard in regression analysis and that we will use in the following sections. Let's start with the case of a dependent variable Y and one independent regressor X. This case is referred to as the *bivariate case* or the *simple linear regression*. Suppose that we are empirically given T pairs of observations of the regressor and the independent variable. In financial econometrics these observations could represent, for example, the returns Y of a stock and the returns X of a factor taken at fixed intervals of time $t = 1, 2,..., T$. Using a notation that is standard in regression estimation, we place the given data in a vector Y and a matrix X:

$$\mathbf{Y} = \begin{pmatrix} Y_1 \\ \vdots \\ Y_T \end{pmatrix}, \mathbf{X} = \begin{pmatrix} 1 & X_1 \\ \vdots & \vdots \\ 1 & X_T \end{pmatrix} \qquad (3.15)$$

The column of 1s represents constant terms. The regression equation can be written as a set of T samples from the same regression equation, one for each moment:

$$Y_1 = \beta_0 + \beta_1 X_1 + \varepsilon_1$$
$$\vdots$$
$$Y_T = \beta_0 + \beta_1 X_T + \varepsilon_T$$

that we can rewrite in matrix form,

$$\mathbf{Y} = \mathbf{X}\boldsymbol{\beta} + \boldsymbol{\varepsilon}$$

where $\boldsymbol{\beta}$ is the vector of regression coefficients,

$$\boldsymbol{\beta} = \begin{pmatrix} \beta_0 \\ \beta_1 \end{pmatrix}$$

and $\boldsymbol{\varepsilon}$ are the residuals.

We now make a set of assumptions that are standard in regression analysis and that we will progressively relax. The assumptions for the linear regression model with normally distributed residuals are:

1. The residuals are zero-mean, normally distributed independent variables $\varepsilon \sim N(0, \sigma_\varepsilon^2 \mathbf{I})$, where σ_ε^2 is the common variance of the residuals and $\mathbf{I}$ is the identity matrix.
2. $\mathbf{X}$ is distributed independently of the residuals $\boldsymbol{\varepsilon}$. $\left.\begin{array}{}\\\\\\\\\end{array}\right\}$ (3.16)

The regression equation can then be written: $E(\mathbf{Y}|\mathbf{X}) = \mathbf{X}\boldsymbol{\beta}$. The residuals form a sequence of independent variables. They can therefore be regarded as a strict white-noise sequence (see Chapter 6 for a discussion of strict white noise). As the residuals are independent draws from the same normal distribution, we can compute the log-likelihood function as follows:

$$\log L = -\frac{T}{2}\log(2\pi) - \frac{T}{2}\log(\sigma_\varepsilon^2) - \sum_{t=1}^{T} \left[\frac{(Y_t - \beta_0 - \beta_1 X_t)^2}{2\sigma_\varepsilon^2} \right] \quad (3.17)$$

The Maximum Likelihood (ML) principle requires maximization of the log-likelihood function. Maximizing the log-likelihood function entails first solving the equations:

$$\frac{\partial \log L}{\partial \beta_0} = 0, \frac{\partial \log L}{\partial \beta_1} = 0, \frac{\partial \log L}{\partial \sigma_\varepsilon^2} = 0$$

These equations can be explicitly written as follows:

$$\sum_{t=1}^{T} (Y_t - \beta_0 - \beta_1 X_t) = 0$$

$$\sum_{t=1}^{T} X_t(Y_t - \beta_0 - \beta_1 X_t) = 0$$

$$T\sigma_\varepsilon^2 - \sum_{t=1}^{T} [(Y_t - \beta_0 - \beta_1 X_t)^2] = 0$$

A little algebra shows that solving the first two equations yields

$$\hat{\beta}_1 = \frac{\overline{XY} - \overline{X}\,\overline{Y}}{\sigma_\varepsilon^2}$$

(3.18)

$$\hat{\beta}_0 = (\overline{Y} - \beta_1 \overline{X})$$

where

$$\overline{X} = \frac{1}{T}\sum_{t=1}^{T} X_t, \quad \overline{XY} = \frac{1}{T}\sum_{t=1}^{T} X_t Y_t$$

and where $\overline{\sigma}_x, \overline{\sigma}_y$ are the empirical standard deviations of the sample variables X, Y respectively. Substituting these expressions in the third equation

$$\frac{\partial \log L}{\partial \sigma_\varepsilon^2} = 0$$

yields the variance of the residuals:

$$\hat{\sigma}_\varepsilon^2 = \frac{1}{T}\sum_{t=1}^{T} \left[\left(Y_t - \hat{\beta}_0 - \hat{\beta}_1 X_t \right)^2 \right]$$

(3.19)

In the matrix notation established above, we can write the estimators as follows:

For parameters: $\hat{\beta} = (X'X)^{-1}X'Y$ (3.20)

For the variance of the regression: $\hat{\sigma}^2 = \frac{1}{T}\left(Y - X\hat{\beta}\right)'\left(Y - X\hat{\beta}\right)$ (3.21)

A comment is in order. We started with T pairs of given data (X_i, Y_i), $i = 1,..., T$ and then attempted to explain these data as a linear regression $Y = \beta_1 X + \beta_0 + \varepsilon$. We estimated the coefficients (β_1, β_2) with Maximum Likelihood Estimation (MLE) methods. Given this estimate of the regression coefficients, the estimated variance of the residuals is given by equation (3.22). Note that equation (3.22) is the *empirical variance of residuals* computed using the estimated regression parameters. A large variance of the residuals indicates that the level of noise in the process (i.e., the size of the unexplained fluctuations of the process) is high.

Generalization to Multiple Independent Variables

The above discussion of the MLE method generalizes to multiple independent variables, N. We are empirically given a set of T observations that we organize in matrix form,

$$Y = \begin{pmatrix} Y_1 \\ \vdots \\ Y_T \end{pmatrix}, \quad X = \begin{pmatrix} X_{11} & \cdots & X_{N1} \\ \vdots & \ddots & \vdots \\ X_{1T} & \cdots & X_{NT} \end{pmatrix}$$ (3.22)

and the regression coefficients and error terms in the vectors,

$$\beta = \begin{pmatrix} \beta_1 \\ \vdots \\ \beta_N \end{pmatrix}, \quad \varepsilon = \begin{pmatrix} \varepsilon_1 \\ \vdots \\ \varepsilon_T \end{pmatrix}$$ (3.23)

The matrix X which contains all the regressors is called the *design matrix*. The regressors X can be deterministic, the important condition being that the residuals are independent. One of the columns can be formed by 1s to allow for a constant term (intercept). Our objective is to explain the data as a linear regression:

$$Y = X\beta + \varepsilon$$

We make the same set of assumptions given by equation (3.17) as we made in the case of a single regressor. Using the above notation, the loglikelihood function will have the form

$$\log L = -\frac{T}{2}\log(2\pi) - \frac{T}{2}\log(\sigma_\varepsilon^2) - \frac{1}{2\sigma_\varepsilon^2}(\mathbf{Y} - \mathbf{X}\boldsymbol{\beta})'(\mathbf{Y} - \mathbf{X}\boldsymbol{\beta}) \qquad (3.24)$$

The maximum likelihood conditions are written as

$$\frac{\partial \log L}{\partial \boldsymbol{\beta}} = 0, \ \frac{\partial \log L}{\partial \sigma_\varepsilon^2} = 0 \qquad (3.25)$$

These equations are called *normal equations*. Solving the system of normal equations gives the same form for the estimators as in the univariate case:

$$\hat{\boldsymbol{\beta}} = (\mathbf{X}'\mathbf{X})^{-1}\mathbf{X}'\mathbf{Y}$$
$$\hat{\sigma}^2 = \frac{1}{T}\Big(\mathbf{Y} - \mathbf{X}\hat{\boldsymbol{\beta}}\Big)'\Big(\mathbf{Y} - \mathbf{X}\hat{\boldsymbol{\beta}}\Big) \qquad (3.26)$$

The variance estimator is not unbiased.[6] It can be demonstrated that to obtain an unbiased estimator we have to apply a correction that takes into account the number of variables by replacing T with $T - N$, assuming $T > N$:

$$\hat{\sigma}^2 = \frac{1}{T-N}\Big(\mathbf{Y} - \mathbf{X}\hat{\boldsymbol{\beta}}\Big)'\Big(\mathbf{Y} - \mathbf{X}\hat{\boldsymbol{\beta}}\Big) \qquad (3.27)$$

The MLE method requires that we know the functional form of the distribution. If the distribution is known but not normal, we can still apply the MLE method but the estimators will be different. We will not here discuss further MLE for nonnormal distributions.

Ordinary Least Squares Method

We now establish the relationship between the MLE principle and the *ordinary least squares* (OLS) method. OLS is a general method to approximate a relationship between two or more variables. We use the matrix notation

---

[6] See Chapter 2 for an explanation of properties of estimators.

defined above for MLE method; that is, we assume that observations are described by the equation (3.23) while the regression coefficients and the residuals are described by equation (3.24).

If we use the OLS method, the assumptions of linear regressions can be weakened. In particular, we need not assume that the residuals are normally distributed but only assume that they are uncorrelated and have finite variance. The residuals can therefore be regarded as a white-noise sequence (and not a strict white-noise sequence as in the previous section). We summarize the linear regression assumptions as follows:

Assumptions for the linear regression model:
1. The mean of the residuals is zero: $E(\varepsilon) = 0$
2. The residuals are mutually uncorrelated:
   $(E(\varepsilon\varepsilon') = \sigma^2 I)$, where σ^2 is the variance of the residuals and I is the identity matrix.
3. X is distributed independently of the residuals ε.

$$(3.28)$$

In the general case of a multivariate regression, the OLS method requires minimization of the sum of the squared residuals. Consider the vector of residuals:

$$\varepsilon = \begin{bmatrix} \varepsilon_1 \\ \vdots \\ \varepsilon_T \end{bmatrix}$$

The *sum of the squared residuals* (SSR) $= (\varepsilon_1^2 + \cdots + \varepsilon_T^2)$ can be written as SSR $= \varepsilon'\varepsilon$. As $\varepsilon = Y - X\beta$, we can also write

$$SSR = (Y - X\beta)'(Y - X\beta)$$

The OLS method requires that we minimize the SSR. To do so, we equate to zero the first derivatives of the SSR:

$$\frac{\partial(Y - X\beta)'(Y - X\beta)}{\partial\beta} = 0$$

This is a system of N equations. Solving this system, we obtain the estimators:

$$\hat{\beta} = (\mathbf{X}'\mathbf{X})^{-1}\mathbf{X}'\mathbf{Y}$$

These estimators are the same estimators obtained with the MLE method; they have an optimality property. In fact, the Gauss-Markov theorem states that the above OLS estimators are the *best linear unbiased estimators* (BLUE). "Best" means that no other linear unbiased estimator has a lower variance. It should be noted explicitly that OLS and MLE are conceptually different methodologies: MLE seeks the optimal parameters of the distribution of the error terms, while OLS seeks to minimize the variance of error terms. The fact that the two estimators coincide was an important discovery.

SAMPLING DISTRIBUTIONS OF REGRESSIONS

Estimated regression parameters depend on the sample. They are random variables whose distribution is to be determined. As we will see in this section, the sampling distributions differ depending on whether the regressors are assumed to be fixed deterministic variables or random variables.

Let's first assume that the regressors are fixed deterministic variables. Thus only the error terms and the dependent variable change from sample to sample. The $\hat{\beta}$ are unbiased estimators and $E[\hat{\beta}] = \beta$ therefore holds. It can also be demonstrated that the following expression for the variance of $\hat{\beta}$ holds

$$E[(\beta - \hat{\beta})(\beta - \hat{\beta})'] = \sigma^2(\mathbf{X}'\mathbf{X})^{-1} \qquad (3.29)$$

where an estimate $\hat{\sigma}^2$ of σ^2 is given by 3.27.

Under the additional assumption that the residuals are normally distributed, it can be demonstrated that the regression coefficients are jointly normally distributed as follows:

$$\hat{\beta} \sim N_N[\beta, \sigma^2(\mathbf{X}'\mathbf{X})^{-1}] \qquad (3.30)$$

These expressions are important because they allow to compute confidence intervals for the regression parameters.

Let's now suppose that the regressors are random variables. Under the assumptions set forth in (3.29), it can be demonstrated that the variance of the estimators $\hat{\beta}$ can be written as follows:

$$V(\hat{\boldsymbol{\beta}}) = E[(\mathbf{X'X})^{-1}]V(\mathbf{X'\boldsymbol{\epsilon}})E[(\mathbf{X'X})^{-1}] \tag{3.31}$$

where the terms $E[(\mathbf{X'X})^{-1}]$ and $V(\mathbf{X'\boldsymbol{\epsilon}})$ are the empirical expectation of $(\mathbf{X'X})^{-1}$ and the empirical variance of $(\mathbf{X'\boldsymbol{\epsilon}})$, respectively.

The following terms are used to describe this estimator of the variance: *sandwich estimator, robust estimator,* and *White estimator.* (These concepts will be expanded in Chapter 12 on robust methods.) The term sandwich estimator is due to the fact that the term $V(\mathbf{X'\boldsymbol{\epsilon}})$ is sandwiched between the terms $E[(\mathbf{X'X})^{-1}]$. These estimators are *robust* because they take into account not only the variability of the dependent variables but also that of the independent variables. Consider that if the regressors are a large sample, the sandwich and the classical estimators are close to each other.

DETERMINING THE EXPLANATORY POWER OF A REGRESSION

The above computations to estimate regression parameters were carried out under the assumption that the data were generated by a linear regression function with uncorrelated and normally distributed noise. In general, we do not know if this is indeed the case. Though we can always estimate a linear regression model on any data sample by applying the estimators discussed above, we must now ask the question: When is a linear regression applicable and how can one establish the goodness (i.e., explanatory power) of a linear regression?

Quite obviously, a linear regression model is applicable if the relationship between the variables is approximately linear. How can we check if this is indeed the case? What happens if we fit a linear model to variables that have non-linear relationships, or if distributions are not normal? A number of tests have been devised to help answer these questions.

Intuitively, a measure of the quality of approximation offered by a linear regression is given by the variance of the residuals. Squared residuals are used because a property of the estimated relationship is that the sum of the residuals is zero. If residuals are large, the regression model has little explanatory power. However, the size of the average residual in itself is meaningless as it has to be compared with the range of the variables. For example, if we regress stock prices over a broad-based stock index, other things being equal, the residuals will be numerically different if the price is in the range of dollars or in the range of hundreds of dollars.

Coefficient of Determination

A widely used measure of the quality and usefulness of a regression model is given by the *coefficient of determination* denoted by R^2 or R-squared. The idea behind R^2 is the following. The dependent variable Y has a total variation given by the following expression:

$$\text{Total variation} = S_Y^2 = \frac{1}{T-1} \sum_{t=1}^{T} (Y_t - \bar{Y})^2 \tag{3.32}$$

where

$$\bar{Y} = \frac{1}{T-1} \sum_{t=1}^{T} Y_t$$

This total variation is the sum of the variation of the variable Y due to the variation of the regressors plus the variation of residuals $S_Y^2 = S_R^2 + S_\varepsilon^2$. We can therefore define the coefficient of determination:

$$\text{Coefficient of determination} = R^2 = \frac{S_R^2}{S_Y^2}$$

$$1 - R^2 = \frac{S_\varepsilon^2}{S_Y^2} \tag{3.33}$$

as the portion of the total fluctuation of the dependent variable, Y, explained by the regression relation. R^2 is a number between 0 and 1: $R^2 = 0$ means that the regression has no explanatory power, $R^2 = 1$ means that the regression has perfect explanatory power. The quantity R^2 is computed by software packages that perform linear regressions.

It can be demonstrated that the coefficient of determination R^2 is distributed as the well known Student F distribution. This fact allows one to determine intervals of confidence around a measure of the significance of a regression.

Adjusted R^2

The quantity R^2 as a measure of the usefulness of a regression model suffers from the problem that a regression might fit data very well in-sample but have no explanatory power out-of-sample. This occurs if the number of regressors is too high. Therefore an adjusted R^2 is sometimes used. The adjusted R^2 is defined as R^2 corrected by a penalty function that takes into account the number p of regressors in the model:

$$\text{Adjusted } R^2 = \frac{T-1}{T-N-1} \frac{S_R^2}{S_Y^2} \qquad (3.34)$$

Relation of R^2 to Correlation Coefficient

The R^2 is the squared *correlation coefficient*. The correlation coefficient is a number between -1 and $+1$ that measures the strength of the dependence between two variables. If a linear relationship is assumed, the correlation coefficient has the usual product-moment expression:

$$r = \sqrt{\frac{\overline{XY} - \overline{X}\,\overline{Y}}{S_y S_x}} \qquad (3.35)$$

USING REGRESSION ANALYSIS IN FINANCE

This section provides several illustrations of regression analysis in finance as well as the data for each illustration. However, in order to present the data, we limit our sample size. The first two illustrations show how to use simple linear regressions (i.e., bivariate regressions) to calculate the characteristic line for common stocks and for mutual funds; the following examples show how to use multiple regressions to estimate empirical duration of common stocks. Further applications are provided in Chapter 5.

Characteristic Line for Common Stocks

The *characteristic line* of a security is the regression of the excess returns of that security on the market excess returns:

$$r_i = \alpha_i + \beta_i r_M$$

where

r_i = the security excess return of a security over the risk-free rate
r_M = the market excess return of the market over the risk-free rate

The characteristic line is discussed in more detail in Chapter 5.

We computed the characteristic lines of two common stocks, Oracle and General Motors (GM), and a randomly created portfolio consisting of 20 stocks equally weighted. We used the S&P 500 Index as a proxy for the market returns and the 90-day Treasury rate as a proxy for the risk-free rate. The return and excess return data are shown in Exhibit 3.1. Note that there are 60 monthly observations used to estimate the characteristic line from December 2000 to November 2005. The 20 stocks comprising the portfolio are shown at the bottom of Exhibit 3.1.

The estimated parameters for the two stocks and the portfolios are reported in Exhibit 3.2. As can be seen from the exhibit, the intercept term is not statistically significant; however, the slope, referred to as the beta of the characteristic line, is statistically significant. Typically for individual stocks, the R^2 ranges from 0.15 to 0.65. For Oracle and GM the R^2 is 0.23 and 0.26, respectively. In contrast, for a randomly created portfolio, the R^2 is considerably higher. For our 20-stock portfolio, the R^2 is 0.79.

Note that some researchers estimate a stock's beta by using returns rather than excess returns. The regression estimated is referred to as the *single-index market model*. This model was first suggested by Markowitz[7] as a proxy measure of the covariance of a stock with an index so that the full mean-variance analysis need not be performed. While the approach was mentioned by Markowitz in a footnote in his book, it was Sharpe who investigated this further.[8] It turns out that the beta estimated using both the characteristic line and the single-index market model do not differ materially. For example, for our 20-stock portfolio, the betas differed only because of rounding off.

Characteristic Line For Mutual Funds[9]

In the previous illustration, we showed how to calculate the characteristic line for two stocks and a portfolio. The same regression model can be estimated for mutual funds. We estimate the characteristic line for two large-cap mutual funds. Since we would prefer not to disclose the name of each fund, we simply refer to them as A and B.[10] Ten years of monthly data were used from January 1, 1995 to December 31, 2004. The data are reported in Exhibit 3.3. Because the two mutual funds are

---

[7] Harry M. Markowitz, *Portfolio Selection: Efficient Diversification of Investments* (New Haven, CT: Cowles Foundation for Research in Economics, 1959).

[8] William F. Sharpe, "A Simplified Model for Portfolio Analysis," *Management Science 9* (January 1963), pp. 277–293.

[9] The data and the regression results in this section were provided by Raman Vardharaj of the *Guardian*. Note that neither of the mutual funds used in the illustrations in this section are managed by the *Guardian*.

[10] Neither fund selected is an index fund and the class A shares were selected.

EXHIBIT 3.1 Return and Excess Return Data for S&P 500, Oracle, GM, and Portfolio[a]: 12/1/2000–11/1/2005

Date	S&P 500 Return	Risk-Free Rate	S&P – Risk Free Rate	Oracle Return	Oracle Excess Return	GM Return	GM Excess Return	Portfolio Return	Portfolio Excess Return
12/1/2000	0.03464	0.00473	0.02990	0.00206	−0.00267	0.05418	0.04945	0.01446	0.00973
1/1/2001	−0.09229	0.00413	−0.09642	−0.34753	−0.35165	−0.00708	−0.01120	−0.07324	−0.07736
2/1/2001	−0.06420	0.00393	−0.06813	−0.21158	−0.21550	−0.02757	−0.03149	−0.07029	−0.07421
3/1/2001	0.07681	0.00357	0.07325	0.07877	0.07521	0.05709	0.05352	0.11492	0.11135
4/1/2001	0.00509	0.00321	0.00188	−0.05322	−0.05643	0.03813	0.03492	0.01942	0.01621
5/1/2001	−0.02504	0.00302	−0.02805	0.24183	0.23881	0.13093	0.12791	−0.03050	−0.03351
6/1/2001	−0.01074	0.00288	−0.01362	−0.04842	−0.05130	−0.01166	−0.01453	−0.03901	−0.04189
7/1/2001	−0.06411	0.00288	−0.06698	−0.32467	−0.32754	−0.13915	−0.14203	−0.08264	−0.08552
8/1/2001	−0.08172	0.00274	−0.08447	0.03030	0.02756	−0.21644	−0.21918	−0.13019	−0.13293
9/1/2001	0.01810	0.00219	0.01591	0.07790	0.07571	−0.03683	−0.03902	0.05969	0.05749
10/1/2001	0.07518	0.00177	0.07341	0.03466	0.03289	0.20281	0.20104	0.11993	0.11816
11/1/2001	0.00757	0.00157	0.00601	−0.01568	−0.01725	−0.02213	−0.02370	0.02346	0.02190
12/1/2001	−0.01557	0.00148	−0.01706	0.24982	0.24834	0.05226	0.05078	0.05125	0.04976
1/1/2002	−0.02077	0.00144	−0.02221	−0.03708	−0.03852	0.03598	0.03454	0.02058	0.01914
2/1/2002	0.03674	0.00152	0.03522	−0.22984	−0.23136	0.14100	0.13948	0.02818	0.02667
3/1/2002	−0.06142	0.00168	−0.06309	−0.21563	−0.21730	0.06121	0.05953	−0.00517	−0.00684
4/1/2002	−0.00908	0.00161	−0.01069	−0.21116	−0.21276	−0.03118	−0.03279	−0.02664	−0.02825
5/1/2002	−0.07246	0.00155	−0.07401	0.19571	0.19416	−0.13998	−0.14153	−0.04080	−0.04235
6/1/2002	−0.07900	0.00149	−0.08050	0.05702	0.05553	−0.12909	−0.13058	−0.05655	−0.05804
7/1/2002	0.00488	0.00142	0.00346	−0.04196	−0.04337	0.02814	0.02673	−0.01411	−0.01553
8/1/2002	−0.11002	0.00133	−0.11136	−0.18040	−0.18173	−0.18721	−0.18855	−0.09664	−0.09797
9/1/2002	0.08645	0.00133	0.08512	0.29644	0.29510	−0.14524	−0.14658	0.06920	0.06787
10/1/2002	0.05707	0.00130	0.05577	0.19235	0.19105	0.19398	0.19268	0.08947	0.08817
11/1/2002	−0.06033	0.00106	−0.06139	−0.11111	−0.11217	−0.07154	−0.07259	−0.04623	−0.04729
12/1/2002	−0.02741	0.00103	−0.02845	0.11389	0.11286	−0.01438	−0.01541	−0.00030	−0.00134
1/1/2003	−0.01700	0.00100	−0.01800	−0.00582	−0.00682	−0.07047	−0.07147	−0.03087	−0.03187
2/1/2003	0.00836	0.00098	0.00737	−0.09365	−0.09463	−0.00444	−0.00543	−0.00951	−0.01049
3/1/2003	0.08104	0.00094	0.08010	0.09594	0.09500	0.07228	0.07134	0.06932	0.06838
4/1/2003	0.05090	0.00095	0.04995	0.09512	0.09417	−0.01997	−0.02092	0.06898	0.06803
5/1/2003	0.01132	0.00090	0.01042	−0.07686	−0.07776	0.01896	0.01806	0.00567	0.00477
6/1/2003	0.01622	0.00077	0.01546	−0.00167	−0.00243	0.03972	0.03896	0.03096	0.03019
7/1/2003	0.01787	0.00079	0.01708	0.07006	0.06927	0.09805	0.09726	0.03756	0.03677
8/1/2003	−0.01194	0.00086	−0.01280	−0.12315	−0.12401	−0.00414	−0.00499	−0.03145	−0.03231
9/1/2003	0.05496	0.00084	0.05412	0.06400	0.06316	0.04251	0.04167	0.07166	0.07082
10/1/2003	0.00713	0.00083	0.00630	0.00418	0.00334	0.00258	0.00174	0.00832	0.00749
11/1/2003	0.05077	0.00085	0.04992	0.10067	0.09982	0.24825	0.24740	0.06934	0.06849
12/1/2003	0.01728	0.00083	0.01645	0.04762	0.04679	−0.06966	−0.07049	0.00012	−0.00070
1/1/2004	0.01221	0.00081	0.01140	−0.07143	−0.07224	−0.03140	−0.03221	0.01279	0.01198
2/1/2004	−0.01636	0.00083	−0.01718	−0.06760	−0.06842	−0.01808	−0.01890	−0.03456	−0.03538
3/1/2004	−0.01679	0.00083	−0.01762	−0.06250	−0.06333	0.00360	0.00277	−0.00890	−0.00972
4/1/2004	0.01208	0.00091	0.01118	0.01333	0.01243	−0.04281	−0.04372	0.02303	0.02212
5/1/2004	0.01799	0.00109	0.01690	0.04649	0.04540	0.02644	0.02535	−0.00927	−0.01036
6/1/2004	−0.03429	0.00133	−0.03562	−0.11903	−0.12036	−0.07405	−0.07538	−0.05173	−0.05307
7/1/2004	0.00229	0.00138	0.00090	−0.05138	−0.05276	−0.04242	−0.04380	−0.00826	−0.00965
8/1/2004	0.00936	0.00143	0.00793	0.13139	0.12996	0.02832	0.02689	0.01632	0.01488

EXHIBIT 3.1   (Continued)

Date	S&P 500 Return	Risk-Free Rate	S&P – Risk Free Rate	Oracle Return	Oracle Excess Return	GM Return	GM Excess Return	Portfolio Return	Portfolio Excess Return
9/1/2004	0.01401	0.00156	0.01246	0.12234	0.12078	–0.09251	–0.09407	0.00577	0.00421
10/1/2004	0.03859	0.00167	0.03693	0.00632	0.00465	0.00104	–0.00063	0.05326	0.05159
11/1/2004	0.03246	0.00189	0.03057	0.07692	0.07503	0.03809	0.03620	0.02507	0.02318
12/1/2004	–0.02529	0.00203	–0.02732	0.00364	0.00162	–0.08113	–0.08315	–0.03109	–0.03311
1/1/2005	0.01890	0.00218	0.01673	–0.05955	–0.06172	–0.03151	–0.03369	0.01225	0.01008
2/1/2005	–0.01912	0.00231	–0.02143	–0.03629	–0.03860	–0.17560	–0.17790	–0.01308	–0.01538
3/1/2005	–0.02011	0.00250	–0.02261	–0.07372	–0.07622	–0.09221	–0.09471	–0.03860	–0.04110
4/1/2005	0.02995	0.00254	0.02741	0.10727	0.10472	0.18178	0.17924	0.04730	0.04476
5/1/2005	–0.00014	0.00257	–0.00271	0.03125	0.02868	0.07834	0.07577	–0.02352	–0.02609
6/1/2005	0.03597	0.00261	0.03336	0.02803	0.02542	0.08294	0.08033	0.04905	0.04644
7/1/2005	–0.01122	0.00285	–0.01407	–0.04274	–0.04559	–0.07143	–0.07428	–0.02185	–0.02470
8/1/2005	0.00695	0.00305	0.00390	–0.04542	–0.04847	–0.10471	–0.10776	0.00880	0.00575
9/1/2005	–0.01774	0.00306	–0.02080	0.02258	0.01952	–0.10487	–0.10793	–0.04390	–0.04696
10/1/2005	0.03519	0.00333	0.03186	–0.00631	–0.00963	–0.20073	–0.20405	0.01649	0.01316
11/1/2005	0.01009	0.00346	0.00663	–0.00714	–0.01060	0.01050	0.00704	0.01812	0.01466

[a] Portfolio includes the following 20 stocks: Honeywell, Alcoa, Campbell Soup, Boeing, General Dynamics, Oracle, Sun, General Motors, Procter & Gamble, Wal-Mart, Exxon, ITT, Unilever, Hilton, Martin Marietta, Coca-Cola, Northrop Grumman, Mercury Interact, Amazon, and United Technologies.

EXHIBIT 3.2   Characteristic Line of the Common Stock of General Motors, Oracle, and Portfolio: 12/1/2000–11/1/2005

Coefficient	Coefficient Estimate	Standard Error	t-statistic	p-value
GM				
α	–0.005	0.015	–0.348	0.729
β	1.406	0.339	4.142	0.00
R^2	0.228			
p-value	0.00			
Oracle				
α	–0.009	0.011	–0.812	0.420
β	1.157	0.257	4.501	0.000
R^2	0.259			
p-value	0.000			
Portfolio				
α	0.003	0.003	1.027	0.309
β	1.026	0.070	14.711	0.000
R^2	0.787			
p-value	0.000			

EXHIBIT 3.3 Data to Estimate the Characteristic Line of Two Large-Cap Mutual Funds

Month	Market Excess Return	Excess Return for Fund A	Excess Return for Fund B
01/31/1995	2.18	0.23	0.86
02/28/1995	3.48	3.04	2.76
03/31/1995	2.50	2.43	2.12
04/30/1995	2.47	1.21	1.37
05/31/1995	3.41	2.12	2.42
06/30/1995	1.88	1.65	1.71
07/31/1995	2.88	3.19	2.83
08/31/1995	−0.20	−0.87	0.51
09/30/1995	3.76	2.63	3.04
10/31/1995	−0.82	−2.24	−1.10
11/30/1995	3.98	3.59	3.50
12/31/1995	1.36	0.80	1.24
01/31/1996	3.01	2.93	1.71
02/29/1996	0.57	1.14	1.49
03/31/1996	0.57	0.20	1.26
04/30/1996	1.01	1.00	1.37
05/31/1996	2.16	1.75	1.78
06/30/1996	0.01	−1.03	−0.40
07/31/1996	−4.90	−4.75	−4.18
08/31/1996	1.71	2.32	1.83
09/30/1996	5.18	4.87	4.05
10/31/1996	2.32	1.00	0.92
11/30/1996	7.18	5.68	4.89
12/31/1996	−2.42	−1.84	−1.36
01/31/1997	5.76	3.70	5.28
02/28/1997	0.42	1.26	−1.75
03/31/1997	−4.59	−4.99	−4.18
04/30/1997	5.54	4.20	2.95
05/31/1997	5.65	4.76	5.56
06/30/1997	4.09	2.61	2.53
07/31/1997	7.51	5.57	7.49
08/31/1997	−5.97	−4.81	−3.70
09/30/1997	5.04	5.26	4.53
10/31/1997	−3.76	−3.18	−3.00
11/30/1997	4.24	2.81	2.52
12/31/1997	1.24	1.23	1.93
01/31/1998	0.68	−0.44	−0.70
02/28/1998	6.82	5.11	6.45
03/31/1998	4.73	5.06	3.45
04/30/1998	0.58	−0.95	0.64
05/31/1998	−2.12	−1.65	−1.70
06/30/1998	3.65	2.96	3.65
07/31/1998	−1.46	−0.30	−2.15
08/31/1998	−14.89	−16.22	−13.87
09/30/1998	5.95	4.54	4.40

EXHIBIT 3.3 (Continued)

Month	Market Excess Return	Excess Return for Fund A	Excess Return for Fund B
10/31/1998	7.81	5.09	4.24
11/30/1998	5.75	4.88	5.25
12/31/1998	5.38	7.21	6.80
01/31/1999	3.83	2.25	2.76
02/28/1999	−3.46	−4.48	−3.36
03/31/1999	3.57	2.66	2.84
04/30/1999	3.50	1.89	1.85
05/31/1999	−2.70	−2.46	−1.66
06/30/1999	5.15	4.03	4.96
07/31/1999	−3.50	−3.53	−2.10
08/31/1999	−0.89	−1.44	−2.45
09/30/1999	−3.13	−3.25	−1.72
10/31/1999	5.94	5.16	1.90
11/30/1999	1.67	2.87	3.27
12/31/1999	5.45	8.04	6.65
01/31/2000	−5.43	−4.50	−1.24
02/29/2000	−2.32	1.00	2.54
03/31/2000	9.31	6.37	5.39
04/30/2000	−3.47	−4.50	−5.01
05/31/2000	−2.55	−3.37	−4.97
06/30/2000	2.06	0.14	5.66
07/31/2000	−2.04	−1.41	1.41
08/31/2000	5.71	6.80	5.51
09/30/2000	−5.79	−5.24	−5.32
10/31/2000	−0.98	−2.48	−5.40
11/30/2000	−8.39	−7.24	−11.51
12/31/2000	−0.01	2.11	3.19
01/31/2001	3.01	−0.18	4.47
02/28/2001	−9.50	−5.79	−8.54
03/31/2001	−6.75	−5.56	−6.23
04/30/2001	7.38	4.86	4.28
05/31/2001	0.35	0.15	0.13
06/30/2001	−2.71	−3.76	−1.61
07/31/2001	−1.28	−2.54	−2.10
08/31/2001	−6.57	−5.09	−5.72
09/30/2001	−8.36	−6.74	−7.55
10/31/2001	1.69	0.79	2.08
11/30/2001	7.50	4.32	5.45
12/31/2001	0.73	1.78	1.99
01/31/2002	−1.60	−1.13	−3.41
02/28/2002	−2.06	−0.97	−2.81
03/31/2002	3.63	3.25	4.57
04/30/2002	−6.21	−4.53	−3.47
05/31/2002	−0.88	−1.92	−0.95
06/30/2002	−7.25	−6.05	−5.42
07/31/2002	−7.95	−6.52	−7.67

EXHIBIT 3.3   (Continued)

Month	Market Excess Return	Excess Return for Fund A	Excess Return for Fund B
08/31/2002	0.52	−0.20	1.72
09/30/2002	−11.01	−9.52	−6.18
10/31/2002	8.66	3.32	4.96
11/30/2002	5.77	3.69	1.61
12/31/2002	−5.99	−4.88	−3.07
01/31/2003	−2.72	−1.73	−2.44
02/28/2003	−1.59	−0.57	−2.37
03/31/2003	0.87	1.01	1.50
04/30/2003	8.14	6.57	5.34
05/31/2003	5.18	4.87	6.56
06/30/2003	1.18	0.59	1.08
07/31/2003	1.69	1.64	3.54
08/31/2003	1.88	1.25	1.06
09/30/2003	−1.14	−1.42	−1.20
10/31/2003	5.59	5.23	4.14
11/30/2003	0.81	0.67	1.11
12/31/2003	5.16	4.79	4.69
01/31/2004	1.77	0.80	2.44
02/29/2004	1.33	0.91	1.12
03/31/2004	−1.60	−0.98	−1.88
04/30/2004	−1.65	−2.67	−1.81
05/31/2004	1.31	0.60	0.77
06/30/2004	1.86	1.58	1.48
07/31/2004	−3.41	−2.92	−4.36
08/31/2004	0.29	−0.44	−0.11
09/30/2004	0.97	1.09	1.88
10/31/2004	1.42	0.22	1.10
11/30/2004	3.90	4.72	5.53
12/31/2004	3.24	2.46	3.27

large cap funds, the S&P 500 was used as the benchmark. The risk-free rate used was the 90-day Treasury bill rate.

The results of the regression for both mutual funds are shown in Exhibit 3.4. The estimated β for both mutual funds is statistically significantly different from zero. If a mutual fund had a β equal to the market, its β would be 1. To test if the estimated β is statistically significantly different from 1, we compute the following t-statistic:

$$\frac{\beta - 1}{\text{Standard error of } \beta}$$

EXHIBIT 3.4 Characteristic Line for Mutual Funds A and B

Coefficient	Coefficient Estimate	Standard Error	t-statistic[a]	p-value
Fund A				
α	−0.206	0.102	−2.014	0.046
β	0.836	0.022	37.176	0.000
R^2	0.92			
p-value	0.00			
Fund B				
α	0.010	0.140	0.073	0.942
β	0.816	0.031	26.569	0.000
R^2	0.86			
p-value	0.000			

[a] Null hypothesis is that β is equal to zero.

From the results in Exhibit 3.3, we compute the previous t-statistic:

	A	B
Estimated β	0.836	0.816
Standard error of β	0.022	0.031
t-statistic	−7.45	−5.94

From the t-statistics, it can be seen that both mutual funds have a β that is statistically significantly different from 1.[11]

As explained in Chapter 5, if the CAPM is assumed to be a valid description of asset pricing, then α in the characteristic is a measure of the performance of the mutual fund manager after adjusting for market risk. This α is referred to as the *Jensen measure*. The α for mutual fund A is negative and statistically significant at the 5% level. This means that if the CAPM is valid, the manager of mutual fund A underperformed the market over the period after adjusting for market risk. The α for mutual fund B is positive but not statistically significant. Hence, the manger of this mutual fund neither outperformed nor underperformed the market over the period after adjusting for market risk.

---

[11] The concepts of p values, t-statistics, and statistical significance are explained in Chapter 2.

Empirical Duration of Common Stock

A commonly used measure of the interest-rate sensitivity of an asset's value is its duration.[12] (See Chapter 5 for a discussion of duration.) Duration can be estimated by using a valuation model or empirically by estimating from historical returns the sensitivity of the asset's value to changes in interest rates. When duration is measured in the latter way, it is called *empirical duration*. Since it is estimated using regression analysis, it is sometimes referred to as *regression-based duration*.

A simple linear regression for computing empirical duration using monthly historical data is[13]

$$y_{it} = \alpha_i + \beta_i x_t + e_{it}$$

where

y_{it} = the percentage change in the value of asset i for month t
x_t = the change in the Treasury yield for month t

The estimated β_i is the empirical duration for asset i.

We will apply this linear regression to monthly data from October 1989 to October 2003 shown in Exhibit 3.5[14] for the following asset indexes:

■ Electric Utility sector of the S&P 500
■ Commercial Bank sector of the S&P 500
■ Lehman U.S. Aggregate Bond Index

The yield change (x_t) is measured by the Lehman Treasury Index. The regression results are shown in Exhibit 3.6. We report the empirical duration (β_i), the t-statistic, the p-value, the R^2, and the intercept term. Negative values are reported for the empirical duration. In practice, however, the duration is quoted as a positive value. For the Electric Utility sector and the Lehman U.S. Aggregate Bond Index, the empirical duration is statistically significant at any reasonable level of significance.

---

[12] Duration is interpreted as the approximate percentage change in the value of an asset for a 100-basis-point change in interest. The concept of duration in financial econometrics is used in another sense, having nothing to do with a measure of interest rate risk. In market microstructure theory, "trade" duration is the time span between two consecutive trades.

[13] See Frank K. Reilly, David J. Wright, and Robert R. Johnson "An Analysis of the Interest Rate Sensitivity of Common Stocks," forthcoming *Journal of Portfolio Management*.

[14] The data were supplied by David Wright of Northern Illinois University.

EXHIBIT 3.5 Data for Empirical Duration Illustration

Month	Change in Lehman Bros Treasury Yield	S&P500 Return	Monthly Returns for		
			Electric Utility Sector	Commercial Bank Sector	Lehman U.S. Aggregate Bond Index
Oct-89	−0.46	−2.33	2.350	−11.043	2.4600
Nov-89	−0.10	2.08	2.236	−3.187	0.9500
Dec-89	0.12	2.36	3.794	−1.887	0.2700
Jan–90	0.43	−6.71	−4.641	−10.795	−1.1900
Feb-90	0.09	1.29	0.193	4.782	0.3200
Mar-90	0.20	2.63	−1.406	−4.419	0.0700
Apr-90	0.34	−2.47	−5.175	−4.265	−0.9200
May-90	−0.46	9.75	5.455	12.209	2.9600
Jun-90	−0.20	−0.70	0.966	−5.399	1.6100
Jul-90	−0.21	−0.32	1.351	−8.328	1.3800
Aug-90	0.37	−9.03	−7.644	−10.943	−1.3400
Sep-90	−0.06	−4.92	0.435	−15.039	0.8300
Oct-90	−0.23	−0.37	10.704	−10.666	1.2700
Nov-90	−0.28	6.44	2.006	18.892	2.1500
Dec-90	−0.23	2.74	1.643	6.620	1.5600
Jan-91	−0.13	4.42	−1.401	8.018	1.2400
Feb-91	0.01	7.16	4.468	12.568	0.8500
Mar-91	0.03	2.38	2.445	5.004	0.6900
Apr-91	−0.15	0.28	−0.140	7.226	1.0800
May-91	0.06	4.28	−0.609	7.501	0.5800
Jun-91	0.15	−4.57	−0.615	−7.865	−0.0500
Jul-91	−0.13	4.68	4.743	7.983	1.3900
Aug-91	−0.37	2.35	3.226	9.058	2.1600
Sep-91	−0.33	−1.64	4.736	−2.033	2.0300
Oct-91	−0.17	1.34	1.455	0.638	1.1100
Nov-91	−0.15	−4.04	2.960	−9.814	0.9200
Dec-91	−0.59	11.43	5.821	14.773	2.9700
Jan-92	0.42	−1.86	−5.515	2.843	−1.3600
Feb-92	0.10	1.28	−1.684	8.834	0.6506
Mar-92	0.27	−1.96	−0.296	−3.244	−0.5634
Apr-92	−0.10	2.91	3.058	4.273	0.7215
May-92	−0.23	0.54	2.405	2.483	1.8871
Jun-92	−0.26	−1.45	0.492	1.221	1.3760
Jul-92	−0.41	4.03	6.394	−0.540	2.0411
Aug-92	−0.13	−2.02	−1.746	−5.407	1.0122
Sep-92	−0.26	1.15	0.718	1.960	1.1864
Oct-92	0.49	0.36	−0.778	2.631	−1.3266
Nov-92	0.26	3.37	−0.025	7.539	0.0228
Dec-92	−0.24	1.31	3.247	5.010	1.5903
Jan-93	−0.36	0.73	3.096	4.203	1.9177
Feb-93	−0.29	1.35	6.000	3.406	1.7492
Mar-93	0.02	2.15	0.622	3.586	0.4183
Apr-93	−0.10	−2.45	−0.026	−5.441	0.6955

EXHIBIT 3.5 (Continued)

Month	Change in Lehman Bros Treasury Yield	S&P500 Return	Monthly Returns for		
			Electric Utility Sector	Commercial Bank Sector	Lehman U.S. Aggregate Bond Index
May-93	0.25	2.70	−0.607	−0.647	0.1268
Jun-93	−0.30	0.33	2.708	4.991	1.8121
Jul-93	0.05	−0.47	2.921	0.741	0.5655
Aug-93	−0.31	3.81	3.354	0.851	1.7539
Sep-93	0.00	−0.74	−1.099	3.790	0.2746
Oct-93	0.05	2.03	−1.499	−7.411	0.3732
Nov-93	0.26	−0.94	−5.091	−1.396	−0.8502
Dec-93	0.01	1.23	2.073	3.828	0.5420
Jan-94	−0.17	3.35	−2.577	4.376	1.3502
Feb-94	0.55	−2.70	−5.683	−4.369	−1.7374
Mar-94	0.55	−4.35	−4.656	−3.031	−2.4657
Apr-94	0.37	1.30	0.890	3.970	−0.7985
May-94	0.18	1.63	−5.675	6.419	−0.0138
Jun-94	0.16	−2.47	−3.989	−2.662	−0.2213
Jul-94	−0.23	3.31	5.555	2.010	1.9868
Aug-94	0.12	4.07	0.851	3.783	0.1234
Sep-94	0.43	−2.41	−2.388	−7.625	−1.4717
Oct-94	0.18	2.29	1.753	1.235	−0.0896
Nov-94	0.37	−3.67	2.454	−7.595	−0.2217
Dec-94	0.11	1.46	0.209	−0.866	0.6915
Jan-95	−0.33	2.60	7.749	6.861	1.9791
Feb-95	−0.41	3.88	−0.750	6.814	2.3773
Mar-95	0.01	2.96	−2.556	−1.434	0.6131
Apr-95	−0.18	2.91	3.038	4.485	1.3974
May-95	−0.72	3.95	7.590	9.981	3.8697
Jun-95	−0.05	2.35	−0.707	0.258	0.7329
Jul-95	0.14	3.33	−0.395	4.129	−0.2231
Aug-95	−0.10	0.27	−0.632	5.731	1.2056
Sep-95	−0.05	4.19	v6.987	5.491	0.9735
Oct-95	−0.21	−0.35	2.215	−1.906	1.3002
Nov-95	−0.23	4.40	−0.627	7.664	1.4982
Dec-95	−0.18	1.85	6.333	0.387	1.4040
Jan-96	−0.13	3.44	2.420	3.361	0.6633
Feb-96	0.49	0.96	−3.590	4.673	−1.7378
Mar-96	0.31	0.96	−1.697	2.346	−0.6954
Apr-96	0.25	1.47	−4.304	−1.292	−0.5621
May-96	0.18	2.58	1.864	2.529	−0.2025
Jun-96	−0.14	0.41	5.991	−0.859	1.3433
Jul-96	0.08	−4.45	−7.150	0.466	0.2736
Aug-96	0.15	2.12	1.154	4.880	−0.1675
Sep-96	−0.23	5.62	0.682	6.415	1.7414
Oct-96	−0.35	2.74	4.356	8.004	2.2162
Nov-96	−0.21	7.59	1.196	10.097	1.7129

EXHIBIT 3.5   (Continued)

Month	Change in Lehman Bros Treasury Yield	S&P500 Return	Monthly Returns for		
			Electric Utility Sector	Commercial Bank Sector	Lehman U.S. Aggregate Bond Index
Dec-96	0.30	–1.96	–0.323	–4.887	–0.9299
Jan-97	0.06	6.21	0.443	8.392	0.3058
Feb-97	0.11	0.81	0.235	5.151	0.2485
Mar-97	0.36	–4.16	–4.216	–7.291	–1.1083
Apr-97	–0.18	5.97	–2.698	5.477	1.4980
May-97	–0.07	6.14	4.240	3.067	0.9451
Jun-97	–0.11	4.46	3.795	4.834	1.1873
Jul-97	–0.43	7.94	2.627	12.946	2.6954
Aug-97	0.30	–5.56	–2.423	–6.205	–0.8521
Sep-97	–0.19	5.48	5.010	7.956	1.4752
Oct-97	–0.21	–3.34	1.244	–2.105	1.4506
Nov-97	0.06	4.63	8.323	3.580	0.4603
Dec-97	–0.11	1.72	7.902	3.991	1.0063
Jan-98	–0.25	1.11	–4.273	–4.404	1.2837
Feb-98	0.17	7.21	2.338	9.763	–0.0753
Mar-98	0.05	5.12	7.850	7.205	0.3441
Apr-98	0.00	1.01	–3.234	2.135	0.5223
May-98	–0.08	–1.72	–0.442	–3.200	0.9481
Jun-98	–0.09	4.06	3.717	2.444	0.8483
Jul-98	0.03	–1.06	–4.566	0.918	0.2122
Aug-98	–0.46	–14.46	7.149	–24.907	1.6277
Sep-98	–0.53	6.41	5.613	2.718	2.3412
Oct-98	0.05	8.13	–2.061	9.999	–0.5276
Nov-98	0.17	6.06	1.631	5.981	0.5664
Dec-98	0.02	5.76	2.608	2.567	0.3007
Jan-99	–0.01	4.18	–6.072	–0.798	0.7143
Feb-99	0.55	–3.11	–5.263	0.524	–1.7460
Mar-99	–0.05	4.00	–2.183	1.370	0.5548
Apr-99	0.05	3.87	6.668	7.407	0.3170
May-99	0.31	–2.36	7.613	–6.782	–0.8763
Jun-99	0.11	5.55	–4.911	5.544	–0.3194
Jul-99	0.11	–3.12	–2.061	–7.351	–0.4248
Aug-99	0.10	–0.50	1.508	–4.507	–0.0508
Sep-99	–0.08	–2.74	–5.267	–6.093	1.1604
Oct-99	0.11	6.33	1.800	15.752	0.3689
Nov-99	0.16	2.03	–8.050	–7.634	–0.0069
Dec-99	0.24	5.89	–0.187	–9.158	–0.4822
Jan-00	0.19	–5.02	5.112	–2.293	–0.3272
Feb-00	–0.13	–1.89	–10.030	–12.114	1.2092
Mar-00	–0.20	9.78	1.671	18.770	1.3166
Apr-00	0.17	–3.01	14.456	–5.885	–0.2854
May-00	0.07	–2.05	2.985	11.064	–0.0459
Jun-00	–0.26	2.47	–5.594	–14.389	2.0803

EXHIBIT 3.5   (Continued)

Month	Change in Lehman Bros Treasury Yield	S&P500 Return	Monthly Returns for		
			Electric Utility Sector	Commercial Bank Sector	Lehman U.S. Aggregate Bond Index
Jul-00	−0.08	−1.56	6.937	6.953	0.9077
Aug-00	−0.17	6.21	13.842	12.309	1.4497
Sep-00	−0.03	−5.28	12.413	1.812	0.6286
Oct-00	−0.06	−0.42	−3.386	−1.380	0.6608
Nov-00	−0.31	−7.88	3.957	−3.582	1.6355
Dec-00	−0.33	0.49	4.607	12.182	1.8554
Jan-01	−0.22	3.55	−11.234	3.169	1.6346
Feb-01	−0.16	−9.12	6.747	−3.740	0.8713
Mar-01	−0.08	−6.33	1.769	0.017	0.5018
Apr-01	0.22	7.77	5.025	−1.538	−0.4151
May-01	0.00	0.67	0.205	5.934	0.6041
Jun-01	0.01	−2.43	−7.248	0.004	0.3773
Jul-01	−0.40	−0.98	−5.092	2.065	2.2357
Aug-01	−0.14	−6.26	−0.149	−3.940	1.1458
Sep-01	−0.41	−8.08	−10.275	−4.425	1.1647
Oct-01	−0.39	1.91	1.479	−7.773	2.0930
Nov-01	0.41	7.67	−0.833	7.946	−1.3789
Dec-01	0.21	0.88	3.328	3.483	−0.6357
Jan-02	0.00	−1.46	−3.673	1.407	0.8096
Feb-02	−0.08	−1.93	−2.214	−0.096	0.9690
Mar-02	0.56	3.76	10.623	7.374	−1.6632
Apr-02	−0.44	−6.06	1.652	2.035	1.9393
May-02	−0.06	−0.74	−3.988	1.247	0.8495
Jun-02	−0.23	−7.12	−4.194	−3.767	0.8651
Jul-02	−0.50	−7.80	−10.827	−4.957	1.2062
Aug-02	−0.17	0.66	2.792	3.628	1.6882
Sep-02	−0.45	−10.87	−8.677	−10.142	1.6199
Oct-02	0.11	8.80	−2.802	5.143	−0.4559
Nov-02	0.34	5.89	1.620	0.827	−0.0264
Dec-02	−0.45	−5.88	5.434	−2.454	2.0654
Jan-03	0.11	−2.62	−3.395	−0.111	0.0855
Feb-03	−0.21	−1.50	−2.712	−1.514	1.3843
Mar-03	0.05	0.97	4.150	−3.296	−0.0773
Apr-03	−0.03	8.24	5.438	9.806	0.8254
May-03	−0.33	5.27	10.519	5.271	1.8645
Jun-03	0.08	1.28	1.470	1.988	−0.1986
Jul-03	0.66	1.76	−5.649	3.331	−3.3620
Aug-03	0.05	1.95	1.342	−1.218	0.6637
Sep-03	−0.46	−1.06	4.993	−0.567	2.6469
Oct-03	0.33	5.66	0.620	8.717	−0.9320
Nov-03	0.13	0.88	0.136	1.428	0.2391
Dec-03	−0.14	5.24	NA	NA	

EXHIBIT 3.6 Estimation of Regression Parameters for Empirical Duration

	Electric Utility Sector	Commercial Bank Sector	Lehman U.S. Aggregate Bond Index
a. Simple Linear Regression			
Intercept			
α_i	0.6376	1.1925	0.5308
t-statistic	1.8251	2.3347	21.1592
p-value	0.0698	0.0207	0.0000
Change in the Treasury yield			
β_i	-4.5329	-2.5269	-4.1062
t-statistic	-3.4310	-1.3083	-43.2873
p-value	0.0008	0.1926	0.0000
R^2	0.0655	0.0101	0.9177
F-value	11.7717	1.7116	1873.8000
p-value	0.0007	0.1926	0.0000
b. Multiple Linear Regression			
Intercept			
α_i	0.3937	0.2199	0.5029
t-statistic	1.1365	0.5835	21.3885
p-value	0.2574	0.5604	0.0000
Change in the Treasury yield			
β_{1i}	-4.3780	-1.9096	-4.0885
t-statistic	-3.4143	-1.3686	-46.9711
p-value	0.0008	0.1730	0.0000
Return on the S&P 500			
β_{2i}	0.2664	1.0620	0.0304
t-statistic	3.4020	12.4631	5.7252
p-value	0.0008	0.0000	0.0000
R^2	0.1260	0.4871	0.9312
F-value	12.0430	79.3060	1130.5000
p-value	0.00001	0.00000	0.00000

A multiple regression model to estimate the empirical duration that has been suggested is

$$y_{it} = \alpha_i + \beta_{1i}x_{1t} + \beta_{2i}x_{2t} + e_{it}$$

where y_{it} and x_{1t} are the same as for the simple linear regression and x_{2t} is the return on the S&P 500. The results for this model are also shown in Exhibit 3.6.

The results of the multiple regression indicate that the returns for the Electric Utility sector are affected by both the change in Treasury rates and the return on the stock market as proxied by the S&P 500. For the Commercial Bank sector, the coefficient of the changes in Treasury rates is not statistically significant, however the coefficient of the return on the S&P 500 is statistically significant. The opposite is the case for the Lehman U.S. Aggregate Bond Index. It is interesting to note that the duration for the Lehman U.S. Aggregate Bond Index as reported by Lehman Brothers was about 4.55 in November 2003. The empirical duration is 4.1.[15]

Predicting the 10-Year Treasury Yield[16]

The U.S. Treasury securities market is the world's most liquid bond market. The U.S. Department of the Treasury issues two types of securities: zero-coupon securities and coupon securities. Securities issued with one year or less to maturity are called *Treasury bills;* they are issued as zero-coupon instruments. Treasury securities with more than one year to maturity are issued as coupon-bearing securities. Treasury securities from more than one year up to 10 years of maturity are called *Treasury notes*; Treasury securities with a maturity in excess of 10 years are called *Treasury bonds*. The U.S. Treasury auctions securities of specified maturities on a regular calendar basis. The Treasury currently issues 30-year Treasury bonds but had stopped issuance of them from October 2001 to January 2006.

An important Treasury coupon bond is the 10-year Treasury note. In this illustration we will try to forecast this rate based on two independent variables suggested by economic theory. A well-known theory of interest rates is that the interest rate in any economy consists of two components.[17] The first is the *expected rate of inflation*. The second is the *real rate of interest*. We use regression analysis to produce a model to forecast the yield on the 10-year Treasury note (simply, the 10-year Treasury yield)—the dependent variable—and the expected rate of inflation (simply, expected inflation) and the real rate of interest (simply, real rate).

---

[15] While the sign of the coefficient that is an estimate of duration is negative (which means the price moves in the opposite direction to the change in interest rates), market participants talk in terms of the positive value of duration for a bond that has this characteristic.

[16] We are grateful to Robert Scott of the Bank for International Settlement for suggesting this illustration and for providing the data.

[17] This relationship is known as Fisher's Law.

The 10-year Treasury yield is observable, but we need a proxy for the two independent variables (i.e., the expected rate of inflation and the real rate of interest at the time) as they are not observable at the time of the forecast. Keep in mind that since we are forecasting, we do not use as our independent variable information that is unavailable at the time of the forecast. Consequently, we need a proxy available at the time of the forecast.

The inflation rate is available from the U.S. Department of Commerce. However, we need a proxy for expected inflation. We can use some type of average of past inflation as a proxy. In our model, we use a 5-year moving average. There are more sophisticated methodologies for calculating expected inflation, but the 5-year moving average is sufficient for our illustration.[18] For the real rate, we use the rate on 3-month certificates of deposit (CDs). Again, we use a 5-year moving average.

The monthly data for the three variables from November 1965 to December 2005 (482 observations) are provided in Exhibit 3.7. The regression results are reported in Exhibit 3.8. As can be seen, the coefficients of both independent variables are positive (as would be predicted by economic theory) and highly significant.

STEPWISE REGRESSION

Stepwise regression is a model-building technique for regression designs. The stepwise regression methodology is based on identifying an initial model and iteratively "stepping," that is, repeatedly altering the model at the previous step by adding or removing a regressor. Addition or removal of regressors is performed in accordance with the "stepping criteria," and terminates when stepping is no longer possible given the stepping criteria, or when a specified maximum number of steps has been reached.

Stepwise regression critically depends on the stepping criteria that must avoid overfitting. We choose the initial model at Step 0. There are two different methodologies for stepwise regression, the *backward stepwise method* and *backward removal method*. Both methods start with a rich model that includes all regressors specified to be included in the design for the analysis. The initial model for these methods is therefore the whole model.

---

[18] For example, one can use an exponential smoothing of actual inflation, a methodology used by the OECD.

EXHIBIT 3.7 Monthly Data for 10-Year Treasury Yield, Expected Inflation, and Real Rate: November 1965–December 2005

Date	10-Yr. Trea. Yield	Exp. Infl.	Real Rate	Date	10-Yr. Trea. Yield	Exp. Infl.	Real Rate	Date	10-Yr. Trea. Yield	Exp. Infl.	Real Rate
1965											
Nov	4.45	1.326	2.739								
Dec	4.62	1.330	2.757								
1966				1969				1972			
Jan	4.61	1.334	2.780	Jan	6.04	2.745	2.811	Jan	5.95	4.959	2.401
Feb	4.83	1.348	2.794	Feb	6.19	2.802	2.826	Feb	6.08	4.959	2.389
Mar	4.87	1.358	2.820	Mar	6.3	2.869	2.830	Mar	6.07	4.953	2.397
Apr	4.75	1.372	2.842	Apr	6.17	2.945	2.827	Apr	6.19	4.953	2.403
May	4.78	1.391	2.861	May	6.32	3.016	2.862	May	6.13	4.949	2.398
June	4.81	1.416	2.883	June	6.57	3.086	2.895	June	6.11	4.941	2.405
July	5.02	1.440	2.910	July	6.72	3.156	2.929	July	6.11	4.933	2.422
Aug	5.22	1.464	2.945	Aug	6.69	3.236	2.967	Aug	6.21	4.924	2.439
Sept	5.18	1.487	2.982	Sept	7.16	3.315	3.001	Sept	6.55	4.916	2.450
Oct	5.01	1.532	2.997	Oct	7.1	3.393	3.014	Oct	6.48	4.912	2.458
Nov	5.16	1.566	3.022	Nov	7.14	3.461	3.045	Nov	6.28	4.899	2.461
Dec	4.84	1.594	3.050	Dec	7.65	3.539	3.059	Dec	6.36	4.886	2.468
1967				1970				1973			
Jan	4.58	1.633	3.047	Jan	7.80	3.621	3.061	Jan	6.46	4.865	2.509
Feb	4.63	1.667	3.050	Feb	7.24	3.698	3.064	Feb	6.64	4.838	2.583
Mar	4.54	1.706	3.039	Mar	7.07	3.779	3.046	Mar	6.71	4.818	2.641
Apr	4.59	1.739	3.027	Apr	7.39	3.854	3.035	Apr	6.67	4.795	2.690
May	4.85	1.767	3.021	May	7.91	3.933	3.021	May	6.85	4.776	2.734
June	5.02	1.801	3.015	June	7.84	4.021	3.001	June	6.90	4.752	2.795
July	5.16	1.834	3.004	July	7.46	4.104	2.981	July	7.13	4.723	2.909
Aug	5.28	1.871	2.987	Aug	7.53	4.187	2.956	Aug	7.40	4.699	3.023
Sept	5.3	1.909	2.980	Sept	7.39	4.264	2.938	Sept	7.09	4.682	3.110
Oct	5.48	1.942	2.975	Oct	7.33	4.345	2.901	Oct	6.79	4.668	3.185
Nov	5.75	1.985	2.974	Nov	6.84	4.436	2.843	Nov	6.73	4.657	3.254
Dec	5.7	2.027	2.972	Dec	6.39	4.520	2.780	Dec	6.74	4.651	3.312
1968				1971				1974			
Jan	5.53	2.074	2.959	Jan	6.24	4.605	2.703	Jan	6.99	4.652	3.330
Feb	5.56	2.126	2.943	Feb	6.11	4.680	2.627	Feb	6.96	4.653	3.332
Mar	5.74	2.177	2.937	Mar	5.70	4.741	2.565	Mar	7.21	4.656	3.353
Apr	5.64	2.229	2.935	Apr	5.83	4.793	2.522	Apr	7.51	4.657	3.404
May	5.87	2.285	2.934	May	6.39	4.844	2.501	May	7.58	4.678	3.405
June	5.72	2.341	2.928	June	6.52	4.885	2.467	June	7.54	4.713	3.419
July	5.5	2.402	2.906	July	6.73	4.921	2.436	July	7.81	4.763	3.421
Aug	5.42	2.457	2.887	Aug	6.58	4.947	2.450	Aug	8.04	4.827	3.401
Sept	5.46	2.517	2.862	Sept	6.14	4.964	2.442	Sept	8.04	4.898	3.346
Oct	5.58	2.576	2.827	Oct	5.93	4.968	2.422	Oct	7.9	4.975	3.271
Nov	5.7	2.639	2.808	Nov	5.81	4.968	2.411	Nov	7.68	5.063	3.176
Dec	6.03	2.697	2.798	Dec	5.93	4.964	2.404	Dec	7.43	5.154	3.086

EXHIBIT 3.7 (Continued)

Date	10-Yr. Trea. Yield	Exp. Infl.	Real Rate	Date	10-Yr. Trea. Yield	Exp. Infl.	Real Rate	Date	10-Yr. Trea. Yield	Exp. Infl.	Real Rate
1975				1978				1981			
Jan	7.5	5.243	2.962	Jan	7.96	6.832	1.068	Jan	12.57	8.520	1.132
Feb	7.39	5.343	2.827	Feb	8.03	6.890	0.995	Feb	13.19	8.594	1.242
Mar	7.73	5.431	2.710	Mar	8.04	6.942	0.923	Mar	13.12	8.649	1.336
Apr	8.23	5.518	2.595	Apr	8.15	7.003	0.854	Apr	13.68	8.700	1.477
May	8.06	5.585	2.477	May	8.35	7.063	0.784	May	14.1	8.751	1.619
June	7.86	5.639	2.384	June	8.46	7.124	0.716	June	13.47	8.802	1.755
July	8.06	5.687	2.311	July	8.64	7.191	0.598	July	14.28	8.877	1.897
Aug	8.4	5.716	2.271	Aug	8.41	7.263	0.482	Aug	14.94	8.956	2.037
Sept	8.43	5.738	2.241	Sept	8.42	7.331	0.397	Sept	15.32	9.039	2.155
Oct	8.15	5.753	2.210	Oct	8.64	7.400	0.365	Oct	15.15	9.110	2.256
Nov	8.05	5.759	2.200	Nov	8.81	7.463	0.322	Nov	13.39	9.175	2.305
Dec	8	5.761	2.186	Dec	9.01	7.525	0.284	Dec	13.72	9.232	2.392
1976				1979				1982			
Jan	7.74	5.771	2.166	Jan	9.1	7.582	0.254	Jan	14.59	9.285	2.497
Feb	7.79	5.777	2.164	Feb	9.1	7.645	0.224	Feb	14.43	9.334	2.612
Mar	7.73	5.800	2.138	Mar	9.12	7.706	0.174	Mar	13.86	9.375	2.741
Apr	7.56	5.824	2.101	Apr	9.18	7.758	0.108	Apr	13.87	9.417	2.860
May	7.9	5.847	2.060	May	9.25	7.797	0.047	May	13.62	9.456	2.958
June	7.86	5.870	2.034	June	8.91	7.821	-0.025	June	14.3	9.487	3.095
July	7.83	5.900	1.988	July	8.95	7.834	-0.075	July	13.95	9.510	3.183
Aug	7.77	5.937	1.889	Aug	9.03	7.837	-0.101	Aug	13.06	9.524	3.259
Sept	7.59	5.981	1.813	Sept	9.33	7.831	-0.085	Sept	12.34	9.519	3.321
Oct	7.41	6.029	1.753	Oct	10.3	7.823	0.011	Oct	10.91	9.517	3.363
Nov	7.29	6.079	1.681	Nov	10.65	7.818	0.079	Nov	10.55	9.502	3.427
Dec	6.87	6.130	1.615	Dec	10.39	7.818	0.154	Dec	10.54	9.469	3.492
1977				1980				1983			
Jan	7.21	6.176	1.573	Jan	10.8	7.825	0.261	Jan	10.46	9.439	3.553
Feb	7.39	6.224	1.527	Feb	12.41	7.828	0.418	Feb	10.72	9.411	3.604
Mar	7.46	6.272	1.474	Mar	12.75	7.849	0.615	Mar	10.51	9.381	3.670
Apr	7.37	6.323	1.427	Apr	11.47	7.879	0.701	Apr	10.4	9.340	3.730
May	7.46	6.377	1.397	May	10.18	7.926	0.716	May	10.38	9.288	3.806
June	7.28	6.441	1.340	June	9.78	7.989	0.702	June	10.85	9.227	3.883
July	7.33	6.499	1.293	July	10.25	8.044	0.695	July	11.38	9.161	3.981
Aug	7.4	6.552	1.252	Aug	11.1	8.109	0.716	Aug	11.85	9.087	4.076
Sept	7.34	6.605	1.217	Sept	11.51	8.184	0.740	Sept	11.65	9.012	4.152
Oct	7.52	6.654	1.193	Oct	11.75	8.269	0.795	Oct	11.54	8.932	4.204
Nov	7.58	6.710	1.154	Nov	12.68	8.356	0.895	Nov	11.69	8.862	4.243
Dec	7.69	6.768	1.119	Dec	12.84	8.446	1.004	Dec	11.83	8.800	4.276

EXHIBIT 3.7   (Continued)

Date	10-Yr. Trea. Yield	Exp. Infl.	Real Rate	Date	10-Yr. Trea. Yield	Exp. Infl.	Real Rate	Date	10-Yr. Trea. Yield	Exp. Infl.	Real Rate
1984				1987				1990			
Jan	11.67	8.741	4.324	Jan	7.08	4.887	4.607	Jan	8.418	4.257	3.610
Feb	11.84	8.670	4.386	Feb	7.25	4.793	4.558	Feb	8.515	4.254	3.595
Mar	12.32	8.598	4.459	Mar	7.25	4.710	4.493	Mar	8.628	4.254	3.585
Apr	12.63	8.529	4.530	Apr	8.02	4.627	4.445	Apr	9.022	4.260	3.580
May	13.41	8.460	4.620	May	8.61	4.551	4.404	May	8.599	4.264	3.586
June	13.56	8.393	4.713	June	8.4	4.476	4.335	June	8.412	4.272	3.589
July	13.36	8.319	4.793	July	8.45	4.413	4.296	July	8.341	4.287	3.568
Aug	12.72	8.241	4.862	Aug	8.76	4.361	4.273	Aug	8.846	4.309	3.546
Sept	12.52	8.164	4.915	Sept	9.42	4.330	4.269	Sept	8.795	4.335	3.523
Oct	12.16	8.081	4.908	Oct	9.52	4.302	4.259	Oct	8.617	4.357	3.503
Nov	11.57	7.984	4.919	Nov	8.86	4.285	4.243	Nov	8.252	4.371	3.493
Dec	12.5	7.877	4.928	Dec	8.99	4.279	4.218	Dec	8.067	4.388	3.471
1985				1988				1991			
Jan	11.38	7.753	4.955	Jan	8.67	4.274	4.180	Jan	8.007	4.407	3.436
Feb	11.51	7.632	4.950	Feb	8.21	4.271	4.149	Feb	8.033	4.431	3.396
Mar	11.86	7.501	4.900	Mar	8.37	4.268	4.104	Mar	8.061	4.451	3.360
Apr	11.43	7.359	4.954	Apr	8.72	4.270	4.075	Apr	8.013	4.467	3.331
May	10.85	7.215	5.063	May	9.09	4.280	4.036	May	8.059	4.487	3.294
June	10.16	7.062	5.183	June	8.92	4.301	3.985	June	8.227	4.504	3.267
July	10.31	6.925	5.293	July	9.06	4.322	3.931	July	8.147	4.517	3.247
Aug	10.33	6.798	5.346	Aug	9.26	4.345	3.879	Aug	7.816	4.527	3.237
Sept	10.37	6.664	5.383	Sept	8.98	4.365	3.844	Sept	7.445	4.534	3.223
Oct	10.24	6.528	5.399	Oct	8.8	4.381	3.810	Oct	7.46	4.540	3.207
Nov	9.78	6.399	5.360	Nov	8.96	4.385	3.797	Nov	7.376	4.552	3.177
Dec	9.26	6.269	5.326	Dec	9.11	4.384	3.787	Dec	6.699	4.562	3.133
1986				1989				1992			
Jan	9.19	6.154	5.284	Jan	9.09	4.377	3.786	Jan	7.274	4.569	3.092
Feb	8.7	6.043	5.249	Feb	9.17	4.374	3.792	Feb	7.25	4.572	3.054
Mar	7.78	5.946	5.225	Mar	9.36	4.367	3.791	Mar	7.528	4.575	3.014
Apr	7.3	5.858	5.143	Apr	9.18	4.356	3.784	Apr	7.583	4.574	2.965
May	7.71	5.763	5.055	May	8.86	4.344	3.758	May	7.318	4.571	2.913
June	7.8	5.673	4.965	June	8.28	4.331	3.723	June	7.121	4.567	2.864
July	7.3	5.554	4.878	July	8.02	4.320	3.679	July	6.709	4.563	2.810
Aug	7.17	5.428	4.789	Aug	8.11	4.306	3.644	Aug	6.604	4.556	2.757
Sept	7.45	5.301	4.719	Sept	8.19	4.287	3.623	Sept	6.354	4.544	2.682
Oct	7.43	5.186	4.671	Oct	8.01	4.273	3.614	Oct	6.789	4.533	2.624
Nov	7.25	5.078	4.680	Nov	7.87	4.266	3.609	Nov	6.937	4.522	2.571
Dec	7.11	4.982	4.655	Dec	7.84	4.258	3.611	Dec	6.686	4.509	2.518

EXHIBIT 3.7 (Continued)

Date	10-Yr. Trea. Yield	Exp. Infl.	Real Rate	Date	10-Yr. Trea. Yield	Exp. Infl.	Real Rate	Date	10-Yr. Trea. Yield	Exp. Infl.
1993				1996				1999		
Jan	6.359	4.495	2.474	Jan	5.58	3.505	1.250	Jan	4.651	2.631
Feb	6.02	4.482	2.427	Feb	6.098	3.458	1.270	Feb	5.287	2.621
Mar	6.024	4.466	2.385	Mar	6.327	3.418	1.295	Mar	5.242	2.605
Apr	6.009	4.453	2.330	Apr	6.67	3.376	1.328	Apr	5.348	2.596
May	6.149	4.439	2.272	May	6.852	3.335	1.359	May	5.622	2.586
June	5.776	4.420	2.214	June	6.711	3.297	1.387	June	5.78	2.572
July	5.807	4.399	2.152	July	6.794	3.261	1.417	July	5.903	2.558
Aug	5.448	4.380	2.084	Aug	6.943	3.228	1.449	Aug	5.97	2.543
Sept	5.382	4.357	2.020	Sept	6.703	3.195	1.481	Sept	5.877	2.527
Oct	5.427	4.333	1.958	Oct	6.339	3.163	1.516	Oct	6.024	2.515
Nov	5.819	4.309	1.885	Nov	6.044	3.131	1.558	Nov	6.191	2.502
Dec	5.794	4.284	1.812	Dec	6.418	3.102	1.608	Dec	6.442	2.490
1994				1997				2000		
Jan	5.642	4.256	1.739	Jan	6.494	3.077	1.656	Jan	6.665	2.477
Feb	6.129	4.224	1.663	Feb	6.552	3.057	1.698	Feb	6.409	2.464
Mar	6.738	4.195	1.586	Mar	6.903	3.033	1.746	Mar	6.004	2.455
Apr	7.042	4.166	1.523	Apr	6.718	3.013	1.795	Apr	6.212	2.440
May	7.147	4.135	1.473	May	6.659	2.990	1.847	May	6.272	2.429
June	7.32	4.106	1.427	June	6.5	2.968	1.899	June	6.031	2.421
July	7.111	4.079	1.394	July	6.011	2.947	1.959	July	6.031	2.412
Aug	7.173	4.052	1.356	Aug	6.339	2.926	2.016	Aug	5.725	2.406
Sept	7.603	4.032	1.315	Sept	6.103	2.909	2.078	Sept	5.802	2.398
Oct	7.807	4.008	1.289	Oct	5.831	2.888	2.136	Oct	5.751	2.389
Nov	7.906	3.982	1.278	Nov	5.874	2.866	2.189	Nov	5.468	2.382
Dec	7.822	3.951	1.278	Dec	5.742	2.847	2.247	Dec	5.112	2.374
1995				1998				2001		
Jan	7.581	3.926	1.269	Jan	5.505	2.828		Jan	5.114	2.368
Feb	7.201	3.899	1.261	Feb	5.622	2.806		Feb	4.896	2.366
Mar	7.196	3.869	1.253	Mar	5.654	2.787		Mar	4.917	2.364
Apr	7.055	3.840	1.240	Apr	5.671	2.765		Apr	5.338	2.364
May	6.284	3.812	1.230	May	5.552	2.744		May	5.381	2.362
June	6.203	3.781	1.222	June	5.446	2.725		June	5.412	2.363
July	6.426	3.746	1.223	July	5.494	2.709		July	5.054	2.363
Aug	6.284	3.704	1.228	Aug	4.976	2.695		Aug	4.832	2.365
Sept	6.182	3.662	1.232	Sept	4.42	2.680		Sept	4.588	2.365
Oct	6.02	3.624	1.234	Oct	4.605	2.666		Oct	4.232	2.366
Nov	5.741	3.587	1.229	Nov	4.714	2.653		Nov	4.752	2.368
Dec	5.572	3.549	1.234	Dec	4.648	2.641		Dec	5.051	2.370

EXHIBIT 3.7 (Continued)

Date	10-Yr. Trea. Yield	Exp. Infl.	Real Rate	Date	10-Yr. Trea. Yield	Exp. Infl.	Real Rate
2002				2004			
Jan	5.033	2.372	2.950	Jan	4.134	2.172	1.492
Feb	4.877	2.372	2.888	Feb	3.973	2.157	1.442
Mar	5.396	2.371	2.827	Mar	3.837	2.149	1.385
Apr	5.087	2.369	2.764	Apr	4.507	2.142	1.329
May	5.045	2.369	2.699	May	4.649	2.136	1.273
June	4.799	2.367	2.636	June	4.583	2.134	1.212
July	4.461	2.363	2.575	July	4.477	2.129	1.156
Aug	4.143	2.364	2.509	Aug	4.119	2.126	1.097
Sept	3.596	2.365	2.441	Sept	4.121	2.124	1.031
Oct	3.894	2.365	2.374	Oct	4.025	2.122	0.966
Nov	4.207	2.362	2.302	Nov	4.351	2.124	0.903
Dec	3.816	2.357	2.234	Dec	4.22	2.129	0.840
2003				2005			
Jan	3.964	2.351	2.168	Jan	4.13	2.131	0.783
Feb	3.692	2.343	2.104	Feb	4.379	2.133	0.727
Mar	3.798	2.334	2.038	Mar	4.483	2.132	0.676
Apr	3.838	2.323	1.976	Apr	4.2	2.131	0.622
May	3.372	2.312	1.913	May	3.983	2.127	0.567
June	3.515	2.300	1.850	June	3.915	2.120	0.520
July	4.408	2.288	1.786	July	4.278	2.114	0.476
Aug	4.466	2.267	1.731	Aug	4.016	2.107	0.436
Sept	3.939	2.248	1.681	Sept	4.326	2.098	0.399
Oct	4.295	2.233	1.629	Oct	4.553	2.089	0.366
Nov	4.334	2.213	1.581	Nov	4.486	2.081	0.336
Dec	4.248	2.191	1.537	Dec	4.393	2.075	0.311

Note:
Expected Infl. (%) = expected rate of inflation as proxied by the 5-year moving average of the actual inflation rate.
Real Rate (%) = real rate of interest as proxied by the 5-year moving average of the interest rate on 3-month certificates of deposit.

The *forward stepwise method* and *forward entry method* begin with a minimal model that typically includes the regression intercept and one or more regressors specified to be forced into the model. Any such effect is not eligible to be removed from the model during subsequent steps. Regressors may also be forced into the model when the backward stepwise and backward removal methods are used. Any such regressors are not eligible to be removed from the model during subsequent steps.

EXHIBIT 3.8   Results of Regression for Forecasting 10-Year Treasury Yield

Regression Statistics

Multiple R^2	0.908318
R^2	0.825042
Adjusted R^2	0.824312
Standard Error	1.033764
Observations	482

Analysis of Variance

	df	SS	MS	F	Significance F
Regression	2	2413.914	1206.957	1129.404	4.8E-182
Residual	479	511.8918	1.068668		
Total	481	2925.806			

	Coefficients	Standard Error	t	Statistics p-value
Intercept	1.89674	0.147593	12.85118	1.1E-32
Expected Inflation	0.996937	0.021558	46.24522	9.1E-179
Real Rate	0.352416	0.039058	9.022903	4.45E-18

With the forward entry method, at each step after Step 0, the entry statistic is computed for each regressor eligible for entry in the model. The regressor with the largest value on the entry statistic is entered into the model provided that the entry statistic exceeds the specified critical value for model entry. If the maximum number of steps is reached or if no statistic exceeds the specified threshold, the process is terminated.

The backward removal method is a strategy which starts from a rich model and progressively removes regressors. At each step after Step 0, the removal statistic is computed for each regressor eligible to be removed from the model. If no regressor has a value on the removal statistic that is less than the critical value for removal from the model, then stepping is terminated; otherwise the effect with the smallest value on the removal statistic is removed from the model. Stepping is also terminated when the maximum number of steps is reached. Mixed strategies are also possible.

Entry or removal criteria are critical. Simplistic criteria based on the average error would lead to overfitting. In general, critical F-values or critical p-values can be specified to control entry and removal of effects from the model. Statistical packages such as Matlab and SAS, for example, offer interactive tools to perform stepwise regressions. At each step, the tool computes all the needed statistics. Alternatively, statistical packages offer tools that perform stepwise regression automatically based on prespecified criteria.

NONNORMALITY AND AUTOCORRELATION OF THE RESIDUALS

In the above discussion we assumed that there is no correlation between the residual terms. Let's now relax these assumptions. The correlation of the residuals is critical from the point of view of estimation. Autocorrelation of residuals is quite common in financial estimation where we regress quantities that are time series.

A time series is said to be autocorrelated if each term is correlated with its predecessor so that the variance of each term is partially explained by regressing each term on its predecessor. These concepts will be explained in Chapter 6.

Recall from the previous section that we organized regressor data in a matrix called the design matrix. Suppose that both regressors and the variable Y are time series data, that is, every row of the design matrix corresponds to a moment in time. The regression equation is written as follows:

$$Y = X\beta + \varepsilon$$

Suppose that residuals are correlated. This means that in general $E[\varepsilon_i \varepsilon_j] = \sigma_{ij} \neq 0$. Thus the variance-covariance matrix of the residuals $\{\sigma_{ij}\}$ will not be a diagonal matrix as in the case of uncorrelated residuals, but will exhibit nonzero off-diagonal terms. We assume that we can write

$$\{\sigma_{ij}\} = \sigma^2 \Omega$$

where Ω is a positive definite symmetric matrix and σ is a parameter to be estimated.

If residuals are correlated, the regression parameters can still be estimated without biases using the formula given by (3.26). However, this estimate will not be optimal in the sense that there are other estimators with lower variance of the sampling distribution. An optimal linear unbiased estimator has been derived. It is called the *Aitken's generalized least squares* (GLS) estimator and is given by

$$\hat{\beta} = (X'\Omega^{-1}X)^{-1}X'\Omega^{-1}Y \tag{3.36}$$

where Ω is the residual correlation matrix.

The GLS estimators vary with the sampling distribution. It can also be demonstrated that the variance of the GLS estimator is also given by the following "sandwich" formula:

$$V(\hat{\beta}) = E((\beta - \hat{\beta})(\beta - \hat{\beta})') = \sigma^2 (X' \Omega^{-1} X)^{-1} \qquad (3.37)$$

This expression is similar to equation (3.28) with the exception of the *sandwiched* term Ω^{-1}. Unfortunately, (3.38) cannot be estimated without first knowing the regression coefficients. For this reason, in the presence of correlation of residuals, it is common practice to replace static regression models with models that explicitly capture autocorrelations and produce uncorrelated residuals.

The key idea here is that autocorrelated residuals signal that the modeling exercise has not been completed. Anticipating what will be discussed in Chapter 6, if residuals are autocorrelated, this signifies that the residuals at a generic time t can be predicted from residuals at an earlier time. For example, suppose that we are linearly regressing a time series of returns r_t on N factors:

$$r_t = \alpha_1 f_{1, t-1} + \cdots + \alpha_N f_{N, t-1} + \varepsilon_t$$

Suppose that the residual terms ε_t are autocorrelated and that we can write regressions of the type

$$\varepsilon_t = \varphi \varepsilon_{t-1} + \eta_t$$

where η_t are now uncorrelated variables. If we ignore this autocorrelation, valuable forecasting information is lost. Our initial model has to be replaced with the following model:

$$r_t = \alpha_1 f_{1, t-1} + \cdots + \alpha_N f_{N, t-1} + \varepsilon_t$$
$$\varepsilon_t = \varphi \varepsilon_{t-1} + \eta_t$$

with the initial conditions ε_0.

Detecting Autocorrelation

How do we detect the autocorrelation of residuals? Suppose that we believe that there is a reasonable linear relationship between two variables, for instance stock returns and some fundamental variable. We then perform a linear regression between the two variables and estimate regression parameters using the OLS method. After estimating the regression parameters, we can compute the sequence of residuals. At this point, we can apply tests such as the Durbin-Watson test or the Dickey-Fuller test to gauge the autocorrelation of residuals. If residuals are auto-correlated, we should modify the model.

PITFALLS OF REGRESSIONS

It is important to understand when regressions are correctly applicable and when they are not. In addition to the autocorrelation of residuals, there are other situations where it would be inappropriate to use regressions. In particular, we analyze the following cases which represent possible pitfalls of regressions:

- Spurious regressions with integrated variables
- Collinearity
- Increasing the number of regressors

Spurious Regressions

The phenomenon of spurious regressions, observed by Yule in 1927, led to the study of cointegration, an econometric tool discussed in Chapter 11. We encounter spurious regressions when we perform an apparently meaningful regression between variables that are independent. A typical case is a regression between two independent random walks. Regressing two independent random walks, one might find very high values of R^2 even if the two processes are independent. More in general, one might find high values of R^2 in the regression of two or more integrated variables, even if residuals are highly correlated.

As we will see in Chapter 11, testing for regressions implies testing for cointegration. Anticipating what will be discussed there, it is always meaningful to perform regressions between stationary variables. When variables are integrated, regressions are possible only if variables are cointegrated. This means that residuals are a stationary (though possibly autocorrelated) process. As a rule of thumb, Granger and Newbold observe that if the R^2 is greater than the Durbin-Watson statistics, it is appropriate to investigate if correlations are spurious.[19]

---

[19] Clive W.J. Granger and P. Newbold, "Spurious Regression in Econometrics," *Journal of Econometrics* 2 (July 1974), pp. 111–120.

Collinearity

Collinearity, also referred to as *multicollinearity*, occurs when two or more regressors have a linear deterministic relationship. For example, there is collinearity if the design matrix

$$\mathbf{X} = \begin{pmatrix} X_{11} & \cdots & X_{N1} \\ \vdots & \ddots & \vdots \\ X_{1T} & \cdots & X_{NT} \end{pmatrix}$$

exhibits two or more columns that are perfectly proportional. Collinearity is essentially a numerical problem. Intuitively, it is clear that it creates indeterminacy as we are regressing twice on the same variable. In particular, the standard estimators given by (3.26) and (3.27) cannot be used because the relative formulas become meaningless.

In principle, collinearity can be easily resolved by eliminating one or more regressors. The problem with collinearity is that some variables might be very close to collinearity, thus leading to numerical problems and indeterminacy of results. In practice, this might happen for many different numerical artifacts. Detecting and analyzing collinearity is a rather delicate problem. In principle one could detect collinearity by computing the determinant of $\mathbf{X}'\mathbf{X}$. The difficulty resides in analyzing situations where this determinant is very small but not zero. One possible strategy for detecting and removing collinearity is to go through a process of orthogonalization of variables.[20]

Increasing the Number of Regressors

Increasing the number of regressors does not always improve regressions. The econometric theorem known as *Pyrrho's lemma* relates to the number of regressors.[21] Pyrrho's lemma states that by adding one special regressor to a linear regression, it is possible to arbitrarily change the size and sign of regression coefficients as well as to obtain an arbitrary goodness of fit. This result, rather technical, seems artificial as the regressor is an artificially constructed variable. It is, however, a perfectly rigorous result; it tells us that, if we add regressors without a proper design and testing methodology, we risk obtaining spurious results.

Pyrrho's lemma is the proof that modeling results can be arbitrarily manipulated in-sample even in the simple context of linear regressions. In fact, by adding regressors one might obtain an excellent fit in-sample

---

[20] See Hendry, *Dynamic Econometrics*.
[21] T.K. Dijkstra, "Pyrrho's Lemma, or Have it Your Way," *Metrica* 42 (1995), pp. 119–225.

though these regressors might have no predictive power out-of-sample. In addition, the size and even the sign of the regression relationships can be artificially altered in-sample.

The above observations are especially important for those financial models that seek to forecast prices, returns, or rates based on regressions over economic or fundamental variables. With modern computers, by trial and error, one might find a complex structure of regressions that give very good results in-sample but have no real forecasting power.

CONCEPTS EXPLAINED IN THIS CHAPTER (IN ORDER OF PRESENTATION)

Dependence
Function
Factorization
Conditioning
Conditional expectation
Linear regression
Regression equation
Regression function
Properties of regression
Spherical and elliptical distributions
t-distribution
Standard assumptions of linear regressions
Linear regression with deterministic regressors
Estimation of linear regressions
Multiple regressions
Design matrix
MLE estimation of regressions
OLS estimation of regressions
Sandwich estimators
Robust estimators
Coefficient of determination (R^2)
Adjusted R^2
Characteristic line of a security
Single-index market model
Jensen measure
Duration
Empirical duration
Stepwise regression
Backward stepwise method
Backward removal method

Forward stepwise method
Forward entry method
Nonnormality of residuals
Autocorrelation of residuals
Aitken's generalized least squares
Spurious regressions
Collinearity
Pyrrho's lemma

CHAPTER 4

Selected Topics in Regression Analysis

In the previous chapter we provided the basics of regression analysis—theory and estimation. There are numerous specialized topics within the area of regression analysis. While we cannot cover all of the specialized topics in this book, in this chapter we cover the following: using categorical and dummy variables in regression models, constrained least squares, and estimation using the method of moments and its generalization. In Chapter 12, we discuss robust estimation of regressions.

CATEGORICAL AND DUMMY VARIABLES IN REGRESSION MODELS

Categorical variables are variables that represent group membership. For example, given a set of bonds, the rating is a categorical variable that indicates to what category—AA, BB, and so on—each bond belongs. A categorical variable does not have a numerical value or a numerical interpretation in itself. Thus the fact that a bond is in category AA or BB does not, in itself, measure any quantitative characteristic of the bond; though quantitative attributes such as a bond's yield spread can be associated with each category.

Making a regression on categorical variables does not make sense per se. For example, it does not make sense to multiply a coefficient times AA or times BB. However, in a number of cases the standard tools of regression analysis can be applied to categorical variables after appropriate transformations. Let's first discuss the case when categorical variables are independent variables and then proceed to discuss models where categorical variables are dependent variables.

Independent Categorical Variables

Categorical input variables are used to cluster input data into different groups.[1] That is, suppose we are given a set of input-output data and a partition of the data set in a number of subsets A_i so that each data point belongs to one and only one set. The A_i represent a categorical input variable. In financial econometrics categories might represent, for example, different market regimes, economic states, ratings, countries, industries, or sectors.

We cannot, per se, mix quantitative input variables and categorical variables. For example, we cannot sum yield spreads and their ratings. However, we can perform a transformation that allows the mixing of categorical and quantitative variables. Let's see how. Suppose first that there is only one categorical input variable D, one quantitative input variable X, and one quantitative output variable Y. Consider our set of quantitative data, that is quantitative observations. We organize data in a matrix form as usual:

$$\mathbf{Y} = \begin{bmatrix} Y_1 \\ \vdots \\ Y_T \end{bmatrix}, \mathbf{X} = \begin{bmatrix} 1 & X_{11} \\ \vdots & \vdots \\ 1 & X_{T1} \end{bmatrix}$$

Suppose data belong to two categories. An explanatory variable that distinguishes only two categories is called a *dichotomous variable*. The key is to represent a dichotomous categorical variable as a numerical variable D, called a *dummy variable*, that can assume the two values 0,1. We can now add the variable D to the input variables to represent membership in one or the other group:

---

[1] We can also say that categorical input variables represent *qualitative* inputs. This last expression, however, can be misleading, insofar as categorical variables represent only the final coding of qualitative inputs in different categories. For example, suppose we want to represent some aspect of market psychology, say confidence level. We can categorize confidence in a number of categories, for example euphoria, optimism, neutrality, fear, panic. The crucial question is how we can operationally determine the applicable category and if this categorization makes sense. A categorical variable entails the ability to categorize, that is, to determine membership in different categories. If and how categorization is useful is a crucial problem in many sciences, especially economics and the social sciences.

$$
\mathbf{X} = \begin{bmatrix} D_1 & 1 & X_{11} \\ \vdots & \vdots & \vdots \\ D_T & 1 & X_{T1} \end{bmatrix}
$$

If $D_i = 0$, the data X_i belong to the first category; if $D_i = 1$, the data X_i belong to the second category.

Consider now the regression equation

$$
Y_i = \beta_0 + \beta_1 X_i + \varepsilon_i
$$

In financial econometric applications, the index i will be time or a variable that identifies a cross section of assets, such as bond issues. Consider that we can write three separate regression equations, one for those data that correspond to $D = 1$, one for those data that correspond to $D = 0$, and one for the fully pooled data. Suppose now that the three equations differ by the intercept term but have the same slope. Let's explicitly write the two equations for those data that correspond to $D = 1$ and for those data that correspond to $D = 0$:

$$
y_i = \begin{cases} \beta_{00} + \beta_{1X_i} + \varepsilon_i, & \text{if } D_i = 0 \\ \beta_{01} + \beta_{1X_i} + \varepsilon_i, & \text{if } D_i = 1 \end{cases}
$$

where i defines the observations that belong to the first category when the dummy variable D assumes value 0 and also defines the observations that belong to the second category when the dummy variable D assumes value 1. If the two categories are recession and expansion, the first equation might hold in periods of expansion and the second in periods of recession. If the two categories are investment-grade bonds and noninvestment-grade bonds, the two equations apply to different cross sections of bonds, as will be illustrated in an example later in this chapter.

Observe now that, under the assumption that only the intercept term differs in the two equations, the two equations can be combined into a single equation in the following way:

$$
Y_i = \beta_{00} + \gamma D(i) + \beta_1 X_i + \varepsilon_i
$$

where $\gamma = \beta_{01} - \beta_{00}$ represents the difference of the intercept for the two categories. In this way we have defined a single regression equation with two independent quantitative variables, X, D, to which we can apply all the usual tools of regression analysis, including the least squares (LS) estimation method and all the tests. By estimating the coefficients of this regression, we obtain the common slope and two intercepts. Observe that we would obtain the same result if the categories were inverted.

Thus far we have assumed that there is no interaction between the categorical and the quantitative variable, that is, the slope of the regression is the same for the two categories. This means that the effects of variables are additive; that is, the effect of one variable is added regardless of the value taken by the other variable. In many applications, this is an unrealistic assumption. An example will be given in the next chapter where we provide applications of regressions.

Using dummy variables, the treatment is the same as that applied to intercepts. Consider the regression equation $Y_i = \beta_0 + \beta_1 X_i + \varepsilon_i$ and write two regression equations for the two categories as we did above:

$$y_i = \begin{cases} \beta_0 + \beta_{10X_i} + \varepsilon_i, & \text{if } D_i = 0 \\ \beta_0 + \beta_{11X_i} + \varepsilon_i, & \text{if } D_i = 1 \end{cases}$$

We can couple these two equations in a single equation as follows:

$$Y_i = \beta_0 + \beta_{10} X_i + \delta(D_i X_i) + \varepsilon_i$$

where $\delta = \beta_{11} - \beta_{10}$. In fact, the above equation is identical to the first equation for $D_i = 0$ and to the second for $D_i = 1$. This regression can be estimated with the usual LS methods.

In practice, it is rarely appropriate to consider only interactions and not the intercept, which is the main effect. We call *marginalization* the fact that the interaction effect is marginal with respect to the main effect. However, we can easily construct a model that combines both effects. In fact we can write the following regression adding two variables, the dummy D and the interaction DX:

$$Y_i = \beta_0 + \gamma D_i + \beta_1 X_i + \delta(D_i X_i) + \varepsilon_i$$

This regression equation, which now includes three regressors, combines both effects.

The above process of introducing dummy variables can be generalized to regressions with multiple variables. Consider the following regression:

$$Y_i = \beta_0 + \sum_{j=1}^{N} \beta_j X_{ij} + \varepsilon_i$$

where data can be partitioned in two categories with the use of a dummy variable:

$$\mathbf{X} = \begin{bmatrix} D_1 & 1 & X_{11} & \cdots & X_{1N} \\ \vdots & \vdots & \vdots & \ddots & \vdots \\ D_T & 1 & X_{T1} & \cdots & X_{TN} \end{bmatrix}$$

We can introduce the dummy D as well as its interaction with the N quantitative variable and thus write the following equation:

$$Y_i = \beta_0 + \gamma_i D_i + \sum_{j=1}^{N} \beta_j X_{ij} + \sum_{j=1}^{N} \delta_{ij}(D_i X_{ij}) + \varepsilon_i$$

The above discussion depends critically on the fact that there are only two categories, a fact that allows one to use the numerical variable 0,1 to identify the two categories. However, the process can be easily extended to multiple categories by adding dummy variables. Suppose there are $K > 2$ categories. An explanatory variable that distinguishes between more than two categories is called a *polytomous variable*.

Suppose there are three categories, A, B, and C. Consider a dummy variable $D1$ that assumes a value one on the elements of A and zero on all the others. Let's now add a second dummy variable $D2$ that assumes the value one on the elements of the category B and zero on all the others. The three categories are now completely identified: A is identified by the values 1,0 of the two dummy variables, B by the values 0,1, and C by the values 0,0. Note that the values 1,1 do not identify any category. This process can be extended to any number of categories. If there are K categories, we need $K - 1$ dummy variables.

How can we determine if a given categorization is useful? It is quite obvious that many categorizations will be totally useless for the purpose of any econometric regression. If we categorize bonds in function of the color of the logo of the issuer, it is quite obvious that we obtain meaningless results. In other cases, however, distinctions can be subtle and important. Consider the question of market regime shifts or structural breaks. These are delicate questions that can be addressed only with appropriate statistical tests.

A word of caution about statistical tests is in order. As observed in Chapter 2, statistical tests typically work under the assumptions of the model and might be misleading if these assumptions are violated. If we try to fit a linear model to a process that is inherently nonlinear, tests might be misleading. It is good practice to use several tests and to be particularly attentive to inconsistencies between test results. Inconsistencies signal potential problems in applying tests, typically model misspecification.

The t-statistic applied to the regression coefficients of dummy variables offer a set of important tests to judge which regressors are significant. Recall from Chapter 2 that the t-statistics are the coefficients divided by their respective squared errors. The p-values associated with each coefficient estimate is the probability of the hypothesis that the corresponding coefficient is zero, that is, that the corresponding variable is irrelevant.

We can also use the F-test to test the significance of each specific dummy variable. To do so we can run the regression with and without that variable and form the corresponding F-test. The *Chow test*[2] is the F-test to gauge if all the dummy variables are collectively irrelevant. The Chow test is an F-test of mutual exclusion, written as follows:

$$F = \frac{[SSR - (SSR_1 + SSR_2)]}{SSR_1 + SSR_2} \frac{[n - 2(k + 1)]}{k + 1}$$

where

SSR_1 = the squared sum of residuals of the regression run with data in the first category without dummy variables

SSR_2 = the squared sum of residuals of the regression run with data in the second category without dummy variables

SSR = the squared sum of residuals of the regression run with fully pooled data without dummy variables

Observe that $SSR_1 + SSR_2$ is equal to the squared sum of residuals of the regression run on fully pooled data but with dummy variables. Thus the Chow test is the F-test of the unrestricted regressions with and without dummy variables.

Illustration: Predicting Corporate Bond Yield Spreads

To illustrate the use of dummy variables, we will estimate a model to predict corporate bond spreads.[3] The regression is relative to a cross section of bonds. The regression equation is the following:

---

[2] Gregory C. Chow, "Tests of Equality Between Sets of Coefficients in Two Linear Regressions," *Econometrica* 28 (1960), pp, 591–605.

[3] The model presented in this illustration was developed by FridsonVision and is described in "Focus Issues Methodology," *Leverage World* (May 30, 2003). The data for this illustration were provided by Greg Braylovskiy of FridsonVision. The firm uses about 650 companies in its analysis. Only 100 observations were used in this illustration.

$$\text{Spread}_i = \beta_0 + \beta_1 \text{Coupon}_i + \beta_2 \text{CoverageRatio}_i + \beta_3 \text{LoggedEBIT}_i + \varepsilon_i$$

where

Spread_i	=	option-adjusted spread (in basis points) for the bond issue of company i
Coupon_i	=	coupon rate for the bond of company i, expressed without considering percentage sign (i.e., 7.5% = 7.5)
CoverageRatio_i	=	earnings before interest, taxes, depreciation and amortization (EBITDA) divided by interest expense for company i
LoggedEBIT_i	=	logarithm of earnings (earnings before interest and taxes, EBIT, in millions of dollars) for company i

The dependent variable, Spread, is not measured by the typically nominal spread but by the option-adjusted spread. This spread measure adjusts for any embedded options in a bond.[4]

Theory would suggest the following properties for the estimated coefficients:

- The higher the coupon rate, the greater the issuer's default risk and hence the larger the spread. Therefore, a positive coefficient for the coupon rate is expected.
- A coverage ratio is a measure of a company's ability to satisfy fixed obligations, such as interest, principal repayment, or lease payments. There are various coverage ratios. The one used in this illustration is the ratio of the *earnings before interest, taxes, depreciation, and amortization* (EBITDA) divided by interest expense. Since the higher the coverage ratio the lower the default risk, an inverse relationship is expected between the spread and the coverage ratio; that is, the estimated coefficient for the coverage ratio is expected to be negative.
- There are various measures of earnings reported in financial statements. Earnings in this illustration is defined as the trailing 12-months *earnings before interest and taxes* (EBIT). Holding other factors constant, it is expected that the larger the EBIT, the lower the default risk and therefore an inverse relationship (negative coefficient) is expected.

We used 100 observations at two different dates, 6/6/05 and 11/28/05; thus there are 200 observations in total. This will allow us to test if there is a difference in the spread regression for investment-grade and

---

[4] See Chapter 17 in Frank J. Fabozzi, *Bond Markets, Analysis, and Strategies*, 6th ed. (Upper Saddle River, NJ: Prentice-Hall, 2006).

noninvestment grade bonds using all observations. We will then test to see if there is any structural break between the two dates. We organize the data in matrix form as usual. Data are shown in Exhibit 4.1. The second column indicates that data belong to two categories and suggests the use of one dummy variable. Another dummy variable is used later to distinguish between the two dates. Let's first estimate the regression equation for the fully pooled data, that is, all data without any distinction in categories. The estimated coefficients for the model and their corresponding t-statistics are shown below:

Coefficient	Estimated Coefficient	Standard Error	t-statistic	p-value
β_0	157.01	89.56	1.753	0.081
β_1	61.27	8.03	7.630	9.98E-13
β_2	-13.20	2.27	-5.800	2.61E-08
β_3	-90.88	16.32	-5.568	8.41E-08

Other regression results are:

SSR: 2.3666e+006
F-statistic: 89.38
p-value: 0
R^2: 0.57

Given the high value of the F-statistic and the p-value close to zero, the regression is significant. The coefficient for the three regressors is statistically significant and has the expected sign. However, the intercept term is not statistically significant. The residuals are given in the first column of Exhibit 4.2.

Let's now analyze if we obtain a better fit if we consider the two categories of investment-grade and below investment-grade bonds. It should be emphasized that this is only an exercise to show the application of regression analysis. The conclusions we reach are not meaningful from an econometric point of view given the small size of the database. The new equation is written as follows:

$$Spread_i = \beta_0 + \beta_1 D1_i + \beta_2 Coupon_i + \beta_3 D1_i Coupon_i + \beta_4 CoverageRatio_i$$
$$+ \beta_5 D1_i CoverageRatio_i + \beta_6 LoggedEBIT_i$$
$$+ \beta_7 D1_i LoggedEBIT_i + \varepsilon_i$$

EXHIBIT 4.1   Regression Data for the Bond Spread Application: 11/28/2005 and 06/06/2005

Issue #	Spread, 11/28/05	CCC+ and Below	Coupon	Coverage Ratio	Logged EBIT	Spread, 6/6/05	CCC+ and Below	Coupon	Coverage Ratio	Logged EBIT
1	509	0	7.400	2.085	2.121	473	0	7.400	2.087	2.111
2	584	0	8.500	2.085	2.121	529	0	8.500	2.087	2.111
3	247	0	8.375	9.603	2.507	377	0	8.375	5.424	2.234
4	73	0	6.650	11.507	3.326	130	0	6.650	9.804	3.263
5	156	0	7.125	11.507	3.326	181	0	7.125	9.804	3.263
6	240	0	7.250	2.819	2.149	312	0	7.250	2.757	2.227
7	866	1	9.000	1.530	2.297	852	1	9.000	1.409	1.716
8	275	0	5.950	8.761	2.250	227	0	5.950	11.031	2.166
9	515	0	8.000	2.694	2.210	480	0	8.000	2.651	2.163
10	251	0	7.875	8.289	1.698	339	0	7.875	8.231	1.951
11	507	0	9.375	2.131	2.113	452	0	9.375	2.039	2.042
12	223	0	7.750	4.040	2.618	237	0	7.750	3.715	2.557
13	71	0	7.250	7.064	2.348	90	0	7.250	7.083	2.296
14	507	0	8.000	2.656	1.753	556	0	8.000	2.681	1.797
15	566	1	9.875	1.030	1.685	634	1	9.875	1.316	1.677
16	213	0	7.500	11.219	3.116	216	0	7.500	10.298	2.996
17	226	0	6.875	11.219	3.116	204	0	6.875	10.298	2.996
18	192	0	7.750	11.219	3.116	201	0	7.750	10.298	2.996
19	266	0	6.250	3.276	2.744	298	0	6.250	3.107	2.653
20	308	0	9.250	3.276	2.744	299	0	9.250	3.107	2.653
21	263	0	7.750	2.096	1.756	266	0	7.750	2.006	3.038
22	215	0	7.190	7.096	3.469	259	0	7.190	6.552	3.453
23	291	0	7.690	7.096	3.469	315	0	7.690	6.552	3.453
24	324	0	8.360	7.096	3.469	331	0	8.360	6.552	3.453
25	272	0	6.875	8.612	1.865	318	0	6.875	9.093	2.074
26	189	0	8.000	4.444	2.790	209	0	8.000	5.002	2.756
27	383	0	7.375	2.366	2.733	417	0	7.375	2.375	2.727
28	207	0	7.000	2.366	2.733	200	0	7.000	2.375	2.727
29	212	0	6.900	4.751	2.847	235	0	6.900	4.528	2.822
30	246	0	7.500	19.454	2.332	307	0	7.500	16.656	2.181
31	327	0	6.625	3.266	2.475	365	0	6.625	2.595	2.510
32	160	0	7.150	3.266	2.475	237	0	7.150	2.595	2.510
33	148	0	6.300	3.266	2.475	253	0	6.300	2.595	2.510
34	231	0	6.625	3.266	2.475	281	0	6.625	2.595	2.510
35	213	0	6.690	3.266	2.475	185	0	6.690	2.595	2.510
36	350	0	7.130	3.266	2.475	379	0	7.130	2.595	2.510
37	334	0	6.875	4.310	2.203	254	0	6.875	5.036	2.155
38	817	1	8.625	1.780	1.965	635	0	8.625	1.851	1.935
39	359	0	7.550	2.951	3.078	410	0	7.550	2.035	3.008
40	189	0	6.500	8.518	2.582	213	0	6.500	13.077	2.479

EXHIBIT 4.1 (Continued)

Issue #	Spread, 11/28/05	CCC+ and Below	Coupon	Coverage Ratio	Logged EBIT	Spread, 6/6/05	CCC+ and Below	Coupon	Coverage Ratio	Logged EBIT
41	138	0	6.950	25.313	2.520	161	0	6.950	24.388	2.488
42	351	0	9.500	3.242	1.935	424	0	9.500	2.787	1.876
43	439	0	8.250	2.502	1.670	483	0	8.250	2.494	1.697
44	347	0	7.700	4.327	3.165	214	0	7.700	4.276	3.226
45	390	0	7.750	4.327	3.165	260	0	7.750	4.276	3.226
46	149	0	8.000	4.327	3.165	189	0	8.000	4.276	3.226
47	194	0	6.625	4.430	3.077	257	0	6.625	4.285	2.972
48	244	0	8.500	4.430	3.077	263	0	8.500	4.285	2.972
49	566	1	10.375	2.036	1.081	839	1	10.375	2.032	1.014
50	185	0	6.300	7.096	3.469	236	0	6.300	6.552	3.453
51	196	0	6.375	7.096	3.469	221	0	6.375	6.552	3.453
52	317	0	6.625	3.075	2.587	389	0	6.625	2.785	2.551
53	330	0	8.250	3.075	2.587	331	0	8.250	2.785	2.551
54	159	0	6.875	8.286	3.146	216	0	6.875	7.210	3.098
55	191	0	7.125	8.286	3.146	257	0	7.125	7.210	3.098
56	148	0	7.375	8.286	3.146	117	0	7.375	7.210	3.098
57	112	0	7.600	8.286	3.146	151	0	7.600	7.210	3.098
58	171	0	7.650	8.286	3.146	221	0	7.650	7.210	3.098
59	319	0	7.375	3.847	1.869	273	0	7.375	4.299	1.860
60	250	0	7.375	12.656	2.286	289	0	7.375	8.713	2.364
61	146	0	5.500	5.365	3.175	226	0	5.500	5.147	3.190
62	332	0	6.450	5.365	3.175	345	0	6.450	5.147	3.190
63	354	0	6.500	5.365	3.175	348	0	6.500	5.147	3.190
64	206	0	6.625	7.140	2.266	261	0	6.625	5.596	2.091
65	558	0	7.875	2.050	2.290	455	0	7.875	2.120	2.333
66	190	0	6.000	2.925	3.085	204	0	6.000	3.380	2.986
67	232	0	6.750	2.925	3.085	244	0	6.750	3.380	2.986
68	913	1	11.250	2.174	1.256	733	0	11.250	2.262	1.313
69	380	0	9.750	4.216	1.465	340	0	9.750	4.388	1.554
70	174	0	6.500	4.281	2.566	208	0	6.500	4.122	2.563
71	190	0	7.450	10.547	2.725	173	0	7.450	8.607	2.775
72	208	0	7.125	2.835	3.109	259	0	7.125	2.813	3.122
73	272	0	6.500	5.885	2.695	282	0	6.500	5.927	2.644
74	249	0	6.125	5.133	2.682	235	0	6.125	6.619	2.645
75	278	0	8.750	6.562	2.802	274	0	8.750	7.433	2.785
76	252	0	7.750	2.822	2.905	197	0	7.750	2.691	2.908
77	321	0	7.500	2.822	2.905	226	0	7.500	2.691	2.908
78	379	0	7.750	4.093	2.068	362	0	7.750	4.296	2.030
79	185	0	6.875	6.074	2.657	181	0	6.875	5.294	2.469
80	307	0	7.250	5.996	2.247	272	0	7.250	3.610	2.119
81	533	0	10.625	1.487	1.950	419	0	10.625	1.717	2.081
82	627	0	8.875	1.487	1.950	446	0	8.875	1.717	2.081

EXHIBIT 4.1   (Continued)

Issue #	Spread, 11/28/05	CCC+ and Below	Coupon	Coverage Ratio	Logged EBIT	Spread, 6/6/05	CCC+ and Below	Coupon	Coverage Ratio	Logged EBIT
83	239	0	8.875	2.994	2.186	241	0	8.875	3.858	2.161
84	240	0	7.375	8.160	2.225	274	0	7.375	8.187	2.075
85	634	0	8.500	2.663	2.337	371	0	8.500	2.674	2.253
86	631	1	7.700	2.389	2.577	654	1	7.700	2.364	2.632
87	679	1	9.250	2.389	2.577	630	1	9.250	2.364	2.632
88	556	1	9.750	1.339	1.850	883	1	9.750	1.422	1.945
89	564	1	9.750	1.861	2.176	775	1	9.750	1.630	1.979
90	209	0	6.750	8.048	2.220	223	0	6.750	7.505	2.092
91	190	0	6.500	4.932	2.524	232	0	6.500	4.626	2.468
92	390	0	6.875	6.366	1.413	403	0	6.875	5.033	1.790
93	377	0	10.250	2.157	2.292	386	0	10.250	2.057	2.262
94	143	0	5.750	11.306	2.580	110	0	5.750	9.777	2.473
95	207	0	7.250	2.835	3.109	250	0	7.250	2.813	3.122
96	253	0	6.500	4.918	2.142	317	0	6.500	2.884	1.733
97	530	1	8.500	0.527	2.807	654	1	8.500	1.327	2.904
98	481	0	6.750	2.677	1.858	439	0	6.750	3.106	1.991
99	270	0	7.625	2.835	3.109	242	0	7.625	2.813	3.122
100	190	0	7.125	9.244	3.021	178	0	7.125	7.583	3.138

Notes:
Spread = option-adjusted spread (in basis points)
Coupon = coupon rate, expressed without considering percentage sign (i.e., 7.5% = 7.5)
Coverage Ratio = EBITDA divided by interest expense for company
Logged EBIT = logarithm of earnings (EBIT in millions of dollars)

There are now seven variables and eight parameters to estimate. The estimated model coefficients and the t-statistics are shown below:

Coefficient	Estimated Coefficient	Standard Error	t-statistic	p-value
β_0	284.52	73.63	3.86	0.00
β_1	597.88	478.74	1.25	0.21
β_2	37.12	7.07	5.25	3.96E-07
β_3	−45.54	38.77	−1.17	0.24
β_4	−10.33	1.84	−5.60	7.24E-08
β_5	50.13	40.42	1.24	0.22
β_6	−83.76	13.63	−6.15	4.52E-09
β_7	−0.24	62.50	−0.00	1.00

EXHIBIT 4.2 Illustration of Residuals and Leverage for Corporate Bond Spread

Issue #	Residuals	Residuals Dummy 1	Residuals Dummy 2	Leverage Point
1	118.79930	148.931400	162.198700	0.013702
2	126.39350	183.097400	200.622000	0.010794
3	−68.57770	−39.278100	−26.716500	0.019632
4	−37.26080	−60.947500	−71.034400	0.025846
5	16.63214	4.419645	−3.828890	0.028057
6	−128.76600	−104.569000	−92.122000	0.012836
7	386.42330	191.377200	217.840000	0.014437
8	73.53972	48.516800	56.58778	0.027183
9	104.15990	146.400600	160.438900	0.008394
10	−124.78700	−98.020100	−71.374300	0.026077
11	−4.28874	73.473220	94.555400	0.017687
12	−117.58200	−88.168700	−82.883100	0.005725
13	−223.61800	−213.055000	−202.748000	0.008469
14	54.13075	99.735710	123.153000	0.017604
15	−29.42160	−132.755000	−179.955000	0.028824
16	27.74192	26.913670	24.308960	0.024891
17	79.04072	63.114850	58.091160	0.021291
18	−8.57759	−3.366800	−5.003930	0.027499
19	18.62462	13.109110	9.664499	0.017078
20	−123.21000	−56.256500	−48.090100	0.022274
21	−181.64800	−140.494000	−118.369000	0.020021
22	26.43157	27.457990	14.487850	0.021077
23	71.79254	84.897050	73.862080	0.025114
24	63.73623	93.025400	84.583560	0.034711
25	−23.09740	−22.603200	−3.106990	0.027129
26	−146.00700	−112.938000	−110.018000	0.008034
27	53.72288	78.075810	78.781050	0.009757
28	−99.29780	−84.003500	−84.749600	0.011686
29	−46.31030	−41.105600	−43.489200	0.008090
30	98.22006	79.285040	96.588250	0.095189
31	32.05062	37.541930	41.075430	0.013795
32	−167.12000	−148.947000	−143.382000	0.008615
33	−127.03400	−129.393000	−127.118000	0.018478
34	−63.94940	−58.458100	−54.924600	0.013795
35	−85.93250	−78.871000	−75.085900	0.012994
36	24.10520	41.795380	47.283410	0.008759
37	12.86740	23.326060	33.884440	0.013293
38	333.53890	101.376800	173.584400	0.013522
39	58.02881	82.472150	77.040360	0.013767
40	−19.14100	−32.550700	−29.298900	0.012888
41	118.41190	67.990200	81.986050	0.171633
42	−169.48100	−90.625700	−64.883800	0.020050
43	−38.74030	13.936980	39.950520	0.019344
44	62.91014	86.397490	80.392250	0.014446
45	102.84620	127.541400	121.729700	0.014750
46	−153.47300	−122.739000	−127.583000	0.016669
47	−30.81510	−32.968700	−41.285200	0.012692

EXHIBIT 4.2   (Continued)

Issue #	Residuals	Residuals Dummy 1	Residuals Dummy 2	Leverage Point
48	−95.711400	−52.572300	−53.631800	0.019541
49	−101.678000	−219.347000	−237.977000	0.051719
50	50.969050	30.496460	14.081700	0.020500
51	57.373200	38.712320	22.587840	0.020222
52	29.717770	34.958870	36.101100	0.013348
53	−56.859100	−12.364200	−4.932630	0.008207
54	−23.959100	−31.659900	−38.650000	0.013002
55	−7.278620	−8.940330	−14.962800	0.013384
56	−65.598100	−61.220800	−66.275700	0.014434
57	−115.386000	−105.573000	−109.757000	0.015949
58	−59.449600	−48.429300	−52.419900	0.016360
59	−69.299000	−43.044000	−23.885700	0.017263
60	15.946800	13.880220	28.513500	0.031493
61	11.362190	−21.353800	−35.607900	0.025113
62	139.148000	129.380400	118.803100	0.014047
63	158.084100	149.524300	139.140600	0.013732
64	−56.785300	−60.952000	−51.339900	0.014753
65	153.651800	194.149900	205.750200	0.009094
66	−15.653600	−28.630900	−40.227500	0.023258
67	−19.612200	−14.472300	−23.166100	0.015577
68	209.488200	144.261600	67.891100	0.063569
69	−185.659000	−100.217000	−63.396000	0.033131
70	−91.541800	−92.646100	−91.015000	0.012423
71	−36.623800	−33.937000	−29.003400	0.016903
72	−65.586300	−51.301800	−59.080100	0.014743
73	39.294110	32.661770	32.391920	0.010000
74	28.197460	14.759650	12.952710	0.015290
75	−73.910000	−28.902200	−22.353300	0.018074
76	−78.608000	−47.733800	−48.902600	0.010866
77	5.711553	30.546620	28.410290	0.010507
78	−10.926100	22.258560	38.888810	0.009622
79	−71.611400	−69.462200	−67.416900	0.007122
80	−10.848000	3.505179	15.383910	0.008845
81	−78.195700	32.775440	61.748590	0.040731
82	123.041000	191.738700	213.938800	0.015223
83	−223.662000	−160.978000	−142.925000	0.011651
84	−58.977600	−47.671100	−33.850800	0.012244
85	203.727300	257.223800	270.556600	0.009014
86	267.904600	−65.208100	89.636310	0.008117
87	220.923600	−4.162260	42.473790	0.019357
88	−12.621600	−142.213000	−168.474000	0.024764
89	31.862060	−127.616000	−134.267000	0.023501
90	−53.593800	−57.028600	−45.579800	0.015906
91	−70.794900	−73.470000	−70.669700	0.011934
92	24.164780	34.342730	62.098550	0.044409
93	−171.291000	−73.744300	−52.943000	0.034539
94	17.439710	−22.092800	−20.420000	0.029392

EXHIBIT 4.2 (Continued)

Issue #	Residuals	Residuals Dummy 1	Residuals Dummy 2	Leverage Point
95	−74.246100	−56.942100	−64.236600	0.014565
96	−42.690600	−42.602900	−31.958300	0.019263
97	114.168900	−66.109500	−66.049500	0.019100
98	114.578500	129.177300	145.600600	0.027901
99	−34.225400	−7.862790	−13.705900	0.015033
100	−6.958960	−10.488100	−13.508000	0.013543
101	81.920940	112.117900	101.420600	0.013887
102	70.515070	127.283800	120.844000	0.010884
103	−18.587600	24.683610	20.132390	0.008541
104	−8.443100	−26.784100	−28.884400	0.018612
105	13.449820	6.582981	6.321103	0.019873
106	−50.430600	−26.617000	−36.781100	0.011579
107	318.056000	133.403000	130.828300	0.020055
108	47.876010	16.919350	5.068270	0.036536
109	64.341610	107.038200	99.281600	0.008974
110	−14.573200	10.557760	3.393970	0.017905
111	−66.995600	11.539420	7.987728	0.017995
112	−113.425000	−82.640800	−88.147800	0.005809
113	−209.054000	−198.177000	−205.892000	0.009238
114	107.522000	152.737700	142.464600	0.016268
115	41.638860	−76.825800	−145.458000	0.028688
116	7.647833	10.327540	9.887700	0.018651
117	33.946630	21.528710	18.669900	0.016205
118	−22.671700	−13.952900	−13.425200	0.020799
119	40.107630	35.729610	24.798540	0.017949
120	−142.727000	−74.636000	−73.956000	0.020301
121	−63.286100	−31.013100	−33.970100	0.015754
122	61.774140	64.481450	64.302480	0.020207
123	87.135110	101.920500	103.676700	0.023941
124	62.078800	93.048860	97.398200	0.033133
125	48.320900	45.935300	36.150130	0.021344
126	−121.736000	−90.029000	−92.609500	0.007491
127	87.253680	111.626800	105.229900	0.009683
128	−106.767000	−91.452500	−99.300700	0.011631
129	−28.566900	−22.540100	−29.135400	0.008184
130	108.560100	98.752280	95.570570	0.067155
131	64.418690	71.586810	60.886980	0.015243
132	−95.752300	−75.902200	−84.570100	0.009928
133	−27.665900	−28.348600	−40.306300	0.020009
134	−19.581300	−12.413200	−23.113000	0.015243
135	−119.564000	−110.826000	−121.274000	0.014425
136	47.473260	66.840260	58.094960	0.010076
137	−61.953700	−53.237800	−64.316600	0.013824
138	149.786400	211.505100	204.226300	0.013863
139	90.609530	118.184700	114.258300	0.014560
140	55.650810	29.860840	23.239180	0.032351
141	126.240500	78.712630	79.050720	0.157105

EXHIBIT 4.2 (Continued)

Issue #	Residuals	Residuals Dummy 1	Residuals Dummy 2	Leverage Point
142	−107.826000	−27.243600	−31.116800	0.020563
143	7.614932	60.121850	50.036220	0.018518
144	−65.174500	−41.979400	−42.794500	0.016334
145	−22.238400	2.164489	1.542950	0.016663
146	−108.558000	−78.116000	−77.769900	0.018707
147	20.679750	19.696850	12.963030	0.011602
148	−88.216600	−43.906700	−43.383600	0.016474
149	165.253100	48.262590	−23.500200	0.054354
150	93.311620	74.519920	70.896340	0.020168
151	73.715770	56.735780	53.402470	0.019845
152	94.629570	100.961000	90.629950	0.014368
153	−62.947300	−17.362000	−21.403800	0.008312
154	14.480140	10.216950	6.659433	0.010802
155	40.160620	41.936480	39.346550	0.010850
156	−115.159000	−107.344000	−108.966000	0.011566
157	−94.946500	−81.696400	−82.447900	0.012781
158	−28.010400	−13.552500	−14.110500	0.013124
159	−110.127000	−85.111400	−96.632900	0.017243
160	9.959282	18.682370	12.662020	0.011670
161	89.889700	57.689740	48.509480	0.025706
162	150.675500	141.424000	135.920500	0.014594
163	150.611600	142.567900	137.258000	0.014276
164	−38.040900	−36.521000	−48.754100	0.018527
165	55.443990	95.437610	88.132530	0.008675
166	−4.652580	−18.233400	−27.698600	0.020882
167	−10.611100	−6.074840	−12.637200	0.012834
168	35.778970	164.163000	162.921500	0.062460
169	−215.328000	−131.013000	−135.422000	0.031092
170	−59.986400	−60.605400	−70.729300	0.012731
171	−74.693600	−66.782400	−69.716200	0.010213
172	−13.734800	0.523639	−3.905600	0.015083
173	45.295840	38.898770	30.164940	0.010233
174	30.476800	13.024800	3.159872	0.014593
175	−67.888500	−25.271900	−23.635500	0.019872
176	−135.061000	−103.830000	−107.375000	0.011204
177	−90.741200	−65.550000	−70.062300	0.010866
178	−28.683300	4.187387	−4.706060	0.010313
179	−103.027000	−97.290000	−106.078000	0.008397
180	−88.975000	−66.845700	−77.367900	0.012101
181	−177.281000	−67.904100	−66.493200	0.041400
182	−43.044700	24.059160	18.696920	0.013532
183	−212.505000	−152.131000	−155.963000	0.011638
184	−38.210800	−25.916400	−34.173800	0.015537
185	−66.764700	−12.702000	−17.886300	0.009148
186	295.611300	−36.578800	106.036400	0.008451
187	176.630300	−47.533000	−13.126100	0.020417

EXHIBIT 4.2   (Continued)

Issue #	Residuals	Residuals Dummy 1	Residuals Dummy 2	Leverage Point
188	324.060100	189.413000	136.666400	0.023978
189	221.951100	76.029960	34.046210	0.023629
190	−58.422000	−59.380500	−70.254000	0.018335
191	−37.907200	−39.303500	−49.850800	0.012962
192	53.841660	65.166450	51.559780	0.025442
193	−166.323000	−68.275700	−66.904900	0.034161
194	−45.521100	−79.888400	−90.959200	0.026897
195	−30.394500	−13.116600	−17.062000	0.014917
196	−42.709500	−33.855500	−50.285700	0.037224
197	257.550200	34.224540	70.337910	0.019013
198	90.307160	102.727000	89.148700	0.022461
199	−61.373800	−35.037300	−37.531400	0.015419
200	−30.310400	−29.889500	−32.034600	0.012067

Notes:
Residuals: residuals from the pooled regression without dummy variables for investment grade.
Residuals Dummy 1: inclusion of dummy variable for investment grade.
Residuals Dummy 2: inclusion of dummy variable to test for regime shift.
Leverage Point: in robust regressions, signals that the corresponding observations might have a decisive influence on the estimation of the regression parameters.

Other regression results are:

SSR: $1.4744e + 006$
F-statistic: 76.83
p-value: 0
$R^2 = 0.73$

The Chow test has the value 16.60. The F-statistic and the Chow test suggest that the use of dummy variables has greatly improved the goodness of fit of the regression, even after compensating for the increase in the number of parameters. The residuals of the model without and with dummy variable D1 are shown, respectively, in the second and third columns of Exhibit 4.2.

Now let's use dummy variables to test if there is a regime shift between the two dates. This is a common use for dummy variables in practice. To this end we create a new dummy variable that has the value 0 for the first date 11/28/05 and 1 for the second date 6/6/05. The new equation is written as follows:

$$\text{Spread}_i = \beta_0 + \beta_1 D2_i + \beta_2 \text{Coupon}_i + \beta_3 D2_i \text{Coupon}_i + \beta_4 \text{CoverageRatio}_i$$
$$+ \beta_5 D2_i \text{CoverageRatio}_i + \beta_6 \text{LoggedEBIT}_i$$
$$+ \beta_7 D2_i \text{LoggedEBIT}_i + \varepsilon_i$$

as in the previous case but with a different dummy variable. There are seven independent variables and eight parameters to estimate. The estimated model coefficients and t-statistics are shown below:

Coefficient	Estimated Coefficient	Standard Error	t-statistic	p-value
β_0	257.26	79.71	3.28	0.00
β_1	82.17	61.63	1.33	0.18
β_2	33.25	7.11	4.67	5.53E-06
β_3	28.14	2.78	10.12	1.45E-19
β_4	−10.79	2.50	−4.32	2.49E-05
β_5	0.00	3.58	0.00	1.00
β_6	−63.20	18.04	−3.50	0.00
β_7	−27.48	24.34	−1.13	0.26

Other regression statistics are:

SSR: $1.5399e + 006$
F-statistic: 72.39
p-value: 0
R^2: 0.71

The Chow test has the value 14.73. The F-statistics and the Chow test suggest that there is indeed a regime shift and that the spread regressions at the two different dates are different. Again, the use of dummy variables has greatly improved the goodness of fit of the regression, even after compensating for the increase in the number of parameters. The residuals of the model with dummy variables D2 are shown in the next-to-the-last column of Exhibit 4.2. (We discuss the last column in the exhibit when we cover the topic of robust regressions in Chapter 12.)

Illustration: Testing the Mutual Fund Characteristic Lines in Different Market Environments

In the previous chapter, we calculated the characteristic line of two large-cap mutual funds. Let's now perform a simple application of the use of dummy variables by determining if the slope (beta) of the two mutual funds is different in a rising stock market ("up market") and a declining stock market ("down market"). To test this, we can write the following multiple regression model:

$$y_{it} = \alpha_i + \beta_{1i}x_t + \beta_{2i}(D_t x_t) + e_{it}$$

where D_t is the dummy variable that can take on a value of 1 or 0. We will let

D_t = 1 if period t is classified as an up market
D_t = 0 if period t is classified as a down market

The coefficient for the dummy variable is β_{2i}. If that coefficient is statistically significant, then for the mutual fund:

In an up market: $\beta_i = \beta_{1i} + \beta_{2i}$
In a down market: $\beta_i = \beta_{1i}$

If β_{2i} is not statistically significant, then there is no difference in β_i for up and down markets.

In our illustration, we have to define what we mean by an up and a down market. We will define an up market precisely as one where the average excess return (market return over the risk-free rate or $(r_M - r_{ft})$) for the prior three months is greater than zero. Then

D_t = 1 if the average $(r_{Mt} - r_{ft})$ for the prior three months > 0
D_t = 0 otherwise

The regressor will then be

$D_t x_t$ = x_t if $(r_M - r_{ft})$ for the prior three months > 0
$D_t x_t$ = 0 otherwise

We use the S&P 500 Index as a proxy for the market returns and the 90-day Treasury rate as a proxy for the risk-free rate. The data are presented in Exhibit 4.3 which shows each observation for the variable $D_t x_t$. The regression results for the two mutual funds are as follows:

Coefficient	Coefficient Estimate	Standard Error	t-statistic	p-value
Fund A				
α	−0.23	0.10	−2.36	0.0198
β_1	0.75	0.03	25.83	4E-50
β_2	0.18	0.04	4.29	4E-05
Fund B				
α	0.00	0.14	−0.03	0.9762
β_1	0.75	0.04	18.02	2E-35
β_2	0.13	0.06	2.14	0.0344

EXHIBIT 4.3 Data for Estimating Mutual Fund Characteristic Line with a Dummy Variable

Month Ended	r_M	r_{ft}	Dummy D_t	$r_M - r_{ft}$ x_t	$D_t x_t$	Mutual Fund A r_t	B r_t	A y_t	B y_t
01/31/1995	2.60	0.42	0	2.18	0	0.65	1.28	0.23	0.86
02/28/1995	3.88	0.40	0	3.48	0	3.44	3.16	3.04	2.76
03/31/1995	2.96	0.46	1	2.50	2.5	2.89	2.58	2.43	2.12
04/30/1995	2.91	0.44	1	2.47	2.47	1.65	1.81	1.21	1.37
05/31/1995	3.95	0.54	1	3.41	3.41	2.66	2.96	2.12	2.42
06/30/1995	2.35	0.47	1	1.88	1.88	2.12	2.18	1.65	1.71
07/31/1995	3.33	0.45	1	2.88	2.88	3.64	3.28	3.19	2.83
08/31/1995	0.27	0.47	1	−0.20	−0.2	−0.40	0.98	−0.87	0.51
09/30/1995	4.19	0.43	1	3.76	3.76	3.06	3.47	2.63	3.04
10/31/1995	−0.35	0.47	1	−0.82	−0.82	−1.77	−0.63	−2.24	−1.10
11/30/1995	4.40	0.42	1	3.98	3.98	4.01	3.92	3.59	3.50
12/31/1995	1.85	0.49	1	1.36	1.36	1.29	1.73	0.80	1.24
01/31/1996	3.44	0.43	1	3.01	3.01	3.36	2.14	2.93	1.71
02/29/1996	0.96	0.39	1	0.57	0.57	1.53	1.88	1.14	1.49
03/31/1996	0.96	0.39	1	0.57	0.57	0.59	1.65	0.20	1.26
04/30/1996	1.47	0.46	1	1.01	1.01	1.46	1.83	1.00	1.37
05/31/1996	2.58	0.42	1	2.16	2.16	2.17	2.20	1.75	1.78
06/30/1996	0.41	0.40	1	0.01	0.01	−0.63	0.00	−1.03	−0.40
07/31/1996	−4.45	0.45	1	−4.90	−4.9	−4.30	−3.73	−4.75	−4.18
08/31/1996	2.12	0.41	0	1.71	0	2.73	2.24	2.32	1.83
09/30/1996	5.62	0.44	0	5.18	0	5.31	4.49	4.87	4.05
10/31/1996	2.74	0.42	1	2.32	2.32	1.42	1.34	1.00	0.92
11/30/1996	7.59	0.41	1	7.18	7.18	6.09	5.30	5.68	4.89
12/31/1996	−1.96	0.46	1	−2.42	−2.42	−1.38	−0.90	−1.84	−1.36
01/31/1997	6.21	0.45	1	5.76	5.76	4.15	5.73	3.70	5.28
02/28/1997	0.81	0.39	1	0.42	0.42	1.65	−1.36	1.26	−1.75
03/31/1997	−4.16	0.43	1	−4.59	−4.59	−4.56	−3.75	−4.99	−4.18
04/30/1997	5.97	0.43	1	5.54	5.54	4.63	3.38	4.20	2.95
05/31/1997	6.14	0.49	1	5.65	5.65	5.25	6.05	4.76	5.56
06/30/1997	4.46	0.37	1	4.09	4.09	2.98	2.90	2.61	2.53
07/31/1997	7.94	0.43	1	7.51	7.51	6.00	7.92	5.57	7.49
08/31/1997	−5.56	0.41	1	−5.97	−5.97	−4.40	−3.29	−4.81	−3.70
09/30/1997	5.48	0.44	1	5.04	5.04	5.70	4.97	5.26	4.53
10/31/1997	−3.34	0.42	1	−3.76	−3.76	−2.76	−2.58	−3.18	−3.00
11/30/1997	4.63	0.39	0	4.24	0	3.20	2.91	2.81	2.52
12/31/1997	1.72	0.48	1	1.24	1.24	1.71	2.41	1.23	1.93
01/31/1998	1.11	0.43	1	0.68	0.68	−0.01	−0.27	−0.44	−0.70
02/28/1998	7.21	0.39	1	6.82	6.82	5.50	6.84	5.11	6.45
03/31/1998	5.12	0.39	1	4.73	4.73	5.45	3.84	5.06	3.45
04/30/1998	1.01	0.43	1	0.58	0.58	−0.52	1.07	−0.95	0.64
05/31/1998	−1.72	0.40	1	−2.12	−2.12	−1.25	−1.30	−1.65	−1.70
06/30/1998	4.06	0.41	1	3.65	3.65	3.37	4.06	2.96	3.65
07/31/1998	−1.06	0.40	1	−1.46	−1.46	0.10	−1.75	−0.30	−2.15
08/31/1998	−14.46	0.43	1	−14.89	−14.89	−15.79	−13.44	−16.22	−13.87

EXHIBIT 4.3   (Continued)

Month Ended	r_M	r_{ft}	Dummy D_t	$r_M - r_{ft}$ x_t	$D_t x_t$	Mutual Fund A r_t	B r_t	A y_t	B y_t
09/30/1998	6.41	0.46	0	5.95	0	5.00	4.86	4.54	4.40
10/31/1998	8.13	0.32	0	7.81	0	5.41	4.56	5.09	4.24
11/30/1998	6.06	0.31	0	5.75	0	5.19	5.56	4.88	5.25
12/31/1998	5.76	0.38	1	5.38	5.38	7.59	7.18	7.21	6.80
01/31/1999	4.18	0.35	1	3.83	3.83	2.60	3.11	2.25	2.76
02/28/1999	−3.11	0.35	1	−3.46	−3.46	−4.13	−3.01	−4.48	−3.36
03/31/1999	4.00	0.43	1	3.57	3.57	3.09	3.27	2.66	2.84
04/30/1999	3.87	0.37	1	3.50	3.5	2.26	2.22	1.89	1.85
05/31/1999	−2.36	0.34	1	−2.70	−2.7	−2.12	−1.32	−2.46	−1.66
06/30/1999	5.55	0.40	1	5.15	5.15	4.43	5.36	4.03	4.96
07/31/1999	−3.12	0.38	1	−3.50	−3.5	−3.15	−1.72	−3.53	−2.10
08/31/1999	−0.50	0.39	0	−0.89	0	−1.05	−2.06	−1.44	−2.45
09/30/1999	−2.74	0.39	1	−3.13	−3.13	−2.86	−1.33	−3.25	−1.72
10/31/1999	6.33	0.39	0	5.94	0	5.55	2.29	5.16	1.90
11/30/1999	2.03	0.36	1	1.67	1.67	3.23	3.63	2.87	3.27
12/31/1999	5.89	0.44	1	5.45	5.45	8.48	7.09	8.04	6.65
01/31/2000	−5.02	0.41	1	−5.43	−5.43	−4.09	−0.83	−4.50	−1.24
02/29/2000	−1.89	0.43	1	−2.32	−2.32	1.43	2.97	1.00	2.54
03/31/2000	9.78	0.47	0	9.31	0	6.84	5.86	6.37	5.39
04/30/2000	−3.01	0.46	1	−3.47	−3.47	−4.04	−4.55	−4.50	−5.01
05/31/2000	−2.05	0.50	1	−2.55	−2.55	−2.87	−4.47	−3.37	−4.97
06/30/2000	2.46	0.40	1	2.06	2.06	0.54	6.06	0.14	5.66
07/31/2000	−1.56	0.48	0	−2.04	0	−0.93	1.89	−1.41	1.41
08/31/2000	6.21	0.50	0	5.71	0	7.30	6.01	6.80	5.51
09/30/2000	−5.28	0.51	1	−5.79	−5.79	−4.73	−4.81	−5.24	−5.32
10/31/2000	−0.42	0.56	0	−0.98	0	−1.92	−4.84	−2.48	−5.40
11/30/2000	−7.88	0.51	0	−8.39	0	−6.73	−11.00	−7.24	−11.51
12/31/2000	0.49	0.50	0	−0.01	0	2.61	3.69	2.11	3.19
01/31/2001	3.55	0.54	0	3.01	0	0.36	5.01	−0.18	4.47
02/28/2001	−9.12	0.38	0	−9.50	0	−5.41	−8.16	−5.79	−8.54
03/31/2001	−6.33	0.42	0	−6.75	0	−5.14	−5.81	−5.56	−6.23
04/30/2001	7.77	0.39	0	7.38	0	5.25	4.67	4.86	4.28
05/31/2001	0.67	0.32	0	0.35	0	0.47	0.45	0.15	0.13
06/30/2001	−2.43	0.28	1	−2.71	−2.71	−3.48	−1.33	−3.76	−1.61
07/31/2001	−0.98	0.30	1	−1.28	−1.28	−2.24	−1.80	−2.54	−2.10
08/31/2001	−6.26	0.31	0	−6.57	0	−4.78	−5.41	−5.09	−5.72
09/30/2001	−8.08	0.28	0	−8.36	0	−6.46	−7.27	−6.74	−7.55
10/31/2001	1.91	0.22	0	1.69	0	1.01	2.30	0.79	2.08
11/30/2001	7.67	0.17	0	7.50	0	4.49	5.62	4.32	5.45
12/31/2001	0.88	0.15	1	0.73	0.73	1.93	2.14	1.78	1.99
01/31/2002	−1.46	0.14	1	−1.60	−1.6	−0.99	−3.27	−1.13	−3.41
02/28/2002	−1.93	0.13	1	−2.06	−2.06	−0.84	−2.68	−0.97	−2.81
03/31/2002	3.76	0.13	0	3.63	0	3.38	4.70	3.25	4.57
04/30/2002	−6.06	0.15	0	−6.21	0	−4.38	−3.32	−4.53	−3.47
05/31/2002	−0.74	0.14	0	−0.88	0	−1.78	−0.81	−1.92	−0.95
06/30/2002	−7.12	0.13	0	−7.25	0	−5.92	−5.29	−6.05	−5.42

EXHIBIT 4.3   (Continued)

Month Ended	r_M	r_{ft}	Dummy D_t	$r_M - r_{ft}$ x_t	$D_t x_t$	Mutual Fund A r_t	B r_t	A y_t	B y_t
07/31/2002	−7.80	0.15	0	−7.95	0	−6.37	−7.52	−6.52	−7.67
08/31/2002	0.66	0.14	0	0.52	0	−0.06	1.86	−0.20	1.72
09/30/2002	−10.87	0.14	0	−11.01	0	−9.38	−6.04	−9.52	−6.18
10/31/2002	8.80	0.14	0	8.66	0	3.46	5.10	3.32	4.96
11/30/2002	5.89	0.12	0	5.77	0	3.81	1.73	3.69	1.61
12/31/2002	−5.88	0.11	1	−5.99	−5.99	−4.77	−2.96	−4.88	−3.07
01/31/2003	−2.62	0.10	1	−2.72	−2.72	−1.63	−2.34	−1.73	−2.44
02/28/2003	−1.50	0.09	0	−1.59	0	−0.48	−2.28	−0.57	−2.37
03/31/2003	0.97	0.10	0	0.87	0	1.11	1.60	1.01	1.50
04/30/2003	8.24	0.10	0	8.14	0	6.67	5.44	6.57	5.34
05/31/2003	5.27	0.09	1	5.18	5.18	4.96	6.65	4.87	6.56
06/30/2003	1.28	0.10	1	1.18	1.18	0.69	1.18	0.59	1.08
07/31/2003	1.76	0.07	1	1.69	1.69	1.71	3.61	1.64	3.54
08/31/2003	1.95	0.07	1	1.88	1.88	1.32	1.13	1.25	1.06
09/30/2003	−1.06	0.08	1	−1.14	−1.14	−1.34	−1.12	−1.42	−1.20
10/31/2003	5.66	0.07	1	5.59	5.59	5.30	4.21	5.23	4.14
11/30/2003	0.88	0.07	1	0.81	0.81	0.74	1.18	0.67	1.11
12/31/2003	5.24	0.08	1	5.16	5.16	4.87	4.77	4.79	4.69
01/31/2004	1.84	0.07	1	1.77	1.77	0.87	2.51	0.80	2.44
02/29/2004	1.39	0.06	1	1.33	1.33	0.97	1.18	0.91	1.12
03/31/2004	−1.51	0.09	1	−1.60	−1.6	−0.89	−1.79	−0.98	−1.88
04/30/2004	−1.57	0.08	1	−1.65	−1.65	−2.59	−1.73	−2.67	−1.81
05/31/2004	1.37	0.06	0	1.31	0	0.66	0.83	0.60	0.77
06/30/2004	1.94	0.08	0	1.86	0	1.66	1.56	1.58	1.48
07/31/2004	−3.31	0.10	1	−3.41	−3.41	−2.82	−4.26	−2.92	−4.36
08/31/2004	0.40	0.11	0	0.29	0	−0.33	0.00	−0.44	−0.11
09/30/2004	1.08	0.11	0	0.97	0	1.20	1.99	1.09	1.88
10/31/2004	1.53	0.11	0	1.42	0	0.33	1.21	0.22	1.10
11/30/2004	4.05	0.15	1	3.90	3.9	4.87	5.68	4.72	5.53
12/31/2004	3.40	0.16	1	3.24	3.24	2.62	3.43	2.46	3.27

Notes:
1. The following information is used for determining the value of the dummy variable for the first three months:

	r_m	r_f	$r_m - r_f$
Sep–94	−2.41	0.37	−2.78
Oct–94	2.29	0.38	1.91
Nov–94	−3.67	0.37	−4.04
Dec–94	1.46	0.44	1.02

2. The dummy variable is defined as follows:
$D_t x_t = x_t$ if $(r_M - r_{ft})$ for the prior three months > 0
$D_t x_t = 0$ otherwise

The adjusted R^2 is 0.93 and 0.83 for mutual funds A and B, respectively.

For both funds, β_{2i} is statistically significantly different from zero. Hence, for these two mutual funds, there is a difference in the β_i for up and down markets.[5] From the results reported above, we would find that:

	Mutual Fund A	Mutual Fund B
Down market β_i (= β_{1i})	0.75	0.75
Up market β_i (=β_{1i} + β_{2i})	0.93 (= 0.75 + 0.18)	0.88 (= 0.75 + 0.13)

Dependent Categorical Variables

Thus far we have discussed models where the independent variables can be either quantitative or categorical while the dependent variable is quantitative. Let's now discuss models where the dependent variable is categorical.

Recall that a regression model can be interpreted as a conditional probability distribution. Suppose that the dependent variable is a categorical variable Y that can assume two values, which we represent conventionally as 0 and 1. The probability distribution of the dependent variable is then a discrete function:

$$\begin{cases} P(Y = 1) = p \\ P(Y = 0) = q = 1 - p \end{cases}$$

A regression model where the dependent variable is a categorical variable is therefore a probability model; that is, it is a model of the probability p given the values of the independent variables $\mathbf{X}$:

$$P(Y = 1 | \mathbf{X}) = f(\mathbf{X})$$

In the following sections we will discuss three probability models: the linear probability model, the logit regression model, and the probit regression model.

Linear Probability Model

The *linear probability model* assumes that the function $f(\mathbf{X})$ is linear. For example, a linear probability model of default assumes that there is a linear relationship between the probability of default and the factors that determine default.

---

[5] We actually selected funds that had this characteristic so one should not infer that all mutual funds exhibit this characteristic.

$$P(Y = 1 | \mathbf{X}) = f(\mathbf{X})$$

The parameters of the model can be obtained by using ordinary least squares applying the estimation methods of multiple regression models discussed in the previous chapter. Once the parameters of the model are estimated, the predicted value for P(Y) can be interpreted as the event probability such as the probability of default in our previous example. Note, however, that when using a linear probability model, the R^2 is used as described in the previous chapter only if all the independent variables are also binary variables.

A major drawback of the linear probability model is that the predicted value may be negative. In the probit regression and logit regression models described below, the predicted probability is forced to be between 0 and 1.

Probit Regression Model

The *probit regression model* is a nonlinear regression model where the dependent variable is a binary variable. Due to its nonlinearity, one cannot estimate this model with least squares methods. We have to use Maximum Likelihood (ML) methods as described below. Because what is being predicted is the standard normal cumulative probability distribution, the predicted values are between 0 and 1.

The general form for the probit regression model is

$$P(Y = 1 \mid X_1, X_2, ..., X_K) = N(a + b_1 X_1 + b_2 X_2 + ... + b_K X_K)$$

where N is the cumulative standard normal distribution function.

To see how ML methods work, consider a model of the probability of corporate bond defaults. Suppose that there are three factors that have been found to historically explain corporate bond defaults. The probit regression model is then

$$\begin{cases} P(Y = 1 | X_1, X_2, X_3) = N(\beta_0 + \beta_1 X_1 + \beta_2 X_2 + \beta_3 X_3) \\ P(Y = 0 | X_1, X_2, X_3) = 1 - N(\beta_0 + \beta_1 X_1 + \beta_2 X_2 + \beta_3 X_3) \end{cases}$$

The likelihood function is formed from the products

$$\prod_i N(\beta_0 + \beta_1 X_{1i} + \beta_2 X_{2i} + \beta_3 X_{3i})^{Y_i} (1 - N(\beta_0 + \beta_1 X_{1i} + \beta_2 X_{2i} + \beta_3 X_{3i}))^{1 - Y_i}$$

extended to all the samples, where the variable Y assumes a value of 0 for defaulted companies and 1 for nondefaulted companies. Parameters are estimated by maximizing the likelihood.

Suppose that the following parameters are estimated:

$$\beta = -2.1 \quad \beta_1 = 1.9 \quad \beta_2 = 0.3 \quad \beta_3 = 0.8$$

Then

$$N(a + b_1X_1 + b_2X_2 + b_3X_3) = N(-2.1 + 1.9X_1 + 0.3X_2 + 0.8X_3)$$

Now suppose that the probability of default of a company with the following values for the independent variables is sought:

$$X_1 = 0.2 \quad X_2 = 0.9 \quad X_3 = 1.0$$

Substituting these values we get

$$N(-2.1 + 1.9(0.2) + 0.3(0.9) + 0.8(1.0)) = N(-0.65)$$

The standard normal cumulative probability for $N(-0.65)$ is 25.8%. Therefore, the probability of default for a company with this characteristic is 25.8%.

Logit Regression Model

As with the probit regression model, the *logit regression model* is a nonlinear regression model where the dependent variable is a binary variable and the predicted values are between 0 and 1. The predicted value is also a cumulative probability distribution. However, rather than being a standard normal cumulative probability distribution, it is standard cumulative probability distribution of a distribution called the *logistic distribution*.

The general formula for the logit regression model is

$$P(Y = 1 | X_1, X_2, ..., X_N) = F(a + b_1X_1 + b_2X_2 + ... + b_NX_N)$$
$$= 1/[1 + e^{-W}]$$

where $W = a + b_1X_1 + b_2X_2 + ... + b_NX_N$.

As with the probit regression model, the logit regression model is estimated with ML methods.

Using our previous illustration, $W = -0.65$. Therefore

$$1/[1 + e^{-W}] = 1/[1 + e^{-(-0.65)}] = 34.3\%$$

The probability of default for the company with these characteristics is 34.3%.

CONSTRAINED LEAST SQUARES

The *constrained least squares* (or *restricted least squares*) *method* uses least squares estimation methods subject to constraints. Consider, for simplicity, a linear model with only one independent variable:

$$y = \beta_0 + \beta_1 x + \varepsilon$$

Given N observations (y_i, x_i), $i = 1, 2, \ldots, N$ the constrained least squares method seeks to minimize the sum of squared residuals

$$\sum_{i=1}^{N} (y_i - \beta_0 - \beta_1 x_i)^2$$

as in ordinary least squares method, but assumes that solutions must respect some constraint that we can represent with the following equation: $\varphi(\beta_0, \beta_1) = 0$.

Constrained problems of this type can be solved with the technique of Lagrange multipliers. This technique transforms a constrained problem into an unconstrained problem by adding one variable, the Lagrange multiplier. To apply the method of Lagrange multipliers, let's form the function:

$$L(\beta_0, \beta_1, \lambda) = \sum_{i=1}^{N} (y_i - \beta_0 - \beta_1 x_i)^2 - \lambda\varphi(\beta_0, \beta_1)$$

Now we determine the unconstrained minimum of the function L by setting its first derivatives to zero:

$$\frac{\partial L}{\partial \beta_0} = 0, \frac{\partial L}{\partial \beta_1} = 0, \frac{\partial L}{\partial \lambda} = 0$$

It can be demonstrated that the solutions of this unconstrained minimization problem also satisfy the original constrained problem.

Illustration: Curve Fitting to Obtain the Spot Rate Curve

An important relationship in the valuation of fixed income securities and option-type instruments on fixed income securities is the term structure of interest rates. The term structure of interest rates shows the relationship between zero-coupon interest rates on some benchmark security and maturity. Unlike the yield curve which shows the relationship between coupon and zero-coupon benchmark security and maturity, the term structure of interest rates is based on zero-coupon rates. Another term for a zero-coupon rate is a *spot rate*. Hence, the graphical depiction of the term structure of interest rates is referred to as the *spot rate curve*. The spot rate curve is not observable in the market and therefore must be estimated.

Participants in the fixed income market typically want to estimate a default-free spot rate curve. Consequently, the benchmark interest rates used are U.S. Treasury securities because they are viewed as default-free securities. The estimated spot rate curve is then used to value non-Treasury securities such as corporate securities by adding an appropriate credit spread to the spot rate curve. Models to value options on Treasury securities begin with the spot rate curve because these models must be calibrated to the market.[6] Calibration to the market is also required in models for valuing bonds with embedded options.[7] Portfolio managers will also use the estimated spot rate curve for rich-cheap analysis.[8]

Within the U.S. Treasury market, there are several possible benchmark securities that can be used. These include (1) Treasury coupon strips, (2) on-the-run Treasury issues, (3) on-the-run Treasury issues and selected off-the-run Treasury issues, and (4) all Treasury coupon securities and bills.[9]

Once the benchmark securities that are to be included in the estimation of the spot rate curve are selected, the methodology for estimating the spot rate curve must be selected. The simplest technique using on-the-run Treasury issues is called *bootstrapping*; this methodology is

---

[6] Fischer Black, Emanuel Derman, and William Toy, "A One Factor Model of Interest Rates and Its Application to the Treasury Bond Options," *Financial Analyst Journal 46* (January–February 1990), pp. 33–39.
[7] Andrew Kalotay, George Williams, and Frank J. Fabozzi, "A Model for the Valuation of Bonds and Embedded Options," *Financial Analyst Journal 49* (May–June 1993), pp. 35–46.
[8] See H. Gifford Fong and Frank J. Fabozzi, *Fixed Income Portfolio Management* (Homewood, IL: Dow Jones-Irwin, 1985).
[9] For a discussion of the advantages and disadvantages of each benchmark, see Chapter 5 in Frank J. Fabozzi, *Bond Markets, Analysis, and Strategies* (Upper Saddle River, NJ: Prentice Hall, 2006).

based purely on arbitrage arguments.[10] The curve fitting methodology we illustrate here employs restricted least squares regression analysis and is called the *spline method*.

A spline is a functional estimation of a curve using pieces that are joined together to give more flexibility in fitting the curve. Ordinary least squares can be used to estimate the curve. However, in joining together the pieces of the spot rate curve, it is necessary to connect the points where one part of the curve ends and another begins. This requirement calls for the use of restricted least squares.

The price of a bond is equal to the present value of its expected cash flows. Let P denote the price of a bond with a par of $100, that matures in T periods, and whose cash flow in period t is equal to $CF(t)$. Let z_t denote the spot rate for the cash flow to be received at time t. Then the price of the bond is

$$P = \frac{CF(1)}{(1 + z_1)^1} + \frac{CF(2)}{(1 + z_2)^2} + \ldots + \frac{CF(T)}{(1 + z_T)^T}$$

We refer to the equation above as the "price equation."

Let

$$D_t = 1/(1 + z_t)^t$$

The D_t's are called *discount functions* and can be used to rewrite the price equation as follows:

$$P = CF(1)D_1 + CF(2)D_2 + \ldots + CF(T)D_T$$

or equivalently,

$$P = \Sigma CF(t)D_t$$

The discount function for each maturity can be approximated. A simple functional form that can be used is the cubic spline given by

$$D_t = b_0 + b_1 t + b_2 t^2 + b_3 t^3$$

Substituting the above into the price equation, we have

---

[10] For an illustration of the procedure, see Chapter 5 in *Bond Markets, Analysis, and Strategies*.

$$P = \Sigma CF(t)[b_0 + b_1 t + b_2 t^2 + b_3 t^3]$$
$$P = b_0[\Sigma CF(t)] + b_1[\Sigma t CF(t)] + b_2[\Sigma t^2 CF(t)] + b_3[\Sigma t^3 CF(t)]$$

There are four parameters, b_0, b_1, b_2, and b_3. If there are five bonds, the above equation can be estimated using OLS. Call ε_i the residual of the i-th bond, that is the difference between the observed and estimated price of the ith bond. Using OLS, we determine the minimum of the sum of squared residuals:

$$\text{Find: } \min\left(\sum \varepsilon_i^2 \right)$$

A spline can be estimated for arbitrarily selected segments of the zero-coupon curve. In our illustration, we will use four segments. The arbitrary points at which the segments are divided are called *knot points*. When there are four segments, there will be five knot points—the first point on the first segment (the shortest maturity), the last point on the fourth segment (the longest maturity), and three points adjoining the segments. Exhibit 4.4 shows four hypothetical segments. Notice that the curve is not continuous across the entire maturity spectrum—there are jumps and discontinuities. To make the curve continuous and twice differentiable with no visible jumps at the knot points, we require that, at each knot point, not only that the level (i.e., the spot rate) match but also that the first and second derivatives match.

EXHIBIT 4.4 Four-Segment Spline without Restrictions

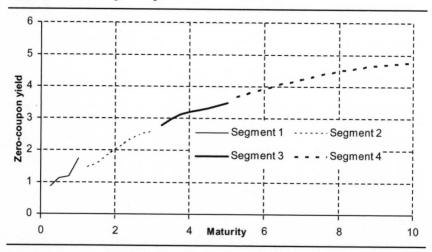

Source: Graph provided by Robert Scott of the Bank for International Settlements.

We will denote the knot points by k. For the four segments there will be five knot points k_1, k_2, k_3, k_4, and k_5. The knot points are typically denominated in years. In our illustration, we use the following knot points: $k_1 = 0$, $k_2 = 1$, $k_3 = 3$, $k_4 = 5$, and $k_5 = 10$. The $D(t)$ can be estimated from the following set of equations for each segment where we use CF instead of $CF(t)$:

$$b_{0,1}CF + b_{1,1}[tCF] + b_{2,1}[t^2CF] + b_{3,1}[t^3CF] \quad \text{for } k_1 < t, k_2 \quad \text{Segment 1}$$

$$b_{0,2}CF + b_{1,2}[tCF] + b_{2,2}[t^2CF] + b_{3,3}[t^3CF] \quad \text{for } k_2 < t, k_3 \quad \text{Segment 2}$$

$$b_{0,3}CF + b_{1,3}[tCF] + b_{2,3}[t^2CF] + b_{3,3}[t^3CF] \quad \text{for } k_3 < t, k_4 \quad \text{Segment 3}$$

$$b_{0,4}CF + b_{1,4}[tCF] + b_{2,4}[t^2CF] + b_{3,4}[t^3CF] \quad \text{for } k_4 < t, k_5 \quad \text{Segment 4}$$

The restrictions required for the estimated curve to be continuous are the following:[11]

Restriction 1: At each knot point, the level of the discount factors must be equal; that is, j = 1, 2, and 3

$$b_{0,j} + b_{1,j}k_{j+1} + b_{2,j}k_{j+1}^2 + b_{3,j}k_{j+1}^3$$
$$= b_{0,j+1} + b_{1,j+1}k_{j+1} + b_{2,j}k_{j+1}^2 + b_{3,j+1}k_{j+1}^3$$

Restriction 2: At each knot point, the first derivative must be equal; that is, for j = 1, 2, and 3

$$b_{1,j} + 2b_{2,j}k_{j+1} + 3b_{3,j}k_{j+1}^2$$
$$= b_{1,j+1} + 2b_{2,j+1}k_{j+1} + 3b_{3,j}k_{j+1}^2 + b_{3,j+1}k_{j+1}^3$$

Restriction 3: At each knot point, the second derivative must be equal; that is, for j = 1, 2, and 3

$$2b_{2,j}k_j + 6b_{3,j}k_{j+1} = 2b_{2,j+1}k_{j+1} + 6b_{3,j+1}$$

[11] The restrictions are provided in G. S. Shea, "Pitfalls in Smoothing Interest Rate Term Structure Data: Equilibrium Models and Spline Approximations," *Journal of Financial and Quantitative Analysis* 19 (September 1984), pp. 253–269.

Restriction 4: When t is equal to zero, the discount factor must be equal to 1 because the present value of \$1 today is \$1; that is,

$$b_{01} = 1$$

Let's call **R** the following matrix:

$$\mathbf{R} = \begin{bmatrix} -1 & -k_2 & -k_2^2 & -k_2^3 & 1 & k_2 & k_2^2 & k_2^3 & 0 & 0 & 0 & 0 & 0 & 0 & 0 & 0 \\ 0 & 0 & 0 & 0 & -1 & -k_3 & -k_3^2 & -k_3^3 & 1 & k_3 & k_3^2 & k_3^3 & 0 & 0 & 0 & 0 \\ 0 & 0 & 0 & 0 & 0 & 0 & 0 & 0 & -1 & -k_4 & -k_4^2 & -k_4^3 & 1 & k_4 & k_4^2 & k_4^3 \\ 0 & -1 & -2k_2 & -3k_2^2 & 0 & 1 & 2k_2 & 3k_3^2 & 0 & 0 & 0 & 0 & 0 & 0 & 0 & 0 \\ 0 & 0 & 0 & 0 & 0 & -1 & -2k_3 & -3k_3^2 & 0 & 1 & 2k_3 & 3k_3^2 & 0 & 0 & 0 & 0 \\ 0 & 0 & 0 & 0 & 0 & 0 & 0 & 0 & 0 & -1 & -2k_4 & -3k_4^2 & 0 & 1 & 2k_4 & 3k_4^2 \\ 0 & 0 & -2 & -6k_2 & 0 & 0 & 2 & 6k_2 & 0 & 0 & 0 & 0 & 0 & 0 & 0 & 0 \\ 0 & 0 & 0 & 0 & 0 & 0 & -2 & -6k_3 & 0 & 0 & 2 & 6k_3 & 0 & 0 & 0 & 0 \\ 0 & 0 & 0 & 0 & 0 & 0 & 0 & 0 & 0 & 0 & -2 & -6k_4 & 0 & 0 & 2 & 6k_4 \\ 1 & 0 & 0 & 0 & 0 & 0 & 0 & 0 & 0 & 0 & 0 & 0 & 0 & 0 & 0 & 0 \end{bmatrix}$$

and let's call **b′** the vector of unknown parameters:

$$\mathbf{b'} = \begin{bmatrix} b_{0,1} & b_{1,1} & b_{2,1} & b_{3,1} & b_{0,2} & b_{1,2} & b_{2,1} & b_{3,2} & b_{0,3} & b_{1,3} & b_{2,2} & b_{3,3} & b_{0,4} & b_{1,4} & b_{2,3} & b_{3,4} \end{bmatrix}$$

The constrained LS problem is then written as follows:

$$\text{Find: } \min\left(\sum_i \varepsilon_i^2\right)$$

subject to

$$\mathbf{Rb} = 0$$

Let's estimate the spot rate curve for April 19, 2005. The second column in Exhibit 4.5 shows the Treasury coupon securities used (i.e., the benchmark securities). There were 110 Treasury issues.[12] The price

---

[12] We are grateful to Robert Scott of the BIS for providing the data and the regression results.

EXHIBIT 4.5 Treasury Issues and Worksheet for the Curve Fitting Illustration Using Constrained Least Squares

Issue	CUSIP	Coupon (%)	Years	Dirty Price	Segment 1 CF	tCF	t^2CF	t^3CF
1	US 4.625% 5YR May 2006	4.6250	1.07123	103.389	106.938	111.020	118.023	125.953
2	US 2.0000% Treas May 2006	2.0000	1.07123	99.516	103.000	108.767	116.079	124.093
3	US 6.875% 10YR Note May 06	6.8750	1.07123	106.692	110.313	112.951	119.690	127.548
4	US 2.500% May 2006	2.5000	1.11507	100.085	103.750	113.730	126.202	140.371
5	US 2.7500% Jun 2006	2.7500	1.19726	100.149	104.125	122.520	145.839	174.100
6	US 7.000% 10YR Note Jul 06	7.0000	1.23836	106.212	110.500	131.513	160.628	197.625
7	US 2.75% 2YR Treas Jul 2006	2.7500	1.28219	99.834	104.125	131.361	167.392	213.952
8	US 2.3750% Treas Aug 2006	2.3750	1.32329	99.131	103.563	135.174	177.882	234.701
9	US 2.3750% Treas Aug 2006	2.3750	1.36712	98.985	103.563	139.681	189.873	258.785
10	US 2.5000% Treas Sep 2006	2.5000	1.44932	98.858	103.750	148.385	213.753	308.770
11	US 6.500% 10YR Bond Oct 06	6.5000	1.49041	104.528	109.750	158.585	232.993	344.647
12	US 2.5000% Treas Oct 2006	2.5000	1.53425	99.812	105.000	157.221	239.675	366.439
13	US 3.50% 5YR Nov 2006	3.5000	1.57534	101.619	107.000	163.185	254.761	399.459
14	US 2.6250% Treas Nov 2006	2.6250	1.57534	99.899	105.250	161.746	253.028	397.132
15	US 2.8750% Treas Nov 2006	2.8750	1.61644	100.227	105.750	166.500	267.020	429.859
16	US 2.8750% Treas Dec 2006	3.0000	1.70137	100.146	106.000	175.704	296.329	501.906
17	US 3.1250% Treas Jan 2007	3.1250	1.78630	100.078	106.250	184.967	327.284	581.784
18	US 2.2500% Treas Feb 2007	2.2500	1.82740	98.246	104.500	187.450	340.087	619.112
19	US 6.250% 10YR Note Feb 07	6.2500	1.82740	106.033	112.500	196.047	351.830	637.114
20	US 3.3750% Treas Feb 2007	3.3750	1.86301	100.273	106.750	193.668	357.040	661.567
21	US 3.7500% 2YR Mar 2007	3.7500	1.94795	100.685	107.500	203.634	391.999	758.848
22	US 3.1250% May 2007	3.1250	2.07123	100.599	107.813	215.358	441.295	908.902
23	US 4.3750% Treas May 2007	4.3750	2.07123	103.606	110.938	218.708	446.447	917.769
24	US 6.625% 10YR Note May 07	6.6250	2.07123	109.031	116.563	224.739	455.722	933.728
25	US 2.7500% Treas Aug 2007	2.7500	2.32329	98.740	106.875	241.272	554.513	1281.044
26	US 3.2500% Treas Aug 2007	3.2500	2.32329	99.944	108.125	242.927	557.328	1286.423
27	US 6.125% 10YR Note Aug 07	6.1250	2.32329	106.819	115.313	252.444	573.517	1317.352
28	US 3.0000% Treas Nov 2007	3.0000	2.57534	99.906	109.000	269.259	684.632	1751.410
29	US 3.0000% Treas Feb 2008	3.0000	2.82740	98.882	109.000	296.715	827.191	2321.741
30	US 5.500% 10YR Note Feb 08	5.5000	2.82740	106.054	116.500	308.522	851.247	2376.831
31	US 3.3750% Treas Feb 2008	3.3750	2.82740	99.960	110.125	298.486	830.800	2330.005
32	US 5.625% 10YR Note May 08	5.6250	3.07397	108.115	119.688	338.142	1011.992	3068.097
33	US 2.6250% Treas May 2008	2.6250	3.07397	98.178	109.188	321.632	975.536	2977.768
34	US 3.2500% Treas Aug 2008	3.2500	3.32603	99.237	111.375	353.125	1153.957	3803.139
35	US 3.1250% Treas Sep 2008	3.1250	3.41096	98.488	110.938	361.709	1212.547	4098.721
36	US 3.1250% Treas Oct 2008	3.1250	3.49315	98.170	110.938	370.833	1272.765	4405.060
37	US 3.3750% Treas Nov 2008	3.3750	3.57808	100.333	113.500	382.170	1341.103	4750.265
38	US 4.750% 10YR Note Nov 2008	4.7500	3.57808	105.531	119.000	392.195	1366.601	4823.095
39	US 3.3750% Treas Dec 2008	3.3750	3.66027	99.990	113.500	391.511	1404.709	5088.740
40	US 3.2500% Treas Jan 2009	3.2500	3.74521	99.197	113.000	400.131	1469.284	5446.840
41	US 3.0000% Treas Feb 2009	3.0000	3.83014	97.909	112.000	407.647	1532.401	5812.557
42	US 2.6250% Treas Mar 2009	2.6250	3.90685	96.237	110.500	413.053	1586.832	6145.281
43	US 3.1250% Treas Apr 2009	3.1250	3.99178	97.734	112.500	426.895	1670.339	6598.187
44	US 3.8750% May 2009	3.8750	4.07397	102.088	15.500	28.252	71.860	205.247
45	US 05.500% 10YR Note May 09	5.5000	4.07397	108.975	22.000	40.100	101.994	291.319
46	US 4.7500% Jun 2009	4.0000	4.15890	102.252	16.000	30.500	79.149	231.007
47	US 3.6250% Treas Jul 2009	3.6250	4.24110	100.328	14.500	28.851	76.456	227.965

EXHIBIT 4.5 (Continued)

Issue	CUSIP	Coupon (%)	Years	Dirty Price	Segment 1 CF	tCF	t^2CF	t^3CF
48	US 3.5000% Treas Aug 2009	3.5000	4.32603	99.531	14.000	29.044	78.649	239.511
49	US 6.000% 10YR Note Aug 2009	6.0000	4.32603	109.836	24.000	49.791	134.827	410.590
50	US 3.3750% Treas Sep 2009	3.3750	4.41096	98.615	13.500	29.102	80.451	249.826
51	US 3.3750% Treas Oct 2009	3.3750	4.49315	98.249	13.500	30.229	85.415	270.658
52	US 3.5000% Treas Nov 2009	3.5000	4.57808	100.219	14.000	25.518	64.906	185.385
53	US 3.5000% Treas Dec 2009	3.5000	4.66027	99.800	14.000	26.687	69.255	202.131
54	US 3.6250% Treas Jan 2010	3.6250	4.74521	100.021	14.500	28.851	76.456	227.965
55	US 3.5000% Treas Feb 2010	3.5000	4.83014	99.154	14.000	29.044	78.649	239.511
56	U.S. 6.5% 10 YR Note Feb 2010	6.5000	4.83014	112.772	26.000	53.940	146.062	444.806
57	US 4.0000% Treas Mar 2010	4.0000	4.90685	101.082	16.000	34.491	95.350	296.090
58	US 10YR 5.75% Aug 2010	5.7500	5.32603	109.939	23.000	47.716	129.209	393.482
59	US 5.0% 10YR Feb 2011	5.0000	5.83014	106.447	20.000	41.492	112.356	342.158
60	US 5.0% 10YR August 2011	5.0000	6.32603	106.575	20.000	41.492	112.356	342.158
61	US 4.875% 10YR Feb 2012	4.8750	6.83014	106.018	19.500	40.455	109.547	333.604
62	US 4.3750% Treas Aug 2012	4.3750	7.32877	102.996	17.500	36.306	98.311	299.389
63	US 4.0000% Treas Nov 2012	4.0000	7.58082	101.392	16.000	29.164	74.178	211.868
64	US 3.8750% Treas Feb 2013	3.8750	7.83288	99.267	15.500	32.156	87.076	265.173
65	US 3.6250% Treas May 2013	3.6250	8.07671	98.654	14.500	26.430	67.224	192.005
66	US 4.2500% Treas Aug 2013	4.2500	8.32877	101.524	17.000	35.268	95.502	290.835
67	US 4.2500% Treas Nov 2013	4.2500	8.58082	102.495	17.000	30.986	78.814	225.110
68	US 4.0000% Treas Feb 2014	4.0000	8.83288	99.455	16.000	33.194	89.884	273.727
69	US 4.7500% Treas May 2014	4.7500	9.07671	106.217	19.000	34.632	88.086	251.593
70	US 4.2500% Treas Aug 2014	4.2500	9.32877	101.095	17.000	35.268	95.502	290.835
71	US 4.2500% Treas Nov 2014	4.2500	9.58082	102.073	17.000	30.986	78.814	225.110
72	US 11.250% Bond Feb 15	11.2500	9.83288	158.069	45.000	93.357	252.800	769.856
73	US 4.0000% Treas Feb 2015	4.0000	9.83288	99.090	16.000	33.194	89.884	273.727
74	US 10.625% Bond Aug 15	10.6250	10.32877	154.718	42.500	88.171	238.756	727.087
75	US 9.875% Bond Nov 15	9.8750	10.58082	151.455	39.500	71.998	183.126	523.049
76	US 9.250% Bond Feb 16	9.2500	10.83288	144.158	37.000	76.760	207.858	632.993
77	US 7.250% Bond May 16	7.2500	11.07945	128.571	29.000	52.859	134.447	384.011
78	US 7.500% Bond Nov 16	7.5000	11.58356	131.533	30.000	54.682	139.083	397.253
79	US 8.750% Bond May 17	8.7500	12.07945	144.314	35.000	63.795	162.264	463.461
80	US 8.875% Bond Aug 17	8.8750	12.33151	143.801	35.500	73.649	199.431	607.331
81	US 9.125% Bond May 18	9.1250	13.07945	150.157	36.500	66.529	169.218	483.324
82	US 9.000% Bond Nov 18	9.0000	13.58356	149.730	36.000	65.618	166.900	476.703
83	US 8.875% Bond Feb 19	8.8750	13.83562	146.493	35.500	73.649	199.431	607.331
84	US 8.125% Bond Aug 19	8.1250	14.33151	139.325	32.500	67.425	182.578	556.007
85	US 8.500% Bond Feb 20	8.5000	14.83562	144.091	34.000	70.537	191.004	581.669
86	US 8.750% Bond May 20	8.7500	15.08219	149.484	35.000	63.795	162.264	463.461
87	US 8.750% Bond Aug 20	8.7500	15.33425	147.697	35.000	72.611	196.622	598.777
88	US 7.875% Bond Feb 21	7.8750	15.83836	138.390	31.500	65.350	176.960	538.899
89	US 8.125% Bond May 21	8.1250	16.08219	143.610	32.500	59.239	150.674	430.357
90	US 8.125% Bond Aug 21	8.1250	16.33425	141.881	32.500	67.425	182.578	556.007
91	US 8.000% Bond Nov 21	8.0000	16.58630	142.774	32.000	58.327	148.356	423.736
92	US 7.250% Bond Aug 22	7.2500	17.33425	132.587	29.000	60.164	162.916	496.130
93	US 7.625% Bond Nov 22	7.6250	17.58630	139.296	30.500	55.593	141.401	403.873
94	US 7.125% Bond Feb 23	7.1250	17.83836	131.405	28.500	59.126	160.107	487.576

EXHIBIT 4.5 (Continued)

Issue	CUSIP	Coupon (%)	Years	Dirty Price	Segment 1			
					CF	tCF	t^2CF	t^3CF
95	US 6.250% Bond Aug 23	6.2500	18.33425	120.892	25.000	51.865	140.444	427.698
96	US 7.500% Bond Nov 24	7.5000	19.58904	139.855	30.000	54.682	139.083	397.253
97	US 7.625% 30YR Bond Feb 25	7.6250	19.84110	139.862	30.500	63.275	171.342	521.792
98	US 6.875% 30YR Bond Aug 25	6.8750	20.33699	130.356	27.500	57.052	154.489	470.468
99	US 6.000% 30YR Bond Feb 26	6.0000	20.84110	118.897	24.000	49.791	134.827	410.590
100	US 6.750% 30YR Bond Aug 26	6.7500	21.33699	129.388	27.000	56.014	151.680	461.914
101	US 6.500% 30YR Bond Nov 26	6.5000	21.58904	127.805	26.000	47.391	120.539	344.286
102	US 6.625% 30YR Bond Feb 27	6.6250	21.84110	128.021	26.500	54.977	148.871	453.360
103	US 6.375% 30YR Bond Aug 27	6.3750	22.33699	124.877	25.500	52.902	143.253	436.252
104	US 6.125% 30YR Bond Nov 27	6.1250	22.58904	123.101	24.500	44.657	113.585	324.423
105	US 5.50% 30YR Bond Aug 2028	5.5000	23.33973	113.052	22.000	45.641	123.591	376.374
106	US 5.25% 30YR Bond Nov 2028	5.2500	23.59178	110.811	21.000	38.277	97.358	278.077
107	US 5.250% 30YR Bond Feb 2029	5.2500	23.84384	109.584	21.000	43.567	117.973	359.266
108	US 6.125% 30YR Bond Aug 2029	6.1250	24.33973	122.528	24.500	50.828	137.636	419.144
109	US 6.25% 30 YR Bond May 2030	6.2500	25.08767	126.605	25.000	45.568	115.903	331.044
110	US 5.375% 30YR Feb 2031	5.3750	25.84384	113.573	21.500	44.604	120.782	367.820

Issue	Segment 2				Segment 3			
	CF	tCF	t^2CF	t^3CF	CF	tCF	t^2CF	t^3CF
1	0.000	0.000	0.000	0.0000	0.0000	0.0000	0.0000	0.0000
2	0.000	0.000	0.000	0.0000	0.0000	0.0000	0.0000	0.0000
3	0.000	0.000	0.000	0.0000	0.0000	0.0000	0.0000	0.0000
4	0.000	0.000	0.000	0.0000	0.0000	0.0000	0.0000	0.0000
5	0.000	0.000	0.000	0.0000	0.0000	0.0000	0.0000	0.0000
6	0.000	0.000	0.000	0.0000	0.0000	0.0000	0.0000	0.0000
7	0.000	0.000	0.000	0.0000	0.0000	0.0000	0.0000	0.0000
8	0.000	0.000	0.000	0.0000	0.0000	0.0000	0.0000	0.0000
9	0.000	0.000	0.000	0.0000	0.0000	0.0000	0.0000	0.0000
10	0.000	0.000	0.000	0.0000	0.0000	0.0000	0.0000	0.0000
11	0.000	0.000	0.000	0.0000	0.0000	0.0000	0.0000	0.0000
12	0.000	0.000	0.000	0.0000	0.0000	0.0000	0.0000	0.0000
13	0.000	0.000	0.000	0.0000	0.0000	0.0000	0.0000	0.0000
14	0.000	0.000	0.000	0.0000	0.0000	0.0000	0.0000	0.0000
15	0.000	0.000	0.000	0.0000	0.0000	0.0000	0.0000	0.0000
16	0.000	0.000	0.000	0.0000	0.0000	0.0000	0.0000	0.0000
17	0.000	0.000	0.000	0.0000	0.0000	0.0000	0.0000	0.0000
18	0.000	0.000	0.000	0.0000	0.0000	0.0000	0.0000	0.0000
19	0.000	0.000	0.000	0.0000	0.0000	0.0000	0.0000	0.0000
20	0.000	0.000	0.000	0.0000	0.0000	0.0000	0.0000	0.0000
21	0.000	0.000	0.000	0.0000	0.0000	0.0000	0.0000	0.0000
22	0.000	0.000	0.000	0.0000	0.0000	0.0000	0.0000	0.0000
23	0.000	0.000	0.000	0.0000	0.0000	0.0000	0.0000	0.0000
24	0.000	0.000	0.000	0.0000	0.0000	0.0000	0.0000	0.0000
25	0.000	0.000	0.000	0.0000	0.0000	0.0000	0.0000	0.0000
26	0.000	0.000	0.000	0.0000	0.0000	0.0000	0.0000	0.0000
27	0.000	0.000	0.000	0.0000	0.0000	0.0000	0.0000	0.0000
28	0.000	0.000	0.000	0.0000	0.0000	0.0000	0.0000	0.0000
29	0.000	0.000	0.000	0.0000	0.0000	0.0000	0.0000	0.0000
30	0.000	0.000	0.000	0.0000	0.0000	0.0000	0.0000	0.0000
31	0.000	0.000	0.000	0.0000	0.0000	0.0000	0.0000	0.0000

EXHIBIT 4.5   (Continued)

Issue	Segment 2				Segment 3			
	CF	tCF	t^2CF	t^3CF	CF	tCF	t^2CF	t^3CF
32	0.000	0.000	0.000	0.0000	0.0000	0.0000	0.0000	0.0000
33	0.000	0.000	0.000	0.0000	0.0000	0.0000	0.0000	0.0000
34	0.000	0.000	0.000	0.0000	0.0000	0.0000	0.0000	0.0000
35	0.000	0.000	0.000	0.0000	0.0000	0.0000	0.0000	0.0000
36	0.000	0.000	0.000	0.0000	0.0000	0.0000	0.0000	0.0000
37	0.000	0.000	0.000	0.0000	0.0000	0.0000	0.0000	0.0000
38	0.000	0.000	0.000	0.0000	0.0000	0.0000	0.0000	0.0000
39	0.000	0.000	0.000	0.0000	0.0000	0.0000	0.0000	0.0000
40	0.000	0.000	0.000	0.0000	0.0000	0.0000	0.0000	0.0000
41	0.000	0.000	0.000	0.0000	0.0000	0.0000	0.0000	0.0000
42	0.000	0.000	0.000	0.0000	0.0000	0.0000	0.0000	0.0000
43	0.000	0.000	0.000	0.0000	0.0000	0.0000	0.0000	0.0000
44	101.938	415.006	1689.567	6878.5391	0.0000	0.0000	0.0000	0.0000
45	102.750	418.314	1703.034	6933.3650	0.0000	0.0000	0.0000	0.0000
46	102.000	423.918	1761.827	7322.2544	0.0000	0.0000	0.0000	0.0000
47	101.813	431.501	1828.785	7750.7423	0.0000	0.0000	0.0000	0.0000
48	101.750	439.872	1901.596	8220.7253	0.0000	0.0000	0.0000	0.0000
49	103.000	445.276	1924.957	8321.7170	0.0000	0.0000	0.0000	0.0000
50	101.688	448.232	1975.781	8709.1250	0.0000	0.0000	0.0000	0.0000
51	101.688	456.585	2050.099	9205.0985	0.0000	0.0000	0.0000	0.0000
52	103.500	472.626	2158.649	9861.0953	0.0000	0.0000	0.0000	0.0000
53	103.500	481.131	2237.025	10402.8713	0.0000	0.0000	0.0000	0.0000
54	103.625	490.472	2321.929	10994.0877	0.0000	0.0000	0.0000	0.0000
55	103.500	498.695	2403.307	11583.8821	0.0000	0.0000	0.0000	0.0000
56	106.500	512.420	2466.288	11873.7575	0.0000	0.0000	0.0000	0.0000
57	104.000	508.972	2491.370	12197.1550	0.0000	0.0000	0.0000	0.0000
58	108.625	573.846	3034.930	16066.1717	0.0000	0.0000	0.0000	0.0000
59	110.000	633.361	3655.046	21130.7216	0.0000	0.0000	0.0000	0.0000
60	112.500	698.720	4356.943	27250.0012	0.0000	0.0000	0.0000	0.0000
61	114.625	764.070	5123.792	34509.2102	0.0000	0.0000	0.0000	0.0000
62	13.125	73.162	417.396	2433.3767	102.1875	748.3958	5481.0643	40141.9494
63	12.000	63.869	348.683	1948.9719	104.0000	786.8583	5953.8248	45053.6046
64	11.625	64.801	369.694	2155.2765	103.8750	812.1071	6349.6327	49649.4952
65	10.875	57.881	315.994	1766.2558	105.4375	848.2960	6827.1401	54960.9744
66	12.750	71.072	405.471	2363.8517	106.3750	882.1896	7318.7275	60735.8337
67	12.750	67.860	370.476	2070.7827	108.5000	923.9938	7875.8845	67183.9592
68	12.000	66.891	381.619	2224.8016	108.0000	947.2854	8315.4818	73045.8589
69	14.250	75.844	414.062	2314.4042	111.8750	1002.9148	9007.2259	81017.7446
70	12.750	71.072	405.471	2363.8517	110.6250	1020.6882	9432.3066	87279.9807
71	12.750	67.860	370.476	2070.7827	112.7500	1063.5455	10059.1871	95347.3426
72	33.750	188.131	1073.305	6257.2544	133.7500	1272.0192	12161.5548	116787.4847
73	12.000	66.891	381.619	2224.8016	112.0000	1085.5140	10546.4228	102665.8117
74	31.875	177.680	1013.677	5909.6292	137.1875	1360.3303	13586.7278	136502.1520
75	29.625	157.676	860.812	4811.5245	139.5000	1405.8556	14306.5706	146711.8667
76	27.750	154.686	882.495	5144.8536	137.0000	1418.3066	14814.4908	155834.9165
77	21.750	115.762	631.989	3532.5117	132.6250	1403.1814	14998.4163	161569.0154
78	22.500	119.754	653.781	3654.3224	137.5000	1507.1732	16736.2749	187658.8192
79	26.250	139.713	762.745	4263.3761	148.1250	1667.8080	19101.7163	221564.6986

EXHIBIT 4.5   (Continued)

	Segment 2				Segment 3			
Issue	CF	tCF	t^2CF	t^3CF	CF	tCF	t^2CF	t^3CF
80	26.625	148.415	846.718	4936.2785	148.8125	1711.8725	20019.3751	237021.2729
81	27.375	145.700	795.434	4446.0923	159.3125	1904.4908	23309.2357	290182.5220
82	27.000	143.704	784.538	4385.1869	163.0000	2007.7673	25395.3973	327348.1710
83	26.625	148.415	846.718	4936.2785	162.1250	2039.5712	26315.7787	345775.3867
84	24.375	135.873	775.164	4519.1282	160.9375	2091.7907	27935.4991	380274.1773
85	25.500	142.144	810.941	4727.7033	168.0000	2235.6194	30680.6200	430217.7182
86	26.250	139.713	762.745	4263.3761	70.0000	757.5907	8571.0165	100809.9876
87	26.250	146.324	834.793	4866.7534	70.0000	775.2225	8957.1049	107431.9629
88	23.625	131.692	751.313	4380.0781	63.0000	697.7002	8061.3944	96688.7666
89	24.375	129.733	708.263	3958.8493	65.0000	703.4771	7958.8010	93609.2742
90	24.375	135.873	775.164	4519.1282	65.0000	719.8494	8317.3117	99758.2513
91	24.000	127.737	697.367	3897.9439	64.0000	692.6543	7836.3579	92169.1316
92	21.750	121.240	691.685	4032.4528	58.0000	642.3272	7421.6012	89015.0550
93	22.875	121.749	664.678	3715.2278	61.0000	660.1862	7469.0286	87848.7035
94	21.375	119.150	679.760	3962.9278	57.0000	631.2526	7293.6426	87480.3126
95	18.750	104.517	596.280	3476.2524	50.0000	553.7303	6397.9321	76737.1163
96	22.500	119.754	653.781	3654.3224	60.0000	649.3634	7346.5855	86408.5608
97	22.875	127.511	727.462	4241.0280	61.0000	675.5510	7805.4771	93619.2819
98	20.625	114.969	655.908	3823.8777	55.0000	609.1034	7037.7253	84410.8280
99	18.000	100.337	572.429	3337.2024	48.0000	531.5811	6142.0148	73667.6317
100	20.250	112.879	643.983	3754.3526	54.0000	598.0287	6909.7667	82876.0857
101	19.500	103.786	566.610	3167.0794	52.0000	562.7817	6367.0408	74887.4194
102	19.875	110.789	632.057	3684.8276	53.0000	586.9541	6781.8080	81341.3433
103	19.125	106.608	608.206	3545.7775	51.0000	564.8049	6525.8907	78271.8587
104	18.375	97.799	533.921	2984.3633	49.0000	530.3135	5999.7115	70566.9913
105	16.500	91.975	524.727	3059.1022	44.0000	487.2827	5630.1802	67528.6624
106	15.750	83.828	457.647	2558.0257	42.0000	454.5544	5142.6099	60485.9926
107	15.750	87.795	500.876	2920.0521	42.0000	465.1335	5374.2630	64459.1777
108	18.375	102.427	584.355	3406.7274	49.0000	542.6557	6269.9734	75202.3740
109	18.750	99.795	544.818	3045.2687	50.0000	541.1362	6122.1546	72007.1340
110	16.125	89.885	512.801	2989.5771	43.0000	476.2081	5502.2216	65993.9201

	Segment 4					Segment 4			
Issue	CF	tCF	t^2CF	t^3CF	Issue	CF	tCF	t^2CF	t^3CF
1	0.0000	0.0000	0.0000	0.0000	14	0.0000	0.0000	0.0000	0.0000
2	0.0000	0.0000	0.0000	0.0000	15	0.0000	0.0000	0.0000	0.0000
3	0.0000	0.0000	0.0000	0.0000	16	0.0000	0.0000	0.0000	0.0000
4	0.0000	0.0000	0.0000	0.0000	17	0.0000	0.0000	0.0000	0.0000
5	0.0000	0.0000	0.0000	0.0000	18	0.0000	0.0000	0.0000	0.0000
6	0.0000	0.0000	0.0000	0.0000	19	0.0000	0.0000	0.0000	0.0000
7	0.0000	0.0000	0.0000	0.0000	20	0.0000	0.0000	0.0000	0.0000
8	0.0000	0.0000	0.0000	0.0000	21	0.0000	0.0000	0.0000	0.0000
9	0.0000	0.0000	0.0000	0.0000	22	0.0000	0.0000	0.0000	0.0000
10	0.0000	0.0000	0.0000	0.0000	23	0.0000	0.0000	0.0000	0.0000
11	0.0000	0.0000	0.0000	0.0000	24	0.0000	0.0000	0.0000	0.0000
12	0.0000	0.0000	0.0000	0.0000	25	0.0000	0.0000	0.0000	0.0000
13	0.0000	0.0000	0.0000	0.0000	26	0.0000	0.0000	0.0000	0.0000

EXHIBIT 4.5 (Continued)

	Segment 4					Segment 4		
Issue	CF	tCF	t^2CF	t^3CF	Issue	CF	tCF	t^2CF	t^3CF
27	0.0000	0.0000	0.0000	0.0000	69	0.0000	0.0000	0.0000	0.0000
28	0.0000	0.0000	0.0000	0.0000	70	0.0000	0.0000	0.0000	0.0000
29	0.0000	0.0000	0.0000	0.0000	71	0.0000	0.0000	0.0000	0.0000
30	0.0000	0.0000	0.0000	0.0000	72	0.0000	0.0000	0.0000	0.0000
31	0.0000	0.0000	0.0000	0.0000	73	0.0000	0.0000	0.0000	0.0000
32	0.0000	0.0000	0.0000	0.0000	74	0.0000	0.0000	0.0000	0.0000
33	0.0000	0.0000	0.0000	0.0000	75	0.0000	0.0000	0.0000	0.0000
34	0.0000	0.0000	0.0000	0.0000	76	0.0000	0.0000	0.0000	0.0000
35	0.0000	0.0000	0.0000	0.0000	77	0.0000	0.0000	0.0000	0.0000
36	0.0000	0.0000	0.0000	0.0000	78	0.0000	0.0000	0.0000	0.0000
37	0.0000	0.0000	0.0000	0.0000	79	0.0000	0.0000	0.0000	0.0000
38	0.0000	0.0000	0.0000	0.0000	80	0.0000	0.0000	0.0000	0.0000
39	0.0000	0.0000	0.0000	0.0000	81	0.0000	0.0000	0.0000	0.0000
40	0.0000	0.0000	0.0000	0.0000	82	0.0000	0.0000	0.0000	0.0000
41	0.0000	0.0000	0.0000	0.0000	83	0.0000	0.0000	0.0000	0.0000
42	0.0000	0.0000	0.0000	0.0000	84	0.0000	0.0000	0.0000	0.0000
43	0.0000	0.0000	0.0000	0.0000	85	0.0000	0.0000	0.0000	0.0000
44	0.0000	0.0000	0.0000	0.0000	86	104.3750	1573.1263	23709.9526	357353.2898
45	0.0000	0.0000	0.0000	0.0000	87	104.3750	1599.4165	24509.0599	375570.7275
46	0.0000	0.0000	0.0000	0.0000	88	107.8750	1705.4097	26962.0017	426275.7204
47	0.0000	0.0000	0.0000	0.0000	89	112.1875	1796.9131	28785.9768	461214.1253
48	0.0000	0.0000	0.0000	0.0000	90	112.1875	1825.1711	29698.3156	483309.9636
49	0.0000	0.0000	0.0000	0.0000	91	116.0000	1910.6694	31483.9861	518989.4955
50	0.0000	0.0000	0.0000	0.0000	92	118.1250	2028.1235	34845.7841	599079.4100
51	0.0000	0.0000	0.0000	0.0000	93	122.8750	2130.8166	36997.0288	643093.3485
52	0.0000	0.0000	0.0000	0.0000	94	121.3750	2136.9042	37665.0672	664572.7504
53	0.0000	0.0000	0.0000	0.0000	95	121.8750	2200.2053	39782.3140	720311.0848
54	0.0000	0.0000	0.0000	0.0000	96	137.5000	2607.1732	49651.0456	949106.6662
55	0.0000	0.0000	0.0000	0.0000	97	138.1250	2652.7912	51167.5063	990584.4838
56	0.0000	0.0000	0.0000	0.0000	98	137.8125	2706.3013	53410.9393	1058592.1141
57	0.0000	0.0000	0.0000	0.0000	99	136.0000	2733.3771	55244.1476	1121776.5355
58	0.0000	0.0000	0.0000	0.0000	100	143.8750	2936.2320	60350.8368	1247825.0018
59	0.0000	0.0000	0.0000	0.0000	101	145.5000	2991.1170	62005.3443	1294225.7691
60	0.0000	0.0000	0.0000	0.0000	102	146.3750	3044.0188	63826.8429	1347457.2413
61	0.0000	0.0000	0.0000	0.0000	103	147.8125	3132.2185	66991.8944	1443738.5287
62	0.0000	0.0000	0.0000	0.0000	104	149.0000	3179.6715	68577.3775	1491742.2641
63	0.0000	0.0000	0.0000	0.0000	105	146.7500	3235.7981	72138.4313	1622437.2998
64	0.0000	0.0000	0.0000	0.0000	106	147.2500	3270.5674	73540.8474	1669681.0825
65	0.0000	0.0000	0.0000	0.0000	107	147.2500	3307.6571	75197.7856	1725876.8432
66	0.0000	0.0000	0.0000	0.0000	108	158.1875	3585.8525	82466.1589	1918296.0767
67	0.0000	0.0000	0.0000	0.0000	109	165.6250	3824.3241	89895.8341	2142728.7115
68	0.0000	0.0000	0.0000	0.0000	110	159.1250	3799.0938	92322.6340	2274259.0269

used in the calculation is the issue's dirty price which is the price including accrued interest and is shown in the fifth column. Notice that the maturity of each issue (shown in the fourth column) is the number of years to maturity and is shown in whole years plus fraction of a year.

A time consuming aspect of the data preparation is the calculation for each security of $[\Sigma CF(t)]$, $[\Sigma\, tCF(t)]$, $[\Sigma\, t^2 CF(t)]$, and $[\Sigma\, t^3 CF(t)]$. For the 110 benchmark securities, these four values are shown in Exhibit 4.5.

There are 16 coefficients to be estimated. The computed coefficients of the restricted least squares regression are reported in Exhibit 4.6.[13] The resulting spot rate curve is shown in Exhibit 4.7.

THE METHOD OF MOMENTS AND ITS GENERALIZATIONS

In a number of cases, the OLS and MLE estimators cannot be used. This occurs, for example, if the residuals are correlated with the independent variables, that is, if the condition $E(Z\varepsilon) = 0$ does not hold. The method of

EXHIBIT 4.6 Estimated Coefficients for the Spline Using Constrained Least Squares Regression

$b_{0,1}$	1.00110432
$b_{0,2}$	−0.032328308
$b_{0,3}$	−0.001064404
$b_{0,4}$	0.000104015
$b_{1,1}$	1.005474867
$b_{1,2}$	−0.034418089
$b_{1,3}$	−0.000644522
$b_{1,4}$	6.39845E-05
$b_{2,1}$	0.977444303
$b_{2,2}$	−0.024192565
$b_{2,3}$	−0.001497796
$b_{2,4}$	6.46978E-05
$b_{3,1}$	0.819502692
$b_{3,2}$	−0.012242924
$b_{3,3}$	−0.001103864
$b_{3,4}$	3.14722E-05

---

[13] Excel can be used to estimate the parameters for the regression model. See Robert Scott, "A Real-Time Zero-Coupon Yield Curve Cubic Spline in Excel," BIS Banking Paper, October 2005.

EXHIBIT 4.7   Estimated Spot Rate Curve on April 19, 2005 using Constrained Least Squares

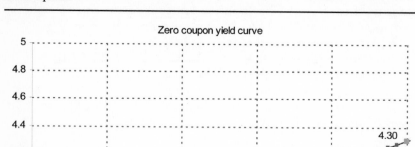

moments, the generalized method of moments, and its generalizations, the linear instrumental variables method and the generalized method of moments, are powerful estimation methods that are often used in financial econometrics when the least squares and the maximum likelihood methods are not applicable. Though the applications involve a number of technical points, the general ideas are simple. We now discuss the method of moments and the method of linear instrumental variables.

Method of Moments

Let's start with the *method of moments* (MM). Suppose that

1. n observations $(Y_1, ..., Y_T)$ of a random variable Y are given.
2. These observations are extracted from a population with a distribution $f(y; \lambda_1, ..., \lambda_N)$ that depends on a vector Λ of N parameters $\Lambda = (\lambda_1, ..., \lambda_N)'$.
3. The k parameters $(\lambda_1, ..., \lambda_N)$ are functions of the first N moments of the distribution: $\Lambda = \mathbf{F}(m_1, ..., m_N)$, where the moments are defined as usual:

$$m_1 = E(Y), \cdots, m_N = E(Y^k) \tag{4.1}$$

The moments m_1, ..., m_k can be estimated with the corresponding empirical moments:

$$\overline{m}_1 = \frac{1}{n} \sum_{i=1}^{n} Y_i, \cdots, \overline{m}_k = \frac{1}{n} \sum_{i=1}^{n} Y_i^k \tag{4.2}$$

The idea of the method of moments is to estimate the parameters (λ_1, ..., λ_k) using the function **F** of the corresponding estimates of moments: $\overline{\Lambda} = \mathbf{F}(\overline{m}_1, ..., \overline{m}_k)$. For example, consider n independent random samples from an exponential distribution with density $f(y) = \lambda e^{-\lambda y}$, $y > 0$. The mean of an exponentially distributed variable is the reciprocal of the distribution parameter: $E(Y) = 1/\lambda$. The method of moments computes the parameters λ as follows:

$$\lambda = \frac{1}{E(\overline{Y})} = \frac{1}{\overline{Y}} = \frac{n}{\displaystyle\sum_{i=1}^{n} Y_i}$$

Method of Linear Instrumental Variables

The method of linear instrumental variables is a generalization of the method of moments. Suppose that:

1. There is a linear relationship between a dependent variable Y and k independent variables X_i, $i = 1, ..., k$:

$$Y = \sum_{i=1}^{k} \lambda_i X_i + \varepsilon$$

2. There are n observations given by

$$Y_j = \sum_{i=1}^{k} \lambda_i X_{j,i} + \varepsilon_j, j = 1, ..., n \tag{4.3}$$

The vector $\Lambda = (\lambda_1, ..., \lambda_k)'$ represents the *true* value of the parameters. Equation (4.3) is a linear regression and could not be estimated with the estimators (**HH.20**) and (**HH.21**) because the regression assumptions are not satisfied. However, suppose that T observations of other variables are available. In particular, suppose that we have h variables Z_i, $i = 1, ..., h$ that might eventually include some of the variables X_i.

To simplify, suppose that all the variables

$$(u_j, X_{j,1}, ..., X_{j,k}, Z_{i,1}, ..., Z_{j,h}), j = 1, ..., T$$

are (1) independent, (2) follow the same distribution, and (3) have finite first- and second-order moments. A variable Z_i is called an *instrumental variable* or an *instrument* if $E(Z_i u) = 0$, that is, if it is uncorrelated with the noise terms. The system of variables Z_i, $i = 1, ..., h$ is called a *system of instrumental variables* if each variable is an instrument. In other words, a system of instrumental variables is a system of variables orthogonal to the noise terms.

We can now express the orthogonality condition in terms of the observables. In fact, we can write the noise terms as

$$u = Y - \sum_{i=1}^{k} \lambda_i X_i \tag{4.4}$$

and rewrite the orthogonality condition as

$$E(Z_j Y) = \sum_{i=1}^{k} \lambda_i E(Z_j X_i), j = 1, ..., h$$

We have now to distinguish three cases.

If $h < k$, that is, if the number of instruments Z is less than the number of explanatory variables X, then the estimation process is not feasible. If $h = k$, then the number of instruments is equal to the number of explanatory variables and the above system will in general admit a unique solution. If we stack the observations and the instruments in matrix form as we did in the case of regressions, it can be demonstrated that the linear instrumental variables estimator can be written as follows:

$$\bar{\Lambda} = (Z'X)^{-1}Z'Y \tag{4.5}$$

Observe that if we choose $Z = X$, we find the same estimation formula that we have determined in the case of regressions (equations (3.20) and

(3.21) in Chapter 3). In this case, the instrumental variables coincide with the regressors.

In the case where $h > k$, the problem is in general impossible to solve exactly because there are more equations than unknown variables. This fact will in general result in incompatible equations if we replace theoretical moments with estimated moments. The number of equations has to be reduced by choosing a subset of instruments. Alternatively, one could try to find an approximate solution by minimizing the following quadratic form:

$$\left[\frac{1}{n}\mathbf{u}'\mathbf{Z}\right]\mathbf{W}_n\left[\frac{1}{n}\mathbf{u}'\mathbf{Z}\right]'$$

where $\mathbf{W}_n$ is a weighting matrix that needs to be estimated. The solution for $\overline{\mathbf{\Lambda}}$ becomes

$$\overline{\mathbf{\Lambda}} = (\mathbf{X}'\mathbf{H}\mathbf{W}_n\mathbf{H}'\mathbf{Z}'\mathbf{X})^{-1}\mathbf{X}'\mathbf{H}\mathbf{W}_n\mathbf{H}'\mathbf{Z}'\mathbf{Y}$$

The rigorous justification of this procedure is quite technical.[14]

In order to study the asymptotic distribution of the instrumental variables estimators, additional conditions are required. If the conditional mean of the residuals given the instruments is zero and if the residuals have constant variance, that is, if $E(\mathbf{u}|\mathbf{Z}) = 0$, $\text{Var}(\mathbf{u}|\mathbf{Z}) = \sigma_0^2$, then the estimator is asymptotically normally distributed with

$$N(0, \sigma_0^2 E[\mathbf{Z}'\mathbf{X}]^{-1} E(\mathbf{Z}'\mathbf{Z}) E[\mathbf{X}'\mathbf{Z}]^{-1})$$

**CONCEPTS EXPLAINED IN THIS CHAPTER
(IN ORDER OF PRESENTATION)**

Categorical variables
Dummy variables
Marginalization
Chow test
Dependent categorical variables

---

[14] See Chapter 9 in Christian Gourieroux and Alain Monfort, *Statistics and Econometric Models, Volume 1: General Concepts, Estimation, Prediction, and Algorithms* (Cambridge: Cambridge University Press, 1995).

Linear probability models
Probit regression model
Logit regression model
Logistic distribution
Constrained least squares method
Spot rate
Spot rate curve
Spline
Discount function
Method of moments
Method of linear instrumental variables

CHAPTER 5

Regression Applications in Finance

Regression analysis is the econometric tool most commonly used by asset managers in four of the five steps of the investment management process described in the appendix to Chapter 1. It is used in setting investment policy, selecting a portfolio strategy, selecting specific assets, and measuring and evaluating performance. We begin this chapter with an overview of the use of regression analysis in each of these steps. We then provide illustrations of specific applications, namely (1) a test of strong-form pricing efficiency; (2) tests of the capital asset pricing model; (3) using the capital asset pricing model to evaluate manager performance; (4) constructing Sharpe benchmarks for performance evaluation; and (5) various uses in bond portfolio management. Regression analysis also plays an important role in the construction of multifactor models. However, because the construction of multifactor models draws on several additional econometric tools, the construction of these models is treated separately in Chapter 13.

APPLICATIONS TO THE INVESTMENT MANAGEMENT PROCESS

In this section we provide an overview of the use of regression analysis in four steps of the investment management process.

Setting an Investment Policy

Setting an investment policy or policy guidelines begins with the asset allocation decision: how the funds to be invested should be distributed among the major classes of assets. An asset allocation model is used to provide guidance in making this decision. While there are many asset allocation models proposed, the critical input in all of them is the expected return for an asset class.

The expected return for an asset class is estimated using regression analysis. The process begins with the selection of an asset pricing or asset return model. As explained in Chapter 1, these models belong to three different families: (1) general equilibrium models, (2) econometric models, and (3) arbitrage pricing models. The first two models rely on the econometric tools discussed in this book. The most well-known general equilibrium model is the *capital asset pricing model* (CAPM). We discuss later how regression analysis has been used to test the validity of this model.

Econometric models of prices or returns establish links between prices and returns and their lagged values and exogenous variables. These variables are referred to as "factors." When a factor is a measure of risk, it is referred to as a "risk factor." The justification of econometric models is empirical, that is, they are valid insofar as they fit empirical data. They are not derived from economic theory, although economic theory might suggest econometric models. While preliminary work in identifying the factors in these models is regression analysis, this book also describes other econometric techniques used for identifying factors. As will be seen, pricing models are also used in each step of the investment management process.

Selecting a Portfolio Strategy

Clients can request a money manager for a particular asset class to pursue an active or passive strategy. An active portfolio strategy uses available information and forecasting techniques to seek a better performance than a portfolio that is simply diversified broadly. A passive portfolio strategy involves minimal expectational input, and instead relies on diversification to match the performance of some market index. There are also hybrid strategies.[1]

Whether clients select an active or passive strategy depends on their belief that the market is efficient for an asset class; if it is not efficient, whether the manager engaged will be able to outperform the benchmark for that asset class believed to be inefficient. In fact, in marketing its services, a money management firm will point to its historical performance in trying to convince a client that it can outperform the market as proxied by a benchmark.

---

[1] An example is where the portfolio manager minimizes the tracking error versus a benchmark but at the same time in the constraint set bounds from above the volatility of the portfolio return. In this way, if the benchmark is volatile, the portfolio manager requires that the portfolio's volatility is bounded.

There is a long list starting in the 1960s of academic papers that have examined the efficiency of capital markets. By far, most studies have focused on the pricing efficiency of the equity markets. Pricing efficiency refers to a market where prices at all times fully reflect all available information that is relevant to the valuation of securities. When a market is price-efficient, strategies pursued to outperform a broad-based market index will not consistently produce superior returns after adjusting for both risk and transactions costs.

In his seminal review article on pricing efficiency, Eugene Fama points out that in order to test whether the stock market is price-efficient, two definitions are necessary.[2] First, it is necessary to define what it means for prices to "fully reflect" information. Second, the "relevant" set of information that is assumed to be "fully reflected" in prices must be defined. Fama defines "fully reflect" in terms of the expected return from holding a security. The expected return over some holding period is equal to expected cash flow (e.g., dividends for a stock) plus the expected price change all divided by the initial price. The price formation process defined by Fama (and others) is that the expected return one period from now is a stochastic (i.e., random) variable that already takes into account the "relevant" information set.

In defining the "relevant" information set that prices should reflect, Fama classified the pricing efficiency of the stock market into three forms: (1) weak form, (2) semistrong form, and (3) strong form. The distinction among these forms lies in the relevant information that is hypothesized to be impounded in the price of the security. *Weak efficiency* means that the price of the security reflects the past price and trading history of the security. *Semistrong efficiency* means that the price of the security fully reflects all public information (which, of course, includes but is not limited to historical price and trading patterns). *Strong efficiency* exists in a market where the price of a security reflects all information, whether or not it is publicly available.

Regression analysis is used in most tests of the pricing efficiency of the market. These tests examine whether it is possible to generate abnormal returns. An abnormal return is defined as the difference between the actual return and the expected return from an investment strategy. The expected return used in empirical tests is the return predicted from a pricing model after adjustment for transaction costs. The pricing model itself adjusts for risk.

If a strategy can be shown to consistently outperform the market, then the market is not price-efficient. To show price inefficiency, earning

---

[2] Eugene F. Fama, "Efficient Capital Markets: A Review of Theory and Empirical Work," *Journal of Finance* 25 (May 1970), pp. 383–417.

an abnormal return must be shown to be statistically significant. This is not sufficient to conclude that the investment strategy that produced the positive abnormal return can outperform the market in the future. The reason is that the empirical test depends critically on the expected return calculated from an assumed pricing model. However, this model may be misspecified for two reasons. First, it may fail to consider the appropriate measure of risk. Second, the risk measures may not be estimated properly. In either instance, the results are questionable. Hence, tests of market efficiency are *joint tests* of both the efficiency of the market and the validity of the pricing model employed in the study.

Studies of the semistrong form of pricing efficiency have tested whether investors can outperform the market by selecting securities on the basis of fundamental security analysis (i.e., analyzing financial statements, the quality of management, and the economic environment of a company). The key is the use of information that is publicly available prior to the implementation of any strategy seeking to outperform the market. It is from such studies that factors have been identified that could potentially outperform the market—at least until these factors are well known by other investors. Once they are well known, the market will price these factors into the price of a security and the outperformance capability of the strategy will cease.

One of the main empirical tests of strong-form pricing efficiency has been the study of the performance of professional money managers: mutual fund managers and pension fund managers. The rationale is that professional managers have access to better information than the general public and therefore should outperform the market. How regression analysis is used to evaluate performance of mutual funds is described later in this chapter.

Selecting the Specific Assets

Given a portfolio strategy, portfolio construction involves the selection of the specific assets to be included in the portfolio. As with the asset allocation distribution among the major asset classes, this step in the investment management process requires an estimate of expected returns as well as the variance and correlation of returns. In constructing a portfolio for a given asset class, a money manager can use these inputs to construct Markowitz mean-variance efficient portfolios. While economic theory tells us that this is the way investors should behave, in practice portfolio managers will rely more on relative value analysis (i.e., the ranking of securities by expected return after adjusting for risk) in selecting securities.

As noted earlier, an asset pricing model can be an equilibrium model such as the CAPM or an econometric model. Regression analysis is used to identify the factors. Alternatively, factors can be derived from one of two econometric techniques, principal components analysis or factor analysis, both of which we discuss in Chapter 13. These factors, referred to as *statistical factors*, are then linked to observable factors.

In addition, regression analysis is used to estimate parameters to control the risk of a portfolio. For example, a portfolio manager may want to hedge a position in an individual security or hedge the entire portfolio. In bond portfolio management, a key measure of the interest rate exposure of a security or portfolio is duration, a measure discussed in the previous chapter and discussed further later in this chapter. While duration is typically estimated from a bond valuation model, regression-based or empirical durations are calculated for some securities. Portfolio managers who want an estimate of the interest rate sensitivity of a portfolio consisting of both equity and bonds would have to estimate the duration of the equity position in the portfolio. Regression-based or empirical duration for equities can be estimated and we demonstrated this in the previous chapter as one of calculation illustrations. The importance of measuring duration for equity portfolios lies in the need for sponsors of defined-benefit pension funds to match the duration of their asset portfolio to the duration of their pension liabilities.

Measuring and Evaluating Performance

In evaluating the performance of a money manager, one must adjust for the risks accepted by the manager in generating return. Asset pricing models such as the CAPM or a multifactor model provide the expected return after adjusting for risk. Subtracting the portfolio's actual return from the expected return gives the *excess return* or the *active return*. From the excess return, various measures have been used to assess performance, one of which is discussed later in this chapter.

Today, the CAPM is not the typical asset pricing model used by professional money manager. Rather, multifactor models are used. Money management firms will either develop proprietary multifactor models or use those vendors such as MSCI Barra and Northfield Information Services. The multifactor models used to construct a portfolio are then used to evaluate performance.

A multifactor model provides more than just the excess return. A multifactor model can be used to show where a money manager took risks relative to the benchmark and if those bets paid off. The process of decomposing the performance of a money manager relative to each factor is called *return attribution analysis*.

A TEST OF STRONG-FORM PRICING EFFICIENCY

As support for the position of strong-form pricing efficiency, many studies have compared the performance of equity mutual fund managers against a suitable stock market index to assess the performance of fund managers in general. For example, it is common to compare the average large-cap mutual fund's performance to that of the S&P 500 Index. But this is not a fair comparison because it ignores risk. Specifically, the risk parameters of the average mutual fund may be different than that of the benchmark, making a simple direct comparison of the mutual fund's performance and that of the benchmark inappropriate.

Robert Jones analyzed the performance of the average large-cap mutual fund adjusted for risk.[3] As noted earlier, tests of market efficiency are joint tests of the assumed asset pricing model. Jones used a model similar to the three-factor model proposed by Eugene Fama and Kenneth French that we will describe later in this chapter. The variables in his regression model are

Y_t = the difference between the returns on a composite mutual fund index and the S&P 500 in month t

$X_{1,t}$ = the difference between the S&P 500 return and the 90-day Treasury rate for month t

$X_{2,t}$ = the difference between the returns on the Russell 3000 Value Index and the Russell 3000 Growth Index for month t

$X_{3,t}$ = the difference between the returns on the Russell 1000 Index (large-cap stocks) and the Russell 2000 Index (small-cap stocks) for month t

The dependent variable, (Y_t), is obtained from indexes published by Lipper, a firm that constructs performance indexes for mutual funds classified by investment category. Specifically, the dependent variable in the study was the average of the return on the Lipper Growth Index and the Lipper Growth and Income Index each month minus the return on the S&P 500. Y_t is the active return.

The first independent variable $(X_{1,t})$ is a measure of the return of the market over the risk-free rate and is therefore the excess return on the market in general. The second independent variable $(X_{2,t})$ is a proxy for the difference in performance of two "styles" that have been found to be important in explaining stock returns: value and growth. (We describe this further later in this chapter.) In the regression, the indepen-

---

[3] Robert C. Jones, "The Active versus Passive Debate: Perspectives of an Active Quant," Chapter 3 in Frank J. Fabozzi (ed.), *Active Equity Portfolio Management* (Hoboken, NJ: John Wiley & Sons, 1998).

dent variable $X_{2,t}$ is the excess return of value style over growth style. Market capitalization is another style factor. The last independent variable $(X_{3,t})$ is the difference in size between large-cap and small-cap stocks and therefore reflects size.

The regression was run over 219 months from January 1979 through March 1997. The results are reported below with the t-statistic for each parameter shown in parentheses:

$$\hat{Y}_t = \begin{array}{cccc} -0.007 & - \, 0.083\,X_{1,\,t} & - \, 0.071\,X_{2,\,t} & - \, 0.244\,X_{3,\,t} \\ (-0.192) & (-8.771) & (-3.628) & (-17.380) \end{array}$$

Let's interpret the results. The t-statistics of the betas are statistically significant for all levels of significance. The regression results suggest that relative to the S&P 500, the average large-cap mutual fund makes statistically significant bets against the market, against value, and against size. The adjusted R^2 is 0.63. This means that 63% of the variation in the average large-cap mutual fund's returns is explained by the regression model. The intercept term, α, is -0.007 (-7 basis points) and is interpreted as the average active return after controlling for risk (i.e., net of market, value, and size). Statistically, the intercept term is not significant. So, the average active return is indistinguishable from zero. Given that the return indexes constructed by Lipper are net of fees and expenses, the conclusion of this simple regression model is that the average large-cap mutual funds covers its costs on a risk-adjusted basis.

TESTS OF THE CAPM

As noted earlier, the CAPM is an equilibrium model of asset pricing. While portfolio managers do not devote time to testing the validity of this model since few have to be convinced of its limitation, there has been more than 35 years of empirical testing of the validity of this model and the primary tool that has been used is regression analysis. While there have been extensions of the CAPM first developed by William Sharpe in 1964,[4] we will only discuss the tests of the original model.

Review of the CAPM
The CAPM is derived from a set of assumptions. It is an abstraction of the real-world capital markets. Although some of the assumptions are

---

[4] William F. Sharpe, "Capital Asset Prices," *Journal of Finance* 19 (September 1964), pp. 425–442.

unrealistic, they simplify matters a great deal and make the CAPM more tractable from a mathematical standpoint. The assumptions fall into two general categories: (1) the way investors make decisions and (2) characteristics of the capital market. With respect to investor decision-making, it is assumed that investors are risk averse and make investment decisions over a one-period horizon based on the expected return and the variance of returns. With respect to capital markets, it is, among other "technical" assumptions, assumed that is perfectly competitive and that there is a risk-free asset at which investors can invest and borrow.

Based on the above assumptions, the CAPM is

$$E(R_i) - R_f = \beta_i [E(R_M) - R_f] \tag{5.1}$$

where

$E(R_i)$ = expected return for asset i
R_f = risk-free rate
$E(R_M)$ = expected return for the market portfolio
β_i = the index of systematic risk of asset i

The index of systematic risk of asset i, β_i, popularly referred to as *beta,* is the degree to which an asset covaries with the market portfolio and for this reason is referred to as the asset's *systematic risk.* More specifically, systematic risk is the portion of an asset's variability that can be attributed to a common factor. Systematic risk is the risk that results from general market and economic conditions that cannot be diversified away. The portion of an asset's variability that can be diversified away is the risk that is unique to an asset. This risk is called *nonsystematic risk, diversifiable risk, unique risk, residual risk,* and *company-specific risk.* We calculated the beta for individual securities in the previous chapter.

The CAPM states that, given the assumptions, the expected return on asset is a positive linear function of its index of systematic risk as measured by beta. The higher the β_i or beta is, the higher the expected return. There are no other factors that should significantly affect an asset's expected return other than the index of systematic risk.

Estimating Beta with Regression Analysis

The beta for an asset can be estimated using the following simple linear regression:

$$r_{it} - r_{ft} = \alpha_i + \beta_i [r_{Mt} - r_{ft}] + e_{it} \tag{5.2}$$

where

r_{it} = observed return on asset i for time t
r_{ft} = observed return on the risk-free asset for time t
r_{Mt} = observed return on the market portfolio for time t
e_{it} = error term for time t

The regression equation (5.2) is called the *characteristic line*. Since there is only one independent variable, $r_{Mt} - r_{ft}$, there is a simple linear regression. Letting

$$x_t = r_{Mt} - r_{ft}$$

and

$$y_t = r_{it} - r_{ft}$$

the characteristic line can be rewritten as

$$y_t = \alpha_i + \beta_i x_t + \varepsilon_{it}$$

The parameters to be estimated are the coefficients α_i and β_i and the standard deviation of the error term, ε_i. The parameter β_i is the focus of interest in this section. Later in this chapter, when we provide an illustration of how regression analysis is used in performance measurement, we will see the economic meaning of the intercept term, α_i.

To estimate the characteristic line for an asset using regression analysis, we consider three time series of returns for (1) the asset, (2) the market portfolio, and (3) the risk-free rate. In our illustration, in the previous chapter we estimated the characteristic line for Oracle, General Motors, and a stock portfolio consisting of 20 stocks using 60 monthly returns from 12/1/2000 to 11/1/2005. For the market portfolio we used the Standard & Poor's 500 (S&P 500) and for risk-free rate we used the returns for the one-month Treasury bill rate.

Clearly, the beta estimates will vary with the particular market index selected as well as with the sample period and frequency used.

Methodology for Testing the CAPM

Typically, a methodology referred to as a *two-pass regression* is used to test the CAPM. The first pass involves the estimation of beta for each security from its characteristic line. The betas from the first-pass regression are then used to form portfolios of securities ranked by portfolio beta.

The portfolio returns, the return on the risk-free asset, and the portfolio betas are then used to estimate the second-pass regression. Then the following second-pass regression which is the empirical analogue of the CAPM is estimated:

$$R_p - R_F = b_0 + b_1 \beta_p + e_p \qquad (5.3)$$

where the parameters to be estimated are b_0 and b_1, and e_p is the error term for the regression.

Unlike the estimation of the characteristic line which uses time series data, the second-pass regression is a cross-sectional regression. The return data are frequently aggregated into five-year periods for this regression.

According to the CAPM, the following should be found:

1. b_0 should not be significantly different from zero. This can be seen by comparing equations (5.1) and (5.3)
2. b_1 should equal the observed risk premium $(R_M - R_F)$ over which the second-pass regression is estimated. Once again, this can be seen by comparing equations (5.1) and (5.2).
3. The relationship between beta and return should be linear. That is, if, for example, the following multiple regression is estimated,

$$R_p - R_F = b_0 + b_1 \beta_p + b_2 (\beta_p)^2 + e_p$$

the parameters b_0 and b_2 should not be significantly different from zero.
4. Beta should be the only factor that is priced by the market. That is, other factors such as the variance or standard deviation of the returns, and variables that we will discuss in later chapters such as the price-earnings ratio, dividend yield, and firm size, should not add any significant explanatory power to the equation.

Findings of CAPM Tests

The general results of the empirical tests of the CAPM are as follows:

1. The estimated intercept term b_0, is significantly different from zero and consequently different from what is hypothesized for this value.
2. The estimated coefficient for beta, b_1, has been found to be less than the observed risk premium $(R_M - R_F)$. The combination of this and the previous finding suggests that low-beta stocks have higher returns than the CAPM predicts and high-beta stocks have lower returns than the CAPM predicts.

3. The relationship between beta and return appears to be linear; hence the functional form of the CAPM is supported.
4. Beta is not the only factor priced by the market. Several studies have discovered other factors that explain stock returns. These include a price-earnings factor, a dividend factor, a firm-size factor, and both a firm-size factor and a book-market factor.

It is the last of these findings that has fostered the empirical search for other factors using econometric models.

It should be noted that in 1977 Richard Roll criticized the published tests of the CAPM.[5] He argued that while the CAPM is testable in principle, no correct test of the theory had yet been presented. He also argued that there was practically no possibility that a correct empirical test would ever be accomplished in the future. We will not discuss these arguments here. Basically, Roll argues that there is only one potentially testable hypothesis associated with the CAPM, namely, that the true market portfolio lies on the Markowitz efficient frontier (i.e., it is mean-variance efficient). Furthermore, because the true market portfolio must contain all worldwide assets, the value of most of which cannot be observed (e.g., human capital), the hypothesis is in all probability untestable. Empirical tests after 1977 have attempted to address Roll's criticisms in testing the CAPM.

USING THE CAPM TO EVALUATE MANAGER PERFORMANCE: THE JENSEN MEASURE

One of the early methodologies for evaluating manager performance was proposed in 1968 by Michael Jensen. Jensen used a simple linear regression model to analyze performance of mutual fund managers.[6] Specifically, the *Jensen measure* (also called the *Jensen index*) is a risk-adjusted performance measure that uses the CAPM to empirically determine whether a portfolio manager outperformed a market index. Using time-series data for the return on the portfolio and the market index, this is done by estimating the same regression as the characteristic line. The intercept term, α_i, is interpreted as the *unique return* realized by the portfolio manager and is the estimated value of the Jensen measure. If

---

[5] Richard Roll, "A Critique of the Asset Pricing Theory: Part I. On the Past and Potential Testability of the Theory," *Journal of Financial Economics* 5 (March 1977), pp. 129–176.

[6] Michael C. Jensen, "The Performance of Mutual Funds in the Period 1945–1964," *Journal of Finance* 23 (May 1968), pp. 389–416.

the estimated intercept term is not statistically different from zero, there is no unique return. A statistically significant intercept term that is positive means that the portfolio manager outperformed the market; a negative value means that the portfolio manager underperformed the market. The Jensen measure is appropriate only when the portfolio is diversified. Hence, there are limitations in applying this measure to hedge funds, for example. In the previous chapter we estimated the characteristic line for two large-cap mutual funds.

When Jensen proposed the model for measuring performance, in his regression model the Greek letter alpha was used to represent the intercept term in equation (5.3). Hence the Jensen measure is also called the "Jensen alpha." Consequently, the market often refers to the "alpha" of a portfolio manager as a measure of performance. However, alpha as the concept is used today is not the Jensen measure but rather the average active return over a period of time. The active return is the difference between the return of a portfolio and the benchmark index. Notice that unlike the Jensen measure or Jensen alpha, measuring performance by the average active return does not adjust for market risk.

EVIDENCE FOR MULTIFACTOR MODELS

Regression-based tests seeking to dispute the CAPM have helped identify factors that have been found to be statistically significant in explaining the variation in asset returns. Employing regression analysis, Robert Jones of Goldman Sachs Asset Management has reported factors found in the U.S. stock market.[7] For the period 1979 through 1996, he regressed monthly stock returns against the following factors: "value" factors, "momentum" factors, and risk factors. The value factors included four ratios: book/market ratio, earnings/price ratio, sales/price ratio, and cash flow/price ratio. The three momentum factors included estimate revisions for earnings, revisions ratio, and price momentum. Three risk factors were used. The first is the systematic risk or beta from the CAPM.[8] The second is the residual risk from the CAPM; this is the risk not explained by the CAPM. The third risk is an uncertainty estimate measure. The factors are beginning-of-month values that are properly lagged where necessary.[9]

---

[7] Jones, "The Active versus Passive Debate: Perspectives on an Active Quant."

[8] As explained later, in the calculation of the CAPM a proxy for the market portfolio is needed. Jones used the Russell 1000 Index. This index includes large-cap stocks.

[9] Lagging is required because certain financial information is reported with lag. For example, year-end income and balance sheet information for a given year is not reported until three months after the corporation's year end.

EXHIBIT 5.1   Factors Found for U.S. Equity Market: Regression Results

	U.S. Results (1979–1996)	
	Coefficient	t-Statistic
Value Factors		
Book/market	0.24	2.96
Earnings/price	0.40	5.46
Sales/price	0.28	4.25
Cash flow/price	0.38	5.28
Momentum Factors		
Estimate revisions	0.56	13.22
Revisions ratio	0.55	14.72
Price momentum	0.61	7.17
Risk Factors		
CAPM beta	−0.17	−1.83
Residual risk	−0.42	−4.05
Estimate uncertainty	−0.33	−6.39

Source: Adapted from Exhibit 5 in Robert C. Jones, "The Active versus Passive Debate: Perspectives on an Active Quant," Chapter 3 in Frank J. Fabozzi (ed.), *Active Equity Portfolio Management* (Hoboken, NJ: John Wiley & Sons, 1998).

Jones calculated the average monthly regression coefficient and t-statistic for the series. Exhibit 5.1 shows the estimated coefficient for each factor and the t-statistic. All of the factors are highly significant. The lowest t-statistic is that of the CAPM beta. The conclusion from the regression results reported in Exhibit 5.1 is that there are factors other than the CAPM beta that explain returns.

Application of Linear Regression to Factor Models

Consider a random vector $\mathbf{X} = (X_1, \ldots, X_N)'$, a vector of factors $f = (f_1, \ldots, f_K)'$, a random vector of errors $\varepsilon = (\varepsilon_1, \ldots, \varepsilon_N)'$, and a $N \times K$ matrix of fixed real numbers $\beta = \{\beta_{ij}\}$. Linear factor models are regression models of the following type:

$$X_i = \alpha_i + \sum_{j=1}^{K} \beta_{ij} f_j + \varepsilon_i$$

The β_{ij} are the *factor loadings* that express the influence of the j-th factor on the i-th variable. We will describe in Chapter 13 how factors are determined.

Using the notation established in Chapter 3, we can write the factor model in matrix form as

$$X = \beta F + \varepsilon$$

Suppose that factors are known time series. A factor model is a multiple regression where the X_i are regressed on the factors f_j. The regression coefficients are the factor loadings. If we assume the standard assumptions of factor models, we can also assume that the usual conditions of regression models are verified. In fact, in a factor model, residuals are assumed to be serially uncorrelated terms, uncorrelated with the factors, and mutually uncorrelated (see Chapter 13). We also assume that the factors follow a multivariate normal distribution and that the residuals are Gaussian as well. In addition, factor models assume that both the factors and the variables are stationary so that regressions are meaningful.[10]

To estimate the regression equations, assuming that factors are known, we can use the standard OLS estimators minimizing the sum of squared residuals. Recall that the regression coefficients are estimated, for each variable X_i through the formulas

$$\bar{\beta} = (F'F)^{-1}F'W$$

where F is the design matrix of the regressors, that is the factors, that includes a column of ones to allow for a nonzero intercept α_i,

$$F = \begin{pmatrix} 1 & f_{11} & \cdots & f_{1K} \\ \vdots & \vdots & \ddots & \vdots \\ 1 & f_{T1} & \cdots & f_{TK} \end{pmatrix}$$

and the vector $\bar{\beta}_i$ includes both the intercept and the factor loadings,

$$\bar{\beta}_i = \begin{bmatrix} \alpha_1 & \beta_{11} & \cdots & \beta_{1K} \end{bmatrix}$$

In practice, it makes a considerable difference if the intercept term is zero or not. The intercept term gives the excess return that a manager is able to produce, the Jensen alpha discussed below, while the other regression coefficients represent the exposure to different factors (i.e., the sensitivities to different factors). Suppose factors are portfolios and that there is a risk-free rate. Let's write a factor model in terms of the excess return

---

[10] Dynamic factor models do not assume stationarity but assume that regressions are meaningful.

Z, defined as the difference between real returns and the risk-free asset, and the factors f are excess risk-factor returns.

$$Z_i = \alpha_i + \sum_{j=1}^{K} \beta_{ij} f_j + \varepsilon_i$$

An *exact factor pricing model* is a factor model where the intercepts are all zeros. The Arbitrage Pricing Theory (APT)[11] prescribes that only a finite number of assets might exhibit an α different from zero. That is, according to the APT, it is impossible that all assets in a large economy have nonzero intercept.

Let's call μ_f the f-vector of the factor means. Suppose that the factor model is not constrained, that is, we estimate the intercepts from market data. From the regression formulas, it can be demonstrated that we can write the following estimates for the intercepts

$$\hat{\alpha} = \hat{\mu} - \hat{\beta}\hat{\mu}_f$$

where

$$\hat{\mu} = \frac{1}{T}\sum_{t=1}^{T} Z_t, \quad \hat{\mu}_f = \frac{1}{T}\sum_{t=1}^{T} \mathbf{f}_{ft}$$

In practice, estimates of the intercepts are very delicate as they require very long time series.

Suppose now that we want to apply a strict factor structure; that is, we impose the requirement that the intercepts are all zero. This restriction might be imposed either to test the alternative hypothesis of no intercept or because, in practice, we are primarily interested in evaluating factor exposure. In this case, to estimate the factor loadings, we apply the general regression coefficients estimation formula

$$\hat{\beta} = (\mathbf{ff}')^{-1}\mathbf{f}'\mathbf{X}$$

without demeaning factors and variables.

The general setting of factor models is such that in the model regression equation both the dependent variables and the factors are random

---

[11] Stephen A. Ross, "The Arbitrage Theory of Capital Asset Pricing," *Journal of Economic Theory* 16 (December 1976), pp. 343–362.

variables. If we want to compute the variance of the regression parameters, we have to use the sandwich estimators introduced in Chapter 3 when regressors are random variables. These concepts also are discussed when estimating a robust regression model in Chapter 12.

Some well known factor models for the equity market are the models developed by Chen, Roll, and Ross,[12] Fama and French,[13] MSCI Barra, and Northfield. The MSCI Barra model is explained in Chapter 13.

BENCHMARK SELECTION: SHARPE BENCHMARKS

Because of the difficulty of classifying a money manager into any one of the generic investment styles for purposes of performance evaluation, William Sharpe suggested that a benchmark can be constructed using multiple regression analysis from various specialized market indexes.[14] The rationale is that potential clients can buy a combination of specialized index funds to replicate a style of investing. A benchmark can be created using regression analysis that adjusts for a manager's index-like tendencies. Such a benchmark is called a *Sharpe benchmark*.

The 10 mutually exclusive indexes suggested by Sharpe to provide asset class diversification are (1) the Russell Price-drive Stock Index (an index of large value stocks); (2) the Russell Earnings-growth Stock Index (an index of large growth stocks); (3) the Russell 2000 Small Stock Index; (4) a 90-Day Bill Index; (5) the Lehman Intermediate Government Bond Index; (6) the Lehman Long-Term Government Bond Index; (7) the Lehman Corporate Bond Index; (8) the Lehman Mortgage-Backed Securities Index; (9) the Salomon Smith Barney Non-U.S. Government Bond Index; and (10) the Financial Times Actuaries Euro-Pacific Index.[15]

---

[12] See the following articles by Eugene F. Fama and Kenneth French, "Common Risk Factors in the Returns on Stocks and Bonds," *Journal of Financial Economics* 33 (1993), pp. 3–56; "Size and Book-to-Market Factors in Earnings and Returns," *Journal of Finance* 50 (1995), pp. 131–155; "Multifactor Explanations of Asset Pricing Anomalies," *Journal of Finance* 51 (1996), pp. 55–84, and; "Value versus Growth: The International Evidence," *Journal of Finance* 53 (1998), pp. 1975–1999.

[13] Nai-fu Chen, Richard Roll, and Stephen A. Ross, "Economic Forces and the Stock Market," *Journal of Business* 59 (July 1986), pp. 383–403.

[14] William F. Sharpe, "Determining A Fund's Effective Asset Mix," *Investment Management Review* 9 (September–October 1988), pp. 16–29.

[15] At the time that Sharpe introduced his model, the bond indexes were published by Shearson-Lehman (now Lehman) and Salomon Brothers (now Salomon Smith Barney).

Sharpe benchmarks are determined by regressing periodic returns (e.g., monthly returns) on various market indexes. The Sharpe benchmark was reported for one portfolio management firm based on performance from the period January 1981 through July 1988 using monthly returns.[16] The resulting Sharpe benchmark based on monthly observations was

$$\text{Sharpe benchmark} = 0.43 \times (\text{FRC Price-driven index})$$
$$+ 0.13 \times (\text{FRC Earnings-growth index})$$
$$+ 0.44 \times (\text{FRC 2000 index})$$

where FRC is an index produced by the Frank Russell Company.

The three indexes were selected because they were the only indexes of the 10 that were statistically significant. Notice that the sum of the three coefficients is equal to one. This is done by estimating a constrained regression as explained in the previous chapter. The coefficient of determination for this regression was 97.6%. The intercept term for this regression is 0.365%, which represents the average excess monthly return and is a statistic similar to Jensen's measure explained earlier.

By subtracting the style benchmark's monthly return from the manager's monthly portfolio return, performance can be measured. This difference, which we refer to as "added value residuals," is what the manager added over the return from three "index funds" in the appropriate proportions. For example, suppose that in some month the return realized by this manager is 1.75%. In the same month, the return for the three indexes were as follows: 0.7% for the FRC Price-driven index, 1.4% for the FRC Earnings-growth index, and 2.2% for the FRC 2000 index. The added value residual for this month would be calculated as follows. First, calculate the value of the Sharpe benchmark:

$$\text{Sharpe benchmark} = 0.43 \times (0.7\%) + 0.13 \times (1.4\%) + 0.44 \times (2.2\%)$$
$$= 1.45\%$$

The added value residual is then:

Added value residual = Actual return − Sharpe benchmark return

Since the actual return for the month is 1.75%,

Added value residual = 1.75% − 1.45% = 0.3%.

---

[16] See H. Russell Fogler, "Normal Style Indexes—An Alternative to Manager Universes?" in *Performance Measurement: Setting the Standards, Interpreting the Numbers*, p. 102.

Notice that if this manager had been benchmarked against a single investment style index such as the FRC Price-driven index, the manager would have outperformed the benchmark by a wide margin (1.05%). In contrast, if the FRC 2000 index is used as the benchmark, the manager would have underperformed by 0.45%.

One interpretation of the results of a Sharpe benchmark that has arisen in practice is that if the R^2 is low, this is an indication that the portfolio is actively managed because it is not associated with any particular style. However, this need not be the case as pointed out by Dor and Jagannathan.[17] One of the reasons could be due to inadequate asset class indexes. Dor and Jagannathan illustrate the importance of including adequate asset class indexes using the Putnam Utilities Growth and Income, a mutual fund. Exhibit 5.2 reports the Sharpe benchmark based on regression analysis of returns from January 1992 through August 2001.

There are two models reported. The first, denoted "Basic Model," uses 12 asset class indexes selected by Dor and Jagannathan. As can be seen, the R^2 is 66.9%. However, Putnam Utilities Growth and Income is a sector-oriented fund. In creating a Sharpe benchmark for sector-oriented funds, it is important to use relevant sector indexes. The "Extended Model" reported in Exhibit 5.2 includes three sector indexes: Dow Jones Utilities, Dow Jones Communications, and Dow Jones Energy. Notice that not only does the R^2 increase from 66.9%, the weights (regression coefficients) change dramatically. For example, a 56.8% weight in the basic model is assigned to Large-Cap Value but only 14.7% in the extended model. Look also at the Treasury 10+ year asset class index. This is the second largest weight in the basic model; however, in the extended model it has no weight assigned to it.

RETURN-BASED STYLE ANALYSIS FOR HEDGE FUNDS

The use of the Sharpe benchmark is typical for evaluating nonhedge fund managers. The difficulty with employing the Sharpe benchmark for hedge funds is attributable to the wide range of assets in which they are free to invest and the dynamic nature of their trading strategy (i.e., flexibility of shifting among asset classes, the higher leverage permitted, and the ability to short sell).

---

[17] Arik Ben Dor and Ravi Jagannathan, "Style Analysis: Asset Allocation and Performance Evaluation," Chapter 1 in T. Daniel Coggin and Frank J. Fabozzi (eds.), *The Handbook of Equity Style Management: Third Edition* (Hoboken, NJ: John Wiley & Sons, 2003).

EXHIBIT 5.2 Sharpe Benchmark for Putnam Utilities Growth and Income (January 1992–August 2001)

Asset Class	Basic Model	Extended Model
Bills	0	3.4%
Treasury 1–10 yrs	11.9%	0
Treasury 10+ yrs	20.5%	0
Corporate Bonds	0	0
Large-Cap Value	56.8%	14.7%
Large-Cap Growth	0	0
Small-Cap Value	0	4.4%
Small-Cap Growth	0	0
Developed Countries	0	0
Japan	0	0
Emerging Markets	0	0
Foreign Bonds	10.8%	10.6%
Dow Jones Utilities	—	44.6%
Dow Jones Communications	—	16.5%
Dow Jones Energy	—	5.9%
R^2	0.669	0.929

Source: Exhibit 1.10 in Arik Ben Dor and Ravi Jagannathan, "Style Analysis: Asset Allocation and Performance Evaluation," Chapter 1 in T. Daniel Coggin and Frank J. Fabozzi (eds.), *The Handbook of Equity Style Management: Third Edition* (Hoboken, NJ: John Wiley & Sons, 2003).

Dor and Jagannathan illustrate this difficulty using four hedge funds.[18] Two of the hedge funds are directional funds and two are non-directional funds. The former employ strategies seeking to benefit from broad market movements and the latter employ strategies seeking to exploit short-term pricing discrepancies between related securities but at the same time maintain market exposure to a minimum. Nondirectional funds are referred to as *market-neutral funds*. The directional funds are Hillsdale U.S. Market Neutral Fund (Hillside fund) and The Nippon Performance Fund (Nippon fund); the nondirectional funds are Axiom Balanced Growth Fund (Axiom fund) and John W. Henry & Company—Financial and Metals Portfolio (CTA fund).

---

[18] Dor and Jagannathan, "Style Analysis: Asset Allocation and Performance Evaluation."

Exhibit 5.3 reports two regression results for the four hedge funds. The first regression (referred to as the "Basic Model" in the exhibit) uses 12 asset classes. The explanatory power (R^2) is lower for these hedge funds than for mutual funds for the reason cited earlier regarding the wide range of strategies available to hedge funds. Note, however, that the R^2 of the nondirectional funds (i.e., market-neutral funds) is higher than that of the directional funds.

Theory and empirical evidence can help us identify factors to improve upon the explanatory power of hedge fund returns. Several researchers have argued that hedge funds pursue strategies that have option-like (nonlinear) payoffs and this occurs even if an option strategy is not pursued.[19] Consequently, Dor and Jagannathan add four S&P 500 index strategies to the 12 asset classes. This second regression, referred to as the "Basic Strategy + Options Strategy," shows that by adding the four option indexes, the R^2 increases significantly for each hedge fund.

Dor and Jagannathan show how the style analysis can be further improved by including peer-group performance as measured by hedge fund indexes created by several organizations. Three examples of such organizations are Hedge Fund Research Company (HFR), CSFB/Tremont, and MAR Futures. The five hedge fund indexes that are used by Dor and Jagannathan in their illustration are (1) Market Neutral, (2) Emerging Markets, (3) Managed Futures, (4) Fixed Income, and (5) Event Driven. A total of 21 explanatory variables then can be used in the style analysis: 12 asset classes, five hedge fund indexes, and four of the S&P 500 option strategies. Because of the large number of variables and their high correlations, Dor and Jagannathan employ stepwise regression analysis—the process of adding and deleting explanatory variables sequentially depending on the F-value, as described in Chapter 4—to determine the explanatory variables that should be included. The results are shown in Exhibit 5.4. In implementing the stepwise regression, Dor and Jagannathan specify a 10% significance level for deleting or adding an explanatory variable in the stepwise regression procedure.

---

[19] See, Lawrence A. Glosten and Ravi Jagannathan, "A Contingent Claim Approach to Performance Evaluation," *Journal of Empirical Finance* 1 (1994), pp. 133–160; Mark Mitchell and Todd Pulvino, "Characteristics of Risk in Risk Arbitrage," *Journal of Finance* 56 (December 2001), pp. 2135–2175; and William Fung and David A. Hsieh, "The Risks in Hedge Fund Strategies: Theory and Evidence From Trend Followers," *Review of Financial Studies* 14 (2001), pp. 313–341; Philip H. Dybvig and Stephen A. Ross, "Differential Information and Performance Measurement using a Security Market Line," *Journal of Finance* 40 (1985), pp. 383–399; and Robert C. Merton, "On Market Timing and Investment Performance I: An Equilibrium Theory of Values for Markets Forecasts," *Journal of Business* 54 (1981), pp. 363–406.

EXHIBIT 5.3 Hedge Funds Style Analysis (I)

	Basic Model				Basic Model + Options Strategy			
	Hillsdale	Nippon	Axiom	CTA	Hillsdale	Nippon	Axiom	CTA
Bills	161.9	219.0	257.5	9.2	137.7	295.7	393.7	-432.0
Treasury 1–10 yrs	-161.4	-281.6	-324.8	676.0	-223.1	-404.0	-450.0	698.5
Treasury 10+ yrs	44.0	-6.6	-21.9	85.3	32.4	8.8	-35.5	-4.5
Corporate Bonds	22.9	177.6	216.8	-297.0	79.8	215.1	240.1	-166.1
Large Value	27.4	-22.3	-24.8	14.0	40.6	-33.5	-44.4	7.6
Large Growth	21.1	10.0	-5.0	-32.6	48.9	-12.3	-23.0	-7.0
Small Value	-3.4	28.3	50.1	24.4	2.2	20.8	89.0	19.5
Small Growth	7.7	-11.3	-23.9	-9.8	0.3	-4.8	-38.2	-12.5
Developed Countries	-14.8	2.4	14.3	0.2	-8.9	4.3	19.5	8.8
Japan	6.7	25.8	25.5	-30.4	10.2	19.7	38.9	-53.3
Emerging Markets	-36.7	-16.7	37.9	30.8	-38.4	-15.5	21.8	28.7
Foreign Bonds	27.4	-24.7	-94.4	-15.0	16.7	4.4	-107.2	8.5
C_{at}	—	—	—	—	0.1	3.3	-0.1	5.9
P_{at}	—	—	—	—	-2.0	2.9	-12.7	11.2
C_{out}	—	—	—	—	-0.8	-1.7	-0.8	-4.3
P_{out}	—	—	—	—	4.1	-3.3	9.0	-9.1
R^2	28.3	29.6	55.4	37.5	32.2	39.8	77.3	55.4

Note: This exhibit reports the results of style analysis for three hedge funds and a CTA during March 1997 to November 2001. The coefficients are not constrained to be nonnegative due to the use of leverage and short-sales, but the sum of the coefficients is constrained to one. All figures in the table are in percents. The columns titled "Basic Model" report the results for the set of 12 asset classes. The next four columns show the results of reestimating the coefficients for each fund using the 12 asset classes and returns on four S&P 500 options strategies. At-the-money call (put) options are denoted as $C_{at}(P_{at})$ and out-of-the-money call (put) option as $C_{out}(P_{out})$.

Source: Exhibit 1.11 in Arik Ben Dor and Ravi Jagannathan, "Style Analysis: Asset Allocation and Performance Evaluation," Chapter 1 in T. Daniel Coggin and Frank J. Fabozzi (eds.), *The Handbook of Equity Style Management, 3rd ed.* (Hoboken, NJ: John Wiley & Sons, 2003).

EXHIBIT 5.4 Hedge Funds Style Analysis Using Stepwise Regression

This exhibit reports for each fund, the results of a stepwise estimation using 12 asset classes, five hedge funds indexes and four option strategies. The analysis is repeated separately for each hedge fund database. Stepwise regression involves adding and/or deleting variables sequentially depending on the F value. We specify a 10% significance level for deleting a variable in the stepwise regression procedure. The single (*) and double (**) asterisks denote significantly different than zero at the 5% and 1% level, respectively.

	Hillsdale Market Neutral			Nippon Market Neutral			Axiom Emerging Markets			CTA		
	HFR	TRE	MAR	HFR	TRE	MAR	HFR	TRE	MAR	HFR	TRE	MAR
Bills	-23.36*						31.9**		23.36			
Treasury 1–10 yrs												
Treasury 10+ yrs							-7.32**	-4.58**	-6.07**			
Corporate Bonds							3.11**	1.75**	2.62**	2.86**		-0.37
Large-Cap Value				-0.21	-0.24*	-0.37*						
Large-Cap Growth		0.38**	0.35**			-0.29*						
Small-Cap Value											0.47**	0.52**
Small-Cap Growth							-0.39**	-0.18*	-0.26**		-0.17	-0.23*
Developed countries											-0.29	
Japan		-0.33**	-0.33**				0.23**		0.15		-0.33**	-0.19**
Emerging Markets	1.86**						0.36**					
Foreign Bonds	-0.51**						-0.58**			-0.23*		
Market Neutral		0.32			0.98*	2.49**		1.44**	3.01*	0.60	0.49*	0.72**
Emerging Markets							1.89**	0.32**	0.81**			
Managed Futures												-0.17
Fixed Income				0.81*							1.28**	1.51**
Event Driven					0.85**		1.47**	1.82**				
At-the-money call	-0.10*			0.014*	0.012*	0.02**					0.02**	-0.10**
At-the-money put	0.08*								-0.12		0.08	
Out-of-the-money put						-0.02				0.2**	-0.08	0.09**
R^2	0.46	0.27	0.22	0.21	0.33	0.29	0.82	0.82	0.80	0.19	0.68	0.77

Source: Exhibit 1.13 in Arik Ben Dor and Ravi Jagannathan, "Style Analysis: Asset Allocation and Performance Evaluation," Chapter 1 in T. Daniel Coggin and Frank J. Fabozzi (eds.), *The Handbook of Equity Style Management*, 3rd ed. (Hoboken, NJ: John Wiley & Sons, 2003).

The results of the stepwise regression results show a higher ability to track the returns of the two directional funds relative to the two nondirectional funds by including the five hedge fund indexes (i.e., peer groups).[20]

In Chapter 13 where we discuss principal component and factor analysis, we will see an application of these tools to extract factors to explain hedge fund returns.

HEDGE FUND SURVIVAL

An illustration of probit regression is provided by Malkiel and Saha who use it to calculate the probability of the demise of a hedge fund.[21] The dependent variable in the regression is 1 if a fund is defunct (did not survive) and 0 if it survived. The explanatory variables, their estimated coefficient, and the standard error of the coefficient using hedge fund data from 1994 to 2003 are given below:

Explanatory Variable	Coefficient	Standard Deviation
1. Return for the first quarter before the end of fund performance.	−1.47	0.36
2. Return for the second quarter before the end of fund performance.	−4.93	0.32
3. Return for the third quarter before the end of fund performance.	−2.74	0.33
4. Return for the fourth quarter before the end of fund performance.	−3.71	0.35
5. Standard deviation for the year prior to the end of fund performance.	17.76	0.92
6. Number of times in the final three months the fund's monthly return fell below the monthly median of all funds in the same primary category.	0.00	0.33
7. Assets of the fund (in billions of dollars) estimated at the end of performance.	−1.30	−7.76
Constant term	−0.37	0.07

---

[20] Also note that the results suggest that each hedge fund appears to use option strategies in different ways. We have not discussed these option strategies above. A discussion is provided in Dor and Jagannathan, "Style Analysis: Asset Allocation and Performance Evaluation."

[21] Burton G. Malkiel and Atanu Saha, "Hedge Funds: Risk and Return," *Financial Analysts Journal* 22 (November–December 2005), pp. 80–88.

For only one explanatory variable, the sixth one, the coefficient is not statistically significant from zero. That explanatory variable is a proxy for peer comparison of the hedge fund versus similar hedge funds. The results suggest that there is a lower probability of the demise of a hedge fund if there is good recent performance (the negative coefficient of the first four variables above) and the more assets under management (the negative coefficient for the last variable above). The greater the hedge fund performance return variability, the higher the probability of demise (the positive coefficient for the fifth variable above).

BOND PORTFOLIO APPLICATIONS

We have focused a good deal so far on applications to equity portfolio management. In this section we will present a few applications to bond portfolio management.

Rich/Cheap Analysis for the Mortgage Market

Regression analysis has long been used to attempt to identify rich and cheap sectors of the bond market.[22] In the previous chapter, we discussed a model for predicting corporate bond spreads. Here we will use a relative value regression model developed by the Mortgage Strategy Group of UBS. The dependent variable is the mortgage spread, a variable measured as the difference between the current coupon mortgage[23] and the average swap rate. The average swap rate is measured by the average of the 5-year swap rate and 10-year swap rate.

There are three explanatory variables in the model that have historically been found to affect mortgage pricing:

1. The level of interest rates
2. The shape of the yield curve
3. The volatility of interest rates

The level of interest rates is measured by the average of the 5-year swap rate and 10-year swap rate. The shape of the yield curve is measured by the spread between the 10-year swap rate and 2-year swap rate. The volatility measure is obtained from swaption prices.

---

[22] See H. Gifford Fong and Frank J. Fabozzi, *Fixed Income Portfolio Management* (Homewood, IL: Dow Jones-Irwin, 1985).

[23] More specifically, it is what UBS calls the "perfect current coupon mortgage," which is a proxy for the current coupon mortgage.

The multiple regression model is[24]

$$\text{Mortgage spread} = \alpha + \beta_1(\text{Average swap rate})$$
$$+ \beta_2(\text{10-year/2-year swap spread})$$
$$+ \beta_3(\text{10-year/2-year swap spread})^2$$
$$+ \beta_4(\text{Swaption volatility}) + e$$

Two years of data were used to estimate the regression model. While the R^2 for the estimated model is not reported, Exhibit 5.5 shows the actual mortgage spread versus the spread projected by the regression model for the Fannie Mae 30-year mortgage passthrough security, one type of *mortgage-backed security* (MBS).

Let's see how the model is used. The analysis was performed in early March 2004 to assess the relative value of the MBS market. If the spread predicted by the model (i.e., model spread) exceeds the actual spread, the market is viewed as rich; it is viewed as cheap if the model spread is less than actual spread. The market is fairly priced if the two

EXHIBIT 5.5   Mortgage Spreads: Actual versus Model

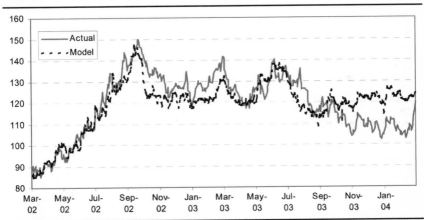

Source: Figure 4 in "Mortgages—Hold Your Nose and Buy," *UBS Mortgage Strategist*, 9 March 2004, p 19. Reprinted with permission.

---

[24] See "Mortgages—Hold Your Nose and Buy," *UBS Mortgage Strategist*, 9 March 2004, pp. 15–26. UBS has argued in other issues of its publication that with this particular regression model the richness of mortgages may be overstated because the model does not recognize the reshaping of the mortgage market. Alternative regression models that do take this into account are analyzed by UBS but the results are not reported here.

spreads are equal. The predicted and actual spreads for March 2004 are the last ones shown in Exhibit 5.5. While the model suggests that the market is rich, it is less rich in comparison to the prior months. In fact, on at the close of March 9, 2004 when the article was written, it was only 5 basis points.

Empirical Duration

Duration is the approximate percentage change in the value of a security or a portfolio to a change in interest rates. For most bonds, duration is estimated from a valuation model by changing interest rates and approximating the percentage price change based on the new prices generated by the model. An alternative approach is to use historical prices to the estimate duration for complex bonds. The resulting duration is referred to as *empirical duration* (also called regression-based duration and implied duration). Empirical duration has been used for estimating duration for complex bonds such as mortgage securities. (In the previous chapter we illustrated an application to the estimation of empirical duration for equities.)

For mortgage securities, several approaches based on observed market prices are used to calculate duration. These market-based approaches are empirical duration, coupon curve duration, and option-implied duration. In this section we discuss empirical duration because it is estimated using regression analysis.[25]

Empirical duration is the sensitivity of a mortgage security as estimated empirically from historical prices and yields. This approach was first suggested in 1986 by Scott Pinkus and Marie Chandoha[26] and then in the 1990s by Paul DeRossa, Laurie Goodman, and Mike Zazzarino[27] and Lakbir Hayre and Hubert Chang.[28]

Laurie Goodman and Jeffrey Ho provided more information on the methodology used at PaineWebber (now UBS).[29] On a daily basis the

---

[25] For a more detailed discussion of regression-based models for measuring mortgage securities, see Bennett W. Golub, "Measuring the Duration of Mortgage-Related Securities," Chapter 34 in Frank J. Fabozzi (ed.), *The Handbook of Mortgage-Backed Securities*, 6th ed. (New York: McGraw Hill, 2006).

[26] The first attempt to calculate empirical duration was by Scott M. Pinkus and Marie A. Chandoha, "The Relative Price Volatility of Mortgage Securities," *Journal of Portfolio Management* 12 (Summer 1986), pp. 9–22.

[27] Paul DeRosa, Laurie Goodman, and Mike Zazzarino, "Duration Estimates on Mortgage-Backed Securities," *Journal of Portfolio Management* 18 (Winter 1993), pp. 32–37.

[28] Lakbir Hayre and Hubert Chang, "Effective and Empirical Duration of Mortgage Securities," *Journal of Fixed Income* 7 (March 1997), pp. 17-33.

following regression is used to calculate 2-week, 4-week, and 8-week empirical duration for 30-year mortgage securities:

$$\text{Change in mortgage price} = \alpha + \beta(\Delta_{10yrPrice})$$

where $\Delta_{10yrPrice}$ = change in the price of the 10-year Treasury note.
The empirical duration is then calculated as follows:

$$\text{Empirical duration} = \frac{(D_{10yr})(P_{10yr})\hat{\beta}}{P_{Mort}}$$

where

D_{10yr} = duration of the 10-year Treasury note
P_{10yr} = price of the 10-year Treasury note
P_{Mort} = price of the mortgage security
$\hat{\beta}$ = estimated parameter fro the change in mortgage price regression

For 15-year mortgage securities, instead of the 10-year Treasury note, the 5-year Treasury note is used in the regression to estimate β and in the empirical duration formula.

Exhibit 5.6 compares empirical duration and measures based on non-statistical models (cash flow duration, effective duration or OAS duration, and option-implied duration)[30] several mortgage securities (more specifically, mortgage passthroughs securities) issued by Ginnie Mae (30-year issues denoted by GNSF in the exhibit) and Fannie Mae (30-year issues denoted by FNCL and 15-year issues denoted by FNCI in the exhibit). The mortgage securities reported in the exhibit were the actively traded coupons based on prices from July 1, 1993 through May 12, 1998.

Goodman and Ho present another regression-based model to derive duration. This model takes into account several factors that impact the price of an MBS: level of rates, shape of the yield curve, and expected interest rate volatility. The price model that they present allows not only for an estimate of the sensitivity of the price to changes in the level of rates, but also to the other factors.

---

[29] Laurie S. Goodman and Jeffrey Ho, "An Integrated Approach to Hedging and Relative Value Analysis," Chapter 15 in Frank J. Fabozzi (ed.), *Advances in the Valuation and Management of Mortgage-Backed Securities* (Hoboken, NJ: John Wiley & Sons, 1999).

[30] For a discussion of these duration measures, see Golub, "Measuring the Duration of Mortgage-Related Securities."

EXHIBIT 5.6   Comparison of Empirical, Effective (OAS), Cash Flow, Option Implied, and Price Model Durations

	5/12/98 Price	Cash Flow Duration	OAS Duration	Empirical Duration	Option Implied Duration	Price Model Duration
GNSF 6.0	96:26	6.27	6.57	5.32	5.53	5.75
GNSF 6.5	99:02	5.82	5.98	4.36	4.52	4.97
GNSF 7.0	101:05+	5.59	5.25	3.55	3.62	4.01
GNSF 7.5	102:24+	4.88	4.31	2.20	3.01	2.95
GNSF 8.0	103:28	3.98	3.32	1.41	2.59	1.74
GNSF 8.5	105:18+	3.03	2.54	0.44	0.00	1.03
FNCL 6.0	96:17+	5.55	5.88	5.10	5.22	5.29
FNCL 6.5	98:30+	5.64	5.29	4.19	4.19	4.68
FNCL 7.0	101:02+	5.28	4.55	3.39	3.32	3.79
FNCL 7.5	102:20+	4.35	3.66	2.03	2.69	2.64
FNCL 8.0	103:24	3.72	2.84	1.23	2.32	1.48
FNCL 8.5	104:18	2.90	2.26	0.46	0.00	0.59
FNCI 6.0	98:16	4.33	4.31	3.77	3.85	6.12
FNCI 6.5	100:11	4.11	3.90	2.92	3.03	5.07
FNCI 7.0	101:25	3.66	3.31	2.10	2.46	3.80
FNCI 7.5	102:28+	2.98	2.69	1.10	2.00	2.28
FNCI 8.0	103:03	2.42	2.24	0.55	1.85	0.72

Note: Hedge ratios versus 10-year Treasury for 30-year mortgages; 5-year Treasury for 15-year mortgages.
Source: Exhibit 3 in Laurie S. Goodman and Jeffrey Ho, "An Integrated Approach to Hedging and Relative Value Analysis," Chapter 15 in Frank J. Fabozzi (ed.), *Advances in the Valuation and Management of Mortgage-Backed Securities* (Hoboken, NJ: John Wiley & Sons, 1999), p. 223.

In their price model, the 10-year Treasury yield is used as a proxy for the level of rates, the spread between the 10-year and 2-year Treasury yields is used as a proxy for the shape of the yield curve, and the implied 3-month yield volatility on the 10-year Treasury note is used as a proxy for expected interest rate volatility. The price model involves estimating the following regression:

$$\text{Price} = a + b(\text{10-year yield}) + c(\ln[\text{10-year yield}]) \\ + d(\text{10-year/2-year spread}) + e(\text{Volatility})$$

where ln[10-year yield] means the natural logarithm of the 10-year Treasury yield.

Exhibit 5.7 reports the price model results estimated using regression for each of the actively traded coupons mortgage securities—30-year Ginnie Maes (denoted GN in the exhibit), 30-year Fannie Maes (denoted FN in the exhibit), and 15-year Fannie Maes (denoted DW in the exhibit). Goodman and Ho used prices from July 1, 1993 through May 12, 1998 to estimate the regression. (Note that the reported standard error of the regression in ticks.)

As can be seen from Exhibit 5.7, the R^2 of the regression is above 97.5% for all of the mortgage securities. For example, for the R^2 is 99.3% and the standard error is 9 ticks FNMA 7.0% regression (FN 7.0 in the exhibit). All the *t*-statistics are highly significant.

Given the estimates for the parameters above, duration (called by Goodman and Ho *price model duration*) is found as follows:

Price model duration = –[*b* + *c*/(10-year Treasury yield)]

For example, for the FN 7.0 price model regression, the regression estimate for *b* was –11.89 and the regression estimate for *c* was 45.87. On the close of May 12, 1998, the 10-year Treasury yield was 5.70%. Therefore, the price model duration was:

Price model duration = –[–11.89 + (45.87/5.7)] = 3.84

The last column in Exhibit 5.6 shows the price model duration. In the exhibit, the FN 7.0 is shown as FNCL 7.0. Note that the value shown in the exhibit's last column for duration is 3.79; this differs from the value of 3.84 computed above due to rounding.

There are advantages and disadvantages of the regression-based approach to estimating duration.[31] First the advantages. The duration estimate does not rely on any theoretical formulas or analytical assumptions. Second, the estimation of the required parameters is easy to compute using regression analysis. Finally, only two inputs are needed: a reliable price series and Treasury yield series.

As for the disadvantages. First, a reliable price series for a mortgage security may not be available. For example, there may be no price series available for a thinly traded mortgage derivative security or the prices may be matrix-priced or model-priced rather than actual transaction prices. Second, an empirical relationship does not impose a structure for the options embedded in a mortgage-backed security; this can distort the empirical duration. Third, the price history may lag current market

---

[31] For a more detailed discussion, see Golub, "Measuring the Duration of Mortgage-Related Securities."

EXHIBIT 5.7 Price Model Regression Results

Cpn	R-Sqr	S.E.	Coefficients (T-Stats)				
			a: intercept	b: 10yr	c: ln(10yr)	d: 10/2	e: vol
GN 6.0	99.2	0:13	93.38 (52.1)	−14.88 (46.2)	52.96 (25.4)	−0.0008 (2.5)	−0.23 (27.2)
GN 6.5	99.3	0:11	88.01 (56.2)	−15.25 (54.2)	58.73 (32.2)	0.0027 (11.7)	−0.25 (36.5)
GN 7.0	99.3	0:10	77.89 (57)	−15.98 (65.1)	67.84 (42.6)	0.0065 (32.3)	−0.24 (39.4)
GN 7.5	99.2	0:09	65.18 (49.9)	−16.81 (71.7)	78.43 (51.6)	0.0095 (49.7)	−0.21 (36.4)
GN 8.0	98.8	0:09	47.4 (35.6)	−18.36 (76.8)	94.25 (60.8)	0.0118 (60.3)	−0.2 (33.5)
GN 8.5	98.2	0:09	50.05 (40.9)	−16.04 (73)	85.17 (59.7)	0.0078 (43.2)	−0.13 (23)
FN 6.0	99.3	0:10	109.98 (80.4)	−9.53 (38.7)	25.19 (15.8)	0.0009 (4)	−0.17 (27.3)
FN 6.5	99.3	0:09	106.24 (79.7)	−9.93 (41.5)	30.12 (19.4)	0.0047 (24.1)	−0.2 (34.3)
FN 7.0	99.3	0:09	91.92 (74.5)	−11.89 (53.7)	45.87 (31.9)	0.0072 (39.6)	−0.21 (37.8)
FN 7.5	99.1	0:08	70.63 (59.4)	−14.62 (68.5)	67.81 (49)	0.0085 (48.6)	−0.2 (36.9)
FN 8.0	98.7	0:09	50.05 (41.6)	−16.97 (78.6)	87.89 (62.7)	0.0097 (54.9)	−0.19 (34.9)
FN 8.5	97.8	0:09	41.56 (33.3)	−16.92 (75.6)	92.86 (64)	0.0093 (50.9)	−0.16 (29.1)
DW 5.5	98.8	0:10	92.68 (62.6)	−10.08 (37.9)	36.54 (21.2)	0.0035 (14.2)	−0.13 (18.3)
DW 6.0	99.1	0:09	94.6 (76)	−9.79 (43.8)	35.67 (24.6)	0.0056 (30.7)	−0.14 (25.1)
DW 6.5	99.2	0:08	85.77 (79.7)	−10.94 (56.6)	45.36 (36.2)	0.0079 (49.7)	−0.14 (28.5)
DW 7.0	99.2	0:07	73.79 (75.5)	−12.39 (70.6)	57.64 (50.7)	0.0098 (68)	−0.13 (29.6)
DW 7.5	99.0	0:07	59.25 (62.8)	−13.91 (82.1)	71.39 (65)	0.0099 (71.4)	−0.11 (26.4)
DW 8.0	98.3	0:07	47.07 (49.4)	−14.75 (86.2)	81.52 (73.5)	0.0097 (69.4)	−0.11 (24.8)

Note: Price = $a + b$(10-year yield) + c(ln(10-year yield)) + d(10/2 spread) + e(vol), $\frac{dP}{dy} = b + \frac{c}{y}$, y = 10-year note, s = 10/2, v = implied 3-month yield volatility on 10-year note

Source: Exhibit 1 in Laurie S. Goodman and Jeffrey Ho, "An Integrated Approach to Hedging and Relative Value Analysis," Chapter 15 in Frank J. Fabozzi (ed.), *Advances in the Valuation and Management of Mortgage-Backed Securities* (Hoboken, NJ: John Wiley & Sons, 1999), p. 219.

conditions. This may occur after a sharp and sustained shock to interest rates has been realized. Finally, the volatility of the spread to Treasury yields can distort how the price of a mortgage-backed security reacts to yield changes.

CONCEPTS EXPLAINED IN THIS CHAPTER (IN ORDER OF PRESENTATION)

Factors
Market efficiency
Market efficiency tests
Excess return
Active return
Return attribution analysis
Diversifiable risk
Jensen measure
Jensen alpha and alpha
Factor models
Factor loadings
Exact factor pricing models
Strict factor structure
Sharpe benchmark
Directional funds
Market neutral funds
Style analysis
Empirical duration
Price model duration

CHAPTER 6

Modeling Univariate Time Series

In this chapter we discuss techniques for modeling univariate time series. These techniques are, for example, employed for short-term prediction of asset prices or returns or to test the market-efficiency hypothesis. We restrict the discussion to linear times series models and focus on the class of *autoregressive moving average* (ARMA) models Although financial time series typically exhibit structures that are more complex than those provided by ARMA processes, ARMA models are a first starting point and often serve as a benchmark against more complex approaches.

We start by introducing some technical background, definitions, properties of ARMA processes, and various models belonging to this class. The practical steps for deriving a model from data using the Box-Jenkins approach are presented in the next chapter.

DIFFERENCE EQUATIONS

In linear time series analysis it is commonly assumed that a time series to be modeled can be represented or approximated by a linear difference equation. In this section, we introduce the notation for linear difference equations and approaches to their solutions.

Notation

Consider a situation where the value of a time series at time t, y_t, is a linear function of the last p values of y and of exogenous terms, denoted by ε_t. We write

$$y_t = a_1 y_{t-1} + a_2 y_{t-2} + \cdots + a_p y_{t-p} + \varepsilon_t \qquad (6.1)$$

201

Expressions of type (6.1) are called difference equations. If the exogenous terms are zero, (6.1) is called an *homogenous difference equation*. If the exogenous term is a white noise, expression (6.1) represents an autoregressive process of order p, which will be detailed later.

Let's now introduce the lag operator notation. The *lag operator*, denoted by L, is an operator that shifts the time index backward by one unit.[1] Applying the lag operator to a variable at time t, we obtain the value of the variable at time $t - 1$:

$$Ly_t = y_{t-1}$$

Applying L^2 amounts to lagging the variable twice. i.e., $L^2 y_t = L(Ly_t) = Ly_{t-1} = y_{t-2}$.

More formally, the lag operator transforms one time series, say

$$\{y_t\}_{t=-\infty}^{\infty}$$

into another series, say

$$\{x_t\}_{t=-\infty}^{\infty}$$

where $x_t = y_{t-1}$. A constant c can be viewed as a special series, namely series

$$\{y_t\}_{t=-\infty}^{\infty}$$

with $y_t = c$ for all t, and we can apply the lag operator to a constant obtaining $Lc = c$. Note that by raising L to a negative power, we obtain a *delay* (or *lead*) *operator*:

$$L^{-k} y_t = y_{t+k}$$

The *difference operator* Δ is used to express the difference between consecutive realizations of a time series. With Δy_t we denote the first difference of y_t:

$$\Delta y_t = y_t - y_{t-1}$$

It follows that $\Delta^2 y_t = \Delta(\Delta y_t) = \Delta(y_t - y_{t-1}) = (y_t - y_{t-1}) - (y_{t-1} - y_{t-2}) = y_t - 2y_{t-1} + y_{t-2}$, etc.

---

[1] The lag operator is also called *backward shift* operator and sometimes denoted by B.

The difference operator can be expressed in terms of the lag operator because $\Delta = 1 - L$. Hence, $\Delta^2 = (1 - L)^2 = 1 - 2L + L^2$ and, in general, $\Delta^n = (1 - L)^n$. From

$$(a + b)^n = \sum_{k=0}^{n} \binom{n}{k} a^{n-k} b^k \qquad (6.2)$$

it follows that

$$\Delta^n = (1 - L)^n = \sum_{k=0}^{n} \binom{n}{k} (-L)^k \qquad (6.3)$$

The lag operator enables us to express higher-order difference equations more compactly in form of polynomials in lag operator L. For example, the difference equation

$$y_t = a_1 y_{t-1} + a_2 y_{t-2} + a_3 y_{t-3} + c$$

can be written as

$$y_t = a_1 L y_t + a_2 L^2 y_t + a_3 L^3 y_t + c$$

$$(1 - a_1 L - a_2 L^2 - a_3 L^3) y_t = c$$

or, in short,

$$a(L) y_t = c$$

where $a(L)$ stands for the third-degree polynomial in the lag operator L, i.e., $a(L) = 1 - a_1 L - a_2 L^2 - a_3 L^3$. This notation allows us to express higher-order difference equation, in a very compact fashion. We write the p-th order equation (6.1) as $(1 - a_1 L - a_2 L^2 - \cdots - a_p L^p) y_t = \varepsilon_t$ or more compactly as $a(L) y_t = \varepsilon_t$ where $a(L)$ is the polynomial $(1 - a_1 L - a_2 L^2 - \cdots - a_p L^p)$. The lag operator L is a linear operator (i.e., for any value y_t it holds $L^i y_t = y_{t-i}$). For lag operators, the distributive law and the associative law of multiplication holds.

Replacing in polynomial $a(L)$ lag operator L by variable λ and setting it equal to zero, we obtain the *reverse characteristic equation* associated with the difference equation (6.1):

$$a(\lambda) = 0 \qquad (6.4)$$

Any value of λ which satisfies the reverse characteristic equation (6.4) is called a root of polynomial $a(\lambda)$. A polynomial of degree p has p roots λ_k, $k = 1,\ldots,p$. In general, roots are complex numbers:

$$\lambda_k = a_k \pm b_k i$$

with a_k and b_k being real numbers, and $i = \sqrt{-1}$. Complex roots come in the form of conjugate pairs (a_i, b_i) and for any such pair, a solution to the homogeneous equation is $c_1(a_1 + ib_1) + c_2(a_1 - ib_1)$, where c_1 and c_2 are arbitrary constants.

The roots of the polynomial associated with difference-equation representation of time series turn out to be important determinants of the behavior of the time series.

Solving a Difference Equation

Expression (6.4) represents the so-called *coefficient form* of a reverse characteristic equation, which is for a polynomial of degree p

$$1 - a_1\lambda - \ldots - a_p\lambda^p = 0$$

An alternative is the *root form* given by

$$(\lambda_1 - \lambda)(\lambda_2 - \lambda) \cdots (\lambda_p - \lambda) = \prod_{i=1}^{p} (\lambda_i - \lambda) = 0$$

The latter form reveals the roots directly, that is, the values of λ, for which the reverse characteristic equation is satisfied.

For example, consider a *difference equation*

$$y_t = \frac{3}{2}y_{t-1} - \frac{1}{2}y_{t-2} + \varepsilon_t$$

The reverse characteristic equation in coefficient form is given by

$$1 - \frac{3}{2}\lambda + \frac{1}{2}\lambda^2 = 0$$

or

$$2 - 3\lambda + 1\lambda^2 = 0$$

that can be written in *root form* as

$$(1 - \lambda)(2 - \lambda) = 0$$

Here, $\lambda_1 = 1$ and $\lambda_2 = 2$ represent the set of possible solutions for λ satisfying the reverse characteristic equation

$$1 - \frac{3}{2}\lambda + \frac{1}{2}\lambda^2 = 0$$

Consider a homogeneous difference equation

$$y_t - a_1 y_{t-1} - a_2 y_{t-2} - \cdots - a_p y_{t-p} = 0 \tag{6.5}$$

where

$$a(\lambda) = \left(1 - \frac{\lambda}{\lambda_1}\right)\left(1 - \frac{\lambda}{\lambda_2}\right)\cdots\left(1 - \frac{\lambda}{\lambda_p}\right)$$

and where we assume that $\lambda_1, \lambda_2. \ldots, \lambda_p$ are distinct. Then the general solution of (6.5) at time t, when referring to an origin at time t_0, is given by

$$y_t = \alpha_1 \frac{1}{\lambda_1^{t-t_0}} + \alpha_2 \frac{1}{\lambda_2^{t-t_0}} + \cdots + \alpha_p \frac{1}{\lambda_p^{t-t_0}} \tag{6.6}$$

where α_i, $i = 1, \ldots, p$, are constants.

To see that (6.6) does satisfy (6.5), we can substitute (6.6) in (6.5) to obtain

$$a(\lambda)\left(\alpha_1 \frac{1}{\lambda_1^{t-t_0}} + \alpha_2 \frac{1}{\lambda_2^{t-t_0}} + \cdots + \alpha_p \frac{1}{\lambda_p^{t-t_0}}\right) = 0 \tag{6.7}$$

Now we consider

$$a(\lambda)\frac{1}{\lambda_i^{t-t_0}} = (1 - a_1\lambda - a_2\lambda^2 - \cdots - a_p\lambda^p)\frac{1}{\lambda_i^{t-t_0}}$$

$$= \frac{1}{\lambda_i^{t-t_0-p}}\left(\frac{1}{\lambda_i^p} - a_1\frac{1}{\lambda_i^{p-1}} - \cdots - a_p\right)$$

We observe that

$$a(\lambda)\frac{1}{\lambda_i^{t-t_0}}$$

disappears for each value of i if

$$\frac{1}{\lambda_i^p} - a_1\frac{1}{\lambda_i^{p-1}} - \cdots - a_p = 0$$

that is, if

$$\lambda = \frac{1}{\lambda_i}$$

is the root of $a(\lambda) = 0$. Since

$$a(\lambda) = \left(1 - \frac{\lambda}{\lambda_1}\right)\left(1 - \frac{\lambda}{\lambda_2}\right)\cdots\left(1 - \frac{\lambda}{\lambda_p}\right)$$

implies that the roots of $a(\lambda) = 0$ are

$$\lambda = \frac{1}{\lambda_i}$$

it follows that

$$a(\lambda)\frac{1}{\lambda_i^{t-t_0}}$$

is zero for all i and thus (6.7) holds, confirming that (6.6) is a general solution of (6.5).

If we have only $r < p$ distinct roots and each root has multiplicity p_i (i.e., the root is repeated p_i times), where

$$\sum_{j=1}^{r} p_i = p$$

then it can be demonstrated that

$$y_t = \frac{1}{\lambda_1^{t-t_0}} \sum_{j=0}^{p_1-1} \alpha_{1j}(t-t_0)^j + \cdots + \frac{1}{\lambda_r^{t-t_0}} \sum_{j=0}^{p_r-1} \alpha_{rj}(t-t_0)^j$$

where α_{ij} are constants.[2] Note that roots are generally complex numbers.

TERMINOLOGY AND DEFINITIONS

Autoregressive (AR) and *moving average* (MA) models are widely used linear time series models. In this section, we introduce the notion of the white noise process as the building block of the AR and MA processes, following with description of the AR and MA processes. Finally, we introduce the ARMA models.

White-Noise Process and Martingale Difference
The sequence of random variables $X_1, X_2, \ldots$ is called IID noise if the observations of the time series are independent and identically distributed (IID) random variables with zero mean. This implies that time series contain no trend or seasonal components and that there is no dependence between observations.

We assume that ε_t, $t = \pm 0, \pm 1, \pm 2, \ldots$, is a zero-mean, IID sequence $\{\varepsilon_t\}$ with

$$E(\varepsilon_t) = 0, \quad E(\varepsilon_s \varepsilon_t) = \begin{cases} \sigma^2, & \text{if } s = t \\ 0, & \text{if } s \neq t \end{cases}$$

---

[2] George E. P. Box, Gwilym M. Jenkins, and Gregory C. Reinsel, *Time Series Analysis Forecasting and Control*, 3rd ed. (Englewood Cliffs, NJ: Prentice Hall, 1994).

for all t and s. Sequence $\{\varepsilon_t\}$ is called a purely random process, *IID noise* or simply *strict white noise* and we write $\varepsilon_t \sim \text{IID}(0, \sigma^2)$. If we require the sequence $\{\varepsilon_t\}$ only to be uncorrelated and not necessarily independent, then $\{\varepsilon_t\}$ is sometimes known as a *uncorrelated white noise process* or *white noise*. In this case, we write $\varepsilon_t \sim \text{WN}(0, \sigma^2)$. Every $\text{IID}(0, \sigma^2)$ sequence is $\text{WN}(0, \sigma^2)$ but the converse does not hold. If successive values follow a normal (Gaussian) distribution, then zero correlation implies independence so that Gaussian white noise is a strict white noise and we denote it

$$\varepsilon_t \sim \text{IID}\,N(0, \sigma^2) \quad \text{or} \quad \varepsilon_t \overset{\text{IID}}{\sim} N(0, \sigma^2)$$

However, when successive values deviate from normal distribution, zero correlation need not imply independence and white noise and strict white noise do not coincide.

An additional useful concept is the *martingale* difference. A series of random variables, $\{X_t\}$, with finite first absolute moment, is called a *martingale* if

$$E_t(X_{t+1}|\Im_t) = X_t$$

where $\Im_t = \{X_t, X_{t-1}, \dots\}$ is the information set available to time t including X_t.[3] If we define $\{Y_t\}$ as the first differences of a martingale, $Y_t = X_t - X_{t-1}$, then a series $\{Y_t\}$ is called a *martingale difference*. A martingale process implies that Y_t is a "fair game" (i.e., a game which is in favor of neither opponents), so that

$$E_t(X_{t+1} - X_t|\Im_t) = 0$$

X_t is a martingale if and only if $(X_t - X_{t-1})$ is a fair game.[4]

If X_t represents an asset's price at date t, then the martingale process implies that tomorrow's price is expected to be equal to today's price, given the information set containing price history of an asset. Also, the martingale difference process says that conditional on the asset's price history, the asset's expected price changes (e.g., changes in prices adjusted for dividends) are zero. In this sense, information $\Im_t$ contained in past prices is instantly and fully reflected in the asset's current price and hence useless in predicting rates of return. The hypothesis that

---

[3] As explained in Chapter 2, in more rigorous terms we condition with respect to a σ-algebra. Informally, we condition with respect to an information set formed by the past values of all relevant variables.

[4] Due to this reason, fair games are sometimes called martingale differences.

prices fully reflect available information is widely known in finance as the "efficient market hypothesis." Broadly speaking, in an efficient market,[5] trading on the information contained in the prior asset's prices will not generate profit.

A martingale difference[6] is similar to uncorrelated white noise except that it need not have constant variance and that its conditional mean is zero. A martingale difference with the conditional mean equal to zero and a constant variance (i.e., $E(X_t|X_s, s < t) = 0$, $\text{Var}(X_t) = \sigma^2$, for all t) is called a *homoskedastic martingale difference*. Here we have assumed that the original process and the difference process generate the same information set, which is often the case. A martingale difference with the conditional mean equal to zero and a nonconstant variance (i.e., $E(X_t|X_s, s < t) = 0$, $\text{Var}(X_t|X_s, s < t) = \sigma^2$) is called a *conditional white noise*. In the case that successive values follow a normal (Gaussian) distribution, a martingale difference with constant variance is a strict white noise.

Uncorrelated white noise and martingale differences have constant mean and zero autocorrelations. Note that definitions do not specify the nonlinear properties of such sequences. Specifically, although $\{X_t\}$ may be uncorrelated white noise or a martingale difference, the series of squared observations $\{X_t^2\}$ need not be. Only if $\{X_t\}$ is a strict white noise then $\{X_t^2\}$ will be uncorrelated white noise.

Consideration of time-series models for white noise and martingale processes that differ in certain characteristics allow treatment of different levels of dependence between subsequent observations and play a role in describing the dynamics of a financial series or checking the validity of fitted models by inspecting the residuals from the model. To

---

[5] Fama defines three types of capital market efficiency with regards to definition of what is the relevant information set: *weak-form* market efficiency if information set includes past prices and returns alone, *semistrong-form* efficiency if information set includes all public information, and *strong-form* efficiency if information set includes any public as well as private information. Strong-form efficiency implies semistrong-form efficiency, which in turn implies weak-form efficiency, but the reverse implications do not follow. (Eugene F. Fama, "Efficient Capital Markets: A Review of Theory and Empirical Work," *Journal of Finance* 25 (1970), pp. 383–417.)

[6] The martingale process is a special case of the more general submartingale process. Specifically, X_t is a "submartingale" if it has the property that $E_t(X_{t+1}|\Im_t) \geq X_t$. In terms of the $(X_{t+1} - X_t)$ process, the submartingale model implies that $E_t(X_{t+1} - X_t|\Im_t) \geq 0$. For further details on the submartingale model and associated concept of a superfair game, see for example, William A. Barnett and Apostolos Serletis, "Martingales, Nonlinearity, and Chaos," *Journal of Economic Dynamics and Control* 24 (2000), pp. 703–724.

summarize the relations between white noise and martingale processes, we sketch here how they relate to each other:

- Uncorrelated white noise → Homoskedastic martingale difference
- Gaussian white noise → Strict white noise → Conditional white noise

where → stands for implication.

Autoregressive Processes

An *autoregressive process* (AR) of order p, or briefly an AR(p) process, is a process where realization y_t is a weighted sum of past p realizations, i.e., $y_{t-1}, y_{t-2}, ..., y_{t-p}$, plus a disturbance term, denoted by ε_t. The process can be represented by the p-th order difference equation

$$y_t = a_1 y_{t-1} + a_2 y_{t-2} + ... + a_p y_{t-p} + \varepsilon_t \tag{6.8}$$

where $\varepsilon_t \sim WN(0, \sigma^2)$. Using the lag operator L, the AR(p) process (6.8) can be expressed as

$$(1 - a_1 L - a_2 L^2 - ... - a_p L^p) y_t = \varepsilon_t$$

or, more compactly,

$$a(L) y_t = \varepsilon_t \tag{6.9}$$

where the autoregressive polynomial $a(L)$ is defined by $a(L) = 1 - a_1 L - a_2 L^2 - ... - a_p L^p$.

Moving Average Processes

A *moving average* (MA) *process* of order q, in short, an MA(q) process, is the weighted sum of the preceding q lagged disturbances plus a contemporaneous disturbance term, i.e.,

$$y_t = b_0 \varepsilon_t + b_1 \varepsilon_{t-1} + ... + b_q \varepsilon_{t-q} \tag{6.10}$$

or

$$y_t = b(L) \varepsilon_t \tag{6.11}$$

where $\varepsilon_t \sim WN(0, \sigma^2)$, $b_0, ..., b_q$ are constants and $b(L) = b_0 + b_1 L + b_2 L^2 + ... + b_q L^q$ denotes a moving average polynomial of degree q with $b_0 \neq 0$.

Usually, if not mentioned otherwise, and without loss of generality, we assume that $b_0 = 1$. Also we assume that $b_q \neq 0$. Otherwise, we would deal with an MA($q - 1$) process.

By allowing $b_0 \neq 1$, we can in fact restrict the noise variance to be unity, because

$$y_t = b_0\varepsilon_t + b_1\varepsilon_{t-1} + \ldots + b_q\varepsilon_{t-q}, \quad \text{Var}(\varepsilon_t) = \sigma^2$$

can be rewritten in terms of standardized errors, $u_t = \varepsilon_t/\sigma$:

$$y_t = \sigma u_t + b_1\sigma u_{t-1} + \ldots + b_q\sigma u_{t-q}, \quad \text{Var}(u_t) = 1$$

Thus either restriction $b_0 = 1$ or restriction $\text{Var}(\varepsilon_t) = \sigma^2 = 1$ should be imposed. Otherwise parameters b_0 and σ^2 will not be identified when estimating autoregressive moving average models.

Autoregressive Moving Average Processes

The AR and MA processes just discussed can be regarded as special cases of a mixed *autoregressive moving average* (ARMA) *process*, in short, an ARMA(p,q) process, given by

$$y_t = a_1 y_{t-1} + a_2 y_{t-2} + \ldots + a_p y_{t-p} + \varepsilon_t + b_1\varepsilon_{t-1} + \ldots + b_q\varepsilon_{t-q} \quad (6.12)$$

or

$$a(L)y_t = b(L)\varepsilon_t \quad (6.13)$$

Clearly, ARMA(p, 0) and ARMA(0, q) processes correspond to pure AR(p) and MA(q) processes, respectively.

The advantage of ARMA process relative to AR and MA processes is that it gives rise to a more parsimonious model with relatively few unknown parameters. Instead of capturing the complex structure of time series with a relatively high-order AR or MA model, the ARMA model which combines the AR and MA presentation forms can be used.

ARMA Processes with Exogenous Variables

ARMA processes that also include current and/or lagged, exogenously determined variables are called *ARMA processes with exogeneous variables* and denoted by *ARMAX processes*. Denoting the exogenous variable by x_t, an ARMAX process has the form

$$a(L)y_t = b(L)\varepsilon_t + g(L)x_t \quad (6.14)$$

The degree of polynomial $g(L) = g_0 + g_1L + \ldots + g_nL^n$ specifies the extent to which past values of the exogenous variable, x_t, affect the endogenous variable, y_t. If more than one exogenous variable, say the r variables $x_{1,t}, x_{2,t}, \ldots, x_{r,t}$, affect y_t, then (6.14) can be generalized to

$$a(L)y_t = b(L)\varepsilon_t + \sum_{i=1}^{r} g_i(L)x_{i,t}$$

where $g_i(L)$ is the lag polynomial of degree n_i that is associated with variable $x_{i,t}$.

ARMA Processes with Deterministic Components

The processes presented so far can be generalized by introducing additional deterministic components, that is, components that are not random variables. Adding, for example, the constant term c to ARMA process (6.13) we obtain

$$a(L)y_t = c + b(L)\varepsilon_t \tag{6.15}$$

If the ARMA process y_t has mean $\mu = E(y_t)$ for all t, it can be transformed into a zero-mean process by *centering* (or *de-meaning*); that is, by defining the centered process $\tilde{y}_t = y_t - \mu$. Then, we have

$$a(L)\tilde{y}_t = b(L)\varepsilon_t \tag{6.16}$$

which is a zero-mean process. To see this, note that

$$E(y_t) = c + E\left(\sum_{i=1}^{p} a_i y_{t-i}\right) + E\left(\sum_{j=0}^{q} b_j \varepsilon_{t-j}\right)$$

with $E(y_{t-i}) = \mu$ and $E(\varepsilon_{t-j}) = 0$, which implies

$$\mu = c + \sum_{i=1}^{p} a_i \mu$$

or

$$\mu = \frac{c}{1 - \sum\limits_{i=1}^{p} a_i} \qquad (6.17)$$

Alternatively, writing

$$a(L)(y_t - \mu) = b(L)\varepsilon_t$$

it follows that

$$a(L)y_t = a(L)\mu + b(L)\varepsilon_t$$

and because $L\mu = \mu$,

$$a(L)\mu = \left(1 - \sum_{i=1}^{p} a_i\right)\mu$$

and from (6.17), we obtain $a(L)\mu = c$.

In addition to having a constant term, there could be a deterministic (linear or polynomial) time trend present. For example, with an additional linear trend component, (6.15) becomes

$$a(L)y_t = c_0 + c_1 t + b(L)\varepsilon_t$$

Under suitable conditions we could remove such more general deterministic trends from the process, and we typically neglect them in theoretical discussions of the ARMA process. However, in practice we generally include a constant term when estimating ARMA models.

Integrated ARMA Processes

Very often we observe that the mean and/or variance of economic time series, y_t, change over time. In this case, we say the series are nonstationary—a concept that will be more formally defined and discussed later. Generally, a nonstationary time series may exhibit a systematic change in mean, variance or both. However, the series of the *changes* from one period to the next, that is, the differenced series Δy_t, may have a mean and variance that do not change over time. In this case, it will be more convenient to model the differenced series, Δy_t, rather than the original level series. It is conceivable that higher-order differencing ($\Delta^d y_t$) may be necessary to obtain a constant mean and variance.

An ARMA process is called an *autoregressive integrated moving average* (ARIMA) *process*, with order of differencing *d*, or an ARIMA(*p*, *d*, *q*) process, if it has the following form

$$a(L)\Delta^d y_t = b(L)\varepsilon_t \tag{6.18}$$

with $\Delta^0 = 1$.

Defining $z_t = \Delta^d y_t$ we deal, in terms of z_t, with a standard ARMA model, namely $a(L)z_t = b(L)\varepsilon_t$. The original level data y_t are recovered from the differenced series by appropriate summation ("integration"):

$$\Delta^{d-1} y_t = \Delta^{d-1} y_0 + \sum_{i=0}^{t-1} \Delta^d y_{t-1}, \quad d = 1, 2, \ldots$$

Standard analysis of financial time series considers the case when the order of differencing, *d*, has an integer value, and is either 0 or 1. However, we can also consider *d* to be a noninteger in which case we say that y_t is said to be fractionally integrated. The properties and implications of this type of processes will be introduced later, after we tackle and explore the concepts of stationarity and linear processes.

STATIONARITY AND INVERTIBILITY OF ARMA PROCESSES

In simple terms, stationarity describes a property of the process to achieve a certain state of statistical equilibrium so that the distribution of the process does not change much. Stationarity thus guarantees that that the essential properties of a time series remain constant over time. Features that do not vary over time can be captured to systematically model time series. Depending on whether we focus on all characteristics or only some particular ones, we distinguish different types of stationarity. Time series

$$\{y_t\}_{t=-\infty}^{\infty}$$

is called *strictly stationary* if the joint distribution of any stretch $y_t, y_{t-1}, \ldots, y_{t-k}$ does not vary over time, with *k* being a finite positive integer. More formally, strict stationarity requires that

$$F_{y_t, y_{t-1}, \ldots, y_{t-k}}(x_0, x_1, \ldots, x_k) = F_{y_{t-\tau}, y_{t-\tau-1}, \ldots, y_{t-\tau-k}}(x_0, x_1, \ldots, x_k)$$

holds for all τ and all k, where $F_{y_t, y_{t-1}, \ldots, y_{t-k}}(x_0, x_1, \ldots, x_k)$ denotes a $(k + 1)$-dimensional joint cumulative distribution function.

Some of the elementary implications of strictly stationary time series are[7]

1. The random variables y_t are identically distributed,
2. $(y_t, y_{t+h})' \stackrel{d}{=} (y_1, y_{1+h})'$ for all integers t and h.[8]

An IID sequence is an example of a strictly stationary process.

Strict stationarity is often too restrictive since it requires that the time series is completely invariant over time—that is, all moments are constant over time. A less restrictive and in many applications sufficient concept of stationarity is that of *weak stationarity*. Weak stationarity focuses solely on the first and second moments of a time series. Time series $\{y_t\}_{t=-\infty}^{\infty}$ is said to be weakly stationary if for all t and $t - k$

1. The mean of y_t is constant over time:

$$E(y_t) = E(y_{t-k}) = \mu, \text{ with } |\mu| < \infty$$

2. The variance of y_t is constant over time:

$$\text{Var}(y_t) = E[(y_t - \mu)^2] = \text{Var}(y_{t-k}) = \sigma_y^2 < \infty$$

3. The covariance of y_t and y_{t-k} does not vary over time, but may depend on the lag k:

$$\text{Cov}(y_t, y_{t-k}) = E[(y_t - \mu)(y_{t-k} - \mu)]$$
$$= \text{Cov}(y_{t-j}, y_{t-j-k}) = \gamma_k, \text{ with } |\gamma_k| < \infty$$

μ, σ_y^2, and all γ_k are constants and finite. For $k = 0$, γ_0 is equivalent to the variance of y_t. In other words, a time series is weakly stationary if its mean and all autocovariances are not affected by a change of time origin. An implication of the above definitions of the stationarity is that the strict stationarity implies weak stationarity provided first and second moments exist. Generally, the opposite is not true except in the case of a normal distribution. Throughout this chapter, unless stated otherwise, we will rely on the concept of weak stationarity which we mean whenever relating to "stationarity."

---

[7] See Peter J. Brockwell and Richard A. Davis, *Introduction to Time Series and Forecasting*, 2nd ed. (New York: Springer, 2002).

[8] The symbol $\stackrel{d}{=}$ denotes equality in distribution.

Let $\{y_t\}$ be a stationary process. We introduce the following concepts

1. $\gamma(k) = \text{Cov}(y_t, y_{t-k})$ is called the autocovariance function.
2. $\rho(k) = \gamma(k)/\gamma(0)$, $k = 0, 1, 2, \ldots$, is called the autocorrelation function.

For a weakly stationary series, γ_0 and γ_k are time independent. A consequence is that the autocorrelation coefficients, $\rho(k)$, are also time-independent. For stationary processes, both functions $\gamma(\cdot)$ and $\rho(\cdot)$ should decay to zero quite rapidly. This can be an indication of the so called *short-term memory* behavior of the time series. This property will be explained later in this chapter. The autocovariance and autocorrelation functions are important for characterization and classification of time series and later in the chapter we will discuss how to use them to model time series as an ARMA process.

Consider the AR(p) process

$$a(L)y_t = \varepsilon_t$$

with $\text{E}(\varepsilon_t) = 0$ and $\text{Var}(\varepsilon_t) = \sigma^2 < \infty$. This process is called stable if the absolute values (or magnitude) of all the roots, λ_i, $i = 1, \ldots, p$, of the reverse characteristic equation $a(\lambda) = 0$ are greater than one.[9] Note that the absolute value of a complex root, $\lambda_k = a_k + b_k i$, is computed by

$$|\lambda_k| = \sqrt{a_k^2 + b_k^2}$$

It can be demonstrated that a stable process is weakly stationary. The converse, however, is not true: a stationary process need not be stable. Conceptually, stability and stationarity are different properties. However, in practice, stability conditions are often referred to as stationarity conditions. Often we are given the coefficients and not the roots of the AR polynomial. It becomes infeasible to express the stationarity conditions of higher-order AR polynomials in terms of the AR coefficients. It is convenient to use the so-called Schur criterion, to determine stationarity in terms of the AR coefficients.[10] For the AR polynomial $a(L) = 1 - a_1 L - a_2 L^2 - \ldots - a_p L^p$, the Schur criterion requires the construction of two lower-triangu-

---

[9] This concept of stable processes should not be confused with the concept of stable Paretian or Lévy-stable processes. As explained in Chapter 14, Lévy-stable processes are processes such that all finite distributions are Lévy-stable distributions.

[10] The Schur theorem gives the necessary and sufficient conditions for stability. See, for example, Chapter 1 in Walter Enders, *Applied Econometric Time Series, 1st Edition* (New York: John Wiley & Sons, 1995).

lar Toeplitz matrices, A_1 and A_2, whose first columns consists of the vectors $(1, -a_1, -a_2, ..., -a_{p-1})'$ and $(-a_p, -a_{p-1}, ..., -a_1)'$, respectively. That is,

$$
A_1 = \begin{bmatrix}
1 & 0 & \cdots & 0 & 0 \\
-a_1 & 1 & & & 0 \\
-a_2 & -a_1 & \ddots & & \vdots \\
\vdots & -a_2 & & & \\
& & & & 0 \\
-a_{p-1} & -a_{p-2} & \cdots & -a_1 & 1
\end{bmatrix}
$$

$$
A_2 = \begin{bmatrix}
-a_p & 0 & \cdots & 0 & 0 \\
-a_{p-1} & -a_p & & & 0 \\
-a_{p-2} & -a_{p-1} & \ddots & & \vdots \\
\vdots & -a_{p-2} & & & \\
& & & & 0 \\
-a_1 & -a_2 & \cdots & -a_{p-1} & -a_p
\end{bmatrix}
$$

Then, the AR(p) process is covariance stationary if and only if the so-called Schur matrix, defined by

$$S_a = A_1 A_1' - A_2 A_2' \tag{6.19}$$

is positive definite.

For an AR(1) process, the Schur condition for weak stationarity requires that

$$|a_1| < 1$$

and for an AR(2) process covariance stationarity requires that the AR coeffcients satisfy

$$
\begin{aligned}
|a_2| &< 1 \\
a_2 + a_1 &< 1 \\
a_2 - a_1 &< 1
\end{aligned} \tag{6.20}
$$

It turns out that the stationarity property of the mixed ARMA process

$$a(L)y_t = b(L)\varepsilon_t \tag{6.21}$$

does not depend on the MA parameters; it depends solely on the AR parameters. Therefore the stationarity results for AR processes apply directly to mixed ARMA processes. A pure MA process of finite order is always stationary, because its AR "polynomial" is equal to 1, which has no roots (i.e., no roots can be on or inside the unit circle in the complex plane).

An ARMA process is called *invertible* if the magnitude of all roots of the MA polynomial exceeds unity. Thus invertibility is the counterpart to stationarity for the MA part of the process.

If a mixed ARMA process is stationary, it has an infinite moving average, in short, an MA(∞) representation. It is obtained by dividing both sides of $a(L)y_t = b(L)\varepsilon_t$ by $a(L)$, i.e.,[11]

$$y_t = \frac{b(L)}{a(L)}\varepsilon_t = c(L)\varepsilon_t = \sum_{j=0}^{\infty} c_j \varepsilon_{t-j} \qquad (6.22)$$

where polynomial $c(L) = c_0 + c_1 L + c_2 L^2 + \ldots$, is generally, of infinite degree. The coefficients of the MA(∞) representation can be computed recursively by

$$c_0 = b_0$$
$$c_1 = b_1 + a_1 c_0$$
$$c_2 = b_1 + a_1 c_1 + a_2 c_0$$

$$c_k = \begin{cases} b_k + \sum_{i=1}^{m} a_i c_{k-i}, & \text{if } k \le q \\ \sum_{i=1}^{m} a_i c_{k-i}, & \text{if } k > q \end{cases} \qquad (6.23)$$

where $m = \max(k, p)$. This representation shows explicitly the impact of the past shocks $\varepsilon_{t-j}(j > 0)$ on the current value y_t (e.g., return y_t). We can say that the output y_t and input ε_t are linked by a linear filter (6.22) and $c(L)$ is called the *transfer function*. The linear filter (6.22) is stable if the series $c(L) = c_0 + c_1 L + c_2 L^2 + \cdots$ converges for $|L| \le 1$. The coefficients $\{c_j\}$ are also referred to as the *impulse response function* of the ARMA process. For a stationary ARMA model, the shock ε_{t-j} does not have a permanent impact on the series.

---

[11] It can be demonstrated that we can operate with lag operator polynomials as if they were algebraic polynomials. In particular, we can formally divide lag operator polynomials

Analogously, an invertible mixed ARMA process has an infinite autoregressive, in short, an AR(∞) representation, which is given by

$$\frac{a(L)}{b(L)}y_t = d(L)y_t = \varepsilon_t \quad \text{or} \quad y_t = \sum_{i=1}^{\infty} d_i y_{t-i} + \varepsilon_t \qquad (6.24)$$

This representation shows the dependence of the current value y_t (e.g., return y_t) on the past values y_{t-i}, where $i > 0$. The coefficients are referred to as the *d-weights of an ARMA model*. A stationary, invertible ARMA model effectively has three representation forms: (6.21), (6.22), and (6.24). Each of these presentations can shed a light on the model from a different perspective, leading to a better understanding of the model. For example, we can analyze the stationarity properties, estimation of parameters, and compute forecasts using different representation forms.

LINEAR PROCESSES

The linear time series models include ARMA models and are useful to analyze stationary processes. The time series

$$\{y_t\}_{t=-\infty}^{\infty}$$

is a linear process if it has the following form

$$y_t = \sum_{j=-\infty}^{\infty} c_j \varepsilon_{t-j} \qquad (6.25)$$

for all t, where $\varepsilon_t \sim \text{WN}(0, \sigma^2)$, and $\{c_j\}$ is a sequence of constants with

$$\sum_{j=-\infty}^{\infty} |c_j| < \infty \qquad (6.26)$$

The (6.25) can be written as $y_t = c(L)\varepsilon_t$, where

$$c(L) = \sum_{j=-\infty}^{\infty} c_j L^j$$

Observing expression (6.25) we can say that a linear process is called a moving average or MA(∞) if $c_j = 0$ for all $j < 0$, that is, if

$$y_t = \sum_{j=0}^{\infty} c_j \varepsilon_{t-j}$$

The condition (6.26) ensures that the infinite sum in (6.25) converges (with probability one), since $E|\varepsilon_t| \le \sigma$ and

$$E|y_t| \le \sum_{j=-\infty}^{\infty} (|c_j| E|\varepsilon_{t-j}|) \le \left(\sum_{j=-\infty}^{\infty} |c_j| \right) \sigma < \infty$$

As already noted, the operator $c(L)$ mimics the function of a linear filter, which takes the white noise series $\{\varepsilon_t\}$ as input and produces the series $\{y_t\}$ as output. A linear filter applied to any stationary input series, produces a stationary output series.[12,13]

Fractionally Integrated ARMA Processes

In the presentation of the ARIMA processes in (6.18), we only considered integer values of d. When d takes a noninteger value, y_t is said to be fractionally integrated[14] and resulting models for such values of d are referred to as FARIMA models. The fractional-difference operator $(1 - L)^d$ is formally defined by the binomial expansion

$$(1 - L)^d = \sum_{j=0}^{\infty} \pi_j L^j$$

---

[12] See Proposition 2.2.1 in Brockwell and Davis, *Introduction to Time Series and Forecasting*, 2nd ed.

[13] In practice, many financial time series exhibit behavior not shown by linear processes, so it is necessary to establish and specify more general models beyond those satisfying (6.25) with white noise. Deviation from linearity property in time series can be seen by observing the sample path. For example, financial time series can contain bursts of outlying values which cannot be reconciled with Gaussian linear processes. Especially important is the observation of the periods of low and high volatility in the time series. The type of models to describe such behavior include models for modeling changing volatility; they are explained in the Chapter 8. Some other nonlinear processes include bilinear models, autoregressive models with random coefficients, and threshold models.

[14] Clive W.J. Granger and R. Joyeux, "An Introduction to Long-Memory Time Series Models and Fractional Differences," *Journal of Time Series Analysis* 1 (1980), pp. 15–39.

where

$$\pi_j = \prod_{0 < k \le j} \frac{k - 1 - d}{k}, \quad j = 1, 2, \ldots$$

Thus FARIMA processes are more specifically ARIMA(p, d, q) processes with $0 < |d| < 0.5$, that satisfy difference equations of the form

$$(1 - L)^d a(L) y_t = b(L) \varepsilon_t \tag{6.27}$$

where $a(L)$ and $b(L)$ are polynomials of degree p and q, respectively, satisfying,

$$a(z) \ne 0 \quad \text{and} \quad b(z) \ne 0 \quad \text{for all } z \text{ such that } |z| \le 1$$

L is the lag operator, and $\{\varepsilon_t\}$ is a white noise sequence with mean 0 and finite variance σ^2.

What are the important properties of the FARIMA processes and what distinguishes them from the ARMA processes? Compared to stationary ARMA process ($d = 0$), FARIMA processes with $d \in (-\frac{1}{2}, \frac{1}{2})$ are stationary processes with different properties of the decay of the autocorrelation function. Generally, autocorrelations from FARIMA processes with $d \in (0, \frac{1}{2})$ remain markedly positive at very high lags, long after the autocorrelations from $I(0)$ processes have declined or reached zero. Consequently, FARIMA processes with $d \in (0, \frac{1}{2})$ are said to exhibit "long memory." In contrast, the autocorrelation function of stationary ARMA processes converges to 0 rapidly, so that ARMA processes are said to have "short memory." (Formal definitions of these concepts will be given later in this chapter when we discuss short- and long-range dependence structure of the time series.) For $d \in (\frac{1}{2}, \infty)$, the variance of the process $\{y_t\}$ generated by the model (6.27) is infinite, and so the process is nonstationary.

A fractionally integrated ARIMA(p, d, q) process can be regarded as an ARMA(p, q) process driven by fractionally integrated noise. To obtain this representation, equation (6.27) can be replaced by the two equations

$$a(L) y_t = b(L) u_t \tag{6.28}$$

and

$$(1 - L)^d u_t = \varepsilon_t \tag{6.29}$$

The process $\{u_t\}$ is called *fractionally integrated noise* and has variance and autocorrelations given by

$$\gamma_u(0) = \sigma^2 \frac{\Gamma(1-2d)}{\Gamma^2(1-d)} \tag{6.30}$$

and

$$\rho_u(h) = \sigma^2 \frac{\Gamma(h+d)\Gamma(1-d)}{\Gamma(h-d+1)\Gamma(d)} = \prod_{0 < k \le h} \frac{k-1+d}{k-d}, \quad h = 1, 2, \ldots \tag{6.31}$$

respectively, where $\Gamma(\cdot)$ is the gamma function.[15]

The exact autocovariance function of the ARIMA(p, d, q) process $\{y_t\}$ defined by the (6.30) can be expressed as

$$\gamma_y(h) = \sum_{j=0}^{\infty} \sum_{k=0}^{\infty} \psi_j \psi_k \gamma_u(h+j-k) \tag{6.32}$$

where

$$\sum_{i=0}^{\infty} \psi_i z^i = \frac{b(z)}{a(z)}, \quad |z| \le 1$$

and $\gamma_u(\cdot)$ is the autocovariance function of fractionally integrated white noise with parameters d and σ^2, such that

$$\gamma_u(h) = \gamma_u(0)\rho_u(h)$$

with $\gamma_u(0)$ and $\rho_u(h)$ as in (6.30) and (6.31). The series (6.32) converges rapidly as long as $a(z)$ does not have zeros with absolute values close to 1.

---

[15] Γ is the gamma function defined as

$$\Gamma(\alpha) = \int_0^{\infty} x^{\alpha-1} e^{-x} dx$$

where α is positive. When α is a positive integer then $\Gamma(\alpha) = (\alpha-1)!$ with 0! defined to be 1.

IDENTIFICATION TOOLS

To identify the appropriate time series model, the unknown parameters and the unknown orders p and q of the ARMA(p, q) model need to be specified or identified and then estimated. The orders of the model can be specified by inspecting the sample autocorrelation and partial auto-correlation function and comparing them with theoretical values. These parameters can be then estimated using several statistical procedures.

Autocovariance and Autocorrelation Function

The infinite sequence of the autocovariances

$$\gamma_k = \text{Cov}(y_t, y_{t-k}), \quad k = 0, 1, \dots \tag{6.33}$$

is called the *autocovariance function* (AcovF) for time series y_t. By scaling by the variance, $\text{Var}(y_t) = \gamma_0$, of the time series we obtain the auto-correlation function (ACF)

$$\rho_k = \text{Corr}(y_t, y_{t-k}) = \frac{\gamma_k}{\gamma_0} \tag{6.34}$$

Recall that for a weakly stationary process we have $\gamma_k = \gamma_{-k}$ and $\rho_k = \rho_{-k}$.

The first step in deriving an ARMA model from stationary time series data is the determination of the appropriate autoregressive order, p, and the moving average order, q.[16] Procedures for identifying these parameters make use of the empirically estimated *sample autocovariance function* (SACovF) or *sample autocorrelation function* (SACF). Specifically, to draw inferences about p and q from a given SACovF or SACF, it is important to first understand the relationship between the parameters of an ARMA process and the theoretical autocovariance function AcovF and theoretical *autocorrelation function* (ACF) implied by these parameters.

Let y_t be generated by the zero-mean stationary ARMA(p, q) process

$$a(L)y_t = b(L)\varepsilon_t \tag{6.35}$$

where ε_t is the usual white-noise process with $E(\varepsilon_t) = 0$ and $\text{Var}(\varepsilon_t) = \sigma^2$; and $a(L)$ and $b(L)$ are polynomials defined by $a(L) = 1 - a_1 L - a_2 L^2 - \dots - a_p L^p$

---

[16] In the case of nonstationary time series, we first perform a stationarity inducing transformation of the data, such as differencing or detrending. Not all nonstationary series can be made stationary

and $b(L) = b_0 + b_1L + b_2L^2 + \ldots + b_qL^{q17}$. From the definition of the autocovariance, $\gamma_k = \text{Cov}(y_t, y_{t-k}) = \text{E}(y_t y_{t-k})$, it follows that

$$\begin{aligned}
\gamma_k = {} & a_1\gamma_{k-1} + a_2\gamma_{k-2} + \ldots + a_p\gamma_{k-p} + \\
& + \text{E}(b_0\varepsilon_t y_{t-k} + b_1\varepsilon_{t-1}y_{t-k} + \ldots + b_q\varepsilon_{t-q}y_{t-k})
\end{aligned} \tag{6.36}$$

Replacing y_{t-k} by its moving average representation, $y_{t-k} = b(L)/a(L)\varepsilon_{t-k}$ $= c(L)\varepsilon_{t-k}$, where $c(L) = c_0 + c_1L + c_2L^2 + \ldots$, we obtain

$$E(\varepsilon_{t-i}y_{t-k}) = \begin{cases} c_{i-k}\sigma^2, & \text{if } i = k, k+1, \ldots, q \\ 0 & \text{otherwise} \end{cases}$$

Therefore,

$$\gamma_k = \begin{cases} \displaystyle\sum_{i=1}^{p} a_i\gamma_{k-i} + \sigma^2\sum_{j=k}^{q} b_j c_{j-k}, & \text{if } k = p+1, p+2, \ldots, q \\ \displaystyle\sum_{i=1}^{p} a_i\gamma_{k-i}, & \text{if } k = q+1, q+2, \ldots \end{cases} \tag{6.37}$$

where we recall that $\gamma_{-k} = \gamma_k$.

For an AR(p) process (6.37) reduces to

$$\gamma_k = a_1\gamma_{k-1} + a_2\gamma_{k-2} + \ldots + a_p\gamma_{k-p}, \quad k = 1, 2, \ldots, \tag{6.38}$$

which carries over to the ACF, namely,

$$\rho_k = a_1\rho_{k-1} + a_2\rho_{k-2} + \ldots + a_p\rho_{k-p}, \quad k = 1, 2, \ldots, \tag{6.39}$$

Thus, the ACovF (ACF) follow the same autoregressive recursions as the time series itself. Relations established by the expressions (6.38) and (6.39) are called *Yule-Walker equations*. The AR(p) process is consequently described by a gradual decay of the ACF for lags greater than p.

In the case of a pure MA process, (6.37) simplifies to

---

[17] We allow $b_0 \neq 1$.

$$\gamma_k = \begin{cases} \sigma^2 \displaystyle\sum_{j=k}^{q} b_j b_{j-k}, & \text{if } k = 0, 1, \ldots, q \\ 0, & \text{if } k > q \end{cases} \qquad (6.40)$$

since $a_i = 0$ and $c_j = b_j$. This implies that for an MA(q) process the autocovariances and autocorrelations of orders higher than q, i.e., γ_k and ρ_k respectively, with $k = q + 1, q + 2, \ldots$, are always zero. In contrast to the AR(p) process, the ACF of the MA(q) process vanishes for lags greater than q. Thus, MA(q) process has no memory beyond q periods.

More generally, for an ARMA(p,q) process, expression (6.37) implies

$$\gamma_k = a_1\gamma_{k-1} + a_2\gamma_{k-2} + \ldots + a_p\gamma_{k-p}, \quad k = q + 1, q + 2, \ldots, \qquad (6.41)$$

or

$$\rho_k = a_1\rho_{k-1} + a_2\rho_{k-2} + \ldots + a_p\rho_{k-p}, \quad k = q + 1, q + 2, \ldots, \qquad (6.42)$$

The latter recursions are sometimes called *extended Yule-Walker equations*. Relations (6.39) and (6.42) entail that the ACF of a pure AR or an ARMA process does not cut off but gradually dies out as k increases.

The stationarity and invertibility conditions of the ARMA(p, q) process will depend on those of the respective AR and MA processes forming it. Beyond a certain number of lags, that is $q - p$, the ACF displays the shape of that of an AR(p) process.

Considering the fractionally integrated series, their ACF properties are markedly different from the ACF of the standard ARMA ($d = 0$) process. While the ACF of the standard ARMA process exhibits exponential decay, the ACF of the FARIMA process for $0 < d < \frac{1}{2}$ declines at a much slower rate (i.e., hyperbolically to zero). Generally, autocorrelations from FARIMA processes remain markedly positive at very high lags, long after the autocorrelations from stationary processes have declined to (almost) zero.

Partial Autocorrelation Function

The *partial autocorrelation function* (PACF) represents another tool for identifying the properties of an ARMA process. It is particularly useful in determining the order of pure AR processes. A partial correlation coefficient adjusts the correlation between two random variables at different lags for the correlation this pair may have with the intervening lags. The ACF ρ_k, $k = 0, 1, 2, \ldots$, represents the *unconditional correla-*

tion between y_t and y_{t-k} which does not take the influence of the intervening realizations, $y_{t-1}, y_{t-2}, ..., y_{t-k+1}$, into account.

The PACF, denoted by α_k, $k = 1, 2, ...$, is the sequence of conditional correlations

$$\alpha_k = \text{Corr}(y_t, y_{t-k} \mid y_{t-1}, ..., y_{t-k+1}) \quad k = 1, 2, ..., \quad (6.43)$$

and reflects the association between y_t and y_{t-k} over and above the association of y_t and y_{t-k} caused by the association with the intervening variables $y_{t-1}, y_{t-2}, ..., y_{t-k+1}$.

To compute the PACF, let's view it as the sequence of the k-th autoregressive coefficients in a k-th order autoregression. Letting a_{kl} denote the l-th autoregressive coefficient of an AR(k) process, that is,

$$y_t = a_{k1}y_{t-1} + a_{k2}y_{t-2} + ... + a_{kk}y_{t-k} + \varepsilon_{k,t}$$

then,

$$\alpha_k = a_{kk}, \quad k = 1, 2, ...$$

The k Yule-Walker equations for the ACF,

$$\rho_l = a_{k,1}\rho_{l-1} + ... + a_{k,k-1}\rho_{l-k+1} + a_{k,k}\rho_{l-k}, \quad l = 1, 2, ..., k \quad (6.44)$$

give rise to the system of linear equations

$$
\begin{bmatrix}
1 & \rho_1 & \cdots & \rho_{k-1} \\
\rho_1 & 1 & & \rho_{k-2} \\
\rho_2 & \rho_1 & & \rho_{k-3} \\
\vdots & & \ddots & \vdots \\
\rho_{k-2} & & & \rho_1 \\
\rho_{k-1} & \rho_{k-2} & \cdots & 1
\end{bmatrix}
\begin{bmatrix}
a_{k1} \\
a_{k2} \\
a_{k3} \\
\vdots \\
a_{k,k-1} \\
a_{kk}
\end{bmatrix}
=
\begin{bmatrix}
\rho_1 \\
\rho_2 \\
\rho_3 \\
\vdots \\
\rho_{k-1} \\
\rho_k
\end{bmatrix}
$$

or, in short

$$P_k a_k = \rho_k \quad k = 1, 2, ... \quad (6.45)$$

Using Cramer's rule to successively solve (6.45) for a_{kk}, $k = 1, 2, ...$, we have

$$\alpha_{kk} = \frac{|\mathbf{P}_k^*|}{|\mathbf{P}_k|}, \quad k = 1, 2, \dots \tag{6.46}$$

where $|\cdot|$ denotes the determinant of a matrix and matrix $\mathbf{P}_k^*$ is obtained by replacing the last column of matrix $\mathbf{P}_k$ by vector $\boldsymbol{\rho}_k = (\rho_1, \rho_2, \dots, \rho_k)'$, that is,

$$\mathbf{P}_k^* = \begin{bmatrix} 1 & \rho_1 & \cdots & \rho_{k-2} & \rho_1 \\ \rho_1 & 1 & & \rho_{k-3} & \rho_2 \\ \rho_2 & \rho_1 & & \rho_{k-4} & \rho_3 \\ \vdots & & \ddots & \vdots & \vdots \\ \rho_{k-2} & & & 1 & \rho_{k-1} \\ \rho_{k-1} & \rho_{k-2} & \cdots & \rho_1 & \rho_k \end{bmatrix}$$

From the Yule-Walker equations it is evident that

$$|\mathbf{P}_k^*| = 0$$

for an AR process whose order is less than k, since the last column of matrix $\mathbf{P}_k^*$ can always be obtained from a linear combination of the first $k - 1$ (or less) columns of $\mathbf{P}_k^*$. Hence, the theoretical PACF of an AR(p) will be different from zero for the first p terms and exactly zero for higher order terms. This property allows us to identify the order of a pure AR process from its PACF. On the other hand, for MA or mixed ARMA processes the PACF will gradually die out. This property prevents us from identifying the autoregressive order of mixed processes by simply examining sample PACFs.

Estimation of ACF and PACF

Sample Autocorrelation Function
Given a sample of T observations, $y_1, y_2, \dots, y_T$, the estimated or sample autocorrelation function (SACF) as an estimator of the ACF, denoted by $\hat{\rho}_k$, $k = 1, 2, \dots$, is computed by

$$\hat{\rho}_k = \frac{\displaystyle\sum_{i=k+1}^{T} (y_i - \hat{\mu})(y_{i-k} - \hat{\mu})}{\displaystyle\sum_{i=1}^{T} (y_i - \hat{\mu})^2} \tag{6.47}$$

where $\hat{\mu}$ is the sample mean given by

$$\hat{\mu} = \frac{1}{T}\sum_{i=1}^{T} y_i \qquad (6.48)$$

It should be noted that (6.47) assumes that the elements of the sample autocovariance function (SACovF) are estimated by

$$\hat{\gamma}_k = \frac{1}{T}\sum_{i=k+1}^{T} (y_i - \hat{\mu})(y_{i-k} - \hat{\mu}), \quad k = 0, 1, \ldots, \qquad (6.49)$$

rather than by

$$\hat{\gamma}_k = \frac{1}{T-k}\sum_{i=k+1}^{T} (y_i - \hat{\mu})(y_{i-k} - \hat{\mu}), \quad k = 0, 1, \ldots, \qquad (6.50)$$

although only $T - k$ and not T terms enter the summation. It turns out that (6.50) may lead to a SACovF that is not positive semidefinite—that is, it is associated with a nonstationary ARMA process. For this reason, (6.49) is commonly used although it introduces a bias. However, for large samples, i.e., large T, and reasonably small values for k the bias will be small.

As discussed above, the SACF helps to identify a suitable ARMA model. For an MA(q) process, we have established that the theoretical ACF cuts off after lag q. Thus, if the SACF exhibits such a pattern, we suspect that the data are generated by an MA(q) process. However, in practice we will not observe that the autocorrelations $\hat{\rho}_{q+i}$, $i = 1, 2, \ldots$, will be exactly zero, because they are *estimates* from given data sample and not theoretical values. It is therefore important to assess whether or not deviations from zero are statistically significant. To that purpose, we compute confidence intervals for the SACF. If, for $k > n$, the population value ρ_k is 0, Bartlett[18] showed that the sample autocorrelations $\hat{\rho}_{k+i}$, $i = 1, 2, \ldots$, are jointly normally distributed with mean zero and that the covariance between $\hat{\rho}_k$ and $\hat{\rho}_{k-s}$ can be approximated by

[18] M.S. Bartlett, "On the Theoretical Specification and Sampling Properties of Autocorrelated Time-Series," *Journal of Royal Statistical Society* B8 (1946), pp. 27–41.

$$Cov(\hat{\rho}_k, \hat{\rho}_{k-s}) = \frac{1}{T} \sum_{i=-n+s}^{T} \hat{\rho}_i \hat{\rho}_{i-s} \tag{6.51}$$

Setting, in (6.51), $s = 0$ and recalling that $\rho_0 = 1$ and $\rho_k = \rho_{-k}$, we obtain

$$Var(\hat{\rho}_k) = \frac{1}{T}\left(1 + 2\sum_{i=1}^{T} \hat{\rho}_i^2\right), \quad \text{for } k > n \tag{6.52}$$

Therefore, if $\hat{\rho}_k$ lies outside the confidence interval $\pm 1.96 \sqrt{Var(\hat{\rho}_k)}$, it is considered to be significantly different from zero at the 5% significance level. In practice, the confidence interval of $\hat{\rho}_k$ is often approximated by $\pm 2/\sqrt{T}$. This leads to tighter confidence intervals than those computed by Bartlett's formula (6.52).

A stationary series will often exhibit short-term correlation where a large value of ρ_1 is followed by a few smaller correlations which gradually decay. In an alternating series, $\hat{\rho}_k$ alternates between positive and negative values. For example, an AR(1) model with a negative coefficient, $y_t = -a_1 y_{t-1} + \varepsilon_t$, where a_1 is a positive coefficient and ε_t are IID random variables. If $\hat{\rho}_k$ does not decay for large values of k, it is an indication of nonstationarity that may be caused by many factors.

For visual inspection of the sample autocorrelation function, we typically use a *correlogram*, which is a plot of $\hat{\rho}_k$ versus k.[19]

Sample Partial Autocorrelation Function

To estimate the sample PACF (SPACF), we follow the procedure for computing the theoretical PACF described earlier, but replace theoretical autocorrelations, ρ_i, by their estimates, $\hat{\rho}_i$.

This yields, analogous to equation (6.46),

$$\hat{\alpha}_k = \hat{a}_{kk} = \frac{|\hat{P}_k^*|}{|\hat{P}_k|}, \quad k = 1, 2, \ldots \tag{6.53}$$

where

---

[19] By definition, $\rho_0 = 1$.

$$
\hat{\mathbf{P}}_k = \begin{bmatrix}
1 & \hat{\rho}_1 & \cdots & \hat{\rho}_{k-1} \\
\hat{\rho}_1 & 1 & & \hat{\rho}_{k-2} \\
\hat{\rho}_2 & \hat{\rho}_1 & & \hat{\rho}_{k-3} \\
\vdots & & & \vdots \\
\hat{\rho}_{k-2} & & & \hat{\rho}_1 \\
\hat{\rho}_{k-1} & \hat{\rho}_{k-2} & \cdots & 1
\end{bmatrix}
$$

and

$$
\hat{\mathbf{P}}_k^* = \left[\begin{array}{cccc|c}
1 & \hat{\rho}_1 & \cdots & \hat{\rho}_{k-2} & \hat{\rho}_1 \\
\hat{\rho}_1 & 1 & & \hat{\rho}_{k-3} & \hat{\rho}_2 \\
\hat{\rho}_2 & \hat{\rho}_1 & & \hat{\rho}_{k-4} & \hat{\rho}_3 \\
\vdots & & & \vdots & \vdots \\
\hat{\rho}_{k-2} & & 1 & & \hat{\rho}_{k-1} \\
\hat{\rho}_{k-1} & \hat{\rho}_{k-2} & \cdots & \hat{\rho}_1 & \hat{\rho}_k
\end{array}\right]
$$

A computationally more efficient procedure for estimating the SPACF is the following recursion for $k = 1, 2, \ldots$[20]

$$
\hat{a}_{kk} = \frac{\hat{\rho}_k - \sum_{l=1}^{k-1} \hat{\alpha}_{k-1,l}\hat{\rho}_{k-l}}{1 - \sum_{l=1}^{k-1} \hat{a}_{k-1,l}\hat{\rho}_k}
\tag{6.54}
$$

$$
\hat{a}_{kl} = \hat{a}_{k-1,l} - \hat{a}_{kk}\hat{a}_{k-1,k-l}, \quad l = 1, 2, \ldots, k
\tag{6.55}
$$

with $\hat{a}_{ij} = 0$, for $i, j < 1$.

For large samples and values of k sufficiently large, the PACF is approximately normally distributed with variance[21]

---

[20] The comma is placed between the subscripts of the partial autocorrelations whenever it may not be clear where the first subscripts ends.

[21] See M.H. Quenouille, "Approximate Tests of Correlation in Time Series," *Journal of Royal Statistical Society,* B11 (1949), pp. 68–84.

$$Var(\hat{a}_k) \approx \frac{1}{T} \tag{6.56}$$

Thus, the 95% confidence interval can be approximated by $\pm 2/\sqrt{T}$.

Illustration: Analysis of the DAX Stock Index Return Series

We illustrate the concepts discussed thus far in this chapter by analyzing the return series for the German stock index Deutscher Aktienindex (DAX). Exhibit 6.1 shows the daily closing values of the DAX for the period 01/1965–12/2005. Exhibit 6.2 reports the SACF and SPACF (up to lag $k = 20$) of the index price (level) series. It is evident from the column in Exhibit 6.2 that the series is very persistent, with the autocorrelation function dying away very slowly. The first partial autocorrelation function coefficient appears to be significant. Thus the slow decay of the ACF for the DAX price series is evident.

Exhibit 6.3 shows the time plot of daily returns of the DAX index from January 1, 1965 to December 30, 2005. The mean of this series is 2.27E-04 and standard deviation 0.0116. The correlogram, the plot of sample ACF is

EXHIBIT 6.1 DAX Daily Price Series from January 1, 1965 to December 31, 2005

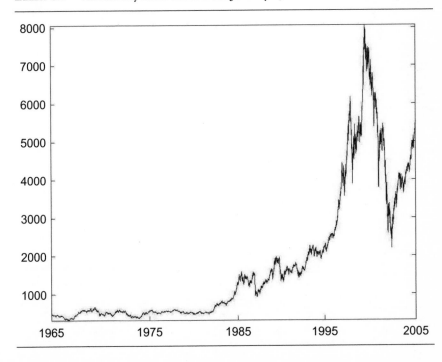

EXHIBIT 6.2   Sample Autocorrelation Function and Partial Autocorrelation Function of the DAX Index Price Series Data from January 1, 1965 to December 31, 2005

Period k	SACF	SPACF
1	0.9996	1.0000
2	0.9991	−0.0013
3	0.9987	0.0144
4	0.9982	0.0294
5	0.9978	−0.0355
6	0.9974	0.0030
7	0.9969	0.0523
8	0.9965	0.0122
9	0.9961	−0.0308
10	0.9957	0.0049
11	0.9953	0.0012
12	0.9949	−0.0065
13	0.9945	0.0136
14	0.9941	0.0063
15	0.9936	−0.0591
16	0.9932	−0.0378
17	0.9927	−0.0005
18	0.9923	0.0254
19	0.9919	0.0061
20	0.9915	0.0261

Notes: k denotes the number of lags

shown in Exhibit 6.4. Exhibit 6.5 reports the SACF and SPACF (up to lag k = 20) of the index price return.

Recall from (6.52) that if the autocorrelation coefficient $\hat{\rho}_k$ lies outside the confidence interval $\pm 1.96\sqrt{T}$, where T is the number of observations, it is considered to be significantly different from zero at the 5% significance level. From (6.56), the same applies to the partial autocorrelation coefficient. In the DAX case presented here, the significant value for the autocorrelation coefficient for 10,654 observations is 0.019. The DAX return series has seven significant autocorrelations (at lags 1, 2, 4, 6, 8, 11, and 14) and eight significant partial autocorrelations (at the same lags as the autocorrelation function and at lag 20) for the first 20 lags. In the first 20 values of the autocorrelation coefficients we can expect one significant value on average if the data are really random.

EXHIBIT 6.3 Time Series Plot of the Daily Log DAX Index Returns from January 1, 1965 to December 31, 2005

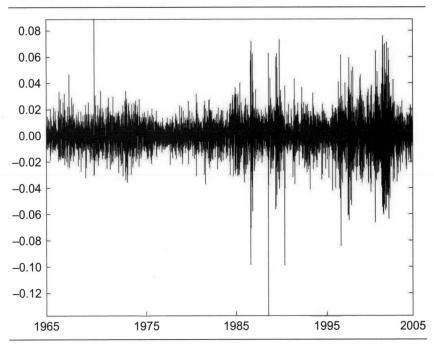

The results for the autocorrelations suggest that the DAX return series is not random. The Ljung-Box Q-statistic (a portmanteau statistic for detecting departures from zero autocorrelations in either direction and at all lags) for returns is also computed to verify the results on the auto-correlation structure. (This statistic is described in the next chapter.) The Q-statistic rejects the null hypothesis of no autocorrelation at the 1% level for all the lags considered. The results of the autocorrelation and partial autocorrelation function suggest that the DAX return series might be modeled by some ARMA process.

Short-Range and Long-Range Dependence Structure

Time series processes can be roughly classified into two general classes based on their dependence structure: *short-range dependent* (or *short memory*) and *long-range dependent* (or *long memory*). These two classes can be distinguished by observing the behavior of the autocorrelation function $\rho(\cdot)$ of the process when the lags increase. While short-range dependence is a property of stationary processes that exhibit fast (e.g., exponential) decay of autocorrelations, long-range dependence is a

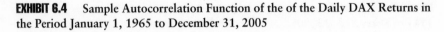

EXHIBIT 6.4 Sample Autocorrelation Function of the of the Daily DAX Returns in the Period January 1, 1965 to December 31, 2005

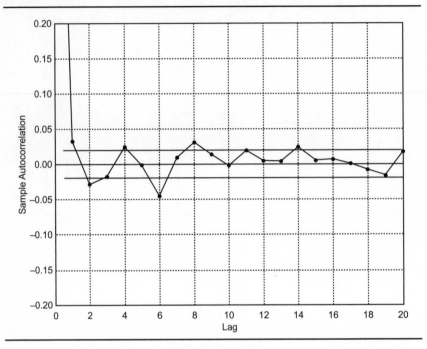

property of certain stationary stochastic processes that has been associated historically with (1) slow decay of autocorrelations and (2) certain type of scaling that is connected to self-similar processes. These properties of the long-range dependence can be traced back to work of Benoit Mandelbrot and his co-authors from the 1960s and 1970s,[22] explaining the Hurst phenomenon.[23]

In the academic literature, there is no commonly accepted definition of long-range dependence. A stationary process with autocorrelation function $\rho(k)$ is said to be a long-memory process if

---

[22] Benoit Mandelbrot and J. Van Ness, "Fractional Brownian Motions, Fractional Noises and Applications," *SIAM Review* 10 (1968), pp. 422–437.

[23] Harold Hurst noted that natural phenomena such as river discharges, rainfalls and temperatures follow a biased random walk, which is a trend with noise. The rescaled range statistics has been used to detect long-range dependence is these series and financial data. Harold E. Hurst, "Long-Term Storage Capacity of Reservoirs," *Transactions of the American Society of Civil Engineers* 116 (1968), pp. 770–808.

EXHIBIT 6.5   Sample Autocorrelation Function, Partial Autocorrelation Function, and Ljung-Box Statistics of the DAX Index Return Data from January 1, 1965 to December 31, 2005

Period k	$\hat{\rho}_k$	$\hat{\rho}_{kk}$	Q-stat.	Q-stat cv.
1	0.0324*	0.0324*	11.2018	3.8415
2	−0.0292*	−0.0302*	20.2643	5.9915
3	−0.0181	−0.0162	23.7597	7.8147
4	0.024*	0.0244*	29.9208	9.4877
5	−0.0016	−0.0042	29.9487	11.0705
6	−0.0452*	−0.044*	51.7262	12.5916
7	0.0091	0.0128	52.6036	14.0671
8	0.0305*	0.0268*	62.5458	15.5073
9	0.0134	0.0106	64.4549	16.9190
10	−0.0021	0.0011	64.5027	18.3070
11	0.019*	0.0202*	68.3733	19.6751
12	0.0042	0.0000	68.5576	21.0261
13	0.0039	0.0053	68.7222	22.3620
14	0.0242*	0.0274*	74.9640	23.6848
15	0.0048	0.003	75.2121	24.9958
16	0.0064	0.0065	75.6435	26.2962
17	0.0004	0.0021	75.6456	27.5871
18	−0.0084	−0.0095	76.3910	28.8693
19	−0.0166	−0.0168	79.3427	30.1435
20	0.0176	0.0197*	82.6447	31.4104

Note: k denotes the number of lags * indicates significance at the 5% level

$$\sum_{k=0}^{\infty} |\rho(k)|$$

does not converge. More formally, a weakly stationary process has long memory if its autocorrelation function $\rho(\cdot)$ has a hyperbolic decay $\rho(k) \sim L(k)k^{2d-1}$ as $k \to \infty$, $0 < d < 0.5$, and $L(k)$ is a slowly varying function.[24] In contrast,

---

[24] $L(x)$ is a slowly varying function as $x \to \infty$, if for every constant $c > 0$,

$$\lim_{x \to \infty} \frac{L(cx)}{L(x)}$$

exists and is equal to 1.

a short memory time series will have an autocorrelation function geometrically bounded as follows, $|\rho(k)| \le Cr^{|k|}$ for some $C > 0$, $0 < r < 1$.

Thus, the obvious way to measure the length of memory in a stochastic process is by analyzing the rate at which its correlations decay with lag. Let us first analyze the autocorrelation function $\rho(\cdot)$ of an ARMA process at lag k. Such function converges rapidly to zero as $k \to \infty$ in the sense that there exists $r > 1$ such that

$$r^k \rho(k) \to 0 \quad \text{as } k \to \infty \tag{6.57}$$

For ARMA processes, the correlations decay exponentially fast with k.

On the other hand, the autocorrelation function $\rho(k)$ at lag k of a FARIMA(p, d, q) process with $0 < |d| < 0.5$ has the property

$$\rho(k)k^{1-2d} \to c \quad \text{as } k \to \infty \tag{6.58}$$

This implies that $\rho(k)$ converges to zero as $k \to \infty$ at a much slower rate than $\rho(k)$ for an ARMA process. Thus, based on this property, FARIMA processes are said to exhibit long memory and ARMA processes are said to have short memory.

In practice, it is difficult to distinguish between a long-memory (stationary) process and a *nonstationary* process. Both models share the property that their empirical autocorrelation function will die out slowly. If the data set exhibits this property, the candidate models include FARIMA model with $0 < d < 1$ and ARIMA model with $d = 1$.

Let us now observe the implications of the absolute summability of the autocorrelations. Formally, let X_n, $n = 0, 1, 2, \ldots$ be a stationary stochastic process with mean $\mu = E(X_0)$ and $0 < \sigma^2 = \text{Var } X_0 < \infty$. Let ρ_n be the autocorrelation function. Consider the partial sum process

$$S_n = X_1 + X_2 + \ldots + X_n, \quad n \ge 1, S_0 = 0 \tag{6.59}$$

Then the variance of the process (6.59) is

$$\begin{aligned}
VarS_n &= \sum_{i=1}^{n} \sum_{j=1}^{n} \text{Cov}(X_i, X_j) = \sigma^2 \sum_{i=1}^{n} \sum_{j=1}^{n} \rho_{|i-j|} \\
&= \sigma^2 \left(n + 2 \sum_{i=1}^{n-1} (n-i)\rho_i \right)
\end{aligned} \tag{6.60}$$

For most of the "usual" stationary stochastic models including ARMA processes and many Markov processes,[25] the autocorrelations are absolutely summable

$$\sum_{n=0}^{\infty} |\rho_n| < \infty \qquad (6.61)$$

Then, observing the limiting behavior of (6.60) divided by n,

$$\lim_{n \to \infty} \frac{Var\ S_n}{n} = \sigma^2 \left(1 + 2 \sum_{i=1}^{\infty} \rho_i \right) \qquad (6.62)$$

and so the partial sums appear to grow at the rate $S_n \sim \sqrt{n}$ of the central limit theorem. In other words, if the autocorrelations are absolutely summable, this guarantees that the variance of the partial sums S_n, $n \geq 0$, cannot grow more than linearly fast, which says, that we do not expect to see S_n to be more than $\sqrt{n}$ away from its mean $n\mu$. What Mandelbrot actually realized almost three decades ago is that the behavior of the particular statistic (the so-called rescaled range, R/S, statistic) applied to the Nile River by Hurst might be explained if the variance of the partial sums could grow faster than linearly fast.[26] However, this implies that

$$\sum_{n=0}^{\infty} |\rho_n| = \infty$$

---

[25] The stochastic process $\{X_t\}$ is a Markov process if it satisfies the property that, given the value of X_t, the values of X_h, $h > t$, do not depend on the values X_s, $s < t$. In other words, $\{X_t\}$ is a Markov process if its conditional distribution function satisfies $P(X_h|X_s, s \leq t) = P(X_h|X_t, s \leq t)$, $h > t$.

[26] The R/S statistic, originally developed by Hurst, is given by

$$(R/S)_n = \frac{1}{S_n} [\max_{1 \leq k \leq n} \sum_{j=1}^{k} (x_j - \mu) - \min_{1 \leq k \leq n} \sum_{j=1}^{k} (x_j - \mu)]$$

where x_j is an observation in the sample, n is the number of the observations in the sample, and μ and S_n are the mean and the standard deviation of the sample, respectively. The range refers to the difference between the maximum and minimum (over k) of the partial sums of the first k deviations of a time series from its mean. The R/S statistic is able to detect long-range dependence in highly non-Gaussian time series exhibiting high skewness and/or kurtosis.

which is often taken as the definition of long memory.[27]

On the other hand, we can also assume that the autocorrelations are regularly varying:

$$\rho_n \sim n^{-d} L(n), \, n \to \infty, \, 0 < d < 1 \qquad (6.63)$$

with a slowly varying function L. Then we obtain[28]

$$\lim_{n \to \infty} \frac{Var \, S_n}{n^2 \rho_n} = \frac{2\sigma^2}{(1-d)(2-d)} \qquad (6.64)$$

In this case, the partial sums appear to grow at the rate $S_n \sim n^{1-d/2} \sqrt{L(n)}$, which is faster than the rate of the central limit theorem. This can be a possible explanation of the Hurst phenomenon. Based on this observation, one of the following postulations can be used as a definition of a process with long-range dependence:

■ Lack of summability of autocorrelations

$$\sum_{n=0}^{\infty} |\rho_n| = \infty$$

■ Autocorrelations are regularly varying at infinity with exponent $-1 < d \le 0$. Note that this assumption implies lack of summability of autocorrelations.

Many empirically observed time series data in hydrology, physics, computer telecommunications, and finance, although satisfying the stationarity assumption, were found to be strongly dependent over large time lags. In these cases, the classical short-range dependent models such as ARMA or ARIMA are inappropriate whereas long-range dependent models are appropriate.

---

[27] This definition seems to originate with D. Cox, "Long-Range Dependence: A Review," in H. David and H. David (eds.), *Statistics: An Appraisal* (Ames, IA: Iowa State University Press, 1984), pp. 55–74.

[28] The result is obtained by the Karamata theorem.

CONCEPTS EXPLAINED IN THIS CHAPTER
(IN ORDER OF PRESENTATION)

Difference equation
Homogeneous difference equations
Lag operator
Difference operator
Reverse characteristic equation
   Coefficient form
   Root form
Solution of a difference equation
White noise
   Strict
   Conditional
Martingale
Martingale difference
   Homoskedastic
Auroregressive (AR) process
Moving average (MA) process
Autoregressive moving average (ARMA) process
Linear filter
ARMAX process
ARMA process with deterministic components
Centering or de-meaning
Integrated processes
Stationary process
   Strictly
   Weakly
Autocovariance function (ACovF)
Autocorrelation function (ACF)
Short-term memory process
Schur criterion
Invertible process
Transfer function
Impulse response function
Linear processes
Fractionally integrated ARMA process (FARIMA)
Long memory process
Fractionally integrated noise
Model identification
Sample autocovariance function (SAcovF)
Sample autocorrelation function (SACF)

Yule-Walker equations
Partial autocorrelation function (PACF)
Bartlett's formula
Short-range dependence
Long-range dependent (LRD) models

CHAPTER 7

Approaches to ARIMA Modeling and Forecasting

The specification and estimation of the conditional mean (i.e., mean estimate given a certain history of time series observations) is essential in the analysis of a time series. This is, in a first step, typically done in form of an autoregressive (AR) or autoregressive moving average (ARMA) model described in the previous chapter. In case of nonstationarity, we consider autoregressive integrated moving average (ARIMA)(p, d, q) models given by (6.18). To do so, we difference the original level series, possibly nonstationary, until it becomes stationary and model the differenced series in the standard ARMA framework. The original level data can be recovered from the differenced series by integration.

There are two basic approaches to provide methods (procedures) for assessing the appropriateness of ARIMA models to describe a given time series. The first approach is attributed to Box and Jenkins.[1] In essence, the Box-Jenkins approach involves inspecting the computed sample autocorrelation functions (SACFs) and sample partial autocorrelation functions (SPACFs) of the time series and comparing them with the theoretical autocorrelation functions (ACFs) and partial autocorrelation functions (PACFs). Once a good match is observed, respective parameters are computed. The major advantage of this approach lies in its systematic application of steps in model building. The disadvantage is that the visual examination of SACFs and SPACFs is rather subjective.

The second approach is to select a set of possible (p, q) combinations and estimate the parameters of the corresponding ARMA(p,q)

---

[1] G. E. P. Box and G. M. Jenkins, *Time Series Analysis: Forecasting and Control,* rev. ed. (San Francisco: Holden-Day, 1976).

models accordingly. The model for which a certain selection criterion attains its minimum is chosen as an optimal one. Typical selection criteria are the Akaike information criterion (AIC) and the so-called Bayesian or the Schwartz criterion.

In this chapter, we discuss methods for model selection and estimation and, given a model, how to forecast future values of a time series.

OVERVIEW OF BOX-JENKINS PROCEDURE

Box and Jenkins presented a comprehensive set of procedures for deriving ARIMA models from time series data. Their approach has become popular in a wide range of fields and is commonly referred to as the *Box-Jenkins approach*. In contrast to conventional econometric modeling strategies, which rely on (economic) theory to specify models, the Box-Jenkins approach adopts an atheoretical or black-box modeling strategy, which relies predominantly on statistical considerations. With some experience, it often enables an analyst to construct a statistical model that approximates an observed time series.

The Box-Jenkins method consists of three steps (see Exhibit 7.1): *identification, estimation* and *diagnostic checking*.[2] The application—typically forecasting—of the derived model represents an additional step. Often, the three steps are applied repeatedly until a satisfactory model is obtained. Each of these steps serves a specific purpose:

> *Step 1.* The purpose of the *identification step* in the Box-Jenkins approach is to first determine the order of differencing, d, necessary to induce stationarity and then the autoregressive order, p, and the moving average order, q.
>
> The first step, identification, is to "guess" the degree of integration. Given d, the ARMA orders p and q for the differenced time series $\Delta^d y_t$ have to be identified.

---

[2] The names of model building stages here follow the original terminology of Box, Jenkins, and Reinsel. See G. E. P. Box, G. M. Jenkins, and G. C. Reinsel, *Time Series Analysis: Forecasting and Control*, 3rd ed. (Englewood Cliffs, NJ: Prentice-Hall, 1994). However, some researchers use different terms to denote model building stages. For example, the first stage is also called *model specification* or *model formulation* (see C. Chatfield, *The Analysis of Time Series: An Introduction*, 5th ed. (London: Chapman & Hall, 1996), the second stage can also be called *model fitting*. Chan uses *term model identification* for the second stage which contradicts the original notation (N. H. Chan, *Time Series: Applications to Finance* (Hoboken, NJ: John Wiley & Sons, 2002). The third stage is also called *model validation*.

EXHIBIT 7.1 The Box-Jenkins Approach to Time Series Modeling

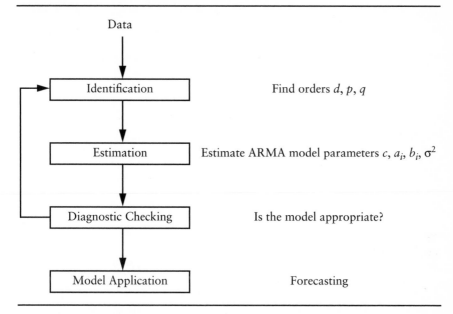

These initial guesses are typically not final values for these orders, but they are used to specify one or more tentative (competing) models. Upon examining the adequacy of a tentative model in the diagnostic–checking step, we may decide to keep the initial choices or to choose alternative orders until a (hopefully) satisfactory model is found.

The identification step may also indicate the need for additional data transformations, such as seasonal differencing.

Step 2. Given values for d, p and q from the identification step, the parameters of the ARIMA(p, d, q) model are derived in the *estimation step*. It delivers estimates of the ARMA coefficients c, a_1, a_2, ..., a_p, b_1, b_2, ..., b_q, for ARMA model formulations (6.15) and (6.18) discussed in the previous chapter and the residual variance σ^2.

Step 3. In the *diagnostic–checking step* we examine the adequacy of the estimated model. Here, the main objective is to determine whether or not all relevant information has been "extracted" from the data. If so, the estimated residuals, the deviation of the model's predictions from the actually observed sample, should not have any systematic pattern which allows one to "predict" the residuals. In other words, the residuals should resemble white noise.

If an estimated model fails one or more diagnostic tests, an alternative model, that is, an alternative set of p-, d-, and q-values, should be identified.

To each of the described steps 1, 2 and 3, the specific corresponding tools or procedures are assigned and used:

1. ARIMA, procedures for detrending and removing seasonal components, SACFs and SPACFs explained in the previous chapter.
2. Estimation methods such as least squares estimation (LSE) and maximum likelihood estimation (MLE) that are explained later in this chapter.
3. Analysis of residuals using *portmanteau* tests, such as Ljung-Box statistic, described later in this chapter.

The most widely accepted criterion for validating a model is its forecasting performance—especially when forecasting is the modeling objective. To judge the forecasting accuracy of a model, one can fit it to various subperiods of the complete data sample, beyond which there are observations available. A comparison of the forecasting performance of alternative models over several postsample (or holding-out) periods may help to find the most suitable model—or at least, eliminate some inappropriate ones. Ultimately, the goodness of a model will be determined and established by its actual operational (i.e., "real-life") performance. This relates to forecasting performance for newer data samples. For this reason, the accuracy of any model in operation should be evaluated regularly to check its adequacy. This is especially important when operating in a changing environment.

The next section details the steps of the Box-Jenkins approach—identification, estimation, diagnostic checking, and application in forecasting.

IDENTIFICATION OF DEGREE OF DIFFERENCING

Here, we discuss two techniques for determining the appropriate degree of differencing of a time series sample:

- Visual inspection of the sample autocorrelation function (SACF)
- Testing for unit roots

Examination of SACF

The shape of the SACF can indicate whether or not a time series is integrated. To show this, we use the extended Yule–Walker equations introduced in the previous chapter. They imply that for stationary ARMA(p, q) processes[3]

$$a(L)\rho_k = 0, \quad k > q \tag{7.1}$$

Using results on homogeneous, linear difference equations, polynomial $a(L)$ can be rewritten in factorized form as

$$(\lambda_1 - L)(\lambda_2 - L) \cdots (\lambda_p - L) = 0$$

where the λ_i's, $i = 1, \ldots, p$ are the roots of the AR polynomial. Assuming distinct roots, result (6.6) in the previous chapter implies that (7.1) has the solution

$$\rho_k = \alpha_1 \frac{1}{\lambda_1^k} + \alpha_2 \frac{1}{\lambda_2^k} + \cdots + \alpha_p \frac{1}{\lambda_p^k} \tag{7.2}$$

Stationarity implies that all λ_i's lie outside the unit circle in the complex plane. If all roots are well outside the unit circle, ρ_k approaches zero rather quickly as k increases. Hence, for a stationary process the ACF will die out rapidly.

Suppose now one real root of $a(L)$, say root λ_i, approaches unity, i.e., $\lambda_i = 1 + \delta$, $\delta > 0$, then because for small δ's $1/(1 + \delta) \approx 1 - \delta$, we have for moderate values of k

$$\rho_k \sim \alpha_i \frac{1}{\lambda_i^k} \sim \alpha_i(1 - k\delta) \tag{7.3}$$

This implies that the ACF will decline rather slowly and in almost linear fashion.

In practice, the SACF of data generated by a nonstationary ARMA process will exhibit a similar behavior. We use this to determine how many times a data series has to be differenced in order to induce stationarity. If the SACF of y_t indicates nonstationarity (i.e., slow and almost linear decay), we difference y_t and analyze the SACF of Δy_t. If also the SACF of Δy_t appears to be nonstationary, we keep differencing until the SACF of $\Delta^k y_t$, $d = 0, 1, \ldots$, decays sufficiently fast indicating stationarity. The first k-value for which we obtain stationarity will be the value we (tentatively) choose for d, the order of differencing of the ARIMA(p, d, q) model to be estimated.

---

[3] Box and Jenkins, *Time Series Analysis: Forecasting and Control*, rev. ed.

Differencing a time series more often than is necessary to induce stationarity is referred to as *overdifferencing*. This practice should be avoided, because it complicates the model by introducing additional, noninvertible MA components which may cause estimation problems. However, as we will see next, one potential consequence of overdifferencing can be utilized to identifying the appropriate order of differencing.

For example, let y_t follow the process

$$y_t = 2y_{t-1} - y_{t-2} + \varepsilon_t \qquad (7.4)$$

From conditions given by (6.20) in previous chapter,[4] it follows that this process is nonstationary. Taking the first difference, we obtain

$$
\begin{aligned}
\Delta y_t &= (2y_{t-1} - y_{t-2} + \varepsilon_t) - y_{t-1} \\
&= y_{t-1} - y_{t-2} + \varepsilon_t \\
&= \Delta y_{t-1} + \varepsilon_t
\end{aligned}
$$

which is a *nonstationary AR(1) process* because the AR coefficient is one. Second-order differencing yields a stationary process—because

$$
\begin{aligned}
\Delta^2 y_t &= \Delta y_{t-1} - \Delta y_{t-2} \\
&= \varepsilon_t
\end{aligned}
$$

The last result implies that (7.4) is an ARIMA(0,2,0) process. Differencing the process once more yields

$$
\begin{aligned}
\Delta^3 y_t &= \Delta^2 y_t - \Delta^2 y_{t-1} \\
&= \varepsilon_t - \varepsilon_{t-1}
\end{aligned}
$$

which is also stationary. However, the third difference is not invertible—because $b_1 = -1$, i.e., the MA polynomial has a root on the unit circle.

Unit-Root Test

Rather than relying on visual checking of the SACF, a formal test is often preferred. A natural approach to test, for example, whether the AR(1) process

---

[4] Recall that an AR(2) process is weakly stationary if its coefficients satisfy $|a_2| < 1$, $a_2 + a_1 < 1$, and $a_2 - a_1 < 1$.

$$y_t = ay_{t-1} + \varepsilon_t, \qquad \varepsilon_t \overset{IID}{\sim} (0, \sigma^2) \tag{7.5}$$

is stationary or a random walk[5] (i.e., $|a| < 1$ versus $a = 1$), would be to obtain the first ordinary least squares (OLS) estimate of a, denoted by $\hat{a}$. Then, we can perform a t-test of $\hat{a}$ to check whether it is significantly different from 1. The problem with this strategy is that if $a = 1$, the OLS estimate turns out to be biased toward zero. Moreover, the standard t-distribution is no longer the appropriate distribution for $\hat{a}$. Therefore the tabulated significance levels of the t-statistic are not valid.

To investigate this problem, Fuller[6] and Dickey and Fuller[7] subtract y_{t-1} from both sides of (7.5), yielding

$$\Delta y_t = (a - 1)y_{t-1} + \varepsilon_t \tag{7.6}$$

so that the test amounts to

$$H_0: a - 1 = 0 \quad \text{and} \quad H_1: a - 1 < 0 \tag{7.7}$$

Dickey and Fuller use Monte Carlo simulations to generate the critical values for the nonstandard t-distribution arising under the null hypothesis. A test of (7.7) by assessing the significance of the t-statistic in (7.6) using critical values tabulated by Dickey and Fuller is called the *Dickey-Fuller* (DF) *test*.

Dickey and Fuller consider, in fact, the more general model

$$\Delta y_t = f(t) + (a - 1)y_{t-1} + \varepsilon_t \tag{7.8}$$

where $f(t)$ is a deterministic function of time. It turns out that the critical values vary with the choice of $f(t)$. They provide critical values for the three cases:

Case 1: pure random walk where $f(t) = 0$
Case 2: random walk with constant drift where $f(t) = c$
Case 3: random walk with a deterministic linear trend where $f(t) = c_0 + c_1 t$

In Case 1, we are testing the model (7.7) for $H_0: a = 1$ as to whether we have a stationary AR(1) process or a pure (driftless) random walk.

---

[5] A random walk series is also called a unit-root nonstationary time series.
[6] W.A. Fuller, *Introduction to Statistical Time Series* (New York: John Wiley & Sons, 1976).
[7] D.A. Dickey, and W.A. Fuller, "Distribution of Estimators for Autoregressive Time Series with a Unit Root," *Journal of the American Statistical Association* 74 (1979), pp. 427–431.

In Case 2, we are testing the model

$$y_t = c + ay_{t-1} + \varepsilon_t \qquad (7.9)$$

If $c \neq 0$, then the t-ratio for testing H_0: $a = 1$ is asymptotically normal. If $c = 0$, then the t-ratio for testing will converge to another nonstandard asymptotic distribution. If $\{\varepsilon_t\}$ is a white noise series with finite moments of order slightly greater than 2, then the Dickey-Fuller statistic converges to a functional of the standard Brownian motion[8] as the sample size approaches infinity.[9]

If in Case 2 there is a unit root, that is,

$$y_t = c + y_{t-1} + \varepsilon_t \qquad (7.10)$$

then the constant c acts like a linear trend. In each period the level of y_t shifts, on average, by the amount c. A process of this type is said to have a stochastic trend and to be a *difference stationary* (DS).

In Case 3 with a unit root, that is,

$$y_t = c_0 + c_1 t + y_{t-1} + \varepsilon_t \qquad (7.11)$$

we refer to $c_1 t$ as *deterministic trend*, and the process becomes *trend stationary* (TS) after differencing.

The difference stationary model (7.10) and trend stationary model

$$y_t = c_0 + c_1 t + \varepsilon_t \qquad (7.12)$$

can be used to represent nonstationary time series with a change in mean level where the ε_t are usually correlated but stationary. Although both representations feature time series that increase in the mean level over time, the substantial difference between them relates to the process to render them stationary. While for the model (7.10) a stationary process $\{\varepsilon_t\}$ is obtained after differencing, for the model (7.12) a stationary process $\{\varepsilon_t\}$ is obtained after detrending. To note the distinction, we inappropriately difference the model (7.11) and obtain

---

[8] A standard Brownian motion or Wiener process is a continuous-time stochastic process $\{W_t\}$ if the following holds: (1) $\Delta W_t = \varepsilon(\sqrt{\Delta t})$ and, (2) ΔW_t is independent of W_j for all $j \leq t$, where ε is a standard normal random variable and $\Delta W_t = W_{t+\Delta} - W_t$ is a small change associated with a small increment Δt in time. In the limit, as $\Delta \to 0$, the equation $\Delta W_t = \varepsilon(\sqrt{\Delta t})$ is interpreted as a continuous-time approximation of the random walk model.

[9] Peter C. B. Phillips, "Time Series Regression with a Unit Root," *Econometrica* 55 (1987), pp. 227–301.

$$\Delta y_t = c_1 + \Delta \varepsilon_t$$

As a consequence, a process $\{\Delta \varepsilon_t\}$ is stationary but noninvertible which is not convenient. The consideration of general model (7.8) helps to distinguish between two models. Thus, for $a = 1$, we obtain a differenced stationary series and for $a < 1$ a trend stationary series.

The critical values Dickey and Fuller derive from their Monte-Carlo simulations for each of the three cases are reproduced in Exhibit 7.2.

A practical problem with the AR(1) based unit-root test is that the residuals obtained from (7.8) tend to be autocorrelated. To circumvent this, one can add sufficiently many lagged Δy_{t-i} on the right-hand side

EXHIBIT 7.2   Critical Values for Dickey-Fuller Test

Sample Size	Probability of a Smaller Sample Value							
	0.01	0.025	0.05	0.10	0.90	0.95	0.975	0.99
Case 1: No constant and no time trend								
25	−2.66	−2.26	−1.95	−1.60	0.92	1.33	1.70	2.16
50	−2.62	−2.25	−1.95	−1.61	0.91	1.31	1.66	2.08
100	−2.60	−2.24	−1.95	−1.61	0.90	1.29	1.64	2.03
250	−2.58	−2.23	−1.95	−1.62	0.89	1.29	1.63	2.01
300	−2.58	−2.23	−1.95	−1.62	0.89	1.28	1.62	2.00
∞	−2.58	−2.23	−1.95	−1.62	0.89	1.28	1.62	2.00
Case 2: With constant but no time trend								
25	−3.75	−3.33	−3.00	−2.62	−0.37	0.00	0.34	0.72
50	−3.58	−3.22	−2.93	−2.60	−0.40	−0.03	0.29	0.66
100	−3.51	−3.17	−2.89	−2.58	−0.42	−0.05	0.26	0.63
250	−3.46	−3.14	−2.88	−2.57	−0.42	−0.06	0.24	0.62
300	−3.44	−3.13	−2.87	−2.57	−0.43	−0.07	−0.24	0.61
∞	−3.43	−3.12	−2.86	−2.57	−0.44	−0.07	0.23	0.60
Case 3: With constant and with linear time trend								
25	−4.38	−3.95	−3.60	−3.24	−1.14	−0.80	−0.50	−0.15
50	−4.15	−3.80	−3.50	−3.18	−1.19	−0.87	−0.58	−0.24
100	−4.04	−3.73	−3.45	−3.15	−1.22	−0.90	−0.62	−0.28
250	−3.99	−3.69	−3.43	−3.13	−1.23	−0.92	−0.64	−0.31
300	−3.98	−3.68	−3.42	−3.13	−1.24	−0.93	−0.65	−0.32
∞	−3.96	−3.66	−3.41	−3.12	−1.25	−0.94	−0.66	−0.33

of (7.8) until the residuals appear to be white. If the unit-root test described above is based on the OLS-estimated coefficient of y_{t-1} in

$$\Delta y_t = f(t) + (a-1)y_{t-1} + \sum_{i=1}^{p} a_i \Delta y_{t-i} + \varepsilon_t \tag{7.13}$$

then one refers to this test as the *augmented Dickey-Fuller* (ADF) *test*. The ADF test, which is the most widely used unit-root test, relies on the same critical values as the DF test.

If the hypothesis H_0: $a - 1 = 0$ cannot be rejected, we conclude that $y_t \sim I(d)$ with $d \geq 1$. To test whether the order of integration exceeds 1, we perform a unit-root test for Δy_t and repeat this until we reject H_0. For economic time series, we typically find $d = 0$, 1 or, at most, $d = 2$ to be sufficient.

IDENTIFICATION OF LAG ORDERS

Having decided the degree of differencing, the next step is to choose the orders p and q for the autoregressive and moving average components of the time series. The choice is facilitated by investigating the sample autocorrelations and partial autocorrelations of the time series as well as applying model selection criteria.

Inspection of SACF and SPACF

Exhibit 7.3 summarizes the behavior of the ACF and PACF for AR, MA, and ARMA processes. For MA models, the ACF is useful in specifying the order because ACF cuts off at lag q for an MA(q) series. For AR models, the PACF is useful in order determination because PACF cuts off at lag p for an AR(p) process. If both the ACF and PACF tail off, a mixed ARMA process is suggested. However, because the evaluation of patterns is based on estimated quantities, it is not effective to check whether the SACF (or SPACF, and so on) cuts off somewhere and

EXHIBIT 7.3 Patterns for Identifying ARMA Processes

	Model		
	AR(p)	MA(q)	ARMA(p, q)
ACF	Tails off	Cuts off after q	Tails off
PACF	Cuts off after p	Tails off	Tails off

exactly assumes a value of zero. It is required to check at what lag the SACF or SPACF accordingly stops being significantly different from zero, using the confidence intervals for estimated ACF and PACF as discussed in the previous chapter.

Model Selection Criteria

A useful criterion for model selection reflects the idea that it is always possible to more or less trade off p versus q in selecting the order of an ARMA model by assigning an informational cost to the number of parameters, to be minimized along with the goodness of fit of the model. An obvious criterion for the goodness of fit of competing models is the residual variance.

Let the residuals of an estimated ARMA(p, q) model be denoted by $\hat{\varepsilon}_t(p, q)$. The estimate of the corresponding residual variance, denoted by $\hat{\sigma}^2_{p, q}$, is

$$\hat{\sigma}^2_{p, q} = \frac{1}{T} \sum_{i = 1}^{T} \hat{\varepsilon}^2_t(p, q)$$

However, a naive in-sample comparison of the residual variances of competing models would favor models with many parameters over simple, low-order models. Larger models tend to fit in-sample better, because each estimated parameter provides additional flexibility in approximating a data set of a given size. However, if we use too many parameters we fit noise and obtain poor forecasting capabilities. This phenomenon is called overfitting. As we are primarily concerned with out-of-sample forecasting, we need to constrain model dimensionality in order to avoid overfitting.

In the extreme, we could achieve a perfect fit by fitting a "model" that has as many parameters as observations. In that case, $\hat{\varepsilon}_t = 0$, for $t = 1, ...,$ T, and so that $\hat{\sigma}^2 = 0$. However, what we obtain is not appropriately categorized as a "model," (i.e., a simplified representation of reality) because we express the T observations in terms of some other T numbers. This simply amounts to a transformation of the original data, but not to a reduction to a smaller set of parameters. Although this is an extreme example, it illustrates that model selection solely based on the residual variance is inappropriate because it leads to overparameterized models. Such models *overfit* the data by also capturing nonsystematic features contained in the data. In general, overparameterized models tend to be unreliable.

Several model-selection criteria attempting to overcome the overparameterization problem have been proposed in the literature. Here we will briefly provide definitions of the most widely used criteria: Akaike information criterion, Bayesian information criterion, and corrected Akaike information criterion.

The *Akaike Information Criterion* (AIC) is given by

$$\text{AIC}_{p,q} = \ln\hat{\sigma}^2_{p,q} + \frac{2}{T}(p+q) \tag{7.14}$$

The (p, q)–combination that minimizes the AIC should be selected. The first term in (7.14), $\hat{\sigma}^2_{p,q}$, measures a model's goodness of fit in terms of the estimated error variance; the second term, $2T^{-1}(p+q)$, penalizes for selecting models with a large number of parameters. The purpose of the penalty term is to avoid overfitting. However, this criterion may give more than one minimum and depends on assumption that the data are normally distributed. Furthermore, Monte Carlo simulations[10] indicate that, despite the penalty term, the AIC tends to overparameterize.

The *Bayesian Information Criterion* (BIC)[11] is given by

$$\text{BIC}_{p,q} = \ln\hat{\sigma}^2_{p,q} + \frac{\ln T}{T}(p+q) \tag{7.15}$$

This criterion imposes a more severe penalty for each additional parameter and thereby tends to select lower-order models than the AIC.

The *Corrected Akaike Information Criterion* (AICC) given by[12]

$$\text{AICC}_{p,q} = \ln\hat{\sigma}^2_{p,q} + \frac{2}{T-p-q-2}(p+q+1) \tag{7.16}$$

attempts to correct the bias of the AIC that is causing the overparameterization problem and is especially designed for small samples. Asymptotically, as T increases, both criteria are equivalent. However, for small sample sizes, it tends to select different models.

---

[10] See R. H. Jones "Fitting Autoregressions," *Journal of the American Statistical Association* 70 (1975), pp. 590–592 and R. Shibata, "Selection of the Order of an Autoregressive Model by Akaike's Information Criterion," *Biometrika* 63 (1976), pp. 147–164.

[11] G. Schwarz, "Estimating the Dimension of a Model," *Annals of Statistics* 6 (1978), pp. 461–464.

[12] AICC has been defined in C.M. Hurvich and C. L. Tsai, "Regression and Time Series Model Selection in Small Samples," *Biometrika* 76 (1989), pp. 297–307.

The AICC imposes a penalty that is somewhere between that of the AIC and BIC. Let k be the number of estimated parameters of a model as recommended by an information criterion. Due to the different penalty terms we have $k_{AIC} \geq k_{AICC} \geq k_{BIC}$. The BIC is *strongly consistent* in selecting the orders of a process; namely, it determines the true model asymptotically. This means if the data are truly generated by an ARMA(p, q) process, the BIC will recover the correct orders p and q as the sample size approaches infinity. In contrast, AIC will always determine an overreparameterized model, independent of the length of the sample. Although consistency is an attractive property, real data are typically not generated by a specific ARMA(p, q) process and are of limited sample size. Therefore the consistency is of less practical importance than it may appear.

In practice, final model selection should not be based exclusively on any of these information criteria. They basically measure the goodness of fit, which is an important but typically not the only relevant criterion for choosing a model. As pointed out by Box, Jenkins, and Reinsel,[13] use of information criteria should be viewed as supplementary guidelines to assist in the model selection process rather than as a complete substitute for a thorough inspection of characteristics of the sample ACF and sample PACF.

As discussed here, different information criteria may recommend different models. But even if we decide to use only one of the criteria, there may be several models that produce criterion values that are very close to the minimum value. Whenever one encounters conflicting recommendations or only small differences, all reasonable models should remain candidates for the final selection and be subjected to further diagnostic checks. A test for whiteness of the residuals is an important diagnostic check, which should be passed by the residuals of an estimated model.

MODEL ESTIMATION

There are several approaches to estimating ARMA models. They are:

1. The *Yule-Walker estimator* uses the Yule-Walker equations explained in the previous chapter with $k = 1, ..., p$ and estimates the AR parameters of pure AR models from the SACF. For mixed ARMA models, in principle the extended Yule-Walker equations could be used to estimate

---

[13] Box, Jenkins, and Reinsel, *Time Series Analysis: Forecasting and Control*, 3rd ed.

the AR coefficients. The MA coefficients need to be estimated by other means.

2. The *least squares estimator* (LSE) finds the parameter estimates that minimize the sum of the squared residuals. For pure AR models, the LSE leads to the linear OLS estimator. If moving average components are present, the LSE becomes nonlinear and has to be solved with numerical methods.

3. The *maximum likelihood estimator* (MLE) maximizes the (exact or approximate) log-likelihood function associated with the specified model. To do so, explicit distributional assumption for the disturbances, ε_t, has to be made. Typically, we assume a normal distribution (i.e., $\varepsilon_t \overset{IID}{\sim} N(0, \sigma^2)$).

We discuss each approach briefly below.

Yule-Walker Estimation

Yule-Walker (YW) equations can be used for parameter estimation of pure AR models. YW equations for $AR(p)$ process are of the following form

$$\rho_k = a_1\rho_{k-1} + \cdots + a_p\rho_{k-p}, \quad k = 1, 2, \ldots. \tag{7.17}$$

Using sample autocorrelations and collecting the first p equations in matrix form we obtain

$$\begin{bmatrix} 1 & \hat{\rho}_1 & \cdots & \hat{\rho}_{p-1} \\ \hat{\rho}_1 & 1 & & \hat{\rho}_{p-2} \\ \hat{\rho}_2 & \hat{\rho}_1 & \cdots & \hat{\rho}_{p-3} \\ \vdots & & \ddots & \vdots \\ \hat{\rho}_{p-2} & & & \hat{\rho}_1 \\ \hat{\rho}_{p-1} & \hat{\rho}_{p-2} & \cdots & 1 \end{bmatrix} \begin{bmatrix} a_1 \\ a_2 \\ a_3 \\ \vdots \\ a_{p-1} \\ a_p \end{bmatrix} = \begin{bmatrix} \hat{\rho}_1 \\ \hat{\rho}_2 \\ \hat{\rho}_3 \\ \vdots \\ \hat{\rho}_{p-1} \\ \hat{\rho}_p \end{bmatrix} \tag{7.18}$$

or, in short,

$$\hat{T}a = \hat{\rho}_p \tag{7.19}$$

YW estimator is then given by

$$\hat{a} = \hat{T}^{-1}\hat{\rho}_p \qquad (7.20)$$

If SACF is estimated by (see (6.47) in the chapter 6)

$$\hat{\rho}_k = \frac{\displaystyle\sum_{i=k+1}^{T} (y_i - \bar{\mu})(y_{i-k} - \bar{\mu})}{\displaystyle\sum_{i=1}^{T} (y_i - \bar{\mu})^2}$$

all roots of the YW-estimated AR polynomial $1 - \hat{a}_1 L - \cdots - \hat{a}_p L^p$ will be greater than unity. That is, the estimated AR model will be stationary.

The YW estimator as presented above is derived by solving exactly identified systems of linear equations (i.e., there are as many equations as unknowns). One can also specify *overidentified systems* of equations by using more than the minimal number of p (or q) YW recursions.

To illustrate, let's use the first four YW equations to estimate an AR(2) model:

$$\begin{bmatrix} 1 & \hat{\rho}_1 \\ \hat{\rho}_1 & 1 \\ \hat{\rho}_2 & \hat{\rho}_1 \\ \hat{\rho}_3 & \hat{\rho}_2 \end{bmatrix} \begin{bmatrix} a_1 \\ a_2 \end{bmatrix} \approx \begin{bmatrix} \hat{\rho}_1 \\ \hat{\rho}_2 \\ \hat{\rho}_3 \\ \hat{\rho}_4 \end{bmatrix}$$

or, in short,

$$\hat{T}_4 a \approx \hat{\rho}_4$$

The overidentified YW estimator is then given by the least squares solution for a:

$$\hat{a} = \left(\hat{T}_4' \hat{T}_4\right)^{-1} \hat{T}_4' \hat{\rho}_4$$

Overidentification makes use of information contained in higher-order sample autocorrelations. However, higher-order SACF terms tend to be noisier and therefore may lead to less reliable estimates.

The YW estimator is consistent but not efficient[14] and is typically used as initial estimate for more elaborate iterative estimation methods such as LSE or MLE.

Least Squares Estimator

The LSE finds the values for the model parameters which minimize the sum of the squares residuals. Writing the ARMA equations (6.12 in the previous chapter)

$$
y_t = a_1 y_{t-1} + a_2 y_{t-2} + \cdots + a_p y_{t-p} + \varepsilon_t + b_1 \varepsilon_{t-1} + \cdots + b_q \varepsilon_{t-q}
$$
$$
= \sum_{i=1}^{p} a_i y_{t-i} + \varepsilon_t + \sum_{j=1}^{q} b_j \varepsilon_{t-j}
$$

for the T observations $y = (y_1,\ldots,y_T)'$, we obtain

$$
\mathbf{A}y = \mathbf{A}^* y^* + \mathbf{B} e + \mathbf{B}^* e^* \tag{7.21}
$$

where e denotes the vector of residuals $e = (e_1,\ldots,e_T)'$; the asterisk refers to pre-sample values $y^* = (y_0, y_{-1},\ldots,y_{-p+1})'$ and $e^* = (e_0, e_{-1},\ldots,e_{-q+1})'$. The matrices are given by

$$
\mathbf{A} = \begin{bmatrix}
1 & 0 & & \cdots & & 0 \\
-a_1 & 1 & & & & \\
-a_2 & -a_1 & & & & \\
 & -a_2 & \ddots & & & \\
\vdots & & & \ddots & & \vdots \\
-a_p & -a_{p-1} & & & & \\
0 & -a_p & & & & \\
\vdots & \vdots & \ddots & & & 0 \\
0 & 0 & \cdots & -a_p & \cdots & -a_1 \; 1
\end{bmatrix}
$$

---

[14] A consistent estimator is one that is bound to give an accurate estimate of the population characteristic if the sample is large enough. An efficient estimator is one for which the probability density function is as concentrated as possible around the true value. Generally, an efficient estimator is the estimator with the smallest variance.

$$
\mathbf{B} = \begin{bmatrix}
1 & 0 & & & \cdots & & & 0 \\
-b_1 & 1 & & & & & & \\
-b_2 & -b_1 & & & & & & \\
\vdots & -b_2 & \ddots & & & \ddots & & \vdots \\
-b_q & -b_{q-1} & & & & & & \\
0 & -b_q & & & & & & \\
\vdots & \vdots & \ddots & & & \ddots & & \\
& & & & & & & 0 \\
0 & 0 & \cdots & & -b_p & \cdots & -b_1 & 1
\end{bmatrix}
$$

$$
\mathbf{A}^* = \left[\begin{array}{cccc}
a_1 & a_2 & \cdots & a_p \\
a_2 & \cdots & a_p & 0 \\
\vdots & a_p & & \vdots \\
a_p & 0 & \cdots & 0 \\
\hline
0 & \cdots & \cdots & 0
\end{array}\right]
$$

$$
\mathbf{B}^* = \left[\begin{array}{cccc}
b_1 & b_2 & \cdots & b_q \\
b_2 & \cdots & b_q & 0 \\
\vdots & b_q & & \vdots \\
b_q & 0 & \cdots & 0 \\
\hline
0 & \cdots & \cdots & 0
\end{array}\right]
$$

Solving (7.21) for $\mathbf{e}$ provides

$$
\mathbf{e} = \mathbf{B}^{-1}(\mathbf{Ay} - \mathbf{A}^*\mathbf{y}^* - \mathbf{B}^*\mathbf{e}^*) \tag{7.22}
$$

Letting $\mathbf{a} = (a_1,\ldots, a_p)$ and $\mathbf{b} = (b_1,\ldots, b_q)$, the sum of squared residual,

$$
S(\mathbf{a},\mathbf{b}) = \mathbf{e}'\mathbf{e}
$$

can be written as

$$
S(\mathbf{a}, \mathbf{b}) = (\mathbf{Ay} - \mathbf{A}^*\mathbf{y}^* - \mathbf{B}^*\mathbf{e}^*)'(\mathbf{BB}')^{-1}(\mathbf{Ay} - \mathbf{A}^*\mathbf{y}^* - \mathbf{B}^*\mathbf{e}^*) \tag{7.23}
$$

Minimization of (7.23) with respect to coefficient vectors **a** and **b** yields the LSE of **a** and **b**.

To minimize (7.23), presample values have to be known. The following three approaches can be used to deal with this problem.

1. Set presample values **y*** and **e*** equal to the unconditional expectations, using

$$E(y_t) = 0, \quad E(\varepsilon_t) = 0, \quad t \leq 0$$

   Assumption $E(y_t) = 0$, $t \leq 0$, is questionable when the AR polynomial has a root close to the unit circle and could lead to a severe bias. With an increasing sample size, the impact of the zero initial-value assumption will, however, diminish.

2. Compute the sum of squares starting at $t = p + 1$ instead of $t = 1$. Then, the p "presample" values $y_1, \ldots, y_p$ are known and only the initial disturbances will be set to zero. This method leads to *conditional sum of squares*, since it is conditioned on $y_1, \ldots, y_p$. Again, for large samples the effects of setting $\varepsilon_t = 0$ for $p - q < t < q$ will be negligible.

3. Treat $\varepsilon_{p-q}, \ldots, \varepsilon_p$ as unknown parameters that have to be jointly estimated with the ARMA parameters. To do so, one can consider them like unknown parameters with respect to which we minimize the sum of squared residuals or by *backcasting* (i.e., *forecasting backward*). The backcasting procedure uses the fact that, if y_t is generated by a stationary process,

$$a(L^{-1})y_t = b(L^{-1})v_t$$

where L^{-1} represents the lead operator, then v_t has the same mean and variance as ε_t.

Since (7.23) is not quadratic in the MA coefficients, the first-order conditions obtained in the optimization will not be linear. Thus we will not have a closed-form solution but rather require iterative numerical solutions.

Given estimates $\hat{\mathbf{a}}$ and $\hat{\mathbf{b}}$, fitted residuals are given by

$$\hat{\mathbf{e}} = \hat{\mathbf{B}}^{-1}\left(\hat{\mathbf{A}}\mathbf{y} - \hat{\mathbf{A}}^*\mathbf{y}^* - \hat{\mathbf{B}}^*\mathbf{e}^*\right) \tag{7.24}$$

from which we can derive the estimate of the residual variance by

$$\hat{\sigma}^2 = \frac{1}{T}\hat{e}'\hat{e} \qquad (7.25)$$

Maximum Likelihood Estimator

The method of maximum likelihood (ML) is another statistical procedure that obtains an estimate that minimizes some form of the sum of squared errors. The likelihood procedure searches for the parameter values that are most "suitable" for the set of observations.

Recall the standard situation in ML estimation—assume random variables are IID and drawn from distribution $f(\cdot; \theta)$ with the probability density function (pdf). For example, if all y_t's are drawn from $N(\mu, \sigma^2)$, then θ is a parameter vector that summarizes estimates of the mean and variance, $\theta = (\mu, \sigma^2)'$.

Given θ, the joint *pdf* of $Y_T = (y_0, \ldots y_T)$ is written as

$$f(Y_T; \theta) = \prod_{t=0}^{T} f(y_t; \theta), \quad \theta \in \Theta \qquad (7.26)$$

where Θ denotes the set of admissible parameter values. For a given sample Y_T, the joint pdf $f(Y_T; \theta)$ can be viewed as a function of θ. Then, for different choices of θ, the value of $f(Y_T; \theta)$ is an indication of the "plausibility" of a particular θ for the data set Y_T.

The likelihood function of model $f(\cdot; \theta)$ for data set Y_T can be defined as

$$L(\theta; Y_T) \propto f(Y_T; \theta)$$

where $\propto$ stands for "is proportional to." Any function positively proportional to $f(Y_T; \theta)$ is a valid likelihood function—which includes the joint pdf itself. The MLE of θ, $\hat{\theta}_{ML} \in \Theta$, has the property that for any other estimator, $\hat{\theta} \in \Theta$,

$$L\left(\hat{\theta}_{ML}; Y_T\right) \geq L\left(\hat{\theta}; Y_T\right)$$

The MLE $\hat{\theta}$ of θ is obtained by finding the value of θ that maximizes (7.26). That means that we aim to find the value of the unknown parameter that maximizes the likelihood (probability) computed for a given set of observations $y_1, \ldots, y_T$. This procedure has a general character and the IID assumption can be relaxed.

If Y_T is a sample of time series, the y_t's will generally be dependent. Consequently, their joint density function cannot be written as a product of individual pdf values $f(y_t, \theta)$ as in (7.26). However, the joint density function of two dependent random variables can be decomposed as[15]

$$f(x_2, x_1) = f(x_2|x_1)f(x_1) \qquad (7.27)$$

where $f(x_2|x_1)$ represents the conditional density of x_2 given the value of x_1. Accordingly, for three dependent random variables:

$$f(x_3, x_2, x_1) = f(x_3|x_2, x_1)f(x_2, x_1) \qquad (7.28)$$

Substituting (7.27) for $f(x_2, x_1)$ yields

$$f(x_3, x_2, x_1) = f(x_3|x_2, x_1)f(x_2|x_1)f(x_1) \qquad (7.29)$$

Then, for time series data $Y_T = (y_0, \dots y_T)$, the joint pdf can be written as

$$f(Y_T) = f(y_T|Y_{T-1}) \, f(y_{T-1}|Y_{T-2}) \, \cdots \, f(y_0) \qquad (7.30)$$

and the likelihood function becomes

$$L(\theta; Y_T) = f(y_0) \prod_{t=1}^{T} f(y_t | Y_{t-1}) \qquad (7.31)$$

Maximizing $L(\theta; Y_T)$ is equivalent to maximizing the log-likelihood function

$$\ln L(\theta; Y_T) = \ln f(y_0) + \sum_{t=1}^{T} \ln f(y_t | Y_{t-1}) \qquad (7.32)$$

which is typically maximized in practice.

We will now illustrate the idea through the example. Consider an AR(1) process $y_t = a_1 y_{t-1} + \varepsilon_t$ with $\varepsilon_t \sim N(0, \sigma^2)$, IID. Then, the conditional pdf of y_t given y_{t-1} is normal with (conditional) mean $a y_{t-1}$ and variance σ^2. Thus, $f(y_T|Y_{T-1}) \sim N(a y_{t-1}, \sigma^2)$ or

---

[15] The parameter vector θ is omitted as an argument in the density function whenever it is clear from the context.

$$f(y_t|Y_{t-1}) = \frac{1}{\sqrt{2\pi}\sigma}\exp\left\{-\frac{(y_t - ay_{t-1})^2}{2\sigma^2}\right\}, \quad t = 1, 2, ..., T$$

Combining this with (7.32) yields

$$L(a, \sigma^2; Y_T) = f(y_0)\prod_{t=1}^{T}(2\pi\sigma^2)^{-1/2}\exp\left\{-\frac{(y_t - ay_{t-1})^2}{2\sigma^2}\right\}$$

$$= f(y_0)(2\pi\sigma^2)^{-\frac{T}{2}}\prod_{t=1}^{T}\exp\left\{-\frac{(y_t - ay_{t-1})^2}{2\sigma^2}\right\}$$

The log-likelihood function is

$$\ln L(a, \sigma^2; Y_T) = \ln f(y_0) - \frac{T}{2}\ln(2\pi) - \frac{T}{2}\ln\sigma^2 - \frac{1}{2\sigma^2}\sum_{t=1}^{T}(y_t - ay_{t-1})^2 \quad (7.33)$$

The unconditional pdf of initial value y_0 is normal with mean 0 and variance $\sigma^2/(1-a^2)$:

$$y_0 \sim N\left(0, \frac{\sigma^2}{1-a^2}\right)$$

Therefore

$$\ln f(y_0) = -\frac{1}{2}\ln(2\pi) + \ln(1-a^2) - \ln\sigma^2 - \frac{y_0^2(1-a^2)}{2\sigma^2} \quad (7.34)$$

Substitution of equation (7.34) into (7.33) gives exact likelihood function for the AR(1) model. Maximization with respect to a and σ^2 yields exact maximum likelihood estimates.

For higher-order AR models, we have to specify the unconditional joint pdf of the pre-sample values $y_0, ..., y_{-p+1}$. In practice, it is often omitted from the log-likelihood function because its (1) influence on the parameter estimates becomes negligible for large samples and (2) derivation is a nontrivial computational problem.

Conditional MLE is obtained by conditioning $y_1,..., y_T$ on presample realizations $y_0, ..., y_{-p+1}$. Conditional log-likelihood function of general ARMA(p, q) model with constant c and $\varepsilon_t \sim N(0, \sigma^2)$, IID:

$$\ln L(\theta, \sigma^2; Y_T) = -\frac{T}{2}\ln(2\pi) - \frac{T}{2}\ln\sigma^2 - \frac{1}{2\sigma^2}\sum_{t=1}^{T}\varepsilon_t^2$$

where

$$\theta = (c, a_1, ..., a_p, b_1, ..., b_q)'$$

and

$$\varepsilon_t = y_t - c - \sum_{i=1}^{p}a_i y_{t-i} - \sum_{j=1}^{q}a_j\varepsilon_{t-j}$$

DIAGNOSTIC CHECKING

After estimating an ARIMA model, the next step in the Box-Jenkins approach is to check the adequacy of that model. Ideally, a model should extract all systematic information from the data. The part of the data unexplained by the model (i.e., the residuals) should be small and not exhibit any systematic or predictable patterns, i.e., white noise, since any information useful for prediction should be captured by the model and not left in the residuals. With these desirable properties for the residuals in mind, most diagnostic checks involve analyses of the residuals of the estimated model.

In addition to analyzing residuals, one could design diagnostic checking procedures that take the modeling objectives explicitly into account. If the model is intended for forecasting, given sample $y_1, ..., y_T$, one could use only observations $y_1, ..., y_{T-K}$ in the estimation step and generate out-of-sample forecasts for the hold-out sample $y_{T-K+1}, ..., y_T$. A comparison of actual and predicted values for the hold-out sample indicates the predictive performance of the estimated model and allows one to judge its adequacy in terms of the modeling objective.

The evaluation of the predictive performance of a model is not considered here but will be discussed later in this chapter. We present next various diagnostic-checking devices that are based on residual analysis.

Testing for Whiteness of the Residuals

A standard assumption in ARIMA modeling is that the disturbances ε_t, the unexplained part of y_t given past information $y_{t-1}, y_{t-2}, \ldots$ and ε_{t-1}, $\varepsilon_{t-2}, \ldots$, cannot be (fully or partially) explained or predicted from this past information. This is reflected in the white noise assumption explained in the previous chapter

$$
E(\varepsilon_t) = 0, \qquad E(\varepsilon_s \varepsilon_t) = \begin{cases} \sigma^2, & \text{if } s = t \\ 0, & \text{if } s \neq t \end{cases} \tag{7.35}
$$

In accordance with this assumption, the residuals of an estimated model should exhibit white noise-like behavior. Any departure from whiteness indicates that the residuals still contain information that the model has not extracted from the data.

A simple plot of the residuals may exhibit systematic patterns and reveal the inadequacy of the estimated model. A more systematic way of checking the whiteness is to subject the residuals to the standard identification procedures employed in the identification step of model building. If the SACF and SPACF of the residuals have no significant elements, we conclude that they resemble white noise; otherwise, there is still information in the residuals.

One problem with checking the significance of individual elements of any of the identification functions is that each element might be individually insignificant, but all (or a subset) of the elements taken together may be jointly significant. For example, the residual SACF could exhibit a systematic pattern within the 95% confidence interval—indicating that the residuals may contain relevant information—although, for each k, we cannot reject the null hypothesis $\rho_{\varepsilon,k} = 0$.

Portmanteu Tests

Several diagnostic goodness of fit tests have been proposed based on the residual autocorrelation coefficients. A popular goodness of fit test is the *Box-Pierce Q-statistic*, also known as the *portmanteau test*,[16] which tests the joint hypothesis H_0: $\rho_{\varepsilon,1} = \rho_{\varepsilon,2} = \ldots = \rho_{\varepsilon,K} = 0$. The Q-statistic is computed by

---

[16] G. E. P. Box and D. A. Pierce, "Distribution of Residual Autocorrelations in Autoregressive Moving Average Time Series Models," *Journal of the American Statistical Association* 65 (1970), pp. 1509–1526.

$$Q = T \sum_{k=1}^{K} \hat{\rho}_{\varepsilon, k}^2 \qquad (7.36)$$

where $\hat{\rho}_{\varepsilon, k}$ is the k-th order sample autocorrelation of the residuals and T is the sample size. K in (7.36) is chosen sufficiently large so that the effect of higher-order autocorrelations, which are assumed to approach zero, can be neglected. In practice, one can compute Q for several values of K. The sum of squared autocorrelations is intended to capture deviations from zero in either direction and at all lags K.

For data generated by a white noise process, Q has an asymptotic chi-square (χ^2) distribution with $(K - p - q)$ degrees of freedom. If Q exceeds the tabulated critical value associated with the chosen significance level, we reject the null hypothesis of uncorrelated residuals.

The Q test is only asymptotically valid and may perform rather poorly for small and moderate samples,[17] for which the distribution of Q can be quite different from the χ^2 distribution. In view of this, Ljung and Box[18] adapt the Box-Pierce test for finite sample by modifying the Q-statistic to obtain the Q^*-statistic, such that

$$Q^* = T(T+2) \sum_{k=1}^{K} (T-k)^{-1} \hat{\rho}_{\varepsilon, k}^2 \qquad (7.37)$$

which constitutes the *Ljung–Box test*. However, for moderate sample sizes, also the Ljung-Box test has low power and may fail to detect model misspecifications.

Both versions of the portmanteau test check only for *uncorrelatedness* of the residuals and not for *independence* or "true" whiteness. If the data are generated by a nonlinear process, we may find a linear ARMA model that extracts all autocorrelations from the data. Then, the residuals would be uncorrelated and both the residual SACF and a Q test would indicate that the estimated ARMA model is adequate. However, more complex temporal dependencies may still be present in the residuals. The detection of such dependencies in the absence of autocorrelations indicates that the class of linear ARMA models is inappropriate for the data

---

[17] This is pointed out in N. Davies and P. Newbold, "Some Power Studies of a Portmanteau Test of Time Series Model Specification," *Biometrika* 66 (1979), pp. 153–155.

[18] G. M. Ljung and G. E. P. Box, "On a Measure of a Lack of Fit in Time Series Models," *Biometrika* 65 (1978), pp. 297–303.

at hand. Granger and Anderson,[19] for example, present several examples where the residuals are uncorrelated whereas the squared residuals are significantly correlated. Adapting the Ljung-Box test, McLeod and Li[20] test the joint hypothesis $H_0 : \rho_{\varepsilon^2, 1} = \rho_{\varepsilon^2, 2} = \cdots = \rho_{\varepsilon^2, K} = 0$ by performing a Q test on the squared residuals. They compute

$$Q_2^* = T(T+2) \sum_{k=1}^{K} (T-k)^{-1} \hat{\rho}_{\varepsilon^2, K}^2 \tag{7.38}$$

where $\hat{\rho}_{\varepsilon^2, K}$ denotes the kth order sample autocorrelation of the squared residuals. They show that under the null hypothesis of no autocorrelation, Q_2^* has a χ^2 distribution with K degrees of freedom.

Alternatively, a goodness of fit test based on residual partial autocorrelation can be used. If $\hat{\psi}_{\varepsilon, k}$ is the k-th order residual partial autocorrelation coefficients, then the statistic

$$Q_M = T(T+2) \sum_{k=1}^{K} (T-k)^{-1} \hat{\psi}_{\varepsilon, k}^2$$

is asymptotically χ^2 distributed with $(K - p - q)$ degrees of freedom if the model fitted is appropriate.[21] Simulation results of Monti indicates that the empirical sizes of Q_M are adequate in moderate sample sizes. The finite sample behavior of the portmanteau tests based on residual autocorrelations and residual partial autocorrelations can also be affected by the choice of the estimation method (e.g., maximum likelihood estimator or least squares estimator). Although the estimators are asymptotically equivalent, they may differ markedly from one another in finite samples. A consequence is that the finite-sample properties of the goodness of fit tests which are based on the residual autocorrelation or partial autocorrelation coefficients are likely to depend on how model parameters are estimated.

Note that the literature offers a variety of alternative tests for whiteness.[22]

---

[19] Clive W. J. Granger, and A. P. Andersen, *An Introduction to Bilinear Time Series Models* (Göttingen: Vandenhoeck and Ruprecht, 1978).

[20] A. J. McLeod and W. K. Li, "Diagnostic Checking ARMA Time Series Models using Squared-Residual Correlations," *Journal of Time Series Analysis* 4 (1983), pp. 269–273.

[21] A. C. Monti, "A Proposal for a Residual Autocorrelation Test in Linear Models," *Biometrika* 81 (1994), pp. 776–780.

[22] For a discussion of these approaches, see M. G. Kendall and A. Stuart, *The Advanced Theory of Statistics*, vol. 3 (London: Griffin, 1976).

Testing for Normality

If the MLE is used to estimate the model, a specific distribution has to be assumed for the disturbances ε_t. As part of the diagnostic check, one should examine whether the residuals are compatible with this distributional assumption. Thus, in the common case of a normal assumption, the residuals have to be tested for normality. The *Jarque-Bera test* accomplishes this. It is based on the third and fourth sample moments of the residuals. Since the normal distribution is symmetric, the third moment, denoted by μ_3, should be zero; and the fourth moment μ_4, should satisfy $\mu_4 = 3\sigma^4$ where σ^2 is the variance.

The measure of third moment or skewness, $\hat{S}$, of residual distribution can be calculated as

$$\hat{S} = \frac{1}{T} \sum_{t=1}^{T} \frac{\hat{\varepsilon}_t^{\,3}}{\hat{\sigma}^3}$$

and the measure of fourth moment or kurtosis, $\hat{K}$, as

$$\hat{K} = \frac{1}{T} \sum_{t=1}^{T} \frac{\hat{\varepsilon}_t^{\,4}}{3\hat{\sigma}^4} - 1$$

where T is the number of observations, and $\hat{\sigma}$ is the estimator of the standard deviation. Under the assumptions of normality, $\hat{S}$ and $\hat{K}$ would have a mean zero asymptotic normal distribution with variances $6/T$ and $8/3 \cdot T$, respectively.

The Jarque-Bera test tests the null hypothesis

$$H_0 : \frac{\mu_3}{\sigma^3} = 0 \quad \text{and} \quad \frac{\mu_4}{\sigma^4} - 3 = 0$$

The sample statistics

$$\lambda_1 = \frac{1}{6T} \sum_{t=1}^{T} \left(\frac{\hat{\varepsilon}_t^3}{\hat{\sigma}^3} \right)^2 \tag{7.39}$$

and

$$\lambda_2 = \frac{1}{24T} \sum_{t=1}^{T} \left(\frac{\hat{\varepsilon}_t^4}{\hat{\sigma}^4} - 3 \right)^2 \tag{7.40}$$

are asymptotically $\chi^2(1)$ distributed, respectively. The null hypothesis, H_0, as stated above consists of a joint test for λ_1 and λ_2 being zero and can be tested via

$$\lambda_3 = \lambda_1 + \lambda_2$$

which is asymptotically $\chi^2(2)$ distributed.

It should be noted the χ^2 distribution will only be valid for large samples. The small sample properties of the sample moments may deviate considerably from their theoretical counterparts. Thus, for small samples, results of the Jarque-Bera test must be interpreted with caution.

Illustration: Modeling Individual Stock Returns Using Simple ARMA Model

To illustrate a simple ARMA model, we will use a time series of daily returns of Commerzbank, one of the major German banks, for the period January 1, 1999 to December 31, 2002. For closing price series p_t, daily returns (in %) are defined as $y_t = 100[\ln(p_t) - \ln(p_{t-1})]$. Descriptive characteristics for the return series are given in Exhibit 7.4. The Commerzbank return series displays statistical properties associated with nonnormal data as far as the third and fourth moments are concerned. More specifically, the return series are skewed negatively and the frequent number of large absolute returns (either positive or negative) lead to a large degree of kurtosis.

Descriptive graphs for the level of prices and daily return series are given in Exhibits 7.5 and 7.6. The plot in Exhibit 7.5 suggests that the data are nonstationary in the mean. Exhibits 7.7 and 7.8 show the ACF

EXHIBIT 7.4 Descriptive Statistics for the Daily Returns on Commerzbank Stock

Mean	−0.00140
Std. Dev.	0.022
Skewness	−0.4729
Kurtosis	6.8196
Min	−0.1322
Max	0.0753

EXHIBIT 7.5   Commerzbank Stock Daily Closing Price Series from January 1, 1999
to December 31, 2002

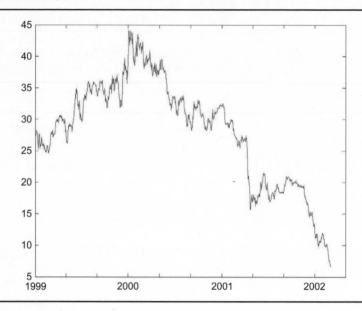

EXHIBIT 7.6   Commerzbank Stock Daily Returns from January 1, 1999 to
December 31, 2002

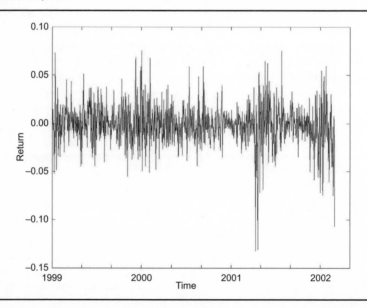

EXHIBIT 7.7   Time Series Plot of the Sample Autocorrelation Function of the Return Series up to 20 Lags[a]

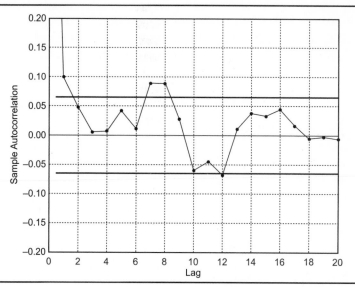

[a] The bold lines reflect the approximate confidence interval.

EXHIBIT 7.8   Time Series Plot of the Partial Sample Autocorrelation Function of the Return Series up to 20 Lags[a]

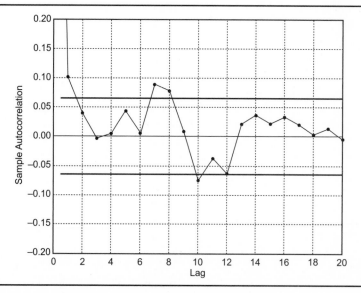

[a] The bold lines reflect the approximate confidence interval.

and PACF estimates given as the correlogram plot respectively. The pattern of SACF shows that there is a strong correlation at lag 7 and 8.

The results for the behavior of the autocorrelation and partial autocorrelation function suggest that the Commerzbank return series can be modeled by some ARMA process. For example, the order of the process may be determined by using the information criteria for model selection.

Fitting an ARMA(1,1) model

$$y_t = a_1 y_{t-1} + b_1 \varepsilon_{t-1} + \varepsilon_t$$

we obtain the coefficients $\hat{a}_1 = 0.3792$ with standard error of 0.2191 (t-statistic = 1.7304), and $\hat{b}_1 = -0.2782$ with standard error of 0.2313 (t-statistic = -1.2029).

To evaluate the validity of the model, we perform diagnostic checks on the residuals with inspection of the structure of the SACF and SPACF of the residuals. The residuals from the fitted model are shown in Exhibit 7.9. Diagnostic plots of the SACF of the residuals from the fitted ARMA(1,1) model are shown in Exhibit 7.10. The first four values of autocorrelations of residuals are very close to zero and only values at lags 7 and 8 appear significant.

EXHIBIT 7.9   Time Series Plot of the Residuals from the Fitted ARMA(1,1) Model

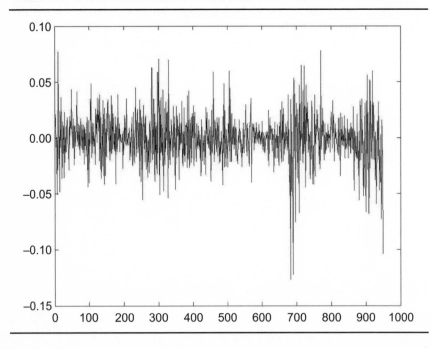

EXHIBIT 7.10   Diagnostic Plot of the ACF of the Residuals from the ARMA(1,1) Model up to 20 Lags[a]

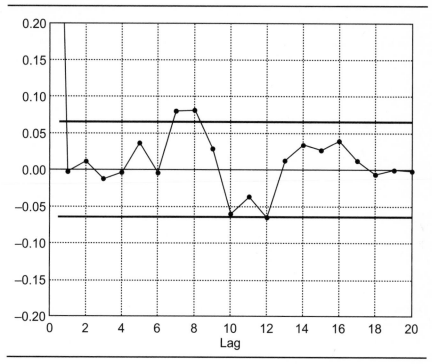

[a] The bold lines reflect the approximate confidence interval.

FORECASTING

Let the data observed up to period t be collected in the information set[23]

$$I_t = \{y_\tau : \tau \le t\}$$

Having observed a time series up to period t, we would like to forecast a future value y_{t+h}. Then, the objective of the forecasting is to predict future realizations of y_t given a specific model. After estimating the model, the estimate of future value y_{t+h} at time t is denoted by $\hat{y}_t(h)$. We distinguish between the one-step-ahead predictor, $\hat{y}_t(1)$, and the multi-step-ahead predictor, $\hat{y}_t(h)$, given the forecasting horizon h and forecasting origin t.

---

[23] Note that I_t contains only information about y_t. In principle, other variables could enter (e.g., in case of ARMAX models).

To characterize the forecasts, three quantities are used:

- Forecast function $\hat{y}_t(h)$
- Forecast error $\hat{\varepsilon}_t(h)$
- Variance of the forecast error

These quantities characterize the quality of forecasts given the underlying forecasting model that has been estimated.

Loss Function

Instead of considering the "true cost" of wrong predictions, we consider a purely statistical criterion, namely, the *mean-squared prediction error* (MSE). Given the information set, we can also define the *conditional expectation* of y_{t+h}:

$$E_t(y_{t+h}): = E(y_{t+h}|I_t) = E(y_{t+h}|y_t, y_{t-1}, \ldots)$$

We would like to find the estimate of y_{t+h}, $\hat{y}_t(h)$, which has the smallest possible MSE:

$$
\begin{aligned}
\mathrm{MSE}(\hat{y}_t(h)) &= E[(y_{t+h} - \hat{y}_t(h))^2] \\
&= E[(y_{t+h} - E_t(y_{t+h}) + E_t(y_{t+h}) - \hat{y}_t(h))^2]
\end{aligned}
\tag{7.41}
$$

Squaring the expression in brackets and using the fact that

$$E[(y_{t+h} - E_t(y_{t+h}))(E_t(y_{t+h}) - \hat{y}_t(h))] = 0 \tag{7.42}$$

which is due to the property that $y_{t+h} - E_t(y_{t+h})$ depends only on ε_{t+1}, ..., ε_{t+h} and $E_t(y_{t+h}) - \hat{y}_t(h)$ only on $y_t, y_{t-1}, \ldots$, then, we obtain

$$\mathrm{MSE}(\hat{y}_t(h)) = \mathrm{MSE}(E_t(y_{t+h})) + E[E_t(y_{t+h}) - \hat{y}_t(h))^2]$$

We see quantity $\mathrm{MSE}(\hat{y}_t(h))$ is minimized, if

$$\hat{y}_t(h) = E_t(y_{t+h})$$

In other words, $E_t(y_{t+h})$, the conditional mean of y_{t+h} given the historical time series observations, is the best estimator in terms of the mean square error.

Best Linear Predictor

We confine ourselves to linear predictions, that is, linear predictions of y_{t+h} given $y_t, y_{t-1},...$ and $\varepsilon_t, \varepsilon_{t-1}, ...$ Assuming a stationary and invertible model (i.e., it has pure AR and MA representations), we have[24]

$$y_{t+h} = \sum_{i=0}^{\infty} c_i \varepsilon_{t+h-i}$$

where $\{c_i\}$ is a sequence of constants with

$$\sum_{i=0}^{\infty} |c_i| < \infty$$

Predictor $\hat{y}_t(h)$ is linear and uses only information $y_t, y_{t-1},...$ or $\varepsilon_t, \varepsilon_{t-1}, ...$ Therefore

$$\hat{y}_t(h) = \sum_{j=0}^{\infty} \tilde{c}_j \varepsilon_{t-j}$$

We obtain the weights $\tilde{c}_i$ that minimize $\mathrm{MSE}(\hat{y}_t(h))$, from the following computation

$$
\begin{aligned}
\mathrm{MSE}(\hat{y}_t(h)) &= E[(y_{t+h} - \hat{y}_t(h))^2] \\
&= E\left[\left(\sum_{i=0}^{\infty} c_i \varepsilon_{t+h-i} - \sum_{j=0}^{\infty} \tilde{c}_j \varepsilon_{t-j} \right)^2\right] \\
&= E\left[\left(\sum_{i=0}^{h-1} c_i \varepsilon_{t+h-i} + \sum_{j=0}^{\infty} (c_{j+h} - \tilde{c}_j)\varepsilon_{t-j} \right)^2\right] \\
&= \sum_{i=0}^{h-1} c_i^2 \sigma^2 + \sum_{j=0}^{\infty} (c_{j+h} - \tilde{c}_j)^2 \sigma^2
\end{aligned}
\tag{7.43}
$$

From (7.33) it follows that $\mathrm{MSE}(\hat{y}_t(h))$ is minimized for

$$\tilde{c}_i = c_{j+h}$$

---

[24] Recall from Chapter 6 that this is the condition for $M(\infty)$ to be a linear process.

and the minimum-MSE h-step predictor for y_{t+h}, that is $E_t(y_{t+h}) = \hat{y}_t(h)$, is given by

$$\hat{y}_t(h) = \sum_{j=0}^{\infty} c_{h+j}\varepsilon_{t-j} = \sum_{j=h}^{\infty} c_j\varepsilon_{t+h-j} \qquad (7.44)$$

The h-step prediction error is then

$$\hat{\varepsilon}_t(h) := y_{t+h} - E_t(\hat{y}_t(h))$$

$$= \sum_{i=0}^{\infty} c_i\varepsilon_{t+h-i} - \sum_{j=h}^{\infty} c_j\varepsilon_{t+h-j}$$

$$= \sum_{j=0}^{h-1} c_j\varepsilon_{t+h-j}$$

and the variance of the h-step prediction error is

$$\text{Var}(\hat{\varepsilon}_t(h)) := \sum_{j=0}^{h-1} c_j^2\sigma^2 = \text{MSE}(\hat{y}_t(h)) \qquad (7.45)$$

There are four points to note:

1. $\text{Var}(\hat{\varepsilon}_t(h)) \overset{h\to\infty}{\to} \gamma_0 = \text{Var}(y_t)$ Thus, the variance of the h-step prediction error approaches the unconditional variance of y_t as $h \to \infty$.
2. Given a_i and b_i, the c_i coefficients can be computed recursively so that (7.44) can be used for prediction. However, for this we require all ε_{t-i}, $i = 0, 1, \ldots$, unless we have a pure MA model, for which ε_{t-i}, $i = 0, 1, \ldots, q$ suffice.
3. For $t = 1, 2, \ldots, T$, we obtain the ε_t's from

$$\varepsilon_t = y_t - \sum_{i=1}^{p} a_i y_{t-i} - \sum_{j=1}^{q} b_i \varepsilon_{t-j}, \qquad t = 1, \ldots, T$$

Setting the initial values of $y_0, y_{-1}, \ldots,$ and $\varepsilon_0, \varepsilon_{-1}, \ldots$ deserves special consideration. For a stationary and invertible model, we have

$$c_j \overset{j\to\infty}{\to} 0$$

in (7.44). Thus, the c_j can be ignored for sufficiently large j.

4. Instead of infinite sum (7.44), we can use the ARMA recursion for multistep prediction:

$$\hat{y}_t(h) = \sum_{i=1}^{p} a_i \hat{y}_t(h-i) + \sum_{j=0}^{q} b_j \hat{\varepsilon}_t(h-j), \quad h = 1, 2, \ldots$$

where

$$\hat{y}_t(h-i) = y_{t+h-i}, \quad i \geq h$$

$$\hat{\varepsilon}_t(h-i) = \begin{cases} \varepsilon_{t+h-j}, & j \geq h \\ 0, & j = 0, 1, \ldots, h-1 \end{cases}$$

Prediction Intervals

The predictor $\hat{y}_t(h)$ derived above yields a point forecast for y_{t+h}. To assess the uncertainty associated with this prediction, we compute the confidence or prediction interval. It is calculated assuming that the fitted model holds true in the future or on an empirical basis from the fitted errors.

Since predictor $\hat{y}_t(h)$ is a linear combination of disturbances ε_t, the distributions of $\hat{y}_t(h)$ and prediction error $\hat{\varepsilon}_t(h)$ are determined by the distribution of the ε_t. Assuming

$$\varepsilon_t \overset{\text{IID}}{\sim} N(0, \sigma^2)$$

we have from (7.45),

$$\hat{\varepsilon}_t(h) \sim N\left(0, \sum_{j=0}^{h-1} c_j^2 \sigma^2\right)$$

Thus the prediction error is normally distributed. Note, however, that $\hat{\varepsilon}_t(h)$, $h = 1, 2, \ldots$, are not independent. The distribution of the normalized prediction error is

$$\frac{\hat{\varepsilon}_t(h)}{\sigma(h)} \sim N(0, 1)$$

where

$$\sigma(h) = \sqrt{\sigma^2 \sum_{j=0}^{h-1} c_j^2}$$

The h-step prediction interval at a specified confidence level $(1 - \alpha)$ of the standard normal distribution can be obtained by observing the normalized prediction error within bounds derived from an $\alpha \times 100\%$ quantile of the standard normal distribution.

Formally, let $z_{(\alpha)}$ denote $\alpha \times 100\%$ quantile of standard normal distribution. Due to the symmetry of standard normal distribution, we have $z_{(\alpha/2)} = -z_{(1-\alpha/2)}$. Then

$$1 - \alpha = \Pr\left\{-z_{(1-\alpha/2)} \le \frac{\hat{\varepsilon}_t(h)}{\sigma(h)} \le z_{(1-\alpha/2)}\right\}$$

$$= \Pr\left\{-z_{(1-\alpha/2)} \le \frac{y_{t+h} - \hat{y}_t(h)}{\sigma(h)} \le z_{(1-\alpha/2)}\right\}$$

$$= \Pr\{\hat{y}_t(h) - z_{(1-\alpha/2)}\sigma(h) \le y_{t+h} \le \hat{y}_t(h) + z_{(1-\alpha/2)}\sigma(h)\}$$

Interval

$$\hat{y}_t(h) \pm z_{(1-\alpha/2)}\sigma(h)$$

or

$$[\hat{y}_t(h) - z_{(1-\alpha/2)}\sigma(h), \hat{y}_t(h) + z_{(1-\alpha/2)}\sigma(h)]$$

is called the $(1 - \alpha) \times 100\%$ *h-step prediction interval*.

Usually, for α the values of 0.05 or 0.01 are chosen. The length of the prediction-error interval increases as h increases, because $\sigma(h)$ increases with h.

CONCEPTS EXPLAINED IN THIS CHAPTER
(IN ORDER OF PRESENTATION)

The Box-Jenkins methodology
Identification
Estimations
Diagnostics
Overdifferencing
Unit root test
Dickey-Fuller test (DF test)
Stochastic trend
Difference stationary process
Augmented Dickey-Fuller test (ADF test)
Akaike information criterion (AIC)
Bayesian information criterion (BIC) or Schwartz criterion
Corrected Akaike information criterion (AICC)
Least squares (LS) estimation
Maximum likelihood (ML) estimation
Testing whiteness of residuals
Box-Pierce Q test
Liung-Box test
McLeod-Li test
Jarque-Bera test
Forecast function
Forecast error
Mean squared prediction error
Prediction intervals
Loss function
Linear predictors

CHAPTER **8**

Autoregressive Conditional Heteroskedastic Models

In linear regression analysis, a standard assumption is that the variance of all squared error terms is the same. This assumption is called *homoskedasticity* (constant variance). However, many time series data exhibit *heteroskedasticity*, where the variances of the error terms are not equal, and in which the error terms may be expected to be larger for some observations or periods of the data than for others. The issue is then how to construct models that accommodate heteroskedasticity so that valid coefficient estimates and models are obtained for the variance of the error terms. *Autoregressive conditional heteroskedasticity* (ARCH) models are the topic of this chapter. They have proven to be very useful in finance to model return variance or volatility of major asset classes including equity, fixed income, and foreign exchange. Understanding the behavior of the variance of the return process is important for forecasting as well as pricing option-type derivative instruments since the variance is a proxy for risk.

Although asset returns, such as stock and exchange rate returns, appear to follow a martingale difference sequence, observation of the daily return plots shows that the amplitude of the returns varies across time. A widely observed phenomenon in finance confirming this fact is the so-called *volatility clustering*. This refers to the tendency of large changes in asset prices (either positive or negative) to be followed by large changes and small changes to be followed by small changes. Hence, there is temporal dependence in asset returns. Typically, they are not even close to being independently and identically distributed (IID). This pattern in the volatility of asset returns was first reported by Mandelbrot.[1] Time-varying vola-

---

[1] Benoit B. Mandelbrot, "The Variation of Certain Speculative Prices," *Journal of Business* 36 (1963), pp. 394–419.

tility and heavy tails found in daily asset returns data are two of the typical *stylized facts* associated with financial return series.[2]

The ARCH model and its generalization, the *generalized autoregressive conditional heteroskedasticity* (GARCH) model, provide a convenient framework to study the problem of modeling volatility clustering. While these models do not answer the question of what causes this phenomenon, they model the underlying time-varying behavior so that forecasts models can be developed. As it turns out, ARCH/GARCH models allow for both volatility clustering and unconditional heavy tails. The ARCH model is one of the pivotal developments in the financial econometrics field and seems to be purposely built for applications in finance.[3] It was introduced in the initial paper by Engle to model inflation rates. Since the seminal papers of Engle[4] in 1982 and Bollerslev[5] in 1987, a large number of variants of the initial ARCH and GARCH models have been developed. They all have the common goal of modeling time-varying volatility, but at the same time they allow extensions to capture more detailed features of financial time series. In addition to ARCH/GARCH models, there are other models of time-varying volatility, such as stochastic-volatility models, which are beyond our objectives here.

In this chapter, we will focus on basic ARCH and GARCH models, discuss their structural properties, their estimation, and how they can be used in forecasting. Additionally, we will discuss important variants of these models along with the relevance for practical use.

ARCH PROCESS

The ARCH process describes a process in which volatility changes in a particular way. Consider an ARCH(q) model for y_t

---

[2] The term stylized facts is used to describe well-known characteristics or empirical regularities of financial return series. For example, daily stock index returns display volatility clustering, fat tails, and almost no autocorrelation. These three major stylized facts can be explained by the ARCH family of models. Additional stylized facts include leverage effect and long memory effect described later in the chapter.

[3] Tim Bollerslev, "The Financial Econometrics: Past Developments and Future Challenges," *Journal of Econometrics* 100 (2001), pp. 41–51.

[4] Robert F. Engle, "Autoregressive Conditional Heteroscedasticity with Estimates of the Variance of U.K. Inflation," *Econometrica* 50 (1982), pp. 987–1008.

[5] Tim Bollerslev, "A Conditionally Heteroscedastic Time-Series Models for Security Prices and Rates of Return Data," *Review of Econometrics and Statistics* 69 (1987), pp. 542–547.

$$y_t = \varepsilon_t \tag{8.1}$$

$$\varepsilon_t = \sqrt{h_t}\eta_t, \quad \eta_t \overset{\text{IID}}{\sim} N(0, 1) \tag{8.2}$$

$$h_t = a_0 + \sum_{i=1}^{q} a_i \varepsilon_{t-i}^2 \tag{8.3}$$

where h_t is the variance of ε_t conditional on the information available at time t. h_t is called the *conditional variance of* ε_t. The sequence $\{\varepsilon_t\}$ is the error process to be modeled. Expression (8.1) is typically extended to the so-called mean equation for y_t that can be more complex and involve additional explanatory variables or at least a constant. The focus of ARCH models is equation (8.3) describing how h_t varies conditionally on past ε_{t-i}^2 (Process $\{\varepsilon_{t-i}^2\}$ is referred to as the noise process.). The random variable η_t is an innovation term which is typically assumed to be IID with mean zero and unit variance. If $\{\eta_t\}$ has the standardized Gaussian distribution (i.e., IID $\eta_t \sim N(0, 1)$), the random variable ε_t is conditionally normal. For this case, we use the term *normal ARCH* model. The Gaussian assumption for η_t is not critical. We can relax it and allow for more heavy-tailed distributions, such as the Student's t-distribution, as is typically required in finance.

Let $\Im_t$ denote the filtration information until time t.[6] Then

$$E(\varepsilon_t^2 | \Im_{t-1}) = E(h_t \eta_t^2 | \Im_{t-1}) = h_t E(\eta_t^2 | \Im_{t-1}) = h_t$$

This implies that the conditional variance of ε_t evolves according to previous realizations of ε_t^2. Thus, we can write $\varepsilon_t | \Im_{t-1} \sim N(0, h_t)$.

In order to have a well-defined process described by (8.3), conditions on the coefficients need to be imposed to avoid negative h_t values. To ensure this, the parameters in the conditional variance equation (8.3) should satisfy $a_0 > 0$ and $a_i \geq 0$ for $i = 1, 2, ..., q$.

In its simplest form, an ARCH(q) model represents the asset return series $\{y_t\}$ with the process $\{\varepsilon_t\}$ as in (8.1). As stated earlier, in practice, equation (8.1) takes a more complex form and describes how y_t varies over time. For example, y_t could have a conditionally varying mean, μ_t, arising, for example, from an ARMA structure, and $\varepsilon_t = y_t - \mu_t$ then represents a shock in the asset return process. The generalized model of y_t

---

[6] More formally, $\Im_{t-1} = \sigma(\varepsilon_{t-1}, \varepsilon_{t-2}, ...)$ denotes the sigma field generated by past information until time t. $\sqrt{h_t}$ in (8.2) is a positive, time-varying, and measurable function with respect to σ-algebra $\Im_{t-1}$.

incorporating more complex structures is discussed later in this chapter in the section ARMA-GARCH models.

Properties of ARCH Processes

The structure of the ARCH model implies that the conditional variance of ε_t, h_t, evolves according to the most recent realizations of ε_t^2 analogous to an autoregressive AR(q) model. Large past squared shocks imply a large conditional variance for ε_t. As a consequence, ε_t tends to assume a large value which in turn implies that a large shock tends to be followed by another large shock.

Let us now take a closer look at the ARCH(1) model for process $\{\varepsilon_t\}$. Equation (8.3) for an ARCH(1) model becomes $h_t = a_0 + a_1\varepsilon_{t-1}^2$ capturing the effect that a large value in ε_t leads to a larger variance (volatility) in the following period. By recursive substitution of (8.3) into (8.2) for ARCH(1) case, we obtain

$$
\begin{aligned}
\varepsilon_t^2 &= h_t\eta_t^2 \\
&= \eta_t^2(a_0 + a_1\varepsilon_{t-1}^2) \\
&= a_0\eta_t^2 + a_1\varepsilon_{t-1}^2\eta_t^2 \\
&= a_0\eta_t^2 + a_1\eta_t^2(h_{t-1}\eta_{t-1}^2) \\
&= a_0\eta_t^2 + a_1\eta_t^2\eta_{t-1}^2(a_0 + a_1\varepsilon_{t-2}^2) \\
&\vdots \\
&= a_0\sum_{i=0}^{n}a_1^i\eta_t^2\cdots\eta_{t-i}^2 + a_1^{n+1}\eta_t^2\eta_{t-1}^2\cdots\eta_{t-n}^2\varepsilon_{t-n-1}^2
\end{aligned}
\tag{8.4}
$$

If $a_1 < 1$, the last term of the expression above tends to zero as n tends to ∞, and we obtain

$$
\varepsilon_t^2 = a_0\sum_{i=0}^{\infty}a_1^i\eta_t^2\cdots\eta_{t-i}^2
\tag{8.5}
$$

Therefore, ε_t is a nonlinear function of $(\eta_t, \eta_{t-1}, \ldots)$ with the following properties:

1. The unconditional mean of ε_t is zero, since

$$
E(\varepsilon_t) = E(E(\varepsilon_t|\mathfrak{I}_{t-1})) = E(E(\sqrt{h_t}\eta_t|\mathfrak{I}_{t-1})) = E(\sqrt{h_t}E(\eta_t)) = 0
$$

where $\Im_{t-1}$ denotes the information set available at time $t-1$.

2. The conditional variance of ε_t is

$$E(\varepsilon_t^2 | \Im_{t-1}) = E(h_t \eta_t^2 | \Im_{t-1}) = h_t E(\eta_t^2 | \Im_{t-1}) = h_t = a_0 + a_1 \varepsilon_{t-1}^2$$

3. The unconditional variance of ε_t is obtained as[7]

$$Var(\varepsilon_t) = E(\varepsilon_t^2) = E[E(\varepsilon_t^2 | \Im_{t-1})] = E(a_0 + a_1 \varepsilon_{t-1}^2)$$

$$= a_0 + a_1 E(\varepsilon_{t-1}^2) = a_0 / (1 - a_1)$$

4. The kurtosis of ε_t, K_ε, is given by

$$K_\varepsilon = \frac{E(\varepsilon_t^4)}{[Var(\varepsilon_t)]^2} = \frac{E(\varepsilon_t^4)}{E(\varepsilon_t^2)^2} = 3 \frac{1 - a_1^2}{1 - 3a_1^2} > 3$$

where we assume that the ε_t has a finite fourth moment.[8] The ARCH model with a conditionally normal distribution ε_t leads to heavy tails in the unconditional distribution. In other words, the excess kurtosis of ε_t is positive and the tail distribution of ε_t is heavier than that of the normal distribution.

Thus, the ARCH(1) process has a mean of zero, a constant unconditional variance, and a time-varying conditional variance. The ε_t is a stationary process for which $0 \le a_1 < 1$ is satisfied, since the variance of ε_t must be positive. Additional constraints on a_1 may be imposed if the higher-order moments of ε_t need to exist. For example, to examine the tail behavior of ε_t in Property 4, a requirement of the finite fourth moment of ε_t is imposed. It turns out that Properties (1) through (4) also hold for higher order ARCH models but the relevant formulas become more involved.

The ARCH model provides a useful framework for modeling volatility of returns since it partially captures the phenomenon that—in absolute terms—large returns would be again followed by large returns. However, ARCH models possess some drawbacks in practical applications:

---

[7] This follows from the fact that ε_t is a stationary process with $E(\varepsilon_t) = 0$ and deriving $Var(\varepsilon_t) = Var(\varepsilon_{t-1}) = E(\varepsilon_{t-1}^2)$.
[8] We also assume the condition $0 \le a_1 \le 1$ that guarantees stationarity. For the derivation, see for example, Ruey S. Tsay, *Analysis of Financial Time Series* (New York: John Wiley & Sons, 2002).

- Due to the structure of the model, only the squared ε_{t-i} affect the current volatility, $\sqrt{h_t}$. This may be unrealistic since in practice, volatility may respond differently to positive and negative values of ε_t (e.g., positive and negative shocks may be interpreted as good and bad news, respectively, that may impact the volatility differently).
- It might be difficult to determine the order of q, the number of lags of the squared residuals in the model.
- The impact of a large shock lasts only for q periods.

GARCH PROCESS

In Chapter 6 we started with the analysis of an AR model and extended it to include MA component, giving rise to a general ARMA model. Analogously, we can extend the concept of an ARCH model to a generalized ARCH (GARCH) model. Next, we consider the GARCH(p, q) process for the time series ε_t

$$\varepsilon_t = \sqrt{h_t}\eta_t, \quad \eta_t \overset{\text{IID}}{\sim} N(0, 1) \tag{8.6}$$

$$h_t = a_0 + \sum_{i=1}^{q} a_i\varepsilon_{t-i}^2 + \sum_{j=1}^{p} b_j h_{t-j} \tag{8.7}$$

where, again, h_t is the conditional variance of ε_t (conditional on the information available at time t), and η_t are IID with mean 0 and variance 1. Thus the GARCH(p,q) model relates the conditional variance, h_t, to a linear function of past squared errors and past conditional variances. Difference from the ARCH model is that GARCH model allows the conditional variance to be modeled by past values of itself in addition to the past shocks. For process (8.7) to be well defined and to ensure that the conditional variance of ε_t is stationary, the conditions on the parameters a's and b's need to be imposed. This can be quite involved and we will show some technical aspects of the problem in the next section. For now, we assume that the parameters $(a_0, a_1, ..., a_q, b_1, ..., b_p)$ are restricted such that $h_t > 0$ for all t, which is ensured when $a_0 > 0$, $a_i \geq 0$ for $i = 1, 2, ..., q$, and $b_j \geq 0$ for $j = 1, 2, ..., p$. We also assume that the fourth moment of η_t exists.

It is important to note that not only the ε_{t-i}^2 but also the h_{t-j} are unobservable. h_{t-j} can be estimated from the initial sample of the data but it is better to reparameterize (8.7) and rewrite it as an ARMA process. Rewriting the equation for h_t in (8.7) considering the squared random variable ε_t at time t relative to the conditional variance and by substituting for $u_t = \varepsilon_t^2 - h_t$, we obtain an ARMA($r$, p) representation for ε_t^2:

$$\varepsilon_t^2 = a_0 + \sum_{i=1}^{r} (a_i + b_i)\varepsilon_{t-i}^2 + u_t - \sum_{j=1}^{p} b_j u_{t-j}$$

where $r = \max(p, q)$. $\{u_t\}$ is a martingale difference series (i.e., $E(u_t) = 0$ and $\text{Cov}(u_t, u_{t-i}) = 0$ for $i \geq 1$). However, $\{u_t\}$ in general is not an IID sequence. In compact representation, we can write the ARMA representation as

$$\Phi(L)\varepsilon_t^2 = a_0 + b(L)u_t \tag{8.8}$$

where L is the lag (backward shift) operator,

$$\Phi(L) = 1 - \sum_{i=1}^{r} \Phi_i L^i$$

$\Phi_i = a_i + b_i$, $r = \max(p, q)$, and

$$b(L) = 1 - \sum_{i=1}^{p} b_i L^i$$

It is clear that $a_i = 0$ for $i > q$ and $b_i = 0$ for $i > p$. Thus, by defining $u_t = \varepsilon_t^2 - h_t$, process $\{\varepsilon_t^2\}$ can be viewed as an ARMA(r,p) process driven by the noise u_t.

Note that the Gaussian assumption of η_t is not always realistic. If the distribution of the historical innovations $\eta_{t-n}, \ldots, \eta_t$ is heavier tailed than the normal, one can modify the model and allow heavy-tailed distributions such as the Student's t-distribution. We address this issue in more detail later in this chapter and in the Chapter 14 where we discuss stable Paretian distributions.

Let us now consider the simple GARCH(1,1) model, which is the most popular for modeling asset-return volatility. We write this model as

$$\varepsilon_t = \sqrt{h_t}\eta_t, \quad \eta_t \sim N(0,1)$$

$$h_t = a_0 + a_1 \varepsilon_{t-1}^2 + b_1 h_{t-1} \tag{8.9}$$

The conditional variance in (8.9) is modeled by the past shock ε_{t-1}^2 and its own lagged value h_{t-1}. For $a_0 \geq 0$, $a_1 > 0$, $b_1 > 0$ and $a_1 + b_1 < 1$,

$\{(\varepsilon_t, \sqrt{h_t})\}$ is a strict stationary solution of (8.9). The sum $a_1 + b_1$ measures the persistence of the conditional variance to shocks. It approaches infinity as $a_1 + b_1$ approaches one from below.[9] Considering (8.8), if ε_t satisfies (8.9), then ε_t^2 has the ARMA(1,1) representation

$$\varepsilon_t^2 = a_0 + (a_1 + b_1)\varepsilon_{t-1}^2 + u_t - b_1 u_{t-1}$$

where $u_t = \varepsilon_t^2 - h_t$ and the expectation and variance conditional on $\Im_{t-1}$ are $E_{t-1}(u_t) = 0$ and $\text{Var}_{t-1}(u_t) = h_t^2 E[(\varepsilon_t^2 - 1)^2]$, respectively. It is also assumed that ε_t and $\sqrt{h_t}$ have finite fourth moments, which requires that $3a_1^2 + 2a_1 b_1 + b_1^2 \geq 1$.

As in the ARCH case, GARCH processes with a conditional normal return distribution imply unconditional distributions that have heavier tails than the normal distribution. Thus, the ARCH/GARCH models allow for both volatility clustering and (unconditional) heavy tails.

The relationship between the kurtosis of $\{\varepsilon_t\}$ and the volatility clustering and conditional nonnormality (non-Gaussian innovations) can be further explored since both volatility clustering and conditional nonnormality can induce the leptokurtosis typically observed in financial return series. Bai, Russel, and Tiao[10] consider the ARMA(r,q) representation of the GARCH(p,q) process (8.8) and analyze the relationships between (1) the excess kurtosis of η_t, called the *IID kurtosis* and denoted by K_η, (2) the excess kurtosis of ε_t, called the *overall kurtosis* and denoted by K_ε if it exists, and (3) the excess kurtosis of the normal GARCH process, called the *GARCH kurtosis* and denoted by $K_\varepsilon^{(g)}$ if it exists. They make two additional assumptions to ensure that u_t's are uncorrelated with zero mean and finite variance and that the $\{\varepsilon_t^2\}$ proccess is weakly stationary.[11] Obviously, if η_t follows a normal distribution, $K_\eta = 0$ and

---

[9] Robert F. Engle and Tim Bollerslev, "Modelling the Persistence of Conditional Variances," *Econometric Reviews* 5 (1986), pp. 1–50.

[10] Xuezheng Bai, Jeffrey R. Russel, and George C. Tiao, "Kurtosis of GARCH and Stochastic Volatility Models with Non-Normal Innovations," *Journal of Econometrics* 114 (2003), pp. 349–360.

[11] Specifically, they assume

A1: All the zeroes of the polynomial $\Phi(L)$ in (8.8) are lying outside the unit circle
A2: $0 < (K_\eta + 2)k_1 < 1$, with

$$k_1 = \sum_{i=1}^{\infty} \psi_i^2$$

where

$$\psi(L) = 1 + \sum_{i=1}^{\infty} \psi_i L^i = b(L)/\Phi(L).$$

process (8.7) is a normal GARCH(p,q) process. Their results show that if ε_t follows the GARCH(p,q) process specified by (8.7) and satisfies the additional two assumptions, the following holds:

$$K_\varepsilon^{(g)} = \frac{6k_1}{1 - 2k_1} \tag{8.10a}$$

$$K_\varepsilon = \frac{K_\varepsilon^{(g)} + K_\eta + (5/6)K_\varepsilon^{(g)}K_\eta}{1 - (1/6)K_\varepsilon^{(g)}K_\eta} \tag{8.10b}$$

Expression (8.10a) for $K_\varepsilon^{(g)}$ relates the normal GARCH kurtosis to the GARCH parameters a_i's and b_i's in (8.7) and characterizes the fact that volatility clustering introduces leptokurtosis.

For a normal GARCH(1,1) model, (8.10a) reduces to

$$K_\varepsilon^{(g)} = \frac{6a_1^2}{1 - (a_1 + b_1)^2 - 2a_1^2}$$

which shows that coefficient a_1 plays an important role in determining the tail behavior of ε_t. If $a_1 = 0$, then $K_\varepsilon^{(g)} = 0$ and there are no heavy tails, and if $a_1 > 0$ then the $\{\varepsilon_t\}$ process has heavy tails. The kurtosis of ε_t exists if $1 - 2a_1^2 - (a_1 + b_1)^2 > 0$.[12]

The empirical results of Bai, Russel, and Tiao, considering the autocorrelation function of $\{\varepsilon_t^2\}$ for a normal GARCH(1,1) model, indicate that the implied GARCH kurtosis, $K_\varepsilon^{(g)}$, takes values which are substantially below the sample excess kurtosis found in the return data. Thus the normal GARCH(1,1) model is not capable of matching the large leptokurtosis typically found in the data. This motivated Bollerslev[13] to suggest the use of the Student's t-distribution to match excessive sample kurtosis.

The expression (8.10b) for the overall kurtosis K_ε suggests that $K_\varepsilon^{(g)}$ (GARCH kurtosis induced by time-varying volatility), and K_η (kurtosis of the IID innovation process), contribute symmetrically to the increase of the overall kurtosis. The experiments of Bai, Russel, and Tiao show that a nonnormal GARCH model fits well the time-varying volatility relation and matches the sample kurtosis much better.

---

[12] See Tim Bollerslev, "Generalized Autoregressive Conditional Heteroscedasticity," *Journal of Econometrics* 31 (1986), pp. 307–327.
[13] Bollerslev, "Generalized Autoregressive Conditional Heteroscedasticity."

Properties of GARCH Processes

The structural properties of GARCH processes relate to conditions for the existence of a stationary solution and higher-order moments. The necessary and sufficient condition for strict stationarity and ergodicity of the GARCH(1,1) model in (8.9) is obtained as follows

$$E[\ln(b_1 + a_1\eta_t^2)] < 0 \tag{8.11}$$

Condition (8.11) allows $a_1 + b_1$ to be 1, or slightly larger than 1, in which case $E(\varepsilon_t^2) = 0$. The derivation of (8.11) is given in this chapter's appendix. For the general model (8.6) and (8.7), the necessary and sufficient condition for second-order stationarity is

$$\sum_{i=1}^{q} a_i + \sum_{i=1}^{p} b_i < 1 \tag{8.12}$$

The necessary and sufficient condition for strict stationarity and ergodicity of the general model (8.6) and (8.7) was established by Bougerol and Picard[14] as follows:

$$\sum_{i=1}^{q} a_i + \sum_{i=1}^{p} b_i \leq 1 \tag{8.13}$$

Ling and McAleer[15] established the necessity and sufficiency of the condition for the existence of the fourth and higher moments for the GARCH(p, q) model. He and Terasvirta[16] observe the following general class of GARCH(1,1) model:

$$\varepsilon_t = z_t h_t, \quad h_t^\delta = g(z_{t-1}) + c(z_{t-1})h_{t-1}^\delta \tag{8.14}$$

where $\Pr\{h_t^\delta > 0\} = 1$, $\delta > 0$, z_t is a sequence of IID random variables with mean zero and variance 1, and $g(x)$ and $c(x)$ are nonnegative func-

---

[14] P. Bougerol and N. Picard, "Stationarity of GARCH Processes and of Some Nonnegative Time Series," *Journal of Econometrics* 52 (1992), pp. 115–127.

[15] Shiqing Ling and Michael McAleer, "Necessary and Sufficient Moment Conditions for the GARCH(r,s) and Asymmetric Power GARCH(r,s) Models," *Econometric Theory* 18 (2002), pp. 722–729.

[16] C. He and Timo Terasvirta, "Properties of Moments of a Family of GARCH Processes," *Journal of Econometrics* 92 (1999), pp. 173–192.

tions. The necessary condition for the $m\delta$-th unconditional moment of model (8.14) to exist is

$$E[c(z_t)]^m < 1 \qquad (8.15)$$

where m is a positive integer and $\delta = 1$ or 2. The result is derived under the assumption of the conditional process (e.g., the process started at some finite value infinitely many periods ago). Although result (8.15) is a useful one, it cannot be verified in practice, so it is an axiom rather than assumption. Ling and McAleer[17] obtain the sufficient conditions for the strict stationarity of model (8.14) without invoking the assumption of the conditional model.[18] They establish two propositions dealing with expression (8.14). In the first, they establish that for some real $\alpha \in (0,1]$, there exists a unique $\alpha\delta$-order stationary solution to (8.14) if $E|z_t|^{\alpha\delta} < \infty$, $E[g(z_t)]^\alpha < \infty$ and $E[c(z_t)]^\alpha < 1$. In the second proposition, they postulate that the necessary and sufficient condition for the existence of the $m\delta$th moment of the solution for $\{\varepsilon_t\}$ in Proposition 1 is $E[c(z_t)]^{m\delta} < 1$, where m is a positive integer if the conditions $|z_t|^{m\delta} < \infty$ and $E[g(z_t)]^{m\alpha} < \infty$ are satisfied.

For example, when $g(z_{t-1}) \equiv a_0 > 0$ and $c(z_{t-1}) \equiv a_1 z_{t-1}^2 + b_1$, we have a GARCH(1,1) process and condition $E[c(z_t)]^\alpha < 1$ for some $\alpha \in (0,1]$ is equivalent to condition $E[\ln[c(z_t)]] < 0$, which is the necessary and sufficient condition established in (8.11).

ESTIMATION OF THE GARCH MODELS

A main obstacle for estimating GARCH models is that the conditional variance in (8.7) is an unobserved variable, which must itself be explicitly estimated along with the parameters of the model.

Maximum Likelihood Estimation
Engle[19] suggested two possible methods for estimating the parameters in model (8.1)–(8.3), namely the *least squares estimator* (LSE) and the *maximum likelihood estimator* (MLE). The LSE is given as

---

[17] Shiqing Ling and Michael McAleer, "Stationarity and the Existence of Moments of a Family of GARCH Processes," *Journal of Econometrics* 106 (2002), pp. 109–117.

[18] They show that model (8.14) in fact, did start infinitely many periods ago, but they argue this is the consequence of the existence of the unique stationary solution and is not an assumption.

[19] Engle, "Autoregressive Conditional Heteroscedasticity with Estimates of the Variance of U.K. Inflation."

$$\hat{\delta} = \left(\sum_{t=2}^{T} \tilde{\varepsilon}_{t-1} \tilde{\varepsilon}'_{t-1} \right)^{-1} \sum_{t=2}^{T} \tilde{\varepsilon}_{t-1} \varepsilon_t^2 \tag{8.16}$$

where $\hat{\delta} = (a_0, a_1, ..., a_p)'$ and $\tilde{\varepsilon}_t = (1, \varepsilon_t^2, ..., \varepsilon_{t-p+1}^2)'$. The $\hat{\delta}$ is consistent and asymptotically normal if $E(\varepsilon_t^8) < \infty$ which is a strong condition.

We will briefly discuss the method of maximum likelihood estimation. Recall the assumption of the ARCH model that $\varepsilon_t = \sqrt{h_t} \eta_t$ with $\eta_t \sim N(0, 1)$ IID. Then, the likelihood, l_t, of ε_t is

$$l_t = \frac{1}{\sqrt{2\pi h_t}} \exp\left(-\frac{1}{2h_t} \varepsilon_t^2 \right)$$

which is the conditional probability function of $f(\varepsilon_t | \mathfrak{S}_{t-1})$ where $\mathfrak{S}_{t-1} = \sigma(\varepsilon_{t-1}, \varepsilon_{t-2}, ...)$.[20] By iterating this conditional argument, we obtain

$$f(\varepsilon_T, ..., \varepsilon_1 | \varepsilon_0) = f(\varepsilon_T | \varepsilon_{T-1}, ..., \varepsilon_0) \cdots f(\varepsilon_2 | \varepsilon_1, \varepsilon_0) f(\varepsilon_1 | \varepsilon_0) = \prod_{t=1}^{T} f(\varepsilon_t | \mathfrak{S}_{t-1})$$

The joint likelihood of the entire sample of T observations is

$$L = \prod_{t=1}^{T} l_t$$

and for the log likelihood we obtain

$$\log f(\varepsilon_T, ..., \varepsilon_1 | \varepsilon_0) = \sum_{t=1}^{T} \log f(\varepsilon_t | \mathfrak{S}_{t-1})$$

$$= -\frac{T}{2} \log 2\pi + \sum_{t=1}^{T} -\frac{1}{2} \log h_t - \frac{1}{2} \sum_{t=1}^{T} \frac{\varepsilon_t^2}{h_t} \tag{8.17}$$

The conditional log-likelihood function can thus be written as

---

[20] Recall that σ denotes the sigma algebra generated by ε_t. The choice of logarithm is convenient as it replaces products with sums and maximizing the logarithm of a function is equivalent to maximizing the function itself as the logarithm is a monotone, increasing function.

$$L(\theta) = -\frac{1}{2} \sum_{t=1}^{T} \left(\log 2\pi + \log h_t(\theta) + \frac{\varepsilon_t^2(\theta)}{h_t(\theta)} \right) \qquad (8.18)$$

where $\theta = (a_0, a_1, ..., a_q, b_1, ..., b_p)$. The value of θ which maximizes $L(\theta)$ is referred to as maximum likelihood estimates or MLEs. Under certain technical assumptions, MLEs are consistent and asymptotically normal. Hence, with infinitely many observations the parameter estimates would converge to their true values and the variance of the estimates would be the smallest possible.

The MLE of a GARCH model is obtained by numerically maximizing the log-likelihood function using iterative optimization methods like Gauss-Newton or Newton-Raphson. The log-likelihood function may have many local maxima and different algorithms could end up in different local maxima of function (8.18). To determine parameter vector estimate $\hat{\theta}$, the Berndt, Hall, Hall, and Hausmann (BHHH) algorithm[21] is often used but it may encounter convergence problems if the initial values are not sufficiently close to the final solutions. The information matrix of function (8.18) is block-diagonal so that the parameters in the conditional-mean and the conditional-variance equation can be estimated separately without loss of asymptotic efficiency. The residuals from the estimated conditional mean equation can be used to estimate the conditional variances.

Starting values for the parameters in θ and initialization of the two series ε_t^2 and h_t need to be specified for iterative ML optimization. Econometric software packages use conditional maximum likelihood to estimate the model, that is, the estimation is conducted conditional upon the pre-sample initializations of ε and h.[22] The usual default solution to parameter initializations is to set parameter values in the mean equal to those estimated using a "first pass" LS estimation, and the parameters (except a_0) in the conditional-variance equation to zero. For the conditional variance h_t, a common initialization is to set each element to the average mean-adjusted sum of squares of the data, i.e., the residual sum of squares from a linear regression of the dependent vari-

---

[21] E. Berndt, B. Hall, R. Hall, and J. Hausmann, "Estimation and Inference in Non-linear Structural Models," *Annals of Economic and Social Measurement* 3 (1974), pp. 653–665.
[22] For a detailed description of the procedure and comparison of nine software packages with particular reference to estimation accuracy of GARCH models, see Chris Brooks, Simon P. Burke, and Gita Persand, "Benchmarks and the Accuracy of GARCH Model Estimation," *International Journal of Forecasting* 17 (2001), pp. 45–56.

able on a constant, divided by the number of observations. Differences in parameter initialization of the packages may yield different results.

Quasi-Maximum Likelihood Estimation

When the innovation process is not normal or the conditional distribution is not perfectly known, one may still use Gaussian MLE methods due to the property of asymptotic parameter efficiency. Such estimates are known as pseudo- or quasi-MLE (PMLE or QMLE). QMLE is consistent and asymptotically normal if $E(\varepsilon_t^2) < \infty$.[23] The QMLE estimates are in general less precise than those from MLE, provided that the η_t are indeed Gaussian.

Recently, it has been established[24] for a nonstationary ARCH(1) model (i.e., $E[\ln(b_1 + a_1\eta_t^2)] \geq 0$ holds with $b_1 = 0$) and IID $(0,1)$ innovation process $\{\eta_t\}$ with finite variance $\mathrm{Var}(\eta_t^2) = E(\eta_t^4 - 1) = \zeta$, that as $T \to \infty$ then the sequence of QMLE estimators $\hat{\delta}_T$ is consistent and asymptotically normal,

$$\sqrt{T}\left(\hat{\delta}_T - \delta\right) \xrightarrow{d} N(0, \sigma^2)$$

where[25]

$$\sigma^2 = \zeta a^2 > 0$$

In other words, for the ARCH(1) model the QMLE is always asymptotically normal as long as the fourth-order moment of the innovations η_t is finite. This is surprising in the absence of strict stationarity. More importantly, these results hold for the GARCH(1,1) model as well.[26] Thus, whether or not the process is stationary, asymptotic normality holds.

The local QMLE for GARCH(p, q) is consistent and asymptotically normal if $E(\varepsilon_t^4) < \infty$. For the global QMLE the condition $E(\varepsilon_t^2) < \infty$ is sufficient for consistency and $E(\varepsilon_t^6) < \infty$ is sufficient for asymptotic normality. The QMLE is efficient only if η_t is normal. When η_t is not normal, adaptive estimation is useful to obtain efficient estimators.

Another alternative approach to estimation is the generalized method of moments which is beyond the scope of the coverage here.

---

[23] Shiqing Ling and Michael McAleer, "Asymptotic Theory for a Vector ARMA-GARCH Model," *Econometric Theory* 19 (2003), pp. 278–308.
[24] S.T. Jensen and A. Rahbek, "Asymptotic Normality of the QMLE Estimator of ARCH in the Nonstationary Case," *Econometrica* 72 (2004), pp. 641–646.
[25] Note that if z_t is Gaussian, then $\sigma^2 = 2a^2$.
[26] S. T. Jensen and A. Rahbek, "Asymptotic Normality for Non-Stationary, Explosive GARCH," Preprint No. 4, Department of Applied Mathematics and Statistics (2003), University of Copenhagen.

STATIONARY ARMA-GARCH MODELS

In the initial definition of the ARCH process given by (8.1) through (8.3), the observed process was simply assumed to be the error process $\{\varepsilon_t\}$. While the purpose of the ARCH/GARCH models is to analyze and model the second moment or volatilities of financial and economic data, the specification of the conditional mean is still important. If the conditional mean is not specified adequately, then the construction of consistent estimates of the true conditional variance process would not be possible and statistical inference and empirical analysis might be wrong. This means that we have to capture the conditional mean of the data with an adequate model so that the residuals obtained from this model satisfy the assumptions for the white-noise sequence $\{\varepsilon_t\}$ which enters the conditional variance. This establishes in essence a joint estimation of two models, the conditional-mean and the conditional-variance model.

For asset returns, the conditional mean is typically captured by an AR or ARMA model. We define the joint ARMA-GARCH model by

$$y_t = \sum_{i=1}^{p} a_i y_{t-i} + \sum_{i=1}^{q} b_i \varepsilon_{t-i} + \varepsilon_t \tag{8.19a}$$

$$\varepsilon_t = \sqrt{h_t}\,\eta_t, \quad h_t = \alpha_0 + \sum_{i=1}^{r} \alpha_i \varepsilon_{t-i}^2 + \sum_{i=1}^{s} \beta_i h_{t-i} \tag{8.19b}$$

where η_t is a sequence of IID random variables, with mean zero and variance one. We also say that the observations $y_1, \ldots, y_T$ are generated by the ARMA model with errors generated by the GARCH process. When $s = 0$, the ARMA-GARCH model reduces to the ARMA-ARCH model.

If all the roots of

$$\phi(z) = z^p - \sum_{i=1}^{p} a_i z^{p-i}$$

lie outside the unit circle, the ARMA-GARCH process y_t is strictly stationary if ε_t is strictly stationary, and y_t is $2m$-th order stationary if ε_t is $2m$-th stationary.[27] If the characteristic polynomial has one unit root taking the value +1, with other roots lying outside the unit circle, (8.19a) and (8.19b) is nonstationary.

---

[27] W. K. Li, Shiqing Ling, and Michael McAleer, "Recent Theoretical Results for Time Series Models with GARCH Errors," *Journal of Economic Surveys* 16 (2002), pp. 245–269.

The parameters of an ARMA-GARCH model can be jointly estimated via MLE. Alternatively, a two-step procedure can be adopted:

1. Estimate the parameters of the conditional mean in (8.19a).
2. From residuals of (8.19a), estimate the parameters of the GARCH model using the methods described in the previous sections.

The latter is sometimes referred to as GARCH estimation after linear filtering or removing linear dependence.[28]

LAGRANGE MULTIPLIER TEST

In order to determine whether or not an ARCH specification is necessary, one needs to test the residuals of the conditional-mean equation for ARCH effects. The squared series $\{\varepsilon_t^2\}$ can be examined to check for heteroskedasticity, as is done in the *Lagrange multiplier test* (LM test) developed by Engle. The test is based upon the score under the null and the information matrix under the null.

This LM test checks the hypothesis that $\{\varepsilon_t\}$ is an IID white noise against the alternative that is an ARCH(q) process. The testing problem can be formulated as the test of the null hypothesis that the ARCH coefficients are all zero, i.e.,

$$H_0: a_1 = a_2 = \dots = a_q = 0$$

against the alternative,

$$H_1: a_i > 0 \text{ for at least one } i = 1, 2, \dots, q \tag{8.20}$$

Consider the ARCH model with $h_t = h(z_t a)$ where h is some differentiable function and $z_t = (1, \hat{e}_{t-1}^2, \dots, \hat{e}_{t-q}^2)$ where e_t are the mean-equation residuals, and $a = (a_0, a_1, \dots, a_q)'$. Under the null, h_t is a constant denoted h^0.

The LM statistic is given by

---

[28] The ARMA-GARCH models are examples of models that are linear in mean and nonlinear in variance. Other combinations of models for mean and variance are possible, such as models that are nonlinear in mean but linear in variance (e.g., bicorrelation models), or models that are nonlinear in both mean and variance (e.g., threshold models).

$$\zeta^* = \frac{1}{2} f' Z (Z'Z)^{-1} Z' f \qquad (8.21)$$

where

$$Z' = (z'_1, z'_2, ..., z'_T), f' = (\hat{f}_1, \hat{f}_2, ..., \hat{f}_T),$$

$$\hat{f}_t = \frac{\hat{e}_t^2}{\hat{\sigma}^2} - 1, \hat{\sigma}^2 = \frac{1}{T} \sum_{t=1}^{T} \hat{e}_t^2$$

The LM statistic does not depend on the linear form of the conditional variance function h_t in equation (8.3)[29] which implies that the test statistic for any specification of h_t depends only on the past squared errors $\{\varepsilon_{t-i}^2 : i = 1, 2, ..., q\}$. Under the assumption of conditional normality of the errors $\{\varepsilon_t\}$, an asymptotically equivalent statistic is given by

$$\zeta = \frac{T f' Z (Z'Z)^{-1} Z' f}{f' f} = TR^2 \qquad (8.22)$$

where R^2 is the squared multiple correlation between f and Z^{30} or the R^2 of the regression of $\hat{e}_t^2$ on a constant and q lagged values of $\hat{e}_t^2$. Under the null hypothesis of no ARCH effect, the LM statistic ζ asymptotically follows the χ_q^2 distribution.[31]

In summary, the test procedure is performed by first obtaining the residuals from the ordinary least squares regression of the conditional-mean equation and then regressing the squared residuals on a constant and q lags, where q can be chosen arbitrarily. TR^2 is evaluated against χ_q^2 distribution. This is asymptotically locally most powerful test.

Illustration: Fitting a GARCH(1,1) Model

We examine the behavior of the DAX index return series using a GARCH(1,1) model. The autocorrelation structure present in the second-order moments of returns on the DAX index indicates some form of heteroskedasticity. We estimate a GARCH(1,1) model jointly with a mean model given by a constant

---

[29] Engle, "Autoregressive Conditional Heteroscedasticity with Estimates of the Variance of U.K. Inflation."
[30] f is the column vector of $(e_t^2 / h^0 - 1)$.
[31] Engle, "Autoregressive Conditional Heteroscedasticity with Estimates of the Variance of U.K. Inflation."

$$y_t = c + \varepsilon_t$$
$$\varepsilon_t = \sqrt{h_t}z_t, \quad z_t \sim N(0, 1)$$
$$h_t = a_0 + a_1\varepsilon_{t-1}^2 + b_1 h_{t-1}$$

where y_t is the return at time t, h_t the conditional variance at time t, and z_t the standardized residual. The residuals conditional on past information are assumed to be normally distributed.

The maximum likelihood estimates for the GARCH(1,1) model for the DAX return series are given in Exhibit 8.1. The coefficients of all three terms in the conditional variance equation, are highly significant as measured by their t-statistics. Note the high significance of the coefficient b_1 which is associated with the variance of the previous period.

Process $\{\varepsilon_t\}$ will be stationary if $a_1 + b_1 < 1$; in that case the unconditional variance is given by $a_0/(1 - a_1 - b_1)$. The sum $a_1 + b_1$ measures the persistence in volatility and, as is typical for financial return data, is very close to unity. From the results, it seems that the DAX returns have high persistence in volatility with $a_1 + b_1 = 0.9698$. The high persistence implies that average variance will remain high since increases in the conditional variance due to shocks will decay slowly. This would also imply that multi-step forecasts from the model will approach the unconditional variance of the return series quite slowly. The variance intercept term is very small, while the coefficient on the lagged conditional variance is close to 0.9. The estimated mean lag of the variance expression can be calculated as $1/(1 - b_1)$ and equals approximately 8 days for the DAX series.

Exhibit 8.2 shows the plot of the fitted model that consists of the return series, conditional standard deviations and estimated innovations over the in-sample period.

EXHIBIT 8.1   GARCH Estimation Results for the DAX Return Series in the Period 1997 through 2001 (1,034 observations)

	Estimate	Std. error	t-statistic
c	0.0012216	0.0004374	2.7930
a_0	7.6552e-006	2.775e-006	2.7586
a_1	0.097243	0.015967	6.0904
b_1	0.87256	0.022564	38.6700
$a_1 + b_1$	0.969803		
Max. Likelihood	2908.5263		

EXHIBIT 8.2   Returns, Conditional Standard Deviations and Estimated Innovations from a GARCH(1,1) Fitted in the Period 1997 through 2001

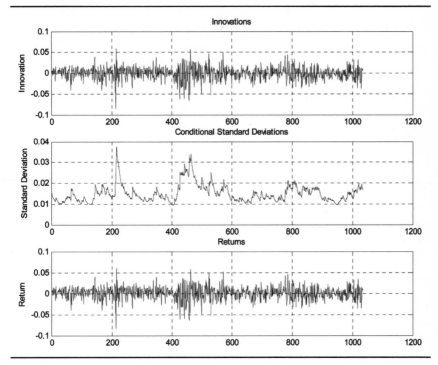

EXHIBIT 8.3   GARCH Estimation Results for the DAX Return Series in the Period 2001 through 2005 (1,272 observations)

	Estimate	Std. error	t-statistic
c	0.00057404	0.00032216	1.7818
a_0	1.3608e-006	5.7394e-007	2.3710
a_1	0.097243	0.015967	6.0904
b_1	0.85113	0.026065	32.6543
$a_1 + b_1$	0.948373		
Max. Likelihood	3646.9956		

To compare the goodness of fit for different periods, we examine the most recent 2001–2005 period containing 1,272 observations. We fit the GARCH specification defined in the first two equations of our illustration and obtain the estimates shown in Exhibit 8.3. The t-statistics for all the coefficients of the conditional variance equation are again significant.

EXHIBIT 8.4 Returns, Conditional Standard Deviations, and Estimated Innovations from a GARCH(1,1) Fitted in the Period 2001 through 2005

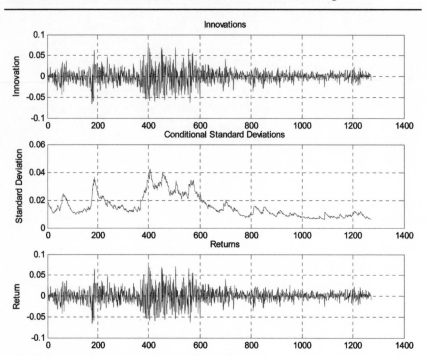

Similar to the result for the 1997–2001 period, the DAX returns have high persistence in volatility with $a_1 + b_1 = 0.9484$.

Exhibit 8.4 shows the returns, conditional standard deviations and estimated innovations of the GARCH model over the entire in-sample 2001–2005 period. Note the different behavior of these series compared to that in the period 1997 through 2001, especially evident in the second half of the sample.

VARIANTS OF THE GARCH MODEL

A variety of different specifications for the conditional variance equation, generalizing the standard ARCH/GARCH model have been proposed. These extensions were motivated by the need to more effectively model some particular features observed in financial data or by concerns regarding computational simplicity.

In the following, we describe empirically relevant variants of the GARCH model that are able to accomodate particular features of asset return series by introducing

- Conditional nonnormality of the error process $\{\varepsilon_t\}$ to better explain the leptokurtosis of the return series (i.e., applying nonnormal innovations η_t).
- Asymmetric responses to negative and positive return innovations to model the asymmetry in the reaction of conditional volatility to the arrival of different news.
- Long-memory,[32] i.e., variances generated by fractionally integrated processes.

GARCH MODEL WITH STUDENT'S T-DISTRIBUTED INNOVATIONS

As discussed in this chapter, time-varying volatility models with Gaussian distributed innovations are capable of capturing the unconditional nonnormality in the data. However, GARCH models with conditionally normal errors fail to sufficiently capture the leptokurtosis common in asset returns. In other words, the shortcoming of the GARCH model with Gaussian innovations is that the assumption of conditional normality for $\{\varepsilon_t\}$ usually does not hold. The error term or residual ε_t is conditionally normal if the *standardized residual*

$$\hat{\eta}_t = \frac{\hat{\varepsilon}_t}{\sqrt{h_t}}$$

is normally distributed. Typically, the standard normality tests applied to standardized residuals indicate that they are not normal—they are leptokurtic although less so than the residuals ε_t. Thus, the GARCH

---

[32] Recall that models with a long memory property have dependency between observations of a variable for a large number of lags so that $\mathrm{Cov}[y_{t+n}, y_{t-j}, j \geq 0]$ does not tend to zero as n gets large. In contrast, if the dependency between observations of a variable disappears for a small number of lags n, such as for stationary ARMA process, then the model is described as having a short-memory property and $\mathrm{Cov}[y_{t+n}, y_{t-j}, j \geq 0] \to 0$. Formally, long memory is defined for a weakly stationary process if its autocovariance function $\gamma(j)$ has a hyperbolic decay structure: $\gamma(j) \sim C_j^{2d-1}$ as $j \to \infty$, $C \neq 0$, $0 < d < 0.5$.

model is only able to capture partially the leptokurtosis in the unconditional distribution of asset returns.

To model the nonnormality in conditional returns, we need to employ a distribution that reflects the specific features of the data better than the normal distribution. For paramater estimation, we then need to construct the likelihood function with the chosen distributional alternative. For example, we can estimate a GARCH model with the Student's t-distribution or generalized exponential distribution (GED). Both of these distributions are symmetric, and allow excess kurtosis. The Student's t-distribution or the standardized $t(d)$ distribution has only one parameter, d, and its density is

$$f_{t(d)}(\eta;d) = \frac{\Gamma((d+1)/2)}{\Gamma(d/2)\sqrt{\pi(d-2)}}\left(\frac{1+\eta^2}{d-2}\right)^{-(1+d)/2}$$

where $d > 2$, η denotes the random variable with zero mean and unit standard deviation and $\Gamma(\cdot)$ represents the gamma function. The distinctive property of the density of the standardized $t(d)$ distribution is that it is a power function of the random variable η, rather than an exponential function as in the normal distribution. This allows the standardized $t(d)$ distribution to have fatter tails than the normal distribution.

This distribution is symmetric around zero and the mean, variance, skewness, and excess kurtosis are 0, 1, 0, and $6/(d-4)$, respectively. For the kurtosis to be well defined, d must be larger than 4. It can be shown that the standardized $t(d)$ distribution converges to the standard normal distribution as d goes to infinity. For the values of d above 50, the standardized $t(d)$ distribution is very close to the standard normal distribution.

When using the assumption that $\eta_t \sim t(d)$ in the GARCH model, the estimation can be done by quasi maximum likelihood estimation. We call the linear GARCH model combined with the Student's t-distribution a GARCH-t model. The GARCH(1,1)-t model has been found to outperform the normal GARCH(1,1) model for high-frequency stock returns.

To accommodate asymmetric distributions, we may use the exponential generalized beta distribution of the second kind (EGB2) that is able to accommodate both fat tails and asymmetry. Wang et al. favor the GARCH-EGB2 model over the GARCH-t model in the context of daily exchange-rate series.[33]

---

[33] Kai-Li Wang, Christopher Fawson, Christopher B. Barret, and James B. McDonald, "A Flexible Parametric GARCH Model with an Application to Exchange Rates," *Journal of Applied Econometrics* 16 (2001), pp. 521–536.

Exponential GARCH Model

Next we consider an asymmetric GARCH process. Since future return volatility tends to respond asymmetrically with respect to negative or positive shocks, the common GARCH model is not appropriate. To overcome this limitation, a nonlinear *exponential GARCH* (EGARCH) specification was proposed by Nelson.[34]

Specifically, the asymmetric behavior of asset returns is modeled as an asymmetric, nonlinear specification of the conditional variance process and a symmetric distribution (such as Gaussian or the Student's *t*-distribution) for the conditional error. Instead of (8.7), the conditional variance h_t is now specified as

$$\log(h_t) = a_0 + \sum_{i=1}^{q} a_i g(\eta_{t-i}) + \sum_{i=1}^{p} b_i \log(h_{t-i}) \tag{8.23}$$

where $\varepsilon_t = \sqrt{h_t}\eta_t$ and $g(\eta_t) = \theta\eta_t + \gamma[|\eta_t| - E|\eta_t|]$ are the weighted innovations that model asymmetric effects between positive and negative asset returns, and θ and γ are constants. Both η_t and $|\eta_t| - E(|\eta_t|)$ are zero mean IID sequences with continuous distribution. Thus $E[g(\eta_t)] = 0$.

The function $g(\eta_t)$ can be rewritten as

$$g(\eta_t) = \begin{cases} (\theta + \gamma)\eta_t - \gamma E(|\eta_t|) & \text{if } \eta_t \geq 0 \\ (\theta - \gamma)\eta_t - \gamma E(|\eta_t|) & \text{if } \eta_t < 0 \end{cases} \tag{8.24}$$

so that $\theta + \gamma$ and $\theta - \gamma$ reflect the asymmetry in response to positive and negative innovations. Obviously, the model is nonlinear if $\gamma \neq 0$. If $\theta < 0$ a positive return shock or surprise will increase volatility less than a negative one of the same magnitude. This phenomenon is referred to as the *leverage effect*.[35]

For a standard Gaussian random variable η_t, $E(|\eta_t|) = \sqrt{2/\pi}$; for the standardized Student's *t*-distribution we have

---

[34] Daniel Nelson, "Conditional Heteroskedasticity in Asset Returns: A New Approach," *Econometrica* 59 (1991), pp. 347–370.

[35] This term dates to Fischer Black, "Studies of Stock Market Volatility Changes," *Proceedings of the American Statistical Association, Business and Economic Statistics Section*, 1976. Black noted that volatilities tend to be higher after negative shocks than after positive shocks of the similar size. This phenomenon has come to be referred to as "leverage effect" since it links the equity value of the firm to the risk of the market.

$$E(|\eta_t|) = \sqrt{d}\Gamma[0.5(d-1)]/\sqrt{d}\Gamma[0.5d]$$

where d is the number of degrees of freedom.

In summary, the EGARCH model has two advantages over the common GARCH specification:

- Function g enables the model to respond asymmetrically to positive and negative lagged values of ε_t.
- Use of the log-conditional variance in EGARCH specification relaxes the constraint of positive model coefficients (even in the case of negative parameters, h_t will be positive).

Integrated GARCH Model

The estimation of ARCH processes on log-return data yields the similar pattern in the results:

- For longer samples, the estimated parameters $a_1, ..., a_q$ and $b_1,...,b_p$ of the model (8.2)–(8.3) and (8.7) sum up to values that are typically close to one.
- For shorter samples, the sum of the estimated coefficients, although not small, stays away from 1.

These two observed facts are known as the *integrated GARCH (IGARCH) effect*. Thus, the IGARCH effect builds up when the sample size increases. This effect has been linked to the persistence in the autocorrelation for absolute returns.

Based on these observed facts, Engle and Bollerslev[36] introduced the integrated GARCH(p, q) (IGARCH(p, q)) process for which

$$a_0 > 0 \quad \text{and} \quad \sum_{i=1}^{q} a_i + \sum_{j=1}^{p} b_j = 1 \qquad (8.25)$$

Under the assumptions of the general ARCH model, in particular, the $E(\eta^2) = 1$, the IGARCH model has a strictly stationary solution (h_t), and therefore $\{\varepsilon_t\}$ is strictly stationary as well, but ε_t's do not have a finite second moment. This can be verified by taking the expectations in the formal definition (8.25) and observing that $E(h) = E(\varepsilon^2)$:

---

[36] Engle and Bollerslev, "Modelling the Persistence of Conditional Variances."

$$E(h) = a_0 + \sum_{i=1}^{q} a_i E(\varepsilon^2) + \sum_{i=1}^{p} b_i E(h) = a_0 + E(h)$$

Since $a_0 > 0$ is necessary for strict stationarity, it follows $E(h) = \infty$.
We can also rewrite the GARCH(1,1) model given by (8.9) as

$$(1 - a_1 L - b_1 L)\varepsilon_t^2 = a_0 + (1 - b_1 L)(\varepsilon_t^2 - h_t)$$

where L denotes the lag operator (i.e., $Lh_t = h_{t-1}$). If the polynomial $1 - a_1 L - b_1 L$ contains a unit root (i.e., when $a_1 + b_1 = 1$), we obtain the IGARCH model of Engle and Bollerslev.[37]

As pointed out by Mikosh and Starica,[38] the name integrated can be misleading from an ARCH perspective. The name integrated suggests that there is a unit root problem (as for integrated ARMA processes) concerning the stationarity of such GARCH processes. However, this does not apply for the GARCH (8.2), (8.3), (8.6), and (8.7) models because, if (8.25) holds, they have unique strictly stationary solution. Thus, for the GARCH case, integrated is not synonymous for nonstationarity.

The stationary GARCH(1,1) process is nonpersistent in variance if and only if $a_1 + b_1 < 1$ (i.e., when ε_t has finite variance), so that shocks to conditional variance disappear at the exponential rate $(a_1 + b_1)^t$. On the other hand, the stationary IGARCH(1,1) model with $a_1 + b_1 = 1$ is persistent in variance so that shocks to conditional variance never die out.

Fractionally Integrated GARCH Model

The clear distinction between GARCH and IGARCH models has been criticized. An obvious generalization is to allow for fractional orders of integration such that

$$(1 - a_1 L - b_1 L)\varepsilon_t^2 = \phi(L)(1 - L)^d$$

leading to the *fractionally integrated* GARCH (FIGARCH) model. This model was first suggested by Bailie, Bollerslev, and Mikkelsen[39] to

---

[37] Engle and Bollerslev, "Modeling the Persistence of Conditional Variances."

[38] T. Mikosch and Catalin Starica, "Long Range Dependence Effects and ARCH Modeling," Technical Report (2000), University of Groningen.

[39] R. T. Bailie, T. Bollerslev, and H.O. Mikkelsen (1996) "Fractionally Integrated Generalized Autoregressive Conditional Heteroscedasticity," *Journal of Econometrics* 74 (1996). pp. 3-30.

accommodate empirical regularities concerning evidence of fractional integration for a time-series of daily index returns. A FIGARCH(p, d, q) process is defined by

$$a(L)(1 - L)^d \varepsilon_t^2 = a_0 + b(L)u_t \qquad (8.26)$$

where $u_t \overset{\Delta}{=} \varepsilon_t^2 - h_t,$[40] $a_0 \in (0,\infty)$, and $(1 - L)^d$ a fractional-difference operator. The fractional-difference operator is formally defined by its infinite Maclaurin series expansion,

$$(1 - L)^d = 1 - \sum_{k=1}^{\infty} d \cdot \frac{\Gamma(k - d)}{\Gamma(1 - d)\Gamma(k + 1)} L^k \qquad (8.27)$$

where $\Gamma(\cdot)$ is the gamma function.

The leverage effect introduced in the EGARCH section is not generated by the FIGARCH model. Analogous to the extension of GARCH model to EGARCH model to account for this effect, we can generalize the FIGARCH model to a FIEGARCH model.[41]

Specifically, the FIEGARCH model takes the form $\varepsilon_t = \sqrt{h_t}\eta_t$ where the $\{\eta_t\}$ are IID with zero mean and a symmetric distribution, and

$$\log h_t = \omega + \sum_{i=1}^{\infty} a_i g(\eta_{t-i}) \qquad (8.28)$$

is the conditional variance with $g(x) = \theta x + \gamma(|x| - E|\eta_t|)$, $\omega > 0$, $\theta > 0$, $\gamma \in \mathfrak{R}$, and constants a_i such that the process $\log h_t$ has long memory with parameter $d \in (0, 0.5)$. If θ is nonzero, the model allows for a so-called leverage effect, whereby the sign of the current return may have impact on the future volatility.

By replacing the apparent unit root in the estimated EGARCH model with the fractional differencing operator, the FIEGARCH model nests the conventional EGARCH model for $d = 0$, and the integrated EGARCH model for $d = 1$. For $0 < d < 1$ the effect of shock to the forecast of dissipates at a slow hyperbolic rate of decay.

---

[40] Symbol $\overset{\Delta}{=}$ is used to indicate equality by definition, so that $\{v_t\}$ is by construction a martingale-difference sequence relative to the σ–field generated by the $\{\varepsilon_s, s \leq t\}$.
[41] Tim Bollerslev and H.O. Mikkelsen, "Modeling and Pricing Long-Memory in Stock Market Volatility," *Journal of Econometrics* 73 (1996), pp. 151–184.

Long-Memory GARCH Model

A common finding in much of the empirical literature on the second-order structure of high-frequency[42] financial time series is that sample autocorrelations for squared or absolute-valued observations tend to decay very slowly and remain fairly large at long lags.[43] As a consequence, extensions of GARCH models have been proposed which can produce such long-memory behavior.

A class of *long-memory GARCH* (LMGARCH) processes that belong to the family of conditionally heteroskedastic processes proposed by Robinson are very closely related to the FIGARCH processes and share some of the features of fractional ARIMA processes.[44] In particular, shocks to the conditional variance of an LMGARCH process eventually die away to zero (in a forecasting sense), at a slow hyperbolic rate rather than the faster geometric rate that is characteristic of weakly stationary GARCH processes.

The LMGARCH process can be represented by using the definitions of the generalized class of GARCH processes. Generalized GARCH processes allow $\{\varepsilon_t^2\}$ to satisfy the equation

$$\varepsilon_t = \omega + \Omega(L)u_t \tag{8.29}$$

for some $\omega \in (0,\infty)$ and

$$\Omega(L) = \sum_{j=0}^{\infty} \omega_j L^j, \ 0 < \sum_{j=0}^{\infty} \omega_j^2 < \infty$$

---

[42] For high-frequency data the time horizon of observations is very short—for example, for stock market data we deal with 5 or 10 minute intervals or with tick-by-tick intervals in the interbank foreign exchange market. In this context, we discuss the intradaily data as opposed to interdaily data. Large intraday price variations occur more and more frequently in stock and foreign exchange markets so that the modelling of intraday price movements and volatilities becomes an important task for active traders and market makers. As liquid assets are traded many times during a day, there is potentially useful information in the intraday prices about the variance.

[43] See for example, Z. Ding and C. Granger, "Modeling Volatility Persistence of Speculative Returns: A New Approach," *Journal of Econometrics* 73 (1996), pp. 185–215.

[44] P. M. Robinson, "Testing for Strong Serial Correlation and Dynamic Conditional Heteroscedasticity in Multiple Regression," *Journal of Econometrics* 47 (1991), pp. 67–84.

where $u_t \overset{\Delta}{=} \varepsilon_t^2 - h_t$.[45]

The specification in (8.29) also includes processes for which the autocorrelations $\{\rho_n(\varepsilon_t^2), n \geq 1\}$ decay at a rate slower than geometric. One possibility is to allow the coefficients $\{\omega_j, j \geq 0\}$ to decay hyperbolically so that $\omega_j \sim Cj^{-\delta}$ as $j \to \infty$ for some $\delta \in (0,1)$. One specific parameterization of $\Omega(L)$ that allows for such behavior is

$$\Omega(L) = \frac{b(L)}{a(L)(1-L)^d} \tag{8.30}$$

for some $d \in (0, 0.5)$ with the lag polynomials

$$a(L) = 1 - \sum_{j=1}^{q} a_j L^j \text{ and } b(L) = 1 - \sum_{j=1}^{p} b_j L^j$$

being such that $|a(z) > 0|$ and $|b(z) > 0|$ for all complex-valued z on the closed unit disk.[46] The fractional-difference operator is defined as in (8.27).

From (8.29) and (8.30), it follows that the stochastic volatility h_t is given by equation

$$h_t = \omega\Psi(1) + [1 - \Psi(L)]\varepsilon_t^2 \tag{8.31}$$

where

$$\Psi(L) = 1 - \sum_{j=1}^{\infty} \psi_j L^j = \frac{a(L)(1-L)^d}{b(L)} = \frac{1}{\Omega(L)}$$

with $\psi_j \geq 0 (j \geq 1)$ and ω defined as in (8.29).

---

[45] A strictly stationary GARCH(p, q) process is a special case of (8.29) with the coefficients $\{\omega_j, j \geq 0\}$ declining towards zero geometrically fast. When $E(\varepsilon_t^4) < \infty$, the geometric decay of $\{\omega_j, j \geq 0\}$ implies that the autocorrelations $\{\rho_n(\varepsilon_t^2) = Corr(\varepsilon_{t+n}^2, \varepsilon_t^2), n \geq 1\}$ are also geometrically decaying. Therefore $\{\varepsilon_t^2\}$ exhibits short memory in the sense that the series

$$\sum_{n=0}^{\infty} \rho_n(\varepsilon_t^2)$$

is absolutely convergent.

[46] See P. M. Robinson and M. Henry, "Long and Short Memory Conditional Heteroscedasticity in Estimating the Memory Paramater of Levels," *Economic Theory* 15 (1999), pp. 299–336.

Under (8.29) and (8.30), the coefficients $\{\omega_j, j \geq 0\}$ decay at a slow hyperbolic rate so that $\omega_j \sim Cj^{d-1}$ as $j \to \infty$. This in turn implies that the autocorrelations $\{\rho_n(\varepsilon_n^2), n \geq 1\}$ satisfy[47]

$$\rho_n(\varepsilon_t^2) = \frac{\displaystyle\sum_{j=0}^{\infty} \omega_j \omega_{j+n}}{\displaystyle\sum_{j=0}^{\infty} \omega_j^2} \sim Cn^{2d-1} \quad \text{as} \quad n \to \infty \tag{8.32}$$

provided that $E(\varepsilon_t^4) < \infty$. Thus, when the fourth moment of the $E(\varepsilon_t^4) < \infty$ exists, $\{\varepsilon_t^2\}$ is a weakly stationary process which exhibits long memory for all $d \in (0, 0.5)$, in the sense that series

$$\sum_{n=0}^{\infty} \left| \rho_n(\varepsilon_t^2) \right|$$

is properly divergent. For this reason, a process satisfying (8.29) and (8.30) is referred to as an LMGARCH(p, d, q) process. The exact properties of processes satisfying (8.29) and (8.30) are not yet established.

Forecasting with GARCH Models

GARCH models describe evolution of the conditional variance of ε_t, which can be linked with the evolution of the conditional variance of variable y_t under investigation

$$Var(y_t | y_{t-1}, y_{t-2}, \ldots) = Var(\varepsilon_t | \varepsilon_{t-1}, \varepsilon_{t-2}, \ldots) \tag{8.33}$$

Thus appropriate modeling of h_t provides models and forecasts for the variance of y_t as well. Once the parameters of the GARCH models or its variants have been estimated using data for $t = 1, \ldots, \tau$, variance forecasts can be generated for $\tau + n$, $n \geq 1$. A clear advantage of GARCH models is that the one-step ahead forecast of the variance $h_{\tau+1}$ is given directly by the model.

Formally, consider GARCH(1,1) model given by (8.9) and let τ be the forecast origin. The 1-step ahead forecast is

---

[47] M. Karanasos, Z. Psaradakis, and M. Sola, "On the Autocorrelation Properties of Long-Memory GARCH Processes," *Journal of Time Series Analysis* 25 (2004), pp. 265–281.

$$h_\tau(1) = h_{\tau+1} = a_0 + a_1\varepsilon_\tau^2 + b_1 h_\tau \qquad (8.34)$$

where the estimated parameters $\hat{a}_0, \hat{a}_1, \hat{b}_1$ and values h_τ and ε_τ^2 at the forecast origin are known. We are also interested to obtain the forecasts of $h_{\tau+2}|\mathfrak{I}_\tau, ..., h_{\tau+n}|\mathfrak{I}_\tau$ where $\mathfrak{I}_\tau$ denotes all the information available up to and including observation τ. To obtain multistep ahead forecasts, (8.34) is updated by recursive substitution for h_τ. In this way, for the GARCH(1,1) model, the n-step ahead forecast can be written as

$$h_\tau(n) = h_{\tau+n} = \hat{a}_0\left(1 + \sum_{i=1}^{n-2}\left(\hat{a}_1 + \hat{b}_1\right)^i\right) + \hat{a}_0 + \hat{a}_1\varepsilon_\tau^2 + \hat{b}_1 h_\tau \qquad (8.35)$$

for any $n \geq 2$ where the quantities on the right-hand side are known. This is obtained by considering $\varepsilon_t^2 = h_t\eta_t^2$ and rewriting (8.9) as

$$h_{t+1} = a_0 + (a_1 + b_1)h_t + a_1 h_t(\eta_t^2 - 1)$$

which becomes $h_{\tau+2} = a_0 + (a_1 + b_1)h_{\tau+1}$ for $t = \tau + 1$ since $E(\eta_{t+1}^2 - 1|\mathfrak{I}_\tau) = 0$. This can be extended to general recursion form

$$h_\tau(n) = a_0 + (a_1 + b_1)h_\tau(n-1), n > 1 \qquad (8.36)$$

The out-of-sample forecasts are obtained by using (8.35) given the estimates of the parameters based on the in-sample data. For the GARCH(1,1) model, given that $(\hat{a}_1 + \hat{b}_1) < 1$, the n-step ahead forecast is obtained by repeated substitution in (8.36)

$$h_{\tau+n} = \hat{a}_0\frac{1 - (\hat{a}_1 + \hat{b}_1)^{n-1}}{1 - \left(\hat{a}_1 + \hat{b}_1\right)} + (\hat{a}_1 + \hat{b}_1)^{n-1}\hat{h}_{\tau+1}, n \geq 2$$

where $\hat{h}_{\tau+1}$ is the one-step ahead forecast given by (8.34). As the forecast horizon grows, the long-term prediction (i.e., obtained by letting $n \to \infty$) will tend towards the unconditional volatility:

$$\hat{h} \to \frac{\hat{a}_0}{1 - (\hat{a}_1 + \hat{b}_1)}, \text{ as } n \to \infty$$

To measure forecast errors, we use usual summary statistics based directly on the deviation between forecasts and realizations (actual values) such as the *root mean squared error* (RMSE), the *mean absolute error* (MAE) and the *mean absolute percentage error* (MAPE). Let $\sqrt{\hat{h}_\tau}$ be the actual and $\sqrt{h_\tau}$ the forecast volatility at time τ, with a forecast period going from $\tau + 1$ to $\tau + n$. Then the forecast error statistics are respectively

■ $\text{RMSE} = \left[\dfrac{1}{n} \displaystyle\sum_{\tau = t+1}^{t+n} \left(\sqrt{\hat{h}_\tau} - \sqrt{h_\tau} \right)^2 \right]^{1/2}$

■ $\text{MAE} = \dfrac{1}{n} \displaystyle\sum_{\tau = t+1}^{t+n} \left| \sqrt{\hat{h}_\tau} - \sqrt{h_\tau} \right|$

■ $\text{MAPE} = \dfrac{1}{n} \displaystyle\sum_{\tau = t+1}^{t+n} \left| \dfrac{(\sqrt{\hat{h}_\tau} - \sqrt{h_\tau})}{\sqrt{h_\tau}} \right|$

The RMSE and the MAE statistics are scale-dependent measures but provide a basis to compare volatility forecasts across the different models used. The MAPE statistics are independent of the scale of the variables.

In practice, when we test the ability of models to predict future volatility, out-of-sample estimations of conditional volatility are compared to some simple benchmark. To that purpose, we can calculate variance forecasts using a constant volatility assumption or some form of a moving average estimator of a variance. A constant volatility assumption benchmark has the form

$$ h_{\tau+n} = \frac{1}{\tau - 1} \sum_{t=1}^{\tau} \left(r_t - \frac{1}{\tau} \sum_{j=1}^{\tau} r_j \right)^2 $$

for all n, and an n-day moving average estimator

$$ h_{\tau+n} = \frac{1}{n-1} \sum_{t=\tau-n-1}^{\tau} \left(r_t - \frac{1}{n} \sum_{j=\tau-n-1}^{\tau} r_j \right)^2 $$

for all n, where r_t are return series in the observed period. These simple benchmarks use the fact that squared returns are a proxy for variance.

In practice, daily volatility forecasts can be obtained by the following general procedure:

1. Estimate the models using the in-sample data set ($t = 1, ..., \tau$) and calculate the volatility forecasts for the next m trading days $\tau + 1, ..., \tau + m$.[48]
2. Move k days forward in time and reestimate the models using observations $t = 1, ..., \tau + k$ (k is usually chosen to be 1, 5, or 10) and generate a new set of volatility forecasts.
3. Repeat the second step until the point where there are m days left until the end of complete data set, giving a total of $(T - m - \tau)/k$ prediction dates ($\tau + k, \tau + 2k, ...$) where T is the number of observations in a complete data set.
4. Average the calculated volatility forecasts over each of the forecast horizons of m days (at each of the prediction dates).
5. Calculate the forecast error statistics RMSE, MAE, and MAPE for the forecasted average volatilities for each of the forecast horizons m.

The models along with benchmarks can be evaluated for different forecast horizons ranging from 1-week (5 days) to half a year trading period (approximately 120 days). The accuracy of the volatility prediction from the models will be measured by the chosen forecast error statistic and related to the length of the forecast horizon. Fair comparison of the out-of-sample performance of the different models can be subsequently done by investigating the statistical significance of the observed difference in specific error statistic between the models. This can be done by using the bootstrap technique, a methodology that is beyond the scope of this chapter.

Illustration: Forecasting with the GARCH Model

In our previous illustration, we have examined how the GARCH(1,1) model fits the DAX returns. Since we performed the fit with the entire observed data period, this was so-called in-sample fit. Now we examine the forecasting ability of the GARCH(1,1) model for the DAX returns in the same period. In this case, we split the data in two sets: in-sample data set on which the model is fitted to obtain parameter estimates and out-of-sample set which is used for forecasting and performance evaluation. In the first step, we fit the GARCH(1,1) model as shown in the previous illustration. In the second step we perform one-step ahead forecasts in that we update the forecast using the estimated coefficients.

For the period 1997 through 2001, the model is fitted using the first 800 data points and the rest of the data (234 data points) is used for evaluating the forecasting performance. Exhibit 8.5 shows the maximum likelihood estimates for joint estimation of the GARCH(1,1) model and ARMA(1,1) model using the in-sample data set of 800 observations.

---

[48] Length m is called the *forecasting horizon*.

EXHIBIT 8.5 ARMA-GARCH Estimation Results for the DAX Return Series Using the In-Sample Data Set of 800 Observations

	Estimate	Std. Error	t-Statistic
a_1	–0.58438	0.16331	–3.5784
b_1	0.66483	0.15136	4.3923
Max. Likelihood	2186.4322		
α_0	9.6526e-006	3.5103e-006	2.7498
α_1	0.1066	0.019818	5.3793
β_1	0.85537	0.0283	30.2245
$\alpha_1 + \beta_1$	0.96197		
Max. Likelihood	2248.3835		

EXHIBIT 8.6 Forecasts of the ARMA(1,1)–GARCH(1,1) Model in the Forecasting Interval (the last 234 Observations in the Period 1997 through 2001)

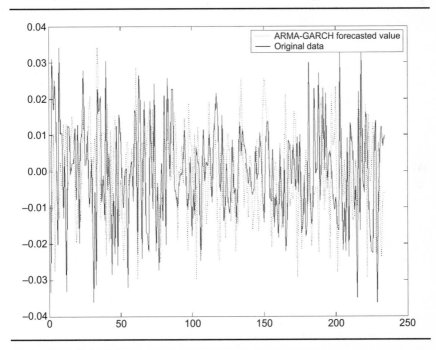

Exhibit 8.6 shows the plots of the actual and predicted returns in the out-of-sample forecasting interval. The forecast error statistics of volatility forecasts for out-of-sample data set are 0.003, 0.0026 and 0.1762 for RMSE, MAE, and MAPE respectively.

Illustration: Forecasting for Value-at-Risk Models

Broadly speaking, Value-at-Risk (VaR) is a quantitative technique with an aim to evaluate possible losses related to the trading of financial assets over a given time period. It has been endorsed by financial regulators and bank supervisory committees as a tool designed to quantify and forecast market risk.[49] Due to the tremendous growth in trading activity and the volatility of the global financial markets, VaR models have become a standard tool for risk managers. They are important for characterizing short-term risk regarding daily and intradaily trading positions. VaR provides a simple answer to the following question: with a given probability α, what is the predicted financial loss over a given time horizon? The answer is the VaR at level α, which gives an amount in the currency of the traded assets, and since it is a single number it is easily comprehensible. However, VaR is not a perfect measure and its drawbacks are well documented in the risk management literature.

The statistical definition of the VaR at level α for sample of returns is simply the corresponding empirical quantile at $(1 - \alpha) \times 100\%$. Empirically, the computation of the VaR for a sample of returns will require the computation of the empirical quantile at level $(1 - \alpha)$ of the distribution of the returns of the portfolio. Because quantiles are direct functions of the variance in parametric models, ARCH class models immediately translate into conditional VaR models. The basic concept underlying the original ARCH model (8.1) through (8.3) is that for a forecast of the distribution of ε_t (where for example ε_t represents log-returns of asset prices for $t \geq 1$) we need to know only two components: $\sqrt{h_t}$ and the distribution of innovation η_t. For example, if η_t is normal $N(0,1)$, then given the past observations of the time series, $\varepsilon_t \sim N(0,h_t)$. Thus, conditionally upon $\varepsilon_{t-1}, \varepsilon_{t-2}, \varepsilon_{t-q}$, the present value ε_t may assume values in $[-1.96 \sqrt{h_t}, 1.96 \sqrt{h_t}]$ with 95% probability. Similarly, there is a 5% chance for the log-return to fall below the threshold $-1.64 \sqrt{h_t}$. The 5%-quantile of the log-return distribution is considered a measure of risk for underlying asset, namely, the VaR. This simple example show the applicability of models of ARCH type and explain their popularity.

---

[49] Regulatory changes have two implications: the imposition of minimum capital requirements for financial institutions as designed by the Basel Committee on Banking Supervision and the adoption of the VaR method of assessing capital adequacy as a risk management technique. According to the Basel Capital Accord, the VaR level at a 10-day horizon is directly related to the amount of capital required for the bank to cushion possible market losses. For general information on VaR techniques see Philippe Jorion, *Value-at-Risk* (New York: McGraw-Hill, 2000).

For a sample of daily returns, y_t, with $t = 1, ..., T$ we can characterize the model of asset returns using conditional mean equation. For example, we can fit an $AR(n)$ structure of the series for all specifications

$$a(L)(y_t - c) = \varepsilon_t$$

where $a(L) = 1 - a_1 L - ... - a_n L^n$ is an AR lag polynomial of order n. Accordingly, the conditional mean of y_t, is

$$\mu_t = c + \sum_{j=1}^{n} a_j(y_{t-j} - \mu)$$

For the conditional variance of ε_t, we can also consider several specifications. We will now show the application of the usual parametric VaR model of RiskMetrics.[50] In the basic RiskMetrics model, the conditional variance is estimated by a GARCH(1,1) model given by (8.9) with zero constant ($a_0 = 0$) and parameters a_1 and b_1 summing to unity.

$$h_t = (1 - \lambda)\varepsilon_{t-1}^2 + \lambda h_{t-1}$$

where $\varepsilon_t = \sqrt{h_t} \eta_t$ with $\eta_t \overset{IID}{\sim} N(0, 1)$. Compared to the simple volatility unconditional estimators that use an equally weighted moving average, the RiskMetrics approach uses exponential weights, so that more recent observations weigh more heavily. The rate of decline of the exponential weights depends on the decay factor λ, thus expressing the persistence with which a shock will decay. The RiskMetrics specification is for daily data $\lambda = 0.94$ and for monthly data $\lambda = 0.97$. The advantage of this approach is that only the one parameter λ is needed to be estimated, facilitating estimation and providing more robustness against estimation error.

Daily VaR is defined as the VaR level for long positions so that losses are incurred for negative returns. How good a model is at predicting long VaR is thus related to its ability to model large negative returns.[51] For short positions, the performance of VaR is measured by its ability to predict large positive returns. For the RiskMetrics model, the one-step ahead VaR computed in $t - 1$ for long trading position is given by

---

[50] Riskmetrics, or more specifically the RiskMetrics Group, is a commercial vendor of tools for investment and risk management. Riskmetrics was originally part of JPMorgan and in 1998 spun off from that firm.

[51] See for example, S. Mittnik and M. Paolella, "Conditional Density and Value-at-Risk Prediction of Asian Currency Exchange Rates," *Journal of Forecasting* 19 (2000), pp. 313–333.

$$\mu_t + \eta_\gamma \sqrt{h}_t$$

and for short trading positions it is equal to

$$\mu_t + \eta_{1-\gamma} \sqrt{h}_t$$

with η_γ being the quantile at $(1 - \gamma) \times 100\%$ for the normal distribution. When computing the VaR, μ_t and $\sqrt{h}_t$ are evaluated by replacing the unknown parameters in the previous equation by their maximum likelihood estimates. Note that $\eta_\gamma = -\eta_{1-\gamma}$ for the normal distribution, so that the predicted long and short level VaR will be equal in both cases.[52]

In practice, VaR models are used to deliver out-of-sample forecasts, where the model is estimated from observed returns (for example, up to time τ) and the VaR forecast is made for period $(\tau + 1, \tau + m)$ where m is the time horizon of the forecasts. The model can be reestimated every, say, 50 days to update the parameters. It is of interest to calculate failure rates for the short or long forecasted $VaR_{\tau+1}$ with the observed return y_t for all days in the out-of-sample period for values of the empirical quantile at level $(1 - \alpha)$ typically equal to 5%, 2.5%, 1%, 0.5%, and 0.25%. The failure rate is the number of times returns exceed (in absolute value) the predicted VaR. For the correctly specified VaR model, the failure rate should be equal to the prespecified VaR level.

MULTIVARIATE GARCH FORMULATIONS

Because volatilities of asset returns of market indexes move together in time, considering GARCH independently for every asset is not sufficient. The multivariate analysis of the movement of covariances over time or time-varying correlations adds additional challenge to "univariate stylized facts" such as volatility clustering, fat tails and skewness. The issue is important, since there is empirical evidence to show that markets become more closely interrelated during periods of higher volatility or market crashes. In particular, in view of applying GARCH to asset allocation, multivariate modeling becomes necessary. Several different models have been proposed in the literature including the VECH and the diagonal VECH model which we briefly discuss here.

We assume r_t to be a n-dimensional vector of asset returns. Then the multivariate return model is given by

---

[52] For examples of VaR forecasts with other distributions see, Pierre Giot and Sébastien Laurent, "Value-at-Risk for Long and Short Trading Positions," *Journal of Applied Econometrics* 18 (2003), pp. 641–664.

$$r_t = \bar{r} + \varepsilon_t \qquad (8.37)$$

$$\varepsilon_t = \Sigma_t^{\frac{1}{2}}\eta_t, \quad \eta_t. \sim N(0,I) \qquad (8.38)$$

with a constant conditional mean factor $\bar{r}$ and a covariance matrix Σ_t.[53]

The multivariate GARCH model of Bollerslev, Engle, and Wooldridge[54] accounts for both varying correlations and changes in volatility. For a symmetric matrix H, let $vech(H)$ denote the column stacking operator applied to the lower portion of the symmetric matrix H. The model takes the general form (8.37) and

$$vech(\Sigma_t) = C + Avech(\varepsilon_{t-1}\varepsilon'_{t-1}) + Bvech(\Sigma_{t-1}) \qquad (8.39)$$

where C is a $n(n+1)/2$ vector of constants and A and B are $n(n+1)/2 \times n(n+1)/2$ matrices. For the model, it is evident that the conditional variances and conditional covariances depend on the lagged values of all of the conditional variances of, and conditional covariences between, all of the asset returns in the series, as well as the lagged squared errors and the errors cross-products.

The VECH model has two major disadvantages. First, estimation of such a model is a daunting task, even for only several assets since (8.39) contains $n(n+1)/2 + 2(n(n+1)/2)^2$ unknown parameters that have to be estimated. For example, for $n = 5$, this corresponds to 465 parameters. Second, the conditions needed for the model to ensure that Σ_t stays positive definite are difficult to establish. In practice, it remains that some simplifying assumptions need to be imposed.

To restrict the VECH's model conditional variance-covariance matrix, the diagonal multivariate GARCH model was introduced, where the matrices A and B are both taken to be diagonal. Therefore the conditional variances and covariances depend on their own lagged moments their respective component in the product of $\varepsilon'_{t-1}\varepsilon_{t-1}$. An alternative representation of the multivariate GARCH model, which guarantees that the conditional covariance matrix stays positive definite, is introduced by Engle and Kroner.[55] Their model is written as

---

[53] The square root of a matrix is its Cholesky decomposition.
[54] Tim Bollerslev, Robert F. Engle, and Jeffery M. Wooldridge, "A Capital Asset Pricing Model with Time-Varying Covariances," *Journal of Political Economy* 96 (1988), pp. 116–131.
[55] Robert F. Engle and Kenneth F. Kroner, "Multivariate Simultaneous Generalized ARCH," *Econometric Theory* 11 (1995), pp. 122–150.

$$\Sigma_t = VV' + \sum_{k=1}^{K} A'_k \varepsilon_{t-1} \varepsilon'_{t-1} A_k + \sum_{k=1}^{K} B'_k \Sigma_{t-1} B_k$$

where V, A_k, B_k, $k = 1,...,K$ are all $n \times n$ matrices. As in (8.39), this formulation involves many unknown parameters, namely $(1 + 2K)n^2$, which is large even if $K = 1$). Yet another way to extend GARCH to a multivariate model is to assume constant correlations. The conditional covariances can be obtained by taking the product of the corresponding standard deviations multiplied with the correlation. Variances are modeled as in (8.9) for every component. Explicitly, this amounts to the specification given by (8.38) and

$$h_{t,i} = \gamma_i + a_i \varepsilon^2_{t-1,i} + b_i h_{t-1,i} \quad i = 1, ..., n \qquad (8.40)$$

$$h^{\frac{1}{2}}_{t,i,j} = \rho_{i,j} h^{\frac{1}{2}}_{t,i} h^{\frac{1}{2}}_{t,j} \quad i = 1, ..., n, \quad i = 1, ..., n \qquad (8.41)$$

where $\rho_{i,j}$ is the constant conditional correlation coefficient between the residuals $\varepsilon_{t,i}$ and $\varepsilon_{t,j}$. In principle, the model consists of n univariate return processes, which define the changes in the covariance matrix only by the changing variances. Hence the properties derived for the univariate GARCH(1,1) model can be transferred to this multivariate case.

The estimation in the multivariate case is, in principle, a straightforward extension from the univariate case. The one-dimensional function of the sample observations is simply replaced by its multidimensional counterpart.

APPENDIX: ANALYSIS OF THE PROPERTIES OF THE GARCH(1,1) MODEL

Nelson[56] investigated the properties of the GARCH(1,1) in detail. He defines the model GARCH(1,1) from (8.7)

$$\varepsilon_t = \sqrt{h_t} z_t$$

$$h_t = a_0 + a_1 \varepsilon^2_{t-1} + b_1 h_{t-1} \qquad (A8.1)$$

---

[56] Daniel B. Nelson, "Stationarity and Persistence in the GARCH(1,1) Model," *Econometric Theory* 6 (1990), pp. 318–334.

where $a_0 \geq 0$, $b_1 \geq 0$, $a_1 > 0$,

$$\{z_t\}_{t = -\infty, \infty} \sim IID, \ z_t^2 \text{ is nondegenerate}, \ P[-\infty < z_t < \infty] = 1 \quad \text{(A8.2)}$$

and

$$E[\ln(b_1 + a_1 z_t^2)] \text{ exists.} \quad \text{(A8.3)}$$

It is important to note that the requirement (A8.3) does not require that $E[\ln(b_1 + a_1 z_t^2)]$ be finite, only that the expectations of the positive and negative parts of $[\ln(b_1 + a_1 z_t^2)]$ are not both infinite. For example, (A8.3) always hold if $b_1 > 0$. By substituting in (A8.1), we obtain for $t \geq 2$[57]

$$h_t = h_0 \prod_{i = 1}^{t} (b_1 + a_1 z_{t-i}^2) + a_0 \left[1 + \sum_{k = 1}^{t-1} \prod_{i = 1}^{k} (b_1 + a_1 z_{t-i}^2) \right] \quad \text{(A8.4)}$$

To fully define the model (A8.4) requires the definition of the probability measure μ_0 for the starting value h_0[58] or the assumption that the system extends infinitely far into the past. In the first case, the start of the system at time 0 requires that h_0 is strictly positive and finite with probability one, and h_0 and $\{z_t\}_{t = 0, \infty}$ are independent. The obtained model $\{h_t, \varepsilon_t\}_{t = 0, \infty}$ is the *conditional* model. In the second case, by extending the process infinitely far into the past, we obtain the *unconditional* model $\{_u h_t, {}_u \varepsilon_t\}_{t = 0, \infty}$ defined by assumptions (A8.2), with

---

[57] It can be shown that equation (A8.4) holds for $t = 1$ as well.

[58] Probability measure is a mapping from arbitrary sets to nonnegative real number R^+ and is associated with possible values of random variable in infinitesimally small intervals. This measure is typically denoted by the symbol $dP(t)$ where z_t is the random variable. It holds

$$\int_{-\infty}^{+\infty} dP(z_t) = 1$$

The expected value of z_t is

$$E(z_t) = \int_{-\infty}^{+\infty} z_t dP(z_t)$$

and its variance

$$E(z_t - E(z_t)^2) = \int_{-\infty}^{+\infty} (z_t - E(z_t))^2 dP(z_t)$$

The expected value and variance have geometric interpretation as the *center* of the probability mass and the *spread* of the probability mass around the center.

$$_u h_t = a_0 \left[1 + \sum_{k=1}^{\infty} \prod_{i=1}^{k} (b_1 + a_1 z_{t-i}^2) \right] \qquad (A8.5)$$

and $_u \varepsilon_t \equiv \sqrt{_u h_t} z_t$. If $a_0 = 0$, $_u h_t \equiv {_u z_t} \equiv 0$ for all t. If $_u h_t = \infty$ and $z_t = 0$, define $_u \varepsilon_t \equiv \infty \cdot 0 \equiv 0$. Without further restrictions, there is no guarantee that $_u h_t$ and $_u \varepsilon_t$ are finite.

Thus, under the assumption $b_1 < 0$, the necessary and sufficient condition for the existence of the unique stationary solution for GARCH(1,1) specified in (A8.1) is

$$E[\ln(b_1 + a_1 z_t^2)] < 0 \qquad (A8.6)$$

This condition can be obtained by analyzing the conditions for stationarity for the two cases distinguished by the choice of a_0 in (A8.5):

- Case $a_0 = 0$: In this case $_u h_t = \infty$ for all t and we consider only the conditional model. It is established that $h_t \to \infty$ almost surely if $E[\ln(b_1 + a_1 z_t^2)] > 0$, $h_t \to 0$ almost surely if $E[\ln(b_1 + a_1 z_t^2)] < 0$, and if $E[\ln(b_1 + a_1 z_t^2)] > 0$, $\ln(h_t)$ is a driftless random walk after time 0.
- Case $a_0 > 0$: If $E[\ln(b_1 + a_1 z_t^2)] \geq 0$, then $h_t \to \infty$ almost surely and $_u h_t \to \infty$ almost surely for all t. If $E[\ln(b_1 + a_1 z_t^2)] < 0$, then $a_0/(1 - b_1) \leq {_u h_t} < \infty$ for all t almost surely and $_u h_t$ is strictly stationary and ergodic.[59]

The log-moment condition (A8.6) allows $a_1 + b_1$ to be slightly larger than 1, in which case the variance is not finite (i.e., $E(\varepsilon_t^2) = 0$). The condition is however, not easy to apply in practice as it is the mean of a function of an unknown random variable with unknown parameters.

When $a_0 = 0$, h_t is a martingale. Regarding the behavior of its conditional expectation, h_t with $a_0 > 0$ and $a_0 = 0$ is analogous to a random walk with and without drift, respectively. However, the behavior of h_t in other respects is markedly different from that of a random walk; for example, the structure of the higher moments of h_t when $a_1 + b_1 = 1$ and $a_0 = 0$ implies that the distribution of h_t becomes more and more concentrated around zero with fatter and fatter tails, which is not the case for a random walk.

---

[59] The process is strictly stationary with a well-defined probability measure.

CONCEPTS EXPLAINED IN THIS CHAPTER
(IN ORDER OF PRESENTATION)

Homoskedasticity
Heteroskedasticity
Autoregressive conditional heteroskedasticity (ARCH)
Volatility clustering
Generalized autoregressive conditional heteroskedasticity (GARCH) model
Conditional variance
Overall kurtosis
Stationarity of ARCH/GARCH processes
Maximum likelihood estimation of ARCH/GARCH models
Pseudo (or quasi) maximum likelihood estimation of ARCH/GARCH models
Berndt, Hall, Hall, and Hausmann (BHHH) algorithm
Lagrange multiplier test
GARCH models with Student's t distributed innovations
Exponential GARCH (EGARCH) models
Integrated GARCH (IGARCH) models
Fractionally integrated GARCH (FIGARCH) models
Fractionally integrated exponential GARCH (FIEGARCH) models
Long memory GARCH (LMGARCH) processes
Forecasting with GARCH models
Root mean square error (RMSE)
Mean absolute error (MAE)
Mean absolute percentage error (MAPE)
Multivariate GARCH models
VECH model

CHAPTER 9

Vector Autoregressive Models I

In this and the following two chapters we discuss vector autoregressive models. Here we provide the formal background of VAR models and discussing their statistical properties. The next chapter addresses the estimation of VAR models.

VAR MODELS DEFINED

Vector autoregressive (VAR) models are, as suggested by their name, models of vectors of variables as autoregressive processes, where each variable depends linearly on its own lagged values and those of the other variables in the vector. This means that the future values of the process are a weighted sum of past and present values plus some noise (and, possibly, exogenous variables). For example, it is known that there are equity price "leaders" and equity price "laggards" in the sense that the returns of some portfolios of large-cap stocks anticipate the returns of large portfolios of small-cap stocks.[1] An analyst who wants to exploit this relationship for a specific pair of leader-laggard portfolios might fit a bivariate VAR to model the returns of the leader and laggard portfolios.

Suppose, for example, that portfolio A is a leader portfolio and portfolio B a laggard portfolio. The analyst can write the following model for returns:

---

[1] See John Y. Campbell, Andrew W. Lo, and A. Craig MacKinlay, *The Econometrics of Financial Markets* (Princeton, NJ: Princeton University Press, 1997); and Angelos Kanas and George P. Kouretas, "A Cointegration Approach to the Lead-Lag Effect Among Sized-Sorted Equity Portfolios," Working Paper, Department of Economics, University of Crete, 2001.

$$R_A(t+1) = R_A(t) + \varepsilon_A(t+1)$$
$$R_B(t+1) = aR_A(t) + \varepsilon_B(t+1)$$

where $R_A(t)$ and $R_B(t)$ are the returns of the two portfolios, respectively, and ε_A and ε_B are independent white-noise terms (IID zero-mean variables). The first equation states that the price-leader portfolio follows a random walk; the second equation states that the laggard portfolio tends to follow the leader with a delay of one period.

The above is a simple example of a multivariate extension of the autoregressive (AR) model. A vector autoregressive model of order p [VAR(p)] has the following general form:

$$\mathbf{x}_t = \mathbf{A}_1\mathbf{x}_{t-1} + \mathbf{A}_2\mathbf{x}_{t-2} + \cdots + \mathbf{A}_p\mathbf{x}_{t-p} + \mathbf{s}_t + \boldsymbol{\varepsilon}_t$$

where $\mathbf{x}_t = (x_{1,t}, ..., x_{n,t})'$ is a multivariate stochastic time series in vector notation; $\mathbf{A}_i$, $i = 1, 2, ..., p$ are deterministic $n \times n$ matrices; $\boldsymbol{\varepsilon}_t = (\varepsilon_{1,t}, ..., \varepsilon_{n,t})'$ is a multivariate white noise with variance-covariance matrix $\boldsymbol{\Omega}$; and $\mathbf{s}_t = (s_{1,t}, ..., s_{n,t})'$ is a vector of deterministic terms.

Using the lag-operator L notation, a VAR(p) model can be written in the following form:

$$\mathbf{x}_t = (\mathbf{A}_1 L + \mathbf{A}_2 L^2 + ... + \mathbf{A}_p L^p)\mathbf{x}_t + \mathbf{s}_t + \boldsymbol{\varepsilon}_t$$

In most applications, the deterministic term will consist of constant intercept terms, i.e., $\mathbf{s}_t = \mathbf{v}$ or a linear function. A deterministic term formed by a constant can produce a linear trend while a deterministic term formed by a linear trend can produce either a quadratic or a linear trend.

Let us first examine the stationarity and stability conditions of VAR models.

Stationarity, Stability, and Invertibility

Recall that a stochastic process is called *weakly stationary* or covariance-stationary if the expectation of x_t, $E(x_t)$, and the autocovariances, $\text{Cov}(x_t, x_{t-k})$, do not vary with time and are finite. A process is called *strictly stationary* if all finite-dimensional distributions are time-invariant. However, in real-life applications, processes start at a given time.

We call weakly asymptotically stationary a process that starts at a time origin and is such that its first and second moments (i.e., expectations and variances-covariances) converge to finite limits.

Stationarity imposes a lot of structure on a stochastic process. In 1938, the Swedish mathematician Herman Ole Andreas Wold proved a fundamental theorem, known as the *Wold decomposition theorem*[2] for multivariate time series, which proposes

> Any zero-mean, covariance stationary process $y_t = (y_{1,t}, ..., y_{n,t})'$ can be represented in a unique way as the sum of a stochastic process and a linearly predictable deterministic process, that is,

$$y_t = \mu_t + \Psi(L)\varepsilon_t$$

where the stochastic part is represented as an infinite moving average,

$$\Psi(L) = \sum_{i=0}^{\infty} \Psi_i \varepsilon_{t-i} \quad \Psi_0 = I_n$$

subject to the condition

$$\sum_{i=0}^{\infty} \Psi_i \Psi_i' < \infty$$

to ensure that the series is summable. The ε_t are the one-step-ahead linear forecast errors and the deterministic part is a linear deterministic process.

Note also that the Wold representation is the unique representation of a covariance stationary time series in terms of linear predictors; however, other representations based on nonforecast errors are perfectly possible.

Consider a VAR(p) model

$$x_t = (A_1 L + A_2 L^2 + ... + A_p L^p)x_t + v + \varepsilon_t, \, t = \pm 0, \pm 1, \pm 2, ...$$

where the deterministic term is a constant; ε_t is a sequence of zero-mean, finite-variance IID variables; and time extends from $-\infty$ to $+\infty$. Defining the matrix polynomial

$$A(z) = I - A_1 z - A_2 z^2 - \cdots - A_p z^p$$

where z is a complex number, the equation

---

[2] Herman Ole Andreas Wold, *A Study in the Analysis of Stationary Time Series* (Stockholm: Almqvist and Wiksell, 1938).

$$\det(\mathbf{A}(z)) = 0$$

is called the *reverse characteristic equation* of the VAR model. It is the multivariate equivalent of the univariate reverse characteristic equation. Alternatively, defining the matrix polynomial,

$$\mathbf{B}(z) = \mathbf{I}z^p - \mathbf{A}_1 z^{p-1} - \mathbf{A}_2 z^{p-2} - \cdots - \mathbf{A}_p, z \in \mathbb{C}$$

the equation

$$\det(\mathbf{B}(z)) = 0$$

is called the *characteristic equation* of the VAR model. As in the univariate case, its solutions are the reciprocal of the solutions of the reverse characteristic equation.

Consider the characteristic equation of an n-variate VAR(p) model with p distinct solutions λ_i. The characteristic equation can then be written as follows:

$$(z - \lambda_1) \cdots (z - \lambda_s) = 0 \,^3$$

If the roots of the reverse characteristic equation are strictly outside of the unit circle, then the VAR process is said to be *stable*. Formally, we can write the *stability conditions* as follows:

$$\det(\mathbf{A}(z)) \neq 0 \text{ for } |z| \leq 1$$

It can be demonstrated that, if the stability conditions are satisfied, the relative VAR process is stationary if it extends on the entire time axis and is asymptotically stationary if it starts from initial conditions. However, the converse is not true: there are stationary processes that are not stable.

To understand the meaning of the stability conditions, consider that the solutions of a VAR model are linear combinations of terms of the type λ^t, $\rho^t \cos(wt + \varphi)$ where λ, ρ are respectively the reciprocal of the solution or the modulus of the reciprocal of the solution of the reverse characteristic equation $\det(\mathbf{A}(z)) = 0$. If the roots of the reverse char-

---

[3] Here we assume that roots are all distinct. The analysis remains the same in the case of multiple roots but the mathematics is more cumbersome. In practice, roots will all be distinct.

acteristic equation are outside the unit circle, all past shocks (i.e., noise terms) decays exponentially over time.

If a VAR process satisfies the stability conditions and is stationary, then the process is *invertible* in the sense that the process

$$(I - A_1 L - A_2 L^2 - \ldots - A_p L^p)x_t = v + \varepsilon_t$$

can be written in an *infinite moving average* representation as follows:

$$x_t = (I - A_1 L - A_2 L^2 - \ldots - A_p L^p)^{-1}(v + \varepsilon_t)$$

$$= \left(\sum_{i=0}^{\infty} \Phi_i L^i \right)(v + \varepsilon_t)$$

$$\Phi_0 = I$$

where the Φ_i are $n \times n$ constant matrices.

It can be demonstrated that, if the process is stable, the matrix sequence Φ_i is *absolutely summable*. Therefore the process

$$\left(\sum_{i=0}^{\infty} \Phi_i L^i \right)\varepsilon_t$$

is a well-defined process. We can rewrite the above process as

$$x_t = u + \left(\sum_{i=0}^{\infty} \Phi_i L^i \right)\varepsilon_t$$

where

$$u = \left(\sum_{i=0}^{\infty} \Phi_i \right)v$$

is the constant mean of the process

$$u = E[x_t]$$

The concept of stable process as used here must not be confused with the concept of stable Paretian processes that will be defined in Chapter 14. If the process is not stable, then the mean is a function of time—as we will see later, in the section on the solutions of VAR processes. The above considerations show that, in the case of a VAR(p) process, the Wold decomposition coincides with the infinite moving average representation obtained by inverting the process and the shocks ε_t are the linear forecast errors.

Solutions of VAR(p) Models

We now present the explicit solutions for multivariate VAR(p) models. These solutions provide the necessary intuition for the concepts of cointegration, error correction, and dynamic factors that are introduced in Chapter 11.

As for any other linear model, solutions to a VAR model are the sum of a deterministic part plus a stochastic part. The deterministic part depends on the initial conditions and deterministic terms; the stochastic part depends on random shocks. The stochastic part of the solution is a weighted sum of past shocks. If the process is stable, then shocks in the distant past have only a negligible influence and the stochastic part is a weighted sum of the most recent shocks. If the process is integrated, then the effects of shocks never decay; the stochastic part is thus the cumulation of all past shocks. If the process is explosive, then shocks are amplified as time passes.

Equivalence of VAR(p) and VAR(1)

In order to compute explicit solutions of VAR(p) models, we make use of the key fact that any VAR(p) model is equivalent to some VAR(1) model after introducing appropriate additional variables. This is an important simplification as VAR(1) models can be characterized with simple intuitive formulas.

To illustrate this point, first write down a bivariate model of order one in matrix notation, that is,

$$\mathbf{x}_t = \mathbf{A}_1 \mathbf{x}_{t-1} + \mathbf{s}_t + \varepsilon_t$$

$$\begin{bmatrix} x_{1,t} \\ x_{2,t} \end{bmatrix} = \begin{bmatrix} a_{11} & a_{12} \\ a_{21} & a_{22} \end{bmatrix} \begin{bmatrix} x_{1,t-1} \\ x_{2,t-1} \end{bmatrix} + \begin{bmatrix} s_{1,t} \\ s_{2,t} \end{bmatrix} + \begin{bmatrix} \varepsilon_{1,t} \\ \varepsilon_{2,t} \end{bmatrix}$$

and explicitly

$$x_{1,t} = a_{11} x_{1,t-1} + a_{12} x_{2,t-1} + s_{1,t} + \varepsilon_{1,t}$$
$$x_{2,t} = a_{21} x_{1,t-1} + a_{22} x_{2,t-1} + s_{1,t} + \varepsilon_{2,t}$$

We observe that any VAR(1) model becomes an arithmetic multivariate random walk if $\mathbf{A}_1$ is an identity matrix and s_t is a constant vector. In particular, in the bivariate case, a VAR(1) is a random walk if

$$\begin{bmatrix} a_{11} & a_{12} \\ a_{21} & a_{22} \end{bmatrix} = \begin{bmatrix} 1 & 0 \\ 0 & 1 \end{bmatrix}$$

and $\mathbf{s}_t = (s_1, s_2)$.

Consider now a bivariate VAR(2) model of order two:

$$\begin{bmatrix} x_{1,t} \\ x_{2,t} \end{bmatrix} = \begin{bmatrix} a_{11} & a_{12} \\ a_{21} & a_{22} \end{bmatrix} \begin{bmatrix} x_{1,t-1} \\ x_{2,t-1} \end{bmatrix} + \begin{bmatrix} b_{11} & b_{12} \\ b_{21} & b_{22} \end{bmatrix} \begin{bmatrix} x_{1,t-2} \\ x_{2,t-2} \end{bmatrix} + \begin{bmatrix} s_{1,t} \\ s_{2,t} \end{bmatrix} + \begin{bmatrix} \varepsilon_{1,t} \\ \varepsilon_{2,t} \end{bmatrix}$$

Let us introduce a new vector variable $\mathbf{z}_t = \mathbf{x}_{t-1}$. The VAR(2) model can then be rewritten as follows:

$$x_{1,t} = a_{11}x_{1,t-1} + a_{12}x_{2,t-1} + b_{11}z_{1,t-1} + b_{12}z_{2,t-1} + s_{1,t} + \varepsilon_{1,t}$$
$$x_{2,t} = a_{21}x_{1,t-1} + a_{22}x_{2,t-1} + b_{21}z_{1,t-1} + b_{22}z_{2,t-1} + s_{1,t} + \varepsilon_{2,t}$$
$$z_{1,t} = x_{1,t-1}$$
$$z_{2,t} = x_{2,t-1}$$

or in matrix form

$$\begin{bmatrix} x_{1,t} \\ x_{2,t} \\ z_{1,t} \\ z_{2,t} \end{bmatrix} = \begin{bmatrix} a_{11} & a_{12} & b_{11} & b_{12} \\ a_{21} & a_{22} & b_{21} & b_{22} \\ 1 & 0 & 0 & 0 \\ 0 & 1 & 0 & 0 \end{bmatrix} \begin{bmatrix} x_{1,t-1} \\ x_{2,t-1} \\ z_{1,t-1} \\ z_{2,t-1} \end{bmatrix} + \begin{bmatrix} 1 & 0 & 0 & 0 \\ 0 & 1 & 0 & 0 \\ 0 & 0 & 0 & 0 \\ 0 & 0 & 0 & 0 \end{bmatrix} \begin{bmatrix} s_{1,t} \\ s_{2,t} \\ 0 \\ 0 \end{bmatrix} + \begin{bmatrix} \varepsilon_{1,t} \\ \varepsilon_{2,t} \\ 0 \\ 0 \end{bmatrix}$$

The above considerations can be generalized. Any AR(p) or VAR(p) model can be transformed into a first-order VAR(1) model by adding appropriate variables.[4] In particular, an n-dimensional VAR(p) model of the form

$$\mathbf{x}_t = (\mathbf{A}_1 L + \mathbf{A}_2 L^2 + \dots + \mathbf{A}_p L^p)\mathbf{x}_t + \mathbf{s}_t + \varepsilon_t$$

is transformed into the following np-dimensional VAR(1) model

---

[4] The theory of VAR models parallels the theory of systems of linear differential equations and of systems of linear stochastic differential equations.

$$\mathbf{X}_t = \mathbf{AX}_t + \mathbf{S}_t + \mathbf{W}_t$$

where

$$
\mathbf{X}_t = \begin{bmatrix} \mathbf{x}_t \\ \mathbf{x}_{t-1} \\ \vdots \\ \mathbf{x}_{t-p+1} \end{bmatrix}, \quad
\mathbf{A} = \begin{bmatrix} \mathbf{A}_1 & \mathbf{A}_2 & \dots & \mathbf{A}_{p-1} & \mathbf{A}_p \\ \mathbf{I}_n & 0 & \dots & 0 & 0 \\ 0 & \mathbf{I}_n & \dots & 0 & 0 \\ 0 & 0 & \ddots & \vdots & \vdots \\ 0 & 0 & \dots & \mathbf{I}_n & 0 \end{bmatrix}, \quad
\mathbf{S}_t = \begin{bmatrix} \mathbf{s}_t \\ 0 \\ \vdots \\ 0 \end{bmatrix}, \quad
\mathbf{W}_t = \begin{bmatrix} \varepsilon_t \\ 0 \\ \vdots \\ 0 \end{bmatrix}
$$

$\mathbf{X}_t$, $\mathbf{S}_t$, and $\mathbf{W}_t$ are $np \times 1$ vectors and $\mathbf{A}$ is a $np \times np$ square matrix. In order to compute explicit solutions of higher-order VAR processes, we have therefore only to consider VAR(1) models.

It can be demonstrated that the reverse characteristic equation of this VAR(1) system and that of the original VAR(p) system have the same roots.

Solving Stable VAR(1) Processes

We can now proceed to show how solutions to stable VAR models can be computed. Given the equivalence between VAR(1) and VAR(p) we will only consider VAR(1) models. We first consider stable processes that start in the infinite past and then move to possibly unstable processes that start at a given point in time from some initial conditions.

Consider an n-dimensional VAR(1) model,

$$\mathbf{x}_t = \mathbf{Ax}_{t-1} + \mathbf{v} + \varepsilon_t, \, t = 0, \pm 1, \pm 2, \dots$$

where the deterministic term, $\mathbf{v}$, is a constant vector. Suppose that the roots of its characteristic equation

$$\det(\mathbf{I}z - \mathbf{A}) = 0$$

lie inside the unit circle. The solutions of this equation are the eigenvalues of the matrix $\mathbf{A}$. Therefore, in the case of a stable process, all the eigenvalues of the matrix $\mathbf{A}$ have modulus less than one. Note that we here express the stability condition in terms of the characteristic equation, while in a previous section we used the reverse characteristic equation.

As the VAR operator is stable, the process is stationary and invertible. Being that it is a VAR(1) process, the infinite moving average polynomial is given by

$$(\mathbf{I} - \mathbf{A}L)^{-1} = \sum_{i=0}^{\infty} \mathbf{A}^i L^i \qquad \mathbf{A}^0 = \mathbf{I}$$

As we saw above in our discussion of stability, stationarity, and invertibility, an invertible process can be represented as follows:

$$\mathbf{x}_t = \mathbf{u} + \left(\sum_{i=0}^{\infty} \mathbf{A}^i L^i \right) \varepsilon_t$$

where

$$\mathbf{u} = \left(\sum_{i=0}^{\infty} \mathbf{A}^i \right) \mathbf{v}$$

is the constant mean of the process

$$\mathbf{u} = E[\mathbf{x}_t]$$

We now compute the autocovariances of the process. It can be demonstrated that the time-invariant autocovariances of the process are

$$\Gamma_h = E[(\mathbf{x}_t - \mathbf{u})(\mathbf{x}_{t-h} - \mathbf{u})'] = \sum_{i=0}^{\infty} \mathbf{A}^{i+h} \Omega (\mathbf{A}^i)'$$

where Ω is the variance-covariance matrix of the noise term. This expression involves an infinite sum of matrices. While it is not convenient for practical computations, it can be demonstrated that the following recursive matrix equations hold:

$$\Gamma_h = \mathbf{A} \Gamma_{h-1}$$

These equations are called *Yule-Walker equations*. They are the *multivariate* equivalent of the Yule-Walker equations that we defined for univariate ARMA processes.

Yule-Walker equations can be used to compute the process autocovariances (see chapters 6 and 7 for the definition of these terms) recursively—provided that we know Γ_0. Note that Γ_0 is the variance-covariance matrix of the *process*, which is different from the variance-covariance matrix Ω of the noise term. It can demonstrated that Γ_0 satisfies

$$\Gamma_0 = A\Gamma_0 A' + \Omega$$

which allows to compute Γ_0 via

$$\text{vec}(\Gamma_0) = (I - A \otimes A)^{-1}\text{vec}(\Omega)$$

The vec operation and the Kronecker product $\otimes$ are defined in the appendix to this chapter.

To explicitly compute solutions, consider separately the case of distinct roots and the case of at least two coincident roots. Suppose first that the matrix A has distinct eigenvalues $(\lambda_1, ..., \lambda_n)$ (see the appendix to this chapter for a definition of eigenvalues) and distinct eigenvectors $(\xi_1, ..., \xi_n)$. The matrix A is thus nonsingular and can be represented as: $A = \Xi\Lambda\Xi^{-1}$ where $\Xi = [\xi_1, ..., \xi_n]$ is a nonsingular matrix whose columns are the eigenvectors and

$$\Lambda = \begin{pmatrix} \lambda_1 & & 0 \\ & \ddots & \\ 0 & & \lambda_n \end{pmatrix}$$

is a diagonal matrix whose diagonal elements are the eigenvalues of A.

Consider the process solution

$$x_t = u + \left(\sum_{i=0}^{\infty} A^i L^i\right)\varepsilon_t$$

The infinite matrix series on the right-hand side converges as the eigenvalues of the matrix A have modulus less than one. In fact we can write

$$A = \Xi\Lambda\Xi^{-1}$$

$$A^i = \overbrace{\Xi\Lambda\Xi^{-1} \dots \Xi\Lambda\Xi^{-1}}^{i \text{ times}} = \Xi\Lambda^i\Xi^{-1}$$

$$
\Lambda^i = \begin{pmatrix} \lambda_1^i & & 0 \\ & \ddots & \\ 0 & & \lambda_n^i \end{pmatrix}
$$

and

$$
(I - AL)^{-1} = \sum_{i=0}^{\infty} A^i L^i = \sum_{i=0}^{\infty} \Xi \Lambda^i \Xi^{-1} L^i
$$

The process solution can therefore be written as

$$
x_t = u + \left(\sum_{i=0}^{\infty} \Xi \Lambda^i \Xi^{-1} L^i \right) \varepsilon_t
$$

The process can be represented as a constant plus an infinite moving average of past noise terms weighted with exponential terms.

Solving Stable and Unstable Processes with Initial Conditions

In the previous section we considered stable, stationary systems defined on the entire time axis. In practice, however, most models start at a given time. If the system starts at a given moment with given initial conditions, it need be neither stable nor stationary. Consider an n-dimensional VAR(1) model

$$
x_t = A x_{t-1} + s_t + \varepsilon_t, \quad t = 1, 2, \ldots
$$

together with initial conditions.

Suppose the VAR(1) model starts at $t = 0$ and suppose that the initial conditions x_0 are given. *The solution of the model is the sum of the general solution of the associated homogeneous system with the given initial conditions plus a particular solution.* The *general* solution can be written as follows:

$$
x_G(t) = \Xi \Lambda^t c = c_1 \lambda_1^t \xi_1 + \ldots + c_n \lambda_n^t \xi_n
$$

with constants c determined in function of initial conditions. A *particular* solution can be written as

$$
x_t = \sum_{i=0}^{t-1} \Xi \Lambda^i \Xi^{-1} (s_{t-i} + \varepsilon_{t-i})
$$

All solutions are a sum of a particular solution and the general solution. We can also see that the solution is a sum of the deterministic and stochastic parts:

$$\mathbf{x}_t = \overbrace{\Xi\Lambda^t\mathbf{c} + \sum_{i=0}^{t-1}\Xi\Lambda^i\Xi^{-1}\mathbf{s}_{t-i}}^{\text{Deterministic part}} + \overbrace{\sum_{i=0}^{t-1}\Xi\Lambda^i\Xi^{-1}\boldsymbol{\varepsilon}_{t-i}}^{\text{Stochastic part}}$$

From the above formulas, we can see that the modulus of eigenvalues dictates if past shocks decay, persist, or are amplified.

We now discuss the shape of the deterministic trend under the above assumptions. Recall that the deterministic trend is given by the mean of the process. Let us assume that the deterministic terms are either constant intercepts $\mathbf{s}_t = \boldsymbol{\mu}$ or linear functions $\mathbf{s}_t = \boldsymbol{\gamma}t + \boldsymbol{\mu}$. Taking expectations on both sides of the above equation, we can write

$$E[\mathbf{x}_t] = \Xi\Lambda^t\mathbf{c} + \sum_{i=0}^{t-1}\Xi\Lambda^i\Xi^{-1}\boldsymbol{\mu}$$

in the case of constant intercepts, and

$$E[\mathbf{x}_t] = \Xi\Lambda^t\mathbf{c} + \sum_{i=0}^{t-1}\Xi\Lambda^i\Xi^{-1}(\boldsymbol{\gamma}t + \boldsymbol{\mu})$$

in the case of a linear functions.

As the matrix Λ is diagonal, it is clear that the process deterministic trend can have different shapes in function of the eigenvalues. In both cases, the trend can be either a constant, a linear trend, or a polynomial of higher order. *If the process has only one unitary root, then a constant intercept produces a linear trend, while a linear function might produce a constant, linear, or quadratic trend.*

To illustrate the above, consider the following VAR(2) model where we replace the notation x_t with $x(t)$:

$$x(t) = 0.6x(t-1) - 0.1y(t-1) - 0.7x(t-2) + 0.15y(t-2) + \varepsilon_x(t)$$
$$y(t) = -0.12x(t-1) + 0.7y(t-1) + 0.22x(t-2) - 0.8y(t-2) + \varepsilon_y(t)$$

with the following initial conditions at time $t = 1,2$:

$$x(1) = 1 \quad x(2) = 1.2 \quad y(1) = 1.5 \quad y(2) = -2$$

It can be transformed into a VAR(1) model as follows:

$$
\begin{aligned}
x(t) &= 0.6x(t-1) - 0.1y(t-1) - 0.7z(t-1) + 0.15w(t-1) + \varepsilon_x(t) \\
y(t) &= -0.12x(t-1) + 0.7y(t-1) + 0.22z(t-1) - 0.8w(t-1) + \varepsilon_y(t) \\
z(t) &= x(t-1) \\
w(t) &= y(t-1)
\end{aligned}
$$

with the following initial conditions:

$$x(2) = 1.2 \quad y(2) = -2 \quad z(2) = 1 \quad w(2) = 1.5$$

Note that now we have defined four initial conditions at $t = 2$.
The coefficient matrix

$$
\mathbf{A} = \begin{pmatrix}
0.6 & -0.1 & -0.7 & 0.15 \\
-0.12 & 0.7 & 0.22 & -0.8 \\
1 & 0 & 0 & 0 \\
0 & 1 & 0 & 0
\end{pmatrix}
$$

has four complex eigenvalues:

$$
\Lambda = \begin{bmatrix}
0.2654 + 0.7011i & 0 & 0 & 0 \\
0 & 0.2654 - 0.7011i & 0 & 0 \\
0 & 0 & 0.3846 + 0.8887i & 0 \\
0 & 0 & 0 & 0.3846 - 0.8887i
\end{bmatrix}
$$

The corresponding eigenvector matrix (columns are the eigenvectors) is

$$
\Xi = \begin{bmatrix}
0.1571 + 0.4150i & 0.1571 - 0.4150i & -0.1311 - 0.3436i & -0.1311 + 0.3436i \\
0.0924 + 0.3928i & 0.0924 - 0.3928i & 0.2346 + 0.5419i & 0.2346 - 0.5419i \\
0.5920 & 0.5920 & -0.3794 + 0.0167i & -0.3794 + 0.0167i \\
0.5337 + 0.0702i & 0.5337 - 0.0702i & 0.6098 & 0.6098
\end{bmatrix}
$$

The general solution can be written as

$$
\mathbf{x}_G = c_1 0.7497^t \cos(1.2090t + \rho_1) + c_2 0.9684^t \cos(1.1623t + \rho_2)
$$

STATIONARY AUTOREGRESSIVE DISTRIBUTED LAG MODELS

An important extension of pure VAR models is given by the family of *autoregressive distributed lag* (ARDL) models. The ARDL model is essentially the coupling of a regression model and a VAR model. The ARDL model is written as follows:

$$y_t = v + \mathbf{\Phi}_1 y_{t-1} + \cdots + \mathbf{\Phi}_s y_{t-s} + \mathbf{P}_0 x_t + \cdots + \mathbf{P}_q x_{t-q} + \mathbf{\eta}_t$$

$$x_t = \mathbf{A}_1 x_{t-1} + \cdots + \mathbf{A}_p x_{t-p} + \mathbf{\varepsilon}_t$$

In the ARDL model, a variable y_t is regressed over its own lagged values and over the values of another variable x_t, which follows a VAR(p) model. Both the $\mathbf{\eta}_t$ and the $\mathbf{\varepsilon}_t$ terms are assumed to be white noise with a time-invariant covariance matrix.

The previous ARDL model can be rewritten as a VAR(1) model as follows:

$$
\begin{pmatrix} y_t \\ y_{t-1} \\ \vdots \\ y_{t-s+2} \\ y_{t-s+1} \\ x_t \\ \vdots \\ \vdots \\ x_{t-p} \end{pmatrix}
=
\begin{pmatrix} v \\ 0 \\ \vdots \\ 0 \\ 0 \\ 0 \\ 0 \\ \vdots \\ 0 \\ 0 \end{pmatrix}
\begin{pmatrix}
\mathbf{\Phi}_1 & \mathbf{\Phi}_2 & \cdots & \mathbf{\Phi}_{s-1} & \mathbf{\Phi}_s & \mathbf{P}_0 & \mathbf{P}_1 & \cdots & \mathbf{P}_q & \cdots & 0 & 0 \\
\mathbf{I} & 0 & \cdots & 0 & 0 & 0 & 0 & \cdots & 0 & \cdots & 0 & 0 \\
\vdots & \vdots & \ddots & \vdots & \vdots & \vdots & \vdots & \ddots & \vdots & \ddots & \vdots & \vdots \\
0 & 0 & \cdots & \mathbf{I} & 0 & 0 & 0 & \cdots & 0 & \cdots & 0 & 0 \\
0 & 0 & \cdots & 0 & \mathbf{I} & 0 & 0 & \cdots & 0 & \cdots & 0 & 0 \\
0 & 0 & \cdots & 0 & 0 & 0 & \mathbf{A}_1 & \cdots & \mathbf{A}_q & \cdots & \mathbf{A}_{p-1} & \mathbf{A}_p \\
0 & 0 & \cdots & 0 & 0 & 0 & \mathbf{I} & \cdots & 0 & \cdots & 0 & 0 \\
\vdots & \vdots & \ddots & \vdots & \vdots & \vdots & \vdots & \ddots & \vdots & \ddots & \vdots & \vdots \\
0 & 0 & \cdots & 0 & 0 & 0 & 0 & \cdots & 0 & \cdots & 0 & 0 \\
0 & 0 & \cdots & 0 & 0 & 0 & 0 & \cdots & 0 & \cdots & \mathbf{I} & 0
\end{pmatrix}
$$

$$
\begin{pmatrix} y_{t-1} \\ y_{t-2} \\ \vdots \\ y_{t-s+1} \\ y_{t-s} \\ x_t \\ x_{t-1} \\ \vdots \\ x_{t-q} \\ \vdots \\ x_{t-p} \\ x_{t-p-1} \end{pmatrix}
+
\begin{pmatrix} \mathbf{\eta}_t \\ 0 \\ \vdots \\ \vdots \\ 0 \\ \mathbf{\varepsilon}_t \\ 0 \\ \vdots \\ \vdots \\ 0 \end{pmatrix}
$$

The estimation of the ARDL model can therefore be done with the methods used for VAR models. Coefficients can be estimated with OLS methods and the number of lags can be determined with the AIC or BIC criteria discussed in a previous section.

The ARDL model is quite important in financial econometrics: many models of stock returns are essentially ARDL models. In particular, all models where stock returns are regressed over a number of state variables that follow a VAR model are ARDL models.

VECTOR AUTOREGRESSIVE MOVING AVERAGE MODELS

Vector autoregressive moving average (VARMA) models combine an autoregressive part and a moving average part. In some cases, they can offer a more parsimonious modeling option than a pure VAR model. A VARMA(p,q) model without deterministic component is of the form:

$$A(L)\mathbf{x}_t = B(L)\boldsymbol{\varepsilon}_t$$
$$A(L) = \mathbf{I} - \mathbf{A}_1 L - \mathbf{A}_2 L^2 - \cdots - \mathbf{A}_p L^p$$
$$B(L) = \mathbf{I} + \mathbf{B}_1 L + \mathbf{B}_2 L^2 + \cdots + \mathbf{B}_q L^q$$

A VARMA model has two characteristic equations:

$$\det(\mathbf{A}(z)) = 0$$
$$\det(\mathbf{B}(z)) = 0$$

If the roots of the equation $\det(\mathbf{A}(z)) = 0$ are all strictly outside the unit circle, then the process is stable and can be represented as an infinite moving average. If the roots of the equation $\det(\mathbf{B}(z)) = 0$ are all strictly outside the unit circle, then the process is invertible and can be represented as an infinite autoregressive process. Both representations require the process to be defined for $-\infty < t < \infty$.

If the process starts at $t = 0$, the theory developed above in our discussion of VAR models can be applied. The process can be reduced to a VAR(1) model and then solved with the same methods.

Integrated Processes

Recall that a process is strictly stationary if the joint distribution of a finite collection x_t, x_{t-1},..., x_{t-k} does not vary with t; it is covariance-stationary if its first and second moments are time-invariant. Stationarity does not imply weak stationarity as distributions might have infinite first or second moments. A process described by a *vector difference equation* (VDE) is stationary if the VDE is stable, that is, if the solutions of the characteristic equations lie strictly outside the unit circle.

A process is said to be *integrated* of order one if its first differences form a stationary process. Recursively, we can define a process integrated of order n if its first differences are integrated of order $n - 1$. An arithmetic random walk is a process integrated of order one as its differences are stationary. However, not all integrated processes are random walks as the definition of stationarity does not assume that processes are generated as IID sequences. In other words, a stationary process can exhibit autocorrelation.

Consider a multivariate process $\mathbf{x}_t$. The process $\mathbf{x}_t$ is said to be integrated of order d if we can write

$$(I - L)^d \mathbf{x}_t = \mathbf{y}_t$$

where $\mathbf{y}_t$ is a stationary process. Suppose that $\mathbf{x}_t$ can be represented by a VAR process,

$$(\mathbf{I} - \mathbf{A}_1 L - \mathbf{A}_2 L^2 - \cdots - \mathbf{A}_p L^p)\mathbf{x}_t = \Phi(\mathbf{A})\mathbf{x}_t = \boldsymbol{\varepsilon}_t$$

The process $\mathbf{x}_t$ is said to be integrated of order d if we can factorize Φ as follows:

$$\mathbf{A}(L)\mathbf{x}_t = (1 - L)^d \mathbf{C}(L)\mathbf{x}_t = \boldsymbol{\varepsilon}_t$$

where $\Psi(L)$ is a stable VAR process that can be inverted to yield

$$(1 - L)^d \mathbf{x}_t = \mathbf{C}(L)^{-1}\boldsymbol{\varepsilon}_t = \sum_{i=0}^{\infty} \mathbf{C}_i \boldsymbol{\varepsilon}_{t-i}$$

In particular, an integrated process with order of integration $d = 1$ admits the following representation:

$$\Delta \mathbf{x}_t = (1 - L)\mathbf{x}_t = \mathbf{C}(L)^{-1}\boldsymbol{\varepsilon}_t = \left(\sum_{i=0}^{\infty} \Psi_i L^i \right)\boldsymbol{\varepsilon}_t$$

The above definition can be generalized to allow for different orders of integration for each variable.

It is clear from the above definition that the characteristic equation of a process integrated of order d has d roots equal to 1.

Stochastic and Deterministic Trends

An integrated process is characterized by the fact that past shocks never decay. In more precise terms, we can demonstrate that an integrated process can be decomposed as the sum of three components: a deterministic trend, a stochastic trend, and a cyclic stationary process. To see this, consider first a process integrated of order 1 and without a constant intercept, given by

$$\Delta \mathbf{x}_t = \mathbf{\Psi}(L)\mathbf{\varepsilon}_t = \left(\sum_{i=0}^{\infty} \mathbf{\Psi}_i L^i \right) \mathbf{\varepsilon}_t$$

Let's rewrite $\mathbf{\Psi}(L)$ as

$$\mathbf{\Psi}(L) = \mathbf{\Psi} + (1 - L)\left(\sum_{i=0}^{\infty} \mathbf{\Psi}_i^* L^i \right)$$

where $\mathbf{\Psi}(1) = \mathbf{\Psi}$. We can now write the process $\mathbf{x}_t$ as follows:

$$\Delta \mathbf{x}_t = (1 - L)\mathbf{x}_t = \left[\mathbf{\Psi} + (1 - L)\left(\sum_{i=0}^{\infty} \mathbf{\Psi}_i^* L^i \right) \right] \mathbf{\varepsilon}_t$$

or, dividing by $(1 - L)$:

$$\mathbf{x}_t = \frac{\mathbf{\Psi}}{1 - L}\mathbf{\varepsilon}_t + \left(\sum_{i=0}^{\infty} \mathbf{\Psi}_i^* L^i \right) \mathbf{\varepsilon}_t$$

$$\mathbf{x}_t = \mathbf{\Psi} \sum_{i=1}^{t} \mathbf{\varepsilon}_i + \left(\sum_{i=0}^{\infty} \mathbf{\Psi}_i^* L^i \right) \mathbf{\varepsilon}_t$$

The process $\mathbf{x}_t$ is thereby decomposed into a stochastic trend,

$$\mathbf{\Psi} \sum_{i=1}^{t} \mathbf{\varepsilon}_i$$

and a stationary component

$$\left(\sum_{i=0}^{\infty} \mathbf{\Psi}_i^* L^i \right) \boldsymbol{\varepsilon}_t$$

The difference between the two terms should be clearly stated: The stochastic term is a sum of shocks that never decay, while in the stationary term past shocks decay due to the weighting matrices $\mathbf{\Psi}_i^*$.

An eventual deterministic trend is added to the stochastic trend and to the stationary component. A constant intercept produces a linear trend or a constant. In fact, if we add a constant intercept $\mathbf{v}$ we can write

$$\Delta \mathbf{x}_t = (1 - L)\mathbf{x}_t = \mathbf{v} + \left[\mathbf{\Psi} + (1 - L) \left(\sum_{i=0}^{\infty} \mathbf{\Psi}_i^* L^i \right) \right] \boldsymbol{\varepsilon}_t$$

which implies

$$\mathbf{x}_t = \frac{\mathbf{\Psi}}{1 - L} \boldsymbol{\varepsilon}_t + \left(\sum_{i=0}^{\infty} \mathbf{\Psi}_i^* L^i \right) \boldsymbol{\varepsilon}_t + \frac{\mathbf{\Psi}}{1 - L} \mathbf{v}$$

$$\mathbf{x}_t = \mathbf{\Psi} \sum_{i=1}^{t} \boldsymbol{\varepsilon}_i + \left(\sum_{i=0}^{\infty} \mathbf{\Psi}_i^* L^i \right) \boldsymbol{\varepsilon}_t + t\mathbf{u}$$

where $\mathbf{u} = \mathbf{\Psi}\mathbf{v}$. The term $\mathbf{u}$ can be zero even if the intercept $\mathbf{v}$ is different from zero.

A process $\mathbf{x}_t$ is called *trend stationary* if it is the sum of a deterministic trend plus a stationary component, that is if

$$\mathbf{x}_t = \mathbf{s}_t + \mathbf{\Psi}_t$$

A process is called *difference stationary* if it becomes stationary after differencing. A difference-stationary process is the sum of a stochastic trend plus a stationary process.

FORECASTING WITH VAR MODELS

One of the key objectives of financial modeling is forecasting. Forecasting entails a criterion for forecasting as we have to concentrate a probability distribution in a point forecast. A widely used criterion is the minimization of the *mean square error* (MSE). Suppose that a process $\mathbf{y}_t$ is generated by a VAR(p) process. It can be demonstrated that the optimal h-step ahead forecast according to the MSE criterion is the conditional expectation:

$$E_t(\mathbf{y}_{t+h}) \equiv E(\mathbf{y}_{t+h} | \mathbf{y}_s, s \leq t)$$

If the error terms are strict white noise, then the optimal forecast of a VAR model can be computed as follows:

$$E_t(\mathbf{y}_{t+h}) = \mathbf{v} + \mathbf{A}_1 E_t(\mathbf{y}_{t+h-1}) + \cdots + \mathbf{A}_p E_t(\mathbf{y}_{t+h-p})$$

This formula remains valid if the noise term is a martingale difference sequence (see Chapter 6 for a definition). If the error term is white noise, the above forecasting formula will be the best linear predictor.

APPENDIX: EIGENVECTORS AND EIGENVALUES

Consider a square $n \times n$ matrix $\mathbf{A}$ and a n-vector $\mathbf{x}$. We call *eigenvectors* of the matrix $\mathbf{A}$ those vectors such that the following relationship holds

$$\mathbf{A}\mathbf{x} = \lambda\mathbf{x}$$

for some real number λ. Given an eigenvector $\mathbf{x}$ the corresponding λ is called an eigenvalue. Zero is a trivial eigenvalue. Nontrivial eigenvalues are determined by finding the solutions of the equation

$$\det(\mathbf{A} - \lambda\mathbf{I}) = 0$$

where $\mathbf{I}$ is the identity matrix. A $n \times n$ matrix has at most n distinct eigenvalues and eigenvectors.

Vectoring Operators and Tensor Products

We first define the *vec operator*. Given an $m \times n$ matrix,

$$A = \begin{pmatrix} a_{11} & \cdots & a_{1n} \\ \vdots & \ddots & \vdots \\ a_{m1} & \cdots & a_{mn} \end{pmatrix}$$

the vec operator, written as $\text{vec}(\mathbf{A})$,[5] stacks the matrix columns in an $mn \times 1$ vector as follows:

$$
\text{vec}(\mathbf{A}) = \begin{pmatrix} a_{11} \\ \vdots \\ a_{m1} \\ \vdots \\ a_{1n} \\ \vdots \\ a_{mn} \end{pmatrix}
$$

Next it is useful to define the Kronecker product. Given the $m \times n$ matrix,

$$
\mathbf{A} = \begin{pmatrix} a_{11} & \cdots & a_{1n} \\ \vdots & \ddots & \vdots \\ a_{m1} & \cdots & a_{mn} \end{pmatrix}
$$

and the $p \times q$ matrix,

$$
\mathbf{B} = \begin{pmatrix} b_{11} & \cdots & b_{1q} \\ \vdots & \ddots & \vdots \\ b_{p1} & \cdots & b_{pq} \end{pmatrix}
$$

we define the Kronecker product $\mathbf{C} = \mathbf{A} \otimes \mathbf{B}$ as follows:

$$
\mathbf{C} = \mathbf{A} \otimes \mathbf{B} = \begin{pmatrix} a_{11}\mathbf{B} & \cdots & a_{1n}\mathbf{B} \\ \vdots & \ddots & \vdots \\ a_{m1}\mathbf{B} & \cdots & a_{mn}\mathbf{B} \end{pmatrix}
$$

The Kronecker product, also called the *direct product* or *the tensor product*, is an $(mp) \times (nq)$ matrix. It can be demonstrated that the tensor product satisfies the associative and distributive property and that, given any four matrices $\mathbf{A}$, $\mathbf{B}$, $\mathbf{C}$, $\mathbf{D}$ of appropriate dimensions, the following properties hold:

$$
(\mathbf{C}' \otimes \mathbf{A})\text{vec}(\mathbf{B}) = \text{vec}(\mathbf{A} \otimes \mathbf{B} \otimes \mathbf{C})
$$

---

[5] The vec operator should not be confused with the vech operator which is similar but not identical. The vech operator stacks the terms below and on the diagonal.

$$(A \otimes B)(C \otimes D) = (AC) \otimes (BD)$$

$$(A \otimes B)' = (A') \otimes (B')$$

$$\text{Trace}(A'BCD') = (\text{vec}(A))'(D \otimes B)\text{vec}(C)$$

CONCEPTS EXPLAINED IN THIS CHAPTER (IN ORDER OF PRESENTATION)

Vector autoregressive (VAR) models
Wold decomposition theorem
Reverse characteristic equation
Characteristic equation
Stability conditions
Stable processes
Invertible processes
Infinite moving average representation
Absolutely summable sequences
Solutions of a VAR process
Equivalence VAR(p) and VAR(1)
Yule-Walker equations
    Computing autocovariances with Yule-Walker equations
General solutions of a homogeneous system
Particular solutions
Linear and quadratic trends
Autoregressive distributed lag (ARDL) models
Vector autoregressive moving average (VARMA) models
Integrated processes
Vector difference equations (VDE)
Stochastic trends
Trend stationary processes
Difference stationary processes
Forecasting
Mean square error
Eigenvalues and eigenvectors
Vec operator
Kronecker product
Tensor product

CHAPTER 10

Vector Autoregressive Models II

In this chapter we discuss estimation methods for vector autoregressive (VAR) models. We first consider estimation of stable systems. The key result here is that stable VAR systems can be conveniently estimated with least squares methods. We then proceed to the estimation of unstable systems.

ESTIMATION OF STABLE VAR MODELS

When discussing the estimation of regression models in Chapter 3, we introduced two main methods for estimating linear regressions: the least squares method and the maximum likelihood method. These methods apply immediately to unrestricted stable VAR models. Note that models are said to be "unrestricted" if the estimation process is allowed to determine any possible outcome, and "restricted" if the estimation procedure restricts parameters in some way.

Suppose that a time series is given and that the data generating process (DGP) of the series is the VAR(p) model:

$$\mathbf{x}_t = \mathbf{A}_1\mathbf{x}_{t-1} + \mathbf{A}_1\mathbf{x}_{t-1} + \cdots + \mathbf{A}_1\mathbf{x}_{t-1} + \mathbf{v} + \boldsymbol{\varepsilon}_t$$

where $\mathbf{x}_t = (x_{1,t}, \ldots, x_{N,t})'$ is a N–dimensional stochastic time series in vector notation; $\mathbf{A}_i$ are deterministic $N \times N$ matrices; $\boldsymbol{\varepsilon}_t = (\varepsilon_{1,t}, \ldots, \varepsilon_{N,t})'$ is a multivariate white noise with variance-covariance matrix Σ; and $\mathbf{v} = (v_1, \ldots, v_N)'$ is a vector of constants.

Let's first assume that stability condition

$$\det(\mathbf{A}(z)) \neq 0 \text{ for } |z| \leq 1$$

holds, that is, the roots of the reverse characteristic equation are strictly outside of the unit circle. The result is that the VAR(p) model is stable and the corresponding process stationary. We will consider processes that start at $t = 1$, assuming that p initial conditions: $x_{-p+1}, \ldots, x_0$ are given. In this case, stable VAR models yield asymptotically stationary processes.

Recall that the above N-dimensional VAR(p) model is equivalent to the following Np-dimensional VAR(1) model:

$$\mathbf{X}_t = \mathbf{A}\mathbf{X}_{t-1} + \mathbf{V} + \mathbf{U}_t$$

where

$$\mathbf{X}_t = \begin{bmatrix} \mathbf{x}_t \\ \mathbf{x}_{t-1} \\ \vdots \\ \mathbf{x}_{t-p+1} \end{bmatrix}, \mathbf{A} = \begin{bmatrix} \mathbf{A}_1 & \mathbf{A}_2 & \cdots & \mathbf{A}_{p-1} & \mathbf{A}_p \\ \mathbf{I}_N & 0 & \cdots & 0 & 0 \\ 0 & \mathbf{I}_N & \cdots & 0 & 0 \\ 0 & 0 & \ddots & \vdots & \vdots \\ 0 & 0 & \cdots & \mathbf{I}_N & 0 \end{bmatrix},$$

$$\mathbf{V} = \begin{bmatrix} \mathbf{v} \\ 0 \\ \vdots \\ 0 \end{bmatrix}, \mathbf{U}_t = \begin{bmatrix} \boldsymbol{\varepsilon}_t \\ 0 \\ \vdots \\ 0 \end{bmatrix}$$

Matrix $\mathbf{A}$ is called the *companion matrix* of the VAR(p) system.

Given that the VAR(p) model is unrestricted, it can be estimated as any linear regression model. As we consider only consistent estimators, the estimated parameters (in the limit of an infinite sample) satisfy the stability condition. However on a finite sample, the estimated parameters might not satisfy the stability condition.

We will first show how the estimation of a VAR(p) model and its VAR(1) equivalent can be performed with least squares and maximum likelihood methods. To do so we apply the estimation theory developed in Chapter 3, estimating the model coefficients either by the multivariate least squares method or by the maximum likelihood method.

Multivariate Least Squares Estimation

Conceptually, the multivariate *least squares* (LS) estimation method is equivalent to that of a linear regression (see Chapter 3); the notation, however, is more complex. This is because we are dealing with multiple time series and because noise terms are correlated. Similar to what we did in estimating regressions (Chapter 3), we represent the autoregressive process as a single-matrix equation. We will introduce two different but equivalent notations.

Suppose that a sample of T observations of the N-variate variable x_t, $t = 1, \ldots, T$ and a presample of p initial conditions $x_{-p+1}, \ldots, x_0$ are given. We first stack all observations x_t, $t = 1, \ldots, T$ in a vector

$$
\mathbf{x} = \begin{pmatrix} x_{1,1} \\ \vdots \\ x_{N,1} \\ \vdots \\ \vdots \\ x_{1,T} \\ \vdots \\ x_{N,T} \end{pmatrix}
$$

Introducing a notation that will be useful later, we can also write

$$
\mathbf{x} = \mathrm{vec}(\mathbf{X})
$$

$$
\mathbf{X} = (\mathbf{x}_1, \ldots, \mathbf{x}_T) = \begin{pmatrix} x_{1,1} & \cdots & x_{1,T} \\ \vdots & \ddots & \vdots \\ x_{N,1} & \cdots & x_{N,T} \end{pmatrix}
$$

In other words, $\mathbf{x}$ is a $(NT \times 1)$ vector where all observations are stacked, while $\mathbf{X}$ is a $(N \times T)$ matrix where each column represents an N-variate observation.

Proceeding analogously with the noise terms, we stack the noise terms in a $(NT \times 1)$ vector as follows:

$$
\mathbf{u} = \begin{pmatrix} \varepsilon_{1,1} \\ \vdots \\ \varepsilon_{N,1} \\ \vdots \\ \vdots \\ \varepsilon_{1,T} \\ \vdots \\ \varepsilon_{N,T} \end{pmatrix}
$$

We can represent this alternatively as follows:

$$\mathbf{u} = \text{vec}(\mathbf{U})$$

$$\mathbf{U} = \begin{pmatrix} \varepsilon_{1,1} & \cdots & \varepsilon_{1,T} \\ \vdots & \ddots & \vdots \\ \varepsilon_{N,1} & \cdots & \varepsilon_{N,T} \end{pmatrix}$$

where $\mathbf{U}$ is a $(N \times T)$ matrix such that each column represents an n-variate innovation term.

The noise terms are assumed to have a nonsingular covariance matrix,

$$\Sigma = [\sigma_{i,j}] = E[\varepsilon_{i,t}\varepsilon_{j,t}]$$

with $E[\varepsilon_{i,t}\varepsilon_{j,s}] = 0$, $\forall i, j, t \neq s$. The covariance matrix of $\mathbf{u}$, $\Sigma_{\mathbf{u}}$ can be written as

$$\Sigma_{\mathbf{u}} = \mathbf{I}_T \otimes \Sigma = \begin{pmatrix} \Sigma & \cdots & 0 \\ \vdots & \ddots & \vdots \\ 0 & \cdots & \Sigma \end{pmatrix}$$

In other words, the covariance matrix of $\mathbf{u}$ is a block-diagonal matrix where all diagonal blocks are equal to Σ. This covariance structure reflects the assumed white-noise nature of innovations that precludes autocorrelations and cross autocorrelations in the innovation terms.

Using the notation established above, we can now compactly write the VAR(p) model in two equivalent ways as follows:

$$\mathbf{X} = \mathbf{AW} + \mathbf{U}$$

$$\mathbf{x} = \mathbf{w}\beta + \mathbf{u}$$

The first is a matrix equation where the left and right sides are $N \times T$ matrices such that each column represents the VAR(p) equation for each observation. The second equation, which equates the two NT vectors on the left and right sides, can be derived from the first as follows, using the properties of the vec operator and the Kronecker product established in the appendix to Chapter 9

$$\text{vec}(\mathbf{X}) = \text{vec}(\mathbf{AW}) + \text{vec}(\mathbf{U})$$

$$\text{vec}(\mathbf{X}) = (\mathbf{W}' \otimes \mathbf{I}_N)\text{vec}(\mathbf{A}) + \text{vec}(\mathbf{U})$$

$$\mathbf{x} = \mathbf{w}\beta + \mathbf{u}$$

This latter equation is the equivalent of the regression equation established in Chapter 3.

EXHIBIT 10.1 The Regressor Matrix for a N-dimensional VAR(p) model

$$
\mathbf{w} =
\begin{bmatrix}
1 & \cdots & 0 & x_{1,0} & \cdots & 0 & \cdots & x_{N,0} & \cdots & 0 & \cdots & x_{1,1-p} & \cdots & 0 & \cdots & x_{N,1-p} & \cdots & 0 \\
\vdots & \cdots & \vdots & \vdots & \cdots & \vdots & \cdots & \vdots & \cdots & \vdots & \cdots & \vdots & \cdots & \vdots & \cdots & \vdots & \cdots & \vdots \\
0 & \cdots & 1 & 0 & \cdots & x_{1,0} & \cdots & 0 & \cdots & x_{N,0} & \cdots & 0 & \cdots & x_{1,1-p} & \cdots & 0 & \cdots & x_{N,1-p} \\
1 & \cdots & 0 & x_{1,1} & \cdots & 0 & \cdots & x_{N,1} & \cdots & 0 & \cdots & x_{1,2-p} & \cdots & 0 & \cdots & x_{N,2-p} & \cdots & 0 \\
\vdots & \cdots & \vdots & \vdots & \cdots & \vdots & \cdots & \vdots & \cdots & \vdots & \cdots & \vdots & \cdots & \vdots & \cdots & \vdots & \cdots & \vdots \\
0 & \cdots & 1 & 0 & \cdots & x_{1,1} & \cdots & 0 & \cdots & x_{N,1} & \cdots & 0 & \cdots & x_{1,2-p} & \cdots & 0 & \cdots & x_{N,2-p} \\
\vdots & & \vdots & \vdots & & \vdots & & \vdots & & \vdots & & \vdots & & \vdots & & \vdots & & \vdots \\
1 & \cdots & 0 & x_{1,T-2} & \cdots & 0 & \cdots & x_{N,T-2} & \cdots & 0 & \cdots & x_{1,T-p-1} & \cdots & 0 & \cdots & x_{N,T-p-1} & \cdots & 0 \\
\vdots & \cdots & \vdots & \vdots & \cdots & \vdots & \cdots & \vdots & \cdots & \vdots & \cdots & \vdots & \cdots & \vdots & \cdots & \vdots & \cdots & \vdots \\
0 & \cdots & 1 & 0 & \cdots & x_{1,T-2} & \cdots & 0 & \cdots & x_{N,T-2} & \cdots & 0 & \cdots & x_{1,T-p-1} & \cdots & 0 & \cdots & x_{N,T-p-1} \\
1 & \cdots & 0 & x_{1,T-1} & \cdots & 0 & \cdots & x_{N,T-1} & \cdots & 0 & \cdots & x_{1,T-p} & \cdots & 0 & \cdots & x_{N,T-p} & \cdots & 0 \\
\vdots & \cdots & \vdots & \vdots & \cdots & \vdots & \cdots & \vdots & \cdots & \vdots & \cdots & \vdots & \cdots & \vdots & \cdots & \vdots & \cdots & \vdots \\
0 & \cdots & 1 & 0 & \cdots & x_{1,T-1} & \cdots & 0 & \cdots & x_{N,T-1} & \cdots & 0 & \cdots & x_{1,T-p} & \cdots & 0 & \cdots & x_{N,T-p}
\end{bmatrix}
$$

Matrix **w** is shown in Exhibit 10.1; matrices **W** and **A** and vector **B** are given by

$$
\mathbf{W} = \begin{bmatrix}
1 & 1 & \cdots & 1 & 1 \\
\mathbf{x}_0 & \mathbf{x}_1 & \cdots & \mathbf{x}_{T-2} & \mathbf{x}_{T-1} \\
\mathbf{x}_{-1} & \mathbf{x}_0 & \cdots & \mathbf{x}_{T-3} & \mathbf{x}_{T-2} \\
\vdots & \vdots & \ddots & \vdots & \vdots \\
\mathbf{x}_{1-p} & \mathbf{x}_{2-p} & \cdots & \mathbf{x}_{T-p-1} & \mathbf{x}_{T-p}
\end{bmatrix}
$$

$$
= \begin{bmatrix}
1 & 1 & \cdots & 1 & 1 \\
x_{1,0} & x_{1,1} & \cdots & x_{1,T-2} & x_{1,T-1} \\
\vdots & \vdots & \ddots & \vdots & \vdots \\
x_{N,0} & x_{N,1} & \cdots & x_{N,T-2} & x_{N,T-1} \\
x_{1,-1} & x_{1,0} & \cdots & x_{1,T-3} & x_{1,T-2} \\
\vdots & \vdots & \ddots & \vdots & \vdots \\
x_{N,-1} & x_{N,0} & \cdots & x_{N,T-3} & x_{N,T-2} \\
\vdots & \vdots & \ddots & \vdots & \vdots \\
\vdots & \vdots & \ddots & \vdots & \vdots \\
x_{1,1-p} & x_{1,2-p} & \cdots & x_{1,T-p-1} & x_{1,T-p} \\
\vdots & \vdots & \ddots & \vdots & \vdots \\
x_{N,1-p} & x_{N,2-p} & \cdots & x_{N,T-p-1} & x_{N,T-p}
\end{bmatrix} (Np+1) \times T
$$

$$
\mathbf{A} = (\mathbf{v}, \mathbf{A}_1, \ldots, \mathbf{A}_p)
$$

$$
= \begin{pmatrix}
v_1 & a_{11}^1 & \cdots & a_{1N}^1 & \cdots & \cdots & \cdots & a_{11}^p & \cdots & a_{1N}^p \\
\vdots & \vdots & \ddots & \vdots & \vdots & \ddots & \vdots & \vdots & \ddots & \vdots \\
v_N & a_{N1}^1 & \cdots & a_{NN}^1 & \cdots & \cdots & \cdots & a_{N1}^p & \cdots & a_{NN}^p
\end{pmatrix} N \times (Np+1)
$$

$$
\beta = \mathrm{vec}(\mathbf{A}) = \begin{pmatrix}
v_1 \\
\vdots \\
v_N \\
a_{11}^1 \\
\vdots \\
a_{N1}^1 \\
\vdots \\
a_{1N}^p \\
\vdots \\
a_{NN}^p
\end{pmatrix} N(Np+1) \times 1
$$

To estimate the model, we have to write the sum of the squares of residuals as we did for the sum of the residuals in a regression (see Chapter 3). However, as already mentioned, we must also consider the multivariate nature of the noise terms and the presence of correlations.

Our starting point is the regression equation $\mathbf{x} = \mathbf{w}\beta + \mathbf{u}$, which implies $\mathbf{u} = \mathbf{x} - \mathbf{w}\beta$. As the innovation terms exhibit a correlation structure, we have to proceed as in the case of generalized least squares (GLS). We write the weighted sum of squared residuals as

$$S = \mathbf{u}'\Sigma_{\mathbf{u}}^{-1}\mathbf{u} = \sum_{t=1}^{T} \varepsilon_t'\Sigma^{-1}\varepsilon_t$$

For a given set of observations, the quantity S is a function of the model parameters $S = S(\beta)$. The function S admits the following alternative representation:

$$S(\beta) = \text{trace}[\mathbf{U}'\Sigma_{\mathbf{u}}^{-1}\mathbf{U}] = \text{trace}[(\mathbf{X} - \mathbf{A}\mathbf{W})'\Sigma_{\mathbf{u}}^{-1}(\mathbf{X} - \mathbf{A}\mathbf{W})]$$

Since

$$\begin{aligned}
S = \mathbf{u}'\Sigma_{\mathbf{u}}^{-1}\mathbf{u} &= (\text{vec}(\mathbf{U}))'(\mathbf{I}_T \otimes \Sigma)^{-1}\text{vec}(\mathbf{U}) \\
&= (\text{vec}(\mathbf{X} - \mathbf{A}\mathbf{W}))'(\mathbf{I}_T \otimes \Sigma^{-1})\text{vec}(\mathbf{X} - \mathbf{A}\mathbf{W}) \\
&= \text{trace}[(\mathbf{X} - \mathbf{A}\mathbf{W})'\Sigma_{\mathbf{u}}^{-1}(\mathbf{X} - \mathbf{A}\mathbf{W})]
\end{aligned}$$

The least squares estimate of the model parameters $\hat{\beta}$, are obtained by minimizing $S = S(\beta)$ with respect to beta requiring

$$\frac{\partial S(\beta)}{\partial \beta} = 0$$

Equating the vector of partial derivatives to zero yields the so-called *normal equations* of the LS method. From

$$\begin{aligned}
S = \mathbf{u}'\Sigma_{\mathbf{u}}^{-1}\mathbf{u} &= (\mathbf{x} - \mathbf{w}\beta)'\Sigma_{\mathbf{u}}^{-1}(\mathbf{x} - \mathbf{w}\beta) \\
&= \mathbf{x}'\Sigma_{\mathbf{u}}^{-1}\mathbf{x} + \beta'\mathbf{w}'\Sigma_{\mathbf{u}}^{-1}\mathbf{w}\beta - 2\beta'\mathbf{w}'\Sigma_{\mathbf{u}}^{-1}\mathbf{x}
\end{aligned}$$

it follows that the normal equations are given by

$$\frac{\partial S(\beta)}{\partial \beta} = 2\mathbf{w}'\Sigma_u^{-1}\mathbf{w}\beta - 2\mathbf{w}'\Sigma_u^{-1}\mathbf{x} = 0$$

The Hessian matrix turns out as

$$\frac{\partial^2 S(\beta)}{\partial\beta\partial\beta'} = 2\mathbf{w}'\Sigma_u^{-1}\mathbf{w}$$

and is positive definite given our assumptions. Consequently, the LS estimator is

$$\hat{\beta} = (\mathbf{w}'\Sigma_u^{-1}\mathbf{w})^{-1}\mathbf{w}'\Sigma_u^{-1}\mathbf{x}$$

This expression—which has the same form as the Aitkin GLS estimator—is a fundamental expression in LS methods. However, due to the structure of the regressors, further simplifications are possible for a VAR model, namely

$$\hat{\beta} = ((\mathbf{W}\mathbf{W}')^{-1}\mathbf{W} \otimes \mathbf{I}_N)\mathbf{x}$$

are possible. To demonstrate this point, consider the following derivation:

$$\begin{aligned}
\hat{\beta} &= (\mathbf{w}'\Sigma_u^{-1}\mathbf{w})^{-1}\mathbf{w}'\Sigma_u^{-1}\mathbf{x} \\
&= ((\mathbf{W}' \otimes \mathbf{I}_N)'(\mathbf{I}_T \otimes \Sigma)^{-1}(\mathbf{W}' \otimes \mathbf{I}_N))^{-1}(\mathbf{W} \otimes \mathbf{I}_N)(\mathbf{I}_T \otimes \Sigma)^{-1}\mathbf{x} \\
&= ((\mathbf{W} \otimes \mathbf{I}_N)(\mathbf{I}_T \otimes \Sigma^{-1})(\mathbf{W}' \otimes \mathbf{I}_N))^{-1}(\mathbf{W} \otimes \mathbf{I}_N)(\mathbf{I}_T \otimes \Sigma)^{-1}\mathbf{x} \\
&= ((\mathbf{W}\mathbf{I}_T) \otimes (\mathbf{I}_N\Sigma^{-1})(\mathbf{W}' \otimes \mathbf{I}_N))^{-1}(\mathbf{W}\mathbf{I}_T) \otimes (\mathbf{I}_N\Sigma^{-1})\mathbf{x} \\
&= ((\mathbf{W} \otimes \Sigma^{-1})(\mathbf{W}' \otimes \mathbf{I}_N))^{-1}(\mathbf{W} \otimes \Sigma^{-1})\mathbf{x} \\
&= ((\mathbf{W}\mathbf{W}')^{-1} \otimes (\Sigma^{-1}))(\mathbf{W} \otimes \Sigma)\mathbf{x} \\
&= ((\mathbf{W}\mathbf{W}')^{-1}\mathbf{W}) \otimes (\Sigma^{-1}\Sigma)\mathbf{x} \\
&= ((\mathbf{W}\mathbf{W}')^{-1}\mathbf{W} \otimes \mathbf{I}_N)\mathbf{x}
\end{aligned}$$

This derivation shows that, in the case of a stable unrestricted VAR process, the multivariate GLS estimator coincides with the ordinary least squares (OLS) estimator obtained by minimizing the quantity $S = \mathbf{u}'\mathbf{u}$.

We can therefore estimate VAR processes by OLS estimate equation by equation rather than the full N-dimensional system. Computationally, this entails a significant simplification.

We can also write another expression to estimate matrix $\mathbf{A}$. Using $\mathbf{X} = \mathbf{AW} + \mathbf{U}$, we have

$$\hat{\mathbf{A}} = \mathbf{XW}'(\mathbf{WW}')^{-1}$$

The relationship between $\hat{\mathbf{A}}$ and $\hat{\beta}$ is as follows:

$$\hat{\beta} = ((\mathbf{WW}')^{-1}\mathbf{W} \otimes \mathbf{I}_N)\mathbf{x}$$

$$\mathrm{vec}\!\left(\hat{\mathbf{A}}\right) = ((\mathbf{WW}')^{-1}\mathbf{W} \otimes \mathbf{I}_N)\mathrm{vec}(\mathbf{X})$$

$$= \mathrm{vec}(\mathbf{XW}'(\mathbf{WW}')^{-1})$$

To summarize

1. Given a VAR(p) process, the multivariate GLS estimator coincides with the OLS estimator computed equation by equation.
2. The following three expressions for the estimator are equivalent:

$$\hat{\beta} = (\mathbf{w}'\Sigma_{\mathbf{u}}^{-1}\mathbf{w})^{-1}\mathbf{w}'\Sigma_{\mathbf{u}}^{-1}\mathbf{x}$$

$$\hat{\beta} = ((\mathbf{WW}')^{-1}\mathbf{W} \otimes \mathbf{I}_N)\mathbf{x}$$

$$\hat{\mathbf{A}} = \mathbf{XW}'(\mathbf{WW}')^{-1}$$

We next discuss the asymptotic distribution of these estimators.

The Asymptotic Distribution of LS Estimators

In Chapter 2 we stated that estimators depend on the sample and are therefore to be considered random variables. To assess the quality of the estimators, the distribution of the estimators must be determined.

It is difficult to calculate the finite sample distributions of the LS estimators of the stationary VAR model. Finite sample properties of a stationary VAR process can be approximately ascertained using Monte Carlo methods.

Significant simplifications arise as the sample size approaches infinity. The essential result is that the model estimators become normally distributed. The asymptotic properties of the LS estimators can be established under additional assumptions on the white noise. Suppose that the white-noise process has finite and bounded fourth moments and that noise variables at different times are independent and not merely uncorrelated as we have assumed thus far. (Note that these conditions are automatically satisfied by any Gaussian white noise.). Under these assumptions, it can be demonstrated that the following properties hold:

■ The $((Np + 1) \times (Np + 1))$ matrix

$$\mathbf{\Gamma} := \text{plim} \frac{\mathbf{W}\mathbf{W}'}{T}$$

exists and is nonsingular.

■ The $(N(Np + 1) \times 1)$ vector $\hat{\boldsymbol{\beta}}$ of estimated model parameters is jointly normally distributed:

$$\sqrt{T}\left(\hat{\boldsymbol{\beta}} - \boldsymbol{\beta}\right) \xrightarrow{d} N(0, \mathbf{\Gamma}^{-1} \otimes \boldsymbol{\Sigma})$$

The $(N(Np + 1) \times N(Np + 1))$ matrix $\mathbf{\Gamma}^{-1} \otimes \boldsymbol{\Sigma}$ is the covariance matrix of the parameter distribution.

From this it follows that, for large samples, we can approximate matrices $\mathbf{\Gamma}$ and $\boldsymbol{\Sigma}$ by

$$\hat{\mathbf{\Gamma}} = \frac{\mathbf{W}\mathbf{W}'}{T}$$

$$\hat{\boldsymbol{\Sigma}} = \frac{1}{T}\mathbf{X}(\mathbf{I}_T - \mathbf{W}'(\mathbf{W}\mathbf{W}')^{-1}\mathbf{W})\mathbf{X}'$$

Note that these matrices are not needed to estimate the model parameters; they are required only for determining the distribution of the model parameters. If $N = 1$, these expressions are the same as those already established for multivariate regressions. The above estimator of the noise covariance matrix is biased. An unbiased estimator is obtained by multiplying the above by the factor $T/(T - Np - 1)$.

Estimating Demeaned Processes

In previous sections we assumed that the VAR(p) model has a constant intercept and that the process variables have, in general, a nonzero mean. Note that the mean and the intercept are not the same numbers. In fact, given that the process is assumed to be stationary, we can write

$$E(\mathbf{x}_t) = \mathbf{A}_1 E(\mathbf{x}_{t-1}) + \mathbf{A}_2 E(\mathbf{x}_{t-2}) + \cdots + \mathbf{A}_p E(\mathbf{x}_{t-p}) + \mathbf{v}$$

$$\boldsymbol{\mu} - \mathbf{A}_1 \boldsymbol{\mu} - \mathbf{A}_2 \boldsymbol{\mu} - \cdots - \mathbf{A}_p \boldsymbol{\mu} = \mathbf{v}$$

$$\boldsymbol{\mu} = (\mathbf{I}_N - \mathbf{A}_1 - \mathbf{A}_2 - \cdots - \mathbf{A}_p)^{-1} \mathbf{v}$$

We can recast the previous derivation in a different notation, assuming that the process variables are demeaned. In this case, we can rewrite the VAR process in the following form:

$$(\mathbf{x}_t - \boldsymbol{\mu}) = \mathbf{A}_1 (\mathbf{x}_{t-1} - \boldsymbol{\mu}) + \mathbf{A}_2 (\mathbf{x}_{t-2} - \boldsymbol{\mu}) + \cdots + \mathbf{A}_p (\mathbf{x}_{t-p} - \boldsymbol{\mu}) + \boldsymbol{\varepsilon}_t$$

Defining the demeaned vector $\mathbf{y}_t = \mathbf{x}_t - \boldsymbol{\mu}$, the VAR process becomes

$$\mathbf{y}_t = \mathbf{A}_1 \mathbf{y}_{t-1} + \mathbf{A}_2 \mathbf{y}_{t-2} + \cdots + \mathbf{A}_p \mathbf{y}_{t-p} + \boldsymbol{\varepsilon}_t$$

The formulas previously established hold with some obvious changes. We will state them explicitly, as they will be used in the following sections. Defining

$$\mathbf{Y} = (\mathbf{y}_1, \ldots, \mathbf{y}_T)$$
$$\mathbf{U} = (\boldsymbol{\varepsilon}_1, \ldots, \boldsymbol{\varepsilon}_T)$$
$$\mathbf{y} = \mathrm{vec}(\mathbf{Y})$$

$$\mathbf{u} = \mathrm{vec}(\mathbf{U})$$
$$\boldsymbol{\Sigma}_{\mathbf{u}} = \mathbf{I}_T \otimes \boldsymbol{\Sigma}$$
$$\mathbf{A} = (\mathbf{A}_1, \ldots, \mathbf{A}_p)$$
$$\boldsymbol{\alpha} = \mathrm{vec}(\mathbf{A})$$

$$\mathbf{Z} = \begin{pmatrix} \mathbf{y}_0 & \cdots & \mathbf{y}_{T-1} \\ \vdots & \ddots & \vdots \\ \mathbf{y}_{1-p} & \cdots & \mathbf{y}_{T-p} \end{pmatrix}$$

$$\mathbf{z} = (\mathbf{Z}' \otimes \mathbf{I}_N)$$

we have

$$\mathbf{y} = \mathbf{z}\alpha + \mathbf{u}$$

$$\mathbf{Y} = \mathbf{A}\mathbf{Z} + \mathbf{U}$$

The LS estimators are

$$\hat{\alpha} = \left(\mathbf{z}'\boldsymbol{\Sigma}_u^{-1}\mathbf{z}\right)^{-1}\mathbf{z}'\boldsymbol{\Sigma}_u^{-1}\mathbf{y}$$

$$\hat{\alpha} = \left((\mathbf{Z}\mathbf{Z}')^{-1}\mathbf{Z} \otimes \mathbf{I}_N\right)\mathbf{y}$$

$$\hat{\mathbf{A}} = \mathbf{Y}\mathbf{Z}'(\mathbf{Z}\mathbf{Z}')^{-1}$$

It can be demonstrated that the sample mean,

$$\hat{\mu} = \frac{1}{T}\sum_{t=1}^{T}\mathbf{x}_t$$

is a consistent estimator of the process mean and has a normal asymptotic distribution. If we estimate intercept $\hat{\mathbf{v}}$ from the original (non-demeaned) data, the mean $\hat{\mu}$, is estimated by the mean can be estimated with the following estimator:

$$\hat{\mu} = (\mathbf{I}_N - \mathbf{A}_1 - \mathbf{A}_2 - \cdots - \mathbf{A}_p)^{-1}\hat{\mathbf{v}}$$

This is consistent and follows an asymptotic normal distribution.

We now turn our attention to the maximum likelihood estimation of stable VAR models.

Maximum Likelihood Estimators

Under the assumption of Gaussian innovations, *maximum likelihood* (ML) estimation methods coincide with LS estimation methods when we condition on the first p observations. Recall from Chapter 2 that, given a known distribution, ML methods try to find the distribution parameters that maximize the likelihood function (i.e., the joint distribution of the sample computed on the sample itself). In the case of a multivariate mean-adjusted VAR(p) process, the given sample data are T observations of the N-variate variable $\mathbf{y}_t$, $t = 1, \ldots, T$ and a presample of p initial conditions $\mathbf{y}_{-p+1}, \ldots, \mathbf{y}_0$. If we assume that the process is stationary and that innovations are Gaussian white noise, the variables $\mathbf{y}_t$, $t = 1, \ldots, T$ will also be jointly normally distributed. However, it is advantageous to express the joint distribution of the noise terms in function of the data. As the white noise is assumed to be Gaussian, the noise variables at different times are independent. As observed in **Chapter GG**, this allows considerable simplifications for computing the likelihood function.

The noise terms $(\boldsymbol{\varepsilon}_1, \ldots, \boldsymbol{\varepsilon}_T)$ are assumed to be independent with constant covariance matrix $\boldsymbol{\Sigma}$ and, therefore, $\mathbf{u} = \text{vec}(\mathbf{U})$ has covariance matrix $\boldsymbol{\Sigma}_{\mathbf{u}} = \mathbf{I}_T \otimes \boldsymbol{\Sigma}$. Under the assumption of Gaussian noise, $\mathbf{u}$ has the following NT-variate normal density:

$$f_{\mathbf{u}}(\mathbf{u}) = (2\pi)^{-\frac{NT}{2}} |\mathbf{I}_T \otimes \boldsymbol{\Sigma}|^{-\frac{1}{2}} \exp\left(-\frac{1}{2}\mathbf{u}'(\mathbf{I}_T \otimes \boldsymbol{\Sigma}^{-1})\mathbf{u}\right)$$

$$= (2\pi)^{-\frac{NT}{2}} |\boldsymbol{\Sigma}|^{-\frac{T}{2}} \exp\left(-\frac{1}{2}\sum_{t=1}^{T} \boldsymbol{\varepsilon}_t'\boldsymbol{\Sigma}^{-1}\boldsymbol{\varepsilon}_t\right)$$

Using

$$\boldsymbol{\varepsilon}_1 = \mathbf{y}_1 - \mathbf{A}_1\mathbf{y}_0 - \mathbf{A}_2\mathbf{y}_{-1} - \cdots - \mathbf{A}_p\mathbf{y}_{1-p}$$

$$\boldsymbol{\varepsilon}_2 = \mathbf{y}_2 - \mathbf{A}_1\mathbf{y}_1 - \mathbf{A}_2\mathbf{y}_0 - \cdots - \mathbf{A}_p\mathbf{y}_{2-p}$$

$$\cdots\cdots\cdots\cdots\cdots\cdots\cdots\cdots\cdots\cdots\cdots\cdots$$

$$\boldsymbol{\varepsilon}_p = \mathbf{y}_p - \mathbf{A}_1\mathbf{y}_0 - \mathbf{A}_2\mathbf{y}_{p-2} - \cdots - \mathbf{A}_p\mathbf{y}_0$$

$$\boldsymbol{\varepsilon}_{p+1} = \mathbf{y}_{p+1} - \mathbf{A}_1\mathbf{y}_p - \mathbf{A}_2\mathbf{y}_{p-2} - \cdots - \mathbf{A}_p\mathbf{y}_1$$

$$\cdots\cdots\cdots\cdots\cdots\cdots\cdots\cdots\cdots\cdots\cdots\cdots$$

$$\boldsymbol{\varepsilon}_{T-1} = \mathbf{y}_{T-1} - \mathbf{A}_1\mathbf{y}_{T-2} - \mathbf{A}_2\mathbf{y}_{T-3} - \cdots - \mathbf{A}_p\mathbf{y}_{T-p-1}$$

$$\boldsymbol{\varepsilon}_T = \mathbf{y}_T - \mathbf{A}_1\mathbf{y}_{T-1} - \mathbf{A}_2\mathbf{y}_{T-2} - \cdots - \mathbf{A}_p\mathbf{y}_{T-p}$$

written in matrix form

$$
\begin{pmatrix} \varepsilon_1 \\ \varepsilon_2 \\ \vdots \\ \varepsilon_p \\ \varepsilon_{p+1} \\ \vdots \\ \varepsilon_{T-1} \\ \varepsilon_T \end{pmatrix} = \begin{pmatrix} \mathbf{I}_N & 0 & \cdots & 0 & 0 & 0 & \cdots & \cdots & 0 & 0 & \cdots & 0 & 0 \\ -\mathbf{A}_1 & \mathbf{I}_N & \cdots & 0 & 0 & 0 & \cdots & \cdots & 0 & 0 & \cdots & 0 & 0 \\ \vdots & \vdots & \ddots & \vdots & \vdots & \vdots & \ddots & \ddots & \vdots & \vdots & \ddots & \vdots & \vdots \\ -\mathbf{A}_p & -\mathbf{A}_{p-1} & \cdots & -\mathbf{A}_1 & \mathbf{I}_N & 0 & \cdots & \cdots & 0 & 0 & \cdots & 0 & 0 & \cdots \\ 0 & -\mathbf{A}_p & \cdots & -\mathbf{A}_2 & -\mathbf{A}_1 & \mathbf{I}_N & \cdots & \cdots & 0 & 0 & \cdots & 0 & 0 \\ \vdots & \vdots & \ddots & \vdots & \vdots & \vdots & \ddots & \ddots & \vdots & \vdots & \ddots & \vdots & \vdots \\ 0 & 0 & \cdots & 0 & 0 & 0 & \cdots & 0 & -\mathbf{A}_p & -\mathbf{A}_{p-1} & \cdots & \mathbf{I}_N & 0 \\ 0 & 0 & \cdots & 0 & 0 & 0 & \cdots & 0 & 0 & -\mathbf{A}_p & \cdots & -\mathbf{A}_1 & \mathbf{I}_N \end{pmatrix}
$$

$$
\begin{pmatrix} \mathbf{y}_1 \\ \mathbf{y}_2 \\ \vdots \\ \mathbf{y}_p \\ \mathbf{y}_{p+1} \\ \vdots \\ \mathbf{y}_{T-p} \\ \vdots \\ \mathbf{y}_{T-1} \\ \mathbf{y}_T \end{pmatrix} + \begin{pmatrix} -\mathbf{A}_p & -\mathbf{A}_{p-1} & \cdots & -\mathbf{A}_1 \\ 0 & -\mathbf{A}_p & \cdots & -\mathbf{A}_2 \\ \vdots & \vdots & \ddots & \vdots \\ 0 & 0 & \cdots & -\mathbf{A}_p \\ \vdots & \vdots & \ddots & \vdots \\ 0 & 0 & \cdots & 0 \end{pmatrix} \begin{pmatrix} \mathbf{y}_{1-p} \\ \mathbf{y}_{2-p} \\ \mathbf{y}_{-1} \\ \mathbf{y}_0 \end{pmatrix}
$$

and the model equation $\mathbf{y} = \mathbf{z}\alpha + \mathbf{u}$, we can express the density function in terms of the variables

$$
f_y(\mathbf{y}) = \left| \frac{\partial \mathbf{u}}{\partial \mathbf{y}} \right| f_u(\mathbf{u}) = (2\pi)^{-\frac{NT}{2}} \left| \mathbf{I}_T \otimes \mathbf{\Sigma} \right|^{-\frac{1}{2}} \exp\left(-\frac{1}{2}(\mathbf{y} - \mathbf{z}\alpha)'(\mathbf{I}_T \otimes \mathbf{\Sigma}^{-1})(\mathbf{y} - \mathbf{z}\alpha) \right)
$$

We can now write the log-likelihood as follows:

$$
\begin{aligned}
\log(l) &= -\frac{NT}{2}\log(2\pi) - \frac{T}{2}\log|\mathbf{\Sigma_u}| - \frac{1}{2}\sum_{t=1}^{T} \varepsilon_t' \mathbf{\Sigma}^{-1} \varepsilon_t \\
&= -\frac{NT}{2}\log(2\pi) - \frac{T}{2}\log|\mathbf{\Sigma_u}| - \frac{1}{2}(\mathbf{y} - \mathbf{z}\alpha)'(\mathbf{I}_T \otimes \mathbf{\Sigma}^{-1})(\mathbf{y} - \mathbf{z}\alpha) \\
&= -\frac{NT}{2}\log(2\pi) - \frac{T}{2}\log|\mathbf{\Sigma_u}| - \frac{1}{2}\text{trace}(\mathbf{U}'\mathbf{\Sigma_u}^{-1}\mathbf{U}) \\
&= -\frac{NT}{2}\log(2\pi) - \frac{T}{2}\log|\mathbf{\Sigma_u}| - \frac{1}{2}\text{trace}((\mathbf{Y} - \mathbf{AZ})'\mathbf{\Sigma_u}^{-1}(\mathbf{Y} - \mathbf{AZ}))
\end{aligned}
$$

Equating the partial derivatives of this expression to zero, we obtain the very same estimators as with the LS method. In the case of Gaussian noise, LS/OLS methods and ML methods yield the same result.

ESTIMATING THE NUMBER OF LAGS

In the previous sections, we assumed that the order p of the model (i.e., the number of lags in the model) is known. The objective of this section is to establish criteria that allow determining *a priori* the correct number of lags. This idea has to be made more precise. We assume, as we did in the previous sections on the estimation of the model coefficients, that the true data generation process is a VAR(p) model. In this case, we expect that the correct model order is exactly p, that is, we expect to come out with a consistent estimate of the model order. This is not the same problem as trying to determine the optimal number of lags to fit a VAR model to a process that is not be generated by a VAR data generating process. We assume that the type of model is correctly specified and discuss methods to estimate the model order under this assumption.

In general, increasing the model order will reduce the size of residuals but tends to reduce the forecasting ability of the model. By increasing the number of parameters, we improve the in-sample accuracy but tend to worsen the out-of-sample forecasting ability. In this section we consider only linear models under the assumption that the data generation process is linear and autoregressive with unknown parameters.

To see how increasing the number of lags can reduce the forecasting ability of the model, consider that the forecasting ability of a linear VAR model can be estimated. Recall from Chapter 9 that the optimal forecast of a VAR model is the conditional mean. This implies that the optimal one-step forecast given the past p values of the process up to the present moment is

$$\hat{\mathbf{x}}_{t+1} = \mathbf{A}_1\mathbf{x}_t + \mathbf{A}_2\mathbf{x}_{t-1} + \cdots + \mathbf{A}_p\mathbf{x}_{t-p+1} + \mathbf{v}$$

The forecasting *mean square error* (MSE) can be estimated. It can be demonstrated that an approximate estimate of the one-step MSE is

$$\boldsymbol{\Sigma}_{\mathbf{x}}(1) = \frac{T+Np+1}{T}\boldsymbol{\Sigma}(p)$$

where $\Sigma(p)$ is the residual covariance matrix of a model of order p and $\Sigma_x(1)$ is the covariance matrix of the forecasting errors. Based on $\Sigma_x(1)$, Akaike suggested a criterion to estimate the model order.[1] First, we have to replace $\Sigma(p)$ with its estimate. In the case of a zero-mean process, we can estimate $\Sigma(p)$ as

$$\hat{\Sigma}(p) = \frac{1}{T}X(I_T - W'(WW')^{-1}W)X'$$

The quantity

$$\text{FPE}(p) = \left[\frac{T + Np + 1}{T - Np + 1}\right]^N \det(\hat{\Sigma}(p))$$

is called the *final prediction error* (FPE). In 1969, Akaike proposed to determine the model order by minimizing the FPE.[2] Four years later, he proposed a different criterion based on information theoretic considerations. The latter criterion, commonly called the *Akaike information criterion* (AIC), proposes to determine the model order by minimizing the following expression:

$$\text{AIC}(p) = \log\left|\hat{\Sigma}(p)\right| + \frac{2pN^2}{T}$$

Neither the FPE nor the AIC estimators are consistent estimators in the sense that they determine the correct model order in the limit of an infinite sample. Different but consistent criteria have been proposed. Among them, the *Bayesian information criterion* (BIC) is quite popular. Proposed by Schwartz, the BIC chooses the model that minimizes the following expression:[3]

$$\text{BIC}(p) = \log\left|\hat{\Sigma}(p)\right| + \frac{\log T}{T}2pN^2$$

---

[1] Hirotugu Akaike, "Fitting Autoregressive Models for Prediction," *Annals of the Institute of Statistical Mathematics* 21 (1969), pp. 243–247.

[2] Hirotugu Akaike, "Information Theory and an Extension of the Maximum Likelihood Principle," B. Petrov and F. Csaki (eds.), *Second International Symposium on Information Theory* (Budapest: Akademiaio Kiado, 1973).

[3] G. Schwarz, "Estimating the Dimension of a Model," *Annals of Statistics* 6 (1978), pp. 461–464.

There is a vast literature on model selection criteria. The justification of each criterion impinges on rather complex considerations of information theory, statistics, and learning theory.[4]

AUTOCORRELATION AND DISTRIBUTIONAL PROPERTIES OF RESIDUALS

The validity of the LS method does not depend on the distribution of innovations provided that their covariance matrix exists. However, the LS method might not be optimal if innovations are not normally distributed. The ML method, in contrast, critically depends on the distributional properties of innovations. Nevertheless, both methods are sensitive to the autocorrelation of innovation terms. Distributional properties are critical in applications such as asset allocation, portfolio management, and risk management. Therefore, once the model order and parameters are estimated, it is important to check the absence of autocorrelation in the residuals and to ascertain deviations from normal distributions.

There is a range of tests for the autocorrelation and normality of residuals. In particular, the autocorrelation of residuals can be tested with the multivariate Ljung-Box test. The multivariate Ljung-Box test (or Q-test) is a generalization of the Ljung-Box test described in Chapter 7. The null hypothesis of the Ljung-Box test is that all noise terms at different lags up to lag s are uncorrelated. Given a n-dimensional VAR(p) model, the Q-test statistics, in the form introduced by Hosking,[5] is the following:

$$LB(s) = T(T+2) \sum_{j=1}^{s} \frac{1}{T-j} tr[\mathbf{C}_{0j} \mathbf{C}_{00}^{-1} \mathbf{C}_{0j}' \mathbf{C}_{00}^{-1}]$$

where

$$\mathbf{C}_{0j} = T^{-1} \sum_{t=j+1}^{T} \boldsymbol{\varepsilon}_t \boldsymbol{\varepsilon}_{t-j}'$$

---

[4] See, for example, D. P. Foster and R. A. Stine, "An Information Theoretic Comparison of Model Selection Criteria," Working Paper 1180, 1997, Northwestern University, Center for Mathematical Studies in Economics and Management Science.
[5] J.R.M. Hosking, "The Multivariate Portmanteau Statistic," *Journal of American Statistical Association* 75 (1980), pp. 602–608.

and T is the sample size. Under the null hypothesis, if $s > p$, the distribution of this statistic is approximately a Chi-square distribution with $n^2(s - p)$.

In the case of stationary models, the normality of distributions can be tested with one of the many tests for normality discussed in Chapter 7. These tests are available on most statistical computer packages.

VAR ILLUSTRATION

Let's now illustrate step by step the process of estimating a VAR model. As stated in Chapter 9, VAR models have been proposed to model asset returns. If asset returns, especially indexes, can be represented as VAR models, then future returns can be predicted from past returns. The objective of this exercise is not to investigate the econometric validity of this assumption but to show how to estimate VAR models and perform diagnostic checks. Specifically, we will show how to:

■ Select the number of lags.
■ Assess the significance of VAR regression equations (in particular the significance of individual coefficients).
■ Assess the causal relationships among the variables.

This information is important both as a model diagnostic and as a tool to help the economic interpretation of the model.

We fit a VAR model to the monthly returns of three stock market indexes: Wilshire capitalization weighted (y_1), Wilshire equal weighted (y_2,), and S&P 500 (y_3,). The time period covered is from October 1989 to January 2003; the data set includes 160 monthly returns. We first model the three indexes as an unrestricted VAR process. Later, we explore the existence of cointegrating relationships. The three series of returns are shown in Exhibit 10.2.

Given that the return series are not integrated, the first task is to determine the number of lags of the VAR model. In practice one compares different models estimated with a different number of lags. To see how this is done, we compare models with one and two lags. We use the following notation:

Wilshire Capitalization Weighted (y_1): WCW
Wilshire Equal Weighted (y_2): WEW
S&P 500 (y_3): S&P

A hyphen following the index abbreviation identifies the number of lags.

EXHIBIT 10.2 Monthly Returns for the Wilshire Capitalization Weighted, Wilshire Equal Weighted, and S&P 500: October 1989–January 2003

Month/ Year	Wilshire Cap Weighted (y_1)	Wilshire Equal Weighted (y_2)	S&P 500 (y_3)	Month/ Year	Wilshire Cap Weighted (y_1)	Wilshire Equal Weighted (y_2)	S&P 500 (y_3)
Oct-89	−2.92	−5.19	−2.33	Oct-92	1.21	2.34	0.36
Nov-89	1.77	−0.53	2.08	Nov-92	4.15	7.93	3.37
Dec-89	1.82	−1.18	2.36	Dec-92	1.78	4.55	1.31
Jan-90	−7.34	−5.10	−6.71	Jan-93	1.23	6.72	0.73
Feb-90	1.59	2.45	1.29	Feb-93	0.41	−1.12	1.35
Mar-90	2.50	2.74	2.63	Mar-93	2.57	3.32	2.15
Apr-90	−2.88	−2.70	−2.47	Apr-93	−2.76	−1.67	−2.45
May-90	9.13	5.21	9.75	May-93	3.13	4.32	2.70
Jun-90	−0.48	0.94	−0.70	Jun-93	0.46	1.36	0.33
Jul-90	−0.97	−2.78	−0.32	Jul-93	−0.01	1.34	−0.47
Aug-90	−9.41	−11.86	−9.03	Aug-93	3.86	4.01	3.81
Sep-90	−5.49	−7.87	−4.92	Sep-93	0.20	3.14	−0.74
Oct-90	−1.34	−6.53	−0.37	Oct-93	1.67	4.38	2.03
Nov-90	6.82	4.79	6.44	Nov-93	−1.62	−2.35	−0.94
Dec-90	3.17	0.58	2.74	Dec-93	1.80	1.40	1.23
Jan-91	4.86	8.63	4.42	Jan-94	3.15	5.01	3.35
Feb-91	7.78	15.58	7.16	Feb-94	−2.24	−0.43	−2.70
Mar-91	3.05	9.41	2.38	Mar-94	−4.53	−4.28	−4.35
Apr-91	0.32	3.83	0.28	Apr-94	0.96	−0.93	1.30
May-91	4.01	4.13	4.28	May-94	0.98	−0.18	1.63
Jun-91	−4.47	−3.03	−4.57	Jun-94	−2.67	−2.60	−2.47
Jul-91	4.70	3.71	4.68	Jul-94	2.97	1.37	3.31
Aug-91	2.76	3.58	2.35	Aug-94	4.42	4.08	4.07
Sep-91	−1.15	1.18	−1.64	Sep-94	−1.94	0.76	−2.41
Oct-91	1.84	3.40	1.34	Oct-94	1.63	0.13	2.29
Nov-91	−3.82	−2.17	−4.04	Nov-94	−3.66	−4.23	−3.67
Dec-91	10.98	4.80	11.43	Dec-94	1.35	−0.75	1.46
Jan-92	−0.20	17.04	−1.86	Jan-95	2.16	2.00	2.60
Feb-92	1.38	6.37	1.28	Feb-95	3.98	3.34	3.88
Mar-92	−2.48	−1.43	−1.96	Mar-95	2.64	1.92	2.96
Apr-92	1.34	3.75	2.91	Apr-95	2.48	2.52	2.91
May-92	0.61	0.94	0.54	May-95	3.39	1.99	3.95
Jun-92	−2.04	−2.80	−1.45	Jun-95	3.19	5.47	2.35
Jul-92	4.05	3.03	4.03	Jul-95	4.11	5.96	3.33
Aug-92	−2.11	−2.49	−2.02	Aug-95	0.97	3.41	0.27
Sep-92	1.19	1.53	1.15	Sep-95	3.81	2.98	4.19

EXHIBIT 10.2 (Continued)

Month/ Year	Wilshire Cap Weighted (y_1)	Wilshire Equal Weighted (y_2)	S&P 500 (y_3)	Month/ Year	Wilshire Cap Weighted (y_1)	Wilshire Equal Weighted (y_2)	S&P 500 (y_3)
Oct-95	−1.00	−4.51	−0.35	Dec-98	6.40	2.08	5.76
Nov-95	4.24	1.80	4.40	Jan-99	3.68	8.50	4.18
Dec-95	1.63	1.04	1.85	Feb-99	−3.62	−4.40	−3.11
Jan-96	2.68	3.02	3.44	Mar-99	3.86	−0.41	4.00
Feb-96	1.75	4.05	0.96	Apr-99	4.79	8.40	3.87
Mar-96	1.09	2.78	0.96	May-99	−2.19	4.30	−2.36
Apr-96	2.47	6.43	1.47	Jun-99	5.18	4.41	5.55
May-96	2.73	8.05	2.58	Jul-99	−3.21	0.82	−3.12
Jun-96	−0.82	−3.19	0.41	Aug-99	−0.93	−3.51	−0.50
Jul-96	−5.40	−8.41	−4.45	Sep-99	−2.61	−1.64	−2.74
Aug-96	3.20	4.55	2.12	Oct-99	6.36	−0.39	6.33
Sep-96	5.32	3.44	5.62	Nov-99	3.35	9.64	2.03
Oct-96	1.40	−2.23	2.74	Dec-99	7.59	8.62	5.89
Nov-96	6.63	2.03	7.59	Jan-00	−4.15	10.35	−5.02
Dec-96	−1.13	0.48	−1.96	Feb-00	2.24	15.95	−1.89
Jan-97	5.35	6.66	6.21	Mar-00	5.94	0.78	9.78
Feb-97	−0.05	−1.41	0.81	Apr-00	−5.21	−10.14	−3.01
Mar-97	−4.42	−4.86	−4.16	May-00	−3.49	−6.91	−2.05
Apr-97	4.36	−2.66	5.97	Jun-00	4.41	8.65	2.47
May-97	7.09	9.51	6.14	Jul-00	−2.04	−1.96	−1.56
Jun-97	4.59	4.89	4.46	Aug-00	7.26	5.64	6.21
Jul-97	7.69	5.25	7.94	Sep-00	−4.67	−3.91	−5.28
Aug-97	−3.76	3.54	−5.56	Oct-00	−2.12	−7.10	−0.42
Sep-97	5.90	8.97	5.48	Nov-00	−9.95	−13.18	−7.88
Oct-97	−3.33	−2.11	−3.34	Dec-00	1.78	−1.67	0.49
Nov-97	3.27	−2.02	4.63	Jan-01	3.83	26.88	3.55
Dec-97	1.85	−2.15	1.72	Feb-01	−9.48	−7.75	−9.12
Jan-98	0.54	1.75	1.11	Mar-01	−6.73	−7.28	−6.33
Feb-98	7.28	6.86	7.21	Apr-01	8.23	7.45	7.77
Mar-98	5.00	5.66	5.12	May-01	1.00	7.86	0.67
Apr-98	1.19	3.01	1.01	Jun-01	−1.68	1.28	−2.43
May-98	−2.66	−4.09	−1.72	Jul-01	−1.65	−2.96	−0.98
Jun-98	3.51	−2.69	4.06	Aug-01	−6.05	−4.00	−6.26
Jul-98	−2.19	−5.17	−1.06	Sep-01	−8.98	−13.02	−8.08
Aug-98	−15.57	−19.79	−14.46	Oct-01	2.54	8.39	1.91
Sep-98	6.53	3.80	6.41	Nov-01	7.65	7.61	7.67
Oct-98	7.44	3.62	8.13	Dec-01	1.80	6.19	0.88
Nov-98	6.30	8.68	6.06	Jan-02	−1.24	2.69	−1.46

EXHIBIT 10.2   (Continued)

Month/ Year	Wilshire Cap Weighted (y_1)	Wilshire Equal Weighted (y_2)	S&P 500 (y_3)
Feb-02	−2.06	−3.72	−1.93
Mar-02	4.38	8.97	3.76
Apr-02	−4.88	−0.22	−6.06
May-02	−1.18	−2.05	−0.74
Jun-02	−7.03	−6.79	−7.12
Jul-02	−8.07	−11.37	−7.80
Aug-02	0.59	0.74	0.66
Sep-02	−10.03	−8.46	−10.87
Oct-02	7.65	4.29	8.80
Nov-02	6.03	13.28	5.89
Dec-02	−5.54	−4.48	−5.88
Jan-03	−2.52	1.26	−2.62

We will first estimate and discuss each model separately and then compare the two models. Let's start with the one lag case, that is, represent our three index time series as the following VAR model:

WCW-1 $y_1(t) = c_1 + a_{11,1} y_1(t-1) + a_{12,1} y_2(t-1) + a_{13,1} y_3(t-1) + \varepsilon_1(t)$

WEW-1 $y_2(t) = c_2 + a_{21,1} y_1(t-1) + a_{22,1} y_2(t-1) + a_{23,1} y_3(t-1) + \varepsilon_2(t)$

S&P-1 $y_3(t) = c_3 + a_{31,1} y_1(t-1) + a_{32,1} y_2(t-1) + a_{33,1} y_3(t-1) + \varepsilon_3(t)$

We treat each equation as a regression equation and compute the t-statistics for each coefficient to assess its significance. We also compute the Q-statistics to assess if residuals are autocorrelated and the Granger causality probability to assess causal links between variables.

Note that for a VAR(p) model and sample size T we have at most $T - p$ observations for estimation. Thus, with $p = 1$ and $T = 160$, we can use 159 observations.

For each equation, there are three independent regressors plus a constant so that $k = 4$ coefficients need to be estimated. Least-squares estimation results are reported for each equation in the three panels in Exhibit 10.3. The Granger causality probabilities are summarized in Exhibit 10.4. The three panels in Exhibit 10.5 show the predicted versus the actual values of the three variables.

Let us look at the estimated coefficients for equation WCW-1. Again, keep in mind that this is only an exercise on how to apply modeling tools, we do not claim any general validity for the results.

EXHIBIT 10.3 Estimates of the Three Equations of a VAR Model with One Lag
Panel A. Equation Estimated: WCW-1

Variable	Coefficient	t-statistic	t-probability
y_1 lag1	$a_{11,1} = 1.679106$	2.825664	0.005340
y_2 lag1	$a_{12,1} = -0.233356$	-2.148203	0.033251
y_3 lag1	$a_{13,1} = -1.489729$	-2.802706	0.005715
Constant	$c_1 = 1.040901$	2.881954	0.004513

$R^2 = 0.0497$
Adjusted $R^2 = 0.0313$
$\hat{\sigma}_1^2 = \hat{e}'\hat{e}/(n-k) = \hat{e}'\hat{e}/155 = 19.0604$
Q-statistic = 0.0323

Panel B. Equation Estimated: WEW-1

Variable	Coefficient	t-statistic	t-probability
y_1 lag1	$a_{21,1} = 3.382911$	4.445398	0.000017
y_2 lag1	$a_{22,1} = -0.312517$	-2.246509	0.026084
y_3 lag1	$a_{23,1} = -2.817606$	-4.139312	0.000057
Constant	$c_2 = 1.424466$	3.079692	0.002452

$R^2 = 0.1578$
Adjusted $R^2 = 0.1415$
$\hat{\sigma}_1^2 = \hat{e}'\hat{e}/(n-k) = \hat{e}'\hat{e}/155 = 31.2591$
Q-statistic = 0.0076

Panel C. Equation Estimated: S&P-1

Variable	Coefficient	t-statistic	t-probability
y_1 lag1	$a_{31,1} = 1.667135$	2.847066	0.005011
y_2 lag1	$a_{32,1} = -0.237547$	-2.219168	0.027928
y_3 lag1	$a_{33,1} = -1.504514$	-2.872438	0.004644
Constant	$c_3 = 1.099824$	3.090190	0.002372

$R^2 = 0.0529$
Adjusted $R^2 = 0.0345$
$\hat{\sigma}_1^2 = \hat{e}'\hat{e}/(n-k) = \hat{e}'\hat{e}/155 = 18.5082$
Q-statistic = 0.0187

EXHIBIT 10.4 Granger Causality Probabilities

Variable	y_1	y_2	y_3
y_1	0.01	0.03	0.01
y_2	0.00	0.03	0.00
y_3	0.01	0.03	0.00

EXHIBIT 10.5   The Predicted versus the Actual Values of the Three Variables
Panel A: Actual versus Predicted Equation WEW–1. The second graph represents residuals.

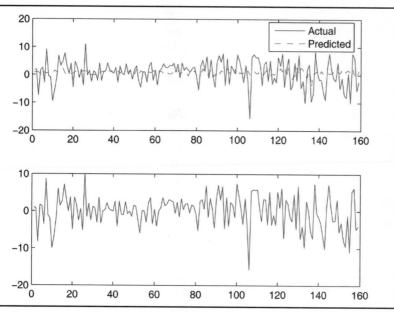

Panel B: Actual versus Predicted Equation WMW–1. The second graph represents residuals.

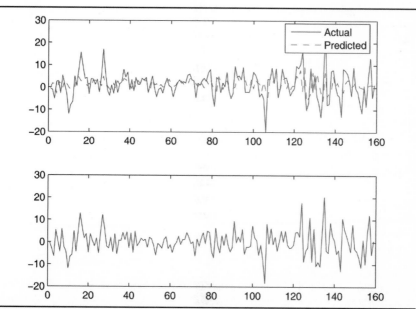

EXHIBIT 10.5   (Continued)

Panel C: Actual versus Predicted Equation S&P–1. The second graph represents residuals.

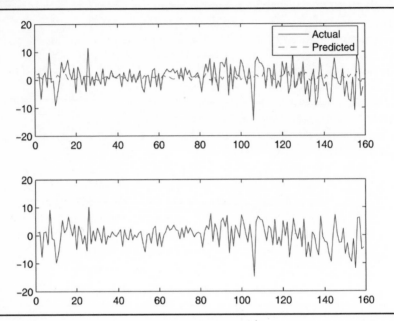

Recall that the t-statistics associated with each coefficient are obtained dividing each coefficient estimate by its respective estimated standard deviation (see Chapter 2) under the assumption that that coefficient is zero. As explained in Chapter 2, the t-statistic of an estimated coefficent represents how many standard deviations that coefficient is far from zero. For example, in equation WCW-1, the coefficient of is 1.679106 and its t-statistic is 2.825664. This means that this estimated coefficient is 2.825664 standard deviations from zero.

The t-probability[6] relative to a coefficient estimates the probability of the null hypothesis that that coefficient is zero; that is, it tests the significance of that coefficient. Small t-values correspond to statistically significant coefficients. For this exercise, we assume that coefficients are significant at 99% (i.e., t-values less than 0.01).The t-probability is the p-value of the t-statistics, that is, the probability of the tail beyond the observed value of the t-statistics of the Student-t distribution with $T - p$

---

[6] Recall from Chapter 2 that the t-probability is the probability that the t-statistic exceeds a given threshold. The p-probability is the probability of the null that all the coefficients be zero.

= 155 degrees of freedom. Exhibit 9.2 shows that only the coefficient of at lag 1 has a nonnegligible probability of being irrelevant. In fact, that coefficient is –2.148203 standard deviations from zero, which corresponds to a tail probability in excess of 3%.[7]

The overall usefulness of the WCW-1 equation can be assessed by the R^2 and the adjusted R^2. Though the null hypothesis that the coefficients of the equation WCW-1 are zero can be rejected, the R^2 shows that only 5% of the variance of variable is explained. The Q-statistic confirms that the residuals have a weak autocorrelation.

We can now repeat the same reasoning for equation WEW-1. Exhibit 9.2 shows that only the coefficient at lag 1 has a nonnegligible probability of being irrelevant. Note that the t-probabilities of coefficients of equation WEW-1 are lower than those of equation WCW-1.

The R^2 and the adjusted R^2 reveal that equation WEW-1 has more explanatory power than equation WCW-1. In fact, nearly 16% of the variance is explained. In addition, the Q-statistic shows that the autocorrelation of the residuals of equation WEW-1 is negligible. As explained in Chapter 7, the Q-statistic tests the autocorrelation coefficient at every lag by forming the sum of the squared autocorrelation coefficients.

The results for equation S&P-1 are very similar to those of equation WCW-1.

Exhibit 10.4 shows the Granger causality probabilities. All the probabilities are small, which implies that there are no clear causal links between the three indexes.

Finally, Exhibit 10.5 shows the predicted versus the actual values of the three variables.

Let's now discuss the VAR model with two lags. That is, we fit the following VAR model to the three index series:

WEW-2 $\quad y_1(t) = c_1 + a_{11,1}y_1(t-1) + a_{12,1}y_2(t-1) + a_{13,1}y_3(t-1)$
$$+ a_{11,2}y_1(t-2) + a_{12,2}y_2(t-2) + a_{13,2}y_3(t-2) + \varepsilon_1(t)$$

WMW-2 $\quad y_2(t) = c_2 + a_{21,1}y_1(t-1) + a_{22,1}y_2(t-1) + a_{23,1}y_3(t-1)$
$$+ a_{21,2}y_1(t-2) + a_{22,2}y_2(t-2) + a_{23,2}y_3(t-2) + \varepsilon_2(t)$$

S&P-2 $\quad y_3(t) = c_3 + a_{31,1}y_1(t-1) + a_{32,1}y_2(t-1) + a_{33,1}y_3(t-1)$
$$+ a_{31,2}y_1(t-2) + a_{32,2}y_2(t-2) + a_{33,2}y_3(t-2) + \varepsilon_3(t)$$

We can now perform the same exercise as with the VAR(1) model with two lags. The sample now includes 158 observations. One might object

---

[7] The threshold for statistical significance is subjective. In addition, some statisticians question the validity of tail probabilities to gauge significance. See Chapter 2.

that we compare models estimated on different data sets (158 versus 159 data points). Though this is true, in practice we have effectively more data to estimate a VAR(1) model with respect to a VAR(2) model. Each regression equation now has six regressors, three variables for each lag.

The least squares estimates are reported for each equation in the three panels in Exhibit 10.6. The Granger causality probabilities are summarized in Exhibit 10.7 while the three panels in Exhibit 10.8 show the predicted versus the actual values of the three variables. Again, keep in mind that this is only an exercise on how to apply modeling tools.

In equation WCW-2, the t-statistics show that at a 99% confidence level we cannot reject the null hypothesis of zero coefficient for variable y_1 at lag 2, for variable y_2 at both lags, and for variable y_3 at lag 2. Equation WCW-2 has little explanatory power, with less than 7% of the variance of y_1 explained by the regression equation. This result is in agreement with the previous case of one lag.

For equation WEW-2, we find that for the coefficients $a_{21,2}$, $a_{22,2}$, $a_{23,2}$ the null hypothesis of zero cannot be rejected (i.e., the null hypothesis that these coefficients are not significant cannot be rejected).

As in the case with one lag (WEW-1), equation WEW-2 has a much higher explanatory power with an R^2 about 16%, but the residuals seem to be slightly autocorrelated.

In equation S&P-2 all first coefficients are significant. The overall significance of equation S&P-2 is similar to that for one lag in equation S&P-1.

EXHIBIT 10.6 Estimates of the Three Equations of a VAR Model with Two Lags
Panel A: Equation Estimated: WCW-2

Variable	Coefficient	t-statistic	t-probability
y_1 lag1	$a_{11,1} = 1.717375$	2.743612	0.006813
y_1 lag2	$a_{11,2} = 0.523684$	0.797806	0.426236
y_2 lag1	$a_{12,1} = -0.242473$	-1.946917	0.053400
y_2 lag2	$a_{12,2} = -0.178097$	-1.591905	0.113497
y_3 lag1	$a_{13,1} = -1.535214$	-2.764817	0.006406
y_3 lag2	$a_{13,2} = -0.343669$	-0.590118	0.555993
constant	$c_1 = 1.155683$	2.991625	0.003242

$R^2 = 0.0675$
Adjusted $R^2 = 0.0305$
$\hat{\sigma}_1^2 = \hat{\mathbf{e}}'\hat{\mathbf{e}}/(n-k) = \hat{\mathbf{e}}'\hat{\mathbf{e}}/155 = 19.1921$
Q-statistic $= 0.0284$

EXHIBIT 10.6 (Continued)
Panel B: Equation Estimated: WEW-2

Variable	Coefficient	t-statistic	t-probability
y_1 lag1	$a_{21,1} = 3.402066$	4.225204	0.000041
y_1 lag2	$a_{21,2} = 0.550829$	0.652368	0.515156
y_2 lag1	$a_{22,1} = -0.309937$	-1.934661	0.054901
y_2 lag2	$a_{22,2} = -0.171607$	-1.192458	0.234952
y_3 lag1	$a_{23,1} = -2.859107$	-4.002905	0.000098
y_3 lag2	$a_{23,2} = -0.420667$	-0.561545	0.575259
constant	$c_2 = 1.581039$	3.181692	0.001778

$R^2 = 0.1659$
Adjusted $R^2 = 0.1328$
$\hat{\sigma}_1^2 = \hat{\mathbf{e}}'\hat{\mathbf{e}}/(n-k) = \hat{\mathbf{e}}'\hat{\mathbf{e}}/155 = 31.7561$
Q-statistic = 0.0948

Panel C: Equation Estimated: S&P-2

Variable	Coefficient	t-statistic	t-probability
y_1 lag1	$a_{31,1} = 1.707183$	2.755778	0.006577
y_1 lag2	$a_{31,2} = 0.410345$	0.631660	0.528564
y_2 lag1	$a_{32,1} = -0.247446$	-2.007572	0.046473
y_2 lag2	$a_{32,2} = -0.130363$	-1.177396	0.240890
y_3 lag1	$a_{33,1} = -1.547094$	-2.815274	0.005524
y_3 lag2	$a_{33,2} = -0.275951$	-0.478782	0.632786
constant	$c_3 = 1.182225$	3.092252	0.002367

$R^2 = 0.0624$
Rbar-squared = 0.0252
$\hat{\sigma}_1^2 = \hat{\mathbf{e}}'\hat{\mathbf{e}}/(n-k) = \hat{\mathbf{e}}'\hat{\mathbf{e}}/155 = 18.7979$
Q-statistic = 0.0775

EXHIBIT 10.7 Granger Causality Probabilities

Variable	y_1	y_2	y_3
y_1	0.03	0.06	0.02
y_2	0.00	0.10	0.00
y_3	0.02	0.09	0.02

Exhibit 10.7 shows the Granger causality probabilities. With two lags, the Granger-causality probability exhibit a weak structure, which might indicate some causal links.

Exhibit 10.8 illustrates graphically the predicted versus the actual values of the three variables.

Let's now compare the two models. The variance of the residuals is slightly smaller in the case of two lags. To see if we should prefer the model with two lags to the model with one lag, let's use the AIC criterion. This criterion requires computing the following expression:

$$n \log \hat{\sigma}_\varepsilon^2 + 2k$$

where $\hat{\sigma}_\varepsilon^2$ is the variance of residuals, n is the number of data points and k the number of parameters. The model with the smallest AIC value has to be preferred. If we consider, for example, equations WCW-1 and WCW-2, in the case of one lag, there are 159 data points and four parameters to estimate, while in the case of two lags there are 158 data points and seven parameters to estimate. Computing the AIC coefficient yields:

EXHIBIT 10.8   Predicted Versus Actual Values of the Three Variables
Panel A: Actual versus Predicted Equation WEW-2. The second graph represents residuals.

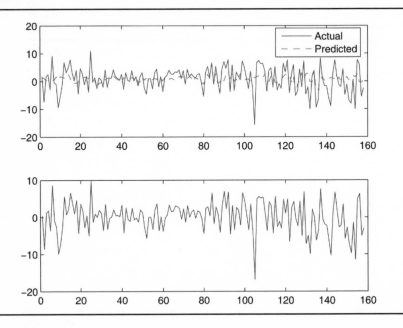

EXHIBIT 10.8 (Continued)

Panel B: Actual versus Predicted Equation WMW-2. The second graph represents residuals.

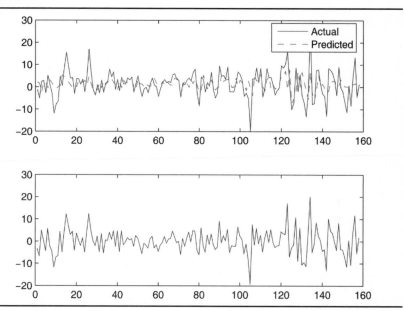

Panel C: Actual versus Predicted Equation S&P-2. The second graph represents residuals.

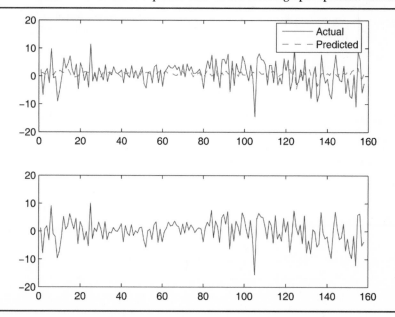

For one lag: $159 \times \log(19.0604) + 2 \times 4 = 476.6704$

For two lags: $158 \times \log(19.1921) + 2 \times 7 = 480.8108$

For the equations WEW-1 and WEW-2, we obtain respectively 555.3274 and 563.8355 and for the equations S&P-1 and S&P-2 471.9960 and 477.5317 respectively. Therefore there should be a slight preference for a model with only one lag.

CONCEPTS EXPLAINED IN THIS CHAPTER (IN ORDER OF PRESENTATION)

Restricted and unrestricted VAR models
Companion matrix
Multivariate least squares estimation
Vec operator
Kronecker product
Normal equations
LS estimators
Asymptotic distributions of LS estimators
Demeaned processes
ML estimators
Likelihood of the VAR model
Mean square error (MSE)
Final prediction error (FPE)
Akaike information criterion (AIC)
Bayesian information criterion (BIC)
Ljung-Box test
Q-test

CHAPTER 11

Cointegration and State Space Models

In this chapter, we introduce the concepts of cointegrated processes and state space models, as well as the relative estimation methods. State space models were introduced in the engineering literature in the 1960s especially through the work of Rudolf E. Kalman. Cointegration analysis is a more recent econometric tool. The first articles to introduce cointegrated models were penned by Engle and Granger in the second half of the 1980s.

Though vector autoregressive (VAR) processes and state space models are equivalent representations of the same processes, deeper insight into the relationship between state space models and cointegration was gained more recently when it was understood that cointegration implies a reduced number of common stochastic trends. The idea behind cointegration that there are feedback mechanisms that force processes to stay close together is therefore intimately related to the idea that the behavior of large sets of processes is driven by the dynamics of a smaller number of variables.

COINTEGRATION

Cointegration is one of the key concepts of modern econometrics. Let's start by giving an intuitive explanation of cointegration and its properties. Two or more processes are said to be *cointegrated* if they stay close to each other even if they "drift about" as individual processes. A colorful illustration is that of the drunken man and his dog: Both stumble about aimlessly but never drift too far apart. Cointegration is an important concept both for economics and financial modeling. It implements the notion that there are feedbacks that keep variables mutually aligned. To introduce the notion of cointegration, recall the concepts of stationary processes and integrated processes.

Key Features of Cointegration

Let's first give an intuitive characterization to the concept of cointegration in the case of two stochastic processes. Cointegration can be understood in terms of its three key features:

- Reduction of order of integration
- Regression
- Common trends

First, consider *reduction of order of integration*. Two or more stochastic processes that are integrated of order one or higher are said to be cointegrated if there are linear combinations of the processes with a *lower* order of integration. In financial econometrics, cointegration is usually a property of processes integrated of order one that admit linear combinations integrated of order zero (stationary). As we will see, it is also possible to define fractional cointegration between fractionally integrated processes.

Second, the concept of cointegration can be also stated in terms of *linear regression*. Two or more processes integrated of order one are said to be cointegrated if it is possible to make a meaningful linear regression of one process on the other(s). In general, it is not possible to make a meaningful linear regression of one integrated process over another. However, regression is possible if the two processes are cointegrated. Cointegration is that property that allows one to meaningfully regress one integrated process on other integrated processes.

Finally, a property of cointegrated processes is the presence of integrated *common trends*. Given n processes with r cointegrating relationships, it is possible to determine $n-r$ common trends. Common trends are integrated processes such that any of the n original processes can be expressed as a linear regression on the common trends. Cointegration entails dimensionality reduction insofar as common trends are the common drivers of a set of processes.

Long-Run Equilibrium

Given n processes integrated of order one, the processes are said to be cointegrated if there is a linear combination of the processes that is stationary. If the processes are stock prices, cointegration means that even if the stock prices are individually integrated of order one—for example arithmetic random walks—there are portfolios that are stationary. The linear relationships that produce stationary processes are called *cointegrating* relationships.

Cointegrated processes are characterized by a short-term dynamics and a long-run equilibrium. Note that this latter property does not mean that cointegrated processes *tend* to a long-term equilibrium. On the contrary, the relative behavior is stationary. Long-run equilibrium is the static regression function, that is, the relationship between the processes after eliminating the short-term dynamics.

In general, there can be many linearly independent cointegrating relationships. Given n processes integrated of order one, there can be a maximum of $n - 1$ cointegrating relationships. Cointegrating relationships are not uniquely defined: In fact, any linear combination of cointegrating relationships is another cointegrating relationship.

More Rigorous Definition of Cointegration

Let's now define cointegration in more rigorous terms. The concept of cointegration was introduced by Granger in the second half of the 1980s.[1] It can be expressed in the following way. Suppose that n time series $x_{i,t}$, integrated of the same order d are given. If there is a linear combination of the series

$$\delta_t = \sum_{i=1}^{n} \beta_i x_{i,t}$$

that is integrated of order $e < d$, then the series are said to be cointegrated. Any linear combination as the one above is called a cointegrating relationship. The most commonly found concept of cointegration in financial econometrics is between processes integrated of order $d = 1$ that exhibit stationary linear combinations ($e = 0$).

The concept of cointegration can be extended to processes integrated of order d where d is a rational fraction. Such processes are called *fractionally integrated processes*. The reduction of the order of integration can be fractional too. For example, processes with order of integration $d = \frac{1}{2}$ are cointegrated if they exhibit linear combinations that are stationary.

Given n time series, there can be from none to at most $n - 1$ cointegrating relationships. The cointegration vectors $[\beta_i]$ are not unique. In fact, given two cointegrating vectors $[\alpha_i]$ and $[\beta_i]$ such that

---

[1] Clive W.J. Granger, "Some Properties of Time Series Data and Their Use in Econometric Model Specification," *Journal of Econometrics* 16 (1981), pp. 121–130.

$$\sum_{i=1}^{n} \alpha_i X_i, \quad \sum_{i=1}^{n} \beta_i X_i$$

are integrated of order e, any linear combination of the cointegrating vectors is another cointegrating vector as the linear combination

$$A \sum_{i=1}^{n} \alpha_i X_i + B \sum_{i=1}^{n} \beta_i X_i$$

is integrated of order e.

Stochastic and Deterministic Cointegration

An important distinction has to be made between stochastic and deterministic cointegration. Following the definition of cointegration given above, a multivariate integrated process is cointegrated if there are stationary linear combinations of its components. Let us now look at how we define cointegration if the integrated process has a deterministic trend.

Suppose that the multivariate stochastic process $\mathbf{x}_t$ has a deterministic trend. The process $\mathbf{x}_t$ is said to be *stochastically cointegrated* if there are linear combinations of the process components, each including its own deterministic trend, that are trend stationary (i.e., stationary plus a deterministic trend). In other words, stochastic cointegration removes stochastic trends but not necessarily deterministic trends.

The process $\mathbf{x}_t$ is said to be *deterministically cointegrated* if there are linear combinations of the process components, each including its own deterministic trend, that are stationary without any deterministic trend. In other words, deterministic cointegration removes both stochastic trends and deterministic trends.

Common Trends

Suppose there are n time series $x_{i,t}$, $i = 1, \dots, n$, and $k < n$ cointegrating relationships. It can be demonstrated that there are $n - k$ integrated time series $u_{j,t}$, $j = 1, \dots, n - k$, called *common trends*, such that every time series can expressed as a linear combination of the common trends plus a stationary disturbance:

$$x_{i,t} = \sum_{j=1}^{n-k} \gamma_j u_{j,t} + \eta_{i,t}$$

In other words, each process can be regressed on the common trends. Common trends are integrated processes; they were first discussed by Stock and Watson.[2]

Let's now analyze how, in a set of cointegrated processes, each process can be expressed in terms of a reduced number of common stochastic trends. The exposition follows the original work of Stock and Watson.[3] Suppose that the n-variate process $\mathbf{x}_t$ has no deterministic trend, is integrated of order 1, and admits $n - k$ linearly independent cointegrating relationships. This means that there are $r = n - k$ vectors of coefficients $\beta_{i,j}$, $i = 1, 2, ..., n$ and $j = 1, 2, ..., r$ such that the processes

$$\sum_{i=1}^{n} \beta_{i,j} x_{i,t}$$

are stationary. Assuming that the process has no deterministic trend, we do not have to make any distinction between stochastic and deterministic cointegration. If $\mathbf{x}_t$ represent logarithms of stock prices, cointegration means that there are r portfolios that are stationary even if each individual price process is a random walk.

We arrange the cointegrating relationships in an $n \times r$ matrix:

$$\beta = \begin{pmatrix} \beta_{1,1} & \cdots & \beta_{1,n-k} \\ \vdots & \ddots & \vdots \\ \beta_{n,1} & \cdots & \beta_{n,n-k} \end{pmatrix}$$

This matrix has rank r given that its columns are linearly independent. Therefore the r-variate process $\beta' \mathbf{x}_t$ is stationary. Recall that the process can be represented as

$$\mathbf{x}_t = \Psi \sum_{i=1}^{t} \varepsilon_i + \left(\sum_{i=0}^{\infty} \Psi_i^* L^i \right) \varepsilon_t + \mathbf{x}_{-1}$$

where x_{-1} represents the constant term. It can be demonstrated that the assumption of r independent cointegrating relationships implies

[2] James H. Stock and Mark W. Watson, "Diffusion Indexes," NBER Working Paper W6702, 1998; James H. Stock and Mark W. Watson, "New Indexes of Coincident and Leading Economic Indications," in O.J. Blanchard and S. Fischer (eds.), *NBER Macroeconomics Annual 1989* (Cambridge, MA: MIT Press, 1989).
[3] James H. Stock and Mark W. Watson, "Testing for Common Trends," *Journal of the American Statistical Association* 83 (December 1988), pp. 1097–1107.

$$\beta'\Psi = 0$$

Therefore, we can write

$$\beta'\mathbf{x}_t = \mathbf{z}_t = \beta'\left(\sum_{i=0}^{\infty} \Psi_i^* L^i\right)\varepsilon_t + \beta'\mathbf{x}_{-1}$$

where $\mathbf{z}_t$ is a r-variate stationary process. The stochastic trends have been removed.

Let's now explicitly express the process $\mathbf{x}_t$ in terms of common stochastic trends. Observe that the assumption of r cointegrating relationships entails that both $\beta'\Psi = 0$ and Ψ has rank $k = n - r$. In fact, if the rank of Ψ were smaller than $k = n - r$, then there would be one or more additional cointegrating relationships. Because Ψ has rank $k < n$ there is an $n \times r$ matrix $\mathbf{H}_1$ such that $\Psi\mathbf{H}_1 = 0$. Furthermore, if $\mathbf{H}_2$ is an $n \times k$ matrix with rank k and columns orthogonal to the columns of $\mathbf{H}_1$ then $\mathbf{A} = \Psi\mathbf{H}_2$ is a $n \times k$ matrix with rank k. The $n \times n$ matrix $\mathbf{H} = [\mathbf{H}_1\mathbf{H}_2]$ is non singular and $\Psi\mathbf{H} = [0\mathbf{A}]$. We can therefore write the representation in terms of common stochastic trends as follows:

$$\mathbf{x}_t = (\Psi\mathbf{H})\left(\mathbf{H}^{-1}\sum_{i=1}^{t}\varepsilon_i\right) + \left(\sum_{i=0}^{\infty} \Psi_i^* L^i\right)\varepsilon_t + \mathbf{x}_{-1} = \mathbf{A}\tau_t + \left(\sum_{i=0}^{\infty} \Psi_i^* L^i\right)\varepsilon_t + \mathbf{x}_{-1}$$

$$\tau_t = \mathbf{H}^{-1}\sum_{i=1}^{t}\varepsilon_i$$

Cointegrated VAR Illustration

Let's now illustrate step by step the process of estimating a cointegrated VAR model. The theory of estimation of cointegrated processes is developed in the next sections. As most advanced econometric software have packages for cointegration estimation that can be used without a detailed knowledge of the theory, we first present the examples. We will use the same data we used for illustrating the VAR modeling, namely monthly return data for the three indexes—Wilshire Capitalization Weighted (WCW), Wilshire Equal Weighted (WEW), and S&P 500 (S&P) index. Returns form stationary time series. Cointegration, however, is a concept that applies to integrated processes. Therefore, our first task is to reconstruct the value P_i of each index from the relative returns.

Returns for each of the three indexes are defined as follows:

$$R_t^i = \frac{V_t^i - V_{t-1}^i}{V_{t-1}^i} = \frac{V_t^i}{V_{t-1}^i} - 1 \,, i = 1, 2, 3$$

Therefore we can write the value of each index as follows:

$$V_t^i = (1 + R_t^i)V_{t-1}^i = V_1^i \prod_{s=2}^{t} (1 + R_s^i)$$

Using this formula we can now compute the values of the three indexes, assuming conventionally that the three indexes have initial unitary value. Assuming returns are a stationary process, the value process is a nonlinear geometrical process. However, if we take the logarithms of values we obtain an integrated process.

Exhibit 11.1 shows the three integrated processes corresponding to the logarithms of the index values. Note that we are considering only the 130 months period from October 1989 to August 2000. The reason

EXHIBIT 11.1   Logarithms of the Index Values

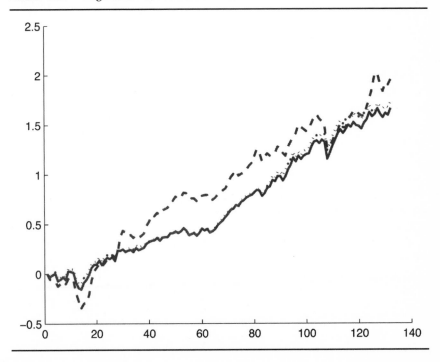

is that it is widely accepted that there was a structural break in year 2000. Structural breaks substantially affect cointegration tests.

Note that the following estimation exercise has the sole purpose of showing how cointegration tests are applied and is not intended to provide general conclusions about the characteristics of financial markets. Because most state-of-the-art econometric packages offer cointegration analysis, the objective of our exercise is to show how results from a typical package should be read and interpreted.

Let's now run the cointegration analysis using the Johansen methodology that will be described in the following sections. We start by determining the number of cointegrating relationships. Then we specify the number of lags. How we determine the number of lags is discussed in the next section on error correction models.

The Johansen methodology offers two tests for testing the number of cointegrating relationships: the trace test and the eigenvalue test. Exhibit 11.2 presents the results of both tests.

The trace test tests the null hypothesis that there are at most r cointegrating relationships. That is, rejecting the null means that there are more than r cointegrating relationships. Panel A of Exhibit 11.2 reports the results of the trace test. The test itself computes the trace statistic, as explained in the previous chapter, and compares it with critical values. Critical values have been computed by several different sources, including Johansen himself. The trace test rejects the null if the trace statistic exceeds the critical value.

EXHIBIT 11.2   Results of Johansen Trace and Eigenvalue Tests
Panel A: Results of Trace Test:

Null Hypothesis	Trace Statistic	Critical Value at		
		90%	95%	99%
$r \leq 0$	38.047	27.067	29.796	35.463
$r \leq 1$	3.890	13.429	15.494	19.935
$r \leq 2$	0.364	2.705	3.841	6.635

Panel B: Results of Eigenvalue Test:

Null Hypothesis	Eigenvalue Statistic	Critical Value at		
		90%	95%	99%
$r \leq 0$	34.157	18.893	21.131	25.865
$r \leq 1$	3.526	12.297	14.264	18.520
$r \leq 2$	0.364	2.705	3.841	6.635

The trace test is performed sequentially. First we test the null hypothesis that there are at most 0 cointegrating relationships; that is, we test the null hypothesis of no cointegration. Then we proceed to test the null of at most 1 or 2 cointegrating relationships. The first line of Panel A in the exhibit tests the null $r \leq 0$. The trace statistic has the value 38.047 which largely exceeds critical values at the 90%, 95%, and 99% confidence levels. Therefore the null hypothesis of no cointegration is rejected at the 99% confidence level.

The second and the third lines in Panel A of Exhibit 11.2 test the null hypothesis that $r \leq 1$ and $r \leq 2$, respectively. The trace statistics 3.526 and 0.364 are well below the respective critical levels at every confidence level. Therefore the null hypothesis of at most 1 or 2 cointegration relationship is accepted. The conclusion is there is one cointegrating relationship.

The eigenvalue test tests the null hypothesis of r versus $r + 1$ cointegrating relationships. The test rejects the null hypothesis if the eigenvalue test statistic exceeds the respective critical value. The results are reported in panel B of Exhibit 11.2. The first line in panel B rejects the null hypothesis of 0 versus 1 cointegrating relationships, while the second and the third lines accept the null hypothesis of 1 versus 2 and 2 versus 3 cointegrating relationships. Both tests therefore conclude that there is one cointegrating relationship.

ERROR CORRECTION MODELS

Having discussed cointegration and cointegrated processes, we now discuss their representation. Granger was able to demonstrate that a multivariate integrated process is cointegrated if and only if it can be represented in the *error correction model* (ECM) form with appropriate restrictions.

First we rewrite a generic VAR model in error correction form. All VAR models can be written in the following error-correction form:

$$\Delta \mathbf{x}_t = (\mathbf{\Phi}_1 L + \mathbf{\Phi}_2 L^2 + \dots + \mathbf{\Phi}_{p-1} L^{p-1})\Delta \mathbf{x}_t + \mathbf{\Pi} L^p \mathbf{x}_t + D \mathbf{s}_t + \mathbf{\varepsilon}_t$$

where there are $p - 1$ terms are in first differences and the last term is in levels. The term in levels can be placed at any lag.

To see how this representation can be obtained, consider, for example, the following transformations of a VAR(2) model:

$$\mathbf{x}_t = \mathbf{A}_1\mathbf{x}_{t-1} + \mathbf{A}_2\mathbf{x}_{t-2} + \mathbf{Ds}_t + \boldsymbol{\varepsilon}_t$$

$$\mathbf{x}_t - \mathbf{x}_{t-1} = (\mathbf{A}_1 - \mathbf{I})\mathbf{x}_{t-1} - (\mathbf{A}_1 - \mathbf{I})\mathbf{x}_{t-2} + (\mathbf{A}_1 - \mathbf{I})\mathbf{x}_{t-2} + \mathbf{A}_2\mathbf{x}_{t-2} + \mathbf{Ds}_t + \boldsymbol{\varepsilon}_t$$

$$\Delta\mathbf{x}_t = (\mathbf{A}_1 - \mathbf{I})\Delta\mathbf{x}_{t-1} + (\mathbf{A}_1 + \mathbf{A}_2 - \mathbf{I})\mathbf{x}_{t-2} + \mathbf{Ds}_t + \boldsymbol{\varepsilon}_t$$

$$\boldsymbol{\Phi}_1 = (\mathbf{A}_1 - \mathbf{I}), \boldsymbol{\Pi} = (\mathbf{A}_1 + \mathbf{A}_2 - \mathbf{I})$$

with the term in level at lag 2, or

$$\mathbf{x}_t = \mathbf{A}_1\mathbf{x}_{t-1} + \mathbf{A}_2\mathbf{x}_{t-2} + \mathbf{Ds}_t + \boldsymbol{\varepsilon}_t$$

$$\mathbf{x}_t - \mathbf{x}_{t-1} = (\mathbf{A}_1 + \mathbf{A}_2 - \mathbf{I})\mathbf{x}_{t-1} - \mathbf{A}_2\mathbf{x}_{t-1} + \mathbf{A}_2\mathbf{x}_{t-2} + \mathbf{Ds}_t + \boldsymbol{\varepsilon}_t$$

$$\Delta\mathbf{x}_t = (-\mathbf{A}_2)\Delta\mathbf{x}_{t-1} + (\mathbf{A}_1 + \mathbf{A}_2 - \mathbf{I})\mathbf{x}_{t-1} + \mathbf{Ds}_t + \boldsymbol{\varepsilon}_t$$

$$\boldsymbol{\Phi}_1 = -\mathbf{A}_2, \boldsymbol{\Pi} = (\mathbf{A}_1 + \mathbf{A}_2 - \mathbf{I})$$

with the term in level at lag 1. Clearly these transformations can be immediately generalized to any number of lags. Note that, though they mix differences and levels, these transformations do not assume any special property of the VAR model: they are simple rearrangements of terms which are always possible. Cointegration is expressed as restrictions on the matrix $\boldsymbol{\Pi}$.

In fact, cointegration is expressed as the ECM representation of a multivariate process in first differences with corrections in levels as follows:

$$\Delta x_t T = \left(\sum_{i=1}^{P-1} AL^i \right) \Delta x_{t-1} + \boldsymbol{\alpha\beta}'\mathbf{x}_{t-1} + \boldsymbol{\varepsilon}_t$$

where $\boldsymbol{\alpha}$ is an $n \times r$ matrix, $\boldsymbol{\beta}$ is an $n \times r$ matrix with $\boldsymbol{\alpha\beta}' = \boldsymbol{\Pi}$.

In the above ECM representation, $\boldsymbol{\beta}'\mathbf{x}_t$ reflect common trends while $\boldsymbol{\alpha}$ contains the loading factors of the common trends. If $r = 0$, there is no common trend and no cointegration exists between the processes; if $r = n$, the processes are stationary; in the other cases $n > r > 0$, processes are integrated and there are cointegrating relationships.

Illustration

Let's illustrate ECM to determine the number of lags for the three indexes in an earlier illustration. Different models have to be run and results compared with the same significance tests used for the VAR model. Let's start with one lag. We use the notation in the previous chapter to denote the number of lags by following the index with a hyphen and the number of lags.

With one lag and one cointegrating relationship, we estimate the following ECM:

WCW-1 $\Delta v_1(t) = c_1 + \alpha_1 w_1(t-1) + a_{11,1}\Delta v_1(t-1) + a_{12,1}\Delta v_2(t-1)$
$$+ a_{13,1}\Delta v_3(t-1) + \varepsilon_1(t)$$

WEW-1 $\Delta v_2(t) = c_2 + \alpha_2 w_1(t-1) + a_{21,1}\Delta v_1(t-1) + a_{22,1}\Delta v_2(t-1)$
$$+ a_{23,1}\Delta v_3(t-1) + \varepsilon_2(t)$$

S&P-1 $\Delta v_3(t) = c_3 + \alpha_3 w_1(t-1) + a_{31,1}\Delta v_1(t-1) + a_{32,1}\Delta v_2(t-1)$
$$+ a_{33,1}\Delta v_3(t-1) + \varepsilon_3(t)$$

where w_1 is the cointegrating variable obtained as a linear combination of

$$v_1(t-1),\ v_2(t-1),\ v_3(t-1)$$

We will first analyze each equation as a regression equation. To do that, we compute the overall R^2 and the t-statistics for each coefficient to assess if that coefficient is significant. Recall that we have already established that there is one cointegrating relationship. In general, estimation software gives the user the option to either impose the number of cointegrating relationships or let the system determine this number.

As the ECM model includes one lag, observations relative to each regression equation require two consecutive values. Therefore, the number of observations is equal to the number of observable values reduced by 1. For our illustration: Number of observations = 130 − 1 = 129.

For each equation, there are four predetermined variables (three differences and one level) and five coefficients to estimate. The results are reported in the three panels in Exhibit 11.3.

The overall usefulness of the WEW-1 equation can be assessed by the R^2 and the adjusted R^2. Although the null hypothesis that the coefficients of the equation WCW-1 are zero can be rejected, the R^2 shows that only 11% of the variance of variable Δv_1 (WCW) is explained.

For equation WEW-1, Exhibit 11.3 shows that the coefficient $a_{22,1}$ of Δv_2 at lag 1, the constant term, and the error correction term are all insignificant.

The R^2 and the adjusted R^2 reveal that equation WCW-1 has more explanatory power than equation WEW-1 with nearly 17% of the variance of Δv_2 (WEW) explained.

The results for equation S&P-1 are very similar to those of equation WCW-1.

EXHIBIT 11.3 Estimates of the Three Equations of the ECM Model with One Lag
Panel A: Equation Estimated: WCW-1

Variable	Coefficient	t-statistic	t-probability
Δv_1 lag1	$a_{11,1} = 1.727977$	0.558256	0.011713
Δv_2 lag1	$a_{12,1} = -0.049972$	-0.364564	0.716053
Δv_3 lag1	$a_{13,1} = -1.734178$	-2.910603	0.004272
w_1 term	$\alpha_1 = 0.009380$	2.807155	0.005800
Constant	$c_1 = -0.010369$	-1.038562	0.301013

$R^2 = 0.1121$
Adjusted $R^2 = 0.0837$
$\hat{\sigma}_1^2 = \hat{\mathbf{e}}'\hat{\mathbf{e}}/(n-k) = \hat{\mathbf{e}}'\hat{\mathbf{e}}/125 = 0.0015$

Panel B: Equation Estimated: WEW-1

Variable	Coefficient	t-statistic	t-probability
Δv_1 lag1	$a_{21,1} = 2.729288$	3.185647	0.001824
Δv_2 lag1	$a_{22,1} = -0.012120$	-0.069707	0.944538
Δv_3 lag1	$a_{23,1} = -2.464786$	-3.261450	0.001429
w_1 term 1	$\alpha_2 = 0.006277$	1.480869	0.141158
Constant	$c_2 = -0.003075$	-0.242773	0.808579

$R^2 = 0.1736$
Adjusted $R^2 = 0.1472$
$\hat{\sigma}_1^2 = \hat{\mathbf{e}}'\hat{\mathbf{e}}/(n-k) = \hat{\mathbf{e}}'\hat{\mathbf{e}}/125 = 0.0023$

Panel C: Equation Estimated: S&P-1

Variable	Coefficient	t-statistic	t-probability
Δv_1 lag1	$a_{31,1} = 1.649616$	2.465139	0.015053
Δv_2 lag1	$a_{32,1} = -0.081206$	-0.597991	0.550928
Δv_3 lag1	$a_{33,1} = -1.670842$	-2.830593	0.005416
w_1 term 1	$\alpha_3 = 0.007235$	2.185528	0.030714
Constant	$c_3 = -0.003537$	-0.357536	0.721294

$R^2 = 0.0959$
Adjusted $R^2 = 0.0670$
$\hat{\sigma}_1^2 = \hat{\mathbf{e}}'\hat{\mathbf{e}}/(n-k) = \hat{\mathbf{e}}'\hat{\mathbf{e}}/125 = 0.0014$

Cointegrating vector: $\hat{\beta}' = (-156.3260, 16.9512, 132.3237)$

THEORY AND METHODS OF ESTIMATION OF NONSTATIONARY VAR MODELS

In this and the following sections, we examine the theory behind the estimation of nonstationary and nonstable processes. In a nonstationary process, the averages, variances, or covariances may vary with time. A somewhat surprising fact is that least-squares methods can be applied to the nonstationary case although other methods are more efficient.

Consider the following VAR process:

$$\mathbf{x}_t = \mathbf{A}_1\mathbf{x}_{t-1} + \mathbf{A}_2\mathbf{x}_{t-2} + \cdots + \mathbf{A}_p\mathbf{x}_{t-p} + \mathbf{v} + \boldsymbol{\varepsilon}_t$$

The process can be rewritten in the following error correction form:

$$\Delta\mathbf{x}_t = -\mathbf{\Pi}\mathbf{x}_{t-1} + \mathbf{F}_1\Delta\mathbf{x}_{t-1} + \mathbf{F}_2\Delta\mathbf{x}_{t-2} + \cdots + \mathbf{F}_{p-1}\Delta\mathbf{x}_{t-p+1} + \mathbf{v} + \boldsymbol{\varepsilon}_t$$

$$\mathbf{F}_i = -\sum_{q=i+1}^{p}\mathbf{A}_i, \mathbf{\Pi} = \mathbf{I} - \mathbf{A}_1 - \mathbf{A}_2 - \cdots - \mathbf{A}_p$$

The cointegration properties of the VAR model depend on the rank r of the matrix $\mathbf{\Pi}$. If $r = 0$, then the VAR model does not exhibit any cointegration relationship and it can be estimated as a stable process in first differences. In this case, the process in first differences can be estimated with LS or MLE techniques for estimation of stable VAR processes as discussed in the previous sections.

If $r = n$, that is, if the matrix $\mathbf{\Pi}$ is of full rank, then the VAR model itself is stable and can be estimated as a stable process. If the rank r is intermediate $0 < r < n$, then the VAR process exhibits cointegration. In this case, we can write the matrix $\mathbf{\Pi}$ as the product $\mathbf{\Pi} = \boldsymbol{\alpha}\boldsymbol{\beta}'$ where both $\boldsymbol{\alpha}$ and $\boldsymbol{\beta}$ are $n \times r$ matrices of rank r. The r columns of the matrix $\boldsymbol{\beta}$ are the cointegrating vectors of the process.

Next we discuss different estimation methods for cointegrated VAR models, starting with the LS estimation method.

Estimation of a Cointegrated VAR with Unrestricted LS Methods

In this section on the estimation of nonstationary VAR processes, we assume for simplicity $\mathbf{v} = 0$, that is, we write a VAR process as follows:

$$\mathbf{x}_t = \mathbf{A}_1\mathbf{x}_{t-1} + \mathbf{A}_2\mathbf{x}_{t-2} + \cdots + \mathbf{A}_p\mathbf{x}_{t-p} + \boldsymbol{\varepsilon}_t$$

The cointegration condition places a restriction on the model. In fact, if we assume that the model has r cointegrating relationships, we have to impose the restriction rank$(\mathbf{\Pi}) = r$, where $\mathbf{\Pi} = \mathbf{I} - \mathbf{A}_1 - \mathbf{A}_2 - \cdots - \mathbf{A}_p$. This restriction precludes the use of standard LS methods. However, Sims, Stock, and Watson[4] and Park and Phillips[5] demonstrated that, if we estimate the above model as an unconstrained VAR model, the estimators thus obtained are consistent and have the same asymptotic properties as the ML estimators that are discussed in the next section.

To write down the estimators, we define, as in the case of stable VAR, the following notation:

$$\mathbf{X} = (\mathbf{x}_1, ..., \mathbf{x}_T)$$

$$\mathbf{A} = (\mathbf{A}_1, ..., \mathbf{A}_p)$$

$$\mathbf{Z} = \begin{pmatrix} \mathbf{x}_0 & \cdots & \mathbf{x}_{T-1} \\ \vdots & \ddots & \vdots \\ \mathbf{x}_{1-p} & \cdots & \mathbf{x}_{T-p} \end{pmatrix}$$

Using this notation, we can write the estimators of the cointegrated VAR model as the usual LS estimator of VAR models as discussed in Chapter 10, that is, we can write

$$\hat{\mathbf{A}} = \mathbf{XZ}'(\mathbf{ZZ}')$$

It has also be demonstrated that this estimator has the same asymptotic properties of the ML estimators that we discuss next. Note that in the illustration earlier in this chapter, we imposed one cointegrating relationship. In the previous chapter, we estimated the same data in first differences (i.e., we imposed the zero cointegrating relationship). In this section, however, we discuss unconstrained estimation of an integrated VAR system. The three estimates are not identical.

ML Estimators

The ML estimation procedure has become the state-of-the-art estimation method for systems of relatively small dimensions, where it outper-

---

[4] Christopher A. Sims, James H. Stock, and Mark W. Watson. 1990. "Inference in Linear Time Series Models with Some Unit Roots," *Econometrica* 58 (1), pp. 161–182.

[5] J. Y. Park and P. C. B. Phillips, "Statistical Inference in Regressions with Integrated Processes. Part 2," *Econometric Theory* 5 (1989), pp. 95–131.

forms other methods. The ML estimation methodology was developed primarily by Søren Johansen,[6] hence it is often referred to as the Johansen method. We will assume, following Johansen, that innovations are independent identically distributed (IID) multivariate, correlated, Gaussian variables. The methodology can be extended to nonnormal distributions for innovations but computations become more complex and depend on the distribution. We will use the ECM formulation of the VAR model, that is, we will write our cointegrated VAR as follows:

$$\Delta \mathbf{x}_t = -\Pi \mathbf{x}_{t-1} + \mathbf{F}_1 \Delta \mathbf{x}_{t-1} + \mathbf{F}_2 \Delta \mathbf{x}_{t-2} + \cdots + \mathbf{F}_{p-1} \Delta \mathbf{x}_{t-p+1} + \boldsymbol{\varepsilon}_t$$

We first describe the ML estimation process for cointegrated processes as introduced by Banerjee and Hendry.[7] We then make the connection with original *reduced rank regression* method of Johansen.

The method of Banerjee and Hendry is based on the idea of *concentrated likelihood*. Concentrated likelihood is a mathematical technique through which the original likelihood function (LF) is transformed into a function of a smaller number of variables, called the *concentrated likelihood function* (CLF). The CLF is also known in statistics as the *profile likelihood*. To see how CLF works, suppose that the LF is a function of two separate sets of parameters:

$$L = L(\vartheta_1, \vartheta_2)$$

In this case, the MLE principle can be established as follows:

$$\max_{\vartheta_1, \vartheta_2} L(\vartheta_1, \vartheta_2) = \max_{\vartheta_1} \left(\max_{\vartheta_2} L(\vartheta_1, \vartheta_2) \right) = \max_{\vartheta_1} (L^C(\vartheta_1))$$

where $L^C(\vartheta_1)$ is the CLF which is a function of the parameters ϑ_1 only.

To see how this result can be achieved, recall from Chapter 2 that, assuming usual regularity conditions, the maximum of the LF is attained where the partial derivatives of the log-likelihood function l are zero. In particular:

$$\frac{\partial l(\vartheta_1, \vartheta_2)}{\partial \vartheta_2} = 0$$

---

[6] S. Johansen "Estimation and Hypothesis Testing of Cointegration Vectors in Gaussian Vector Autoregressive Models," *Econometrica* 59 (1991): pp. 1551–1581.
[7] A. Banerjee and D. F. Hendry, "Testing Integration and Cointegration: An Overview," *Oxford Bulletin of Economics and Statistics* 54 (1992), pp. 225–255.

If we can solve this system of functional equations, we obtain: $\vartheta_2 = \vartheta_2(\vartheta_1)$. The invariance property of the ML estimators[8] now allows us to conclude that the following relationship must hold between the two sets of estimated parameters:

$$\hat{\vartheta}_2 = \vartheta_2(\hat{\vartheta}_1)$$

We see that the original likelihood function has been *concentrated* in a function of a smaller set of parameters. We now apply this idea to the ML estimation of cointegrated systems. It is convenient to use a notation that parallels that already introduced but is adapted to the special form of the cointegrated VAR model that we adopted as follows:

$$\Delta \mathbf{x}_t = -\mathbf{\Pi} \mathbf{x}_{t-1} + \mathbf{F}_1 \Delta \mathbf{x}_{t-1} + \mathbf{F}_2 \Delta \mathbf{x}_{t-2} + \cdots + \mathbf{F}_{p-1} \Delta \mathbf{x}_{t-p+1} + \mathbf{\varepsilon}_t$$

We define

$$\mathbf{X} = (\mathbf{x}_0, \ldots, \mathbf{x}_{T-1})$$

$$\Delta \mathbf{x}_t = \begin{pmatrix} \Delta x_{1,t} \\ \vdots \\ \Delta x_{n,t} \end{pmatrix}$$

$$\Delta \mathbf{X} = (\Delta \mathbf{x}_1, \ldots, \Delta \mathbf{x}_T) = \begin{pmatrix} \Delta x_{1,1} & \cdots & \Delta x_{1,T} \\ \vdots & \ddots & \vdots \\ \Delta x_{n,1} & \cdots & \Delta x_{n,T} \end{pmatrix}$$

$$\Delta \mathbf{Z}_t = \begin{pmatrix} \Delta \mathbf{x}_t \\ \vdots \\ \Delta \mathbf{x}_{t-p+2} \end{pmatrix},$$

$$\Delta \mathbf{Z} = \begin{pmatrix} \Delta \mathbf{x}_0 & \cdots & \Delta \mathbf{x}_{T-1} \\ \vdots & \ddots & \vdots \\ \Delta \mathbf{x}_{-p+2} & \cdots & \Delta \mathbf{x}_{T-p+1} \end{pmatrix} = \begin{pmatrix} \Delta x_{1,0} & \cdots & \Delta x_{1,T-1} \\ \vdots & \ddots & \vdots \\ \Delta x_{n,0} & \cdots & \Delta x_{n,T-1} \\ \vdots & \ddots & \vdots \\ \Delta x_{1,-p+2} & \cdots & \Delta x_{1,T} \\ \vdots & \ddots & \vdots \\ \Delta x_{n,-p+2} & \cdots & \Delta x_{n,T} \end{pmatrix}$$

[8] Recall that the invariance property of ML estimators states that if parameter a is a function of parameter b then the ML estimator of a is the same function of the ML estimator of b.

$$\mathbf{F} = (\mathbf{F}_1, \mathbf{F}_2, ..., \mathbf{F}_{p-1})$$

Using the matrix notation, as we assume $\Pi = \alpha\beta'$, we can compactly write our model in the following form:

$$\Delta\mathbf{X} = \mathbf{F}\Delta\mathbf{Z} - \alpha\beta'\mathbf{X} + \mathbf{U}$$

Reasoning as we did in the case of stable VAR models, we can write the log-likelihood function as follows:

$$
\begin{aligned}
\log(l) &= -\frac{nT}{2}\log(2\pi) - \frac{T}{2}\log|\Sigma_\mathbf{u}| - \frac{1}{2}\sum_{t=1}^{T}\varepsilon_t'\Sigma^{-1}\varepsilon_t \\
&= -\frac{nT}{2}\log(2\pi) - \frac{T}{2}\log|\Sigma_\mathbf{u}| - \frac{1}{2}\text{trace}(\mathbf{U}'\Sigma_\mathbf{u}^{-1}\mathbf{U}) \\
&= -\frac{nT}{2}\log(2\pi) - \frac{T}{2}\log|\Sigma_\mathbf{u}| - \frac{1}{2}\text{trace}(\Sigma_\mathbf{u}^{-1}\mathbf{U}\mathbf{U}') \\
&= -\frac{nT}{2}\log(2\pi) - \frac{T}{2}\log|\Sigma_\mathbf{u}| \\
&\quad - \frac{1}{2}\text{trace}((\Delta\mathbf{X} - \mathbf{F}\mathbf{Z} + \alpha\beta'\mathbf{X})'\Sigma_\mathbf{u}^{-1}(\Delta\mathbf{X} - \mathbf{F}\mathbf{Z} + \alpha\beta'\mathbf{X}))
\end{aligned}
$$

We now concentrate this log-likelihood function, eliminating Σ and F. As explained above, this entails taking partial derivatives, equating them to zero, and expressing Σ and F in terms of the other parameters. By equating the derivatives with respect to Σ to zero, it can be demonstrated that $\Sigma_C = T^{-1}\mathbf{U}\mathbf{U}'$. Substituting this expression in the log-likelihood, we obtain the concentrated likelihood after removing Σ:

$$
\begin{aligned}
l^{CI} &= K - \frac{T}{2}\log|\mathbf{U}\mathbf{U}'| \\
&= K - \frac{T}{2}\log|(\Delta\mathbf{X} - \mathbf{F}\mathbf{Z} + \alpha\beta'\mathbf{X})(\Delta\mathbf{X} - \mathbf{F}\mathbf{Z} + \alpha\beta'\mathbf{X})'|
\end{aligned}
$$

where K is a constant that includes all the constant terms left after concentrating.

We next eliminate the F terms. This result can be achieved taking derivatives of l with respect to F, equating them to zero, and evaluating them at Σ_C. Performing all the calculations, it can be demonstrated that the evaluation at Σ_C is irrelevant and that the following formula holds:

$$\mathbf{F}_C = (\Delta\mathbf{X} + \alpha\beta'\mathbf{X})\Delta\mathbf{Z}'(\Delta\mathbf{Z}\Delta\mathbf{Z}')^{-1}$$

Substituting this expression in the formula for l^{CI}, that is, the log-likelihood after eliminating Σ_C, we obtain:

$$
\begin{aligned}
l^{C\Pi} &= K - \frac{T}{2}\log|((\Delta\mathbf{X} - ((\Delta\mathbf{X} + \alpha\beta'\mathbf{X})\Delta\mathbf{Z}'(\Delta\mathbf{Z}\Delta\mathbf{Z}')^{-1})\Delta\mathbf{Z} + \alpha\beta'\mathbf{X})) \\
&\qquad (\Delta\mathbf{X} - (\Delta\mathbf{X} + \alpha\beta'\mathbf{X})\Delta\mathbf{Z}'(\Delta\mathbf{Z}\Delta\mathbf{Z}')^{-1}\Delta\mathbf{Z} + \alpha\beta'\mathbf{X})'| \\[4pt]
&= K - \frac{T}{2}\log|(\Delta\mathbf{X} + \alpha\beta'\mathbf{X} - ((\Delta\mathbf{X} + \alpha\beta'\mathbf{X})\Delta\mathbf{Z}'(\Delta\mathbf{Z}\Delta\mathbf{Z}')^{-1})\Delta\mathbf{Z}) \\
&\qquad (\Delta\mathbf{X} + \alpha\beta'\mathbf{X} - (\Delta\mathbf{X} + \alpha\beta'\mathbf{X})\Delta\mathbf{Z}'(\Delta\mathbf{Z}\Delta\mathbf{Z}')^{-1}\Delta\mathbf{Z})'| \\[4pt]
&= K - \frac{T}{2}\log|((\Delta\mathbf{X} + \alpha\beta'\mathbf{X})(\mathbf{I}_T - \Delta\mathbf{Z}'(\Delta\mathbf{Z}\Delta\mathbf{Z}')^{-1}\Delta\mathbf{Z})) \\
&\qquad ((\Delta\mathbf{X} + \alpha\beta'\mathbf{X})(\mathbf{I}_T - \Delta\mathbf{Z}'(\Delta\mathbf{Z}\Delta\mathbf{Z}')^{-1}\Delta\mathbf{Z}))'| \\[4pt]
&= K - \frac{T}{2}\log|(\Delta\mathbf{X} + \alpha\beta'\mathbf{X})\mathbf{M}(\Delta\mathbf{X} + \alpha\beta'\mathbf{X})'| \\[4pt]
&= K - \frac{T}{2}\log|\Delta\mathbf{X}\mathbf{M}\Delta\mathbf{X}' + \alpha\beta'\mathbf{X}\mathbf{M}\Delta\mathbf{X}' + \Delta\mathbf{X}\mathbf{M}(\alpha\beta'\mathbf{X})' + \alpha\beta'\mathbf{X}\mathbf{M}(\alpha\beta'\mathbf{X})'|
\end{aligned}
$$

where $\mathbf{M} = \mathbf{I}_T - \Delta\mathbf{Z}'(\Delta\mathbf{Z}\Delta\mathbf{Z}')^{-1}\Delta\mathbf{Z}$. Matrices of the form $\mathbf{A} = \mathbf{I} - \mathbf{B}'(\mathbf{BB}')^{-1}\mathbf{B}$ are called *projection matrices*. They are idempotent and symmetric, that is $\mathbf{AA} = \mathbf{A}^2 = \mathbf{A}$ and $\mathbf{A} = \mathbf{A}'$. The latter properties were used in the last three steps of the above derivations.

We will rewrite the CLF as follows. Define $\mathbf{R}_0 = \Delta\mathbf{X}\mathbf{M}$, $\mathbf{R}_1 = \mathbf{X}\mathbf{M}$ and

$$\mathbf{S}_{ij} = \frac{\mathbf{R}_i\mathbf{R}_j}{T}, \, i, j = 1, 2$$

We can then rewrite the CLF as follows:

$$l^{C\Pi}(\alpha\beta') = K - \frac{T}{2}\log|\mathbf{S}_{00} - \mathbf{S}_{10}\alpha\beta' - \mathbf{S}_{01}(\alpha\beta')' + \alpha\beta'\mathbf{S}_{11}(\alpha\beta')'|$$

The original analysis of Johansen obtained the same result applying the method of *reduced rank regression*. Reduced rank regressions are multiple regressions where the coefficient matrix is subject to constraints. The Johansen method eliminates the terms $\mathbf{F}$ by regressing $\Delta\mathbf{x}_t$ and $\mathbf{x}_{t-1}$ on $(\Delta\mathbf{x}_{t-1}, \Delta\mathbf{x}_{t-2}, \ldots, \Delta\mathbf{x}_{t-p+1})$ to obtain the following residuals:

$$\mathbf{R}_{0t} = \Delta\mathbf{x}_t + \mathbf{D}_1\Delta\mathbf{x}_{t-1} + \mathbf{D}_2\Delta\mathbf{x}_{t-2} + \cdots + \mathbf{D}_{p-1}\Delta\mathbf{x}_{t-p+1}$$

$$\mathbf{R}_{1t} = \Delta\mathbf{x}_{t-1} + \mathbf{E}_1\Delta\mathbf{x}_{t-1} + \mathbf{E}_2\Delta\mathbf{x}_{t-2} + \cdots + \mathbf{E}_{p-1}\Delta\mathbf{x}_{t-p+1}$$

where

$$\mathbf{D} = (\mathbf{D}_1, \mathbf{D}_2, ..., \mathbf{D}_{p-1}) = \Delta\mathbf{X}\Delta\mathbf{Z}'(\Delta\mathbf{Z}\Delta\mathbf{Z}')^{-1}$$

and

$$\mathbf{E} = (\mathbf{E}_1, \mathbf{E}_2, ..., \mathbf{E}_{p-1}) = \mathbf{X}\Delta\mathbf{Z}'(\Delta\mathbf{Z}\Delta\mathbf{Z}')^{-1}$$

The original model is therefore reduced to the following "simpler model":

$$\mathbf{R}_{0t} = \alpha\beta'\mathbf{R}_{1t} + \mathbf{u}_t$$

The likelihood function of this model depends only on $\mathbf{R}_{0t}$, $\mathbf{R}_{1t}$. It can be written as follows:

$$l(\alpha\beta') = K_1 - \frac{T}{2}\log\left|(\mathbf{R}_0 + \mathbf{R}_1(\alpha\beta'))'(\mathbf{R}_0 + \mathbf{R}_1(\alpha\beta'))\right|$$

where we define $\mathbf{R}_0$, $\mathbf{R}_1$ as above. If we also define $\mathbf{S}_{ij}$ as above, we obtain exactly the same form for the CLF:

$$l^{C\Pi}(\alpha\beta') = K - \frac{T}{2}\log\left|\mathbf{S}_{00} - \mathbf{S}_{10}\alpha\beta' - \mathbf{S}_{01}(\alpha\beta')' + \alpha\beta'\mathbf{S}_{11}(\alpha\beta')'\right|$$

We have now to find the maximum of this CLF. Note that this problem is not well identified because, given any solution α, β' and any nonsingular matrix $\mathbf{G}$, the following relationships hold:

$$\Pi = \alpha\beta' = \alpha\mathbf{G}\mathbf{G}^{-1}\beta' = \alpha^*\beta'^*$$

so that the matrices

$$\alpha^* = \alpha\mathbf{G}$$

$$\beta'^* = \mathbf{G}^{-1}\beta'$$

are also a solution. Additional conditions must therefore be imposed.

If the matrix $\Pi = \alpha\beta'$ were unrestricted, then maximization would yield

$$\Pi = S_{01}S_{11}^{-1}$$

However, our problem now is to find solutions that respect the cointegration condition, that is, the rank r of Π which is the common rank of α, β'. To achieve this goal, we can concentrate the CLF with respect to α and thus solve with respect to β'. By performing the rather lengthy computations, it can be demonstrated that we obtain a solution by solving the following eigenvalue problem:

$$\left|S_{10}S_{00}^{-1}S_{01} - \lambda S_{11}\right| = 0$$

This eigenvalue problem, together with normalizing conditions, will yield n eigenvalues λ_i and n eigenvectors Λ_i. In order to make this problem well determined, Johansen imposed the normalizing conditions: $\Lambda'S_{11}\Lambda = I$. Order the eigenvalues and choose the r eigenvectors Λ_i corresponding to the largest r eigenvalues. It can be demonstrated that a ML estimator of the matrix C is given by

$$\hat{\beta}' = (\hat{\Lambda}_1, ..., \hat{\Lambda}_r)$$

and an estimator of the matrix α by $\hat{\alpha} = S_{00}\hat{C}$. The maximum of the log-likelihood is

$$l_{\max} = K - \frac{T}{2}\log|S_{00}| - \frac{T}{2}\sum_{i=1}^{r}\log(1 - \lambda_i)$$

The solutions of the above eigenvalue problem, that is, the eigenvalues λ_i, can be interpreted as the canonical correlations between Δx_t and x_{t-1}. *Canonical correlations* are the maximum correlations between linear combinations of the Δx_t and x_{t-1}. We therefore see that the cointegrating relationships are those linear combinations of the levels x_{t-1} that are maximally correlated with linear combinations of the Δx_t after conditioning with the remaining terms.

Different types of normalizing conditions have been studied and are described in the literature. A general theory of long-run modeling that considers general nonlinear constraints on the matrix C was developed by Pesaran and Shin.[9] The interested reader should refer to their article.

Estimating the Number of Cointegrating Relationships

The Johansen ML estimation method and its extensions critically depend on correctly estimating the number r of cointegrating relationships. Two tests, in particular, have been suggested in relationship with the Johansen method: the trace test and the maximum eigenvalue test. The *trace test* tests the hypothesis that there are at most r cointegrating vectors while the *maximum eigenvalue test* tests the hypothesis that there are $r + 1$ cointegrating vectors against the hypothesis that there are r cointegrating vectors. The mathematical details are given in the Johansen paper discussed earlier. Lütkepohl, Saikkonen, and Trenkler provide an extensive discussion of the relative merit and power of the various forms of these tests.[10] Here we provide only a brief overview of these tests which are implemented in many standard statistical packages.

The trace test is immediately suggested by the Johansen procedure. Recall from the discussion earlier in this chapter that with the Johansen method the maximum of the log-likelihood function is

$$l_{max} = K - \frac{T}{2}\log|S_{00}| - \frac{T}{2}\sum_{i=1}^{r} \log(1 - \lambda_i)$$

The likelihood ratio test statistics for the hypothesis of at most r cointegrating vectors is

$$\lambda_{trace} = -T \sum_{i=r+1}^{n} \log(1 - \lambda_i)$$

where the sum is extended to the $n - r$ smallest eigenvalues. The likelihood ratio statistics for the maximum eigenvalue test is

$$\lambda_{max} = -T\log(1 - \lambda_{r+1})$$

[9] M. Hashem Pesaran and Yongcheol Shin, "Long-Run Structural Modelling," Chapter 11 in S. Strom (ed.), *Econometrics and Economic Theory in the 20th Century: The Ragnar Frisch Centennial Symposium* (Cambridge: Cambridge University Press, 2001).
[10] H. Lütkepohl, P. Saikkonen, and C. Trenkler, "Maximum Eigenvalue Versus Trace Tests for the Cointegrating Rank of a VAR Process," *Econometrics Journal* 4 (2001), pp. 287–310.

The asymptotic distribution of both test statistics are not normal. They are given by the trace, respectively, the maximum eigenvalue of a stochastic matrix formed with functionals of a Brownian motion. Critical values at different confidence levels have been tabulated and are used in many standard statistical packages.

MI Estimators in the Presence of Linear Trends

The above discussion assumed a zero intercept in the model and therefore no linear trends or nonzero intercepts in the process. If we add an intercept to a VAR model, we might obtain a linear trend in the variables. With cointegrated systems, there is the additional complication that a linear trend might or might not be present in the cointegrated variables. In other words, the cointegrating vectors transform the I(1) variables into stationary variables or into trend-stationary variables.

The original definition of cointegration in Engle and Granger excluded deterministic trends in the cointegrated variables.[11] We now distinguish between stochastic cointegration and deterministic cointegration. A set of I(1) variables is said to be stochastically cointegrated if there are linear combinations of these variables that are trend-stationary (i.e., stationary plus a deterministic trend). A set of I(1) variables are said to be deterministically cointegrated if there exist linear combinations which are stationary without any deterministic trend.

Therefore, when considering deterministic terms in a cointegrated VAR model, we cannot consider only constant intercepts but must include linear trends. Adding a constant term and a linear trend to the model variables as we did in the stable case, the estimation procedure described in the previous section remains valid.

Estimation with Canonical Correlations

The use of *canonical correlation analysis* (CCA) was first proposed by Bossaerts in 1988.[12] In 1995, Bewley and Yang provided a more rigorous foundation for CCA-based methodology which they called *level canonical correlation analysis* (LCCA) because the canonical correlations are computed in levels.[13] Cointegration tests based on CCA are based on the idea that canonical correlations should discriminate those

---

[11] R. F. Engle and C. W. J. Granger, "Cointegration and Error Correction: Representation, Estimation, and Testing," *Econometrica* 55 (1987), pp. 251–276.

[12] Peter Bossaerts, "Common Non-Stationary Components of Asset Prices," *Journal of Economic Dynamics and Control* 12 (1988), pp. 348–364.

[13] Ronald Bewley and Minxian Yang, "Tests for Cointegration Based on Canonical Correlation Analysis," *Journal of the American Statistical Association* 90 (1995), pp. 990–996.

linear combinations of variables that are I(1) from those that are I(0). In fact, integrated variables should be more predictable while stationary components should be less predictable.

Bossaerts proposed performing CCA and the use of the standard Dickey-Fuller (DF) test to identify those canonical variates that are I(1). He considers a model of the type

$$\Delta x_t = \alpha \beta' x_t + \varepsilon_t$$

After performing the CCA between Δx_t and x_t, the canonical variates are tested for unit roots. Bossaerts conjectured, without proof, that one can use the standard critical values of the DF test.

Bewley and Yang extended the methodology, allowing for deterministic trends and other variables explaining short-run dynamics. They proposed new tests, developed the asymptotic theory, and computed the critical values to determine the number of cointegrating vectors.

Computationally, the LCCA methodology of Bewley and Yang is not very different from that of Johansen. Following Bewley and Yang, the LCCA method proceeds as follows. First, if there are additional exogenous variables, they have to be removed regressing x_t and x_{t-1} on those variables. Let R_{0t} and R_{1t} denote the residuals of these regressions and perform the regression:

$$R_{0t} = B R_{1t} + u_t$$

The determination of the canonical correlations between R_{0t} and R_{1t} is formally done as in the Johansen method, that is, solving the following eigenvalue problem:

$$\left| S_{10} S_{00}^{-1} S_{01} - \lambda S_{11} \right| = 0$$

where

$$S_{ij} = \frac{R_i R_j}{T}, \, i, j = 1, 2$$

However, the interpretation of these quantities is different. Here we are seeking canonical correlations between variables in levels while in the Johansen methods we correlate both levels and differences. The LCCA method picks the largest eigenvalues as does the Johansen method. Bewley and Yang developed the asymptotic theory as well as four tests for cointegration, two DF-type tests, a trace test, and a maximum eigenvalue test. For each test they tabulated critical values for up to six-variables systems.

The asymptotic theory developed by Bewley and Yang shows that one can indeed use the standard unit root tests such as the Dickey-Fuller and Phillips tests, but the critical values depend on the number of variables and are not standard. Therefore, one cannot use the DF test with standard critical values, as conjectured by Bossaerts.

Estimation with Principal Component Analysis

Thus far we have discussed methodologies for estimating cointegrated systems based on OLS, ML, and CCA. In this section we analyze another important method based on *Principal Component Analysis* (PCA). PCA is a well-known statistical methodology that, given a set of multidimensional data, finds the directions of maximum variance. PCA-based methods are used in classical factor analysis of stationary returns.

The use of PCA-based methods for integrated variables was originally proposed by Stock and Watson.[14] They were the first to observe that the presence of r cointegrating vectors in n time series implies the presence of r common stochastic trends. This means that there are r independent linear combinations of the variables that are I(1) while the remaining n-r are I(0). In addition, it means that each of the n variables can be expressed as a linear combination of the common stochastic trends plus a stationary process.

Stock and Watson conjectured that those linear combinations that are I(1) must have the largest variance. Therefore, by performing a PCA on the variables in levels, one should be able to determine the cointegrating vectors by picking the largest eigenvalues. The Stock and Watson methodology proceeds as follows.

Suppose the data generation process is our usual VAR(p) model,

$$\mathbf{x}_t = \mathbf{A}_1\mathbf{x}_{t-1} + \mathbf{A}_2\mathbf{x}_{t-2} + \cdots + \mathbf{A}_p\mathbf{x}_{t-p} + \boldsymbol{\varepsilon}_t$$

where we assume for the moment that the intercept term is zero. Suppose also that the number of lags p have been determined independently. Next, perform the PCA of the variables $\mathbf{x}_t$. This entails solving the following eigenvalue problem:

$$\Omega\boldsymbol{\beta} = \mu\boldsymbol{\beta}$$

---

[14] James H. Stock and Mark W. Watson, "Testing for Common Trends," *Journal of the American Statistical Association* 83 (1988), pp. 1097–1107.

where Ω is the empirical covariance matrix of the $\mathbf{x}_t$, defined as

$$\Omega = \frac{1}{T} \sum_{t=1}^{T} \mathbf{x}_t \mathbf{x}_t'$$

and μ and β are respectively the eigenvalues and the eigenvectors to be determined.

Order the eigenvalues and choose the m largest eigenvalues μ_i, $i = 1$, ..., m. The corresponding eigenvectors β_i are the candidate cointegrating vectors. Forming the linear combinations $P_{i,t} = \beta_i \mathbf{x}_t$, we obtain the vector $\mathbf{P}_t = (P_{1,t}, \ldots, P_{m,t})'$ first m principal components. We must now check the hypothesis that these principal components are I(1) series and are not cointegrated among themselves.

In order to do this, the Stock and Watson method estimates the following stable VAR(p) model:

$$\Delta \mathbf{P}_t = \mathbf{A}_1 \Delta \mathbf{P}_{t-1} + \cdots + \mathbf{A}_{p-1} \Delta \mathbf{P}_{t-p+1} + \boldsymbol{\varepsilon}_t$$

and then computes

$$\hat{\mathbf{F}}_t = \mathbf{P}_t - \hat{\mathbf{A}}_1 \Delta \mathbf{P}_{t-1} - \cdots - \hat{\mathbf{A}}_{p-1} \Delta \mathbf{P}_{t-p+1}$$

Regress $\Delta \mathbf{F}_t$ on $\mathbf{F}_{t-1}$, compute the normalized eigenvalues of the regression matrix $\mathbf{B}$, and compare with the critical values tabulated in the Stock and Watson paper to test the null of m common trends against $m-q$ common trends.

If the VAR model exhibits a nonzero intercept, then there might be linear trends in the variables. This fact, in turn, raises the question of stochastic versus deterministic cointegration. The details of the computations are actually quite intricate.[15]

A major advantage of the PCA-based methodologies is that critical values depend only on the number of common trends and not on the number of time series involved. Therefore they can be used to determine a small number of common trends in a large number of time series.

Estimation with the Eigenvalues of the Companion Matrix

A univariate process is called *integrated of order one* if it can be written as: $x_t = \rho x_{t-1} + \eta_t$ where $\rho = 1$, and η_t is a stationary process. Dickey and Fuller established the asymptotic distribution of ρ and tabulated the

---

[15] The interested reader should consult the original Stock and Watson paper.

critical values that now form the basis of the DF and ADF unit root test. Ahlgren and Nyblom[16] developed an equivalent methodology for multivariate processes. They studied a N-variate, VAR(1) process of the form:

$$\mathbf{x}_t = \Pi\mathbf{x}_{t-1} + \boldsymbol{\varepsilon}_t$$

The major result of their work is that the number of cointegrating relationships depends on the eigenvalues of the autoregressive matrix. Ahlgren and Nyblom determined the asymptotic distribution of the eigenvalues of the autoregressive matrix estimated with OLS methods and computed critical values. The methodology can be extended to VAR models of any order by transforming the original model into a VAR(1) model and considering the companion matrix.

STATE-SPACE MODELS

All ARMA and VAR models can be expressed as *State-Space Models*.
The general form of a state-space model is the following:

$$\mathbf{x}_t = \mathbf{C}\mathbf{z}_t + \mathbf{D}\mathbf{u}_t + \boldsymbol{\varepsilon}_t$$
$$\mathbf{z}_{t+1} = \mathbf{A}\mathbf{z}_t + \mathbf{B}\mathbf{u}_t + \boldsymbol{\eta}_t$$
$$t = 1, 2, \dots$$

where

- $\mathbf{x}_t$ is the n-dimensional vector of observable output series
- $\mathbf{z}_t$ is the s-dimensional vector of latent (nonobservable) state variables
- $\mathbf{u}_t$ is a m-dimensional vector of deterministic inputs
- $\boldsymbol{\varepsilon}_t$ is the n-dimensional observation white noise
- $\boldsymbol{\eta}_t$ is the s-dimensional transition equation white noise
- $\mathbf{A}$ is the $n \times s$ observation matrix
- $\mathbf{B}$ is the $n \times m$ input matrix of the observation equation
- $\mathbf{C}$ is the $s \times s$ transition matrix
- $\mathbf{D}$ is the $s \times m$ input matrix of the transition equation

The first equation, called the *observation equation*, is a linear regression of the output variables over the state variables and the input

---

[16] Niklas Ahlgren and Jukka Nyblom, "A General Test for the Cointegrating Rank in Vector Autoregressive Models," Working Paper No 499, 2003, Swedish School of Economics and Business Administration.

variables, while the second equation, called the (*state*) *transition equation* is a VAR(1) model that describes the dynamics of the state variables. In general it is assumed that the system starts from a state z_0 and an initial input u_0.

The joint noise process, $(\varepsilon_t', \eta_t')'$ is a zero-mean, IID sequence with variance-covariance matrix

$$\begin{bmatrix} \Omega_\varepsilon & \Omega_{\varepsilon\eta} \\ \Omega_{\eta\varepsilon} & \Omega_\eta \end{bmatrix}$$

Observe that it is possible to write different variants of state-space models. For example, we could define state-space processes with only one noise process so that $\eta_t = \mathbf{H}\varepsilon_t$. Observe also that it is not restrictive to assume that the transition equation is a VAR(1) model. In fact, all VAR(p) models are equivalent to a larger VAR(1) model obtained adding variables for each additional lag.

Let's now establish the equivalence with ARMA/VAR models. To see the equivalence of state-space and ARMA models, consider the following ARMA(p,q) model:

$$x_t = \sum_{i=1}^{p} \varphi_i x_{t-i} + \sum_{j=0}^{q} \psi_j \varepsilon_{t-j}, \quad \psi_0 = 1$$

This model is equivalent to the following state-space model:

$$x_t = \mathbf{C}z_t$$
$$z_t = \mathbf{A}z_{t-1} + \varepsilon_t$$

where

$$\mathbf{C} = \begin{bmatrix} \varphi_1 \dots \varphi_p & 1 & \psi_1 \dots \psi_q \end{bmatrix}$$

$$z_t = \begin{bmatrix} x_{t-1} \\ \vdots \\ x_{t-p} \\ \varepsilon_t \\ \varepsilon_{t-1} \\ \vdots \\ \varepsilon_{t-q} \end{bmatrix}$$

and

$$
\mathbf{A} = \begin{bmatrix}
\varphi_1 & \cdots & \varphi_p & 1 & \psi_1 & \cdots & \psi_{q-1} & \psi_q \\
1 & \cdots & 0 & 0 & 0 & \cdots & 0 & 0 \\
\vdots & \vdots & \vdots & \vdots & \vdots & \vdots & \vdots & \vdots \\
0 & \cdots & 1 & 0 & 0 & \cdots & 0 & 0 \\
0 & \cdots & 0 & 0 & 0 & \cdots & 0 & 0 \\
\vdots & \vdots & \vdots & \vdots & \vdots & \vdots & \vdots & \vdots \\
0 & \cdots & 0 & 0 & 0 & \cdots & 1 & 0
\end{bmatrix}
$$

The converse also holds. It can be demonstrated that a state-space model admits a VARMA representation.

Neither ARMA nor state-space representations are unique. However, it can be demonstrated that a minimal state-space representation exists for any model that admits an ARMA and state-space representation. A minimal representation is a state-space model of minimal dimension, that is, such that any other equivalent model cannot have state vector of smaller dimension.

The solutions of a state-space model are clearly determined by the transition equation. Therefore solutions of a state-space model are determined by the solutions of a VAR(1) model. We know from our above discussion of VAR models that these solutions are sums of exponentials and/or sinusoidal functions. Exhibit 11.4 shows the solutions of bivariate VAR(2) model. The two variables x and y exhibit oscillating behavior. This VAR(2) model is equivalent to a state-space model with four state variables. Two of the variables are x and y while the other two are their lagged values.

Maximum Likelihood Estimation

The estimation of linear state-space models based on maximum likelihood (ML) principles requires the determination of the log-likelihood, which is a function of observables and hidden variables plus deterministic inputs. Hidden variables, however, can only be estimated, not observed. We use the Kalman filter to replace unknown hidden variables with their best estimates. We describe first the Kalman filter and then show how to compute the log-likelihood function and applying the expected maximization method.

Estimation of the Kalman Filter

The Kalman filter allows us to obtain, filtered, smoothed, or predicted state-variable estimates:

EXHIBIT 11.4   Solutions of a Bivariate VAR(2) Model

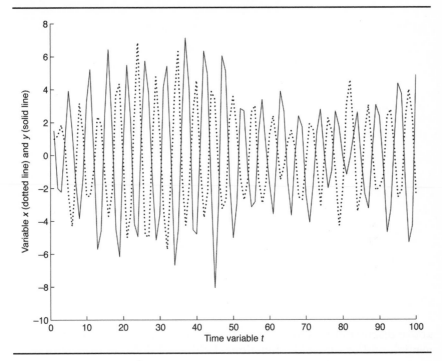

- *Filtering*, which computes the present state conditional to all the observations up to the present time.
- *Smoothing*, which computes the state at intermediate dates conditional on all the observations up to the present date.
- *Forecasting*, which forecasts the state at a future date conditional on all the observations up to the present date.

We first describe the Kalman filter using the state-space model specified above with the additional assumption that the noise terms are normally distributed. The assumption of normality can be relaxed. (We will see later how the filter is modified relaxing the assumption of normality.) We need to introduce the following notation—standard in the Kalman filter literature—to express compactly the various conditional means. We need to define the following four variables:

1. The conditional mean of the state variables at time t given observations up to time t:

$$z_{t|t} = E(z_t | x_1, ..., x_t)$$

2. The conditional mean of the observables and of the state variables at time t given observations up to time $t - 1$:

$$z_{t|t-1} = E(z_t | x_1, ..., x_{t-1})$$
$$x_{t|t-1} = E(x_t | x_1, ..., x_{t-1})$$

3. The mean squared errors of forecasts:

$$\Omega_{z|t} = E((z_t - z_{t|t})(z_t - z_{t|t})')$$
$$\Omega_{z|t-1} = E((z_t - z_{t|t-1})(z_t - z_{t|t-1})')$$
$$\Omega_{x|t-1} = E((x_t - x_{t|t-1})(x_t - x_{t|t-1})')$$

4. The residuals of the regression of the observable on its own past:

$$\tilde{x} = x_t - x_{t|t-1} = x_t - Az_{t|t-1}$$

The Kalman filter is a recursive methodology for computing past, present, and future states given a set of observables up to the present state. Starting from the initial period, the filter computes the conditional mean and the conditional covariance matrix of the states step by step. Let us now look at the four steps of the recursive equations of the Kalman filter: the prediction step, the correction step, the forecasting step, and the smoothing step.

The Prediction Step

The *prediction step* predicts the state and the variables one step ahead for every time $1 \le t \le T$ given the present state:

$$z_{t|t-1} = Az_{t-1|t-1} + Bu_{t-1}$$
$$x_{t|t-1} = Cz_{t|t-1} + Du_t$$

The covariance matrices of the one-step-ahead prediction error of the states and the variables are

$$\Omega_z(t|t-1) = A\Omega_z(t-1|t-1)A' + \Omega_\eta$$
$$\Omega_x(t|t-1) = C\Omega_z(t|t-1)C' + \Omega_\varepsilon$$

The Correction Step

The *correction step* improves the forecast made in the prediction step, taking into account the covariance matrix. The role played by the conditional covariance matrix in improving forecasts was the key intuition of Kalman. The correction step is written as follows:

$$z_{t|t} = z_{t|t-1} + P_t(x_t - x_{t|t-1})$$
$$\Omega_z(t|t) = \Omega_z(t|t-1) - P_t\Omega_x(t|t-1)P'_t$$

where $P_t = \Omega_z(t|t-1)A'\Omega_x(t|t-1)^{-1}$ is called the *filter gain matrix*.

The Forecasting Step

The *forecasting step* forecasts both the state and the variables s steps ahead for every time $t = T + s > T$ given the present state. It is based on the following recursive relationships:

$$z_{t|T} = Az_{t-1|T} + Bu_{t-1}$$
$$x_{t|T} = Cz_{t|T} + Du_t$$

The forecasting step also predicts the covariance matrix of the states and the variables one step ahead:

$$\Omega_z(t|T) = A\Omega_z(t-1|T)A' + \Omega_\eta$$
$$\Omega_x(t|T) = C\Omega_z(t|T)C' + \Omega_\varepsilon$$

The Smoothing Step

The *smoothing step* computes the states at intermediate times $t < T$. It is computed recursively backwards with the following recursive equations:

$$z_{t|T} = z_{t|t} + S_t(z_{t+1|T} - z_{t+1|t})$$
$$\Omega_z(t|T) = \Omega_z(t|t) - S_t[\Omega_z(t+1|t) - \Omega_z(t+1|T)]S'_t$$

where $S_t = \Omega_z(t|t)A'\Omega_z(t+1|t)^{-1}$ is called the *Kalman smoothing matrix*.

The filter is initialized with the initial conditions (i.e., the initial state z_0 and the initial input u_0) and computations are carried out recursively to the desired time.

Note that if the noise terms are not normally distributed but their second order moment still exists, all of the recursion equations remain valid.

The Log-Likelihood Function

To compute the log-likelihood of the model, first arrange all the model parameters, that is the four matrices $\mathbf{A}$, $\mathbf{B}$, $\mathbf{C}$, $\mathbf{D}$, and the covariance matrices, in one parameter vector $\boldsymbol{\theta}$. The model likelihood has the following expression:

$$
\begin{aligned}
f(\mathbf{x}_1, ..., \mathbf{x}_T; \boldsymbol{\theta}) &= f(\mathbf{x}_1; \boldsymbol{\theta}) f(\mathbf{x}_2, ..., \mathbf{x}_T | \mathbf{x}_1; \boldsymbol{\theta}) \\
&= f(\mathbf{x}_1; \boldsymbol{\theta}) f(\mathbf{x}_2 | \mathbf{x}_1; \boldsymbol{\theta}) ... (f(\mathbf{x}_T | \mathbf{x}_1, ..., \mathbf{x}_{T-1}; \boldsymbol{\theta}))
\end{aligned}
$$

Assuming that the noise is normally distributed then

$$
(\mathbf{x}_t | \mathbf{x}_1, ..., \mathbf{x}_{t-1}; \boldsymbol{\theta}) \sim N(\mathbf{x}_{t|t-1}, \boldsymbol{\Omega}_{\mathbf{x}}(t|t-1))
$$

Therefore we can write the log-likelihood as follows:

$$
\begin{aligned}
\log f(\mathbf{x}_1, ..., \mathbf{x}_{t-1}; \boldsymbol{\theta}) = -\frac{NT}{2}\log(2\pi) - \frac{1}{2}\sum_{t=1}^{T} \log|\boldsymbol{\Omega}_{\mathbf{x}}(t|t-1)| \\
-\frac{1}{2}\sum_{t=1}^{T} ((\mathbf{x}_t - \mathbf{x}_{t|t-1})' \boldsymbol{\Omega}_{\mathbf{x}}(t|t-1)^{-1} (\mathbf{x}_t - \mathbf{x}_{t|t-1}))
\end{aligned}
$$

We can see from the above expression that all quantities that appear in the log-likelihood function can be computed using the Kalman filter. The Kalman filter provides a convenient recursive procedure for computing the log-likelihood and performing ML estimates.

CONCEPTS EXPLAINED IN THIS CHAPTER (IN ORDER OF PRESENTATION)

Cointegration
Cointegrated processes
Reduction of order of integration
Common trends
Long-run equilibrium
Fractional cointegration
Stochastic and deterministic cointegration
Error correction models (ECM)
Estimation of cointegrated VAR with LS methods
ML estimators of cointegrated VAR
Johansen method

Concentrated likelihood
Reduced rank regression
Canonical correlations
Trace test
Maximum eigenvalue test
Estimation with linear trends
Canonical correlation analysis (CCA)
Estimation of cointegrated VAR with principal components
Estimation with the eigenvalues of the companion matrix
State-space models
Observation matrix
Transition matrix
Equivalence VARMA state-space
Estimation of state space models with ML methods
Kalman filters
Filtering
Smoothing
Forecasting
Prediction step
Correction step
Forecasting step
Smoothing step
Likelihood of state-space models

CHAPTER 12

Robust Estimation

I n this chapter we discuss methods for *robust estimation*, with particular emphasis on the robust estimation of regressions. Robust estimation is a topic of robust statistics. Therefore we first introduce the
general concepts and methods of robust statistics and then apply them
to regression analysis. In particular, we will introduce robust regression
estimators and robust regression diagnostics.

ROBUST STATISTICS

Robust statistics addresses the problem of making estimates that are
insensitive to small changes in the basic assumptions of the statistical
models employed. The concepts and methods of robust statistics origi-
nated in the 1950s. The technical term "robust statistics" was coined by
G. E. P. Box in 1953. However, the concepts of robust statistics had
been used much earlier, for example by the physicist Arthur Eddington
and the geophysicist Harold Jeffreys.

Statistical models are based on a set of assumptions; the most
important include (1) the distribution of key variables, for example the
normal distribution of errors, and (2) the model specification, for example model linearity or nonlinearity. Some of these assumptions are critical to the estimation process: if they are violated, the estimates become
unreliable. Robust statistics (1) assesses the changes in estimates due to
small changes in the basic assumptions and (2) creates new estimates
that are insensitive to small changes in some of the assumptions. The
focus of our exposition is to make estimates robust to small changes in
the distribution of errors and, in particular, to the presence of outliers.

Robust statistics is also useful to separate the contribution of the
tails from the contribution of the body of the data. We can say that

robust statistics and classical nonrobust statistics are complementary. By conducting a robust analysis, one can better articulate important econometric findings. We will see later examples of how robust statistics sheds new light on a number of well-known empirical findings.[1]

As observed by Peter Huber, *robust, distribution-free,* and *nonparametrical* seem to be closely related properties but actually are not.[2] For example, the sample mean and the sample median are nonparametric estimates of the mean and the median but the mean is not robust to outliers. In fact, changes of one single observation might have unbounded effects on the mean while the median is insensitive to changes of up to half the sample. Robust methods assume that there are indeed parameters in the distributions under study and attempt to minimize the effects of outliers as well as erroneous assumptions on the shape of the distribution.

A general definition of robustness is, by nature, quite technical. The reason is that we need to define robustness with respect to changes in distributions. That is, we need to make precise the concept that small changes in the distribution, which is a function, result in small changes in the estimate, which is a number.[3] Let's first give an intuitive, nontechnical overview of the modern concept of robustness and how to measure robustness.

---

[1] For example, see Anna Chernobai and Svetlozar T. Rachev, "Applying Robust Methods to Operation Risk Modeling," for an application of robust methods to the modeling of the tail behavior in operational risk.

[2] Huber's book is a standard reference on robust statistics: Peter J. Huber, *Robust Statistics* (New York: John Wiley & Sons, Inc., 1981). See also, C. Goodall, "M-Estimators of Location: An Outline of the Theory," in David C. Hoaglin, Frederick Mosteller, and John W. Tukey (eds.), *Understanding Robust and Exploratory Data Analysis* (New York: John Wiley & Sons, 1983), pp. 339–403; F. R. Hampel, E. M. Ronchetti, P. J. Rousseeuw, and W. A. Stahel, *Robust Statistics: The Approach Based on Influence Functions* (New York: John Wiley & Sons, 1986); P. W. Holland and R. E. Welsch, "Robust Regression Using Iteratively Reweighted Least-Squares." *Communications in Statistics: Theory and Methods* A6, 9 (1977), pp. 813–827; L. A. Jaeckel, "Estimating Regression Coefficients by Minimizing the Dispersion of the Residuals," *Annals of Mathematical Statistics* 43 (1972), pp. 1449–1458; R. Koenker and G. Basset Jr., "Regression Quantiles," *Econometrica* 36 (1978), pp. 33–50; P. J. Rousseeuw and A. M. Leroy, *Robust Regression and Outlier Detection* (New York: John Wiley & Sons, 1987); R. A. Maronna, R. D. Martin, and V. J. Yohai, *Robust Statistics: Theory and Methods* (Hoboken, NJ: John Wiley & Sons, 2006); and J. W. Tukey, "A Survey of Sampling from Contaminated Distributions," in I. Olkin, S. G. Ghurye, W. Hoeffding, W. G. Madow, and H. B. Mann (eds.), *Contributions to Probability and Statistics, Essays in Honor of Harold Hotelling* (Stanford, CA: Stanford University Press, 1960), pp. 448–485.

[3] To this end, we need to define topological and metric concepts on the functional space of distributions.

Qualitative and Quantitative Robustness

In this section we introduce the concepts of qualitative and quantitative robustness of estimators. Estimators are functions of the sample data. Given an N-sample of data $\mathbf{X} = (x_1, \ldots, x_N)'$ from a population with a cdf $F(x)$, depending on parameter θ_∞, an estimator for θ_∞ is a function $\hat{\vartheta} = \vartheta_N(x_1, \ldots, x_N)$. Consider those estimators that can be written as functions of the cumulative empirical distribution function:

$$F_N(x) = N^{-1} \sum_{i=1}^{N} I(x_i \le x)$$

where I is the indicator function. For these estimators we can write

$$\hat{\vartheta} = \vartheta_N(F_N)$$

Most estimators, in particular the ML estimators, can be written in this way with probability 1. In general, when $N \to \infty$ then $F_N(x) \to F(x)$ almost surely and $\hat{\vartheta}_N \to \vartheta_\infty$ in probability and almost surely. The estimator $\hat{\vartheta}_N$ is a random variable that depends on the sample. Under the distribution F, it will have a probability distribution $L_F(\vartheta_N)$. Intuitively, statistics defined as functionals of a distribution are robust if they are continuous with respect to the distribution. In 1968, Hampel introduced a technical definition of qualitative robustness based on metrics of the functional space of distributions.[4] The Hampel definition states that an estimator is robust for a given distribution F if small deviations from F in the given metric result in small deviations from $L_F(\vartheta_N)$ in the same metric or eventually in some other metric for any sequence of samples of increasing size. The definition of robustness can be made quantitative by assessing quantitatively how changes in the distribution F affect the distribution $L_F(\vartheta_N)$.

Resistant Estimators

An estimator is called *resistant* if it is insensitive to changes in one single observation.[5] Given an estimator $\hat{\vartheta} = \vartheta_N(F_N)$, we want to understand

---

[4] F. R. Hampel, "A General Qualitative Definition of Robustness," *Annals of Mathematical Statistics* 42 (1971), pp. 1887–1896.

[5] For an application to the estimation of the estimation of beta, see R. Douglas Martin and Timothy T. Simin, "Outlier Resistant Estimates of Beta," *Financial Analysts Journal* (September–October 2003), pp. 56–58. We discuss this application at the end of this chapter.

what happens if we add a new observation of value x to a large sample. To this end we define the *influence curve* (IC), also called *influence function*. The IC is a function of x given ϑ, and F is defined as follows:

$$IC_{\vartheta,\,F}(x) \;=\; \lim_{s \to 0} \frac{\vartheta((1-s)F + s\delta_x) - \vartheta(F)}{s}$$

where δ_x denotes a point mass 1 at x (i.e., a probability distribution concentrated at the single point x). As we can see from its previous definition, the IC is a function of the size of the single observation that is added. In other words, the IC measures the influence of a single observation x on a statistics ϑ for a given distribution F. In practice, the influence curve is generated by plotting the value of the computed statistic with a single point of X added to Y against that X value. For example, the IC of the mean is a straight line. Several aspects of the influence curve are of particular interest:

- Is the curve "bounded" as the X values become extreme? Robust statistics should be bounded. That is, a robust statistic should not be unduly influenced by a single extreme point.
- What is the general behavior as the X observation becomes extreme? For example, does it becomes smoothly down-weighted as the values become extreme?
- What is the influence if the X point is in the "center" of the Y points?.

Let's now introduce concepts that are important in applied work. We then introduce the robust estimators.

Breakdown Bound

The *breakdown* (BD) *bound* or *point* is the largest possible fraction of observations for which there is a bound on the change of the estimate when that fraction of the sample is altered without restrictions. For example, we can change up to 50% of the sample points without provoking unbounded changes of the median. On the contrary, changes of one single observation might have unbounded effects on the mean.

Rejection Point

The *rejection point* is defined as the point beyond which the IC becomes zero. Note that observations beyond the rejection point make no contribution to the final estimate except, possibly, through the auxiliary scale estimate. Estimators that have a finite rejection point are said to be redescending and are well protected against very large outliers. However, a finite rejection point usually results in the underestimation of scale. This is because when the samples near the tails of a distribution are ignored, an insufficient fraction of the observations may remain for the estimation process. This in turn adversely affects the efficiency of the estimator.

Gross Error Sensitivity

The *gross error sensitivity* expresses asymptotically the maximum effect that a contaminated observation can have on the estimator. It is the maximum absolute value of the IC.

Local Shift Sensitivity

The *local shift sensitivity* measures the effect of the removal of a mass at y and its reintroduction at x. For continuous and differentiable IC, the local shift sensitivity is given by the maximum absolute value of the slope of IC at any point.

Winsor's Principle

Winsor's principle states that all distributions are normal in the middle.

M-Estimators

M-estimators are those estimators that are obtained by minimizing a function of the sample data. Suppose that we are given an N-sample of data $\mathbf{X} = (x_1, \ldots, x_N)'$. The estimator $T(x_1, \ldots, x_N)$ is called an M-estimator if it is obtained by solving the following minimum problem:

$$T = \arg \min_t \left\{ J = \sum_{i=1}^{N} \rho(x_i, t) \right\}$$

where $\rho(x_i, t)$ is an arbitrary function. Alternatively, if $\rho(x_i, t)$ is a smooth function, we can say that T is an M-estimator if it is determined by solving the equations:

$$\sum_{i=1}^{N} \psi(x_i, t) = 0$$

where

$$\psi(x_i, t) = \frac{\partial \rho(x_i, t)}{\partial t}$$

When the M-estimator is equivariant, that is $T(x_1 + a, \ldots, x_N + a) = T(x_1, \ldots, x_N) + a, \forall a \in R$, we can write ψ and ρ in terms of the residuals $x - t$. Also, in general, an auxiliary scale estimate, S, is used to obtain the scaled residuals $r = (x - t)/S$. If the estimator is also equivariant to changes of scale, we can write

$$\psi(x, t) = \psi\left(\frac{x - t}{S}\right) = \psi(r)$$

$$\rho(x, t) = \rho\left(\frac{x - t}{S}\right) = \rho(r)$$

ML estimators are M-estimators with $\rho = -\log f$, where f is the probability density. (Actually the name M-estimators means maximum likelihood-type estimators.) LS estimators are also M-estimators.

The IC of M-estimators has a particularly simple form. In fact, it can be demonstrated that the IC is proportional to the function ψ:

$$IC = \text{Constant} \times \psi$$

L-Estimators

Consider an N-sample $(x_1, \ldots, x_N)'$. Order the samples so that $x_{(1)} \leq x_{(2)} \leq \ldots \leq x_{(N)}$. The i-th element $X = x_{(i)}$ of the ordered sample is called the *i-th order statistic*. *L-estimators* are estimators obtained as a linear combination of order statistics:

$$L = \sum_{i=1}^{N} a_i x_{(i)}$$

where the a_i are fixed constants. Constants are typically normalized so that

$$\sum_{i=1}^{N} a_i = 1$$

An important example of an L-estimator is the *trimmed mean*. The trimmed mean is a mean formed excluding a fraction of the highest and/

or lowest samples. In this way the mean, which is not a robust estimator, becomes less sensitive to outliers.

R-Estimators

R-estimators are obtained by minimizing the sum of residuals weighted by functions of the rank of each residual. The functional to be minimized is the following:

$$\arg\min\left\{ J = \sum_{i=1}^{N} a(R_i) r_i \right\}$$

where R_i is the rank of the i-th residual r_i and a is a nondecreasing score function that satisfies the condition

$$\sum_{i=1}^{N} a(R_i) = 0$$

The Least Median of Squares Estimator

Instead of minimizing the sum of squared residuals, as in LS, to estimate the parameter vector, Rousseuw[6] proposed minimizing the median of squared residuals, referred to as the *least median of squares* (LMedS) *estimator*. This estimator effectively trims the $N/2$ observations having the largest residuals, and uses the maximal residual value in the remaining set as the criterion to be minimized. It is hence equivalent to *assuming* that the noise proportion is 50%.

LMedS is unwieldy from a computational point of view because of its nondifferentiable form. This means that a quasi-exhaustive search on all possible parameter values needs to be done to find the global minimum.

The Least Trimmed of Squares Estimator

The *least trimmed of squares* (LTS) *estimator* offers an efficient way to find robust estimates by minimizing the objective function given by

$$\left\{ J = \sum_{i=1}^{h} r_{(i)}^2 \right\}$$

---

[6] P. Rousseuw, "Least Median of Squares Regression," *Journal of the American Statistical Association* 79 (1984), pp. 871–890.

where $r_{(i)}^2$ is the i-th smallest residual or distance when the residuals are ordered in ascending order, that is: $r_{(1)}^2 \le r_{(2)}^2 \le \cdots \le r_{(N)}^2$ and h is the number of data points whose residuals we want to include in the sum. This estimator basically finds a robust estimate by identifying the $N - h$ points having the largest residuals as outliers, and discarding (trimming) them from the dataset. The resulting estimates are essentially LS estimates of the trimmed dataset. Note that h should be as close as possible to the number of points in the data set that we do not consider outliers.

Reweighted Least Squares Estimator

Some algorithms explicitly cast their objective functions in terms of a set of weights that distinguish between inliers and outliers. However, these weights usually depend on a scale measure that is also difficult to estimate. For example, the *reweighted least squares* (RLS) estimator uses the following objective function:

$$\arg \min \left\{ J = \sum_{i=1}^{N} \omega_i r_i^2 \right\}$$

where r_i are robust residuals resulting from an approximate LMedS or LTS procedure. Here the weights ω_i trim outliers from the data used in LS minimization, and can be computed after a preliminary approximate step of LMedS or LTS.

Robust Estimators of the Center

The mean estimates the center of a distribution but it is not resistant. *Resistant estimators* of the center are the following:[7]

■ *Trimmed mean.* Suppose $x_{(1)} \le x_{(2)} \le \ldots \le x_{(N)}$ are the sample order statistics (that is, the sample sorted). The trimmed mean $T_N(\delta, 1 - \gamma)$ is defined as follows:

$$T_N(\delta, 1 - \gamma) = \frac{1}{U_N - L_N} \sum_{j = L_N + 1}^{U_N} x_j$$

$$\delta, \gamma \in (0, 0.5), \ L_N = \text{floor}[N\delta], \ U_N = \text{floor}[N\gamma]$$

---

[7] This discussion draws from Chernobai and Rachev, "Applying Robust Methods to Operation Risk Modeling."

■ *Winsorized mean.* The Winsorized mean $\overline{X}_W$ is the mean of Winsorized data:

$$y_j = \begin{cases} x_{I_N+1} & j \le L_N \\ x_j & L_N+1 \le j \le U_N \\ x_j = x_{U_N+1} & j \ge U_N+1 \end{cases}$$

$$\overline{X}_W = \overline{Y}$$

■ *Median.* The median Med(X) is defined as that value that occupies a central position in a sample order statistics:

$$\text{Med}(\mathbf{X}) = \begin{cases} x_{((N+1)/2)} & \text{if } N \text{ is odd} \\ ((x_{(N/2)} + x_{(N/2+1)})/2) & \text{if } N \text{ is even} \end{cases}$$

Robust Estimators of the Spread

The variance is a classical estimator of the spread but it is not robust. Robust estimators of the spread are the following:[8]

■ *Median absolute deviation.* The median absolute deviation (MAD) is defined as the median of the absolute value of the difference between a variable and its median, that is,

$$\text{MAD} = \text{MED}|X - \text{MED}(X)|$$

■ *Interquartile range.* The interquartile range (IQR) is defined as the difference between the highest and lowest quartile:

$$\text{IQR} = Q(0.75) - Q(0.25)$$

where $Q(0.75)$ and $Q(0.25)$ are the 75th and 25th percentiles of the data.

■ *Mean absolute deviation.* The mean absolute deviation (MeanAD) is defined as follows:

---

[8] This discussion draws from Chernobai and Rachev, "Applying Robust Methods to Operation Risk Modeling."

$$\frac{1}{N} \sum_{j=1}^{N} |x_j - \mathrm{MED}(\mathbf{X})|$$

- *Winsorized standard deviation.* The Winsorized standard deviation is the standard deviation of Winsorized data, that is,

$$\sigma_W = \frac{\sigma_N}{(U_N - L_N)/N}$$

Illustration of Robust Statistics

To illustrate the effect of robust statistics, consider the series of daily returns of Nippon Oil in the period 1986 through 2005 depicted in Exhibit 12.1. If we compute the mean, the trimmed mean, and the median we obtain the following results:

EXHIBIT 12.1 Daily Returns Nippon Oil: 1986–2005

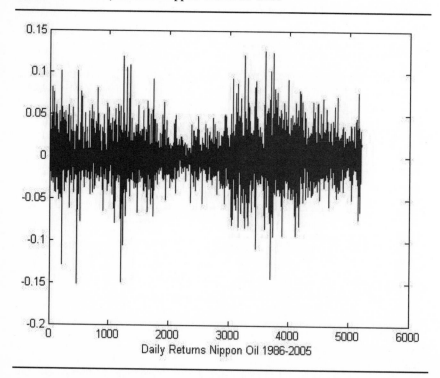

Daily Returns Nippon Oil 1986-2005

Mean $= 3.8396e{-}005$
Trimmed mean $(20\%)^{9}$ $= -4.5636e{-}004$
Median $= 0$

In order to show the robustness properties of these estimators, let's multiply the 10% highest/lowest returns by 2. If we compute again the same quantities we obtain:

Mean $= 4.4756e{-}004$
Trimmed mean (20%) $= -4.4936e{-}004$
Median $= 0$

While the mean is largely affected, the median is not affected and the trimmed mean is only marginally affected by doubling the value of 20% of the points.

We can perform the same exercise for measures of the spread. If we compute the standard deviation, the IQR, and the MAD we obtain the following results:

Standard deviation $= 0.0229$
IQR $= 0.0237$
MAD $= 0.0164$

Let's multiply the 10% highest/lowest returns by 2. The new values are:

Standard deviation $= 0.0415$
IQR $= 0.0237$
MAD $= 0.0248$

The MAD are less affected by the change than the standard deviation while the IQR is not affected. If we multiply the 25% highest/lowest returns by 2 we obtain the following results:

Standard deviation $= 0.0450$
IQR $= 0.0237$ (but suddenly changes if we add/subtract one element)
MAD $= 0.0299$

ROBUST ESTIMATORS OF REGRESSIONS

Let's now apply the concepts of robust statistics to the estimation of regression coefficients, which is sensitive to outliers.

---

[9] Trimmed mean (20%) means that we exclude the 20%/2 = 10% highest and lowest observations.

Identifying robust estimators of regressions is a rather difficult problem. In fact, different choices of estimators, robust or not, might lead to radically different estimates of slopes and intercepts. Consider the following linear regression model:

$$Y = \beta_0 + \sum_{i=1}^{N} \beta_i X_i + \varepsilon$$

If data are organized in matrix form as usual,

$$\mathbf{Y} = \begin{pmatrix} Y_1 \\ \vdots \\ Y_T \end{pmatrix}, \mathbf{X} = \begin{pmatrix} 1 & X_{11} & \cdots & X_{N1} \\ \vdots & \vdots & \ddots & \vdots \\ 1 & X_{1T} & \cdots & X_{NT} \end{pmatrix}, \boldsymbol{\beta} = \begin{pmatrix} \beta_1 \\ \vdots \\ \beta_N \end{pmatrix}, \boldsymbol{\varepsilon} = \begin{pmatrix} \varepsilon_1 \\ \vdots \\ \varepsilon_T \end{pmatrix}$$

then the regression equation takes the form,

$$\mathbf{Y} = \mathbf{X}\boldsymbol{\beta} + \boldsymbol{\varepsilon}$$

The standard nonrobust LS estimation of regression parameters minimizes the sum of squared residuals,

$$\sum_{i=1}^{T} \varepsilon_t^2 = \sum_{i=1}^{T} \left(Y_i - \sum_{j=0}^{N} \beta_{ij} X_{ij} \right)^2$$

or, equivalently, as explained in the previous chapter, solves the system of $N + 1$ equations,

$$\sum_{i=1}^{T} \left(Y_i - \sum_{j=0}^{N} \beta_{ij} X_{ij} \right) X_{ij} = 0$$

or, in matrix notation, $\mathbf{X}'\mathbf{X}\boldsymbol{\beta} = \mathbf{X}'\mathbf{Y}$. The solution of this system is

$$\hat{\boldsymbol{\beta}} = (\mathbf{X}'\mathbf{X})^{-1}\mathbf{X}'\mathbf{Y}$$

The fitted values (i.e, the LS estimates of the expectations) of the $\mathbf{Y}$ are

$$\hat{\mathbf{Y}} = \mathbf{X}(\mathbf{X}'\mathbf{X})^{-1}\mathbf{X}'\mathbf{Y} = \mathbf{H}\mathbf{Y}$$

The **H** matrix is called the *hat matrix* because it puts a hat on, that is, it computes the expectation $\hat{\mathbf{Y}}$ of the **Y**. The hat matrix **H** is a symmetric $T \times T$ projection matrix; that is, the following relationship holds: **HH** = **H**. The matrix **H** has N eigenvalues equal to 1 and $T - N$ eigenvalues equal to 0. Its diagonal elements, $h_i \equiv h_{ii}$ satisfy:

$$0 \le h_i \le 1$$

and its trace (i.e., the sum of its diagonal elements) is equal to N:

$$tr(\mathbf{H}) = N$$

Under the assumption that the errors are independent and identically distributed with mean zero and variance σ^2, it can be demonstrated that the $\hat{\mathbf{Y}}$ are consistent, that is, $\hat{\mathbf{Y}} \to E(\mathbf{Y})$ in probability when the sample becomes infinite if and only if $h = \max(h_i) \to 0$. Points where the h_i have large values are called *leverage points*. It can be demonstrated that the presence of leverage points signals that there are observations that might have a decisive influence on the estimation of the regression parameters. A rule of thumb, reported in Huber,[10] suggests that values $h_i \le 0.2$ are safe, values $0.2 \le h_i \le 0.5$ require careful attention, and higher values are to be avoided.

Thus far we have discussed methods to ascertain regression robustness. Let's now discuss methods to "robustify" the regression estimates, namely, methods based on *M*-estimators and *W*-estimators.

Robust Regressions Based on M-Estimators

Let's first discuss how to make *robust regressions* with Huber *M*-estimators. The LS estimators $\hat{\boldsymbol{\beta}} = (\mathbf{X}'\mathbf{X})^{-1}\mathbf{X}'\mathbf{Y}$ are *M*-estimators but are not robust. We can generalize LS seeking to minimize

$$J = \sum_{i=1}^{T} \rho\left(Y_i - \sum_{j=0}^{N} \beta_{ij} X_{ij} \right)$$

by solving the set of $N + 1$ simultaneous equations

$$\sum_{i=1}^{T} \psi\left(Y_i - \sum_{j=0}^{N} \beta_{ij} X_{ij} \right) X_{ij} = 0$$

---

[10] Huber, *Robust Statistics*.

where

$$\psi = \frac{\partial \rho}{\partial \beta}$$

Robust Regressions Based on W-Estimators

W-estimators offer an alternative form of M-estimators. They are obtained by rewriting M-estimators as follows:

$$\psi \left(Y_i - \sum_{j=0}^{N} \beta_{ij} X_{ij} \right) = w \left(Y_i - \sum_{j=0}^{N} \beta_{ij} X_{ij} \right) \left(Y_i - \sum_{j=0}^{N} \beta_{ij} X_{ij} \right)$$

Hence the $N + 1$ simultaneous equations become

$$w \left(Y_i - \sum_{j=0}^{N} \beta_{ij} X_{ij} \right) \left(Y_i - \sum_{j=0}^{N} \beta_{ij} X_{ij} \right) = 0$$

or, in matrix form

$$\mathbf{X'WX\beta} = \mathbf{X'WY}$$

where $\mathbf{W}$ is a diagonal matrix.

The above is not a linear system because the weighting function is in general a nonlinear function of the data. A typical approach is to determine iteratively the weights through an iterative *reweighted least squares* (RLS) procedure. Clearly the iterative procedure depends numerically on the choice of the weighting functions. Two commonly used choices are the *Huber weighting function* $w_H(e)$, defined as

$$w_H(e) = \begin{cases} 1 & \text{for } |e| \leq k \\ k/|e| & \text{for } |e| > k \end{cases}$$

and the *Tukey bisquare weighting function* $w_T(e)$, defined as

$$w_T(e) = \begin{cases} (1 - (e/k)^2)^2 & \text{for } |e| \leq k \\ 0 & \text{for } |e| > k \end{cases}$$

where k is a tuning constant often set at $1.345 \times$ (standard deviation of errors) for the Huber function and $k = 4.6853 \times$ (standard deviation of errors) for the Tukey function.

ILLUSTRATION: ROBUSTNESS OF THE CORPORATE BOND YIELD SPREAD MODEL

To illustrate robust regressions, let's continue with our illustration of the spread regression used in Chapter 4 to show how to incorporate dummy variables into a regression model. The last column of Exhibit 4.2 represents the diagonal elements of the hat matrix called leverage points. These elements are all very small, much smaller than the safety threshold 0.2. We therefore expect that the robust regression does not differ much from the standard regression.

We ran two robust regressions with the Huber and Tukey weighting functions. The tuning parameter k is set as suggested earlier. The estimated coefficients of both robust regressions were identical to the coefficients of the standard regression. In fact, with the Huber weighting function we obtained the parameters estimates shown in the second column Exhibit 12.2. The tuning parameter was set at 160, that is, 1.345 the standard deviation of errors. The algorithm converged at the first iteration.

With the Tukey weighting function we obtained the following beta parameters in Exhibit 12.2: with the tuning parameter set at 550, that is, 4.685 the standard deviation of errors. The algorithm converged at the second iteration.

Let's illustrate the robustness of regression through another example. Let's create an equally weighted index with the daily returns of 234 Japanese firms. Note that this index is created only for the sake of this illustration; no econometric meaning is attached to this index. The daily returns for the index for period 1986 to 2005 are shown in Exhibit 12.3.

EXHIBIT 12.2 Robust Estimates of Parameters Using Huber and Tukey Weighting Functions

Coefficient	Huber	Tukey
β_0	157.0116	157.0138
β_1	61.2781	61.2776
β_2	–13.2054	–13.2052
β_3	–90.8871	–90.8871

EXHIBIT 12.3   Daily Returns of the Japan Index: 1986–2005

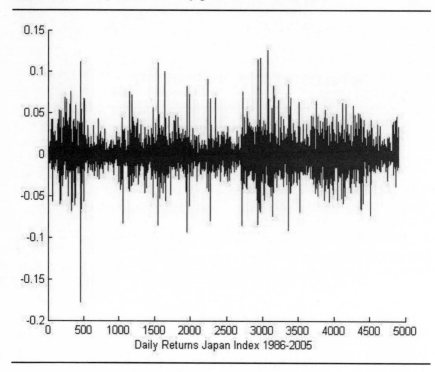

Now suppose that we want to estimate the regression of Nippon Oil on this index; that is, we want to estimate the following regression:

$$R_{NO} = \beta_0 + \beta_1 R_{Index} + \text{Errors}$$

Estimation with the standard least squares method yields the following regression parameters:

R^2: 0.1349
Adjusted R^2: 0.1346
Standard deviation of errors: 0.0213

	beta	t-statistic	p-value
β_0	0.0000	0.1252	0.9003
β_1	0.4533	27.6487	0.0000

When we examined the diagonal of the hat matrix, we found the following results

Maximum leverage $= 0.0189$
Mean leverage $= 4.0783e-004$

suggesting that there is no dangerous point. Robust regression can be applied; that is, there is no need to change the regression design. We applied robust regression using the Huber and Tukey weighting functions with the following parameters:

$$\text{Huber } (k = 1.345 \times \text{standard deviation})$$

and

$$\text{Tukey } (k = 4.685 \times \text{standard deviation})$$

The robust regression estimate with Huber weighting functions yields the following results:

R^2 $= 0.1324$
Adjusted R^2 $= 0.1322$
Weight parameter $= 0.0287$
Number of iterations $= 39$

	beta	*t*-statistic	Change in *p*-value
β_0	−0.000706	−0.767860	0.442607
β_1	0.405633	7.128768	0.000000

The robust regression estimate with Tukey weighting functions yields the following results:

R^2 $= 0.1315$
Adjusted R^2 $= 0.1313$
Weight parameter $= 0.0998$
Number of iterations $= 88$

	beta	*t*-statistic	Change in *p*-value
β_0	−0.000879	−0.632619	0.527012
β_1	0.400825	4.852742	0.000001

We can conclude that all regression slope estimates are highly significant; the intercept estimates are insignificant in all cases. There is a considerable difference between the robust (0.40) and the nonrobust (0.45) regression coefficient.

Robust Estimation of Covariance and Correlation Matrices

Variance-covariance matrices are central to modern portfolio theory. In fact, the estimation of the variance-covariance matrices is critical for portfolio management and asset allocation. Suppose returns are a multivariate random vector written as

$$r_t = \mu + \varepsilon_t$$

The random disturbances ε_t is characterized by a covariance matrix Ω.

$$\begin{aligned} \rho_{X,Y} &= \mathrm{Corr}(X, Y) \\ &= \frac{\mathrm{Cov}(X, Y)}{\sqrt{\mathrm{Var}(X)\mathrm{Var}(Y)}} = \frac{\sigma_{X,Y}}{\sigma_X \sigma_Y} \end{aligned}$$

The correlation coefficient fully represents the dependence structure of multivariate normal distribution. More in general, the correlation coefficient is a valid measure of dependence for elliptical distributions (i.e., distributions that are constants on ellipsoids). In other cases, different measures of dependence are needed (e.g., copula functions).[11]

The empirical covariance between two variables is defined as

$$\hat{\sigma}_{X,Y} = \frac{1}{N-1} \sum_{i=1}^{N} (X_i - \overline{X})(Y_i - \overline{Y})$$

where

$$\overline{X} = \frac{1}{N} \sum_{i=1}^{N} X_i, \quad \overline{Y} = \frac{1}{N} \sum_{i=1}^{N} Y_i$$

are the empirical means of the variables.

The empirical correlation coefficient is the empirical covariance normalized with the product of the respective empirical standard deviations:

---

[11] Paul Embrechts, Filip Lindskog, and Alexander McNeil, "Modelling Dependence with Copulas and Applications to Risk Management," in S. T. Rachev (ed.), *Handbook of Heavy Tailed Distributions in Finance* (Amsterdam: Elsevier/North-Holland, 2003).

$$\hat{\rho}_{X,Y} = \frac{\hat{\sigma}_{X,Y}}{\hat{\sigma}_X \hat{\sigma}_Y}$$

The empirical standard deviations are defined as

$$\hat{\sigma}_X = \frac{1}{N}\sqrt{\sum_{i=1}^{N}(X_i - \overline{X})^2}, \ \hat{\sigma}_Y = \frac{1}{N}\sqrt{\sum_{i=1}^{N}(Y_i - \overline{Y})^2}$$

Empirical covariances and correlations are not robust as they are highly sensitive to tails or outliers. Robust estimators of covariances and/or correlations are insensitive to the tails. However, it does not make sense to robustify correlations if dependence is not linear.

Different strategies for robust estimation of covariances exist; among them are:

- Robust estimation of pairwise covariances
- Robust estimation of elliptic distributions

Here we discuss only the robust estimation of pairwise covariances. As detailed in Huber,[12] the following identity holds:

$$\text{cov}(X, Y) = \frac{1}{4ab}[\text{var}(aX + bY) - \text{var}(aX - bY)]$$

Assume S is a robust scale functional:

$$S(aX + b) = |a|S(X)$$

A robust covariance is defined as

$$C(X, Y) = \frac{1}{4ab}[S(aX + bY)^2 - S(aX - bY)^2]$$

Choose

$$a = \frac{1}{S(X)}, \ b = \frac{1}{S(Y)}$$

---

[12] Huber, *Robust Statistics*.

A robust correlation coefficient is defined as

$$c = \frac{1}{4}[S(aX+bY)^2 - S(aX-bY)^2]$$

The robust correlation coefficient thus defined is not confined to stay in the interval [−1,+1]. For this reason the following alternative definition is often used:

$$r = \frac{S(aX+bY)^2 - S(aX-bY)^2}{S(aX+bY)^2 + S(aX-bY)^2}$$

Applications

As explained in Chapter 4, regression analysis has been used to estimate the market risk of a stock (beta) and to estimate the factor loadings in a factor model. Robust regressions have been used to improve estimates in these two areas.

Martin and Simin provide the first comprehensive analysis of the impact of outliers on the estimation of beta.[13] Moreover, they propose a weighted least-squares estimator with data-dependent weights for estimating beta, referring to this estimate as "resistant beta," and report that this beta is a superior predictor of future risk and return characteristics than the beta calculated using LS. To see the potential dramatic difference between the LS beta and the resistant beta, shown below are the estimates of beta and the standard error of the estimate for four companies reported by Martin and Simin:[14]

	OLS Estimate		Resistant Estimate	
	Beta	Standard Error	Beta	Standard Error
AW Computer Systems	2.33	1.13	1.10	0.33
Chief Consolidated	1.12	0.80	0.50	0.26
Mining Co. Oil City Petroleum	3.27	0.90	0.86	0.47
Metallurgical Industries Co.	2.05	1.62	1.14	0.22

---

[13] Martin and Simin, "Outlier-Resistant Estimates of Beta."
[14] Reported in Table 1 of the Martin-Simin study. Various time periods were used from January 1962 to December 1996.

Martin and Simin provide a feeling for the magnitude of the *absolute* difference between the OLS beta and the resistant beta using weekly returns for 8,314 companies over the period January 1992 to December 1996. A summary of the distribution follows:

Absolute Difference in Beta	No. of Companies	Percent
0.0+ to 0.3	5,043	60.7
0.3+ to 0.5	2,206	26.5
0.5+ to 1.0	800	9.6
Greater than 1.0+	265	3.2

Studies by Fama and French find that market capitalization (size) and book-to-market are important factors in explaining cross-sectional returns.[15] These results are purely empirically based since there is no equilibrium asset pricing model that would suggest either factor as being related to expected return. The empirical evidence that size may be a factor that earns a risk premia (popularly referred to as the "small-firm effect" or "size effect") was first reported by Banz.[16] Knez and Ready reexamined the empirical evidence using robust regressions, more specifically the least-trimmed squares regression discussed earlier.[17] Their results are twofold. First, they find that when 1% of the most extreme observations are trimmed each month, the risk premia found by Fama and French for the size factor disappears. Second, the inverse relation between size and the risk premia reported by Banz and Fama and French (i.e., the larger the capitalization, the smaller the risk premia) no longer holds when the sample is trimmed. For example, the average monthly risk premia estimated using LS is –12 basis points. However, when 5% of the sample is trimmed, the average monthly risk premia is estimated to be +33 basis points; when 1% of the sample is trimmed, the estimated average risk premia is +14 basis points.

---

[15] Eugene F. Fama and Kenneth R. French, "The Cross-Section of Expected Stock Returns," *Journal of Finance* 47 (1992), pp. 427–466 and "Common risk Factors in the Returns on Stocks and Bonds," *Journal of Financial Economics* 33 (1993), pp. 3–56.
[16] Rolf W. Banz, "The Relationship Between Return and Market Value of Common Stocks," *Journal of Financial Economics* 9 (1981), pp. 3–18.
[17] Peter J. Knez and Mark J. Ready, "On the Robustness of Size and Book-to-Market in Cross-Sectional Regressions," *Journal of Finance* 52 (1997), pp. 1355–1382.

CONCEPTS EXPLAINED IN THIS CHAPTER
(IN ORDER OF PRESENTATION)

Robust estimation
Robust statistic
Qualitative robustness
Hampel's qualitative robustness
Quantitative robustness
Resistant estimators
Influence curve/Influence function
Breakdown bound
Rejection point
Redescending estimators
Gross error sensitivity
Local shift sensitivity
Winsor's principle
M-estimators
Equivariant estimators
L-estimators
Trimmed mean
R-estimators
Least median of squares (LMedS)
Least trimmed of squares (LTS)
Reweighted least squares (RLS)
Trimmed mean
Winsorized mean
Median
Median absolute deviation (MAD)
Interquartile range (IQR)
Mean absolute deviation (MeanAD)
Winsorized standard deviation
Hat matrix
Leverage points
Robust regression
Huber weighting function
Tukey weighting function
Resistant beta

CHAPTER 13

Principal Components Analysis and Factor Analysis

In Chapter 5, we described how regression analysis is used to estimate factor models. In our discussion, we stated that the factors used in a factor model can be obtained based on either theory or one of two statistical techniques, namely *principal components analysis* (PCA) or factor analysis. These two statistical techniques provide a tool to (1) reduce the number of variables in a model (i.e., to reduce the dimensionality) and (2) identify if there is structure in the relationships between variables (i.e., to classify variables).

In this chapter, we explain PCA and factor analysis, illustrate and compare both techniques using a sample of stocks. The chapter closes with two examples of principal components analysis applied to stock returns and bond analysis. Before beginning our discussion of PCA and factor analysis let's take a look at factor models, which are the econometric models behind both.

FACTOR MODELS

Factor models are statistical models that try to explain complex phenomena through a small number of basic causes or factors. Factor models serve two main purposes: (1) They reduce the dimensionality of models to make estimation possible; and/or (2) they find the true causes that drive data. Factor models were introduced by Charles Spearman in 1904.[1] A former British Army officer, Spearman was a leading psycholo-

---

[1] Charles Spearman, "General Intelligence, Objectively Determined and Measured," *American Journal of Psychology* 15 (1904), pp. 201–293.

gist who developed many concepts of modern psychometrics. At the turn of the century, in the prevailing climate of "positive science," psychologists were trying to develop quantitative theories of personality. Psychologists had already developed a large number of psychometric tests, including the IQ test invented by the French psychologist Binet. All these tests gave psychologists a vast amount of data.

Spearman was particularly interested in understanding how to measure human intellectual abilities. In his endeavor to do so, he developed the first factor model, known as the Spearman model. The Spearman model explains intellectual abilities through one common factor, the famous "general intelligence" *g* factor, plus another factor *s* which is specific to each distinct ability. Spearman was persuaded that the factor *g* had an overwhelming importance. That is, he thought that any mental ability can be explained quantitatively through a common intelligence factor. According to this theory, outstanding achievements of, say, a painter, a novelist, and a scientist can all be ascribed to a common general intelligence factor plus a small contribution from specific factors.

Some 30 years later, Louis Leon Thurstone developed the first true multifactor model of intelligence. An engineer by training, Thurstone was among the first to propose and demonstrate that there are numerous ways in which a person can be intelligent. Thurstone's Multiple-factors theory identified the following seven primary mental abilities: Verbal Comprehension, Word Fluency, Number Facility, Spatial Visualization, Associative Memory, Perceptual Speed, and Reasoning.[2] The Educational Testing Service presently operates a system based on three important factors of mental ability—verbal, mathematical, and logical abilities—but most psychologists agree that many other factors could be identified as well.

One might question whether factors are only statistical artifacts or if they actually correspond to any reality. In the modern operational interpretation of science, a classification or a factor is "real" if we can make useful predictions using that classification. For example, if the Spearman theory is correct, we can predict that a highly intelligent person can obtain outstanding results in any field. Thus, a novelist could have obtained outstanding results in science. However, if many distinct mental factors are needed, people might be able to achieve great results in some field but be unable to excel in others.

In the early applications of factor models to psychometrics, the statistical model was essentially a conditional multivariate distribution. The raw data were large samples of psychometric tests. The objective was to

---

[2] Louis L. Thurstone, *Primary Mental Abilities* (Chicago: University of Chicago Press, 1938).

explain these tests as probability distributions conditional on the value of one or more factors. In this way, one can make predictions of, for example, the future success of young individuals in different activities.

In economics, factor models are typically applied to time series. The objective is to explain the behavior of a large number of stochastic processes, typically price, returns, or rate processes, in terms of a small number of factors. These factors are themselves stochastic processes. In order to simplify both modeling and estimation, most factor models employed in financial econometrics are static models. This means that time series are assumed to be sequences of temporally independent and identically distributed (IID) random variables so that the series can be thought as independent samples extracted from one common distribution.

In financial econometrics, factor models are needed not only to explain data but to make estimation feasible. Given the large number of stocks presently available—in excess of 15,000—the estimation of correlations cannot be performed without simplifications. Widely used ensembles such as the S&P 500 or the MSCI Europe, include hundreds of stocks and therefore hundreds of thousands of individual correlations. Available samples are insufficient to estimate this large number of correlations. Hence factor models able to explain all pairwise correlations in terms of a much smaller number of correlations between factors.

Linear Factor Models Equations

Linear factor models are regression models of the following type:

$$X_i = \alpha_i + \sum_{j=1}^{K} \beta_{ij} f_j + \varepsilon_i$$

where

X_i = a set of N random variables
f_j = a set of K common factors
ε_i = the noise terms associated with each variable X_i

The β_{ij}'s are called the *factor loadings* or *factor sensitivities;* they express the influence of the j-th factor on the i-th variable.

In this formulation, factor models are essentially static models, where the variables and the factors are random variables without any explicit dependence on time. It is possible to add a dynamics to both the variables and the factors, but that is beyond the scope of this book.

As mentioned above, one of the key objectives of factor models is to reduce the dimensionality of the covariance matrix so that the covariances between the variables X_i is determined only by the covariances between factors. Suppose that the noise terms are mutually uncorrelated, so that

$$E(\varepsilon_i \varepsilon_j) = \begin{cases} 0, & i \neq j \\ \sigma_i^2, & i = j \end{cases}$$

and that the noise terms are uncorrelated with the factors, that is, $E(\varepsilon_i f_j) = 0$, $\forall i,j$. Suppose also that both factors and noise terms have a zero mean, so that $E(X_i) = \alpha_i$. Factor models that respect the above constraints are called *strict factor models*.

Let's compute the covariances of a strict factor model:

$$E((X_i - \alpha_i)(X_j - \alpha_j)) = E\left(\left(\sum_{s=1}^{K} \beta_{is} f_s + \varepsilon_i\right)\left(\sum_{t=1}^{K} \beta_{jt} f_t + \varepsilon_j\right)\right)$$

$$= E\left(\left(\sum_{s=1}^{K} \beta_{is} f_s\right)\left(\sum_{t=1}^{K} \beta_{jt} f_t\right)\right) + E\left(\left(\sum_{s=1}^{K} \beta_{is} f_s\right)(\varepsilon_j)\right)$$

$$+ E\left((\varepsilon_i)\sum_{t=1}^{K} \beta_{jt} f_t\right) + E(\varepsilon_i \varepsilon_j)$$

$$= \sum_{s,t} \beta_{is} E(f_s f_t)\beta_{jt} + E(\varepsilon_i \varepsilon_j)$$

From this expression we can see that the variances and covariances between the variables X_i depend only on the covariances between the factors and the variances of the noise term.

We can express the above compactly in matrix form. Let's write a factor model in matrix form as follows:

$$\mathbf{X} = \boldsymbol{\alpha} + \boldsymbol{\beta}\mathbf{f} + \boldsymbol{\varepsilon}$$

where

$\mathbf{X} = (X_1, \ldots, X_N)'$ = the N-vector of variables
$\boldsymbol{\alpha} = (\alpha_1, \ldots, \alpha_N)'$ = the N-vector of means
$\boldsymbol{\varepsilon} = (\varepsilon_1, \ldots, \varepsilon_N)'$ = the N-vector of idiosyncratic noise terms
$\mathbf{f} = (f_1, \ldots, f_K)'$ = the K-vector of factors

$$\beta = \begin{bmatrix} \beta_{11} & \cdots & \beta_{1K} \\ \vdots & \ddots & \vdots \\ \beta_{N1} & \cdots & \beta_{NK} \end{bmatrix} = \text{the } N \times K \text{ matrix of factor loadings.}$$

Let's define the following:

Σ = the $N \times N$ variance-covariance matrix of the variables X
Ω = the $K \times K$ variance-covariance matrix of the factors
Ψ = $N \times N$ variance-covariance matrix of the error terms ε

If we assume that our model is a strict factor model, the matrix Ψ will be a diagonal matrix with the noise variances on the diagonal, that is,

$$\Psi = \begin{pmatrix} \psi_1^2 & \cdots & 0 \\ \vdots & \ddots & \vdots \\ 0 & \cdots & \psi_N^2 \end{pmatrix}$$

Under the above assumptions, we can express the variance-covariance matrix of the variables in the following way:

$$\Sigma = \beta \Omega \beta' + \Psi$$

In practice, the assumption of a strict factor model might be too restrictive. In applied work, factor models will often be approximate factor models.[3] Approximate factor models allow idiosyncratic terms to be weakly correlated among themselves and with the factors.

As many different factor models have been proposed for explaining stock returns, an important question is whether a factor model is fully determined by the observed time series. In a strict factor model, factors are determined up to a nonsingular linear transformation. In fact, the above matrix notation makes it clear that the factors, which are hidden, nonobservable variables, are not fully determined by the above factor model. That is, an estimation procedure cannot univocally determine the hidden factors and the factor loadings from the observable variables X. In fact, suppose that we multiply the factors by any nonsingular matrix $\mathbf{R}$. We obtain other factors

$$\mathbf{g} = \mathbf{Rf}$$

---

[3] See, for example, Jushan Bai, "Inferential Theory for Factor Models of Large Dimensions," *Econometrica* 71 (2003), pp. 135–171.

with a covariance matrix

$$\Omega_g = R\Omega R^{-1}$$

and we can write a new factor model:

$$X = \alpha + \beta f + \varepsilon = \alpha + \beta R^{-1} R f + \varepsilon = \alpha + \beta_g g + \varepsilon$$

In order to solve this indeterminacy, we can always choose the matrix **R** so that the factors **g** are a set of orthonormal variables, that is, uncorrelated variables (the orthogonality condition) with unit variance (the normality condition). In order to make the model uniquely identifiable, we can stipulate that factors must be a set of orthonormal variables and that, in addition, the matrix of factor loadings is diagonal. Under this additional assumption, a strict factor model is called a *normal factor model*. Note explicitly that under this assumption, factors are simply a set of standardized independent variables. The model is still undetermined under rotation, that is multiplication by any nonsingular matrix such that **RR′ = I**.

In summary, a set of variables has a normal factor representation if it is represented by the following factor model:

$$X = \alpha + \beta f + \varepsilon$$

where factors are orthonormal variables and noise terms are such that the covariance matrix can be represented as follows:

$$\Sigma = \beta\beta' + \Psi$$

where β is the diagonal matrix of factor loadings and Ψ is a diagonal matrix.

How can we explain the variety of factor models proposed given that a strict factor model could be uniquely identified up to a factor linear transformation? As mentioned, the assumptions underlying strict factor models are often too restrictive and approximate factor models have to be adopted. Approximate factor models are uniquely identifiable only in the limit of an infinite number of series. The level of approximation is implicit in practical models of returns.

Types of Factors and Their Estimation

In financial econometrics, the factors used in factor models can belong to three different categories:

- Macroeconomic factors
- Fundamental factors
- Statistical factors

Macroeconomic factors are macroeconomic variables that are believed to determine asset returns.[4] They might be variables such as the GNP, the inflation rate, the unemployment rate, or the steepness of the yield curve. Fundamental factors are variables that derive from financial analysis;[5] statistical factors are factors that derive from a mathematical process as we will shortly explain.

Macroeconomic factors are exogenous factors that must be estimated as variables exogenous to the factor model. They influence the model variables but are not influenced by them. Given factors as exogenous variables, a factor model is estimated as a linear regression model. Obviously this implies that there is indeed a linear relationship between the factors and the model variables. One cannot write an arbitrary factor model with arbitrary factors. More precisely, one can always write a linear model with arbitrary factors and arbitrary factor loadings. However, such a model will have no explanatory power. The variance of each variable that is not explained by common factors appears as noise.

As explained in Chapter 3, adding factors might improve the explanatory power of the model but, in general, worsens the ability to estimate the model because there are more parameters to estimate. Thus, even if factors exhibit genuine linear relationships with the model variables, given the finite and often small size of samples, there is a trade-off between adding explanatory factors and the ability to estimate them (i.e., noise to information ratio).

Note that the ability to find exogenous factors is an empirical question. Given a set of empirical variables, say stock returns, it is an empirical fact that there are other variables of a different nature that are linearly related to them. However, it is conceivable that there are economic factors that have a nonlinear relationship with stock returns. Thus, the decomposition with exogenous factors is dictated by empirical research.

Statistical factors, in contrast, are obtained through a logical process of analysis of the given variables. Statistical factors are factors that are endogenous to the system. They are typically determined with one of two statistical processes; namely, principal component analysis or factor analysis.

---

[4] An example of a macrofactor is the Chen-Roll-Ross model. See Nai-fu Chen, Richard Roll, and Stephen A. Ross, "Economic Forces and the Stock Market," *Journal of Business* 59 (July 1986), pp. 383–403.
[5] Examples are the MSCI Barra model and several models developed by Fama and French.

Note that factors defined through statistical analysis are linear combinations of the variables. That is, if the variables are asset returns, factors are portfolios of assets. They are hidden variables insofar as one does not know the weights of the linear combinations. However, once the estimation process is completed, statistical factors are always linear combinations of variables. If data have a strict factor structure, we can always construct linear combinations of the series (e.g., portfolios of returns) that are perfectly correlated with a set of factors. Often they can be given important economic interpretations. In the following sections we describe the theory and estimation methods of principal components analysis and factor analysis.

PRINCIPAL COMPONENTS ANALYSIS

Principal components analysis (PCA) was introduced in 1933 by Harold Hotelling.[6] Hotelling proposed PCA as a way to determine factors with statistical learning techniques when factors are not exogenously given. Given a variance-covariance matrix, one can determine factors using the technique of PCA.

PCA implements a dimensionality reduction of a set of observations. The concept of PCA is the following. Consider a set of n stationary time series X_i, for example the 500 series of returns of the S&P 500. Consider next a linear combination of these series, that is, a portfolio of securities. Each portfolio P is identified by an n-vector of weights ω_P and is characterized by a variance σ_P^2. In general, the variance σ_P^2 depends on the portfolio's weights ω_P. Lastly, consider a normalized portfolio, which has the largest possible variance. In this context, a normalized portfolio is a portfolio such that the squares of the weights sum to one.

If we assume that returns are IID sequences, jointly normally distributed with variance-covariance matrix σ, a lengthy direct calculation demonstrates that each portfolio's return will be normally distributed with variance

$$\sigma_P^2 = \omega_P^T \sigma \omega_P$$

The normalized portfolio of maximum variance can therefore be determined in the following way:

---

[6] Harold Hotelling, "Analysis of a Complex of Statistical Variables with Principal Components," *Journal of Educational Psychology* 27 (1933), pp. 417–441.

$$\text{Maximize } \omega_P^T \sigma \omega_P$$

subject to the normalization condition

$$\omega_P^T \omega_P = 1$$

where the product is a scalar product. It can be demonstrated that the solution of this problem is the eigenvector ω_1 corresponding to the largest eigenvalue λ_1 of the variance-covariance matrix σ. As σ is a variance-covariance matrix, the eigenvalues are all real.

Consider next the set of all normalized portfolios orthogonal to ω_1, that is, portfolios completely uncorrelated with ω_1. These portfolios are identified by the following relationship:

$$\omega_1^T \omega_P = \omega_P^T \omega_1 = 0$$

We can repeat the previous reasoning. Among this set, the portfolio of maximum variance is given by the eigenvector ω_2 corresponding to the second largest eigenvalue λ_2 of the variance-covariance matrix σ. If there are n distinct eigenvalues, we can repeat this process n times. In this way, we determine the n portfolios P_i of maximum variance. The weights of these portfolios are the orthonormal eigenvectors of the variance-covariance matrix σ. Note that each portfolio is a time series which is a linear combination of the original time series X_i. The coefficients are the portfolios' weights.

These portfolios of maximum variance are all mutually uncorrelated. It can be demonstrated that we can recover all the original return time series as linear combinations of these portfolios:

$$X_j = \sum_{i=1}^{n} \alpha_{j,i} P_i$$

Thus far we have succeeded in replacing the original n correlated time series X_j with n uncorrelated time series P_i with the additional insight that each X_j is a linear combination of the P_i. Suppose now that only p of the portfolios P_i have a significant variance, while the remaining $n-p$ have very small variances. We can then implement a dimensionality reduction by choosing only those portfolios whose variance is significantly different from zero. Let's call these portfolios factors F.

It is clear that we can approximately represent each series X_j as a linear combination of the factors plus a small uncorrelated noise. In fact we can write

$$X_j = \sum_{i=1}^{p} \alpha_{j,i} F_i + \sum_{i=p+1}^{n} \alpha_{j,i} P_i = \sum_{i=1}^{p} \alpha_{j,i} F_i + \varepsilon_j$$

where the last term is a noise term. Therefore to implement PCA one computes the eigenvalues and the eigenvectors of the variance-covariance matrix and chooses the eigenvalues significantly different from zero. The corresponding eigenvectors are the weights of portfolios that form the factors. Criteria of choice are somewhat arbitrary.

Suppose, however, that there is a *strict factor structure*, which means that returns follow a strict factor model as defined earlier in this chapter:

$$r = a + \beta f + \varepsilon$$

The matrix β can be obtained diagonalizing the variance-covariance matrix. In general, the structure of factors will not be strict and one will try to find an approximation by choosing only the largest eigenvalues.

Note that PCA works either on the variance-covariance matrix or on the correlation matrix. The technique is the same but results are generally different. PCA applied to the variance-covariance matrix is sensitive to the units of measurement, which determine variances and covariances. This observation does not apply to returns, which are dimensionless quantities. However, if PCA is applied to prices and not to returns, the currency in which prices are expressed matters; one obtains different results in different currencies. In these cases, it might be preferable to work with the correlation matrix.

We have described PCA in the case of time series, which is the relevant case in econometrics. However PCA is a generalized dimensionality reduction technique applicable to any set of multidimensional observations. It admits a simple geometrical interpretation which can be easily visualized in the three-dimensional case. Suppose a cloud of points in the three-dimensional Euclidean space is given. PCA finds the planes that cut the cloud of points in such a way as to obtain the maximum variance.

Illustration of Principal Components Analysis

Let's now show how PCA is performed. To do so, we will use a subset of the same stocks that we used in Chapter 3 to illustrate the estimation of the characteristic line. The data are monthly observations for the following 10 stocks: Campbell Soup, General Dynamics, Sun Microsystems,

Hilton, Martin Marietta, Coca-Cola, Northrop Grumman, Mercury Interactive, Amazon.com, and United Technologies. The period considered is from December 2000 to November 2005. This book's Data Appendix (following Chapter 15) shows the monthly returns for the stocks. Exhibit 13.1 shows the graphics of the 10 return processes.

As explained earlier, performing PCA is equivalent to determining the eigenvalues and eigenvectors of the covariance matrix or of the correlation matrix. The two matrices yield different results. We perform both exercises, estimating the principal components using separately the covariance and the correlation matrices of the return processes. We estimate the covariance with the empirical covariance matrix. Recall that the empirical covariance σ_{ij} between variables (X_i, X_j) is defined as follows:

EXHIBIT 13.1   Graphics of the 10 Stock Return Processes

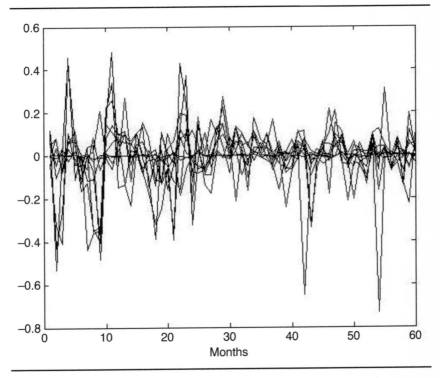

$$\hat{\sigma}_{ij} = \frac{1}{T} \sum_{t=1}^{T} (X_i(t) - \overline{X}_i)(X_j(t) - \overline{X}_j)$$

$$\overline{X}_i = \frac{1}{T} \sum_{t=1}^{T} X_i(t), \ \overline{X}_j = \frac{1}{T} \sum_{t=1}^{T} X_j(t)$$

Exhibit 13.2 shows the covariance matrix.

Normalizing the covariance matrix with the standard deviations, we obtain the correlation matrix. Exhibit 13.3 shows the correlation matrix. Note that the diagonal elements of the correlation matrix are all equal to one. In addition, a number of entries in the covariance matrix are close to zero. Normalization by the product of standard deviations makes the same elements larger.

Let's now proceed to perform PCA using the covariance matrix. We have to compute the eigenvalues and the eigenvectors of the covariance matrix. Exhibit 13.4 shows the eigenvectors (panel A) and the eigenvalues (panel B) of the covariance matrix.

Each column of panel A of Exhibit 13.4 represents an eigenvector. The corresponding eigenvector is shown in panel B. Eigenvalues are listed in descending order; the corresponding eigenvectors go from left to right in the matrix of eigenvectors. Thus the leftmost eigenvector corresponds to the largest eigenvalue. Eigenvectors are not uniquely determined. In fact, multiplying any eigenvector for a real constant yields another eigenvector. The eigenvectors in Exhibit 13.4 are normalized in the sense that the sum of the squares of each component is equal to 1. It can be easily checked that the sum of the squares of the elements in each column is equal to 1. This still leaves an indeterminacy, as we can change the sign of the eigenvector without affecting this normalization.

As explained earlier, if we form portfolios whose weights are the eigenvectors, we can form 10 portfolios that are orthogonal (i.e., uncorrelated). These orthogonal portfolios are called *principal components*. The variance of each principal component will be equal to the corresponding eigenvector. Thus the first principal component (i.e., the portfolio corresponding to the first eigenvalue), will have the maximum possible variance and the last principal component (i.e., the portfolio corresponding to the last eigenvalue) will have the smallest variance. Exhibit 13.5 shows the graphics of the principal components of maximum and minimum variance.

The 10 principal components thus obtained are linear combinations of the original series, $\mathbf{X} = (X_1, \ldots, X_N)'$ that is, they are obtained by multiplying $\mathbf{X}$ by the matrix of the eigenvectors. If the eigenvalues and the corresponding eigenvectors are all distinct, as it is the case in our

EXHIBIT 13.2 The Covariance Matrix of 10 Stock Returns

	SUNW	AMZN	MERQ	GD	NOC	CPB	KO	MLM	HLT	UTX
SUNW	0.02922	0.017373	0.020874	3.38E-05	-0.00256	-3.85E-05	0.000382	0.004252	0.006097	0.005467
AMZN	0.017373	0.032292	0.020262	5.03E-05	-0.00277	0.000304	0.001507	0.001502	0.010138	0.007483
MERQ	0.020874	0.020262	0.0355	-0.00027	-0.0035	-0.00011	0.003541	0.003878	0.007075	0.008557
GD	3.38E-05	5.03E-05	-0.00027	9.27E-05	0.000162	2.14E-05	-0.00015	3.03E-05	-4.03E-05	-3.32E-05
NOC	-0.00256	-0.00277	-0.0035	0.000162	0.010826	3.04E-05	-0.00097	0.000398	-0.00169	-0.00205
CPB	-3.85E-05	0.000304	-0.00011	2.14E-05	3.04E-05	7.15E-05	2.48E-05	-7.96E-06	-9.96E-06	-4.62E-05
KO	0.000382	0.001507	0.003541	-0.00015	-0.00097	2.48E-05	0.004008	-9.49E-05	0.001485	0.000574
MLM	0.004252	0.001502	0.003878	3.03E-05	0.000398	-7.96E-06	-9.49E-05	0.004871	0.00079	0.000407
HLT	0.006097	0.010138	0.007075	-4.03E-05	-0.00169	-9.96E-06	0.001485	0.00079	0.009813	0.005378
UTX	0.005467	0.007483	0.008557	-3.32E-05	-0.00205	-4.62E-05	0.000574	0.000407	0.005378	0.015017

Note: Sun Microsystems (SUNW), Amazon.com (AMZN), Mercury Interactive (MERQ), General Dynamics (GD), Northrop Grumman (NOC), Campbell Soup (CPB), Coca-Cola (KO), Martin Marietta (MLM), Hilton (HLT), United Technologies (UTX).

EXHIBIT 13.3 The Correlation Matrix of the Same 10 Return Processes

	SUNW	AMZN	MERQ	GD	NOC	CPB	KO	MLM	HLT	UTX
SUNW	1	0.56558	0.64812	0.020565	-0.14407	-0.02667	0.035276	0.35642	0.36007	0.26097
AMZN	0.56558	1	0.59845	0.029105	-0.14815	0.20041	0.1325	0.11975	0.56951	0.33983
MERQ	0.64812	0.59845	1	-0.14638	-0.17869	-0.06865	0.29688	0.29489	0.37905	0.37061
GD	0.020565	0.029105	-0.14638	1	0.16217	0.26307	-0.24395	0.045072	-0.04227	-0.02817
NOC	-0.14407	-0.14815	-0.17869	0.16217	1	0.034519	-0.14731	0.054818	-0.16358	-0.16058
CPB	-0.02667	0.20041	-0.06865	0.26307	0.034519	1	0.046329	-0.01349	-0.0119	-0.04457
KO	0.035276	0.1325	0.29688	-0.24395	-0.14731	0.046329	1	-0.02147	0.23678	0.07393
MLM	0.35642	0.11975	0.29489	0.045072	0.054818	-0.01349	-0.02147	1	0.11433	0.047624
HLT	0.36007	0.56951	0.37905	-0.04227	-0.16358	-0.0119	0.23678	0.11433	1	0.44302
UTX	0.26097	0.33983	0.37061	-0.02817	-0.16058	-0.04457	0.07393	0.047624	0.44302	1

Note: Sun Microsystems (SUNW), Amazon.com (AMZN), Mercury Interactive (MERQ), General Dynamics (GD), Northrop Grumman (NOC), Campbell Soup (CPB), Coca-Cola (KO), Martin Marietta (MLM), Hilton (HLT), United Technologies (UTX).

EXHIBIT 13.4 Eigenvectors and Eigenvalues of the Covariance Matrix

Panel A: Eigenvectors

	1	2	3	4	5	6	7	8	9	10
1	-0.50374	0.50099	0.28903	-0.59632	-0.01824	-0.01612	0.22069	-0.08226	0.002934	-0.00586
2	-0.54013	-0.53792	0.51672	0.22686	-0.06092	0.25933	-0.10967	-0.12947	0.020253	0.016624
3	-0.59441	0.32924	-0.4559	0.52998	0.051976	0.015346	0.010496	0.21483	-0.01809	-0.00551
4	0.001884	-0.00255	0.018107	-0.01185	0.013384	0.01246	-0.01398	0.01317	-0.86644	0.4981
5	0.083382	0.10993	0.28331	0.19031	0.91542	-0.06618	0.14532	-0.02762	0.011349	-0.00392
6	-0.00085	-0.01196	0.016896	0.006252	-0.00157	0.01185	-0.00607	-0.02791	-0.49795	-0.86638
7	-0.0486	-0.02839	-0.1413	0.19412	-0.08989	-0.35435	0.31808	-0.8387	-0.01425	0.027386
8	-0.07443	0.19009	0.013485	-0.06363	0.11133	-0.22666	-0.90181	-0.27739	0.010908	0.002932
9	-0.20647	-0.36078	-0.01067	-0.1424	0.038221	-0.82197	0.052533	0.35591	-0.01155	-0.01256
10	-0.20883	-0.41462	-0.5835	-0.46223	0.3649	0.27388	-0.02487	-0.14688	0.001641	-0.00174

Panel B: Eigenvalues of the covariance matrix

1	0.0783
2	0.0164
3	0.0136
4	0.0109
5	0.0101
6	0.0055
7	0.0039
8	0.0028
9	0.0001
10	0.0001

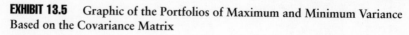

EXHIBIT 13.5   Graphic of the Portfolios of Maximum and Minimum Variance Based on the Covariance Matrix

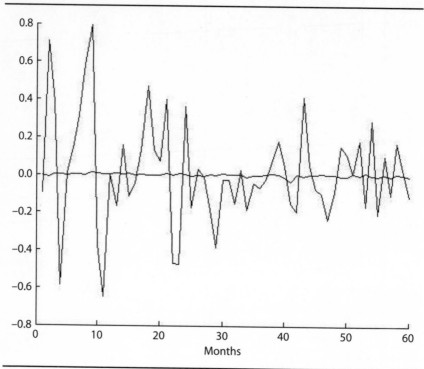

illustration, we can apply the inverse transformation and recover the **X** as linear combinations of the principal components.

PCA is interesting if, in using only a small number of principal components, we nevertheless obtain a good approximation. That is, we use PCA to determine principal components but we use only those principal components that have a large variance as factors of a factor model. Stated otherwise, we regress the original series **X** onto a small number of principal components. In this way, PCA implements a dimensionality reduction as it allows one to retain only a small number of components. By choosing as factors the components with the largest variance, we can explain a large portion of the total variance of **X**.

Exhibit 13.6 shows the total variance explained by a growing number of components. Thus the first component explains 55.2784% of the total variance, the first two components explain 66.8507% of the total variance, and so on. Obviously 10 components explain 100% of the total variance. The second, third, and fourth columns of Exhibit 13.7

show the residuals of the Sun Microsystem return process with 1, 5, and all 10 components, respectively. There is a large gain from 1 to 5, while the gain from 5 to all 10 components is marginal.

EXHIBIT 13.6   Percentage of the Total Variance Explained by a Growing Number of Components Based on the Covariance Matrix

Principal Component	Percentage of Total Variance Explained
1	55.2784%
2	66.8508
3	76.4425
4	84.1345
5	91.2774
6	95.1818
7	97.9355
8	99.8982
9	99.9637
10	100.0000

EXHIBIT 13.7   Residuals of the Sun Microsytem Return Process with 1, 5, and All Components Based on the Covariance Matrix and the Correlation Matrix

Month/ Year	Residuals Based on Covariance Matrix			Residuals Based on Correlation Matrix		
	1 Principal Component	5 Principal Components	10 Principal Components	1 Principal Component	5 Principal Components	10 Principal Components
Dec. 2000	0.069044	0.018711	1.53E-16	0.31828	0.61281	-2.00E-15
Jan. 2001	-0.04723	-0.02325	1.11E-16	-0.78027	-0.81071	1.78E-15
Feb. 2001	-0.03768	0.010533	-1.11E-16	-0.47671	0.04825	2.22E-16
March 2001	-0.16204	-0.02016	2.50E-16	-0.47015	-0.82958	-2.78E-15
April 2001l	-0.00819	-0.00858	-7.63E-17	-0.32717	-0.28034	-5.00E-16
May 2001	0.048814	-0.00399	2.08E-17	0.36321	0.016427	7.22E-16
June 2001	0.21834	0.025337	-2.36E-16	1.1437	1.37	7.94E-15
July 2001	-0.03399	0.02732	1.11E-16	-0.7547	0.35591	1.11E-15
Aug. 2001	0.098758	-0.00146	2.22E-16	1.0501	0.19739	-8.88E-16
Sept. 2001	0.042674	0.006381	-5.55E-17	0.40304	0.28441	2.00E-15
Oct. 2001	0.038679	-0.00813	-5.55E-17	0.50858	0.17217	4.44E-16
Nov. 2001	-0.11967	-0.01624	1.11E-16	-0.89512	-0.8765	-7.77E-16
Dec. 2001	-0.19192	0.030744	1.67E-16	-1.001	0.047784	-1.55E-15
Jan. 2002	-0.13013	-0.00591	5.55E-17	-1.1085	-0.68171	-1.33E-15
Feb. 2002	0.003304	0.017737	0	-0.05222	0.20963	-9.99E-16
March 2002	-0.07221	0.012569	5.55E-17	-0.35765	0.13344	2.22E-16
April 2002l	-0.08211	-0.00916	2.78E-17	-0.38222	-0.47647	-2.55E-15
May 2002	-0.05537	-0.02103	0	-0.45957	-0.53564	4.22E-15

EXHIBIT 13.7 (Continued)

Month/Year	Residuals Based on Covariance Matrix			Residuals Based on Correlation Matrix		
	1 Principal Component	5 Principal Components	10 Principal Components	1 Principal Component	5 Principal Components	10 Principal Components
June 2002	−0.15461	0.004614	1.39E-16	−1.0311	−0.54064	−3.33E-15
July 2002	0.00221	0.013057	8.33E-17	0.24301	0.37431	−1.89E-15
Aug. 2002	−0.12655	0.004691	5.55E-17	−0.8143	−0.30497	2.00E-15
Sept. 2002	−0.07898	0.039666	5.55E-17	−0.25876	0.64902	−6.66E-16
Oct. 2002	0.15839	0.003346	−1.11E-16	0.98252	0.53223	−1.78E-15
Nov. 2002	−0.11377	0.013601	1.67E-16	−0.95263	−0.33884	−2.89E-15
Dec. 2002	−0.06957	0.012352	1.32E-16	−0.10309	0.029623	−4.05E-15
Jan. 2003	0.14889	−0.00118	−8.33E-17	1.193	0.73723	5.00E-15
Feb. 2003	−0.03359	−0.02719	−4.16E-17	−0.02854	−0.38331	4.05E-15
March 2003	−0.05314	−0.00859	2.78E-17	−0.38853	−0.40615	−2.22E-16
April 2003	0.10457	−0.01442	−2.22E-16	0.73075	0.097101	−1.11E-15
May 2003	0.078567	0.022227	−5.55E-17	0.52298	0.63772	−7.77E-16
June 2003	−0.1989	−0.02905	1.39E-16	−1.4213	−1.3836	−3.55E-15
July 2003	−0.0149	−0.00955	0	0.13876	−0.1059	3.44E-15
Aug. 2003	−0.12529	−0.00528	8.33E-17	−0.73819	−0.51792	9.99E-16
Sept. 2003	0.10879	−0.00645	−8.33E-17	0.69572	0.25503	−2.22E-15
Oct. 2003	0.07783	0.01089	−2.78E-17	0.36715	0.45274	−1.11E-15
Nov. 2003	0.038408	−0.01181	−5.55E-17	0.11761	−0.13271	3.33E-16
Dec. 2003	0.18203	0.012593	−1.39E-16	1.2655	0.98182	3.77E-15
Jan. 2004	0.063885	−0.00042	6.94E-18	0.33717	0.038477	0
Feb. 2004	−0.12552	−0.00225	1.11E-16	−0.70345	−0.49379	0
March 2004	−0.01747	0.016836	0	−0.1949	0.35348	−1.94E-16
April 2004	0.015742	0.013764	4.16E-17	0.2673	0.46969	−5.77E-15
May 2004	−0.03556	−0.02072	−6.94E-17	−0.60652	−0.68268	0
June 2004	0.14325	0.008155	−1.94E-16	0.54463	0.59768	3.22E-15
July 2004	0.030731	−0.00285	−4.16E-17	0.13011	0.028779	7.08E-16
Aug. 2004	0.032719	−0.00179	−5.55E-17	0.26793	0.18353	2.05E-15
Sept. 2004	0.083238	0.003664	0	0.58186	0.29544	3.77E-15
Oct. 2004	0.11722	−0.00356	−1.39E-16	0.77575	0.38959	2.22E-16
Nov. 2004	−0.04794	−0.00088	0	−0.47706	−0.35464	−3.13E-15
Dec. 2004	−0.1099	−0.01903	1.11E-16	−0.69439	−0.64663	−2.22E-16
Jan. 2005	0.0479	−0.00573	2.08E-17	0.24203	−0.04065	−4.45E-16
Feb. 2005	−0.015	0.003186	1.39E-17	−0.07198	0.054412	3.28E-15
March 2005	0.005969	−0.0092	−4.16E-17	0.035251	−0.02106	3.83E-15
April 2005l	−0.00742	−0.01241	−4.16E-17	−0.09335	−0.42659	−1.67E-16
May 2005	0.14998	−0.01126	6.25E-17	1.0219	0.034585	−9.05E-15
June 2005	−0.05045	−0.00363	3.47E-17	−0.25655	−0.1229	−4.66E-15
July 2005	0.065302	−0.00421	−5.20E-17	0.56136	0.16602	3.08E-15
Aug. 2005	0.006719	−0.01174	1.39E-17	0.09319	−0.22119	−2.00E-15
Sept. 2005	0.12865	−0.00259	−8.33E-17	0.95602	0.33442	3.50E-15
Oct. 2005	−0.01782	0.011827	−8.33E-17	−0.2249	0.27675	1.53E-15
Nov. 2005	0.026312	−7.72E-05	−1.39E-17	0.26642	0.19725	1.67E-15

We can repeat the same exercise for the correlation matrix. Exhibit 13.8 shows the eigenvectors (panel A) and the eigenvalues (panel B) of the correlation matrix. Eigenvectors are normalized as in the case of the covariance matrix.

Exhibit 13.9 shows the total variance explained by a growing number of components. Thus the first component explains 30.6522% of the total variance, the first two components explain 45.2509% of the total variance and so on. Obviously 10 components explain 100% of the total variance. The increase in explanatory power with the number of components is slower than in the case of the covariance matrix.

The proportion of the total variance explained grows more slowly in the correlation case than in the covariance case. Exhibit 13.10 shows the graphics of the portfolios of maximum and minimum variance. The ratio between the two portfolios is smaller in this case than in the case of the covariance.

The last three columns of Exhibit 13.8 show the residuals of the Sun Microsystem return process with 1, 5, and all components based on the correlation matrix. Residuals are progressively reduced, but at a lower rate than with the covariance matrix.

PCA and Factor Analysis with Stable Distributions

In the previous sections we discussed PCA and factor analysis without making any explicit reference to the distributional properties of the variables. These statistical tools can be applied provided that all variances and covariances exist. Therefore applying them does not require, per se, that distributions are normal, but only that they have finite variances and covariances. Variances and covariances are not robust but are sensitive to outliers. As discussed in Chapter 12, robust equivalent of variances and covariances exist. In order to make PCA and factor analysis insensitive to outliers, one could use robust versions of variances and covariances and apply PCA and factor analysis to these robust estimates.

In many cases, however, distributions might exhibit fat tails and infinite variances. In this case, large values cannot be trimmed but must be taken into proper consideration. However, if variances and covariances are not finite, the least squares methods used to estimate factor loadings cannot be applied. In addition, the concept of PCA and factor analysis as illustrated in the previous sections cannot be applied. In fact, if distributions have infinite variances, it does not make sense to determine the portfolio of maximum variance as all portfolios will have infinite variance and it will be impossible, in general, to determine an ordering based on the size of variance.

EXHIBIT 13.8 Eigenvectors and Eigenvalues of the Correlation Matrix

Panel A: Eigenvectors

	1	2	3	4	5	6	7	8	9	10
1	-0.4341	0.19295	-0.26841	0.040065	-0.19761	0.29518	-0.11161	-0.11759	-0.72535	-0.14857
2	-0.45727	0.18203	0.20011	0.001184	0.013236	0.37606	0.05077	0.19402	0.47275	-0.55894
3	-0.47513	-0.03803	-0.16513	0.16372	-0.01282	0.19087	-0.08297	-0.38843	0.37432	0.61989
4	0.06606	0.63511	0.18027	-0.16941	-0.05974	-0.24149	-0.66306	-0.14342	0.092295	0.02113
5	0.17481	0.33897	-0.21337	0.14797	0.84329	0.23995	0.091628	-0.07926	-0.06105	0.001886
6	-0.00505	0.42039	0.57434	0.40236	-0.15072	-0.05018	0.48758	-0.07382	-0.15788	0.19532
7	-0.18172	-0.397	0.28037	0.58674	0.26063	-0.26864	-0.38592	-0.16286	-0.11336	-0.24105
8	-0.1913	0.26851	-0.55744	0.32448	-0.09047	-0.58736	0.20083	0.19847	0.15935	-0.13035
9	-0.40588	-0.0309	0.20884	-0.20157	0.29193	-0.16641	-0.08666	0.67897	-0.1739	0.37201
10	-0.32773	-0.05042	0.14067	-0.51858	0.24871	-0.41444	0.30906	-0.4883	-0.06781	-0.17077

Panel B: Eigenvalues

1	3.0652
2	1.4599
3	1.1922
4	0.9920
5	0.8611
6	0.6995
7	0.6190
8	0.5709
9	0.3143
10	0.2258

EXHIBIT 13.9   Percentage of the Total Variance Explained by a Growing Number of Components Using the Correlation Matrix

Principal Component	Percentage of Total Variance Explained
1	30.6522%
2	45.2509
3	57.1734
4	67.0935
5	75.7044
6	82.6998
7	88.8901
8	94.5987
9	97.7417
10	100.0000

EXHIBIT 13.10   Graphic of the Portfolios of Maximum and Minimum Variance Based on the Correlation Matrix

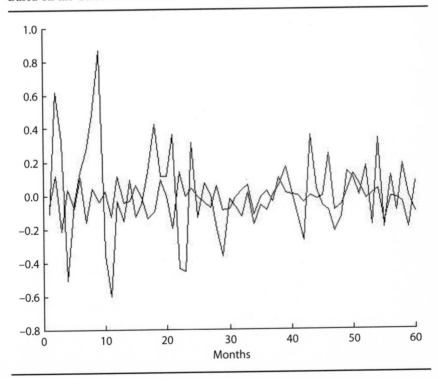

Both PCA and factor analysis as well as the estimation of factor models with infinite-variance error terms are at the forefront of econometric research. We will discuss both topics in Chapter 14 where we discuss stable distributions.

FACTOR ANALYSIS

In the above sections we saw how factors can be determined using principal components analysis. We retained as factors those principal components with the largest variance. In this section, we consider an alternative technique for determining factors: *factor analysis* (FA). Suppose we are given T independent samples of a random vector $\mathbf{X} = (X_1, \ldots, X_N)'$. In the most common cases in financial econometrics, we will be given T samples of a multivariate time series. However, factor analysis can be applied to samples extracted from a generic multivariate distribution. To fix these ideas, suppose we are given N time series of stock returns at T moments, as in the case of PCA.

Assuming that the data are described by a strict factor model with K factors, the objective of factor analysis (FA) consists of determining a model of the type

$$\mathbf{X} = \alpha + \beta f + \varepsilon$$

with covariance matrix

$$\Sigma = \beta\beta' + \Psi$$

The estimation procedure is performed in two steps. In the first step, we estimate the covariance matrix and the factor loadings. In the second step, we estimate factors using the covariance matrix and the factor loadings.

If we assume that the variables are jointly normally distributed and temporally independently and identically distributed (IID), we can estimate the covariance matrix with maximum likelihood methods. Estimation of factor models with maximum likelihood methods is not immediate because factors are not observable. Iterative methods such as the *expectation maximization* (EM) algorithm are generally used.

After estimating the matrices β and Ψ factors can be estimated as linear regressions. In fact, assuming that factors are zero means (an assumption that can always be made), we can write the factor model as

$$\mathbf{X} - \alpha = \beta f + \varepsilon$$

which shows that, at any given time, factors can be estimated as the regression coefficients of the regression of $(\mathbf{X} - \boldsymbol{\alpha})$ onto $\boldsymbol{\beta}$. Using the standard formulas of regression analysis that we established in Chapter 3, we can now write factors, at any given time, as follows:

$$\hat{\mathbf{f}}_t = \left(\boldsymbol{\beta}'\hat{\boldsymbol{\Psi}}^{-1}\boldsymbol{\beta}\right)^{-1}\boldsymbol{\beta}'\hat{\boldsymbol{\Psi}}^{-1}(\mathbf{X}_t - \hat{\boldsymbol{\alpha}})$$

The estimation approach based on maximum likelihood estimates implies that the number of factors is known. In order to determine the number of factors, a heuristic procedure consists of iteratively estimating models with a growing number of factors. The correct number of factors is determined when estimates of q factors stabilize and cannot be rejected on the basis of p probabilities. A theoretical method for determining the number of factors was proposed by Bai and Ng.[7] Given the technical nature of the argument, the interested reader should consult their article.

The factor loadings matrix can also be estimated with *ordinary least squares* (OLS) methods. The OLS estimator of the factor loadings coincide with the principal component estimator of factor loadings. However, in a strict factor model, OLS estimates of the factor loadings are inconsistent when the number of time points goes to infinity but the number of series remains finite, unless we assume that the idiosyncratic noise terms all have the same variance.

The OLS estimators, however, remain consistent if we allow both the number of processes and the time to go to infinity. Under this assumption, we can also use OLS estimators for approximate factor models.[8]

In a number of applications, we might want to enforce the condition $\alpha = 0$. This condition is the condition of asset of arbitrage. OLS estimates of factor models with this additional condition are an instance of constrained OLS methods that we described in Chapter 4.

An Illustration of Factor Analysis

Let's now show how factor analysis is performed. To do so, we will use the same 10 stocks and return data for December 2000 to November 2005 that we used to illustrate principal components analysis.

As just described, to perform factor analysis, we need estimate only the factor loadings and the idiosyncratic variances of noise terms. We

---

[7] Jushan Bai and Serena Ng, "Determining the Number of Factors in Approximate Factor Models," *Econometrica* 70 (January 2002), pp. 191–221.

[8] See Bai, "Inferential Theory for Factor Models of Large Dimensions."

EXHIBIT 13.11   A Factor Loadings and Idiosyncratic Variances

| | Factor Loadings | | | |
	β_1	β_2	β_3	Variance
SUNW	0.656940	0.434420	0.27910	0.301780
AMZN	0.959860	−0.147050	−0.00293	0.057042
MERQ	0.697140	0.499410	−0.08949	0.256570
GD	0.002596	−0.237610	0.43511	0.754220
NOC	−0.174710	−0.119960	0.23013	0.902130
CPB	0.153360	−0.344400	0.13520	0.839590
KO	0.170520	0.180660	−0.46988	0.717500
MLM	0.184870	0.361180	0.28657	0.753250
HLT	0.593540	0.011929	−0.18782	0.612300
UTX	0.385970	0.144390	−0.15357	0.806590

assume that the model has three factors. Exhibit 13.11 shows the factor loadings. Each row represents the loadings of the three factors corresponding to each stock. The last column of the exhibit shows the idiosyncratic variances.

The idiosyncratic variances are numbers between 0 and 1, where 0 means that the variance is completely explained by common factors and 1 that common factors fail to explain variance.

The p-value turns out to be 0.6808 and therefore fails to reject the null of three factors. Estimating the model with 1 and 2 factors we obtain much lower p-values while we run into numerical difficulties with 4 or more factors. We can therefore accept the null of three factors. Exhibit 13.12 shows the graphics of the three factors.

Applying PCA to Bond Portfolio Management

There are two applications in bond portfolio management where PCA has been employed. The first application is explaining the movement or dynamics in the yield curve and then applying the resulting principal components to measure and manage yield curve risk. Several studies suggest that the principal components approach to controlling interest rate risk is superior to using the traditional measure of interest rate risk, duration, coupled with a second-order approximation of price changes known as "convexity."[9] The second application of PCA is to identify risk factors beyond changes in the term structure. For example, given

---

[9] We explained duration in Chapter 5.

EXHIBIT 13.12   Graphics of the Three Factors

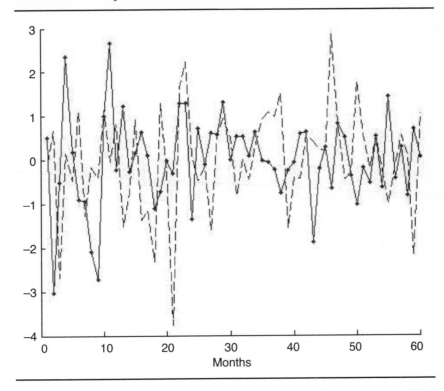

Months

historical bond returns and factors that are believed to affect bond returns, PCA can be used to obtain principal components that are linear combinations of the variables that explain the variation in returns.

Using PCA to Control Interest Rate Risk

Using PCA, several studies have investigated the factors that have affected the historical returns on Treasury portfolios. Robert Litterman and Jose Scheinkman found that three factors explained historical bond returns for U.S. Treasuries zero-coupon securities.[10] The first factor is changes in the *level of rates*, the second factor is changes in the *slope of the yield curve*, and the third factor is changes in the *curvature of the yield curve*.

After identifying the factors, Litterman and Scheinkman use regression analysis to assess the relative contribution of these three factors in

---

[10] Robert Litterman and Jose Scheinkman, "Common Factors Affecting Bond Returns," *Journal of Fixed Income* 1 (June 1991), pp. 54–61.

explaining the returns on zero-coupon Treasury securities of different maturities. On average (i.e., over all maturities), the first principal component explained about 90% of the returns, the second principal component 8%, and the third principal component 2%. Thus, only three principal components were needed to fully explain the dynamics of the yield curve.

Subsequent to the publication of the 1991 Litterman-Scheinkman study, there have been several studies that have examined the yield curve movement using PCA and reported similar results—that is, three principal components and a similar relative contribution to the explanatory power for each principal component. Exhibit 13.13 shows the results of one study by Golub and Tilman for U.S. Treasury securities using the monthly database by RiskMetrics™. Schumacher, Dektar, and Fabozzi found similar results for the U.S. mortgage-backed securities market.[11]

Martellini, Priaulet, and Priaulet investigated both the zero-coupon euro interbank yield curve and zero-coupon Treasury yield curves of the following five countries: France, Germany, Italy, Spain, and the Netherlands.[12] Daily returns are used and the period investigated is January 2, 2001 through August 21, 2002. Five principal components are estimated.[13] Exhibit 13.14 shows for each of the five countries and the euro interbank market, the percentage of the variation in the movement of interest rates explained.

Notice the following for the results reported in Exhibit 13.14 for the five government bond markets. First, the first three principal components explain from 91% to 97% of the change in interest rates. Second, the relative contribution of each principal component has the same relative importance for each country. Third, compared to the U.S. Treasury market, the second and third principal components explain a larger percentage of the change in interest rates in the five non-U.S. government bond markets examined. Since the second and third principal components are typically interpreted as the slope and curvature of the yield curve, these findings suggest that in these five non-U.S. markets nonparallel shifts in the yield curve are more important than in the U.S. Trea-

---

[11] Michael P. Schumacher, Daniel C. Dektar, and Frank J. Fabozzi, "Yield Curve Risk of CMO Bonds," in Frank J. Fabozzi (ed.), *CMO Portfolio Management* (Hoboken, NJ: John Wiley & Sons, 1994).

[12] Lionel Martellini, Philippe Priaulet, and Stephane Priaulet, "The Euro Benchmark Yield Curve: Principal Component Analysis of Yield Curve Dynamics," in Frank J. Fabozzi (ed.), *Professional Perspectives on Fixed Income Portfolio Management: Volume 4* (Hoboken, NJ: John Wiley & Sons, 2003).

[13] In their study, Martellini, Priaulet, and Priaulet refer to the principal components as "factors."

EXHIBIT 13.13 Golub-Tilman Derived Principal Components Implied by RiskMetrics™ Dataset (9/6/96)

		3-Mo.	1-Yr.	2-Yr.	3-Yr.	5-Yr.	7-Yr.	10-Yr.	15-Yr.	20-Yr.	30-Yr.
Annualized ZCB Yield Volume (%)		9.63	16.55	18.33	17.82	17.30	16.62	15.27	14.25	13.26	12.09
One Std. Dev. of ZCB Yields (bps)		52	96	113	112	113	111	104	101	97	83
Correlation Matrix	3-Mo.	1.00	0.80	0.72	0.68	0.65	0.61	0.58	0.54	0.51	0.46
	1-Yr.	0.80	1.00	0.91	0.91	0.89	0.87	0.85	0.81	0.78	0.76
	2-Yr.	0.72	0.91	1.00	0.99	0.97	0.95	0.93	0.89	0.85	0.84
	3-Yr.	0.68	0.91	0.99	1.00	0.99	0.97	0.96	0.92	0.90	0.88
	5-Yr.	0.65	0.89	0.97	0.99	1.00	0.99	0.98	0.96	0.93	0.92
	7-Yr.	0.61	0.87	0.95	0.97	0.99	1.00	0.99	0.98	0.96	0.95
	10-Yr.	0.58	0.85	0.93	0.96	0.98	0.99	1.00	0.99	0.98	0.97
	15-Yr.	0.54	0.81	0.89	0.92	0.96	0.98	0.99	1.00	0.99	0.98
	20-Yr.	0.51	0.78	0.85	0.90	0.93	0.96	0.98	0.99	1.00	0.99
	30-Yr.	0.46	0.76	0.84	0.88	0.92	0.95	0.97	0.98	0.99	1.00

EXHIBIT 13.13   (Continued)

PC No.	Eig. Val.	Vol. PC	Var. Expl.	CVar. Expl.	3-Mo.	1-Yr.	2-Yr.	3-Yr.	5-Yr.	7-Yr.	10-Yr.	15-Yr.	20-Yr.	30-Yr.
									Principal Components					
1	9.24	3.04	92.80	92.80	11.09	28.46	35.69	36.37	36.94	36.30	34.02	32.40	30.33	25.71
2	0.48	0.69	4.80	97.60	43.93	48.66	34.19	20.37	5.23	-9.32	-18.63	-30.09	-37.24	-36.94
3	0.13	0.36	1.27	98.87	42.43	54.93	-44.61	-35.28	-21.02	-8.43	0.31	19.59	27.12	17.76
4	0.06	0.25	0.62	99.49	76.77	-61.47	9.21	-0.18	-0.01	-2.08	-0.65	10.46	11.30	-0.31
5	0.02	0.14	0.20	99.69	12.33	-4.93	-55.03	-3.84	38.06	47.35	33.64	-21.36	-35.74	-14.98
6	0.01	0.10	0.11	99.79	8.94	0.33	18.59	-11.83	-15.02	-2.14	19.64	-44.15	-30.58	77.03
7	0.01	0.09	0.09	99.88	3.02	-0.79	-38.42	49.35	45.01	-48.00	-28.08	-10.93	7.76	27.93
8	0.00	0.07	0.06	99.94	3.26	-1.14	-24.96	66.51	-66.82	17.27	13.02	-0.70	-2.46	-1.38
9	0.00	0.06	0.03	99.97	0.76	-0.46	-1.46	-0.97	0.21	60.38	-72.73	-20.12	19.52	16.59
10	0.00	0.05	0.03	100.00	0.54	0.00	-2.53	1.32	-0.42	5.15	-27.03	67.98	-64.58	21.03

ZCB = Zero-coupon bond
Eig. Val. = Eigenvalues (i.e., principal component variances) × 10,000
Vol. PC = Volatility of principal components × 100
Var. Expl. = Percentage of variance explained
CVar. Expl. = Cumulative percentage of variance explained

Source: Exhibit 11.1 in Bennett W. Golub and Leo M. Tilman, "Measuring Plausibility of Hypothetical Interest Rate Shocks," Chapter 11 in Frank J. Fabozzi (ed.), *Interest Rate, Term Structure, and Valuation Modeling* (Hoboken, NJ: John Wiley & Sons, 2002).

EXHIBIT 13.14   Percentage of Explanation by the First Five Principal Components for Five Non-U.S. Government Bond Markets and the Euro Interbank Market: January 2, 2001–August 21, 2002

France	PC 1	PC 2	PC 3	PC 4	PC 5
% Explained	62.42%	21.87%	6.76%	5.47%	2.22%
% Cumulative	62.42%	84.29%	91.05%	96.52%	98.74%
Germany	PC 1	PC 2	PC 3	PC 4	PC 5
% Explained	66.87%	22.29%	7.91%	1.44%	0.89%
% Cumulative	66.87%	89.16%	97.07%	98.51%	99.40%
Italy	PC 1	PC 2	PC 3	PC 4	PC 5
% Explained	66.12%	22.47%	8.28%	1.69%	0.72%
% Cumulative	66.12%	88.59%	96.87%	98.56%	99.28%
The Netherlands	PC 1	PC 2	PC 3	PC 4	PC 5
% Explained	65.03%	22.30%	7.44%	2.82%	1.49%
% Cumulative	65.03%	87.33%	94.77%	97.59%	99.08%
Spain	PC 1	PC 2	PC 3	PC 4	PC 5
% Explained	62.22%	22.61%	9.60%	2.82%	1.55%
% Cumulative	62.22%	84.83%	94.43%	97.25%	98.80%
Euro Interbank	PC 1	PC 2	PC 3	PC 4	PC 5
% Explained	47.54%	25.63%	10.91%	5.80%	3.46%
% Cumulative	47.54%	73.17%	84.08%	89.88%	93.34%

Source: Adapted from Exhibit 1 in Lionel Martellini, Philippe Priaulet, and Stephane Priaulet, "The Euro Benchmark Yield Curve: Principal Component Analysis of Yield Curve Dynamics," in Frank J. Fabozzi (ed.), *Professional Perspectives on Fixed Income Portfolio Management*, Vol. 4 (Hoboken, NJ: John Wiley & Sons, 2003).

sury market. For the euro interbank market, the first three principal components explain less of the variation in the movement of interest rates than in government bond markets, only 84%. Moreover, nonparallel shifts in the yield curve are even more important compared than for the five government bond markets whose results are reported in Exhibit 13.14 and that the last two principal components explain around 16% of the dynamics of the yield curve.

Once yield curve risk is described in terms of principal components, the factor loadings can be used to:

- Construct hedges that neutralize exposure to changes in the direction of interest rates.
- Construct hedges that neutralize exposure to changes in nonparallel shifts in the yield curve.
- Structure yield curve trades.

Axel and Vankudre illustrate how this is done.[14] They also present evidence that using PCA to measure and control interest rate risk is superior to the traditional approaches using duration/convexity and another widely used measures of the yield curve risk, key rate duration.[15] In the out-of-sample hedges that they performed using PCA, Axel and Vankudre found significantly lower profit and loss variance than for hedges using duration. Similar findings are reported in other studies.[16]

PCA of the dynamics of the yield curve have lead to the use of what is now referred to as *principal component duration*.[17] Moreover, PCA can be used to estimate the probability associated with a given hypothetical interest rate shock so that a bond portfolio manager can better analyze the interest rate risk of a bond portfolio and traders can better understand the risk exposure of a bond trading strategy.[18]

Bond Risk Factors

The discussion of bond risk factors described in the previous application focused on term structure factors for government bond markets and the euro interbank market which has little credit risk. For a bond index that

---

[14] Ralph Axel and Prashant Vankudre, "Managing the Yield Curve with Principal Component Analysis," in Frank J. Fabozzi (ed.), *Professional Perspectives on Fixed Income Portfolio Management*, Vol. 3 (Hoboken, NJ: John Wiley & Sons, 2002).

[15] Thomas S. Y. Ho, "Key Rate Durations: Measures of Interest Rate Risks," *Journal of Fixed Income* 2 (September 1992), pp. 29–44.

[16] See, for example, Lionel Martellini, Philippe Priaulet, Frank J. Fabozzi, and Michael Luo, "Hedging Interest Rate Risk with Term Structure Factor Models," Chapter 11 in Frank J. Fabozzi, Lionel Martellini, and Philippe Priaulet (eds), *Advanced Bond Portfolio Management: Best Practices in Modeling and Strategies* (Hoboken, NJ: John Wiley & Sons, 2006).

[17] See Bennett W. Golub and Leo M. Tilman, "Measuring Yield Curve Risk Using Principal Components Analysis, Value-at-Risk, and Key Rate Durations," *Journal of Portfolio Management* 26 (Summer 1997), pp. 72–84.

[18] Golub and Tilman, "Measuring Plausibility of Hypothetical Interest Rate Shocks."

includes nongovernment securities, there are risk factors other than term structure factors.

Using PCA, Gauthier and Goodman have empirically identified the risk factors that generate nominal excess returns for the Salomon Smith Barney Broad Investment Grade Index (SSB BIG Index) for the period January 1992 to March 2003.[19] Exhibit 13.15 shows the results of their

EXHIBIT 13.15   Principal Component Analysis of the Sectors of the SSB BIG Index: January 1992–March 2003

	Component					
	1	2	3	4	5	6
Nominal Returns						
Agy. Callable	0.28	0.00	0.41	0.16	0.00	0.85
Agy. NC	0.54	0.24	−0.20	0.60	0.46	−0.22
MBS	0.30	0.00	0.75	0.00	−0.34	−0.46
Credit	0.48	−0.82	−0.28	−0.11	0.00	0.00
ABS	0.31	0.15	0.19	−0.73	0.56	0.00
Treasury	0.47	0.49	−0.34	−0.25	−0.60	0.00
Factor contribution (%)	92.7	3.1	2.3	0.9	0.5	—
Cumulative Importance (%)	92.7	95.8	98.1	99	99.5	1
Duration-Adjusted Returns						
Agy. Callable	0.18	0.28	0.76	−0.10	−0.53	−0.12
Agy. NC	0.21	0.52	0.17	0.67	0.45	
MBS	0.23	0.65	−0.23	−0.66	0.21	
Credit	0.91	−0.40	0.00		0.12	
ABS	0.23	0.26	−0.58	0.32	−0.64	−0.18
Treasury	0.00	0.00	0.00		−0.22	0.97
Factor contribution (%)	80.3	12.1	2.9	2.5	1.8	—
Cumulative importance (%)	80.3	92.4	95.3	97.8	99.6	1.0

Source: Adapted from Exhibit 3 in Laurent Gauthier and Laurie Goodman, "Risk/Return Trade-Offs on Fixed Income Asset Classes," in *Professional Perspectives on Fixed Income Portfolio Management*, Vol. 4 (Hoboken, NJ: John Wiley & Sons, 2003).

---

[19] Laurent Gauthier and Laurie Goodman, "Risk/Return Trade-Offs on Fixed Income Asset Classes," in *Professional Perspectives on Fixed Income Portfolio Management*, Vol. 4. In addition to nominal excess returns, Gauthier and Goodman also analyzed duration-adjusted excess returns. Only the results for the nominal excess returns are discussed here.

PCA for the first six principal components for each bond sector of the SSB BIG Index. The values for each principal component reported in the exhibit are the factor loadings. Notice from the last row in the exhibit that the first three principal components explain 98.1% of the variation in nominal excess returns.

The *first* principal component explains 92.7% of the variation. How do we know how to interpret the first principal component or risk factor? First, while we do not report the average duration of each sector of the SSB BIG Index here, it turns out that the order of magnitude of the factor loading on each of the sectors looks very much like the average duration for each sector. To confirm this, Gauthier and Goodman did two things. First they looked at a scatter plot of the return on first principal component versus the change in the 10-year Treasury yield. The first principal component had a very clear, linear relationship to changes in interest rates. Second they looked at the correlation of each of the first three principal components to various market measures (such as the slope of the 2 to 10 spread, 5-year cap volatility, etc.). They found that the 10-year yield had a correlation of −89% to nominal returns.

The second principal component explains 3.1% of nominal excess returns. Gauthier and Goodman identify this factor as the *credit specific factor* because of the high negative factor loadings on the credit index combined with a high positive weighting on Treasuries. They confirm this by looking at the correlation between the second principal component and the S&P 500. The correlation was −0.5. The weight on the credit index is −0.82, indicating that the lower the S&P 500, the lower corporate bond returns will be.

Gauthier and Goodman identify the third principal component as an *optionality factor*. This can be supported by noting that the factor loadings on the assets classes that have *some* optionality (callable Agencies, MBS and ABS) is positive, while the factor loading on the noncallable series (Treasuries, noncallable agencies and credit) is negative. This third principal component, which represents optionality, is consistent with studies of the movements of the yield curve discussed earlier because it reflects market factors such as the shape of the curve and volatility. Gauthier and Goodman show that there is a high positive correlation between the optionality factor and the slope of the yield, but a negative relationship with 5-year cap volatility. This suggests (1) the steeper the yield curve slope, the better a callable series should do and (2) the higher the volatility, the lower the return on the callable series.

PCA AND FACTOR ANALYSIS COMPARED

The two illustrations of PCA and FA are relative to the same data and will help clarify the differences between the two methods. Let's first observe that PCA does not imply, per se, any specific restriction on the process. Given a nonsingular covariance matrix, we can always perform PCA as an exact linear transformation of the series. When we consider a smaller number of principal components, we perform an approximation which has to be empirically justified. For example, in our PCA illustration, the first three components explain 76% of the total variance (based on the covariance matrix, see Exhibit 13.6).

Factor analysis, on the other hand, assumes that the data have a strict factor structure in the sense that the covariance matrix of the data can be represented as a function of the covariances between factors plus idiosyncratic variances. This assumption has to be verified, otherwise the estimation process might yield incorrect results.

In other words, PCA tends to be a dimensionality reduction technique that can be applied to any multivariate distribution and that yields incremental results. This means that there is a trade-off between the gain in estimation from dimensionality reduction and the percentage of variance explained. Consider that PCA is not an estimation procedure: it is an exact linear transformation of a time series. Estimation comes into play when a reduced number of principal components is chosen and each variable is regressed onto these principal components. At this point, a reduced number of principal components yields a simplified regression which results in a more robust estimation of the covariance matrix of the original series though only a fraction of the variance is explained.

Factor analysis, on the other hand, tends to reveal the exact factor structure of the data. That is, FA tends to give an explanation in terms of what factors explain what processes. Factor rotation can be useful both in the case of PCA and FA. Consider FA. In our illustration, to make the factor model identifiable, we applied the restriction that factors are orthonormal variables. This restriction, however, might result in a matrix of factor loadings that is difficult to interpret.

For example, if we look at the loading matrix in Exhibit 13.11, there is no easily recognizable structure, in the sense that the time series is influenced by all factors. Exhibit 13.16 shows graphically the relationship of the time series to the factors. In this graphic, each of the 10 time series is represented by its three loadings.

We can try to obtain a better representation through factor rotation. The objective is to create factors such that each series has only one large loading and thus is associated primarily with one factor. Several proce-

EXHIBIT 13.16   Graphical Representation of Factor Loadings

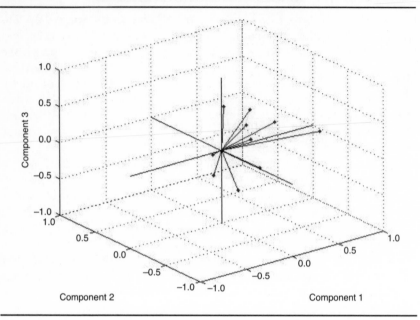

dures have been proposed for doing so.[20] For example, if we rotate factors using the "promax" method, we obtain factors that are no longer orthogonal but that often have a better explanatory power.[21] Exhibit 13.18 shows graphically the relationship of time series to the factors after rotation. The association of the series to a factor is more evident. This fact can be seen from the matrix of new factor loadings in Exhibit 13.17 which shows how nearly each stock has one large loading.

[20] These include the promax, promin, proma, and simplimax.
[21] The promax method was developed in A. E. Hendrickson and P. O. White, "Promax: A Quick Method for Rotation to Orthogonal Oblique Structure," *British Journal of Statistical Psychology* 17 (1964), pp. 65–70.

EXHIBIT 13.17   Factor Loadings after Rotation

	F1	F2	F3
SUNW	0.214020	0.750690	0.101240
AMZN	0.943680	0.127310	0.104990
MERQ	0.218340	0.578050	−0.294340
GD	0.163360	0.073269	0.544220
NOC	−0.070130	−0.003990	0.278000
CPB	0.393120	−0.178070	0.301920
KO	0.032397	−0.100020	−0.545120
MLM	−0.137130	0.561640	0.123670
HLT	0.513660	0.048842	−0.168290
UTX	0.229400	0.133510	−0.204650

EXHIBIT 13.18   Relationship of Times Series to the Factors after Rotation

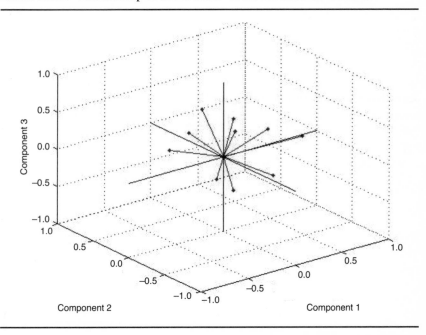

CONCEPTS EXPLAINED IN THIS CHAPTER (IN ORDER OF PRESENTATION)

Factor models
Spearman's model
Thurstone's multiple-factors model
Linear factor models
Factor loadings
Static models
Dynamic models
Strict factor models
Normal factor models
Covariance of a factor models
Fundamental factors
Macroeconomic factors
Statistical factors
Principal components analysis
Strict factor structure
Principal components
Factor analysis
PCA with stable distributions
Principal components duration
Bond risk factors

CHAPTER 14

Heavy-Tailed and Stable Distributions in Financial Econometrics

In August of 1992, powerful hurricane Andrew ravaged through southern Florida and Louisiana, creating insured losses exceeding $16 billion and total losses of more than $30 billion. This single event forced several insurance companies to bankruptcy and significantly depleted the insurance capital available for natural catastrophes. In September 1998, the sudden rise of volatility in the global financial markets, set off by a default in Russia's sovereign debt, led to the hedge fund[1] Long-Term Capital Management (LTCM) incurring losses in excess of 90% of its value. LTCM was highly leveraged, meaning it had more than $125 billion of borrowed funds. This financial mishap caused a serious treat to the stability of the global financial system and a more widespread collapse in the financial markets was only avoided by a $3.6 billion bailout organized by the Federal Reserve Board of the New York. A consequence of this event is that it exposed the vulnerability of financial markets to dealings of hedge funds. What do natural catastrophes such as hurricane Andrew have in common with market crashes and what are the implications of these events? Although the first one relates to natural phenomena and the second one to socioeconomic phenomena, both of these events share the property that laws that govern extreme events may vio-

---

[1] This term denotes a fund whose managers receive performance-related fees and can freely use various active investment strategies to achieve positive absolute returns, involving any combination of leverage, derivatives, long and short positions in securities or any other assets in a wide range of markets. Hedge funds are currently not regulated but monitoring of their activities is increasing. The terms "pooled investment vehicle" and "sophisticated alternative investment vehicles" are used interchangeably.

late the assumptions on which the current prevailing assessment of insurance losses due to extreme weather events and risk management practices in financial markets are built upon. For the hurricane event, the expert commission that reviewed the situation concluded that "the basic assumptions underpinning most of the insurance industry are violated by the laws of nature that apply to climate and tropical cyclones."[2] In the case of LTCM, the review pointed out that LTCM's assessment of the potential for overall losses in a situation of extreme financial risk was built on a basic assumption that did not hold. LTCM appeared to use recent history to estimate risk, assigning a low probability to events such as sovereign defaults and major market crashes such as the October 1987 stock market crash.[3] In both cases, the basic assumption that was rendered invalid is the one of Gaussian law or the popular "bell" curve.

The tails of the distribution describe the regions to either side of a distribution curve that correspond to large fluctuations. The two events described above imply that extreme events take place far more often than one would expect based on the "normal" Gaussian statistics. The extreme events are contained in the tail region and if they appear with higher probability compared to that implied by the Gaussian distribution, we say that such distribution possess "fat tails." In mathematical terms, fat tails or heavy tails are associated with a power-law curve and fall off much slower than the tails of the Gaussian curve.[4] Thus, to appropriately assess the probability of extreme events taking place, we have to consider the assumptions and models that distance themselves from the Gaussian laws, or even better, that generalize them. The heavy-tail behavior has been found in both natural and economic data such as astrophysics, evolutionary biology, internet traffic data, a wide range of financial asset data, and complex business management issues.[5]

Focusing on financial asset data, we have indicated in Chapter 8 that movements in asset prices or equivalently asset returns show certain important characteristics or stylized facts. Leptokurtic property is one of

---

[2] Anthony Michaels, Ann Close, David Malmquist, and Anthony Knapp, "Climate Science and Insurance Risk," *Nature* 389 (1997), pp. 225–227.

[3] Philippe Jorion, "Risk management lessons from Long-Term Capital Management," *European Financial Management* 6 (2000), pp. 277–300.

[4] There are various characterizations of fat tails in the literature. In finance, typically the tails which are heavier than those of the Gaussian distribution are considered "heavy." In some applications of extreme value theory such as the modeling of operational risk, the exponential tails are considered a borderline case separating "thin tails" and "heavy tails."

[5] Mark Buchanan, "Power Laws & the New Science of Complexity Management," *Strategy+Business* 34 (2004), pp. 71–79.

them, indicating that empirical asset return distributions are fat tailed and more peaked around the center compared to normal distribution. This was first noted in the studies of Mandelbrot dealing with cotton futures return data.[6] Subsequently, other asset classes such as bonds and exchange rates have also been observed to exhibit fat tails.[7] Fatter tails imply a higher probability of large losses than the Gaussian distribution would suggest.

Events such as market crashes and bubbles regularly point out the potential effects of fat tails in unconditional return distributions. Empirical research in finance has the goal of precise modeling of such extreme events to provide the basis for asset pricing, trading, and risk management in all market environments. For modeling extreme events, various nonnormal distributions have been suggested in the literature:

- Mixtures of two or more normal distributions
- Student's *t*-distributions, hyperbolic distributions, and other scale mixtures of normal distributions
- Gamma distributions
- Extreme value distributions
- Stable Paretian (Lévy) non-Gaussian distributions
- Smoothly truncated stable distributions
- Tempered stable distributions
- Infinitely divisible (non-Gaussian) distributions

The focus of this chapter is on the stable Paretian or stable distributions that are appropriate for modeling heavy-tailed data. While alternative models utilizing other nonnormal distributions have been proposed and used, stable distributions have unique characteristics that make them a suitable candidate for modeling of financial stochastic processes. One of them is the *stability*, which is not shared by alternative distributions. The stability property implies that any sum of independent and identically stable distributed returns is again stable distributed, and furthermore, the distribution of the properly linearly normalized returns has the same distribution as the individual returns. Stability implies existence of an overall parameter, the index of stability, that governs the main properties of the underlying return distribution and remains unchanged across all scales (e.g., daily, monthly or annual sampling intervals).

---

[6] Benoit B. Mandelbrot, "The Variation of Certain Speculative Prices," *Journal of Business* 36 (1963), pp. 394–419.

[7] For a review of these studies, see Chapter 11 in Svetlozar T. Rachev, Christian Menn, and Frank J. Fabozzi, *Fat-Tailed and Skewed Asset Return Distributions: Implications for Risk Management, Portfolio Selection, and Option Pricing* (Hoboken, NJ: John Wiley & Sons, 2005).

However, the use of stable distributions has its cost. Since, in essence, they describe distributions with *infinite variance*, there is a conceptual difficulty in using them for financial data with bounded range and in estimation. Since the assumption of IID random variables for the stability property may be too restrictive in practice, more advanced models, generalizing the concept of stable distributions, have been developed (smoothly truncated stable distributions[8] and tempered stable distributions),[9] relaxing the stability property but allowing for finite and infinite variance return distributions.

In this chapter, we provide a formal definition of stable distributions, discuss their main properties, and show how they can be applied in financial modeling. In the next chapter, we see how some of the econometric models described in previous chapters (e.g., ARMA and GARCH) are modified to accommodate the assumption that innovation processes are governed by stable Paretian distributions.

BASIC FACTS AND DEFINITIONS OF STABLE DISTRIBUTIONS

Stable Paretian distributions are a class of probability laws that have interesting theoretical and practical properties. They are appealing for financial modeling since they generalize the normal (Gaussian) distribution and allow heavy tails and skewness, properties which are common in financial data. In this section, we present the basic definitions of stable laws. We will be rather informal in coverage by presenting the material without proofs, which can be found in the standard literature on this topic.[10]

Definitions of the Stable Distributions

The key characteristic of stable distributions, and the reason for the term "stable," is that they retain shape (up to scale and shift) under addition: if X_1, X_2 ..., are IDD stable random variables, then for every n

$$X_1 + X_2 + \ldots + X_n \overset{d}{=} c_n X + d_n \tag{14.1}$$

---

[8] Christian Menn and Svetlozar T. Rachev, "A New Class of Probability Distributions and Its Applications to Finance," *Technical Report*, University of California at Santa Barbara, 2004.

[9] J. Rosinski, "Tempered Stable Processes," in O. E. Barndorff–Nielsen (ed.), *Second MaPhySto Conference on Lévy Processes: Theory and Applications* (Aarhus: Ma Physto, 2002), pp. 215–220.

[10] See, for example, Svetlozar T. Rachev and Stefan Mittnik, *Stable Paretian Models in Finance* (Chichester: John Wiley & Sons, 2000).

for some constants $c_n > 0$ and d_n. The symbol $\overset{d}{=}$ means equality in distribution; that is, the right- and left-hand sides of the expression (14.1) have the same distribution. The law is called *strictly stable* if $d_n = 0$ for all n.

For financial modeling, this key characteristic implies that the distribution of the total (cumulative) return of IID, say, daily returns over a period has the same distributional "shape" as the individual daily returns.[11]

The class of all laws that satisfy (14.1) is called stable or α-stable and is described by four parameters:

- *Index of stability* α that determines the tail weight or the distribution's kurtosis with $0 < \alpha \leq 2$.[12]
- *Skewness parameter* β which determines the distribution's skewness and is in the range $-1 \leq 0 \leq 1$.
- *Scale parameter* σ that can be any positive number. (If σ = 0 the distribution is degenerated and the stable random variable is a constant.)
- *Location parameter* μ that the shifts distribution right if μ > 0, and left if μ < 0.

To denote that a stable random variable X is characterized by the four stable parameters, we write $X \sim S_\alpha(\beta,\sigma,\mu)$ where S_α denotes the α-stable distribution. Parameters α and β determine the shape of the distribution. If the index of stability α = 2, then the stable distribution reduces to the normal (Gaussian) distribution. That implies that relative to the normal distribution a higher probability of extreme events exists when α < 2. The impact of α for values less than 2 on the density of the distribution is twofold. First, it has an effect on the tail thickness of the density. Second, it has an effect on the peakedness at the origin relative to the normal distribution. Jointly, these two effects are known as the "leptokurtosis" of the density; consequently, the index of stability α can be interpreted as a measure of leptokurtosis. As the value of α becomes smaller, the more leptokurtic the distribution—the peak of the density becomes higher and the tails heavier. Thus, for α < 2, stable distributions are more peaked around the center than the normal and have fatter tails. In fact, for α < 2 they are so heavy that the variance is infinite; and for $\alpha \leq 1$, even the first moment does not exist.

---

[11] The standard deterministic summation scheme where n is a deterministic integer as in (14.1) produces the stable Paretian distributions. Other schemes are also possible, such as the maximum and minimum schemes that lead to extreme-value distributions. Some authors use the term *sum-stable* to distinguish it from *min-stable* and *max-stable* schemes.

[12] Other names for α are the stable index, characteristic exponent, exponent of stable distribution, and the tail index.

For $\beta = 0$, the distribution is symmetric around the location parameter μ. If $\beta > 0$, the distribution is skewed to the right and if $\beta < 0$, it is skewed toward the left. Larger magnitudes of β indicate greater skewness. A *symmetric stable distribution* is a stable distribution with $\beta = 0$ and $\mu = 0$ and the stable distribution is symmetric around μ if $\beta = 0$.[13]

The scale parameter generalizes the definition of standard deviation and can be interpreted as volatility. It allows any stable random variable X to be expressed as $X = \sigma X_0$, where the distribution of X_0 has a unit scale parameter and the same α and β as X.

Exhibit 14.1 shows the effect of α on the kurtosis of the density for the case of $\beta = 0$, $\mu = 0$, and $\sigma = 1$. Exhibit 14.2 illustrates the impact of β on the skewness of the density function for $\alpha = 1.5$, $\mu = 0$, and $\sigma = 1$.

Inconveniently, stable distributions, in general, do not have closed-form expressions for the density and distribution functions. However, they can be

EXHIBIT 14.1 Influence of α on the Resulting Stable Distribution

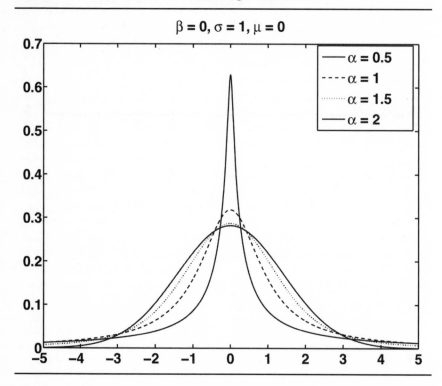

$$\beta = 0, \sigma = 1, \mu = 0$$

——	$\alpha = 0.5$
----	$\alpha = 1$
....	$\alpha = 1.5$
——	$\alpha = 2$

[13] If $\beta = 0$, we say that the distribution is symmetric around μ. In the literature, it is often the case that the symmetry is defined around the value of location parameter equal to zero.

EXHIBIT 14.2 Influence of β on the Resulting Stable Distribution

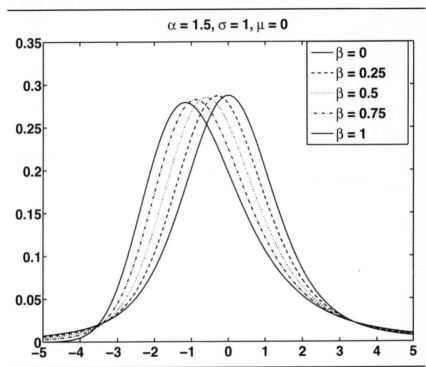

described by their characteristic function, denoted by φ. A characteristic function (ch.f.) uniquely defines a probability distribution, as is the case for cumulative distribution function and the probability density function.

In addition to definition (14.1), another definition of a stable random variable is given by its characteristic function.

A random variable X is said to have a stable distribution if there are parameters $0 < \alpha \le 2$, $\sigma \ge 0$, $-1 \le \beta \le 1$, and μ that are real such that its characteristic function has the following form

$$\varphi(t) = E\exp(itX) = \begin{cases} \exp\left\{-\sigma^{\alpha}|t|^{\alpha}\left(1 - i\beta(\mathrm{sign}\,t)\tan\dfrac{\pi\alpha}{2}\right) + i\mu t\right\} & \text{if } \alpha \neq 1 \\[2mm] \exp\left\{-\sigma|t|\left(1 + i\beta\dfrac{2}{\pi}(\mathrm{sign}\,t)\ln|t|\right) + i\mu t\right\} & \text{if } \alpha = 1 \end{cases} \tag{14.2}$$

where

$$\text{sign} t = \begin{cases} 1 & \text{if } t > 0 \\ 0 & \text{if } t = 0 \\ -1 & \text{if } t < 0 \end{cases}$$

The explicit expression for the logarithm of the characteristic function $\varphi(t)$ of any stable random variable was derived by Paul Lévy in 1925. The characteristic function given by (14.2) is one parameterization that is denoted with $S(\alpha,\beta,\sigma,\mu_1;1)$, $\mu_1 = \mu$. Another parameterization, denoted by $S(\alpha,\beta,\sigma,\mu_0;0)$, is

$$\varphi(t) = E \exp(itX)$$

$$= \begin{cases} \exp\left\{-\sigma^{\alpha}\left(|t|^{\alpha} - it\beta\left(\tan\dfrac{\pi\alpha}{2}\right)(|t|^{\alpha-1} - 1)\right) + i\mu_0 t\right\} & \text{if } \alpha \neq 1 \\ \exp\left\{-\sigma\left(|t| + it\beta\dfrac{2}{\pi}\ln|t|\right) + i\mu_0 t\right\} & \text{if } \alpha = 1 \end{cases} \tag{14.3}$$

The first parameterization is more commonly found in the literature and the second one is used in applications since it facilitates numerical operations. As pointed out in Samorodnitsky and Taqqu,[14] the characteristic function (14.2) is not continuous at $\alpha = 1$ and $\beta \neq 0$. When α is near 1, computing stable densities and cumulatives in this range is numerically difficult. In applications, one prefers the (14.3) parameterization, which is jointly continuous in alpha and beta. By defining the modified location parameter

$$\mu_0 = \begin{cases} \mu + \beta\sigma^{\alpha}\tan\dfrac{\pi\alpha}{2} & \text{if } \alpha \neq 1 \\ \mu & \text{if } \alpha = 1 \end{cases}$$

Zolotarev shows that the characteristic function and therefore the distribution of the new modified variable shifted by μ_0 undergoes no discontinuity as α passes unity.[15] The parameters α, β, and σ have the same meaning in both parameterizations, only the location parameter is differ-

---

[14] Gennady Samorodnitsky and Murad S. Taqqu, *Stable Non-Gaussian Random Processes* (New York: Chapman & Hall, 1994).

[15] See V.M. Zolotarev, *One-Dimensional Stable Laws, Volume 65 of Translations of Mathematical Monographs* (Providence, RI: American Mathematical Society, 1986). Translated from Russian by H.H. McFaden.

ent. A subscript with location parameter is used to distinguish between the two parameterizations: μ_0 for the location parameter in $S(\alpha,\beta,\sigma,\mu_0;0)$ and μ_1 for the location parameter in the $S(\alpha,\beta,\sigma,\mu_1;1)$ parameterization.

They are only three special cases where one can provide closed-form expression for the density and verify directly that they are stable:

- Normal distribution for the case where $\alpha = 2$, $\beta = 0$ and the reparameterization in scale.
- Cauchy distribution for the case where $\alpha = 1$ and $\beta = 0$.
- Lévy distribution for the case where $\alpha = 0.5$ and $\beta = 1$.

The Cauchy distribution has much fatter tails than the normal distribution. The probability mass of the Lévy distribution is concentrated on the interval $(\mu, +\infty)$. The special cases are presented in the following examples:

Normal or Gaussian distribution: $X \sim N(\mu,\sigma^2)$ if it has a density

$$f(x) = \frac{1}{\sqrt{2\pi}\sigma}\exp\left(-\frac{(x-\mu)^2}{2\sigma^2}\right), \quad -\infty < x < \infty \quad (14.4)$$

Gaussian laws are stable: $N(\mu,\sigma^2) = S(2,0,\sigma/\sqrt{2},\mu;0) = S(2,0,\sigma/\sqrt{2},\mu;1)$

Cauchy distribution: $X \sim \text{Cauchy}(\sigma,\mu)$ if it has a density

$$f(x) = \frac{1}{\pi}\frac{\sigma}{\sigma^2 + (x-\mu)^2}, \quad -\infty < x < \infty \quad (14.5)$$

Cauchy laws are stable: $\text{Cauchy}(\sigma,\mu) = S(1,0,\sigma,\mu;1)$

Lévy distributions: $X \sim \text{Lévy}(\sigma,\mu)$ if it has a density

$$f(x) = \sqrt{\frac{\sigma}{2\pi}}\frac{1}{(x-\mu)^{3/2}}\exp\left(-\frac{\sigma}{2(x-\mu)}\right), \quad \mu < x < \infty \quad (14.6)$$

Lévy's laws are stable: $\text{Lévy}(\sigma,\mu) = S(1/2,1,\sigma,\sigma+\mu;1)$

Exhibit 14.3 compares the normal distribution and the Cauchy distribution. From the exhibit the fatter tails of the Cauchy distribution are evident. The expected value of the Cauchy distribution is not well defined, since the integrals

EXHIBIT 14.3 Comparison of Standard Cauchy and Standard Normal Distribution

Panel A: General Shape

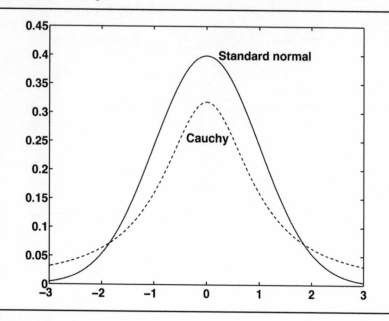

Panel B: Comparison of the Tails

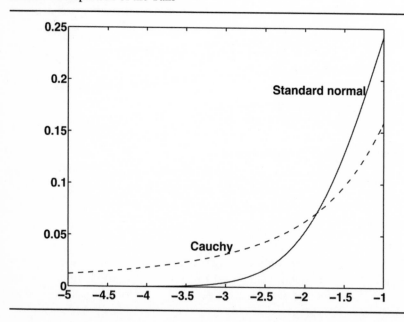

$$\int\limits_{-\infty}^{0} xf(x)dx$$

and

$$\int\limits_{0}^{+\infty} xf(x)dx$$

are individually divergent. The variance and higher moments are also not well defined.

Capturing stylized facts of asset returns, such as skewness and heavy tails, requires the specification of appropriate distributions or models. Clearly, the stable distribution with $\beta \neq 0$ and $\alpha < 2$ is a natural candidate. Increasing β towards +1 results in skewness to the right; decreasing β towards −1 results in skewness to the left; and lower values of α lead to stronger leptokurtosis. When $\alpha > 1$, the location parameter measures the mean of the distribution. In empirical finance α usually takes values in the interval (1,2). This implies the assumption that the asset returns modeled with α-stable laws exhibit finite means but infinite variances. Empirical evidence suggests that financial return data have a finite mean. The assumption of finite variance, however, has to be questioned.

PROPERTIES OF STABLE DISTRIBUTIONS

We now consider several key properties of stable distributions that are appealing in empirical finance. Specifically, we describe the behavior of the tails of the stable distribution and discuss the implications for the p-th absolute moment of the stable distribution.

Important Properties of Stable Models

When $\alpha = 2$, the stable law is identical to the normal law that has light tails and all moments exist. Except for the normal law, all other stable laws have heavy tails following an asymptotic power (Pareto) decay law characterized by

$$\lim_{x \to +\infty} x^{\alpha} P(X > x) = k_{\alpha} \frac{1 + \beta}{2} \sigma^{\alpha} \qquad (14.7)$$

for the right tail and

$$\lim_{x \to +\infty} x^{\alpha} P(X < -x) = k_{\alpha} \frac{1-\beta}{2} \sigma^{\alpha} \tag{14.8}$$

for the left tail, where

$$k_{\alpha} = \frac{1-\alpha}{\Gamma(2-\alpha)\cos(\pi\alpha/2)}, \text{ if } \alpha \neq 1$$

and

$$k_{\alpha} = \frac{2}{\pi}, \text{ if } \alpha = 1$$

When $\beta = -1$, the right tail decays faster than any power. The left tail behavior is similar by the symmetry property.

To see the difference between Gaussian and non-Gaussian stable distributions we compare their tail behavior. The tail behavior of the Gaussian distribution as $x \to \infty$ is specified by

$$P(X < -x) = P(X > x) \sim \frac{1}{2\sqrt{\pi}\sigma x} e^{-\frac{x^2}{4\sigma^2}}$$

which is markedly different from the asymptotic behavior of the tails of stable distributions that follow a power law

$$P(X > x) \sim cx^{-\alpha}, \text{ as } x \to \infty$$

In the (non-Gaussian) stable case, the tail of the stable law approaches zero in form of a power function. It is called "Pareto-like" behavior because the Pareto distribution decays in the same fashion.

One important consequence of the power decay of the tails is that only certain moments exist. This is, however, not a property that exclusively applies to stable laws; any distribution decaying with a power law (e.g., Pareto law) will not have finite moments for certain orders. For a stable random variable, the p-th absolute moment

$$E|X|^p = \int_0^{\infty} P(|X|^p > x) dx \tag{14.9}$$

exists if and only if $p < \alpha$ or $\alpha = 2$, that is, when the integral given by (14.9) converges. If the tails are too heavy, the integral will diverge.[16] Thus, the second moment of any non-Gaussian stable distribution is infinite. One obvious consequence for practical applications in finance is that, since stable distributions have infinite variances, one cannot measure risk in terms of variance and dependence in terms of correlation. Alternative concepts, namely, scale and covariation can be employed instead.

The third important property inherent to stable laws is the *stability* or *additivity property*, allowing us to use stable laws in portfolio analysis. Specifically, the sum of two independent stable random variables follows—up to some adjustment of scale and location—again the same stable distribution. We say the family of stable distributions is closed under convolution.[17] Following (14.1): If X and Y are independent and identically distributed stable random variables, then for any given positive numbers a and b, there exist a positive number c and real number d, such that

$$aX + bY \overset{d}{=} cX + d$$

where c is determined by $a^{\alpha} + b^{\alpha} = c^{\alpha}$, and $\alpha \in (0,2]$ is the index of stability of the stable distribution. For $d = 0$, we obtain the strictly stable distribution of X.

Applicability of Stable Models

Due to their appealing probabilistic properties and the overwhelming empirical evidence that asset returns are fat tailed, stable distributions are natural candidates in financial modeling.[18] Specifically, the unique probabilistic property of the generalized central limit theorem combined with the compelling empirical evidence provide justification for using stable models.

Let us now look at the property of the generalized central limit theorem (GCLT). The classical central limit theorem (CLT) says that the normalized sum of IID random variables with a finite variance con-

---

[16] Note that the sample moments of all orders will exist: one can always compute the variance of the sample. The sample variance under the stable distribution sample will have a limiting distribution after a normalization and this fact can be used in testing the stable hypothesis.

[17] Recall that in Chapter 2 we explained that the distribution of the sum is the convolution of the distributions.

[18] See Chapter 1 in Rachev, Menn, and Fabozzi, *Fat-Tailed and Skewed Asset Return Distributions: Implications for Risk Management, Portfolio Selection, and Option Pricing*.

verges to a normal distribution. This holds (under fairly general conditions) regardless of the forms of the individual probability distribution of independent random variables. This theorem is crucial to probability theory; it asserts that, asymptotically, the Gaussian law rules the center of the distribution or "bell." The CLT also serves as the formal justification for treating measurement errors as Gaussian random variables and holds to the extent that the total error is the sum of a large number of small contributions.[19] However, we also need an alternative that is only concerned with the tail behavior. This alternative is offered in the form of the GCLT. It states that if the finite variance assumption is removed, only the α-stable distribution arises as limiting distribution of sums of IID random variables.

Suppose $X_1, X_2, ..., X_n, ...$ is a sequence of IID random variables with distribution F. If there are sequences of positive numbers $\{a_n\}$, $a_n > 0$, and real numbers $\{b_n\}$, $b_n \in \Re$, such that

$$\frac{X_1 + \cdots + X_n}{a_n} + b_n \Rightarrow X \tag{14.10}$$

for some random variable X, then we say F (or the random sequence $\{X_i\}_{i=1}^{\infty}$) is in the *domain of attraction* of an α-stable law with index $\alpha \in (0,2)$.[20] We write $F \in DA(\alpha)$, where $\alpha \in (0,2]$ is the stable index of the corresponding stable distribution, and we call X a stable distributed

---

[19] Note that the central limit theorem holds in the limit ($n \to \infty$ for n independent random variables) but in practical data analysis it is more important to know to what extent the Gaussian approximation is valid for finite n. Generally, we can say that it holds as long as the sum is built up of a large number of small contributions. Discrepancies arise if, for example, the distributions of the individual contributions have long tails, so that occasional large values make up a large part of the sum. Such contributions lead to non-Gaussian tails in the sum, which can significantly alter the probability to find values with large departures from the mean. See G.R. Grimmett and D.R. Stirzaker, *Probability and Random Processes* (Oxford: Clarendon Press, 1992).

[20] Throughout the text, the symbol "$\Rightarrow$" means convergence in distribution. For example, if we consider the X_i's to be (continuously compounded) daily financial asset returns, we could say that the sum of daily returns is—up to scale and location—distributed as monthly or annual returns. It has been proven that a_n must be of the form $a_n = n^{1/\alpha} h(n)$, where $h(n)$ is a slowly varying function at infinity. Thus

$$\sum_{i=1}^{n} X_i / n^{1/\alpha} h(n) + b_n \Rightarrow X$$

where X is some α-stable distributed random variable. (See Theorem 2.1.1 in I. A. Ibragimov and Yu. V. Linnik, *Independent and Stationary Sequences of Random Variables* (Groningen: Wolters-Noordhoff Publishing, 1971).)

random variable. Note that when the X_i's are IID with finite variance, then (14.10) amounts to the classical central limit theorem. The assumption that X_i's are in the domain of attraction of an α-stable law is more general than assuming that they are α-stable distributed, because the former requires only conditions on the tails of the distribution. The domain of attraction for a stable model contains many distributions with properties close to the specified stable law.

In other words, the GCLT says that the only possible distributions with a domain of attraction are stable ones.[21] Characterizations of distributions in the domain of attraction of α-stable law are in terms of tail probabilities. The implication of this unique property for financial modeling lies in the fact that presuming that movements in asset prices are driven by many, independently occurring small shocks (identically stable distributed with index of stability α), then the only appropriate distributional model for these changes is a stable model with the same stability index α.[22]

Rather than engaging in a dispute whether stable models are appropriate, it is reasonable to use stable models as a realistic alternative in financial econometrics. In practice, statistical tests should determine whether a stable distribution fits the data better than any other candidate.

ESTIMATION OF THE PARAMETERS OF THE STABLE DISTRIBUTION

As already mentioned, stable distributions have, in general, no closed-form expression for their probability density and distribution function. Consequently, methods for estimating the parameters of the stable distribution rely on numerical approximations. Since the stable characteristic function can be written in a closed form, several estimation techniques are based on fitting the sample characteristic function. There are two basic strategies to estimation. The first focuses solely on the estimation of the tail index; the second is to estimate all parameters of the distribution.

---

[21] Mandelbrot has even suggested that the substance of the classical central limit theorem would be better understood if it was referred to as *center* limit theorem. Indeed, that theorem concerns the center of the distribution, while the anomalies concern the tails. In a similar vein, the generalized central limit theorem that yields Lévy stable limits would be better understood if called *tail* limit theorem. See Benoit B. Mandelbrot, "Heavy Tails in Finance for Independent or Multifractal Price Increments," in Svetlozar T. Rachev (ed.), *Handbook of Heavy Tailed Distributions in Finance* (Amsterdam: Elsevier/North-Holland, 2003), pp. 1–34.

[22] This property is a consequence of the domain of attraction of stable distributions defined by (14.10). For further details on this property, see Chapter 2 in Rachev and Mittnik, *Stable Paretian Models in Finance*, pp. 27–28.

Asymptotic Tail Behavior: Where Does the Tail Begin?

One of the most popular estimators of the tail index is the *Hill estimator*,[23] which is a simple nonparametric estimator based on order statistics.[24] Hill proposed a conditional maximum likelihood estimation (MLE) approach by maximizing the conditional likelihood function. Given a sample of n observations, $X_1, ..., X_n$, the Hill estimator is computed by

$$\hat{\alpha}_{\text{Hill}} = \left(\frac{1}{k} \sum_{j=1}^{k} \log X_{n+1-j:n} - \log X_{n-k:n} \right)^{-1} \tag{14.11}$$

with standard error

$$SD(\hat{\alpha}_{\text{Hill}}) = \frac{k \hat{\alpha}_{\text{Hill}}}{(k-1)\sqrt{(k-2)}}$$

where $X_{j:n}$ denotes the j-th order statistic of the sample size n; and k is the number of observations that lie in the right tail of the distribution of interest.

The Hill estimator is strongly consistent[25] and asymptotically normal.[26] Asymptotic normality of the Hill estimator is given by

$$\sqrt{k}(\hat{\alpha}_{\text{Hill}}^{-1} - \hat{\alpha}^{-1}) \sim N(0, \hat{\alpha}^{-2})$$

The Hill estimator depends on the number k of the largest observations chosen to calculate the estimates. The practical choice of the truncation parameter k/n poses a problem with the Hill estimator and its generalizations. k must be sufficiently small so that $X_{n-k:n}$ is in the tail

---

[23] B. M. Hill, "A Simple General Approach to Inference about the Tail of a Distribution," *Annals of Statistics* 3 (1975), pp. 1163–1174.

[24] Let $X_1, X_2, ..., X_n$ be n IID, continuous random variables having a common probability distribution function and distribution function. Define $X_{1:n}$ as the smallest of the n-tuple $(X_1, X_2, , ..., X_n)$, $X_{2:n}$ as the second smallest of the n-tuple $(X_1, X_2, ..., X_n)$, ..., $X_{j:n}$ as the j-th smallest of the n-tuple $(X_1, X_2, ..., X_n)$, ..., and finally $X_{n:n}$ as the largest of the n-tuple $(X_1, X_2, ..., X_n)$. The ordered values $X_{1:n} \leq X_{2:n} \leq \cdots \leq X_{n:n}$ are called order statistics corresponding to the random variables $X_1, X_2, ..., X_n$. In other words, $X_{1:n}, ..., X_{n:n}$ are the ordered values of $X_1, X_2, ..., X_n$. For further details on order statistics, see for example, Sheldon Ross, *A First Course in Probability* (Englewood Cliffs, NJ: Prentice Hall, 1994).

[25] P. Deheuvels, E. Häusler, and D. M. Mason, "Almost Sure Convergence of the Hill Estimator," *Mathematical Proceedings of the Cambridge Philosophical Society* 104 (1988), pp. 371–381.

[26] C. M. Goldie and R. L. Smith, "Slow Variation with Remainder: A Survey of the Theory and its Applications," *Quarterly Journal of Mathematics* 38 (1987), pp. 45–71.

of the distribution; however, it should not be too small because then the estimator will not be accurate. In general, k needs to satisfy

$$k \to \infty \quad \text{and} \quad \frac{k}{n} \to 0 \quad \text{and} \quad n \to \infty \tag{14.12}$$

to achieve strong consistency and asymptotic normality. With the proper choice of the sequence $k = k(n)$, the estimator is consistent and asymptotically normal. However, the rate of convergence of the tail estimators can be very slow.

It should be noted that the Hill estimator and its modifications are highly unreliable to be used in practice. Mittnik, Paolella, and Rachev found that small sample performance of $\hat{\alpha}_{\text{Hill}}$ for IID stable distributed returns does not resemble its asymptotic behavior, even for $n >$ 10,000.[27] To obtain meaningful estimates of α, it is necessary to have an enormous data series; for example, for $\alpha = 1.9$, reasonable estimates are produced only for $n > 100,000$. The implication is that, considering the length of financial data available, no meaningful estimates can be obtained by the Hill method. In practice, one usually plots values of the estimator against the value of k (obtaining the Hill plot) and looks for a stabilization (flat spot) in the graph.

Alternatives to the Hill estimator are the Pickands and the modified unconditional Pickands estimators.[28] In contrast to the Hill estimator, these two estimators are solely based on the k-th, $(2k)$-th, $(3k)$-th, and $(4k)$-th order statistics. Although the tail estimators are not reliable enough to be used in practice, they are the only ones that should be used when attempting to "get an idea" about the behavior far in the tail. Their use requires minimal assumptions (only certain tail behavior of the sample distribution) but an extremely large sample size.

Estimating the Entire Distribution

Methods for estimating stable parameters by fitting the entire distribution include:

1. Quantile approaches
2. Characteristic function techniques
3. Maximum likelihood methods

---

[27] Stefan Mittnik, Marc S. Paolella, and Svetlozar T. Rachev, "A Tail Estimator for the Index of the Stable Paretian Distribution," *Communications in Statistics, Theory and Methods* 27 (1998), pp. 1239–1262.

[28] J. Pickands, "Statistical Inference Using Extreme Order Statistics," *Annals of Statistics* 3 (1975), pp. 119–131.

We discuss each in the following sections.

Quantile Approaches

In essence, the quantile estimator matches sample quantiles and theoretical quantiles. The quantile approach was first suggested by Fama and Roll[29] and is based on observed properties of stable quantiles. Their method was designed for estimating parameters of symmetric stable distributions with an index of stability $\alpha > 1$. This estimator exhibits a small asymptotic bias. McCulloch[30] generalized the quantile procedures of Fama and Roll to the asymmetric case. His method uses a modified quantile technique, which provides consistent and asymptotically normal estimators of all four stable parameters with $\alpha \in [0.6, 2.0]$ and $\beta \in [-1, 1]$. The estimator is based on five sample quantiles, namely the 5%, 25%, 50%, 75%, and 95% quantiles. A disadvantage of the McCulloch method is that it ignores all observations in the tails (below the 5% quantile and above the 95% quantile).

Characteristic Function Techniques

Characteristic function techniques are based on fitting the sample characteristic function to the theoretical characteristic function. The first characteristic function methods proposed were the minimum distance, the minimum r-th mean distance, and the method of moments.[31] Characteristic function estimators are consistent and under certain conditions are asymptotically normal.[32]

Maximum Likelihood Method

The maximum likelihood (ML) method for estimating stable parameters was first proposed by DuMouchel.[33] ML methods differ in the manner in which they compute stable densities. DuMouchel evaluated the density by grouping data applying the fast Fourier transform (FFT) to "cen-

---

[29] Eugene F. Fama and Richard R. Roll, "Parameter Estimates for Symmetric Stable Distributions," *Journal of the American Statistical Association* 66 (June 1971), pp. 331–338.

[30] J. H. McCulloch, "Simple Consistent Estimators of Stable Distribution Parameters," *Communication in Statistics: Simulation Computation* 15 (1986), pp. 1109–1136.

[31] S. J. Press, "Estimation of Univariate and Multivariate Stable Distributions," *Journal of the American Statistical Association* 67 (1972), pp. 842–846.

[32] I. A. Koutrouvelis, "An Iterative Procedure for the Estimation of the Parameters of Stable Laws," *Communications in Statistics: Simulation and Computation* 10 (1981), pp. 17–28.

[33] W. DuMouchel, "Stable Distributions in Statistical Inference: 1. Symmetric Stable Distribution Compared to Other Symmetric Long-Tailed Distributions," *Journal of the American Statistical Association* 68 (1973), pp. 469–477.

ter" values and asymptotic expansions in the tails. He proved that the ML estimator is consistent and asymptotically normal. Mittnik, Rachev, and Paolella[34] suggest an approximate conditional ML procedure where they calculate the density at equally-spaced grid points via an FFT of the characteristic function and at intermediate points by linear interpolation. The FFT method applies an FFT approximation to the probability density function to compute the likelihood. The unconditional ML estimate of $\theta = (\alpha, \beta, \sigma, \mu)$ is obtained by maximizing the logarithm of the likelihood function

$$L(\theta) = \prod_{t=1}^{T} S_{\alpha, \beta}\left(\frac{r_t - \mu}{\sigma}\right)\sigma^{-1} \qquad (14.13)$$

where r_t are, for example, daily asset returns, and T is the number of observations in the sample.

The estimation of all stable models is approximate in the sense that the stable function, $S_\alpha(\beta, \sigma, \mu)$, is approximated via FFT of the stable characteristic function given by expression (14.2).[35] One advantage of the ML approach over most other methods is its ability to handle generalizations to dependent or not identically distributed data arising in financial modeling(e.g.,varioustime-seriesmodelswithstabledisturbances).[36]

Assessing the Goodness of Fit

To compare the goodness of fit between stable distributions and normal or other distributions, we can employ different criteria:

- Kolmogorov-Smirnov distance statistic
- Anderson-Darling statistic
- the log-likelihood values obtained from maximum likelihood estimation

Kolmogorov-Smirnov Distance Statistic

The *Kolmogorov-Smirnov distance statistic* (KS-statistic) is computed according to

---

[34] Stefan Mittnik, Svetlozar T. Rachev, and Marc S. Paollela, "Stable Paretian Modeling in Finance: Some Empirical and Theoretical Aspects," in R. J. Adler et al. (eds). *A Practical Guide to Heavy Tails: Statistical Techniques and Applications* (Boston: Birkhauser, 1998), pp. 79–110.

[35] Details on the tail estimation using FFT is provided in Chapter 3 of Rachev and Mittnik, *Stable Paretian Models in Finance.*

[36] For further references on estimating stable parameters, see Rachev and Mittnik, *Stable Paretian Models in Finance.*

$$KS = \sup_{x \in R} \left| F_S(x) - \hat{F}(x) \right| \tag{14.14}$$

where $F_S(x)$ is the empirical sample distribution and $\hat{F}(x)$ is the cumulative density function of the estimated parametric density.[37] The "sup" denotes the supremum, which is the least upper bound of a set. The KS-statistic turns out to emphasize deviations around the median of the fitted distribution. It is a robust measure in the sense that it focuses only on the maximum deviation between the sample and fitted distributions. The formal definition and use of KS-statistic in comparing probability distributions are described in the appendix.

Anderson-Darling Statistic

Anderson-Darling statistic (AD-statistic)[38] is computed by

$$AD = \sup_{x \in R} \frac{\left| F_S(x) - \hat{F}(x) \right|}{\sqrt{\hat{F}(x)(1 - \hat{F}(x))}} \tag{14.15}$$

The AD-statistic scales the absolute deviations between empirical and fitted distributions with the standard deviation of $F_S(x)$ that is given in the denominator of (14.15). By its construction, the AD-statistic accentuates more the discrepancies in the tails.

Maximum Log-Likelihood Value

The maximum log-likelihood value achieved in an ML estimation may be viewed as an overall measure of goodness of fit and allows us to judge which distribution candidate is more likely to have generated the data. From a Bayesian viewpoint, given large samples and assuming equal prior probabilities for two candidate distributions, the ratio of maximum likelihood values of two competing models represents the posterior odds ratio of one candidate relative to the other.[39]

---

[37] See, for example, Chapter 9 in M.H. DeGroot, *Probability and Statistics*, 3rd ed. (Reading, MA: Addison-Wesley, 1965).

[38] T. W. Anderson, D. A. Darling, "Asymptotic Theory of Certain 'Goodness of Fit' Criteria Based on Stochastic Processes," *Annals of Mathematical Statistics* 23 (1952), pp. 193–212.

[39] Arnold Zellner, *An Introduction to Bayesian Inference in Econometrics* (New York: John Wiley & Sons, 1971).

When comparing the goodness of fit, one has to keep the number of freely estimated parameters in mind. Here, we can employ the information criteria, such as Akaike information criterion (AIC), Bayesian information criterion (BIC), and Corrected Akaike information criterion (AICC) discussed in Chapter 7. For nonnormal data they are based on the log-likelihood. For example, the AIC becomes

$$AIC = -2(\text{loglikelihood}) + 2k$$

with k denoting the number of estimated parameters.

We will now turn to illustrations that investigate alternative unconditional distributional models for the stock returns.

APPLICATIONS TO GERMAN STOCK DATA[40]

Since the initial work in the 1960s by Mandelbrot and Fama, the stable distribution has been applied to modeling both the unconditional and conditional return distributions, as well as providing a theoretical framework for portfolio theory and market equilibrium models.[41] In this section, we apply the probability and statistical concepts of stable distributions to the modeling of financial data. We provide illustrations applied to financial asset returns for individual stocks.

We investigate the distributional behavior of daily logarithmic stock returns constituting the German DAX index in the period January 1, 1988 through September 30, 2002.[42] The returns are corrected for cash dividends, stock splits, and capital adjustments. We would like to examine whether the stable distribution offers a reasonable improvement over the Gaussian distribution. The sample is restricted to 35 stocks that have a minimum of 1,000 observations to ensure that the statistics estimated were generated from sufficient data.

An initial assessment of the nonnormality of the sample is done by computing the kurtosis of the returns. For the normal case, the kurtosis is 3 whereas for heavy-tailed distributions, the values exceed 3. As shown in Exhibit 14.4, for the 35 DAX stocks considered, kurtosis is significantly greater than 3, indicating leptokurtosis for all 35 return series.

---

[40] Markus Hoechstoetter, Svetlozar Rachev, and Frank J. Fabozzi, "Distributional Analysis of the Stocks Comprising the DAX 30," *Probability and Mathematical Statistics* 25, no. 2 (2005), pp. 363–383.

[41] Rachev and Mittnik, *Stable Paretian Models in Finance.*

[42] During the period of observation there were 55 stocks that had been included in the DAX.

EXHIBIT 14.4   Kurtosis and Kolmogorov-Smirnov Test

(1) Company	(2) Kurtosis	(3) H	(4) P	(5) KSSTAT	(6) CV
Adidas-Salomon	5.9	1	$7.25 \cdot 10^{-6}$	7.57	4.11
BASF	6.3	1	$3.37 \cdot 10^{-14}$	6.53	2.23
BMW	9.0	1	$1.43 \cdot 10^{-20}$	7.90	2.23
Continental	6.2	1	$2.74 \cdot 10^{-5}$	5.05	2.90
Daimler Benz	11.0	1	$6.37 \cdot 10^{-9}$	5.98	2.60
Babcock Borsig	40.5	1	$2.25 \cdot 10^{-12}$	8.42	3.08
Degussa	15.2	1	$4.17 \cdot 10^{-15}$	7.78	2.57
Bayer	11.8	1	$1.35 \cdot 10^{-16}$	7.07	2.23
Hoechst	8.1	1	$2.99 \cdot 10^{-11}$	6.50	2.50
MAN	14.2	1	$1.38 \cdot 10^{-11}$	5.88	2.23
Henkel	11.7	1	$9.42 \cdot 10^{-19}$	7.53	2.23
Karstadt Quelle	12.7	1	$8.44 \cdot 10^{-13}$	6.54	2.35
Linde	9.8	1	$3.28 \cdot 10^{-20}$	7.83	2.23
Mannesmann	11.1	1	$1.68 \cdot 10^{-12}$	6.87	2.50
Metallgesellschaft	21.5	1	$3.27 \cdot 10^{-18}$	1.14	3.43
Preussag	9.1	1	$3.96 \cdot 10^{-11}$	6.36	2.46
RWE	11.6	1	$3.46 \cdot 10^{-20}$	8.37	2.38
SAP	8.4	1	$2.63 \cdot 10^{-5}$	6.22	3.56
Schering	6.1	1	$1.99 \cdot 10^{-14}$	6.58	2.23
Siemens	11.0	1	$3.49 \cdot 10^{-13}$	7.09	2.51
Metro	5.4	1	$4.35 \cdot 10^{-3}$	4.49	3.48
Thyssen	7.2	1	$1.11 \cdot 10^{-6}$	5.05	2.56
Veba	7.7	1	$1.46 \cdot 10^{-20}$	7.34	2.07
Viag	15.1	1	$2.55 \cdot 10^{-21}$	8.76	2.42
Volkswagen	8.1	1	$4.06 \cdot 10^{-8}$	4.88	2.23
Kaufhof	13.7	1	$4.74 \cdot 10^{-6}$	5.48	2.93
Bay. Hyp. u. Wechsel-Bank	18.7	1	$1.59 \cdot 10^{-10}$	6.65	2.65
Bay. Hypo- u. Vereinsbank	12.5	1	$3.27 \cdot 10^{-23}$	8.40	2.23
Commerzbank	10.4	1	$2.03 \cdot 10^{-17}$	7.25	2.23
Deutsche Bank	12.2	1	$7.30 \cdot 10^{-14}$	7.26	2.51
Dresdner Bank	14.7	1	$3.41 \cdot 10^{-23}$	9.43	2.50
Deutsche-Lufthansa (common stock)	9.1	1	$7.10 \cdot 10^{-8}$	5.93	2.75
Deutsche Lufthansa (name share)	5.6	0	$9.37 \cdot 10^{-2}$	3.45	3.79
Allianz	9.9	1	$1.01 \cdot 10^{-18}$	7.53	2.23
Muenchener Ruck	6.8	1	$7.20 \cdot 10^{-6}$	6.41	3.48

Notes: Column (2): Kurtosis measurements of the returns with over 1,000 trading days (January 1988–September 2002). Columns (3)–(6): Kolmogorov-Smirnov test results. $H = 0$: normal hypothesis not rejected. $H = 1$: normal hypothesis rejected. P is the significance level, KSSTAT is the value of the KS-statistic, and CV is the critical value.

Source: Adapted from Table 1 in Markus Hoechstoetter, Svetlozar Rachev, and Frank J. Fabozzi, "Distributional Analysis of the Stocks Comprising the DAX 30," *Probability and Mathematical Statistics* 25, no. 2 (2005), pp. 363–383.

The Kolmogorov-Smirnov distance goodness of fit test shows that the Gaussian distribution is clearly rejected for all but one stock at the 95% confidence level.[43] The values for the KS-statistic are given in columns (3) through (6) in Exhibit 14.4.

The estimates of the parameters of the stable distribution are obtained via the ML estimation. The estimates for the index of stability α range from 1.4461 to 1.8168. The values of β imply skewness for the majority of the stocks. Exhibit 14.5 shows the MLE estimates for the four stable parameters. Based on the estimated values for α and β and the values of the KD-statistic, it is safe to say that the data strongly favor the stable distribution over the Gaussian hypothesis for all stocks considered except Lufthansa.

APPENDIX: COMPARING PROBABILITY DISTRIBUTIONS[44]

When examining the empirical distribution of observations, it is not only interesting to fit a representative of a given class of probability distributions to the observations, but it is also quite important to determine how well the fit between the empirical and the theoretical distribution is. The reason why this question is so important is that when estimating the parameters of a given distribution family one determines the best candidate in exactly this distribution class to explain the observations. But it very might be that the real distribution generating the data does not belong to the prespecified distribution family and consequently the estimated distribution will not be able to explain the observed realizations, neither in the past nor in the future. This question leads us to the concept of probability metrics.

Generally speaking a *probability metric*[45] is a function that assigns distances to two given probability distributions. This concept helps in addressing the above mentioned problems because we can proceed in the

---

[43] The use of the KS-statistic to test the Gaussian hypothesis in data is presented in the appendix.

[44] This appendix draws from Svetlozar T. Rachev, Christian Menn, and Frank J. Fabozzi, *Fat-Tailed and Skewed Asset Return Distributions: Implications for Risk Management, Portfolio Selection, and Option Pricing* (Hoboken, NJ: John Wiley & Sons, 2005).

[45] Strictly speaking, one has to distinguish between two types of probability metrics. The so-called "simple probability" metrics (or "simple distances") measure the distance between two probability distributions; whereas the "compound probability" metrics (distances) measure the distance between two (possibly dependent) random variables. For a rigorous description of probability metrics, see Svetlozar T. Rachev, *Probability Metrics and the Stability of Stochastic Models* (Chichester: John Wiley & Sons, 1991).

EXHIBIT 14.5 Parametric Estimation Results: Maximum Likelihood Estimate

(1) Company	(2) α	(3) γ	(4) β	(5) μ	(6) α	(7) γ	(8) β	(9) μ	(10) α	(11) γ	(12) β	(13) μ
	MLE				MCE				CFE			
Adidas-Salomon	1.6182	0.0145	0.0817	-0.0010	1.4871	0.0137	0.0250	0.0003	1.7577	0.0150	0.4577	0.0011
BASF	1.6811	0.0091	-0.0590	0.0007	1.5301	0.0086	-0.0556	0.0001	1.7849	0.0093	0.0185	0.0007
BMW	1.5444	0.0098	0.0470	0.0003	1.4471	0.0094	0.0687	0.0006	1.6623	0.0101	0.1269	0.0010
Continental	1.7370	0.0100	0.1411	-0.0002	1.5511	0.0094	0.0810	0.0005	1.8236	0.0102	0.4648	0.0009
Daimler Benz	1.7014	0.0093	0.0951	0.0002	1.5907	0.0088	0.1129	0.0005	1.7796	0.0094	0.1920	0.0007
Babcock Borsig	1.6590	0.0105	0.1502	-0.0005	1.5079	0.0098	0.1109	0.0008	1.7347	0.0107	0.2990	0.0008
Degussa	1.6113	0.0089	0.0826	0.0001	1.5016	0.0086	0.0760	0.0005	1.7085	0.0092	0.2673	0.0011
Bayer	1.6770	0.0093	-0.1332	0.0008	1.5225	0.0087	-0.0740	0	1.7673	0.0095	-0.1633	0.0002
Hoechst	1.6429	0.0089	0.0983	0.0002	1.5758	0.0087	0.0732	0.0007	1.7482	0.0092	0.2151	0.0010
MAN	1.7214	0.0109	0.0195	0.0002	1.5727	0.0103	-0.0012	0	1.7986	0.0111	-0.0143	0.0002
Henkel	1.9117	0.0288	0.3086	-0.0054	1.4607	0.0080	0.0830	0.0006	1.7145	0.0088	0.1391	0.0006
Karstadt Quelle	1.6642	0.0098	0.1014	-0.0001	1.5298	0.0094	0.0829	0.0005	1.7533	0.0101	0.2704	0.0008
Linde	1.5633	0.0079	0.0259	0.0002	1.44	0.0074	0.0010	0	1.6877	0.0082	0.1071	0.0006
Mannesmann	1.6542	0.0103	0.0302	0.0011	1.5759	0.0100	0.0488	0.0011	1.7342	0.0106	0.0002	0.0011
Metallgesellschaft	1.4605	0.0104	0.0024	-0.0006	1.3975	0.0100	-0.0444	-0.0005	1.5377	0.0107	0.0859	0.0001
Preussag	1.6738	0.0102	-0.0125	0.0001	1.535	0.0097	-0.0149	-0.0001	1.7740	0.0105	-0.0715	-0.0001
RWE	1.5466	0.0081	0.1107	0.0000	1.4195	0.0076	0.0434	0.0003	1.6731	0.0085	0.1602	0.0007
SAP	1.6716	0.0181	-0.0954	0.0020	1.5149	0.0168	-0.1392	0	1.7723	0.0185	-0.1897	0.0008
Schering	1.6366	0.0089	0.0408	0.0005	1.4674	0.0083	0.0211	0.0004	1.7561	0.0092	0.0657	0.0007

EXHIBIT 14.5 (Continued)

(1) Company	(2) α	(3) γ	(4) β	(5) μ	(6) α	(7) γ	(8) β	(9) μ	(10) α	(11) γ	(12) β	(13) μ
Siemens	1.6416	0.0080	0.0370	0.0005	1.5781	0.0077	0.0421	0.0006	1.7118	0.0081	0.0326	0.0006
Metro	1.8217	0.0143	-0.2349	0.0006	1.6935	0.0136	-0.1593	-0.0008	1.8623	0.0143	-0.2041	-0.0001
Thyssen	1.7807	0.0101	0.0884	0.0004	1.6827	0.0096	0.1061	0.0004	1.8327	0.0102	0.1927	0.0008
Veba	1.5851	0.0088	-0.0260	0.0004	1.4715	0.0084	-0.0566	-0.0001	1.7084	0.0091	-0.0786	0.0001
Viag	1.5657	0.0083	0.0817	0.0002	1.4622	0.0078	0.0764	0.0005	1.6652	0.0086	0.0322	0.0004
Volkswagen	1.7218	0.0117	-0.0793	0.0008	1.6684	0.0114	-0.0574	0.0003	1.8055	0.0119	-0.1804	0.0002
Kaufhof	1.7502	0.0093	0.1419	0.0000	1.5893	0.0089	0.1238	0.0006	1.8280	0.0095	0.4307	0.0008
Bay. Hyp. u. Wechsel-Bank	1.6891	0.0079	0.1689	0.0001	1.5673	0.0074	0.1477	0.0006	1.7618	0.0080	0.2513	0.0008
Bay. Hypo- u. Vereinsbank	1.5478	0.0099	-0.0058	0.0003	1.4277	0.0093	0.0002	0	1.6495	0.0102	0.0742	0.0006
Commerzbank	1.6271	0.0092	-0.0135	0.0002	1.4822	0.0085	0.0228	0.0002	1.7225	0.0094	0.0272	0.0003
Deutsche Bank	1.6105	0.0085	0.0372	0.0005	1.5283	0.0083	0.0488	0.0006	1.7137	0.0088	0.1020	0.0009
Dresdner Bank	1.5021	0.0080	0.1207	0.0002	1.4138	0.0076	0.1188	0.0009	1.6198	0.0083	0.2581	0.0015
Deutsche-Lufthansa (common stock)	1.7218	0.0109	0.1965	-0.0002	1.569	0.0102	0.1777	0.0010	1.8090	0.0111	0.3514	0.0009
Deutsche Lufthansa (name share)	1.8506	0.0159	-0.0166	-0.0002	1.8019	0.0157	0.1195	0.0004	1.8828	0.0159	0.3694	0.0003
Allianz	1.6281	0.0098	-0.0338	0.0004	1.5274	0.0094	-0.0376	-0.0002	1.7120	0.0100	-0.0236	0.0003
Muenchener Ruck	1.6863	0.0146	-0.0223	0.0004	1.5244	0.0136	-0.0348	-0.0003	1.7871	0.0148	0.0721	0.0006

Notes:

Columns (2)–(5): Maximum Likelihood Estimates (MLE)

Columns (6)–(9): McCulloch Estimates (MCE)

Columns (10)–(13): Characteristic Function Based Estimation (CFE)

Adapted from Table 3 in Markus Hoechstoetter, Svetlozar Rachev, and Frank J. Fabozzi, "Distributional Analysis of the Stocks Comprising the DAX 30," *Probability and Mathematical Statistics* 25, no. 2 (2005), pp. 363–383.

following way: Given a sample of observations, we can compare the empirical distribution with the presumed distribution in order to determine whether it is plausible that the data were generated by the estimated distribution or not. Another application could be to determine whether the data generating distribution belongs to a certain class of probability distributions such as the class of normal distributions.

Kolmogorov-Smirnov Distance and Quantile-Quantile Plots

One of the most famous (simple) probability distances is the *Kolmogorov-Smirnov distance* (KS-distance). We apply this probability distance in our illustration in the chapter. When used to test a distributional assumption, we refer to the KS-distance as a KS-statistic as we have done in our illustration. Given two probability distributions P and Q on the real line with cumulative distribution functions F and G, we can assess a distance between these two distributions by calculating the highest distance between the values $F(x)$ and $G(x)$ for varying x. Mathematically, this means calculating the supremum distance between F and G:

$$d(P, Q) = \|F - G\|_\infty = \sup_x |F(x) - G(x)|$$

The *supremum* is the least upper bound of a set and is denoted by "sup."

It was understood by statisticians that the distribution of this distance calculated between an empirical distribution function and the theoretical one on the basis of a sample, does not depend on the concrete type of distribution as long as it is a continuous distribution. This fact can be used to perform the famous Kolmogorov-Smirnov test of goodness of fit, which is outlined below.

Given a sample of observations $x = (x_1, ..., x_n)$, the empirical distribution function F_n is given by the following expression

$$F_n(t) = \frac{1}{n} \# \{x_i | x_i \le t\}$$

where #{...} denotes the number of elements contained in the set {...} and F_n defines a discrete probability distribution on the real line and for large values of n the empirical distribution converges to the theoretical one. Under the hypothesis that the sample was generated by a probability distribution with distribution function F, the distribution of the KS-distance between F and F_n is tabulated. That means that depending on the concrete value of n and the observed distance (denoted by d), it is possible to calculate the p-value and to decide whether we should believe in the hypotheses or not.

Sometimes it is helpful to plot the distance between the empirical and theoretical distribution function to illustrate the deviation graphically. In order to generate a maximum of comparability, it is common to standardize the two distributions in the following way: Instead of plotting the x-values versus the difference of distribution function values, we plot the quantiles of the first distribution versus the quantiles of the second. The result is called the *quantile-quantile plot* or simply the *QQ-plot*.

Let us illustrate the concepts presented with an example. Suppose that we are given the sample of 20 observations (e.g., daily stock return data in percent over one trading month) in Exhibit A14.1. We want to determine whether it is reasonable to assume that the underlying distribution is standard normal.

We can use the QQ-plot in Exhibit A14.2, which shows the differences between the empirical distribution and the standard normal distribution.

The line in the exhibit embodies the perfect coincidence, whereas the dots represent the actual observations. We can see that there are notable differences between the corresponding quantiles. In order to interpret these deviations, we calculate additionally the KS-distance. The calculations are shown in Exhibit A14.3. The KS-distance is given by

$$d = \max_{1 \le i \le 20} \left| F_n(x_i) - \Phi(x_i) \right| = 0.1446$$

and the critical value (which can be found in any statistics textbook) for a confidence level of 95% is $d_n = 0.2647$. The latter value can be interpreted as follows: If we draw randomly 20 values from a standard normal distribution and calculate the KS-distance, then we obtain in 95%

EXHIBIT A14.1　　Sample of 20 Observations

i	Observation	i	Observation
1	−2.1	11	0.4
2	0.1	12	0.1
3	0.3	13	−1.1
4	−0.8	14	−0.3
5	1.7	15	0.9
6	1.3	16	0.1
7	0.2	17	−3.1
8	−0.4	18	−0.7
9	0.0	19	−0.2
10	−0.1	20	1.5

EXHIBIT A14.2   Q-Q Plot Illustration

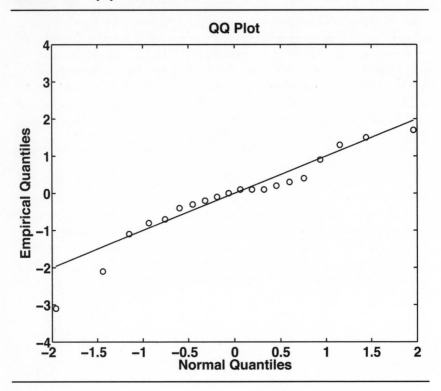

of the cases a value which is below 0.2467 and only in 5% of the cases a value above. Consequently, a value higher than 0.2467 will speak against the hypothesis that the data are generated by a standard normal distribution. In our case, the value is below and we cannot reject the standard normal hypothesis.

Anderson-Darling Distance

Sometimes it is important to assign different weights to the same deviations between two probability distribution functions. In financial applications, for example, one might be interested in estimating the tails of a return distribution very accurately. The reason for that is that the tails are responsible for the unexpected events and if such an unexpected event takes place, we want to know how much money we lose (or win) and, therefore, we need information about the tail of the return distribution. If we assume a certain probability distribution with distribution function F and measure the distance between F and the empirical distri-

EXHIBIT A14.3   Calculation of the KS-Distance

i	x_i	$\Phi(x_i)$	$F_{20}(x_i) = i/n$	$|F_{20}(x_i) - \Phi(x_i)|$
1	−3.1	0.00096767	0.05	0.04903233
2	−2.1	0.01786436	0.1	0.08213564
3	−1.1	0.1356661	0.15	0.0143339
4	−0.8	0.21185533	0.2	0.01185533
5	−0.7	0.24196358	0.25	0.00803642
6	−0.4	0.3445783	0.3	0.0445783
7	−0.3	0.38208864	0.35	0.03208864
8	−0.2	0.42074031	0.4	0.02074031
9	−0.1	0.4601721	0.45	0.0101721
10	0	0.5	0.5	0
11	0.1	0.5398279	0.55	0.0101721
12	0.1	0.5398279	0.6	0.0601721
13	0.1	0.5398279	0.65	0.1101721
14	0.2	0.57925969	0.7	0.12074031
15	0.3	0.61791136	0.75	0.13208864
16	0.4	0.6554217	0.8	0.1445783
17	0.9	0.81593991	0.85	0.03406009
18	1.3	0.90319945	0.9	0.00319945
19	1.5	0.93319277	0.95	0.01680723
20	1.7	0.95543457	1	0.04456543

bution function F_n by the KS-distance, then the same importance is assigned to the tails as to the center. The reason is that the KS-distance measures the uniform distance between the two functions (that is, the maximum deviation regardless where it occurs).

An alternative way is provided by the following empirical variant of the *Anderson Darling statistic* (AD-statistic):

$$AD = \sup_x \frac{|F_n(x) - F(x)|}{\sqrt{F(x)(1 - F(x))}}$$

As with the KS-statistic, the AD-statistic measures the distance between the empirical and theoretical distribution function but is rescaled by dividing the distance through the "standard deviation" of this distance, given by the denominator in the above formula. As can be seen, the denominator becomes small for very large and very small x-values. Thus the same absolute deviation between F and F_n in the tails gets a higher weight as if it occurs in the center of the distribution. The drawback of this approach is the fact that the distribution of the statistic depends on the concrete choice of F and consequently tests about the validity of the assumption cannot be performed as easy as with the KS-distance.

We use the AD-statistic measure in our illustration in Chapter 15.

CONCEPTS EXPLAINED IN THIS CHAPTER (IN ORDER OF PRESENTATION)

Stable Paretian distributions
Strictly stable distributions
Index of stability
Skewness parameter
Scale parameter
Location parameter
Symmetric stable distributions
Characteristic function of stable distributions
Normal, Cauchy, and Lévy distributions
Power law decay of tails
Stability or additivity property
Domain of attraction
Generalized central limit theorem
Estimation of the tail parameters
    Hill estimators
Density estimation
    Quantile approaches
    Characteristic function techniques
    Maximum likelihood method
Kolmogorov-Smirnov distance statistic
Anderson-Darling statistic

CHAPTER 15

ARMA and ARCH Models with Infinite-Variance Innovations

In Chapter 6 we described autoregressive moving average (ARMA) processes and their properties with regards to stationarity and estimation. In the previous chapter we introduced a stable non-Gaussian distributed random variable (exhibiting heavy tails) along with major properties of stability and power law decay of tails which imply that its second moment is infinite.[1] ARMA models can then be extended by considering error terms that follow a stable non-Gaussian distribution, giving rise to "infinite variance autoregressive moving average models." Such heavy-tailed processes are encountered in economics and finance and it is of practical interest to analyze their properties. However, the statistical theory of the infinite variance models is fundamentally different from that of models with finite variances. In this chapter we describe ARMA models and autoregressive conditional heteroskedastic (ARCH) models with infinite variance innovations and outline relevant properties along with estimation approaches.

INFINITE VARIANCE AUTOREGRESSIVE PROCESSES

Recall from equation (6.8) in Chapter 6 that a stationary autoregressive (AR(p)) time series $\{y_t\}$ is represented by difference equation

$$y_t = a_0 + a_1 y_{t-1} + a_2 y_{t-2} + \ldots + a_p y_{t-p} + \varepsilon_t \tag{15.1}$$

---

[1] There are versions of the stable random variables called "modified tempered stable" with finite second moment. Jan Rosinski, "Tempering Stable Processes," in O.E. Barndorff -Nielsen (ed.), *Second MaPhySto Conference on Lévy Processes: Theory and Applications*, 2002, pp. 215–220.

where $\{\varepsilon_t\}$ is a sequence of independent and identically distributed (IID) errors and $\phi = (a_0, a_1, ..., a_p)'$ is an unknown parameter vector with true value ϕ_0. When the second moment of the error term, $E(\varepsilon_t^2)$, is finite, we have shown that various estimators (e.g., least-squares estimators and maximum likelihood estimators) of ϕ_0 are asymptotically normal and several methods are available for statistical inference. When $E(\varepsilon_t^2)$ is infinite, we call the model given by equation (15.1) the *infinite variance autoregressive model* (IVAR model). Such heavy-tailed models have been encountered in economics and finance.[2] A problem with IVAR models is their estimation because the maximum likelihood estimation is very cumbersome.

The condition for strict stationarity of model (15.1) is given as follows:[3]

The characteristic polynomial $1 - a_1\lambda - ... a_p\lambda_p$ has all roots outside the unit circle and $\{\varepsilon_t\}$ are independent and identically distributed with $E|\varepsilon_t|^\delta < \infty$ for some $\delta > 0$.

Regarding estimation of model (15.1), consistency and the limiting distribution of estimators for ϕ_0 are of interest. Various estimators have been applied to estimate the model (15.1). The least squares estimator (LSE) of ϕ_0 has been proven to be strongly consistent with a convergence rate $n^{-1/\delta}$, where n is the sample size, $\delta < \alpha$, and $\alpha \in (0,2)$ is the tail index of ε_t.[4] The *least absolute deviation* (LAD) estimator[5] also has been proven to be strongly consistent with the same convergence rate as for the LSE. The so called *Whittle estimator* that has been applied to standard ARMA processes and a fractionally integrated ARIMA (p,d,q)

---

[2] Svetlozar T. Rachev and Stefan Mittnik, *Stable Paretian Models in Finance* (Chichester: John Wiley & Sons, 2000).

[3] See proposition 13.3.2 in P. J. Brockwell and R. A. Davis, *Time Series: Theory and Methods*, 2nd ed. (New York: Springer, 1996).

[4] E. J. Hannan and M. Kanter, "Autoregressive Processes with Infinite Variance," *Journal of Applied Probability* 14 (1977), pp. 411–415.

[5] The problem in estimation of (15.1) is that the large positive or negative values of ε_t in IVAR models generate y_t which appear to be outliers, and the same generates many leverage points (i.e., the large positive or negative values of y_s, as $s > t$) such that process $\{y_t\}$ itself has heavy tails. Compared with the least squares estimator, the LAD estimator gives less weight to the outliers but it gives basically the same weight to the leverage points. This may result in the covariance matrix failing to be finite and asymptotic normality will not hold. See S. Ling, "Self-Weighted Least Absolute Deviation Estimation for Infinite Variance Autoregressive Models," *Journal of Royal Statistical Society* 67, no. 2 (2005), pp. 381–393.

processes[6] has also been applied to IVAR models. It has been shown that the Whittle estimator converges to a function of a sequence of stable random variables.[7] However, the limiting distributions of these estimators do not have a closed form which implies that they cannot be used for statistical inference in practice. Recently, Ling provides a new approach to handle heavy-tailed time series data based on the approach of robust estimators and introduces a self-weighted LAD (SLAD) estimator.[8] He proves that this estimator is asymptotically normal.

ARMA Process with Infinite-Variance Innovations

We can extend the IVAR models to infinite variance ARMA(p, q) process in the same way that we extended the AR to ARMA processes with finite innovations in Chapter 6. Consider a casual stationary ARMA-process $\{y_t\}_{t \in Z}$ satisfying the difference equation[9]

$$y_t - a_1 y_{t-1} - \ldots - a_p y_{t-p} = \varepsilon_t + b_1 \varepsilon_{t-1} + \ldots + b_q \varepsilon_{t-q} \tag{15.2}$$

for $t \in Z = \{0, \pm 1, \pm 2, \ldots\}$. The innovations $\{\varepsilon_t\}_{t \in Z}$ are IID symmetric random variables in the domain of normal attraction of a symmetric

---

[6] The Whittle estimator is defined to be the value of β which minimizes

$$\hat{\sigma}_n^2(\beta) = \frac{1}{n} \sum_j \frac{I_{n, X}(\lambda_j)}{g(\lambda_j, \beta)}$$

where Σ_j denotes the sum over all nonzero Fourier frequencies $\lambda_j = 2\pi j / n \in (-\pi, \pi)$, and the numerator of the sum terms is the so called *sample periodogramm* of the sequence $\{X_t\}$. In the Gaussian case, the Whittle estimator is related to least squares and maximum likelihood estimators and is a standard estimator for ARMA processes $\{X_t\}$ with finite variance. (See P. Whittle, "Estimation and Information in Stationary Time Series," *Arkiv for Matematik* 2 (1953), pp. 423–434.). When the $\{X_t\}$ is a fractionally integrated ARIMA(p, d, q) process, it is easier to implement the Whittle estimator then maximizing the Gaussian likelihood. For further details, see Chapter 10 in Brockwell and Davis, *Time Series: Theory and Methods, Second Edition.*

[7] T. Mikosch, T. Gadrich, C. Klüppelberg, and R.J. Adler, "Parameter Estimation for ARMA Models with Infinite Variance Innovations," *Annals of Statistics* 23, no. 1 (1995), pp. 305–326.

[8] Shiqing Ling, "Self-Weighted Least Absolute Deviation Estimation for Infinite Variance Autoregressive Models."

[9] See Gennady Samorodnitsky and Murad S. Taqqu, *Stable Non-Gaussian Random Processes: Stochastic Models with Infinite Variance* (New York: Chapman & Hall, 1994); and T. Mikosch, T. Gadrich, C. Klüppelberg, and R. J. Adler, "Parameter Estimation for ARMA Models with Infinite Variance Innovations," *The Annals of Statistics* 23, no. 1 (1995), pp. 305–326.

stable distribution with index $\alpha \in (0,2)$ and scale parameter $\sigma_0 > 0$. That is, as $n \to \infty$,

$$n^{-1/\alpha} \sum_{t=1}^{n} \varepsilon_t \xrightarrow{d} Y \tag{15.3}$$

where ε_0 has characteristic function

$$Ee^{iu\varepsilon_0} = e^{-|\sigma_0 u|^{\alpha}}$$

Expression (15.2) describes an *infinite variance ARMA(p, q) process*.

Properties and Estimation of ARMA Processes with Infinite-Variance Innovations

An estimator for the ARMA coefficients

$$\beta = (a_1, ..., a_p, b_1, ..., b_q)'$$

can be derived by using the *sample periodogramm* of $\{y_t\}$[10] which is defined by

$$I_{n,y}(\lambda) = \left| n^{-1/\alpha} \sum_{t=1}^{n} y_t e^{-i\lambda t} \right|^2, \quad -\pi < \lambda < \pi \tag{15.4}$$

The *self-normalized* periodogramm is obtained by normalizing the expression (15.4) with the sum of the squared terms of the sequence $\{y_t\}$.[11] Sequence $\{y_t\}_{t \in Z}$ has the infinite moving average representation

$$y_t = \sum_{j=0}^{\infty} c_j \varepsilon_{t-j}, \quad t \in Z, c_0 = 1$$

where c_j are specified, for a complex $z \in C$ with norm $|z| \le 1$, by

---

[10] Mikosch, Gadrich, Klüppelberg, and Adler, "Parameter Estimation for ARMA Models with Infinite Variance Innovation."

[11] $\bar{I}_{n,y}(\lambda) = \left| \sum_{t=1}^{n} y_t e^{-i\lambda t} \right|^2 \Big/ \sum_{t=1}^{n} y_t^2, \quad -\pi < \lambda < \pi$

$$1 + c_1 z + c_2 z^2 + \ldots = c(z) := \frac{b(z)}{a(z)}$$

with $a(z) = 1 - a_1 z - a_2 z^2 - \ldots - a_p z^p$ and $b(z) = 1 + b_1 z + \ldots - b_q b^q$. The parameter space for β is defined as C:= $\{\beta \in R^{p+q}: a_p \neq 0, b_q \neq 0, a(z)$ and $b(z)$ have no common errors, $a(z)b(z) \neq 0$ for $|z| \leq 1\}$

The objective function is defined as

$$\sigma_n^2(\beta) = \int_{-\pi}^{\pi} \frac{\bar{I}_{n,y}(\lambda)}{g(\lambda, \beta)} d\lambda$$

where $g(\lambda, \beta)$ is the *power transfer* function corresponding to $\beta \in C$,

$$g(\lambda, \beta) := \left| \frac{b(e^{-i\lambda})}{a(e^{-\lambda})} \right|^2 = \left| c(e^{-i\lambda}) \right|^2$$

Suppose $\beta_0 \in C$ is the true, but unknown, parameter vector. Then, two natural estimators are given by

$$\beta_n = \arg\min_{\beta \in C} \sigma_n^2(\beta) \qquad (15.5)$$

and

$$\bar{\beta}_n = \arg\min_{\beta \in C} \bar{\sigma}_n^2(\beta) = \arg\min_{\beta \in C} \hat{\sigma}_n^2(\beta)$$

Estimator (15.5) is called the Whittle estimator and is given by the value of β that minimizes $\sigma_n^2(\beta)$.

The rate of convergence of this estimator will differ depending on the properties of the ARMA process. While the rate of convergence for the Whittle estimator in the case of the ARMA(p, q) processes with finite variance is $n^{-1/2}$, in the stable case a considerably faster rate of convergence of order $(n/\ln n)^{-1/\alpha}$, $\alpha < 2$, is obtained.

Fractional ARIMA Process with Infinite-Variance Innovations

Recall from Chapter 6 that if the fractionally differenced series $(1 - L)^d y_t$ follows an ARMA(p, q) process, then y_t is called an FARIMA(p, d, q) process, which is a generalized ARIMA model by allowing for non-integer d. The FARIMA for time series $\{y_t\}$ is defined by

$$a(L)y_t = b(L)\Delta^{-d}\varepsilon_t = b(L)(1-L)^{-d}\varepsilon_t \qquad (15.6)$$

where the innovations ε_t have infinite variance and d is a positive fractional number. The notation Δ^d with (for $d = 1, 2, \ldots$) stands for the operator iterated d times, and

$$\Delta^{-d} = (1-L)^{-d} = \sum_{j=0}^{\infty} l_j(-d)L^j \qquad (15.7)$$

with $l_0(-d) := 1$ and

$$l_j(-d) = \frac{\Gamma(j+d)}{\Gamma(d)\Gamma(j+1)} \quad j = 1, 2, \ldots$$

Time series (15.6) exhibits both infinite variance and long-range dependence. One can estimate both d and the coefficients in polynomials $a(L)$ and $b(L)$ by using a variant of Whittle's method.

The innovations ε_t in (15.6) are assumed to be IID zero mean and in the domain of attraction of a stable law with $1 < \alpha < 2$; that is,

$$P(|\varepsilon_t| > x) \sim x^{-\alpha}F(x), \quad \text{as } x \to \infty \qquad (15.8)$$

where F is a slowly varying function, and

$$P(\varepsilon_t > x)/P(|\varepsilon_t| > x) \to i, \, P(\varepsilon_t < -x)/P(|\varepsilon_t| > x) \to j \qquad (15.9)$$

where i and j are nonnegative numbers satisfying $i + j = 1$. Then, there is a unique moving average representation

$$y_t = \sum_{j=0}^{\infty} c_j\varepsilon_{t-j} \qquad (15.10)$$

satisfying (15.6), provided that (1) polynomials $a(L)$ and $b(L)$ have no zeros in the closed unit disk $D = \{z: |z| \leq 1\}$ and no zeros in common and (2) $d < 1-1/\alpha$. The coefficients c_j are defined by

$$\sum_{j=0}^{\infty} c_j z^j = \frac{b(z)}{a(z)(1-z)^d}, \quad |z| \leq 1 \qquad (15.11)$$

The process given by (15.10) is called a *fractional ARIMA process* or, in short, a FARIMA(p, d, q) process.

Similar to the definition of estimators for an ARMA process, we define the vector of true parameters

$$\beta_0 = (a_1, ..., a_p, b_1,..., b_q, d)' \qquad (15.12)$$

where parameter d is now added. Analogous to the ARMA case, we define the Whittle estimator β_n as the value of β minimizing objective function $\sigma_n^2(\beta)$. In the case of a FARIMA process, the expression for the power transfer function $g(\lambda, \beta)$ is more involved than in the ARMA case. As in the ARMA case, the estimator β_n is consistent.

An analysis of the stationary process

$$y_n = \sum_{j=0}^{\infty} c_j \varepsilon_{n-j} \qquad (15.13)$$

with a noise sequence, $\{\varepsilon_t\}_{t \in Z}$, of IID random variables, which may have finite or infinite variance, is useful for characterization of the *long-memory* or *long-range dependence of some process*.[12]

The result of Mikosh et al.[13] on the Whittle estimator for IVAR moving average models was extended by Kokoszka and Taqqu[14] for long memory autoregressive fractionally integrated moving average models.

STABLE GARCH MODELS

In Chapter 8, GARCH and ARMA-GARCH models were described. Here we look at the extension of these models by allowing the distribu-

---

[12] Correlations to distinguish between short and long memory if the variance is infinite cannot be used. Several approaches try to use "correlation-like" notions in that case. In the class of stable processes notions of covariation and codifference have been introduced and their rate of decay for various classes of stationary stable processes computed. (See, for example, A. Astrauskas, J. Levy and M. S. Taqqu, "The Asymptotic Dependence Structure of the Linear Fractional Lévy motion," *Lithuanian Mathematical Journal* 31, no. 1 (1991), pp. 1–28.) Such "surrogate correlations" can be expected to carry even less information than the "real correlations" do in the case when the latter are defined.

[13] Mikosch, Gadrich, Klüppelberg, and Adler, "Parameter Estimation for ARMA Models with Infinite Variance Innovation."

[14] P. Kokoszka and M. S. Taqqu, "Infinite Variance Stable Moving Averages with Long Memory," *Journal of Econometrics* 73, no. 1 (1996), pp. 79–99.

tion of the historical innovations to be heavier-tailed than the normal distribution—more precisely belonging to the family of non-Gaussian stable distributions. Recall that GARCH model is given by

$$y_t \stackrel{d}{=} \sigma_t z_t \tag{15.14}$$

where z_t are IID mean zero and unit variance random variables representing the innovations of the return process; and the conditional variance σ_t^2, follows

$$\sigma_t^2 = a_0 + \sum_{i=1}^{q} a_i y_{t-i}^2 + \sum_{j=1}^{p} b_i \sigma_{t-j}^2 \tag{15.15}$$

Commonly it is assumed that $z_t \sim N(0,1)$, so that the returns are conditionally normal. We observed in Chapter 8 that the GARCH model with a conditionally normal return distribution can lead to heavy tails in the unconditional return distribution. We also introduced in Chapter 8 ARMA-GARCH models where expression (15.14) is replaced by an ARMA expression that captures serial dependence in returns. The ARMA structure is used to model the conditional mean $E(y_t | \mathfrak{S}_{t-1})$ of the return series y_t, i.e.,

$$y_t = \alpha_0 + \sum_{i=1}^{r} \alpha_i y_{t-i} + \varepsilon_t + \sum_{j=1}^{s} \beta_j \varepsilon_{t-j} \tag{15.16}$$

where $\mathfrak{S}_{t-1}$ is the information set up to time $t-1$. The GARCH is again given by

$$\sigma_t^2 = a_0 + \sum_{i=1}^{q} a_i \varepsilon_{t-i}^2 + \sum_{j=1}^{p} b_i \sigma_{t-j}^2 \tag{15.17}$$

with $\varepsilon_t = \sigma_t z_t$ and $z_t \sim N(0,1)$ IID.

If we assume that the distribution of the historical innovations $z_{t-n}, ..., z_t$ is heavier-tailed than the normal, then the GARCH model will exhibit non-Gaussian conditional distribution. In the remainder of this chapter, we consider the heavy-tailed innovation process $\{z_t\}$ with specific focus on a family of non-Gaussian stable distributions.

An ARMA-GARCH model that accommodates heavy-tailed innovation process has been introduced by Panorska, Mittnik, and Rachev[15] and given by an ARMA structure as in (15.16),

$$y_t = \alpha_0 + \sum_{i=1}^{r} \alpha_i y_{t-i} + \varepsilon_t + \sum_{j=1}^{s} \beta_j \varepsilon_{t-j} \qquad (15.18)$$

and a GARCH structure imposed on the scale parameter σ_t,

$$\sigma_t^2 = a_0 + \sum_{i=1}^{q} a_i \varepsilon_{t-i}^2 + \sum_{j=1}^{p} b_i \sigma_{t-j}^2 \qquad (15.19)$$

where $\varepsilon_t = \sigma_t z_t$ and z_t is an IID location zero, unit scale heavy-tailed random variable. For example, for z_t the partially asymmetric Weibull, the Student's t, and the asymmetric stable distributions can be used. Note that in this model, σ_t in expression (15.9) is interpreted as a scale parameter and not necessarily a volatility, since for some distributional choices for z_t, the variance may not exist. Specifically, in the case where z_t are realizations from a stable non-Gaussian distribution, the GARCH model is represented by the modified expression of (15.19).

$$\sigma_t = a_0 + \sum_{i=1}^{q} a_i |\varepsilon_{t-i}| + \sum_{j=1}^{p} b_i |\sigma_{t-j}| \qquad (15.20)$$

and the index of stability α for the stable distribution is constrained to be greater than 1.[16] Expression (15.20) represents a *stable-GARCH model.*

Similar to conventional GARCH models, stable-GARCH models may prove beneficial to model the conditional distribution of asset returns by capturing appropriately temporal dependencies of the return series. To test the goodness of fit of the models, the standard Kolmogorov-Smirnov distance and Anderson-Darling test statistic can be applied. These test statistics are explained in the appendix to Chapter 14.

---

[15] Ania K. Panorska, Stefan Mittnik, and Svetlozar T. Rachev, "Stable GARCH Models for Financial Time Series," *Applied Mathematics Letters* 8, no. 5 (1995), pp. 33–37.

[16] Note that term ε_{t-i}^2 in (15.9) assuming stable innovation process z_t can become infinite, rendering the whole expression meaningless. The condition of $\alpha > 1$ means that we impose a finite mean condition.

Panorska, Mittnik, and Rachev model the conditional distribution for the Nikkei Index using different distributional models for the $\{z_t\}$ process, including Weibull, the Student-t, and the asymmetric stable distribution. All the alternative distributional models for the innovation process outperform the normal assumption for the innovation process in modeling daily asset returns.

In (15.14) to (15.20) we presented the extension of a conventional GARCH process to a stable-GARCH process. The formal definition of a stable-GARCH process is as follows.

Definition of stable-GARCH Process. A sequence of random variables ε_t is said to be a stable GARCH(α, p, q) or S_αGARCH(p, q) process if:

- $\varepsilon_t = \sigma_t z_t$, where z_t are IID random variables distributed as strictly symmetric α-stable random variable[17] with unit scale parameter, $1 < \alpha \le 2$.
- Nonnegative constants a_i, $i = 1, ..., q$, and b_j, $j = 1, 2, ..., p$, and a_0 exist, such that (15.20) holds.

The assumption $1 < \alpha \le 2$ is commonly satisfied in finance, since most return series have finite mean.

In addition to allowing infinite-variance disturbances, the stable-GARCH process can be further generalized by considering asymmetric innovations and processes where the GARCH equation propagates not just conditional moments of order 2, but, more generally, absolute moments of order $\delta > 0$. The process $\{y_t\}$ is called a *stable Paretian power-GARCH process*, in short, an $S_{\alpha,\beta,\delta}$ GARCH(r, s) process, if it is described by

$$y_t = \mu_t + \sigma_t z_t, \quad z_t \overset{iid}{\sim} S_{\alpha,\beta}(0, 1) \tag{15.21}$$

and

$$\sigma_t^\delta = a_0 + \sum_{i=1}^{r} a_i |y_{t-i} - \mu_{t-i}|^\delta + \sum_{j=1}^{s} b_j \sigma_{t-j}^\delta \tag{15.22}$$

---

[17] To obtain strictly symmetric stable random variables, we assume $\beta = \mu = 0$. The characteristic function for symmetric stable random variable with scale parameter σ is $\exp\{-|\sigma t|^\alpha\}$.

where $a_0 > 0$, $a_i \geq 0$, $i = 1, 2, ..., r$, $r \geq 1$, $b_j \geq 0$, $j = 1, 2, ..., s$, $s \geq 0$, and $S_{\alpha,\beta}$ denotes the standard asymmetric stable Paretian distribution[18] with stable index α, skewness parameter $\beta \in [-1,1]$, zero location parameter, and unit scale parameter.[19] The power parameter, δ, satisfies $0 < \delta < \alpha$. By letting the location parameter in (15.21) be time-varying, we permit general mean equations, including, for example, regression and/or ARMA structures.

Properties of Stable GARCH Processes

The sufficient conditions for a unique stationarity solution of the stable power-GARCH process (15.21)–(15.22) driven by stable Paretian innovations have been established with the following proposition:[20]

The sufficient conditions under which the $S_{\alpha,\beta,\delta}$ GARCH(r,s) process defined by (15.21) and (15.22) has a unique strictly stationary solution are: $1 < \alpha \leq 2$, $0 < \delta < \alpha$, $a_0 > 0$, $a_i \geq 0$, $i = 1, 2, ..., r$, $r \geq 1$, $b_j \geq 0$, $j = 1, 2, ..., s$, $s \geq 0$, and

$$\lambda_{\alpha, \beta, \delta} \sum_{i=1}^{r} a_i + \sum_{j=1}^{s} b_j \leq 1 \qquad (15.23)$$

where $\lambda_{\alpha, \beta, \delta} := E|z|^{\delta}$ with $z \sim S_{\alpha,\beta}(0,1)$. The left side of inequality (15.23) is defined as *volatility persistence*, V_S.

Factor $\lambda_{\alpha,\beta,\delta}$ depends on power δ as well as the stable index α and skewness parameter β of the standard stable Paretian distribution and is, for $0 < \delta < \alpha$, of the form[21]

---

[18] Here we employ the same parameterization and notation as in Svetlozar T. Rachev and Stefan Mittnik, *Stable Paretian Models in Finance* (Chichester: John Wiley & Sons, 2000).

[19] As already discussed in Chapter 14, the stable distribution is symmetric for $\beta = 0$ and skewed to the right (left) for $\beta > 0$ ($\beta < 0$). The stable index α, which in general assumes values in the interval $(0,2]$, determines the tail-thickness of the distribution. The tails become thinner as α approaches 2; and for $\alpha = 2$, the standard stable Paretian distribution coincides with the normal distribution $N(0,2)$. For $\alpha < 2$, z_t does not possess moments of order α or higher. Thus, the mean exist only for $\alpha > 1$.

[20] Stefan Mittnik, Marc S. Paolella, and Svetlozar T. Rachev, "Stationarity of Stable Power-GARCH Processes," *Journal of Econometrics* 106, no. 1 (2002), pp. 97–107.

[21] Gennady Samorodnitsky and Murad S. Taqqu, *Stable Non-Gaussian Random Processes, Stochastic Models with Infinite Variance* (New York: Chapman & Hall, 1994).

$$\lambda_{\alpha,\beta,\delta} = E|z|^\delta = \frac{1}{\psi_\delta}\Gamma\left(1-\frac{\delta}{\alpha}\right)(1+\sigma_{\alpha,\beta}^2)^{\delta/2\alpha}\cos\left(\frac{\delta}{\beta}\arctan\tau_{\alpha,\beta}\right) \quad (15.24)$$

where $\tau_{\alpha,\beta} := \beta\tan\alpha\pi/2$ and

$$\psi_\delta = \begin{cases} \Gamma(1-\delta)\cos\dfrac{\pi\delta}{2}, & \text{if } \delta \neq 1 \\[2ex] \dfrac{\pi}{2}, & \text{if } \delta = 1 \end{cases}$$

It is important to note that $\lambda_{\alpha,\beta,\delta}$ increases without bound as δ approaches α. Note that in practice, the restrictions $1 < \alpha \leq 2$, $0 < \delta < \alpha$ need to be satisfied for the examined datasets, which usually consist of various volatile series of exchange rates, stock returns, and stock indices return series. The stationarity conditions for the special stable-GARCH process (15.20) follow by setting $\delta = 1$ and $\beta = 0$.[22]

Analogous to the ordinary normal GARCH model, we say that y_t is an integrated $S_{\alpha,\beta,\delta}$ GARCH(r, s) process, denoted by $S_{\alpha,\beta,\delta}$ IGARCH(r, s), if in (15.23) the volatility persistence is equal to 1. In practice, the estimated volatility persistence, $\hat{V}_S$, tends to be quite close to 1 for a highly volatile series, so that an integrated model might offer a reasonable data description. However, both finite sample and asymptotic properties of $\hat{V}_S$ and the associated likelihood ratio statistics are not known, so that it is not immediately clear how one can test for an integrated process. An alternative approach is to fit both GARCH and IGARCH models and examine the change in various goodness of fit statistics, most notably the Anderson-Darling statistics.

From the analysis performed by Mittnik, Paolella, and Rachev,[23] it follows that the admissible parameter space for parameters in the conditional-volatility equation (15.22), $a_i \geq 0$, $i = 1, 2, ..., r$, and b_j, $j = 1, 2, ..., s$, shrinks, under *ceteris paribus* conditions, as the tails of the inno-

---

[22] If $a_0 > 0$ and

$$\sum_{i=1}^{q} a_i + \sum_{j=1}^{p} b_j \leq 1$$

then the stable GARCH (α, p, q) with $p \geq 2$ or $q \geq 2$, has a unique strictly stationary solution. The case when $p = q = 1$ requires separate treatment because of some technical issues concerning conditions for obtaining a stationary solution. This is beyond the scope of this chapter.

[23] Mittnik, Paolella, and Rachev, "Stationarity of Stable Power-GARCH Processes."

vations became heavier (i.e., $\alpha \downarrow 1$), as the skewness of the innovation increases (i.e., as $\beta \to \pm 1$), and as the power parameter increases (i.e., $\delta \uparrow \alpha$). In the case when $\delta = \alpha$, simulation experiments show extremely erratic behavior of the conditional-volatility process, which is actually not encountered in financial data.

ESTIMATION OF THE STABLE GARCH MODEL

As explained in the previous chapter, estimation of the probability density function (pdf) and subsequently the likelihood function $S_{\alpha,\beta}$, distribution is nontrivial, because it lacks an analytic expression. We describe here the maximum likelihood estimate for a GARCH(r, s) specification with $r = s = 1$ which is commonly sufficient to capture serial dependence in absolute returns.

For a GARCH(1,1) model, (15.21) and (15.22) become

$$y_t = \mu_t + c_t z_t, \quad z_t \overset{iid}{\sim} S_{\alpha,\beta}(0, 1) \tag{15.25}$$

$$c_t^\delta = a_0 + a_1 |y_{t-1} - \mu|^\delta + b_1 c_{t-1}^\delta \tag{15.26}$$

where c_t is the conditionally varying scale parameter of the stable distribution. The goal is to estimate the parameter vector $\theta = (\mu, c_0, a_0, a_1, b_1, \alpha, \beta, \delta)$, where c_0 denotes the unknown initial value of c_t. The ML estimate of θ is obtained by maximizing the logarithm of the likelihood function

$$L(\theta; y_1, \ldots, y_T) = \prod_{t=1}^{T} c_t^{-1} S_{\alpha,\beta}\left(\frac{y_t - \mu}{c_t}\right) \tag{15.27}$$

The ML estimation is *approximate* in the sense that the stable Paretian density $S_{\alpha,\beta}((y_t - \mu)/c_t)$ needs to be approximated. For this purpose, the algorithm of Mittnik, Rachev, Doganoglu, and Chenyao,[24] which approximates the stable Paretian density via *fast Fourier transform* (FFT) of the characteristic function is used. The ML estimator of the parameters of the stable density is consistent and asymptotically normal with the asymptotic covariance matrix being given by the inverse of the Fisher

---

[24] S. Mittnik, S.T. Rachev, T. Doganoglu, and D. Chenyao, "Maximum Likelihood Estimation of Stable Paretian Models," *Mathematical and Computer Modelling* 29 (1999), pp. 275–293.

information matrix.[25] Approximate standard errors of the estimates can be obtained via numerical approximation of the Hessian matrix.

For practical use, three issues are important:

1. How easily the stable ML estimation routine can be implemented.
2. Whether the stable ML estimation routine is numerically well behaved.
3. Performance in terms of computational speed.

The stable ML estimation method can be directly implemented using standard econometric packages and is well behaved.[26] The exception is in cases of grossly misspecified and/or overspecified models, as well as the more general class of ARMA-GARCH models when there is near unit root in the general ARMA structure (which poses a well-known difficulty in ARMA estimation).

As highlighted in Chapter 8, evaluation of the GARCH recursion requires presample values of z_0 and c_0. Instead of treating them as unknown parameters, they can be set to their unconditional expected values

$$\hat{c}_0 = \frac{\hat{a}_0}{1 - \lambda_{\hat{\alpha}, \beta, \delta} \sum_{i=1}^{r} \hat{a}_i - \sum_{j=1}^{s} \hat{b}_j} \quad \text{and} \quad \hat{z}_0 = \hat{\lambda}\hat{c}_0 \tag{15.28}$$

Note that expression (15.28) is not valid in the IGARCH case. To avoid problems for IGARCH and nearly integrated GARCH models, we need to estimate c_0 as an additional parameter rather than setting it to its unconditional expected value.

For the integrated $S_{\alpha,\beta,\delta}$ IGARCH(1,1) model, the restriction $b_1 = 1 - \lambda_{\alpha,\beta,\delta} a_1$ needs to be imposed. This entails the evaluation of volatility persistence,

$$\lambda_{\alpha, \beta, \delta} \sum_{i=1}^{r} a_i + \sum_{j=1}^{s} b_j$$

at each iteration, as b_1 is also dependent on values $\hat{\alpha}$, $\hat{\beta}$, and $\hat{\delta}$.

---

[25] The Fisher information matrix is explained in Chapter 2.
[26] The satisfactory behavior of the algorithm is due to avoidance of explicit numerical integration and the fact that the method can be made arbitrarily accurate by the choice of several tuning constants.

Illustration: Modeling Exchange Rate Returns

To examine the appropriateness of the stable GARCH hypothesis, we present an application reported in Mittnik and Paolella[27] who model exchange rate returns for five daily spot foreign exchange rates against the U.S. dollar, namely the British pound, Canadian dollar, German mark, Japanese yen, and the Swiss franc. The sample covers the period January 2, 1980 to July 28, 1994, yielding series of lengths 3,681, 3,682, 3,661, 3,621, and 3,678, respectively. Since serial correlation was found to be negligible, and, assuming a GARCH(1,1) specification is sufficient to capture serial correlation in absolute returns, the model of the form (15.25) and (15.26) for each of the four currencies was specified.

The approximate ML estimation is used to fit the model (15.25) and (15.26). To avoid problems for IGARCH and nearly integrated GARCH models, Mittnik and Paolella estimate c_0 as an additional parameter rather than to set it to its unconditional expected value. The parameter estimates of the models are shown in Exhibit 15.1.

It is important to note the estimates of the skewness parameter β: all $\hat\beta$ values are statistically different from zero, although those for the British pound and German mark are quite close to zero. Skewness is most pronounced for the Japanese yen, for which $\hat\alpha = 1.81$ and $\hat\beta = -0.418$.

The persistence of volatility is given in the last column of Exhibit 15.1 and reflects the speed with which volatility shocks die out. A $\hat V$ value of persistence measure ($\hat V = \lambda_{\hat\alpha, \hat\beta, \hat\delta} \hat a_1 + \hat b_1$) near 1 is indicative of an integrated GARCH process, in which volatility shocks have persistent effects. The results show that the models for the Canadian dollar and Japanese yen with $\hat V$ values of 1.001 and 1.002 respectively, are very close to being integrated. For the estimates here, we obtain $\hat\delta < \hat\alpha$, which suggest that conditional volatility c_t^δ is a well defined quantity in the sense that $E(c_t^\delta | y_{t-1}, y_{t-2}, \ldots)$ for $V_S < 1$.[28]

---

[27] Stefan Mittnik and Marc S. Paolella, "Prediction of Financial Downside-Risk with Heavy-Tailed Conditional Distributions," in Svetlozar T. Rachev (ed.) *Handbook of Heavy Tailed Distributions in Finance* (Amsterdam: Elsevier Science 2003), pp. 386–404.

[28] It is worthwhile noting that the restriction $\alpha = \delta$, imposed by Liu and Brorsen when estimating stable-GARCH models for the same four currencies is not supported by the presented results. This is important because, if $\delta \geq \alpha$, the unconditional first moments of c_t is infinite for any $\alpha < 2$. The specification $\alpha = \delta$ does not only induce conceptual difficulties, but also leads to a highly volatile evolution of the c_t series in practical work. (See S. Liu and B.W. Brorsen, "Maximum Likelihood Estimation of a GARCH-Stable Model," *Journal of Applied Econometrics* 10 (April 1995), pp. 273–285.)

EXHIBIT 15.1   GARCH Parameter Estimates for Exchange-Rate Return Models[a]

	Intercept μ	GARCH Parameters				Distribution Parameters		Persistence Measure[b]
		θ_0	θ_1	ϕ_1	δ	Shape (α)	Skew (β)	$\hat{V}$
British								
$S_{\alpha,\beta}$	−9.773e-3	8.085e-3	0.04132	0.9171	1.359	1.850	−0.1368	0.984
	(0.012)	(2.39e-3)	(6.42e-3)	(0.0118)	(0.0892)	(0.0245)	(0.0211)	
t	−2.312e-3	0.01190	0.06373	0.9071	1.457	6.218	—	0.976
	(0.010)	(3.56e-3)	(0.0115)	(0.0200)	(0.167)	(0.615)		
Canadian								
$S_{\alpha,\beta}$	5.167e-3	1.034e-3	0.04710	0.9164	1.404	1.823	0.3577	1.001
	(0.0614)	(3.12e-4)	(6.63e-3)	(0.0118)	(0.0143)	(0.0104)	(0.0209)	
t	−2.240e-3	7.774e-4	0.06112	0.9118	1.793	5.900	---	0.992
	(3.83e-3)	(6.90e-4)	(5.98e-3)	(7.27e-3)	(0.0150)	(0.0801)		
German								
$S_{\alpha,\beta}$	2.580e-3	0.01525	0.05684	0.8971	1.101	1.892	−0.06779	0.969
	(0.016)	(1.61e-3)	(3.44e-3)	(7.42e-3)	(9.78e-3)	(0.0216)	(0.0184)	
t	6.643e-3	0.01812	0.07803	0.8938	1.261	7.297	—	0.969
	(9.21e-4)	(2.25e-3)	(6.45e-3)	(4.43e-3)	(0.147)	(0.186)		
Japanese								
$S_{\alpha,\beta}$	−0.01938	4.518e-3	0.06827	0.8865	1.337	1.814	−0.4175	1.002
	(0.0166)	(1.12e-3)	(7.91e-3)	(0.0124)	(0.0132)	(0.0107)	(8.80e-3)	
t	5.318e-3	9.949e-3	0.07016	0.8756	1.816	5.509	—	0.972
	(8.87e-3)	(3.03e-3)	(0.0119)	(0.0205)	(0.162)	(0.461)		
Swiss								
$S_{\alpha,\beta}$	−2.677e-3	0.01595	0.04873	0.9115	1.041	1.902	−0.2836	0.971
	(0.0124)	(3.30e-3)	(6.84e-3)	(0.0132)	(0.144)	(0.0206)	(0.0722)	
t	8.275e-3	0.02099	0.06825	0.9061	1.159	8.294	—	0.968
	(0.0118)	(3.91e-3)	(6.85e-3)	(7.25e-3)	(0.179)	(0.933)		

[a] Estimated models: $r_t = \mu + c_t \varepsilon_t$, $c_t^\delta = \theta_0 + \theta_1 |r_{t-1} - \mu|^\delta + \phi_1 c_{t-1}^\delta$. "Shape" denotes the degrees of freedom parameter ν for the Student's t-distribution and stable index α for the stable Paretian distribution; "Skew" refers to the stable Paretian skewness parameter β. Standard deviations resulting from ML estimation are given in parentheses.

[b] $\hat{V}$ corresponds to $\hat{V}_S$ in the stable Paretian and $\hat{V}_t$ in the Student's t case. $V = 1$ implies an IGARCH model.

Source: Table 1 in Stefan Mittnik and Marc S. Paolella, "Prediction of Financial Downside-Risk with Heavy-Tailed Conditional Distributions," in Svetlozar T. Rachev (ed.), *Handbook of Heavy Tailed Distributions in Finance* (Amsterdam: Elsevier Science 2003).

EXHIBIT 15.2   IGARCH Parameter Estimates for Exchange-Rate Return Models[a]

	Intercept μ	GARCH Parameters				Distribution Parameters	
		θ_0	θ_1	ϕ_1	δ	Shape	Skew
British							
$S_{\alpha,\beta}$	−0.01023	7.050e-3	0.03781	0.9114	1.598	1.846	−0.1340
	(0.0103)	(1.79e-3)	(5.64e-3)	—	(0.0677)	(0.0224)	(0.0147)
t	−3.033e-3	4.237e-3	0.05774	0.9130	1.949	5.543	—
	(0.0101)	(1.68e-3)	(9.83e-3)	—	(0.264)	(0.484)	
Canadian							
$S_{\alpha,\beta}$	5.148e-3	1.115e-3	0.04689	0.9154	1.404	1.823	0.3578
	(3.65e-3)	(2.14e-4)	(5.71e-3)	—	(0.0143)	(0.0105)	(0.0209)
t	−2.098e-3	4.998e-4	0.06468	0.9146	1.796	5.890	—
	(3.48e-3)	(1.37e-4)	(7.54e-3)	—	(0.0226)	(0.838)	
German							
$S_{\alpha,\beta}$	8.959e-3	9.666e-3	0.04518	0.8896	1.676	1.881	0.03944
	(0.0113)	(1.85e-3)	(6.10e-3)	—	(0.662)	(0.0217)	(0.0930)
t	8.851e-3	5.505e-3	0.08124	0.9003	1.741	6.560	—
	(0.0106)	(1.60e-3)	(0.0106)	—	(0.231)	(0.676)	
Japanese							
$S_{\alpha,\beta}$	−0.01932	4.814e-3	0.06768	0.8858	1.336	1.814	−0.4175
	(8.44e-3)	(9.75e-4)	(7.68e-3)	—	(0.0751)	(0.0226)	(0.0151)
t	6.136e-3	5.611e-3	0.06036	08689	2.314	5.066	—
	(8.57e-3)	(1.31e-3)	(0.0112)	—	(0.224)	(0.410)	
Swiss							
$S_{\alpha,\beta}$	3.823e-3	0.01111	0.03700	0.9009	1.724	1.889	−1703
	(0.0127)	(2.65e-3)	(5.40e-3)	—	(0.0419)	(0.0169)	(0.137)
t	9.130e-3	2.047e-3	0.07125	0.9347	1.166	8.194	—
	(0.0119)	(8.34e-4)	(9.13e-3)	—	(9.79e-3)	(0.0996)	

[a] Estimated models: $r_t = \mu + c_t\varepsilon_t$, $c_t^\delta = \theta_0 + \theta_1|r_{t-1} - \mu|^\delta + \phi_1 c_{t-1}^\delta$ with IGARCH condition $\hat{\phi}_1 = 1 - \hat{\lambda}\hat{\theta}_1$ imposed. See footnote to Exhibit 15.1 for further details.

Source: Table 2 in Stefan Mittnik and Marc S. Paolella, "Prediction of Financial Downside-Risk with Heavy-Tailed Conditional Distributions," in Svetlozar T. Rachev (ed.), *Handbook of Heavy Tailed Distributions in Finance* (Amsterdam: Elsevier Science 2003).

For all five exchange rate series, Mittnik and Paolella also estimate models with the IGARCH condition imposed. Exhibit 15.2 shows the resulting parameter estimates. As expected, for those models for which the persistence measure was close to unity, Canadian dollar and Japanese yen, the IGARCH-restricted parameter estimates differ very little. For the remaining models, the greatest changes occur with the power parameter δ and, to a lesser extent, the shape parameter α. The former increases, while the latter decreases under IGARCH restrictions.

To compare the goodness of fit of the candidate models, Mittnik and Paolella employ the maximum log-likelihood value, Anderson-Darling statistic and the AICC described in Chapter 7. The results are shown in Exhibit 15.3. The inference suggested from the maximum log-likelihood value $\mathcal{L}$ and the AICC are identical. For each currency we plot the values of

$$AD_t = \frac{\left|F_S(\hat{z}_{t:T}) - \hat{F}(\hat{z}_{t:T})\right|}{\sqrt{F(z_{t:T})(1 - \hat{F}(\hat{z}_{t:T}))}}$$

EXHIBIT 15.3 Goodness of Fit Measures of Estimated Exchange-Rate Return Models[a]

	$\mathcal{L}$		AICC		SBC		AD	
	$S_{\alpha,\beta}$	t	$S_{\alpha,\beta}$	t	$S_{\alpha,\beta}$	t	$S_{\alpha,\beta}$	t
Britain:								
GARCH	−3842.0	−3828.6	7700.0	7671.2	7684.0	7657.2	0.0375	0.0244
IGARCH	−3842.3	−3837.1	7698.6	7686.2	7684.6	7674.2	0.0417	0.0420
Canada:								
GARCH	−159.92	−152.25	0335.9	0318.5	0319.9	0304.5	0.0532	0.0571
IGARCH	−159.97	−153.71	0334.0	0319.4	0320.0	0307.4	0.0529	0.0633
Germany:								
GARCH	−3986.5	−3986.2	7989.0	7986.4	7973.0	7972.4	0.0368	0.345
IGARCH	−3989.9	−3999.4	7993.8	8010.8	7979.8	7998.8	0.0506	0.200
Japan:								
GARCH	−3178.7	−3333.7	6373.4	6681.4	6357.4	6667.4	0.0401	0.0986
IGARCH	−3178.8	−3334.6	6371.6	6681.2	6357.6	6669.2	0.0394	0.0793
Switzerland:								
GARCH	−4308.6	−4308.1	8633.2	8630.2	8617.2	8616.2	0.0457	0.287
IGARCH	−4314.2	−4325.0	8642.4	8662.0	8628.4	8650.0	0.0460	0.278

[a] $\mathcal{L}$ refers to the maximum log-likelihood value; AICC is the corrected AIC criteria; SBC is the Schwarz Bayesian Criteria; and AD is the Anderson-Darling statistic.

Source: Table 3 in Stefan Mittnik and Marc S. Paolella, "Prediction of Financial Downside-Risk with Heavy-Tailed Conditional Distributions," in Svetlozar T. Rachev (ed.), *Handbook of Heavy Tailed Distributions in Finance* (Amsterdam: Elsevier Science 2003).

$t = 1,...,T$, where T is the sample size and $\hat{z}_{t:T}$ denotes the *sorted* GARCH-filtered residuals. The plots shown in Exhibit 15.4 indicate that in most cases, the maximum absolute value of the AD_t occurs in the left (tail) of the distribution.

PREDICTION OF CONDITIONAL DENSITIES

Under unconditional normality, to obtain predictive conditional density it would be sufficient to simply predict the conditional mean and variance. However, for GARCH processes driven by non-normal, asymmetric, and possibly, infinite-variance innovations, the predictive conditional density, given by

$$\hat{f}_{t+1|t}(y_{t+1}) = f\left(\frac{y_{t+1}-\mu(\hat{\theta}_t)}{c_{t+1}(\hat{\theta}_t)}\middle| y_t, y_{t-1, ...}\right) \tag{15.29}$$

needs to be computed. In (15.29), $\hat{\theta}_t$ refers to the estimated parameter vector using the sample information up to and including period t and $c_{t+1}(\cdot)$ is obtained from the conditional-scale recursion (15.22) using $\hat{\theta}_t$. Multistep density predictions given by

$$\hat{f}_{t+n|t}(y_{t+n}) = f\left(\frac{y_{t+n}-\mu(\hat{\theta}_t)}{c_{t+n}(\hat{\theta}_t)}\middle| y_t, y_{t-1, ...}\right) \tag{15.30}$$

are obtained by recursive application of (15.20), with unobserved quantities being replaced by their conditional expectation.

For one-step predictions over the out-of-sample dataset, the following recursive procedure is used:

1. Evaluate $\hat{f}_{t+1|t}(y_{t+1})$, $t = M, ..., T-1$ for the $S_{\alpha,\beta,\delta}\text{GARCH}(r, s)$ model where M is the beginning of the out-of-sample set used for prediction.
2. Reestimate (via ML estimation) the model parameters at each step.

The overall density forecasting performance of competing models can be compared by evaluating their conditional densities at the future observed value y_{t+1}, i.e., $\hat{f}_{t+1|t}(y_{t+1})$. A model will perform well in such

EXHIBIT 15.4   Comparison of the Variance-Adjusted Differences between the Sample and Fitted Distribution Functions for Exchange-Rate Return Models

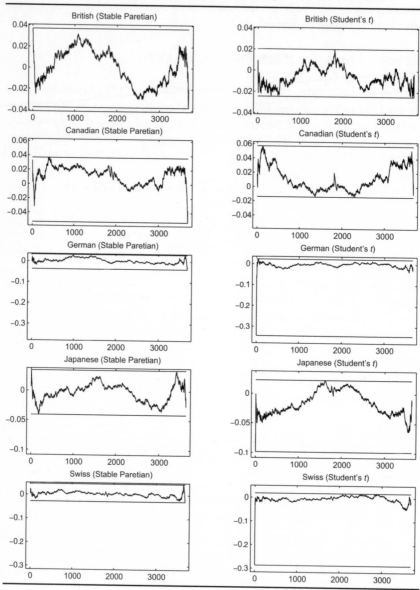

Source: Figure 1 in Stefan Mittnik and Marc S. Paolella, "Prediction of Financial Downside-Risk with Heavy-Tailed Conditional Distributions," in Svetlozar T. Rachev (ed.), *Handbook of Heavy Tailed Distributions in Finance* (Amsterdam: Elsevier Science, 2003).

a comparison if realization y_{t+1} is near the mode of $\hat{f}_{t+1|t}(\cdot)$ and if the mode of the conditional density is more peaked. The conditional densities are determined not only by the specification of the mean and GARCH equations, but also by the distributional choice for the innovations.

Illustration: Forecasting of Densities of Exchange Rate Returns

To illustrate forecasting, let's continue with the Mittnik and Paolella model for exchange-rate returns used in our earlier illustration.[29] They calculate the predictive conditional density for five currencies using the following three models: (1) GARCH(1,1) model with stable innovations ($S_{\alpha,\beta,\delta}$ GARCH(1, 1)), (2) GARCH(1,1) model with heavy-tailed Student's t-distribution innovations ($t_{\nu,\delta}$ GARCH(1, 1)),[30] and (3) conventional GARCH(1,1) model with normal innovations. Exhibit 15.5 presents

EXHIBIT 15.5   Comparison of Overall Forecasting Performance[a]

	British	Canadian	German	Japanese	Swiss
			Mean		
Normal	0.4198	1.1248	0.4064	0.4796	0.3713
t	0.4429	1.1871	0.4258	0.5207	0.3851
$S_{\alpha,\beta}$	0.4380	1.1798	0.4213	0.5173	0.3820
			Standard Deviation		
Normal	0.1934	0.5697	0.1888	0.1988	0.1620
t	0.2325	0.6802	0.2151	0.2782	0.1840
$S_{\alpha,\beta}$	0.2189	0.6482	0.2016	0.2662	0.1771
			Median		
Normal	0.4291	1.0824	0.4178	0.5172	0.3942
t	0.4483	1.1500	0.4452	0.5261	0.4069
$S_{\alpha,\beta}$	0.4493	1.1730	0.4477	0.5242	0.4041

[a] The entries represent average predictive likelihood values, $\sum_{t=2000}^{T-1} \hat{f}_{t+1|t}(r_{t+1})$.

Source: Table 4 in Stefan Mittnik and Marc S. Paolella, "Prediction of Financial Downside-Risk with Heavy-Tailed Conditional Distributions," in Svetlozar T. Rachev (ed.), *Handbook of Heavy Tailed Distributions in Finance* (Amsterdam: Elsevier Science 2003).

---

[29] Mittnik and Paolella, "Prediction of Financial Downside-Risk with Heavy-Tailed Conditional Distributions."

[30] See Chapter 8.

the means, standard deviations, and medians of the density values $\hat{f}_{t+1|t}(y_{t+1})$, $t = 2000, ..., T - 1$ for each currency. Based on the means, values corresponding to the competing stable distribution $S_{\alpha,\beta}$, and Student's t-hypotheses are very close, with the Student's t-values nevertheless larger in each case. Based on the medians, however, the stable Paretian model is (slightly) favored by the British, Canadian, and German currencies. It is noteworthy that these results might be contrary to the model selection based on the applied goodness of fit measures; for example, AD statistics favors use of stable Paretian innovations for the Japanese yen and Student's t-innovations for the British pound. The standard deviations reported in Exhibit 15.5 indicate that the density values of the GARCH-t model fluctuate the most. Overall, the use of stable Paretian models helps to improve forecasting ability.

CONCEPTS EXPLAINED IN THIS CHAPTER (IN ORDER OF PRESENTATION)

Infinite-variance autoregressive models (IVAR)
    Condition for strict stationarity and ergodicity
    Estimation methods
LAD
Whittle estimator
ARMA processes with infinite-variance innovations
Sample periodogram
Self-normalized periodogram
Transfer function
Power transfer function
Fractional ARIMA processes with infinite-variance innovations (FARIMA)
Stable GARCH models
ARMA-GARCH models
Stable Paretian power GARCH processes
Volatility persistence
Maximum likelihood estimates of stable GARCH processes
IGARCH processes
Conditional density forecast

Monthly Returns for 20 Stocks: December 2000 – November 2005

Company	Ticker Symbol
Sun Microsystems	SUNW
Amazon.com	AMZN
Mercury Interactive	MERQ
General Dynamics	GD
Northrop Grumman	NOC
Campbell Soup	CPB
Coca–Cola	KO
Martin Marietta	MLM
Hilton	HLT
United Technologies	UTX
Unilever	UN
ITT	ITT
Exxon Mobile	XOM
Alcoa	AA
Wal–Mart	WMT
Boeing	BA
Procter & Gamble	PG
Honeywell International	HON
Oracle	ORCL
General Motors	GM

Panel A: First 10 Stocks

Month/Year	SUNW	AMZN	MERQ	GD	NOC	CPB	KO	MLM	HLT	UTX
Dec. 2000	0.0921	0.1066	-0.0381	-0.0046	0.0434	0.0041	0.0745	0.0017	0.1201	-0.0474
Jan. 2001	-0.4305	-0.5299	-0.3224	-0.0066	0.0805	0.0038	-0.0454	0.0811	-0.1003	0.0383
Feb. 2001	-0.2568	0.0039	-0.4074	0.0029	-0.0769	0.0075	0.0363	-0.0734	-0.0246	-0.0610
Mar. 2001	0.1078	0.4334	0.4571	0.0025	0.0322	0.0020	-0.0243	0.0710	0.0558	0.0632
April 2001	-0.0387	0.0561	-0.1103	0.0025	-0.0122	0.0034	0.0211	0.0742	0.1145	0.0648
May 2001	-0.0466	-0.1651	0.0111	0.0004	-0.1027	-0.0034	-0.0241	0.0024	-0.0659	-0.1286
June 2001	0.0356	-0.1248	-0.4379	0.0092	0.0016	0.0003	-0.0613	-0.1158	0.0430	0.0019
July 2001	-0.3526	-0.3344	-0.3586	-0.0247	0.0218	-0.0108	0.0864	-0.1097	0.0484	-0.0706
Aug. 2001	-0.3254	-0.4038	-0.3497	0.0063	0.2084	-0.0075	-0.0666	-0.0099	-0.4819	-0.3859
Sept. 2001	0.2048	0.1563	0.2240	0.0092	-0.0105	-0.0052	0.0132	0.0205	0.0866	0.1475
Oct. 2001	0.3386	0.4835	0.2567	-0.0027	-0.0627	-0.0007	-0.0305	0.0626	0.1454	0.1107
Nov. 2001	-0.1465	-0.0452	0.0986	0.0012	0.0712	-0.0042	0.0203	0.0921	0.0981	0.0710
Dec. 2001	-0.1338	0.2711	0.1144	0.0003	0.1018	0.0003	0.1038	-0.1337	0.0943	0.0615
Jan. 2002	-0.2346	-0.0064	-0.1174	-0.0025	-0.0418	0.0003	0.0522	0.0238	0.0692	0.0596
Feb. 2002	0.0358	0.0141	0.1055	0.0079	0.0546	-0.0045	0.1020	0.0112	0.1061	0.0170
Mar. 2002	-0.0753	0.1546	-0.0101	0.0012	0.0651	0.0069	0.0033	-0.0804	0.1346	-0.0558
April 2002	-0.1716	0.0883	-0.0960	-0.0025	0.0054	0.0000	0.0057	0.0263	-0.1416	-0.0187
May 2002	-0.3186	-0.1150	-0.3885	0.0095	0.0300	0.0038	-0.1396	-0.0253	-0.0214	-0.0142
June 2002	-0.2453	-0.1174	0.1096	-0.0258	-0.1215	-0.0097	0.1037	-0.0173	-0.1288	0.0233
July 2002	-0.0605	0.0333	-0.0082	-0.0123	0.1037	0.0003	0.0137	-0.0451	-0.0599	-0.1572
Aug. 2002	-0.3540	0.0642	-0.3926	0.0174	0.0100	0.0066	-0.0307	-0.1178	-0.0114	-0.0501
Sept. 2002	0.1335	0.1950	0.4297	-0.0184	-0.1846	-0.0052	0.1275	-0.1569	0.0777	0.0877
Oct. 2002	0.3711	0.1874	0.2387	-0.0065	-0.0622	-0.0094	0.0715	0.1242	0.1071	0.0129

Panel A: (Continued)

Month/Year	SUNW	AMZN	MERQ	GD	NOC	CPB	KO	MLM	HLT	UTX
Nov. 2002	−0.3217	−0.2120	−0.1215	−0.0044	0.0009	−0.0028	0.1197	−0.0277	−0.0743	−0.0085
Dec. 2002	−0.0065	0.1456	0.1815	0.0129	−0.0594	0.0222	0.0555	−0.0488	−0.0819	0.0261
Jan. 2003	0.1073	0.0073	−0.0897	−0.0030	−0.0529	0.0003	−0.1378	−0.0571	−0.0635	−0.0819
Feb. 2003	−0.0537	0.1678	−0.0908	−0.0022	−0.0104	0.0038	−0.1744	0.0011	0.0549	−0.0138
Mar. 2003	0.0152	0.0973	0.1341	0.0022	0.0247	−0.0017	0.0167	0.0686	0.1374	0.0674
April 2003	0.2732	0.2239	0.1469	−0.0013	−0.0028	0.0017	−0.0111	0.1458	0.0397	0.0991
May 2003	0.0667	0.0119	−0.0141	0.0020	−0.0162	−0.0034	0.0844	−0.0177	−0.0803	0.0371
June 2003	−0.2125	0.1367	0.0199	0.0010	0.0667	0.0017	0.0190	0.1306	0.1324	0.0603
July 2003	0.0366	0.1065	0.1030	0.0065	0.0345	−0.0010	−0.0892	−0.0018	0.0455	0.0646
Aug. 2003	−0.1640	0.0445	0.0396	−0.0005	−0.1020	−0.0031	−0.0164	−0.0477	0.0597	−0.0377
Sept. 2003	0.1768	0.1168	0.0219	0.0026	0.0362	0.0157	0.0086	0.1169	−0.0237	0.0916
Oct. 2003	0.0756	−0.0085	0.0011	−0.0098	0.0355	−0.0014	0.0588	0.0383	0.0323	0.0119
Nov. 2003	0.0481	−0.0253	0.0416	−0.0034	0.0316	0.0010	−0.0132	0.0984	0.0460	0.1006
Dec. 2003	0.1684	−0.0431	−0.0356	−0.0039	0.0115	−0.0065	−0.0405	−0.0209	−0.0682	0.0081
Jan. 2004	0.0038	−0.1586	0.0335	0.0074	0.0445	−0.0044	0.0241	0.0650	0.0019	−0.0366
Feb. 2004	−0.2417	0.0063	−0.0802	0.0148	−0.0270	0.0096	−0.0184	−0.0615	0.0136	−0.0652
Mar. 2004	−0.0669	0.0074	−0.0492	−0.0076	0.0084	0.0085	0.0360	−0.0651	0.0735	−0.0005
April 2004	0.0669	0.1065	0.1146	−0.0018	0.0383	0.0419	0.0489	−0.0098	−0.0080	−0.0193
May 2004	0.0377	0.1148	0.0410	−0.0074	−0.6526	−0.0013	0.0388	0.0344	0.0728	0.0781
June 2004	−0.0919	−0.3349	−0.3097	0.0002	−0.0207	0.0068	−0.0189	−0.0132	−0.0455	0.0218
July 2004	−0.0205	−0.0202	−0.0577	−0.0022	−0.0182	−0.0026	−0.0064	0.0279	0.0011	0.0044
Aug. 2004	0.0430	0.0689	0.0107	−0.0074	0.0320	−0.0065	−0.0419	0.0062	0.0540	−0.0057
Sept. 2004	0.1078	−0.1800	0.2192	0.0021	−0.0301	−0.0137	−0.0217	0.0057	0.0547	−0.0060

Panel A: (Continued)

Month/Year	SUNW	AMZN	MERQ	GD	NOC	CPB	KO	MLM	HLT	UTX
Oct. 2004	0.2097	0.1507	0.0490	−0.0085	0.0848	−0.0076	−0.0084	0.0986	0.0375	0.0500
Nov. 2004	−0.0293	0.1099	−0.0013	0.0126	−0.0356	0.0089	0.0846	0.0657	0.0959	0.0574
Dec. 2004	−0.2121	−0.0245	−0.0399	−0.0192	−0.0467	−0.0010	−0.0628	0.0067	−0.0218	−0.0262
Jan. 2005	−0.0326	−0.2058	0.0471	−0.0049	0.0195	0.0003	0.0007	0.0656	−0.0550	−0.0080
Feb. 2005	−0.0436	−0.0262	0.0322	−0.0038	0.0202	−0.0116	−0.0247	−0.0310	0.0595	0.0177
Mar. 2005	−0.1098	−0.0573	−0.1366	−0.0132	0.0158	−0.0093	−0.0918	−0.0168	−0.0235	0.0006
April 2005	0.0512	0.0929	0.0877	0.0139	0.0159	−0.0057	0.0162	0.1045	0.1043	0.0478
May 2005	−0.0212	−0.0706	−0.1623	0.0012	−0.0085	0.0067	0.0412	0.1242	−0.0158	−0.7314
June 2005	0.0291	0.3108	0.0260	−0.0189	0.0036	0.0060	0.0401	0.0504	0.0370	−0.0127
July 2005	−0.0105	−0.0558	−0.0724	0.0127	0.0115	0.0010	−0.0731	−0.0051	−0.0660	−0.0139
Aug. 2005	0.0336	0.0591	0.0782	−0.0037	−0.0315	0.0063	0.0008	0.0815	−0.0374	0.0361
Sept. 2005	0.0177	−0.1279	−0.1295	0.0225	−0.0130	0.0010	−0.0705	0.0057	−0.1376	−0.0109
Oct. 2005	−0.0592	0.1954	−0.2243	0.0018	0.0670	0.0007	0.0085	−0.0494	0.1196	0.0487
Nov. 2005	0.0592	−0.0019	0.1227	−0.0070	0.0175	0.0007	−0.0359	0.0025	0.0226	0.0595

Panel B: Last 10 Stocks

Month/Year	UN	ITT	XOM	AA	WMT	BA	PG	HON	ORCL	GM
Dec. 2000	-0.1119	0.0280	-0.0326	0.0923	0.0668	-0.1206	-0.0879	-0.0013	0.0021	0.0528
Jan. 2001	-0.0078	0.0174	-0.0375	-0.0270	-0.1257	0.0613	-0.0188	-0.0111	-0.4270	-0.0071
Feb. 2001	-0.0553	-0.0454	-0.0006	0.0053	0.0082	-0.1102	-0.1189	-0.1357	-0.2377	-0.0280
Mar. 2001	0.0458	v0.1255	0.0897	0.1412	0.0243	0.1037	-0.0416	0.1807	0.0758	0.0555
April 2001	0.0238	0.0603	0.0017	0.0414	0.0002	0.0175	0.0674	-0.0099	-0.0547	v0.0374
May 2001	0.1038	-0.0530	-0.0159	-0.0758	-0.0587	-0.1232	-0.0069	-0.3270	0.2166	0.1230
June 2001	-0.0029	0.0034	-0.7380	-0.0194	0.1358	0.0514	0.1072	0.0549	-0.0496	-0.0117
July 2001	0.0000	0.0168	-0.0393	-0.0287	-0.1513	-0.1338	0.0431	0.0105	-0.3926	-0.1498
Aug. 2001	-0.1369	-0.0078	-0.0189	-0.2064	0.0297	-0.4242	-0.0185	-0.3446	0.0299	-0.2439
Sept. 2001	-0.0322	0.0709	0.0013	0.0398	0.0377	-0.0272	0.0135	0.1127	0.0750	-0.0375
Oct. 2001	0.1085	0.0196	-0.0534	0.1791	0.0704	0.0739	0.0487	0.1147	0.0341	0.1847
Nov. 2001	0.0271	0.0293	0.0496	-0.0823	0.0426	0.0997	0.0213	0.0203	-0.0158	-0.0224
Dec. 2001	-0.0167	0.0500	-0.0064	0.0084	0.0414	0.0544	0.0317	-0.0062	0.2230	0.0509
Jan. 2002	0.0256	0.1056	0.0560	0.0469	0.0333	0.1154	0.0374	0.1259	-0.0378	0.0353
Feb. 2002	-0.0573	0.0662	0.0595	0.0045	-0.0115	0.0486	0.0606	0.0039	-0.2612	0.1319
Mar. 2002	0.1424	0.1027	-0.0872	-0.1035	-0.0929	-0.0787	0.0019	-0.0424	-0.2429	0.0594
April 2002	0.0149	-0.0418	-0.0060	0.0275	-0.0320	-0.0447	-0.0079	0.0664	-0.2372	-0.0317
May 2002	-0.0158	0.0523	0.0245	-0.0537	0.0167	0.0536	-0.0028	-0.1068	0.1787	-0.1508
June 2002	-0.0437	-0.1000	-0.1072	-0.2034	-0.1120	-0.0805	-0.0035	-0.0850	0.0555	-0.1382
July 2002	0.0420	0.0622	-0.0363	-0.0752	0.0838	-0.1134	-0.0038	-0.0774	-0.0429	0.0278
Aug. 2002	-0.0003	-0.0868	-0.1055	-0.2624	-0.0826	-0.0826	0.0082	-0.3241	-0.1989	-0.2073

Panel B: (Continued)

Month/Year	UN	ITT	XOM	AA	WMT	BA	PG	HON	ORCL	GM
Sept. 2002	0.0694	0.0416	0.0537	0.1337	0.0839	-0.1374	-0.0105	0.1001	0.2596	-0.1569
Oct. 2002	-0.0955	-0.0751	0.0333	0.1469	0.0065	0.1350	-0.0453	0.0829	0.1759	0.1773
Nov. 2002	0.0743	0.0068	0.0040	-0.1148	-0.0650	-0.0316	0.0165	-0.0804	-0.1178	-0.0742
Dec. 2002	-0.0817	-0.0776	-0.0229	-0.1417	-0.0551	-0.0434	-0.0043	0.0182	0.1079	-0.0145
Jan. 2003	-0.0028	0.0012	-0.0038	0.0363	0.0054	-0.1365	-0.0443	-0.0655	-0.0058	-0.0731
Feb. 2003	0.0526	-0.0515	0.0270	-0.0562	0.0794	-0.0951	0.0842	-0.0692	-0.0983	-0.0045
Mar. 2003	0.0582	0.0876	0.0071	0.1682	0.0792	0.0849	0.0089	0.0997	0.0916	0.0698
April 2003	-0.0831	0.0721	0.0335	0.0707	-0.0681	0.1171	0.0217	0.1045	0.0909	-0.0202
May 2003	-0.1185	0.0437	-0.0136	0.0355	0.0199	0.1124	-0.0292	0.0245	-0.0800	v0.0188
June 2003	0.0273	0.0188	-0.0092	0.0853	0.0409	-0.0356	-0.0148	0.0519	-0.0017	0.0390
July 2003	-0.0113	-0.0246	0.0579	0.0281	0.0567	0.1213	-0.0066	0.0248	0.0677	0.0935
Aug. 2003	0.0601	-0.0839	-0.0296	-0.0878	-0.0577	-0.0854	0.0614	-0.0955	-0.1314	-0.0041
Sept. 2003	-0.0128	0.1277	-0.0005	0.1880	0.0540	0.1144	0.0573	0.1499	0.0620	0.0416
Oct. 2003	0.0300	-0.0309	-0.0104	0.0385	-0.0578	-0.0026	-0.0211	-0.0305	0.0042	0.0026
Nov. 2003	0.0648	0.1185	0.1245	0.1469	-0.0477	0.0932	0.0371	0.1186	0.0959	0.2217
Dec. 2003	0.0373	0.0044	-0.0051	-0.1060	0.0150	-0.0093	0.0119	0.0774	0.0465	-0.0722
Jan. 2004	0.0852	0.0128	0.0333	0.0919	0.1008	0.0381	0.0140	-0.0301	-0.0741	-0.0319
Feb. 2004	-0.0532	0.0109	-0.0138	-0.0771	0.0022	-0.0545	0.0229	-0.0348	-0.0700	-0.0182
Mar. 2004	-0.0465	0.0380	0.0228	-0.1206	-0.0461	0.0387	0.0086	0.0213	-0.0645	0.0036
April 2004	-0.0008	0.0158	0.0163	0.0177	-0.0225	0.0703	0.0190	-0.0258	0.0132	-0.0438
May 2004	0.0340	0.0300	0.0265	0.0538	-0.0597	0.1093	-0.6834	0.0834	0.0454	0.0261

Panel B: (Continued)

Month/Year	UN	ITT	XOM	AA	WMT	BA	PG	HON	ORCL	GM
June 2004	-0.1038	-0.0374	0.0417	-0.0307	0.0097	-0.0067	-0.0430	0.0264	-0.1267	-0.0769
July 2004	-0.0286	-0.0107	-0.0043	0.0109	-0.0064	v0.0286	0.0707	-0.0443	-0.0527	-0.0433
Aug. 2004	-0.0537	0.0112	0.0472	0.0367	0.0100	-0.0116	-0.0336	-0.0033	0.1235	0.0279
Sept. 2004	0.0319	0.0143	0.0182	-0.0330	0.0134	-0.0339	-0.0559	-0.0627	0.1154	-0.0971
Oct. 2004	0.0822	0.0479	0.0404	0.0445	-0.0351	0.0710	0.0440	0.0478	0.0063	0.0010
Nov. 2004	0.0656	-0.0079	0.0002	-0.0786	0.0145	-0.0342	0.0295	0.0023	0.0741	0.0374
Dec. 2004	-0.0314	0.0099	0.0066	-0.0624	-0.0080	-0.0229	-0.0342	0.0160	0.0036	-0.0846
Jan. 2005	0.0132	0.0307	0.2045	0.0848	-0.0152	0.0828	-0.0026	0.0538	-0.0614	-0.0320
Feb. 2005	0.0302	0.0257	-0.0604	-0.0554	-0.0295	0.0616	-0.0017	-0.0202	-0.0370	-0.1931
Mar. 2005	-0.0419	0.0024	-0.0441	-0.0461	-0.0611	0.0180	0.0215	-0.0397	-0.0766	-0.0967
April 2005	0.0285	0.0490	-0.0147	-0.0685	0.0019	0.0710	0.0183	0.0131	0.1019	0.1670
May 2005	-0.0158	0.0273	0.0223	-0.0365	0.0203	0.0323	-0.0445	0.0110	0.0308	0.0754
June 2005	0.0046	0.0860	0.0220	0.0709	0.0236	0.0002	0.0532	0.0698	0.0276	0.0797
July 2005	0.0404	0.0252	0.0194	-0.0460	-0.0932	0.0152	-0.0027	-0.0258	-0.0437	-0.0741
Aug. 2005	0.0381	0.0402	0.0590	-0.0926	-0.0257	0.0138	0.0693	-0.0206	-0.0465	-0.1106
Sept. 2005	-0.0391	-0.1116	-0.1238	-0.0053	0.0766	-0.0499	-0.0601	-0.0921	0.0223	-0.1108
Oct. 2005	-0.0341	0.0681	0.0331	0.1208	0.0261	0.0535	0.0212	0.0662	-0.0063	-0.2241
Nov. 2005	0.0299	-0.0553	-0.0057	0.0407	0.0082	0.0258	0.0235	0.0355	-0.0072	0.0104

Index